BEFORE

YOU CALL THE

DOCTOR

BEFORE YOU CALL THE DOCTOR

Safe, Effective Self-Care for Over 300 Medical Problems

ANNE SIMONS, M.D.

BOBBIE HASSELBRING

MICHAEL CASTLEMAN

FAWCETT COLUMBINE · NEW YORK

A Fawcett Columbine Book
Published by Ballantine Books

Library of Congress Catalog Card Number: 91-73145

ISBN: 0-449-90493-8

Design by Holly Johnson

Printed in the United States of America on acid-free (∞), recycled paper ♻

10 9 8 7 6 5 4 3 2 1

Dedicated to
Medical Self-Care Magazine
1976–1990.
Its spirit lives.

With special thanks
to our medical reviewer,
Elizabeth Johnson, M.D.

CONTENTS

PREFACE

This Empowering Book Will Save You Time and Money

Before You Call the Doctor contains the information you need to become medically empowered. This clear, concise, and friendly guide demystifies the process of diagnosis, allowing you to: manage many common complaints at home, understand when you should consult a health-care provider, and recognize true emergencies which require immediate professional care.

The basic health information in *Before You Call the Doctor* is accurate and valuable, but as a physician, what impresses me most is the way the book helps readers analyze their medical problems, gain perspective on them, and make appropriate decisions about how to proceed. There are three different kinds of patients: those who consult physicians for things they could just as easily manage by themselves at home, those who use the health-care system appropriately, and those who don't consult physicians even when they should. Those in the first group often waste physicians' time and their own time and money. Those in the third group may risk their lives by delaying appropriate professional care. Doctors wish more people were in the middle group, and *Before You Call the Doctor* should help people use the health-care system more wisely by providing the information necessary to make informed decisions. After reading the appropriate section of the book, you'll be able to analyze your symptoms more intelligently and, if you decide to call a physician, describe them more thoroughly, which is a tremendous help to health-care professionals.

People on both sides of the stethoscope should benefit from the medical empowerment of *Before You Call the Doctor*. The book helps consumers stay healthier, feel more confident about their medical judgment, and save time and money because they use the health-care system appropriately. It helps health professionals by informing consumers when they *really should* call a physician. And it helps the nation as a whole because it promotes greater health-care efficiency.

The next time you have a medical problem, before you call the doctor, look it up in *Before You Call the Doctor*. Whether or not you need professional care, it will point you in the right direction.

> —*Melanie Mintzer, M.D., Assistant Professor*
> *Department of Family Medicine, University of North*
> *Carolina School of Medicine, Chapel Hill.*

ACKNOWLEDGMENTS

The authors would like to thank:
- Their editors at Ballantine: Lynn Rosen, Elizabeth Zack, and Elizabeth Rapoport.
- Their agents: Katinka Matson and John Brockman.
- Their medical reviewer: Elizabeth Johnson, M.D.
- Their colleagues at *Medical Self-Care:* Publisher, Carole Pisarczyk; Founder, Tom Ferguson, M.D.; Art Director, Gordon Smith; Associate Editor, Neshama Franklin; Associate Art Director, Charlene Charles; Production Editors: Trisha Giramma and Gregory Reeves; Contributing Editors: David J. Fletcher, M.D., M.P.H., Joe and Teresa Graedon, Sadja Greenwood, M.D., M.P.H., Sheldon Saul Hendler, M.D., Ph.D., Rod Moser, P.A.C., Ph.D., Kenneth Pelletier, M.D., Joan Price, Melanie Scheller, Trisha Thompson, and Terri Wuerthner; Advisory Editors: Michael Lerner, Ph.D., Keith W. Sehnert, M.D., and David Sobel, M.D., Friends: Norma Ashby, Pamela Boyd, Robert Cohen and Associates, Wendy Davis, Ph.D., Dean Edell, M.D., Alex Jean Elizabeth, Harmony Grisman, Kathryn LeMieux, Dewey Livingston, Kim MacLeod, Linda Nolte, Carla Perry, Mara Prokop, Lila Purinton, Trish Ratto, R.D., Paul Selinger, Robert Rodale, Rodale Press, Kerry Tremain, Anne Weaver, and Gretel Elizabeth Weaver.
- And the more than 500 *Medical Self-Care* contributors whose efforts have helped popularize the concept of informed self-care.

NOTE

In addition to physicians (who have an M.D. or D.O. degree), nurse practitioners and physician assistants also provide primary care. We use the terms "doctor" and "physician" for the sake of brevity, but we mean all these health professionals.

The Authors

One time I got so sick . . . I *almost* called the doctor.
—Sam Levinson

BEFORE

YOU CALL THE

DOCTOR

INTRODUCTION

You *Already Are* Your Own "Primary Care Practitioner"

This book has a mission—to help you practice self-care more confidently and effectively. Chances are you're already quite good at taking care of yourself. Every day you make decisions and take steps to keep yourself and your family healthy. Every day you deal with common injuries and illnesses. But if you've read this far, chances are you're interested in becoming more medically self-reliant. We applaud your initiative and welcome you into a book that can guide you along the path to informed self-care and optimal health.

The medical profession has sold Americans on the myth that doctors take care of the nation's health. Nothing could be further from the truth. Doctors are—and have always been—the health care alternative of last resort. The real "primary care practitioners" are nonphysicians, the millions of people who practice informed self-care. These individuals manage their health concerns successfully every day, and they consult health professionals only when the need arises.

The idea that physicians are the medical option of last resort may come as a shock. After all, isn't the family doctor the first person we turn to when we need health care? Family practitioners are the first *doctors* people turn to, but prior to consulting them, the vast majority of Americans deal with their health problems themselves—and usually resolve them without professional assistance.

Many studies show that self-care accounts for more than 80 percent of health care. In the early 1970s, at a time when health information was nowhere near as available to the public as it is today, British family physician Christopher Elliott-Binns, M.D., became fascinated by his patients' medical sophistication and surveyed several hundred on what they'd done about their health problems *before* they'd come to see him. Fully 88 percent responded that they'd practiced at least some self-care, usually with the help of friends and relatives. About 16 percent had also consulted magazines and home medical guides like this one.

Years later, as the amount of consumer health information exploded, family practitioner John D. Williamson, M.D., and Kate Danaher, a health educator, obtained very similar results on this side of the Atlantic. They interviewed several hundred people in family practice waiting rooms and asked what they'd done before they'd called their doctors. More than 90 percent said they'd tried self-care and had come to the doctor only because home treatment had not provided sufficient relief.

Recently, the trade organization that represents the manufacturers of over-the-counter drugs surveyed a representative sample of Americans on how they dealt with their health problems. The average respondent reported a "health concern" every three days—approximately 120 health concerns per year—yet consulted a doctor fewer than ten times a year. What did the respondents do for the other 92 percent of their medical problems? You guessed it—self-care.

A few studies have also investigated what happens when physicians provide even minimal encouragement for medical self-reliance. In a recent report published in the *Journal of the American Medical Association,* a group of family physicians divided their 875-family practice into two groups at the start of the winter cold and flu season. One group received self-care instructions for dealing with colds and flu; the other group received no special instructions. By the following summer, the group encouraged to practice self-care had made 44 percent fewer office visits for upper respiratory infections, saving themselves considerable time and money—without suffering any more complications of colds and flu than the members of the other group, who had visited the doctors almost twice as frequently.

Former Food and Drug Administration Commissioner Frank Young has said, "Pennies for self-care save dollars in health care." We're confident your investment in this book will pay similar dividends, not just because you'll save time and money, but also because you'll gain the personal satisfaction that comes with increased competence in the vital area of personal and family health.

The three authors of this book worked together for ten years on *Medical Self-Care,* the magazine *The Washington Post* called "the encyclopedia of self-care" and the *Los Angeles Times* termed "the self-health Bible." A poster tacked to the wall of our office read: "It's not enough for doctors to stop playing God. The rest of us must get up off our knees." The view that doctors are responsible for the nation's health and that health consumers are simply passive recipients of physicians' wisdom keeps people overly dependent on health professionals—not to mention that it wastes a great deal of time for both patients and physicians and costs tens of millions of dollars a year because of unnecessary medical consultations. But once people get up off their knees and take responsibility for their health and well-being, they become equal partners in their health care, dealing effectively with most health concerns at home and turning to the health care system only when a problem truly requires professional expertise.

Practitioners of enlightened self-care in no way reject doctors or the health care system. Many health problems require professional care, and a key element of informed self-care is to understand the limits of what nonprofessionals can do to treat their health problems. Those who practice good self-care use professional health resources *appropriately*—which usually means not too often.

We've focused on more than three hundred common ailments and other health-related concerns which can be managed partially or entirely at home. We've organized our chapters the way physicians think about the body—by system: skin, respiratory, digestive, eyes, ears, etc. Within each system, we've included both symptoms and specific illnesses to simplify the process of zeroing in on the subject that concerns you. We've also included chapters on staying healthy, home medical necessities, and medical emergencies.

Each topic in the book is divided into three sections:

• "What's Going On?" An overview of the subject.

• "Before You Call the Doctor." How best to deal with it at home.

• And "When to Call the Doctor." How to tell when a health concern really requires professional attention.

Some topics also include a "Red Flag" section, which list the signs of potential emergencies requiring *immediate* professional care. Always check to see if any topic you're interested in has a "Red Flag" section, and if so, read it carefully.

As a general rule, if symptoms do not improve significantly after two weeks of committed self-care, consult a physician. And when in doubt about any health concern, call your doctor.

We hope your copy of this book becomes worn and dog-eared. That means you're using it frequently—and saving yourself and your family time, money, and medical anxiety.

Anne Simons, M.D. • *Bobbie Hasselbring* • *Michael Castleman*

CHAPTER 1

The Seven Keys to
Optimal Health

Health is much more than merely the absence of disease and disability. It is a state of optimal well-being, a condition in which we feel vibrant, energized, excited to be alive. The seven keys to optimal health are: eat and drink right, exercise regularly, don't smoke, get adequate rest, manage your stress load, maintain close social ties, and take prudent precautions to reduce your risk of illness and accidents.

Chances are you've heard some of this advice before—from your mother, spouse, friends, or doctor or from the media. But take a little time to read this chapter. We bet you find one or two important steps you might take right now to improve your health.

EAT AND DRINK RIGHT

Eat Less Fat. An enormous amount of research has accumulated linking the hamburger-fries-and-shake high-fat American diet to an increased risk of cancer and cardiovascular disease, which together account for about two-thirds of all U.S. deaths. Nutrition experts say most Americans eat six to eight tablespoons of fat every day—many times more than anyone needs. Worse yet, much of the fat we eat comes from red meat and dairy products. These foods are high in both cholesterol and saturated fat, a particularly hazardous form of fat. A high-fat, high-cholesterol diet leads to atherosclerosis, or "hardening of the arteries." The arteries don't actually harden. Rather, they become narrowed by cholesterol-rich deposits on their walls ("plaques"), which results in elevated blood pressure and an increased risk of heart attack and stroke.

Dietary fat is also strongly associated with many types of cancer: breast, colorectal, pancreatic, prostatic, and uterine. Oncologists who study the diet-cancer link estimate that as many as 35 percent of all malignancies in the U.S. may be related to diet. For example, in this country, where fat accounts for about 40 percent of calories in the average diet, breast cancer is five to six times more prevalent than in Japan, where fat accounts for only about 20 percent of calories. However, when Japanese women move to the U.S. and adopt the higher-fat American diet, their breast cancer rate rises and soon mirrors ours.

Dietary fat also contributes to obesity, which is strongly associated with stroke, diabetes, heart disease, back problems, kidney and gallbladder disorders, and other complications. Recent research shows that the body converts fat calories to fat tissue much more readily than it turns protein or carbohydrate calories into fat tissue.

The good news is that it's fairly easy to reduce dietary fat from the U.S. average of 40 percent to a healthier level below 30 percent. Simply make three changes in your diet:

• Substitute monounsaturated and polyunsaturated fats for saturated fats. Use margarine, a polyunsaturated fat, instead of butter, which is high in saturated fat. In cooking, use olive oil, a monounsaturated fat, instead of butter and other oils. Mono- and polyunsaturated fats are still "fat," but they don't clog the arteries as much as saturated fats do.

• Reduce the amount of cholesterol in your diet. The body can manufacture cholesterol, but a major proportion of the cholesterol that is found in the plaques that clog our arteries comes from cholesterol in the diet. Cholesterol is not a fat, but fatty foods usually contain a good deal of it. Eggs are also high in cholesterol, which is why many nutrition authorities urge people to eat fewer eggs. We also recommend that you cut back on eggs, but you don't have to give up custards and soufflés—just use egg substitutes. For example, Egg Beaters, which are available in supermarket frozen food sections, have no cholesterol but taste and cook like real eggs.

• Reduce the total amount of fat in your diet. Once you substitute margarine for butter, don't use huge gobs of margarine. And once you sauté with olive oil, use only a tablespoon or so. Even these "better fats" are still fat. In addition:

○ Base your diet on whole grains and fresh fruits and vegetables. Snack on fresh fruits or no-butter popcorn instead of potato chips, corn chips, and other junk snacks. Replace your cookie jar with a fruit bowl. In less time than it takes to order a high-fat pizza or heat a microwave frozen dinner, you can whip up a great salad and microwave a baked potato.

○ Substitute skinless chicken and fish for beef, pork, veal, and lamb. Salmon is not only low in fat, it also is high in omega-3 fatty acids, which help maintain healthy arteries.

○ Eat less cheese. Most recipes don't suffer if you cut the cheese in half. And whenever possible, buy cheeses made from skim milk.

○ Substitute skim, extra light (1 percent), or low-fat (2 percent) milk for whole milk.

○ Eat less ice cream, especially super-high-fat premium ice creams like Häagen-Dazs. Try frozen yogurt instead (and keep the high-fat toppings to a minimum).

○ Watch for hidden sources of saturated fats (palm, palm kernel, and coconut oils) in processed foods and commercial baked goods. Don't get "butter" on your popcorn at the movies— it's not butter but coconut oil, which is even higher in saturated fat than butter.

∘Take a pocket calculator to the supermarket. That allows you to figure out the percentage of calories that come from fat in any food item that contains a nutritional label. Any food with more than 30 percent of calories from fat should not be a regular part of your diet. Some nutrition authorities encourage Americans to reduce dietary fat to 20 percent of calories. On food labels, fat content is typically expressed in grams. One gram of fat contains nine calories. To figure out the percentage of calories from fat, multiply the number of grams of fat by nine to get the number of calories of fat, then divide that number by the total number of calories. Ideally, the number should be .30 or less.

Finally, low-fat eating does *not* have to taste bland and boring. In fact, it can be delicious. The best low-fat, low-cholesterol cookbook we've encountered is *Eater's Choice: A Food Lover's Guide to Lower Cholesterol* by Ron Goor, M.D., and Nancy Goor, whose tasty recipes rarely contain more than 25 percent of calories from fat (see RESOURCES at the end of this chapter).

Eat More Fiber and Complex Carbohydrates.   Dietary fiber, or "roughage," as Grandma used to call it, is the indigestible part of plant cells. Fiber is found in foods containing "complex carbohydrates," including "starches" such as potatoes and pasta, as well as fresh fruits, vegetables, legumes, and whole grains. Foods such as granulated sugar and white flour are also carbohydrates, but they are simple carbohydrates that have had most or all of their fiber removed during processing.

Fiber plays a major role in healthy digestion. It provides bulk, which helps prevent that major American health annoyance—constipation. It also reduces the time it takes for waste products to travel through the colon ("transit time"), which decreases the exposure of the colon's sensitive lining to carcinogenic substances. A recent study published in *The Journal of the National Cancer Institute* showed that adding fiber to the diet can actually shrink precancerous polyps in the intestine, reducing the risk of colon cancer. The American Cancer Society recommends a high-fiber diet to help prevent several cancers, particularly colon cancer, the leading cause of cancer death among nonsmokers.

Many studies show that a high-fiber diet also helps protect against obesity, diabetes, heart disease, and stroke. In addition, soluble fibers such as pectin (in apples), barley, and oat bran have been shown to lower elevated levels of cholesterol.

However, the myth is that high-fiber carbohydrates such as potatoes are "fattening." They aren't. It's not the potatoes and pasta ("starches") that are fattening; it's the butter- and cream-based sauces you add to them. The truth is, complex carbohydrates like potatoes, pastas, and whole grain breads are low in calories and high in fiber. They're more likely to help you lose weight than gain it.

The National Cancer Institute has been urging Americans to *double* their daily intake of fiber. Again, that's not hard to accomplish. Instead of eggs and sausage or bacon for breakfast, try oatmeal or a whole grain muffin, cereal, or bread. Instead of a burger for lunch, try a green salad. And instead of a pizza dripping with cheese for dinner, try whole-grain pasta and a fruit salad.

Eat Plenty of Fruits and Vegetables Rich in Vitamin C, Beta-Carotene, and Indoles.   Foods rich in vitamin C, such as strawberries, cantaloupe, citrus fruits, broccoli, cabbage, and dark green leafy vegetables, have been shown to reduce the incidence of cancers of the stomach and esophagus. Beta-carotene, a form of vitamin A, has been shown to reduce the risk of several cancers, particularly lung cancer. Foods rich in beta-carotene include yellow and orange fruits and various vegetables, such as carrots, cantaloupe, peaches, apricots, sweet potatoes, winter squash, and dark green leafy vegetables. Cruciferous vegetables belonging to the cabbage family, such as kale, broccoli, cauliflower, and brussels sprouts, contain natural cancer-fighting substances called "indoles," which also have been shown to reduce the risk of several cancers.

Limit Your Salt Intake.   The average American consumes more than ten times as much salt as the human body requires for good health. The chemical name for salt is sodium chloride. The sodium causes the problems, and any "sodium" on a food label means salt. An estimated one-third to one-half of the U.S. population is "salt-sensitive." In these persons, high salt intake causes fluid retention, which in turn elevates blood pressure, often contributing to chronic high blood pressure ("hypertension"). High blood pressure is known as "the silent killer" because symptoms rarely appear until the body has already suffered significant harm. Everyone with a personal or family history of high blood pressure, diabetes, glaucoma, heart disease, or stroke should reduce salt (sodium) consumption substantially. Salt restriction is a good idea for everyone.

A century ago, most of the salt in the American diet came from the salt shaker. Not anymore. Today most salt is invisible. It's added to foods during processing.

Fortunately, eating a low-fat, low-cholesterol, high-fiber diet automatically reduces salt intake. Whole grains and fresh fruits and vegetables contain little salt. Processed foods typically contain a great deal. Every time you snack on a banana instead of grabbing a bag of potato chips, you're not only cutting your fat consumption and increasing your fiber intake, you're also shaking the salt habit.

Taste for salt is a habit, a habit that's often hard to break. To wean yourself from salt:

•Don't quit cold turkey. Your food will taste too bland. Cut back slowly over a few months. That way your taste buds have time to adjust.

•Don't reach for the salt shaker right away. Taste your food first, and if you add salt, add it one shake at a time.

•Don't automatically reach for the salt shaker when cooking either. Try herbs and spices instead.

•Try salty-tasting salt alternatives such as No Salt, which contain potassium chloride instead of sodium. However, if you have any chronic medical condition, especially kidney problems, or take any medications regularly, check with your physician before switching to a salt substitute.

Limit Your Consumption of Foods That Contain Nitrites. Processed meats such as bacon, sausages, bologna, and frankfurters contain nitrites, which are added to prolong their shelf life. Cooking and digestion chemically transform nitrites into nitrosamines, which are potent carcinogens. Meats containing nitrites are also typically very high in fat. Therefore, it is important to limit your consumption of these foods.

Drink More Water. The body is more than 80 percent water, and this fluid is vital to just about every body process. People die more quickly from water deprivation than from lack of food. But even when life is not on the line, low-level dehydration impairs mental faculties and physical performance. Next time you feel the pull of the Coke machine, pass up its sugar and caffeine and just have a glass of cool, refreshing water.

Limit Alcohol Intake to No More Than Two Drinks Per Day, Preferably Less. A "drink" is one bottle of beer, one shot of liquor, or one glass of wine. Small amounts of alcohol do no harm, but an estimated 10 percent of Americans are alcoholics. Alcohol is a contributing factor in more than 40,000 automobile accidents each year. Alcohol abusers are also at increased risk for death from being hit by cars. A recent National Highway Transportation Safety Board study showed that *one-*

third of pedestrians killed by cars were legally drunk when they were hit. Alcoholics are at increased risk for liver disease, heart disease, and several cancers. Alcohol is also loaded with calories, so it can sabotage weight-control efforts. Pregnant women who drink risk mental and growth retardation and other problems in their babies ("fetal alcohol syndrome"). Most authorities advise pregnant women not to drink any alcohol. If you're concerned about your alcohol consumption—or use of any other drugs—call the toll-free Alcohol and Drug Helpline (see RESOURCES at the end of this chapter).

If You Are a Woman, Take Calcium Supplements.   If your diet is well-balanced and contains plenty of fresh, nutrient-rich foods, such as whole grains and fresh fruits and vegetables, you probably don't need to take vitamin and mineral supplements, though some authorities recommend a multi-vitamin-and-mineral "insurance formula" just in case. But women should definitely take supplemental calcium. Women need about 1,500 milligrams (mg) of this mineral every day to maintain the health of their bones and reduce their risk of postmenopausal bone-thinning ("osteoporosis"). Most women consume less than half that amount in their daily diet. A daily calcium supplement (calcium carbonate is the most concentrated) starting during the teen years and continuing throughout life can help prevent bone-thinning osteoporosis. See OSTEOPOROSIS in Chapter 16 for more information on calcium supplements.

Eat Breakfast.   Many people have difficulty thinking about food in the morning or making time for it as they rush to shower, dress, and get the kids off to school and themselves off to work. But eating even a small breakfast revs up your metabolism so you can function at your best throughout the day and avoid the temptation of high-fat, high-salt junk snacks when mid-morning snack time rolls around. Build your breakfast around whole-grain or bran breads, muffins, and cereals, fresh fruits, and low-fat milk or yogurt. Instead of butter, try margarine, apple butter, jam, or nonfat yogurt or cheese.

In addition to reducing your risk of cancer and cardiovascular disease, a high-fiber breakfast also helps prevent constipation.

EXERCISE REGULARLY

Regular moderate exercise is as important to good health as a well-balanced diet. According to Duke University researchers, regular moderate exercise reduces stress; elevates mood; improves mental capacities, such as problem-solving and short-term memory; reduces anger, anxiety, and depression; and contributes to better eating habits, reduced cigarette and alcohol consumption, and a better sex life. In short, regular moderate exercise helps you feel great.

In addition, regular exercise can help prevent serious illnesses, such as respiratory problems, diabetes, heart disease, and high blood pressure. It's a key component in weight control, helps protect against osteoporosis, and may even play a part in preventing some types of cancer.

Barbara L. Drinkwater, Ph.D., President of the American College of Sports Medicine, defines physical fitness as the ability "to meet the challenges of everyday living with energy in reserve." In other words, becoming physically fit through regular exercise can help us accomplish our daily tasks and goals without feeling worn out.

But exercise can also feel uncomfortable. Sore muscles, painful joints, heavy sweating, labored breathing, and feeling like you're on the verge of collapse are not much incentive to keep exercising. Here are a few tips to help you start—and maintain—a satisfying, invigorating exercise program.

• *Start Slowly.* This is especially important if you haven't exercised regularly in a while, or if you're beginning an exercise program after an illness or injury. Walking, swimming, and bicycle riding are excellent, fun-filled ways for beginners to start exercising. Start at a level that feels comfortable—even if you can only walk around the block—and slowly increase your exercise toward a goal of at least three half-hour workouts a week.

• *Chart Your Progress.* Even if you can only walk, run, or bike a few minutes or a few blocks the first week, mark it on your calendar, or design a progress chart for yourself. It may sound silly, but you'll be surprised to discover how satisfying it feels to see your progress, and later you'll be able to look back and see how far you've come.

• *Choose a Time to Exercise That Fits Into Your Schedule.* "I just don't have the time." That's the leading excuse for not exercising. But you have time for whatever you *make* time for. Three half-hour exercise sessions a week are rarely a problem—if you're committed to fitting them into your life.

• *Exercise with a Friend or Join a Class.* On days when you don't feel motivated to exercise, other people can help you do it—and stick with it. Exercising with others also provides an enjoyable—and health enhancing—social connection.

• *Choose a Form of Exercise You Enjoy.* This is the most important key to sticking with any exercise program. During the running craze of the

1970s, many people who didn't enjoy jogging did it simply because it was fashionable. Few stuck with it. Your taste in exercise is as personal and individual as your taste in food, clothing, or friends. Forget the fads. Find a form of exercise you enjoy—it doesn't matter what. Just get off the couch and become more active. Studies show that even such ostensibly low-intensity activities as Ping-Pong, housework, and gardening can provide good workouts if you do them vigorously for at least a half-hour at a time. Shop around. Try various fitness activities until you find one (or several) you enjoy and can have fun doing for life.

• *Understand the Three Components of Fitness.* Physiologists separate fitness into three components: muscle strength; cardiorespiratory or "aerobic" fitness, which used to be called stamina or endurance; and flexibility, your ability to move your joints through their full range of motion. As you develop your exercise program, strive to combine all three of these components.

• *Build Strength.* If muscles aren't kept strong and balanced in relationship to each other, they atrophy over time. Think about how weak your muscles feel after you've been confined to bed for a week with a bout of the flu. Keep your muscles strong with a strength-building program. Use them or lose them.

Strengthening exercises can help you tone up and lose inches from your waist and hips—without necessarily losing weight. With well-conditioned muscles, you'll look better, feel better, be better able to resist fatigue, and help protect your joints against the strains and sprains that debilitate millions every year. In addition, recent research at the Oregon Health Sciences University in Portland indicates that a regular strength-building exercise program leads to reduced blood cholesterol levels without dietary changes.

A strength-building exercise program takes only fifteen to thirty minutes three times a week. All you need is an inexpensive set of free weights (dumbbells)—or even large cans of tomato sauce. Strength-building exercises are done in groups ("sets") of repetitions ("reps"). For example, if the directions for a specific exercise call for two sets of six reps, you'd perform the exercise six times (one set), rest for a minute or two, and then repeat the exercise for another set. Most programs suggest beginners start with two sets of six to fifteen reps for any exercise. Most exercise physiologists recommend twenty-four to forty-eight hours between strength-building exercise sessions because it takes the body that long to repair and rebuild the muscle fibers "torn down" during strength-building. Muscle strength increases over time because, when the body rebuilds its muscle fibers, they're rebuilt stronger. If you enjoy weight lifting enough to do it every day, that's fine, just exercise different muscle groups serially, so you give each group a day or two to rebuild.

• **Get Aerobic Exercise.** "Aerobic" means "with air." It describes physical activities that use the large muscle groups for long enough without interruption to stimulate the heart to pump a steady supply of highly oxygenated blood throughout the body. To promote heart and blood vessel ("cardiovascular") fitness, aerobic exercise must be vigorous enough to increase your heart rate to 70 to 80 percent of your age-specific maximum, the so-called "target" or "training heart rate" for your age group. To calculate your target heart rate, subtract your age from 220, then multiply by .7 or .8. This is your personal aerobic heart-rate range. As you exercise, try to stay within this range. Below your target range, you don't get the full benefit of aerobic exercise. Above it, you may strain your heart. Of course, if you have any significant health problem, check with your doctor first before starting any exercise program. To gain aerobic benefit, you must also exercise *continuously* for at least fifteen to twenty minutes three times per week, which is why some activities that require only short bursts of energy, such as softball, aren't aerobic.

One of the biggest problems with aerobic exercise is risk of injury. Two of the biggest offenders are running and aerobic dance. During running, the foot strikes the ground up to 300 times per minute, which may cause all sorts of foot, ankle, shin, knee, and hip injuries. When performed improperly, aerobic dance may also cause problems. Only a few years ago, the American Aerobics Association reported that 80 percent of aerobic dance programs contained dangerous routines.

In response to such problems, many runners have taken up aerobic walking, and many aerobic dance enthusiasts have abandoned high-jumping, high-impact aerobics in favor of low-impact routines, in which one foot stays in contact with the floor at all times and target heart rates are maintained through vigorous use of the arms.

A few simple guidelines can help you have an injury-free aerobic workout:

• Warm up slowly. Do a low intensity routine for five to ten minutes, then stretch thoroughly for about ten minutes.

• Wear correct shoes for your sport. No single athletic shoe is best for all forms of exercise. Without getting too technical, sports that require quick pivoting, such as aerobic dance, racquet sports, and basketball, require shoes that provide good side-to-side ("lateral") support. Sports involving steady foot pounding without much pivoting, such as running, require more front-to-back support. Discuss your fitness activities with athletic shoe store staff.

PROS AND CONS OF VARIOUS RECOMMENDED AEROBIC EXERCISES

Aerobic Dance.   A good aerobic dance program offers a well-rounded program of cardiovascular endurance, fat loss, strength-building, and flexibility. However, for best results, it requires special aerobic shoes, a studio with a wooden floor, an organized class (or video), and a trained instructor. Without these requirements, the risk of injury increases.

Bicycling.   Cycling promotes cardiorespiratory endurance and fat loss. Peddling at a moderate 12 m.p.h., a 150 lb. person burns up to 600 calories an hour. In poor weather, a stationary bike can be used. The disadvantages are that cycling exercises only the legs—although adding small hand weights when on a stationary bike allows an upper-body workout as well. You need a bicycle and safety equipment. And motorists sometimes fail to see cyclists on the road, raising a risk of serious injury.

Rowing.   Like bicycling, rowing can be performed both indoors and out. Rowing rapidly (6 m.p.h.) burns fat and builds strength. It has the advantage of exercising both the arms and legs and causes relatively few injuries; however, those with a history of back trouble should row with caution. As for disadvantages, rowing can be tedious, especially indoors, and it requires a boat or rowing machine.

Running.   Running burns fat and builds leg muscles. At a rate of 6 m.p.h., running burns about 750 calories an hour. Its disadvantages include the need for special shoes (which generally cost at least $50). It's difficult to run in inclement weather unless you have access to an indoor track. Injuries are common. And it only exercises the lower half of the body. Adding small hand weights allows an upper-body workout as well.

Skating.   Ice or roller skating is as aerobic as running and often more fun, but it must be performed longer for comparable results. Skating burns about 700 calories an hour, which helps eliminate body fat, and it builds muscle strength and increases flexibility. The disadvantages include the need for skates and a place to do it, as well as the potential for injuries.

PROS AND CONS *(Continued)*

Cross-country Skiing.   Cross-country skiing can trim fat and build strength and, in some areas, provide breath-taking scenery. At a moderate 4 m.p.h., it burns about 600 calories per hour. However, it's limited to the winter months, requires considerable equipment, and, if you're not careful, may lead to hypothermia and frostbite (see HYPOTHERMIA AND FROSTBITE in Chapter 3). Cross-country ski machines replicate the workout indoors, but they take up space and don't provide comparable views.

Swimming.   Swimming is great exercise for injury-prone fitness buffs. Swimming increases aerobic capacity, promotes fat loss, and increases flexibility. However, it requires access to a pool, and recent research indicates it is not particularly helpful for weight control.

Walking.   Underrated until recently, brisk walking (4 m.p.h.) is a terrific way to start a fitness program, and many people like it so much they just keep doing it instead of switching to more "advanced" athletic activities. Walking requires no special equipment other than a good pair of shoes. You can walk almost anywhere. And it's easily adaptable to most life-styles—you can park your car a little farther from work, school, or shopping and walk part way. One limitation for walking is foul weather, but recently many malls around the country have begun sponsoring Mall Walks so you can walk for health anytime. Adding small hand weights allows an upper-body workout as well.

• Use appropriate safety equipment. If you ride a bicycle, wear a helmet and be sure your bike has adequate reflectors and lights. If you play racquetball or squash, wear safety goggles.

• Progress slowly. Forget the "no pain, no gain" philosophy. If something hurts, stop doing it. Learn to recognize the difference between pain and soreness. Sharp pains that develop during exercise are a clear signal to stop what you're doing and initiate self-care or seek professional treatment. However, the dull muscle aches that develop a day or two after exercise are a message that what you're doing is challenging your muscles and joints in a good way, just a little too much. After your soreness subsides, feel free to return to the activity that caused it—but work out less vigorously.

· Drink plenty of water before, during, and after your workout. Sweating is great, but it costs you water. Replace it. Be particularly aware of the dangers of dehydration, heat exhaustion, and heat stroke during the warm summer months (see HEATSTROKE in Chapter 3).

• ***Build Flexibility.*** Stretching builds flexibility. It helps you feel relaxed and supple, and it helps prevent injuries during exercise. Recent research indicates that it's ineffective—and even dangerous—to stretch muscles when they're "cold." Instead, "warm up" the muscles first with some low-intensity exercise, such as easy walking. After five to ten minutes of low-intensity exercise, your muscles are ready to be stretched.

Another common stretching mistake involves bouncy ("ballistic") exercises, such as traditional toe stretches and hurdler's stretches. Exercise experts now contend that bounce-stretch movements increase the risk of tiny muscle injuries. When these injuries heal, they form scar tissue that eventually reduces the muscle's elasticity and increases the risk of more serious injuries later (see MUSCLE STRAINS and MUSCLE TEARS in Chapter 15).

HOW MANY CALORIES DOES EXERCISE BURN?

This table estimates the number of calories burned by a 150-pound man during a 45-minute workout. A 125-pound woman would burn about 20 percent fewer calories. Note that walking can be tailored to provide a workout at any calorie-consumption level.

Slow walking (2 m.p.h.)	113
Ballroom-style dancing	162
Bicycling (5.5 m.p.h.)	203
Fitness walking (4 m.p.h.)	248
Singles tennis	311
Fitness walking up a 5-percent grade	338
Jogging	455
Brisk fitness walking up a 10-percent grade	541

(Source: *Walking,* Summer 1986, p. 18)

Stretching exercises should be performed *slowly* and smoothly without bouncing. You may feel some tightness, but if you feel any pain, stop doing the stretch. Stretch for at least five to ten minutes before any vigorous exercise and stretch again for ten to fifteen minutes after vigorous exercise.

DON'T SMOKE

Smoking is the number one preventable cause of death in the U.S. It contributes not only to lung cancer but to heart disease, stroke, and several other cancers as well. In addition, even among nonsmokers, exposure to burning cigarettes and exhaled smoke ("passive smoking") increases the risk of lung disease and other health problems, especially among family members and children of smokers. Pregnant women who smoke harm their babies.

If you don't smoke, don't start. If you smoke, quit. Of course, that's much easier said than done. Authorities say smoking is one of the most difficult addictions to break, harder even than heroin. Smoking has become unfashionable, and nonsmokers often villify those who continue to smoke as "bad people." Smokers are not bad people. They simply have a bad habit. Many quit-smoking books and programs are long on guilt and short on support. But we've found one book that truly helps smokers cut down and eventually quit: *The No-Guilt, No-Nag, Do-It-Yourself Guide to Quitting Smoking* by Tom Ferguson, M.D. (see RESOURCES at the end of this chapter).

GET ADEQUATE REST

Everyone needs rest, but what's "adequate" for some may not be enough for others. Most people need seven or eight hours of sleep a night, but others seem to do fine with only four or five. Some people may, in fact, be able to thrive on just five hours of sleep a night, but recent research suggests that the vast majority of people need at least seven hours a night to function at their best.

As people age, many find they require less sleep than they did when they were younger, but they may also sleep less soundly and more fitfully, which becomes a problem.

Insomnia is a major national wellness problem, as the multimillion-dollar sleep-aid industry clearly shows. Chronic insomnia may be a symptom of serious anxiety and/or depression requiring professional help. For most people, however, it's just a manifestation of daily stresses. Before you buy a nonprescription sleep aid at the drug store, and certainly before you call the doctor, see the discussion of INSOMNIA in Chapter 4.

MANAGE YOUR STRESS LOAD

Stress is any perceived threat to well-being. When the body feels stressed it reacts with the "fight-or-flight" reflex. Heart rate increases, blood pressure rises, breathing quickens, muscles become tense, and blood clots more easily and flows away from the internal organs and out to the limbs in preparation for self-defense or escape. The fight-or-flight response evolved because it has clear survival advantages. When prehistoric humans saw saber-toothed tigers charging out of the underbrush, the fight-or-flight response helped them combat the peril or run away.

Today, the fight-or-flight response is still quite useful. For example, it will come into play if you wake up and suddenly realize your house is on fire. But unlike our prehistoric ancestors who had to react physically to most dangers they encountered, today most of our stressors are more subtle: overdue bills, car repairs, family problems, relationships stresses, tensions with the boss. We continue to experience the fight-or-flight response, but we experience it at a lower level and more frequently. Over time, stress builds to the point where it becomes distress, and we may develop headaches, abdominal problems, or other physical or emotional ailments for no apparent reason. If we don't relieve these low-level symptoms of distress, we may suffer more serious stress-related health problems—for example, chronic neck pain.

It seems that the only constant in our pressure-cooker world is change. Since change is stressful, it follows that stress is inevitable. But not all stress is bad. Without stress there would be no roller coasters, surprise parties, or movie thrillers. Even "bad" stress is not always so bad. Losing one's job is certainly stressful, but it may lead to positive career changes. Borrowing large sums can be frightening, but if the loan is a mortgage, the pleasure of enjoying a new home may outweigh the fear and stress. Any change can be stressful, but stresses are "bad" or "good" depending on how we perceive and react to them.

What distinguishes stress that is ultimately harmless from stress that becomes distress? An important element is control. When we feel in control, we can see stress as a challenge. We're stimulated and ready to make the changes required. But when we feel out of control, we often perceive stress as a threat. We may feel frustrated, alienated, powerless, helpless, and hopeless—and our risk increases for stress-related health problems.

Personality plays a major role in how we react to stress. During the late 1950s, Meyer Friedman, M.D., Director of Cardiology Research at the Harold Brunn Institute at Mt. Zion Hospital in San Francisco, and his colleague Ray Rosenman, M.D., coined the term "Type-A behavior" to describe hostile, hard-driving individuals who, their studies showed, were at high risk for serious stress-related illnesses. Their research showed that compared with more relaxed Type-B's, Type-A's were at significantly greater risk for heart attack. Are *you* Type-A? If you have any of the following traits, you have Type-A tendencies. If you have three or more, you're probably Type-A:

• Try to do two things at once, such as reading while eating, or watching TV while talking on the phone.

• Have a mania about being on time, and get annoyed when others are late.

• Have trouble sitting still and doing nothing.

• Yell at the stupidity of other drivers.

• Become irritated waiting in lines.

• Interrupt others frequently.

• Always play to win, even in games with children.

• Have often been told by your spouse, friends, and family to slow down, and dismiss such suggestions as ridiculous or impossible.

Although it's difficult, if not impossible, to change one's basic personality, Dr. Friedman's work with Type-A's shows it's possible to change Type-A behavior to more laid-back Type-B and, along the way, reduce the risk of heart attack and feel much better about life. Dr. Friedman suggests the following exercises for Type-A's interested in mellowing out:

• Listen to your spouse, family, and friends. Stop arguing with requests to slow down. Start planning how you'll comply.

• The next time you see someone doing a task more slowly than you could, do not interfere.

• Never interrupt anyone.

• Read a long novel about a subject far removed from your occupation.

• Purposely choose to wait in the longest line at the supermarket or toll plaza and use the time to reflect on what you enjoy about your life.

• Write a letter to an old friend. Don't mention your job. Use a thesaurus at least once.

• Practice saying "no" to keep from overscheduling your time. Ask yourself whether you'll care about every meeting or engagement in five years. Only attend those you think you'll remember five years from now.

•Develop an imaginary "internal friend" who sits on your shoulder, observes your behavior, and reminds you to relax, slow down, smile, forgive, and focus on what's really important.

•Laugh at yourself at least twice a day.

Whether or not you have a Type-A personality, chances are you have questions about how you're holding up under your own personal stress load. There's no shortage of self-assessment stress tests on the market, but in our experience, most of them are simplistic and hokey. All except StressMap™. Much more than a "what's bothering you?" questionnaire, StressMap™ provides fresh insights into problem areas and spotlights coping skills you might not have realized you even have (see RE-SOURCES at the end of this chapter).

Once you understand how your individual stress load affects you, here are some general coping tips to help you manage it better:

•Eat a balanced diet, exercise regularly, and get adequate rest. A person in good health is better able to deal with life's inevitable stresses and strains. In addition, fatigue, poor diet, and physical flabbiness themselves can become significant stressors. Many studies show that regular exercise is one of the most effective stress reducers. In addition to the mental boost that exercise provides, feeling physically strong may help you feel more powerful and more in control.

•Analyze your problems. Too often, people feel overwhelmed by the apparent enormity of their problems. Some problems are, indeed, catastrophic, for example, the death of a child, but most are not. Try analyzing your problems. Write each one down, then break it into its various components. Small parts of larger problems usually feel more manageable. Once you've broken your big problems down, deal with them one small component at a time.

•Voice your concerns. Sometimes sharing your worries with a spouse, relative, or close friend can lighten your burden. If your problems feel like more than you can handle with the help of friends or relatives, seek a professional therapist.

•Feel your feelings. Often a good cry or yelling as loudly as you can while pounding on a pillow can help release pent-up frustration. Once you've "vented" it's sometimes easier to find solutions.

•Work to accept change as inevitable. In a recent study, psychologists asked a large number of adults over the age of forty what they considered the keys to personal happiness. "Happiness" is really just another way of saying you have your stressors under control. The respondents hardly mentioned such classic psychological notions as early childhood relations with parents. Topping their list was "personal resilience," the ability to accept change. Change is inevitable. If you habitually resist it, you're likely to be plagued with stress-related health problems. Instead, try to follow this precept from Alcoholics Anonymous: God grant me the courage to change what I can, the strength to accept what I can't, and the wisdom to know the difference.

• Fill your life with things that make you happy. Beyond such basic necessities as food, clothing, shelter, and a job, it's life's little pleasures that bring the most happiness. Take the time to enjoy your children. Play with a pet. Listen to music. Work in your garden. Go to a concert, play, or movie. Stroll through a park. Do whatever gives you pleasure, and chances are your stressors won't feel so threatening.

• Vary your mental diet. Changes of scenery often work wonders for one's emotional outlook. Take breaks at work. Take a walk at lunch. Vary your leisure activities. Take classes. Meet new people. Schedule vacations and weekend getaways.

• Practice stress management techniques. Deep breathing is among the most effective stress reducers. When you become stressed, your diaphragm muscles contract and you tend to breath rapidly and shallowly. When you feel tense or under pressure, take a few deep breaths. Fill your entire chest and abdomen, then exhale completely. Chances are, after four or five breaths, you'll feel more relaxed.

Deep breathing is a handy stress reliever even when you don't feel particularly stressed. Schedule quickie deep breathing breaks into your day—for example, whenever you go to the bathroom, have a snack, or hang up the phone.

Deep breathing is a fundamental ingredient in meditation, one of the most ancient forms of stress management. There are dozens of ways to meditate, but they're all fairly similar. Basically, you sit with your eyes closed in a quiet place where you won't be disturbed. Empty your mind of conscious thoughts, and focus on your breathing and/or a word or phrase such as "one" or "peace." Say the word silently to yourself while breathing deeply. If other thoughts enter your mind, observe them, but don't dwell on them. Let them pass on their own, as they arrived. Do this for five to ten minutes twice a day for a week until you become skilled at quieting your mind. Then increase the time to fifteen minutes once or twice a day.

Biofeedback is another way to achieve the mental state induced by meditation. In biofeedback, you get hooked up to a machine and as you relax, a dial moves or lights become illuminated. After a while, most people learn to relax without the aid of the machine. Biofeedback equipment is available at health facilities specializing in stress management. If you have trouble finding it in your area, call some mental health agencies and ask for a referral.

Another effective relaxation technique is progressive relaxation exercises, in which you alternately contract and relax your various muscle groups. Progressive relaxation is a handy way to take mini-breaks at work. Begin with your toes and work upward until your whole body feels relaxed. Hold each contraction for a few seconds, then relax, and repeat it. A full-body session—including the feet, lower legs, thighs, buttocks, hands, arms, back, shoulders, neck, and face—takes about twenty minutes. Finish with several slow, deep breaths.

MAINTAIN STRONG SOCIAL TIES

A popular song once proclaimed: "People who need people are the luckiest people in the world." They're also the healthiest, according to researchers who have studied the relationship between well-being and social ties. Leonard Syme, Ph.D., a professor of Public Health at the University of California at Berkeley, has discovered that good health and longevity correlate strongly with a rich and supportive social environment. People with what Dr. Syme calls "interrupted social ties" exhibit more depression, unhappiness, headaches, pregnancy complications, intestinal upsets, and skin problems as well as higher rates of many serious diseases, including heart disease, cancer, and arthritis. On the other hand, people who have a network of intimate friends are better able to avoid disease and, in general, deal more successfully with life's difficulties.

In a landmark study of more than 4,000 people in Alameda County, California, Dr. Syme and his colleagues found that married people have significantly lower death rates than single people, and that those who have many friends they see frequently have lower death rates than those with fewer friends or those who see their friends less frequently. They found that regardless of age, those who are "socially isolated" have a death rate up to four and a half times higher than their more socially connected counterparts. Other studies have shown that lonely people are more likely to feel depressed and that depression impairs the immune system. Presumably, strong social ties boost the immune system and ability to resist disease.

Other surveys have shown that stable social networks provide an important buffering effect against all manner of disease among those undergoing major life changes. Japanese men who immigrate to the United States are five times more likely to develop heart disease than their counterparts back in Japan. But Japanese immigrants who join Japanese cultural organizations in the U.S. suffer no increased risk of heart disease.

The health benefits of close ties help explain why hard-driving, competitive Type-A's have higher rates of illness and disease. They generally spend little time cultivating close personal relationships. It may also help explain why women live longer than men. Women tend to value family and friends more than men do.

Close relationships need not be limited to people. Many studies show that people who own pets are healthier than their non–pet-owning counterparts. Pets provide a source of unconditional love and an intimate bond with another living creature. University of Pennsylvania researchers have found that pet owners who develop serious heart disease have better survival rates than non–pet-owners.

REDUCE YOUR RISKS

Life is inherently risky. You can eat the most healthful foods, exercise daily, sleep like a baby, be as mellow as Buddha, and have dozens of close social ties—yet still get killed in a car wreck, plane crash, earthquake, hurricane, or some other disaster. Meanwhile, every day the mass media pummel us with new hazards we should worry about: pesticides on our food, radon in our basements, toxic wastes in our landfills, holes in the ozone layer—you name it. Some people react fatalistically. They ignore all the warnings, live their lives as they please, and figure that when their number is up, well, you've got to die sometime. Such sentiments are understandable when you turn on the evening news and discover to your horror that someone just died in a freak accident involving a contaminated food item. No doubt about it: Anyone can be in the wrong place at the wrong time. But the fact is, the major health risks are well known, and those interested in living long and happy lives can take prudent precautions against them.

Understand Your Personal and Family Medical History. Your personal and family medical histories provide invaluable clues to your health, particularly your special health risks. For example, if one of your parents was an alcoholic, substance abuse experts estimate that compared with people from nonalcoholic backgrounds, you are up to *four times* more likely to marry an alcoholic or become one yourself. You're not fated to do so, but to be forewarned is to be forearmed. Many other serious diseases—cancer, diabetes, arthritis, and heart disease—also have hereditary components. By becoming aware of your inherited health risks, you can take steps to reduce those risks (see YOUR PERSONAL MEDI-CAL RECORD in Chapter 2).

If you don't know your immediate family's medical history, by all means *ask*. Asking isn't nosy. It's crucial to your health. It's also a good opportunity to remind family members to do things like having their blood pressure and cholesterol tested.

Get Screened Appropriately.   One effective way to reduce health risks is to have periodic simple screening tests. The testing intervals suggested here are only guidelines. If you have a family history of a particular disease, your physician might advise more frequent testing. Ask what screening interval is right for you.

• *Blood Pressure Testing.*   High blood pressure has been called the silent killer because you can't feel or see it, yet it is a major risk factor for stroke and coronary heart disease. Blood pressure is measured painlessly with a noninvasive blood pressure cuff ("sphygmomanometer"). Reliable home blood pressure monitors are now available for those who need to check their pressure frequently.

Blood pressure is expressed as a fraction—120/80, for example. The first number ("systolic pressure") measures the force the blood exerts on the artery walls when the heart contracts; the second ("diastolic pressure") measures the residual pressure when the heart relaxes. Normal blood pressure is generally considered to fall between 100/60 and 140/90. Blood pressure, especially systolic pressure, normally increases with age, but for simplicity, physicians consider 140/90 the upper limit of normal until age sixty. After age sixty, blood pressure is considered "too high" when it's greater than 160/95. Moderately high blood pressure can often be brought down through weight loss, salt restriction, exercise, and stress management. More serious hypertension is typically treated with drugs.

Individual readings vary widely throughout the day, even from minute to minute. Blood pressure tends to be lower in the morning and higher in the afternoon. It's higher after drinking a cup of coffee, and lower after orgasm.

• *Cholesterol Screening.*   Heart disease is virtually unheard of in people with a cholesterol level of 150 milligrams per deciliter (mg/dl) of blood. Most medical authorities urge Americans to strive for a level below 200, though some say the goal should be 160. Unfortunately, the nation's average cholesterol level is around 240, which translates to significant heart disease risk, and many people have cholesterol levels of 300 or more, which means they are at high risk.

Cholesterol is easy to check with a simple blood test, which costs about $20. People with readings above 200 should have a more detailed ("fractionated") blood test, which gives the ratio of HDL (high density lipoprotein, also known as "good" cholesterol because higher levels mean a lower risk of heart disease) and LDL (low density lipoprotein, or "bad," artery-clogging cholesterol).

According to the National Heart, Lung, and Blood Institute's National Cholesterol Education Program, adults should have a total cholesterol screening once to determine their level, and if it is below 200, every five years thereafter. Those with cholesterol levels above 200 should be tested at least annually. Controversy surrounds the issue of cholesterol screening for children because researchers have little information on what's "too high" in young people or on the effects of treating it. But children with a strong family history of heart disease probably benefit from early detection of genetic high-cholesterol conditions. Early detection allows them to develop heart-healthy diet and exercise habits earlier.

• **Colon and Rectal Exams.**   Colorectal cancer is the nation's third most common cancer (after cancers of the lung and breast) and the leading cause of cancer death among nonsmokers. People with a ten-year history of ulcerative colitis or a family history of colorectal cancer or polyps are at higher risk. Colorectal cancer typically occurs after age fifty, though it may develop much earlier in those with a strong family history of the disease. The American Cancer Society (ACS) recommends a screening rectal exam annually after age forty. At age fifty, the ACS recommends an annual stool test for hidden ("occult") blood, usually the first sign of the disease. Also after age fifty, the ACS recommends sigmoidoscopy every three to five years. This involves inserting a flexible instrument into the colon, which allows direct examination of its lowest twelve to twenty-four inches, the area where tumors are most likely to develop.

• **Breast Exam/Mammogram.**   About 10 percent of American women develop breast cancer at some point in life, and that proportion appears to be increasing. The ACS urges all women over age twenty to perform monthly breast self-exams and to have their breasts examined by a physician annually. In addition, women between thirty-five and forty years of age should have a baseline breast x-ray ("mammogram") taken for later comparison. Between the ages of forty and forty-nine, they should have a mammogram every other year, and after age fifty, every year. However, if your mother or a sister, grandmother, or blood-related aunt has any history of breast cancer—particularly premenopausal breast cancer—you should have all breast screening tests more frequently. Discuss scheduling with your physician.

In the mid-1960s, when mammography was first introduced, the radiation dose was high, and many physicians and women's health advocates charged that the exam might cause as many cancers as it detected.

Today's mammography machines emit only a tiny fraction of the radiation the original machines produced, and authorities agree mammography's benefits now far outweigh any remaining risks.

• *Testicular Exam.*   Cancer of the testicles is relatively rare, accounting for only about 1 percent of cancers in men. However, testicular cancer is the most common solid tumor in men under thirty years of age. Men with undescended testicles are at greatest risk. The ACS urges men to examine their testicles monthly by rolling each one gently between the thumb and fingers. If you feel any firm painless lumps, consult a physician immediately.

• *Pap Smear.*   A Pap smear is the screening test for cancer of the cervix, the neck of the uterus that hangs down into the back of the vagina. Cervical cancer is usually slow growing and can be successfully treated most of the time *if* it's detected early. Pap smears detect 90 to 95 percent of cervical cancers and may also indicate the presence of cervical or vaginal infections. Women's health authorities recommend the test annually, though some say it may be performed less frequently. Discuss this with your physician. Some women should definitely have Paps at least once a year: those who smoke, had first intercourse before age twenty, have multiple sex partners, or have a personal history of genital herpes or venereal warts. Women with venereal warts might need Paps more than once a year (see VENEREAL WARTS in Chapter 18).

• *Skin Cancer Exam.*   Malignant melanoma is now experiencing a greater increase in incidence than any other form of cancer. Those who are fair-skinned, who have moles in areas typically irritated by clothing or shaving, or who have a history of blistering sunburns as children or teens are at increased risk. Other risk factors include a family history of breast, colorectal, prostate, lung, or uterine cancer; a personal history of exposure to carcinogens, such as asbestos, nickel, or vinyl chloride, or exposure to DES (diethylstilbestrol) before birth; and x-ray treatments to the head and neck, particularly x-rays taken with old machines, which delivered high doses of radiation. Most dermatologists recommend regular self-exams to detect any potentially cancerous skin changes. See your doctor if you notice any mole increasing in size or if you discover new moles, especially ones that bleed and won't heal.

To prevent skin cancer: Avoid excessive sun exposure, especially between the hours of 10:00 A.M. and 4:00 P.M. Don't use tanning salons. Although operators of tanning beds, booths, and salons claim their machines produce only "safe" UVA (long-wave untraviolet) radiation, recent evidence strongly suggests that UVA can contribute to precancerous skin changes. Wear sunblock with an SPF (sun protective factor) of at least 15 (up to 30 if you're very fair), and reapply it after sweating and after you emerge from the water. Don't forget to apply sunscreen to your lips. Some sunscreens are now waterproof. Long sleeves and hats provide an SPF of about 20. Sunscreens are particularly important for children, because most people receive the majority of their lifetime sun exposure before adulthood.

• *Prostate Exam.*   During annual rectal exams, physicians should check the prostates of men over forty years of age for tumors and other problems.

Get All Recommended Immunizations.   Most people think "immunizations" conclude with the end of childhood. But they aren't just kids' stuff. If you escaped one or more of the major childhood diseases, or if you're unsure whether or not you were vaccinated, talk with your physician about getting this protection now.

There is no harm in vaccination if you're already immune, either from previous vaccination or from having had the disease, except in the case of pneumococcal pneumonia vaccine (Pneumovax). A second dose of Pneumovax may cause severe pain and swelling at the injection site.

Some potentially fatal diseases—primarily flu ("influenza") and tetanus—require periodic vaccinations throughout life. The Centers for Disease Control recommend the following immunizations for adults.

• *Diphtheria.*   Unprotected adults need a complete three-dose series. Everyone should receive boosters every ten years. Though it's uncommon in North America, diphtheria, a bacterial infection involving the growth of a membrane across the throat and other symptoms, is potentially life-threatening at any age.

• *Tetanus.*   About ninety cases of tetanus are reported each year in the United States. Most cases occur in those fifty years of age or older who failed to keep up their immunizations. Tetanus, also known as "lockjaw," is a bacterial infection that develops in deep lacerations or puncture wounds. To maintain immunity, tetanus boosters are necessary every ten years.

• *German Measles ("Rubella").*   Rubella protection is especially important for women of childbearing age because if a woman develops this disease during pregnancy, her baby can suffer severe birth defects. Women should wait at least three months after being vaccinated before attempting to conceive.

• *Measles.*   Adults born after 1957 who have not had measles or who aren't sure they've been vaccinated should see their physicians and get immunized. In addition, recent unexpected measles outbreaks have caused considerable concern. Public health authorities recommend second doses for all children.

• *Mumps.*   Unvaccinated adults who have not had mumps should receive this vaccination. Mumps vaccine is especially important for men because if mumps develops in adult men it may impair fertility.

• *Influenza.*   Flu epidemics strike every winter. In those over age sixty-five and in anyone with any chronic illness, flu can lead to pneumonia. The combination of flu and pneumonia are the nation's leading cause of death from an infectious disease. Tens of thousands of Americans die of flu-related pneumonia each year. These deaths are largely preventable. The annual flu shot provides good—but not perfect—protection against influenza. Children receive about 90 percent protection, older adults about 70 percent. But if you get the shot and develop the flu, it's usually a mild case that does not progress to pneumonia. The following people should get the annual flu shot every autumn (in October or November): everyone over age sixty-five, and everyone of any age who has a chronic medical condition, especially respiratory problems (asthma, cystic fibrosis, etc.). In addition, those who would rather not risk a week flat on their backs in bed may also get immunized. Pregnant women may receive flu shots after their first trimester.

• *Pneumococcal Pneumonia.*   Pneumococcus is the leading cause of bacterial pneumonia in adults. (Influenza, a virus, is a leading cause of viral pneumonia.) The current vaccine provides protection against more than twenty different strains. It is recommended for everyone over age sixty-five and for anyone without a spleen or with a chonic disease, especially one affecting the lungs (for example, asthma). Pneumococcal vaccine should be administered only once. A second dose may cause severe pain and swelling at the injection site. Other diseases prevented by this vaccine include pneumococcal meningitis and septicemia.

• *Hepatitis B.*   About 10 percent of those who develop this viral infection wind up years later with cirrhosis or liver cancer, which are life-threatening. Among adults, health-care workers, kidney dialysis patients, overseas travelers, sexual partners of hepatitis B carriers, sexually active homosexual men, and those who use intravenous (I.V.) drugs are at risk and should be vaccinated. In addition, all infants should be immunized.

• *Miscellaneous Vaccines for International Travelers.*   Adults who travel to other countries, especially some Third World countries, may need additional vaccines to protect them against various diseases, including cholera, typhoid, hepatitis, and yellow fever. Before you go abroad, call your local health department or the Centers for Disease Control to learn whether additional immunizations are required for your destination (see RESOURCES at the end of this chapter). Be sure to add these and any other immunizations to your Personal Medical Record.

Prevent Accidents.   Nearly 100,000 Americans die each year in accidents. Tragically, most accidental deaths can be prevented.

   • *Motor Vehicle Accidents.*   Automobile accidents account for about half of all accidental deaths. When you drive or ride in a car, *always* wear a seat belt. If you are transporting children who weigh less than forty pounds, they should *always* use car seats. Older children should *always* use seat belts.

   Motorcycles are inherently more dangerous than cars. Other drivers have difficulty seeing them, motorcyclists don't wear seat belts, and motorcycles provide much less protection than automobiles. Health authorities discourage motorcycles, but if you decide to ride one, *always* wear an approved safety helmet and long-legged, long-sleeved clothing, preferably of a heavy material such as leather.

   Never drive or ride with anyone who is under the influence of drugs or alcohol. Many prescription and over-the-counter drugs impair driving, particularly antihistamines, which are widely used for allergies and the common cold. Despite all the advice not to drive after taking over-the-counter antihistamines, a recent survey showed that most people drive anyway, placing themselves—and everyone else on the road—at risk of injury.

   Maintain your vehicle. Regularly replace worn tires, brakes, wiper blades, head, tail, and brake lights, and other safety equipment. Always carry emergency equipment: a flashlight, flares, warning triangles, and a first-aid kit.

   • *Home Accidents.*   You can prevent injury to yourself and your children by taking some simple precautions. Here's a brief checklist. It's by no means complete, but it's a good start:

   _____ Does your home have a working smoke alarm on every floor?

   _____ Have you tested your smoke alarms recently to make sure they all work properly?

   _____ Does your kitchen have a fully charged fire extinguisher within easy reach?

   _____ Have you checked your fire extinguisher recently?

   _____ Are flammable materials, such as paints, gasoline, and kerosene, stored in tightly sealed safety containers in well-ventilated areas away from children?

   _____ Does your family have an escape route planned in case of an emergency?

   _____ Have all family members participated in household fire drills?

_____ Are all your appliances approved by the Underwriters Laboratory (UL)?

_____ Are electrical cords arranged so no one can accidentally trip over them?

_____ Have you checked to make sure that electrical sockets and cords are not overloaded?

_____ Does your tub or shower have a rubber mat or safety decals to prevent slipping?

_____ If you own a pool or hot tub, is it adequately secured with a locked gate and/or lockable cover?

_____ Are potentially poisonous substances properly stored out of the reach of children?

_____ Does your home have ladders the correct height for projects?

_____ If you own firearms, are they stored *unloaded* in a locked cabinet?

_____ Your ammunition should be stored separately. Is it?

_____ If you own firearms, has everyone in the family taken a firearm safety course?

_____ Even if you *don't* own any firearms, half of all U.S. households contain them. Do your children know never to play with guns?

_____ Are emergency numbers for the police, fire department, and poison control center posted near each phone in the house?

_____ If you have young children, or if they ever visit, has your house been adequately childproofed?

For more information on home accident prevention, contact the National Safety Council (see RESOURCES at the end of this chapter).

Take Action against Occupational Risks.   Many Americans work at dangerous jobs. Obviously, police and firefighters are called upon to risk their lives in the course of their duties, but ironically, theirs are not the riskiest occupations. A recent study by San Jose State University researcher J. Paul Leigh, Ph.D., showed that the ten riskiest blue collar jobs, in descending order, are:

- Logger
- Asbestos and insulation worker
- Structural metal worker
- Electrical power-line and cable installer/repairer
- Firefighter
- Garbage collector
- Truck driver
- Bulldozer operator

- Earth driller
- Skilled trade apprentice

The ten most hazardous white collar jobs are:

- Airline pilot
- Office helper/messenger
- Retail manager
- Geologist
- Agricultural scientist
- Vehicle dispatcher
- Physicist/astronomer
- Construction inspector
- Office machine operator
- Engineer

According to the National Safe Workplace Institute in Chicago, more than 200 Americans die every day from job-related accidents or illnesses. That's more than 50,000 deaths every year—approximately the number of Americans killed in the Vietnam War—and it happens *every year*. Because occupational injuries are not always reported as such, most experts believe this figure actually underestimates the problem. Many people have no idea of the possible dangers they face at work.

One of the most insidious work-related health risks involves exposure to disease-causing radiation and chemicals that can result in illness and death years after exposure. For example, hospital workers are routinely exposed to ethylene oxide, a potent compound used to sterilize instruments, which may cause cancer and birth defects. Laboratory workers are exposed to hazardous xylene, mercury, and formaldehyde. Some experts estimate as many as 500,000 people annually suffer from occupational illnesses.

Here's how to start protecting yourself:

- Educate yourself and your coworkers. Learn what hazards you're exposed to. Federal law requires most employers to fill out Material Safety Data Sheets and make them available to employees. Read them. If you are represented by a union, bring any health questions to the attention of its Health and Safety Committee.

- Once you know what you're exposed to, find out what levels are hazardous to your health. Find out what the Permissible Exposure Limits (PEL), Short Term Exposure Limits (STEL), and Action Levels (AL) are for the materials in your industry. See if your exposure levels appear to violate recognized safety limits.

- Check your company's Occupational Injuries and Illness Log This Occupational Health and Safety Administration (OSHA) document must be posted annually by February 1 at worksites with eleven or more employees. Look for trends in the types of injuries or illnesses on your job.

• Suggest that your company start a medical surveillance program. OSHA requires such programs in many industries, but they are advisable at any worksite that uses potentially hazardous materials, for example, dry cleaning establishments.

• Educate management. Share your concerns or encourage your union to make safety an issue in contract negotiations.

• Use protective equipment. Employers are required to provide workers with suitable protective equipment if there is a "reasonable probability" of injuries. But protective equipment only works when it's used. Wear the gloves, goggles, earplugs, respirators, hard hats, steel-toed boots, and other protective equipment appropriate for your industry.

• Call OSHA. If management is unresponsive, notify your state OSHA and the nearest federal OSHA office. Complaints may be registered anonymously.

• Inform your personal physician of your workplace exposures. If you suspect occupational factors in any illness, be sure to mention your job to your physician. Medical training virtually ignores occupational medicine so few physicians are trained in it, and physicians may not ask about it unless you prompt them. You may have to be rather assertive to persuade your physician that your symptoms are occupational. Also, don't forget to mention exposure to hazardous substances used in hobbies, particularly activities like painting, ceramics, sculpture, woodworking, or automotive restoration.

Develop "Street Smarts."   Crime has been an issue since before the dawn of civilization, but in recent years it has become a leading cause of death and disability in many urban areas. Homicide is now the leading cause of death for black men in their twenties. No wonder more than half of Americans say they're reluctant to leave their homes alone at night.

The myth is that everyone is a target for street assault. The reality is much different. Researchers showed videotapes of random pedestrians on New York City streets to inmates at New Jersey's Rahway State Prison who were serving time for street crimes such as mugging, rape, and robbery and asked them to select people they thought were attractive targets. All the prisoners picked the same people, based largely on how they moved on the street. In other words, you can reduce your risk of assault by not looking like an attractive victim. Here are some tips to avoid being the victim of a street crime:

• Pay attention. Be aware of your surroundings. Crime experts say that most victims of street crime are preoccupied with other things—reading, looking at maps, fishing for items in purses—and don't see danger approaching.

• Move confidently. In the Rahway study, the most attractive targets moved in halting, jerky, uncomfortable, "untogether" ways. Those least likely to become victims moved more gracefully. They looked agile and comfortable in their bodies. They moved with assurance and radiated a sense of purpose. Many people believe women and the elderly are automatically at high risk for street assault, but the Rahway prisoners agreed that sex and age, per se, had little to do with selecting an assault target. On the other hand, women in high heels and elderly people with arthritis or other minor disabilities often move in the jerky untogether way that attracts assailants. The bottom line is it's not who you are; it's how you move on the street.

• Dress conservatively in clothing that does not restrict movement. Try not to wear high heels or tight skirts on the street. Don't wear conspicuous jewelry.

• Walk accompanied, if possible. Walking with one other person reduces mugging risk about 70 percent. Walking with two or more people reduces it up to 90 percent. Medium to large dogs are also good attack-deterring companions.

• Walk in populated, well-lighted areas. The mere presence of others is a deterrant to muggers. Avoid empty or near-empty public transportation vehicles.

• When in doubt, walk in the street. If sidewalks appear uncomfortably dark or filled with people who look like trouble, take to the street.

• Keep your hands free. Don't load yourself down with parcels. A small knapsack is preferrable to carrying a purse. If you do carry a purse, shoulder models are best. They should be carried with the flap-side in and cradled in one arm.

• Stay sober. Alcohol and other drugs dull the senses and make you more vulnerable to attack. One study showed that more than 25 percent of rape victims were under the influence of alcohol at the time of the attack.

• Trust your intuition. Pay attention to your hunches. After the fact, many assault victims report having felt "funny" about their attackers or the situations that turned into assaults. You may feel silly crossing a street to avoid someone, but better safe than sorry.

• If you are confronted, stay as calm as possible. Most street criminals just want to take the money and/or other valuables and run. Don't endanger your life for the sake of any property.

• Size up the situation and act on your decision. If you think you can escape without endangering your life, go for it. If you commit to fighting, fight dirty: scream, bite, kick, gouge at the eyes. Street assailants hope for compliant victims. Committed resistance often breaks off the attack. As a last resort, fall down and simply act crazy or act like you're having a seizure. When confronted with the unexpected, many assailants decide the situation has become too weird and they withdraw.

• As a general rule, don't resist anyone with a weapon. That's very likely to get you seriously hurt. The only time resistance is advisable is if the assailant tries to abduct you or if you believe he or she plans to hurt you anyway. Then you have nothing to lose by resisting.

RESOURCES

Eater's Choice: A Food Lover's Guide to Lower Cholesterol by Ron Goor, M.D., and Nancy Goor. (Boston: Houghton Mifflin, 1992, $11.95) Contains hundreds of delicious, easy-to-prepare recipes— including desserts—that contain no more than 25 percent of calories from fat. Our favorite.

Alcohol and Drug Helpline. 1-(800)-252-6465. Provides information about alcohol and drug abuse, and provides referrals to support groups, counseling services, and other resources.

The No-Guilt, No-Nag, Do-It-Yourself Guide to Quitting Smoking by Tom Ferguson, M.D. (New York: Ballantine, 1989, $5.95) This book really lives up to its title.

StressMap™ Self-Assessment Questionnaire. ($16.95 from Essi Systems, Inc., 126 South Park, San Francisco, CA 94107; (415) 541-4911) StressMap™ is divided into four parts: work, coping strengths, inner emotions, and symptoms of distress. You answer several sets of twenty-one questions, which takes about an hour. Then you plot your results on the ingenious scoring grid, and presto—at a glance you can see where your stress problems and coping strengths lie.

Centers for Disease Control Office of International Health Information. (404) 329-3141. This office provides updates on any special vaccinations or other health precautions recommended for various destinations abroad.

National Safety Council. 444 North Michigan Ave., Chicago, IL 60611; (312) 527-4800. The NSC publishes pamphlets and other materials on home accident prevention and other home safety issues.

Health and Fitness Excellence by Robert Cooper, Ph.D. (Boston: Houghton Mifflin, 1989, $19.95) The best compilation of healthy life-style advice we've seen. Comprehensive, thoroughly researched, and well documented.

Your Home Black Bag: Essential Items for a Well-Stocked Medicine Cabinet and Home Medical Tool Kit

To practice good self-care, you need the right tools. A well-provisioned medicine cabinet and home medical tool kit can save you time, money, and anxiety. With a few simple, easy-to-use instruments and supplies, you can treat a surprisingly large number of everyday medical problems at home. You won't have to call your doctor as much, and you won't have to spend your nights waiting to be seen in some crowded, expensive, and alienating emergency room.

Keep your home black bag convenient, dry, and out of the reach of children. In addition, keep first-aid kits in your car, shop, office, backpack, boat, and gym bag.

MEDICINES

Take a look inside your medicine cabinet. How old are those prescription drugs? What is that mysterious ointment without a label? Periodically check your medicine cabinet and throw out any unidentifiable or outdated items.

All drugs can cause side effects ("adverse reactions"). Just because a product is available over-the-counter (OTC) doesn't mean it may be used carelessly. When used incorrectly, many OTCs cause harm. For example, high doses of aspirin can cause stomach ulcers. No medicine should ever be used frivolously. Read labels carefully and follow the instructions. If you have questions, before you call the doctor, call your pharmacist or your local Poison Control Center, listed under "Poison" in the white pages of your phone book.

Before you spring for an expensive brand-name drug, ask your pharmacist if there's a generic substitute. Generics are almost always cheaper. However, the generic forms of a few prescription drugs may not be as reliably potent as the brand-name products. Check with your doctor about the advisability of generic substitutions for heart, hormonal, and anti-seizure medications.

If you take more than one medication at the same time—OTCs, prescription drugs, or combinations of the two—check with your doctor or pharmacist about their interactions. In fact, tell your doctor about *every* medicine you use regularly. Frequently, drugs that cause no problems when taken alone trigger harmful interactions when taken with other medications.

If you have children, or if children ever visit your home:

• Keep all medications out of their reach.

• Store them in childproof containers.

• Unfortunately, childproof containers often cause problems for people with arthritis or other strength- and dexterity-impairing conditions. In such circumstances, keep easy-opening drug containers in a secure cabinet children cannot open.

• Most children's medicines are now formulated to taste like candy. This represents a major difference from the experience of previous generations. Today, many kids *like* to take medications and seek it out. Teach children that medicine is *not* candy and that they should never take any medication without adult supervision.

Following are the drugs every well-stocked medicine cabinet should contain:

• *Aspirin.*   Generic aspirin is just as effective as the brand-name products—and usually much cheaper. Aspirin relieves pain, fever, muscle aches, sprains, menstrual cramps, and inflammations (particularly arthritis), but it upsets some stomachs. To minimize stomach upset, take it after meals or use "enteric coated" aspirin, which does not dissolve until it's out of the stomach. Coated aspirin takes longer to work. Most authorities question the stomach-sparing effectiveness of "buffered aspirin."

▶ **RED FLAGS**   In many ways, aspirin is a wonder drug—regular low doses are now even recommended to prevent heart attacks and strokes—but this potent medication may also cause many adverse reactions:

• Aspirin may cause stomach bleeding. This is usually minor, but people with a history of ulcers should not take it.

• High doses or prolonged use may cause ringing in the ears. If this develops, reduce your dose or stop using it.

• Pregnant women should not take aspirin unless a doctor recommends because it may cause problems with fetal development and delivery.

• In children under sixteen years of age suffering fevers from colds, flu, or chickenpox, aspirin increases the risk of Reye syndrome, a rare but potentially fatal condition affecting the brain and liver. To relieve childhood fevers, use acetaminophen instead.

• Aspirin interferes with blood clotting. This effect helps prevent heart attack, but it may be a problem for those with clotting disorders. Don't take aspirin within ten days of planned surgery.

• People with liver disease should consult their physicians before taking aspirin.

• *Ibuprofen.*   Sold over-the-counter both generically and under brand names, such as Advil and Nuprin, and by prescription both generically and as Motrin, ibuprofen may be substituted for aspirin. It has the same potency and generally causes fewer gastrointestinal side effects, though it does upset some people's stomachs. Many women prefer it to aspirin for relief of menstrual cramping. However, ibuprofen is considerably more expensive than aspirin. It is also available as a children's liquid, but it has no advantages over children's aspirin.

▶ **RED FLAGS**   Ibuprofen may cause drowsiness or dizziness, and prolonged use can cause kidney damage.

Pregnant women and those with liver or kidney disease or a history of ulcers should consult a physician or pharmacist before using ibuprofen.

• *Acetaminophen.*   Sold generically, as APAP, or under brand names, such as Tylenol and Datril, among others, acetaminophen relieves pain and fever and tends not to upset the stomach as much as aspirin or ibuprofen. But unlike aspirin and ibuprofen, it does not reduce inflammation. Acetaminophen is also available in liquid (drops or elixir) for children or those who have difficulty swallowing pills.

▶ **RED FLAGS**   Pregnant women and those with liver disease should consult a physician or pharmacist before using acetaminophen. Prolonged heavy use—more than eight extra-strength tablets every day for two years—can cause permanent kidney damage.

• *Aloe Vera Gel.*   Available at health food stores or taken directly from the cut leaves of the living plant, aloe vera gel is a handy treatment for minor burns, scalds, cuts, and scrapes. Wash the affected area thoroughly with soap and water to disinfect it and remove any debris, then apply a layer of the gel. It dries into a natural bandage and contains chemicals which have been shown to help prevent infection and promote healing.

Keep a potted aloe in your kitchen, the site of most household wounds. When you need it, simply cut off a leaf, slit it open, and scoop out the gel. The plant quickly heals its own wound, and moderate leaf-snipping won't hurt it.

• *Antacids.*   Drug store shelves are crowded with OTC and prescription antacids, but baking soda (sodium bicarbonate) often works just as well for *occasional* treatment of heartburn or indigestion. However, before you open your medicine cabinet, and certainly before you call the doctor, try the nondrug approaches discussed in the HEARTBURN and INDIGESTION sections of Chapter 13.

Don't take baking soda if you're on a salt-restricted diet. Look for antacids that contain aluminum hydroxide, magnesium hydroxide, or a combination of the two.

Don't use baking soda on a regular basis. Overuse can *cause* heartburn. It can also upset the normal acid-base balance of the blood and thereby interfere with many metabolic processes. If you suffer frequent indigestion or heartburn that does not respond to two weeks of committed self-care, consult a physician.

• *Antibacterial/Antifungal Ointment.* OTC products such as Bacitracin, Neosporin, and Mycitracin help prevent and treat minor skin infections. They also keep bandages from sticking to wounds. Wash wounds thoroughly with soap and water, then apply a layer of ointment.

• *Antihistamines.* Antihistamines are useful for temporary suppression of the effects of histamine, the chemical that causes the welts of hives and the stuffed, runny nose and itchy, watery eyes of hayfever-type allergies. (See ALLERGIES in Chapter 4 and HIVES in Chapter 6.) Most multi-symptom cold formulas contain antihistamines for relief of nasal symptoms, but common-cold authorities agree that these symptoms are *not* caused by histamine and therefore not relieved by antihistamines. Popular antihistamines include Chlor-Trimeton (chlorpheniramine) and Benadryl (diphenhydramine).

Antihistamines cause drowsiness, an effect considerably enhanced by simultaneous use of alcohol. Those who take antihistamines should not drive or use things like power tools. Unfortunately, surveys show that about two-thirds of antihistamine users disregard this advice, increasing their risk of auto accidents—and everyone else's risk as well. Antihistamines containing diphenhydramine cause more drowsiness than those containing chlorpheniramine. In fact, diphenhydramine is the active ingredient in most OTC sleep aids. If you must drive, ask your physician for one of the nonsedating antihistamines now available by prescription. They don't cause drowsiness but cost more. People who take sedating antihistamines for long periods often notice that after a few weeks, they no longer cause drowsiness.

Pregnant women should not use antihistamines.

• ***Decongestants.*** These OTCs are effective for the nasal and chest congestion of the common cold and flu or for stuffed ears. Decongestants come in two varieties, sprays and pills. Oral decongestants often contain pseudoephedrine or phenylpropanolamine. Nasal sprays typically contain phenylephrine (short-acting) or oxymetazoline (long-acting).

Don't use decongestant sprays for more than three days in a row or you'll develop "rebound congestion," a stuffed nose caused by the spray that's even worse than the congestion you had to begin with. In addition, don't share inhalers. They can spread cold viruses.

Decongestant pills don't cause rebound congestion, but they often cause insomnia, nervousness, and jitters and raise blood pressure. If you have high blood pressure, diabetes, glaucoma, heart disease, or a history of stroke, don't use them.

Pregnant women should consult a physician before using decongestants.

• ***Anti-itch Products.*** Medically known as "antipruritics," these products are useful for the itch of rashes and insect bites. Some products (Caladryl, Calamine) tend to dry the skin. They work well for insect bites and blistery rashes, such as those caused by poison ivy or chickenpox. Over-the-counter 0.5% hydrocortisone preparations block the inflammation that can cause itching. They are often ineffectively mild in adults, though they lubricate the skin, which may provide some relief. They tend to be more effective in children and in thin-skinned areas—the face and genitals.

• ***Sunblocks.*** Don't keep this one in your medicine cabinet or it won't be at your fingertips when you need it. Keep some in your purse, glove compartment, beach bag, boat, diaper bag, office desk, and fishing tackle box. Authorities recommend a block with a sun protection factor (SPF) of 15 or greater.

• ***Topical Anesthetics.*** Sold as sunburn remedies, they contain benzocaine or lidocaine. The best way to escape sunburn pain is to use sunblock and follow the suggestions in the SUNBURN section of Chapter 6, but topical anesthetics can come in handy for itchy rashes.

Some people are allergic to topical anesthetics. If they aggravate symptoms or seem to cause other reactions, stop using them.

• *Vomiting Inducer.*   An agent that induces vomiting is medically known as an "emetic." The drug of choice is syrup of ipecac. To induce vomiting in case of accidental poisoning, every medicine chest and first-aid kit should contain a bottle of ipecac. However, surveys show that only about 10 percent of households have this potential life-saver on hand. Put this book down *right now* and go check. If you don't have any ipecac, put it on your shopping list. Though ipecac is an absolute household essential, never give it without first calling your local poison control center (listed in the white pages under "Poison") or an emergency room. Ipecac should not be used to treat corrosive poisons, such as lye or acids.

• *Rubbing Alcohol.*   Also known as "isopropyl" alcohol, this all-purpose disinfectant is particularly effective for countertops and objects such as thermometers.

▶ **RED FLAG**   Never ingest rubbing alcohol.

• *Hydrogen Peroxide.*   Another handy disinfectant, it's good for cleansing wounds.
    Don't swallow hydrogen peroxide, but a mouthful may be used as a swish-and-spit rinse for mouth wounds.

• *Vitamin C.*   For prevention and treatment of colds and flu (see COMMON COLD and FLU in Chapter 11).

• *Zinc Lozenges.*   For treatment of colds and flu (see COMMON COLD and FLU in Chapter 11).

• *Zinc Oxide Ointment.*   This soothing ointment acts as a physical barrier between the skin and irritants. It readily absorbs moisture and is useful in treating open or oozing wounds, such as second degree burns, poison ivy rashes, hemorrhoids, and diaper rash.
    If zinc oxide causes a burning sensation, you're probably sensitive to zinc. Stop using it.

• *Fluoride Drops.*   Fluoride is added to drinking water supplies to prevent tooth decay. If you live in an area with unfluoridated water, children in the household should take these prescription drops. In addition, the fluoride in fluoridated water does not enter breast milk, so nursing mothers who breast feed exclusively should also give their babies fluoride until they begin to drink water.

SUPPLIES

Every medicine chest should also have a collection of home medical tools and supplies.

- *Assorted Adhesive Bandages.*   For the treatment of cuts, scrapes, and other wounds. Look for the type with breathable coverings and non-stick gauze pads.
- *Sterile Gauze Pads and Adhesive Tape.*   A must for the treatment of larger wounds or anytime you need absorbency.

Some people are allergic to standard adhesive tape. The alternative is "paper" tape. It doesn't adhere quite as well, but it causes fewer reactions and can be removed less painfully.

- *Moleskin or Molefoam.*   This adhesive cushioning material can be cut to provide protection for blisters, corns, and warts, especially on the feet. Never go hiking or camping without it.
- *Flashlights.*   They provide excellent illumination for looking down throats and into ears and for splinter removal. Take a penlight along in your travel bag. They're also essential when the lights go out during storms or other natural disasters.
- *Nasal Bulb Syringe.*   Families with infants should have nasal bulb syringes to remove mucus from tiny stuffed noses. To use one, squeeze the bulb, then insert the tip gently into one nostril while holding a fingertip over the other nostril. Release the bulb all at once for best suction. Pretreating the nose with salt water nose drops (1/4 teaspoon salt in 8 ounces water) may help loosen mucus.
- *Thermometers.*   The ones made of glass and mercury are still the most accurate. Digital-type thermometers are slightly less accurate, but they're the easiest to use with children. Temperature-sensitive paper strips are not particularly accurate and should be used only as a last resort. It's amazing how many people spend time and money going to doctors for "fevers" without taking their temperatures.

Feeling the forehead is not an accurate way to take a temperature. The forehead is nowhere near the body's "core," the internal organs, site of true body temperature. For a quick temperature "guesstimate," feel the chest or belly. But anytime you suspect a fever or infection, take a temperature (see box).

HOW TO TAKE AN ACCURATE TEMPERATURE

Do it before you call the doctor.

• Shake a glass-mercury thermometer until it reads less than 96° F. When using an electronic thermometer, check the batteries by observing the liquid crystal display. Clear black numbers suggest normal operation. If the numbers seem at all faded or incomplete, replace the batteries or recharge the device.

• Make sure the person has not had any hot or cold liquids for thirty minutes before taking the temperature.

• Place the bulb end of an oral thermometer or the probe end of an electronic model under the tongue and tell the person to close his or her mouth but not to bite the thermometer. Leave it in place for two minutes.

• To take a child's temperature rectally coat the bulb or probe with petroleum jelly and gently insert it *no more than one inch*. Hold the thermometer in place for two to three minutes by cupping the buttocks in the palm of your hand and letting the thermometer rest between your fingers. Leave it in place for two minutes.

• To take an armpit ("axillary") temperature, place the bulb or probe under the arm and press the arm snug against the body. Wait three to four minutes.

• Read a glass-mercury thermometer by slowly rotating it until you can clearly see the line of mercury. The number where the line of mercury ends is the temperature. Normal oral temperature is 98.6°F. Normal rectal temperature is 99.6°F. Normal axillary temperature is 97.6°F.

• After use, clean the thermometer in warm (not hot) soapy water, wipe it with rubbing alcohol, and store it in its container.

• **Tweezers.** This little item is invaluable for removing splinters. You can usually buy a good pair in a pharmacy for less than $5.

• **Scissors.** A small, sharp pair with pointed ends is the best tool for cutting bandages, gauze, and adhesive tape.

• **Vaporizer.** These relatively inexpensive devices are excellent for moistening the air and loosening secretions during upper respiratory infections.

The warm water in vaporizers may become home to a variety of harmful microorganisms. Wash the inside of your vaporizer periodically with household bleach. Cool mist nebulizers are safer than steam vaporizers because there's no risk of scalding. Safety questions have been raised about ultrasonic vaporizers, which may disperse harmful mineral particles into the air. Don't use ultrasonic vaporizers.

 • *Blood Pressure Cuff or Electronic Blood Pressure Monitor.*   If anyone in your family has high blood pressure, one of these is a must.

REFERENCE BOOKS

There are literally thousands of useful books on health, fitness, medical care, and specific health concerns. Here are a few suggestions for home reference books to supplement *Before You Call the Doctor:*

American Red Cross Standard First Aid and Personal Safety Guide. (American Red Cross, revised periodically, $7.95) This is a standard text for dealing with emergencies. Obtain it from your local chapter of the Red Cross. And while you're there, if you haven't taken a CPR class, sign up.

Dr. Spock's Baby and Child Care. (New York: Pocket Books, revised periodically, $4.95) Although some of Dr. Spock's advice is controversial, this book is still the best all-around pediatrics-for-parents Bible.

The Medical Self-Care Book of Women's Health. by Sadja Greenwood, M.D., Bobbie Hasselbring, and Michael Castleman. (New York: Doubleday, 1987, $12.95) This book is a useful reference on women's special health concerns.

Merck Manual. (Rahway, NJ: Merck, Sharp, & Dohme Research Laboratories, revised periodically, $21.50) A relatively technical mini-medical textbook for those who want greater detail than can be found in family medical guides. Be forewarned, you'll probably need a medical dictionary to understand the information. But it's a good resource before you call the doctor—and afterward as well.

The People's Pharmacy. (New York: St. Martin's, 1989, $5.95) Written by pharmacists and syndicated columnists Joe and Teresa Graedon, this book contains outstanding, reader-friendly information on both prescription and over-the-counter drugs.

Physician's Desk Reference (PDR). (Oradell, NJ: Medical Economics Co., revised annually, $49.95) Published by the drug industry for physicians, this highly technical compendium on prescription drugs is a bit unwieldy, but once you become familiar with its several indices and format, it provides information about precautions, side effects, and drug interactions. It can be purchased in bookstores, but the drug industry provides them free each year to physicians. Ask your doctor if you can have last year's edition.

Webster's Medical Desk Dictionary. (Springfield, MA: Merriam-Webster, 1986, $21.95) A good companion to the *Merck Manual* or for anyone who wants to understand medical terminology.

YOUR PERSONAL MEDICAL RECORD

My mother started a spiral-bound "Health Record" for me and each of my siblings at birth. The table of contents read: Record of shots, illnesses, medical check-ups, eye exams, miscellaneous operations, and orthodontia. She covered most of the bases. When I left home for college, I took the Health Record with me and began adding my own entries. When I started medical school, I had to provide proof of immunity to rubella (German measles). I looked in my health record and there was the entry: "Age 3. German measles: red rash, blotchy face, no fever, nodules on back of neck." I've kept my Health Record up to date and I've started one for each of my children. You'll find it's an easy and convenient way to keep track of your health.

ANNE SIMONS, M.D.

A personal medical record can help your peace of mind, enhance communication between you and your doctor, ensure continuity of care when you relocate, and help alert you and your medical providers to any health problems that may run in your family.

Use a loose-leaf notebook to allow easy additions and rearrangements. If you have children, start records for them at birth and pass them on. The "Baby Book" supplied by many clinics and doctor's offices is a convenient way to start, but you'll eventually need to expand it.

Your personal medical record should include:

• *Your Family History.*   List all of the members of your immediate family: parents, grandparents, siblings, and children. List their birth dates, any surgery, serious illnesses, or chronic health conditions, and if they are deceased, the cause of death. Especially note hereditary disorders, such as bleeding disorders, Down's syndrome, G6PD deficiency, and sickle cell trait, as well as health problems that often run in families but are not strictly hereditary, such as alcoholism, Alzheimer's, arthritis (note the type), asthma, cancer (especially breast and colorectal), ulcers, diabetes, seizures, migraines, hayfever, heart disease, high blood pressure, elevated cholesterol, and mental health problems.

• *Immunizations and Screening Tests.*   List all immunizations, including vaccines for DPT (diptheria, pertussis [whooping cough], and tetanus), hepatitis, polio, measles, mumps, rubella, influenza, pneumococcal infection (for bacterial pneumonia and meningitis), and foreign travel protection (typhoid, yellow fever, etc.). Include tests, such as TB (tuberculosis) skin test, breast exam/mammogram, Paps, occult blood tests (for colorectal cancer), cholesterol tests, bone density evaluations (for osteoporosis), electrocardiogram (EKG) and other test results from complete physical exams.

• *Significant Illnesses.*   Note all important or unusual illnesses and include date, symptoms, any relevant tests, and treatment and/or prescriptions.

• *Hospitalizations and Surgeries.*   List all hospitalizations and operations. Note all relevant facts about your condition, treatment, and prognosis.

• *Allergies.*   Record any allergies and note any unusual reactions you have to any medications.

• *Medications.*   List all your prescription and over-the-counter drugs under the particular health condition for which you take them. It's also helpful to have a single list of all your medications, including nutritional supplements.

Whenever you visit any physician, take your Medical Record. In addition to answering many questions, it will impress your health provider that you're an organized, "together" person, someone who takes responsibility for his or her health and is willing to take an active role in preventing and treating illnesses.

Doctors and hospitals generally provide free copies of records to other doctors who request them with the person's consent. You can also obtain a copy yourself, though it may not be free. If there is a charge, you're better off asking for specific items, such as lab reports, EKG tracings, operation reports, and hospital discharge summaries. If you are relocating, take copies of any abnormal x-rays. Get them from the facility where the x-rays were taken rather than from your doctor, who will have only the x-ray report.

Lifesavers:

First Aid for

Common Medical

Emergencies

More than 100,000 accidental deaths occur each year in the U.S., making accidents the fourth leading cause of death (after heart disease, cancer, and stroke). But this overall average obscures an important fact. For people under thirty-five years of age, accidents are the *number one* cause of death, accounting for more than half of all fatalities in young people.

BE PREPARED

Most accidental deaths can be prevented. The key is to be prepared:

• Make sure everyone in your household knows about 911. If you call, stay on the line. Don't hang up unless the operator tells you to. 911 operators don't just dispatch police, firefighters, and ambulances. They can also coach you through first-aid for the kinds of medical emergencies discussed in this chapter. 911 calls are free from pay phones.

• Keep an up-to-date list of emergency phone numbers by your telephone:

○ 911

○ Ambulance (if other than 911)

○ Fire

○ Police

○ Poison Control Center (listed in the white pages under "Poison"). Most, but not all, communities have poison control centers. If yours doesn't, call an emergency room or the police.

○ Doctor

○ Neighbor(s) and/or friend(s) who can be contacted in emergencies.

• Take a CPR class. "CPR" stands for "cardiopulmonary resuscitation," a set of techniques for treating those whose hearts or breathing have stopped. CPR is easy to learn, but you *cannot* learn it from a book, so we make no attempt to teach it here. CPR is something people often mean to learn but never quite get around to. This is a serious mistake. *About 90 percent of the time, people use CPR on close relatives or friends.* If you're not certified in CPR, put this book down *right now* and sign up for a class. Make it a family affair. Everyone in your household should learn this skill. If you're already CPR-trained but feel rusty, take a refresher course. Many organizations offer classes: the Red Cross, the American Heart Association, and many church and civic groups.

•Take the Red Cross first-aid course. In just a few weeks, you can learn how to deal with the full range of medical emergencies. Again, make it a family activity. Everyone should know first aid.

•Always have basic medicines and supplies handy (see Chapter 2). Don't keep them just in your medicine cabinet. Assemble first-aid kits for your shop, office, garden, school, backpack, boat, purse, briefcase, and car.

PLAY IT SAFE

• *Automobiles.*

•Everyone in the car should wear a seat belt all the time. Most states require children to be belted and hold adults legally responsible for this. During the 1970s, when many states adopted laws requiring seat belt use, some "rugged individuals" refused to wear them, leading to awkward situations when they were passengers in cars driven by seat-belt advocates. But in recent years, seat belts have become generally accepted, and few passengers require more than a gentle reminder.

•Never drink and drive.

•Don't drive if you feel sleepy or ill. If you're already on the road and begin to feel sleepy or ill, pull off the road.

•Don't drive in heavy weather. If you must, drive extra cautiously with your lights on.

•Do not drive after taking sedating medications, including antihistamines (unless they are the nonsedating variety).

•Keep your car in good repair. Never drive on bald tires or with worn brakes.

• *Fire.*

•Place a working smoke detector on every floor. Check the batteries periodically. Many people killed in home fires have smoke detectors— with dead batteries.

•Keep working fire extinguishers in your kitchen and anywhere there are open flames. They are sold at hardware and building supply stores. Have fire extinguishers serviced periodically. Make sure everyone in the household knows how to use them.

•Organize periodic household fire drills.

•Cigarettes are the leading cause of house fires. No one should smoke in bed or while drowsy. (No one should smoke at all. For help quitting, see RESOURCES at the end of Chapter 11.)

•Use only flame-resistant materials for curtains and children's sleepwear.

• Fireplaces should have protective screens and aprons.

• Never block fire exits. If you cover windows with metal grillwork for home security reasons, make sure it's the "breakaway" variety—hinged for emergency escapes.

• Use candles cautiously.

• Keep matches away from children. Teach them never to play with matches. Teach them how to use matches safely and appropriately after age seven.

• Make sure the wind can't blow curtains over your range or into electric space heaters.

• Chimneys and flues should be inspected and cleaned annually. This is especially important for wood-burning stoves.

• Keep roll-up fire ladders by the windows of upstairs rooms.

• Place "Tot Finder" stickers in the corners of windows in children's rooms so that fire fighters can quickly see where children might be trapped.

• Store all flammable materials in sealed containers in well ventilated areas, preferably outdoors.

• Keep oily or greasy rags in tightly sealed containers.

• Never store anything flammable near stoves, furnaces, fireplaces, or other heat-generating devices.

• All electrical appliances should be approved by Underwriters Laboratory (UL).

• Never overload electrical circuits.

• Never use a fuse rated for higher amperage than recommended.

• **_Children._** If you have young children or if children _visit_ you, childproof your home:

• Place plastic outlet covers in all electrical outlets.

• Remove household poisons, cleaning items, and other toxics from below sinks, and store them out of children's reach.

• Use gates or doorlocks to deny children access to inherently hazardous rooms—for example, woodshops or photographic dark rooms.

• Secure rugs so children can't slip and fall.

• Keep pot handles turned toward the back of your range so children can't reach up and spill hot liquids on themselves.

• Never leave children unsupervised around swimming pools or power tools.

• **_Guns._**

• If you own firearms, store them unloaded in locked cabinets. Make sure everyone in the household takes a gun safety class to learn proper respect for firearms.

• Even if you don't own any firearms, it's a good idea to enroll your children in a gun safety class. Half of U.S. homes are armed, so it's likely your children will encounter firearms at some point.

● *The Medicine Cabinet.*

• Keep all medicines out of the reach of children.

• Buy medicines in containers with childproof caps if you have young children or if children visit your home.

• Keep medicines in their original containers. Labels always tell the name of the drug, dosage, and expiration date. Prescription medicines also show the date of purchase and the prescribing physician's name.

• Never take medicine in the dark.

• This may sound like a platitude, but it bears repeating: Take medicines only as directed. If you think you need a different dosage, check with a pharmacist or physician.

● *Miscellaneous Precautions.*

• Never handle electrical appliances or wiring with wet hands.

• Never use a portable electric space heater in your bathroom.

• Never use a portable electric hair dryer in or near your bathtub.

• Always wear appropriate eye, ear, hand, and other protective gear on the job or when engaged in hobbies.

• If you live in an area threatened by natural disasters—floods, hurricanes, earthquakes, etc.—take recommended precautions and develop a family response plan.

BLEEDING

Here we mean the kind of massive bleeding caused by knifings, gunshot wounds, and motor vehicle accidents.

Massive bleeding causes two related problems—blood loss and shock, a potentially fatal condition caused by loss of blood supply to the vital organs.

• If there are other people around, ask if any are medical professionals or trained in first aid. If so, defer to them, but let them know you're ready to help. If not, have someone call 911 for help and possibly transportation to an emergency medical facility.

• Most bleeding stops under firm direct pressure. Use the heel of your hand and/or the cleanest cloth available (see illustrations). Large wounds may take a while to stop bleeding. Maintain pressure on the wound(s) until professional help arrives or until you deliver the person to an emergency facility.

• Bleeding from an artery ("arterial bleeding") is harder to control than

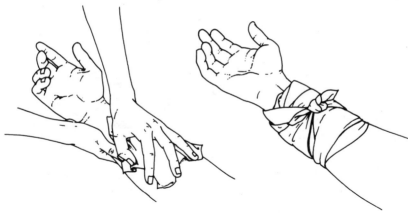

Stopping the bleeding. Left: direct pressure stops most bleeding. If no proper dressing is available, place a piece of clean clothing between the wound and the hand. Right: the dressing may be tied in place if you cannot continue direct hand pressure. (You may also tie it in place when the bleeding stops.) Make sure that you do not remove the original piece of cloth; if necessary, add more layers of cloth on top of it.

bleeding from a vein ("venous bleeding") because arterial blood is under higher pressure. Blood spurts rapidly from severed arteries. This can be frightening, but the treatment is the same—the application of firm, direct pressure.

• Do not apply a tourniquet unless you are specially trained in emergency medicine. Tourniquets can be extremely hazardous. They are appropriate only in cases of otherwise uncontrollable torrential bleeding when you're prepared to sacrifice the limb to save the person's life.

• If any bones or internal organs protrude from the wound or appear injured, touch them as little as possible. Don't push them back inside. Simply cover them with a moistened cloth.

• Meanwhile, talk to the person and look for signs of shock:

  ○ Confusion
  ○ Weakness
  ○ Nausea
  ○ Moist and cool ("clammy") skin
  ○ Rapid, shallow breathing
  ○ Weak, rapid ("thready") pulse

Shock is a life-threatening emergency and may be more dangerous than the wound that caused the bleeding. Treatment requires an emergency medical facility, but first aid can make the difference between the person's life or death:

Treating shock. Raise the feet and keep the accident victim warm to prevent or to treat shock.

• Position the person on his or her back with legs elevated to encourage blood return to the vital organs of the central body and head. (In cases involving a head injury, elevate the head.) (See illustrations.)

• Keep the person as warm as possible. Use blankets and your own clothing if necessary. Be sure to place insulation under as well as over the person and cover the head, neck, and hands, which can radiate a great deal of heat. If necessary, lie down beside the person and hug him or her close to you to share your body heat until professional help arrives or until you reach an emergency medical facility.

BROKEN BONES

Bone breaks ("fractures") usually cause a cracking or snapping sound, with limb deformity and discoloration from bleeding beneath the skin. If you don't hear the characteristic breaking sound and observe the other tip-offs to a fracture, chances are the injury is a muscle, ligament, or tendon problem (see MUSCLE STRAINS, MUSCLE TEARS, SPRAINS, and TENDINITIS in Chapter 15).

Fractures may involve one clean break ("simple fracture") or a shattered bone with many breaks ("comminuted"). They may also cause no breaks in the skin ("closed"), or the broken bone ends may poke through the skin ("compound"). Compound fractures demand extra attention because broken skin means there is an increased risk of infection.

• If there are other people around, ask if any are medical professionals or trained in first aid. If so, defer to them, but let them know you're ready to help. If not, have someone call 911 for help and transportation to an emergency medical facility.

• Make the injured person as comfortable as possible. Place blankets or your own clothing over and under the person for warmth. Be sure to cover the head, neck, and hands, which can radiate a great deal of heat.

• While covering the person, move the broken limb as little as possible.

• If a compound fracture bleeds profusely, apply firm pressure and consider the possibility of shock (see BLEEDING in this chapter).

• Decide whether to wait for help or take the person to an emergency facility. This decision depends on several factors: which bone is fractured, where you are, and how many of you there are. Broken arms leave the injured person more mobile than broken legs, ankles, or feet. Waiting for help is more of an option in a town than it is twenty miles out in the wilderness. And if you're part of a large group, you might be able to carry the injured person or have someone go for help while others remain with the victim.

• Ideally, get the person to an emergency medical facility as quickly as possible. But if emergency transportation is unavailable, follow these additional steps:

• Rinse the wound of a compound fracture gently with clean water to remove obvious dirt, apply antibiotic ointment generously if it's available, and cover the wound gently with sterile gauze or the cleanest cloth available.

• Assuming that the person is conscious, not pregnant, and can swallow, give pain medication. Any pain-reliever will do: aspirin, ibuprofen, or acetaminophen. However, because aspirin and ibuprofen may interfere with blood clotting, these drugs should not be used to treat compound fractures or fractures that may require surgery.

• If you must move the person, prepare to splint the fracture. Before doing so, use a knife or scissors to cut any clothing away from the injured area. Rip it away if necessary. The injured area will swell, possibly a great deal. Clothing acts like a tourniquet, preventing blood flow and possibly threatening the limb. Removing clothing also provides cloth for padding and tying the splint.

• Then "splint 'em as you find 'em," even if the limb is deformed. This rule follows from the idea that broken bones should be moved as little as possible. Splints can be made from anything stiff that's handy: tree or shrub branches, pack frames, fishing poles, walking sticks, and in a pinch, even a tightly rolled up blanket. The splint should extend beyond the joints on either side of the injury. If a leg is broken at the calf, the splint should extend beyond the knee and ankle (see illustrations). Of course, sometimes available splints are not long enough. In that case, do the best with whatever you have.

• Pad and tie the splint securely *but not too tightly*. Fractured limbs swell

Various splinting techniques.

Left: for an ankle, knee, or leg injury. Right: for an ankle or foot injury.

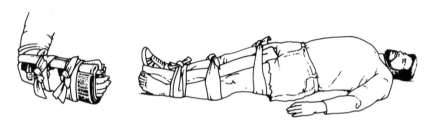

Left: for a wrist or hand injury. Right: for a knee or leg injury.

up, and splints invariably get tighter. As swelling progresses, loosen the bindings to prevent any tourniquet effect. If the person's toes or fingers begin to tingle or feel numb, the splint is too tight. Even if the person does not complain of tingling, numbness, or tightness, check the splint frequently. Don't let the bindings get too tight.

CHOKING

Dozens of Americans die in choking accidents each year. Choking deaths occur suddenly and out of the blue. One minute you're enjoying a great meal and laughing at a companion's jokes, and the next, something gets caught in your throat. If you or someone else doesn't react almost immediately, you're dead.

People often use the term "choking" when they are actually gagging or coughing. In gagging and coughing, some food meant to descend into the stomach along the food tube ("esophagus") instead enters the windpipe ("trachea") and the person gags or coughs it back out, with no interruption of breathing. But in true choking, the food becomes tightly lodged in the vocal cords and the person cannot gag, cough, or even breathe. Unless the food is removed, the person suffocates.

Because choking blocks the vocal cords ("larynx"), chokers cannot talk, so they can't ask for help. Typically, they draw attention to their predicament by clutching at their throats and looking surprised and frightened.

The object blocking the trachea is like a cork in a plastic bottle. If you squeeze the bottle forcefully enough, the air in the bottle—or in this case, in the person's lungs—pops the cork out. That's the theory behind the choking rescue technique known as the "Heimlich maneuver."

• **The Heimlich Maneuver** *(see illustrations).*

• If you see any behavior that might be choking, immediately ask if the person can talk or cough. If so, it's not choking.

• If the person cannot talk or cough, minimize panic and struggling by providing reassurance that you know the Heimlich maneuver and can help.

• Then step behind the person and clasp your hands around his or her abdomen below the ribcage.

• Make a fist with one hand and hold the thumb side in against the person.

• Then grasp the fist with your other hand and thrust your fist forcefully in and up.

• If one forceful thrust does not restore free breathing, repeat the procedure.

• If the victim is pregnant or overweight or simply bigger than you and you're unable to reach all the way around, use the same grasped-fist technique but apply the upward thrusts higher up on the chest.

• If the victim loses consciousness despite your best efforts, lay the person down gently face up and apply upper abdominal thrusts with the heel of your hand. Then turn the person's head sideways and check the mouth for dislodged food.

• If the choker is unconscious by the time the trapped object has been expelled, have someone call 911 for emergency medical help. If the person is not breathing or has no pulse, begin CPR.

Don't slap the choker's back if he or she is over one year old. For years, many first-aid authorities—including the American Red Cross—recommended alternating Heimlich's abdominal up-thrusts with four back blows, which were thought to help dislodge objects trapped in the trachea. However, in recent years, first-aid experts—including Dr. Henry Heimlich, who invented the maneuver—have advised vehemently against back blows, based on studies showing that they may actually lodge the

The Heimlich maneuver. Do not do the Heimlich maneuver if the victim can talk or cough. This indicates that the airway is not completely blocked.

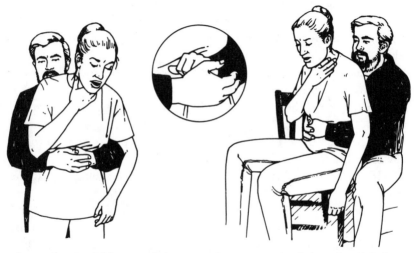

As you thrust quickly upward, be prepared to support the victim, who might lose consciousness and fall to the floor.

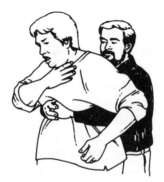

Chest thrust technique for large or pregnant victims and for small children.

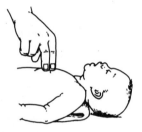

For an infant, use only two fingers.

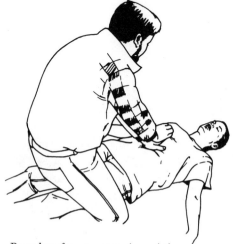

Procedure for an unconscious victim.

Make sure to check the mouth with your fingers after the thrust.

Self-rescue for choking.

object more permanently in the throat. In 1985, the American Red Cross dropped the back-blow recommendation and now advises only the Heimlich maneuver for choking. However, four back blows are still recommended for choking in infants less than one year old.

But what if you start choking and no one notices? Or no one knows the Heimlich maneuver? Not to worry. The Heimlich maneuver can be adapted into a self-rescue technique. Simply lean over the back of a chair and drop your abdomen down onto it. Throwing yourself on a chair accomplishes the same ends as the Heimlich's up-thrusts.

CPR courses (see BE PREPARED in this chapter) teach the Heimlich maneuver.

ELECTROCUTION

(See also FIRE and HEART ATTACK in this chapter and BURNS in Chapter 6)

You need look no farther than the electric chair to know that large jolts of electricity can kill. Electricity passing through the body—from lightning, a downed power line, or a household appliance—can disrupt the heart's rhythmic beating, causing rapid, uncoordinated, quivering contractions ("ventricular fibrillation") and cardiac arrest. The longer the exposure, the greater the risk. But prompt intervention can save a life:

• *Never* touch anyone who is being electrocuted. The human body conducts electricity and if you touch the person, you'll get electrocuted, too.

• If possible, shut off the current by unplugging the appliance. Simply turning it off is often not enough.

• If you can't turn off the current—for example, if the person is wrapped in a downed power line—dry your hands completely and insulate them with dry gloves or a dry cloth. Then stand on an insulating surface—newspapers, wood, clothing or a rubber mat but *not* the earth or anything metal or wet. Using a nonconducting object—a wooden board, broom handle, or ladder—push the person off the wire or push the wire away from the person (see illustration). Once the wire and victim are safely separated, you may touch the person.

• Lightning passes through the body. As soon as it has passed, you may touch the person.

• Check for breathing and pulse, and begin CPR immediately if necessary.

• Send anyone nearby to call 911 for help.

• If there's any possibility of a head or neck injury, don't move the person. Follow the suggestions in HEAD INJURIES in this chapter.

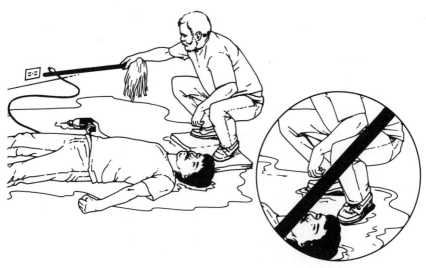

Electrocution. Use a dry wooden or cardboard object—the longer the better—to separate the victim from the current.

• If there's any possibility of shock—cool, moist ("clammy") skin, rapid shallow breathing, confusion—cover the person and raise the legs.

• Wait for help to arrive, or take the person to an emergency medical facility as quickly as possible.

Electric shock burns are often more severe than they appear to be. If an electrical shock leaves any visible skin burn, get the person to an emergency medical facility quickly.

FIRE

More than 70,000 Americans require hospitalization each year because of burns suffered in house fires, and about 10,000 die. Fire injuries are a leading cause of death among children. To save yourself and those you love in a fire emergency:

• Immediately wake up everyone you can reach without endangering your own life and get them out of the house. Fire can consume a home very quickly. Don't waste a moment. Don't get dressed. Don't gather up valuables no matter how much they're worth. Leave immediately.

• Smoke rises. If you're caught in a smoky fire, drop down to your hands and knees and crawl out. It's usually easier to breathe near the floor.

• If exits are blocked by flames or debris, hang roll-up fire ladders or a sheet or blanket out an accessible window and climb down. In a pinch, jump. Jumping risks broken bones and other injuries, but they are less life-threatening than massive burns. If children or the elderly are afraid to jump, jump with them. Just get out as quickly as possible.

• Once everyone is out, call 911. Rouse a neighbor if you have no other phone. Give your address and be as specific as possible about your situation. Is anyone still inside? Is anyone injured? How severely?

• Never go back inside a burning house to save personal property or pets. Your risk of death is quite high.

• If anyone emerges from the building with clothes on fire, roll the person on the ground to smother the flames. If coats or blankets are handy, throw them around the person to help smother the fire.

The same basic rules apply when dealing with rescuing people from burning motor vehicles, except *be sure* to get everyone away from the vehicle. Gasoline explosions are possible.

At theatres, concert halls, and other large public facilities, take a moment to find the fire exit nearest you and the best route to it.

When traveling, beware of hotel fires. Your risk of death is higher in a hotel fire than it is at home, particularly if you live in a nonsmoking household. Someone staying at your hotel is bound to be a smoker, and hotel guests often drink more heavily than they do at home, raising the possibility of a smoker falling asleep while holding a lighted cigarette. Hotel guests' increased alcohol consumption adds to their general disorientation in emergencies. And at a hotel, you may not be familiar with the exit routes. So, when staying at hotels:

• Get yourself oriented. Check for exits near your room and near conference rooms or ballrooms you use.

• Limit your alcohol consumption.

• Fire rules require use of stairs—not elevators—in a fire. Sweeping views are great, but from a fire-safety perspective, you're safer on lower floors, especially if you have any physical problems that make descending stairs difficult.

• If you can't get to a staircase, return to your room, block the door with wet towels, go to the window, and wait for help or instructions from professional firefighters.

• Pack a flashlight. Emergency lighting usually works, but why take chances?

HEAD INJURIES

Head injuries from blows or falls are always potentially dangerous. The main task in first aid is to assess how serious the injury is. If it's not serious, first aid may be all that's necessary. But if it is serious, it's critical to call for emergency professional help as quickly as possible and not aggravate the person's injuries while trying to help.

Head injuries that cause no loss of consciousness are usually not serious unless the person becomes faint or loses consciousness later. But minor head injuries can still be quite frightening because even minor scalp wounds often bleed profusely, unnerving both the victim and first-aiders who do not expect this. Stop any bleeding by applying firm pressure with the heel of your hand or the cleanest cloth available. If the cloth soaks through, leave it in place, apply another on top of it, and continue to apply firm pressure.

Minor scalp blows, cuts, and scrapes may also raise surprisingly large bumps or swellings. To minimize swelling, apply an ice pack. Wrap a few ice cubes in a plastic bag, then wrap the bag in a clean cloth. Press the ice pack into the affected area for twenty minutes, then remove it for ten minutes before reapplying it. An ice substitute may be used instead of ice cubes. Do not apply ice directly to the skin. This may cause the equivalent of frostbite (see HYPOTHERMIA AND FROSTBITE in this chapter). For additional swelling control and to minimize throbbing, keep the head elevated above the level of the heart.

Any blow to the head that causes loss of consciousness suggests a serious head injury. Get the person to an emergency medical facility as quickly as possible. The longer the period of unconsciousness, the more serious the injury is likely to be.

A person who loses consciousness often loses bladder control as well. Wet clothing suggests that the person may have been unconscious, even if he or she is conscious when you arrive.

A potential serious complication of a head injury is a broken neck. If the person is unconscious, assume that the neck is broken and do not move the person. Stop any bleeding, but keep the neck immobile. If the person is conscious but the neck seems deformed, with the head lying at an odd angle, try to keep the person as calm and still as possible until professional emergency help arrives.

Blows or falls may injure the brain itself. These injuries can cause bleeding or swelling inside the skull, which is very serious because the increased pressure inside the skull can interfere with vital brain functions.

In addition to loss of consciousness and possible broken neck, here are the other signs of serious head injuries:

• An increase in the size ("dilation") of the pupil of one eye.

• Clear fluid or blood draining from the nose or ear canal. This suggests a fractured skull.

• Bruises behind one or both ears or around one or both eyes in a "goggle" pattern. This also suggests a fractured skull.

• In infants, any bulging of the soft spot ("fontanelle") on top of the head. (However, this sign may be difficult to judge because ordinary crying may also cause some fontanelle bulging.)

• Vomiting.

• Disorientation and/or drifting in and out of consciousness.

• A pulse of less than 60 beats per minute in adults, or 80 in children.

• Unusual behavior: agitation, lethargy, hostility, or withdrawal.

• Regaining consciousness, then losing it again. This suggests bleeding inside the skull.

To prevent head injuries:

• Always wear a seat belt when driving or riding in a car.

• Always wear an approved helmet when skateboarding or operating or riding as a passenger on a bicycle, motorcycle, or all-terrain vehicle.

• Always wear an approved helmet when boxing or playing football or hockey.

HEART ATTACK

Medically known as "myocardial infarction" or "MI," heart attack is the most dramatic manifestation of heart disease, the nation's leading cause of death. About 1.5 million Americans suffer heart attacks each year and about 500,000 die, often before they reach a hospital. The typical heart-attack death occurs within two hours of the attack. But if more people knew the signs of heart attack, many lives could be saved.

What is an MI? It's the death of a part of the heart muscle caused by a lack of blood supply. Fatty, cholesterol-rich deposits ("atherosclerotic plaques") build up in the arteries that supply oxygen and nourishment to the heart's cells, and when these plaques deny the heart the blood it needs, part of the organ dies.

The myth is that heart attacks are always dramatic—people clutch their chests, look terrified, and keel over. Many heart attacks cause such symptoms, but quite a few do not. Sometimes heart attacks are confused with heartburn (see HEARTBURN in Chapter 13). Common symptoms include:

• Chest pain, which may be mild to crushing or feel more like pressure or squeezing.

• Burning in the chest, indistinguishable from heartburn, which may occur in association with or independent of eating.

• Chest pain that radiates up under the jaw or out to the right or left shoulder or arm (though more commonly, the left side is affected).

- Sweating.
- Nausea.
- Shortness of breath.
- Dizziness.
- A feeling of impending doom, which causes anxiety and agitation.

If you're with someone who has any of these symptoms for more than ten minutes, take action. People often deny or dismiss heart attack symptoms—especially when all they feel is a "funny heartburn"—but if you suspect a heart attack, don't delay. *Get help.* Either take the person to an emergency room or call 911, say "Suspected heart attack," and give your location and the person's symptoms. Then wait for instructions and don't hang up until the 911 operator does.

If the person can swallow without difficulty and is not allergic to aspirin, immediately give him or her one standard tablet. Aspirin helps dissolve the internal blood clots that trigger a heart attack. Studies show that those who take aspirin as soon as they suspect a heart attack have a better chance of surviving than those who don't. (And if it turns out the suspected heart attack was just heartburn, there's still no harm done.)

While waiting for the ambulance or on the way to the emergency room, make the person as comfortable as possible. Loosen a tight collar and other constricting clothing. To relieve nausea, have the person lie down. But don't give the person anything to eat or drink. Choking is a real possibility. Then talk to the person. Reassure him or her that if it is a heart attack, survival chances are very good with prompt emergency medical attention. Reassurance is crucial. Heart attack sufferers often panic, which places considerable strain on their already-damaged hearts.

If the person loses consciousness, check for pulse and breathing, and if necessary, begin CPR.

If convulsions occur, make sure the person's head is protected, and wait until they pass. Then check for breathing and if you don't detect any, start CPR.

Sometimes, after rushing to the emergency room, you find out that the suspected heart attack is, in fact, heartburn or some other relatively minor problem. Don't feel embarrassed. Plenty of physicians experience particularly strong heartburn and become convinced that *they* are having heart attacks. It's better to be safe than sorry, especially if the person has any heart disease risk factors: smoking, obesity, diabetes, high blood pressure, high cholesterol, high stress, sedentary life-style, and/or a personal or family history of heart disease.

Of course the best way to prevent heart attacks is to reduce your risk of heart disease. See Chapter 1 for heart-healthy life-style suggestions.

HEATSTROKE

Also known as "sunstroke," this emergency strikes in hot, very humid weather and usually affects the elderly, those with chronic illnesses, or those taking diuretics for high blood pressure or congestive heart failure or certain drugs ("phenothiazines") for mental health problems.

Symptoms of heatstroke include lethargy, stupor, confusion, agitation, rapid pulse, and hot, red, dry skin. Loss of consciousness is possible.

Heatstroke results from a malfunction in the body's temperature-regulating mechanisms. Sweating, which cools the body, ceases, and internal temperature rises to dangerous levels (104° or higher).

If heatstroke occurs:

• Send someone to call 911 for an ambulance.

• Move the person as quickly as possible to a cool spot, ideally into an air-conditioned building, but if that's not possible, a shady place.

• Cool the person by pouring cold water on his or her clothing and using sheets soaked in cool water as a wrap.

• If a thermometer is handy, keep taking the person's temperature and discontinue the cold-water treatment when his or her temperature declines to 102°.

To prevent heatstroke, use common sense in hot, humid weather:

• Don't overdo outdoor strenuous activities, especially from 10:00 A.M. to 4:00 P.M.

• Wear light clothing.

• Drink plenty of fluids.

• Stay out of the sun.

• If you feel at all woozy, get into a cool or air-conditioned environment and drink fluids.

HYPOTHERMIA AND FROSTBITE

Skiing, sledding, ice skating, hockey, and other winter activities are great fun, but they can cause a major hazard of cold-weather recreation—an inability to maintain adequate body temperature ("hypothermia").

• **Hypothermia.**   The thermometer need not dip below freezing to trigger hypothermia. The condition can occur in temperatures as high as 50° if the cold is accompanied by wind or wetness or if the person is exhausted. The elderly and children under five years of age are particularly susceptible to hypothermia and can develop it even indoors.

Frequently, those who become hypothermic have no idea what's happening to them until it's too late. As the body's inner core becomes progressively chilled, both physical and mental collapse occur. Hypothermia typically begins with an attack of chills, followed by slow, slurred speech and memory lapses. The hands and feet become numb and victims usually feel overwhelmed by exhaustion and drowsiness. They may deny that anything is wrong but already be in serious trouble. Without immediate help, they may slip into a coma and die.

If you suspect hypothermia:

• Taking the person's temperature may not show it. The typical household thermometer does not register below 94°. If the thermometer does not register higher than 96°, assume the person is hypothermic.

• Get the person out of the wind, rain, and/or cold and gently remove all of his or her wet clothing.

• If the person is still conscious and capable of swallowing without choking, give hot drinks and get the person into warm dry clothes, a warm sleeping bag, or under warm blankets. Have another person climb into the sleeping bag with the hypothermia victim to share body heat.

• Never give alcohol to "warm someone up." Alcohol initially feels warming, but physiologically, it increases heat loss by opening up ("dilating") blood vessels near the surface of the skin.

• If the person seems to be losing consciousness, do anything necessary to preserve wakefulness. Talk, slap the person's cheeks, and sandwich the person between two warm bodies.

• If the person stops breathing or if you cannot detect a pulse, begin CPR immediately and keep it up until professional help arrives. If you can't call for help, wrap the person up as warmly as possible—making sure to cover the head, neck, and hands—and transport him or her to emergency medical help. During transport, jostle the person as little as possible.

• Rewarming a person with severe hypothermia is tricky. First-aiders should attempt it only if the person cannot be brought quickly to an emergency medical facility.

To prevent hypothermia:

• Don't drink alcohol out-of-doors in cool or cold wet weather. It decreases stamina and mental acuity and causes heat loss, which can contribute to hypothermia.

• Plan ahead before venturing out for any extended length of time in cold weather. Eat well to keep your strength up and carry snacks as provisions in case of emergency. Always take foul-weather gear, even if the sky is clear. Wear wool clothing, not cotton. Cover your head, neck, and hands. Tents should always be strong, waterproof, and windproof. Carry a gas stove with extra gas. Always carry a reliable fire-starter—a plumber's candle or flammable paste.

• Use your equipment. If you're getting cold and wet, don't hike that last mile. Stop, make camp, and get warm and dry as soon as possible.

• Remember, the elderly and children under five are highly susceptible to hypothermia. Even if you don't feel wet and chilled, they might.

• *Frostbite.*   Frostbite is a painful and potentially serious injury to the skin and the nerves, muscle cells, and blood vessels near the skin surface. Frostbite means that the tissue has become frozen with ice crystals within and between cells. Symptoms include numbness, prickling, and itching. As frostbite progresses, the frozen skin becomes hard to the touch and loses all feeling. Once the skin loses feeling, it appears whitish or yellow. One of the dangers of frostbite is that people may be unaware they are getting it.

Frostbite occurs in severely cold, windy weather. The key to susceptibility is the wind-chill factor, not just the temperature. In high winds, frostbite can occur at relatively high temperatures. At 20° with no wind, frostbite might develop, but it's not much of a risk. But at 20° in a 45-mile-an-hour wind, the wind-chill equivalent temperature is − 40° and frostbite is a real possibility after even a brief exposure.

The body parts most likely to become frostbitten are the nose, ear-lobes, cheeks, fingers, and toes. Risk increases if these body parts are covered by wet clothing or clothing so tight that it restricts blood flow, particularly tight gloves.

Other risk factors for frostbite include a previous history of frostbite, smoking, sensitivity to cold, getting wet, or having drunk alcohol or taken other drugs.

If you suspect frostbite:

• Forget the myths. One myth is: Rub the affected part with snow. Never rub the affected part with snow. Another advises: Massage the frozen part. Wrong. Touch the frozen part as little as possible. A third says: Don't thaw the frozen part rapidly. Wrong again.

• Get to a warm environment as quickly as possible. Walking on frozen toes is much less damaging than staying outdoors.

• Begin rewarming the frostbitten part as soon as the person arrives in a reliably warm environment. Just don't begin rewarming if there's any danger of refreezing.

• Rapidly warm the affected part in a warm—but not hot—water bath. This usually takes twenty to thirty minutes. But don't use the frozen part to gauge the temperature of the water. Frostbitten extremities are insensitive to heat and you'll wind up making the water too hot.

• The application of warm wet towels also helps.

• If warm water is not available, wrap the affected part in wool and get the person into a warm sleeping bag. Drinking hot liquids may also help.

• Don't rub, hit, or bump the frostbitten part during rewarming.

• Thawed parts should be kept warm, dry, and clean. They are quite vulnerable to infection.

• Think twice about going out again. Thawed parts are extra-susceptible to becoming frostbitten again.

• After rewarming, get the person to a medical facility promptly. It's difficult for nonprofessionals to assess the depth and degree of frostbite. If the condition is severe, additional treatment may be necessary.

To prevent frostbite:

• Dress for the weather. In addition to wool socks, water-tight footwear, and warm gloves, wear nose, face, and ear protection.

• Dress in layers. Your outermost layer should be wind- and waterproof.

• Pace your outdoor activities. Don't overexert yourself. Don't become exhausted or drenched in perspiration.

• Never touch bare flesh to cold metal.

• Don't smoke. Smoking decreases blood flow to the extremities.

• Don't drink alcohol before or during cold-weather activities. Alcohol initially feels warming but actually causes heat loss.

LOSS OF CONSCIOUSNESS

(See also BLEEDING, CHOKING, ELECTROCUTION, HEAD INJURIES, HEART ATTACK, HEATSTROKE, HYPOTHERMIA AND FROSTBITE, MOTOR VEHICLE ACCIDENTS, POISONING AND OVERDOSES, and SEIZURES in this chapter and FAINTING AND LIGHTHEADEDNESS and STROKE in Chapter 7)

If you don't know why the person has lost consciousness:

• Start with "A.B.C." Check the person's *A*irway, *B*reathing, and *C*irculation (pulse). Begin CPR if necessary.

• Send someone to call 911. Be specific with the 911 operator. Is the person breathing? Is there a pulse?

• Keep the person warm if the weather is cool, or cool if the weather is hot, but do not move the person unless absolutely necessary.

• Keep the person's head down at or below heart level to improve circulation to the brain, unless you suspect a head injury. If you must move the person to do this, keep the neck from moving by having one person hold the head and neck motionless.

MOTOR VEHICLE ACCIDENTS

(See also BLEEDING, BROKEN BONES, FIRE, and HEAD INJU-
RIES in this chapter)

Your first concern in any motor vehicle accident should be the safety
of the uninjured. Get them away from the wreckage as quickly as possible.
Vehicles generally do not explode except on impact. But they may catch
fire, and if they are carrying any containers of flammable materials, those
items may explode.

Assess the situation before sending anyone to call 911 or to rouse
people who live nearby. Do you or the car(s) involved in the accident have
first-aid kits, flares, blankets, splinting materials, flashlights, or other necessary items? If not, make sure the person you send for help knows to
return with as many needed items as possible.

Help those who are conscious first. If they are trapped inside, do
anything necessary to free them. Tell them to protect their eyes, then
break the windows by any means necessary. Clear away as much glass as
possible, then help or pull them out. They may still get cut by remaining
glass fragments, but minor cuts are preferable to remaining in a vehicle
that might catch fire.

There are two exceptions to the "get them out" rule—people who are
unconscious, and people who might have broken necks. Assess the situation, and if the car or truck does not seem to be at risk of catching fire,
rolling down a hill, or off a cliff, consider leaving the person inside. Any
unnecessary movement may cause a spinal injury and leave the person
paralyzed. Simply cover the person with any available blankets and/or
clothing to conserve body heat and wait for professional assistance.

If you must move an unconscious person or anyone with a suspected
neck injury, the best approach is to position yourself behind the person,
supporting the head and neck against your chest. Then wrap your arms
around the person's trunk under the arms and pull the person backwards,
making every effort not to move the neck. But beware, this type of carry
places considerable strain on the rescuer's back. If you have a history of
back problems, it's not a good idea to attempt this, but you'll have to
decide for yourself.

The next step is to sort ("triage") the injured according to the severity
and treatability of their injuries. Treat those with the most serious *but
treatable* injuries first. In a serious multi-vehicle accident, the number and
gravity of injuries often overwhelms untrained first-aiders. Deal with
those you feel best able to help. If you're faced with a choice between
helping someone with massive injuries pinned under a wreck or one with

severe but controllable bleeding, assist the latter first. If you try to save everyone, you may sacrifice everyone.

Triage is a terrible responsibility, especially for the untrained first-aider. Stay as calm as possible, and do the best you can. Try not to become paralyzed by thoughts of all those you can't help. Instead, focus on those you can, and do your best for them.

When you've decided to help someone, first make sure the person is breathing and has a pulse. If not, begin CPR immediately.

Once you know that those you're helping are breathing and have a pulse, look for bleeding. To stop bleeding use the heel of your hand or any cloth available to apply firm pressure to the wound. If you're dealing with head or limb wounds, raise the injured part above the level of the person's heart. Scalp wounds tend to bleed profusely, even minor ones. Spurting blood means a severed artery and the possible loss of a great deal of blood and shock. But the treatment is the same: the application of firm direct pressure.

A person who appears confused or agitated and has cool, moist ("clammy") skin and a weak, rapid pulse is probably in shock. Elevate the person's feet and arms to encourage blood return to the central body. Lower the head unless you suspect a neck injury. Then cover the person with a blanket, coat, or whatever is available. Be sure to place insulation between the person and the ground as well.

For burns, apply cool wet compresses over the affected area. Do not open any blisters. Protect them. Blisters are nature's bandages. They help keep the injured skin under the blister's fluid from becoming infected. If burns cover an extensive area, cover the person with blankets, coats, or whatever is available.

For possible broken bones ("fractures"), find something like a straight tree or bush branch or a straight piece of wreckage and use it as a splint. Ideally, splints should extend beyond the joints on either side of the suspected fracture. Cut away any clothing around the suspected fracture. Bone breaks swell, and you don't want clothing to become a tourniquet. If bone fragments protrude through the skin, don't push them back in or attempt to straighten the limb. Splint broken bones as you find them. Move them as little as possible. Secure splints with anything that's available: rope, the victim's clothing, or your clothing. Don't tie splints too tight or you risk creating a tourniquet as the injured area swells. Check splints periodically, and as the injury swells, loosen the ties.

What about liability? You've probably heard stories about people who attempted to help, only to be sued for any mistakes they made. In most states, if you render first-aid in good faith and do the best you can, you are protected from lawsuits. If you were in a motor vehicle accident, you'd certainly want people to stop and help and not just drive by.

NEAR DROWNING

Drowning is the fourth leading cause of accidental death, and among those who enjoy swimming, boating, or fishing, it ranks second only to motor vehicle accidents.

Childhood drownings often result from poor supervision, particularly in bathtubs. Never leave a young child unattended in a bathtub, even for a few moments. If you must leave momentarily, insist that any child old enough to talk do so or sing until you return.

Adult drownings typically involve unexpected immersion—falling off a dock or boat—when under the influence of alcohol or other drugs.

Here's how to prevent near-drownings from becoming drownings:

• Size up the situation. Most drownings are the result of panic within reach of safety—docks, boats, etc. The typical victim dies of choking from panic ("asphyxiation") and not from water flooding the lungs. If you hear a cry for help from the water, check to see if anyone else is extending a hand, rope, or life preserver. Yell for someone to call 911. Then ask if anyone nearby is trained in lifesaving. Water rescues are tricky even for trained lifesavers. Those who are untrained often inadvertently risk their own lives in naive attempts to save others. Always defer to trained lifesavers. Authorities advise never risking your own life to save someone else. Of course, if you find yourself observing a near-drowning and the victim is a loved one, you'll have to decide for yourself.

• Follow the sequence: Reach, Throw, Go. First try to reach the victim by staying out of the water and extending a hand, pole, or anything handy. If you can't reach, then try to throw something—a rope or life preserver. If you can neither reach nor throw, then consider whether you should go, that is, enter the water yourself.

• If you decide to go, approach the water very carefully. This is especially true in the ocean, where powerful currents and undertows can overwhelm even strong swimmers.

• Once you're in the water, approach the person very carefully. Shout that you're coming to help, but *don't* approach within arm's length— grabbing distance. Near drownings invariably cause panic. If given the chance, a panicked swimmer always grabs a potential rescuer with an instinctive death-grip bear hug, and both of you may drown. If at all possible, swim out with something the person can grab: a board, paddle, oar, air mattress, or styrofoam float—anything other than your hand.

• From a safe distance, talk to the person. Many people involved in near-drownings can swim, but fatigue, injury, and/or drugs overwhelm them and cause panic. Ask, "Are you okay?" Encourage them to talk. Talking is calming. Then say, "Everything will be all right. Just do as I say." Instruct the person to remove any clothing that might become water-logged and make swimming difficult, particularly jackets, shoes, or boots. Then urge self-help: "Relax. Breathe deeply. Float. I'm right here. The boat's right there. Stop flailing. Relax. Swim toward me." Sometimes, simple reassurance helps the person recover enough to swim to safety unassisted. But if not:

• Approach the person from behind. Announce in advance that you're going to do this and instruct the person to keep arms outstretched away from you. If the person spins around and won't let you approach from behind, *don't* move in. If you do, you're risking your life. If you can approach from behind, grab some clothing, or cup the person's chin in one hand and pull the victim into a back float. Keep up a steady stream of reassurance: "Relax. Breathe deeply. You're okay. You're floating. Everything's going to be fine." Then tow the person to safety. You don't have to be big or strong to do this. Instruct the rescuee to help by using the backstroke. And don't hesitate to shout for assistance from other people.

• If you move in from behind but, at the last minute, the person spins around and lunges for you, break the death grip by any means necessary, then try again to approach safely from behind without being grabbed. If necessary, conserve your own strength and wait until the person has become completely exhausted. This may sound unfeeling, but it's not. Once in a panicked person's death grip, your life is in real jeopardy.

• If you get grabbed, don't fight—dive. A person in the throes of panic can muster unbelievable strength. Avoid the death grip at all costs, but if you get bear-hugged, do anything necessary to submerge as quickly and deeply as you can. Very few near-drowning victims maintain a death grip if doing so drags them under water. Once you've escaped the panicked person's clutches, surface, collect your wits, keep your distance, and try to talk the person into cooperating again.

• If a person pulled from the water is not breathing, initiate CPR immediately.

• Near-drowning rescues often involve friends or loved ones, and rescuers sometimes fear that after being rescued, the person will castigate them for refusing to approach or for using force to break any grips. Don't worry. Near-drowning victims have *no memory* of their actions—or yours—while they were panicked. They may act literally psychotic from panic and lunge at your ferociously, but once safe on shore and calmed down, they typically become sheepish and say, "I guess I got a little tired out there, didn't I?"

POISONING AND OVERDOSES

The moment you suspect a poisoning, call your local Poison Control Center, listed in the white pages of you phone book under "Poison." If it's busy, call 911. Tell the operator as much of the following as you know:
- The substance taken.
- How much was taken.
- When.
- The victim's age and health status.
- Whether the victim has vomited.
- How far you are from emergency medical help.

Then wait for instructions and follow them. If the victim is conscious, you may be told to do one of two things: dilute the poison by giving the victim lots of water or milk, or induce vomiting. To induce vomiting give syrup of ipecac, an "emetic" (vomiting inducer) which every household should have but, surveys show, few actually possess. If you don't have syrup of ipecac, put it on your shopping list *now*.

However, do not give ipecac if you cannot identify the substance swallowed or if the poison is an acid (such as industrial drain cleaner), alkali (such as lye or Drano), or petroleum product (such as gasoline or lighter fluid). In these cases, there is too much damage to the throat or breathing passages from re-exposure to the poison during vomiting, so simply dilute the poison by giving the person plenty of water.

If the person is convulsing, loosen any clothing around the neck and protect the person from self-injury. For additional information, see SEIZURES in this chapter.

If the person is unconscious, check for breathing and pulse. If you don't detect either one or both, begin CPR immediately, and continue it until help arrives or until the person can be taken to an emergency medical facility.

Poisoning is a leading cause of childhood death. Keep all toxic chemicals out of the reach of children.

Common household poisons include:
- Alcohol. An amount that might only get an adult drunk can kill—yes, *kill*—a child.
- Cigarettes.
- All drugs, both over-the-counter and prescription.
- Bleach.

- Toilet cleaner.
- Drain cleaner.
- Oven cleaner.
- Furniture polish.
- Weedkillers.
- Insecticides and insect repellants.
- Paint thinner.
- Paint remover.
- Cosmetics.
- Many houseplants.

SEIZURES

(See also HEAD INJURIES in this chapter and SEIZURES in Chapter 7)

You're standing in line waiting to get into a hit movie. Suddenly, a man in front of you collapses and starts writhing on the sidewalk. He shakes all over, and his right arm flails especially wildly. Other people in line shrink back aghast. Someone says, "It's an epileptic fit!" What should you do?

It's not a "fit." It's a grand mal seizure, the most potentially hazardous manifestation of the many kinds of seizures known as epilepsy (see SEIZURES in Chapter 7). Seizures are electrical "short circuits" in the brain that overwhelm the mechanisms that maintain consciousness. Seizures may be caused by injuries, infection, drug withdrawal, structural abnormalities in the brain, abnormal levels of certain nutrients, or tumors. The causes of many seizures are a mystery. Grand mal seizures involve sudden loss of consciousness, characteristic jerky movements, and possibly serious head and neck injury from falling (see HEAD INJURIES in this chapter).

An estimated two million Americans suffer seizures. Seizures may strike anyone at any age, but about 75 percent of first seizures occur during childhood, and most have no obvious trigger.

There is no first aid to stop grand mal seizures themselves. Most simply stop by themselves within thirty seconds to thirty minutes. When the jerky movements stop, the person wakes up—usually groggy and confused, with no memory of the seizure.

However, seizures require rapid, careful first-aid intervention because loss of consciousness may lead to serious medical problems, possibly even death.

- First, see if any medical professionals or certified first-aiders are nearby. If so, defer to them, but let them know you're available to help.

• If no professionals are available, send someone as quickly as possible to call 911. The caller should give your precise location and, ideally, describe the seizing person's movements as specifically as possible. Seizure movements provide important clues to the type and severity of the problem. If a phone is available nearby, keep the line open and follow the operator's instructions. If not:

• Check your watch to time the episode. This may seem odd, but it's very important. Seizure duration is crucial to accurate diagnosis and treatment.

• Then determine if the episode is really a seizure. In a typical grand mal seizure, the person suddenly loses consciousness, falls down (often with a guttural cry), becomes stiff for a few seconds, then jerks spasmodically with drooling and snoring-type breathing noises. The jerky movements last thirty seconds to thirty minutes, sometimes punctuated with periods of rest. If the person can talk to you and understand simple commands, the episode is *not* a seizure. Suspect a traumatic injury such as a blow to the head or a drug or alcohol problem. In case of a true seizure:

• Protect the airway and restore breathing. Airway obstruction is a leading cause of death in cases of head injury. It frequently results from vomiting during unconsciousness. If the person vomits, do your best to clear the mouth and nose of debris. Try not to use your fingers. You might get bitten. (If you do, see BITE WOUNDS in Chapter 6.) Simply keep the head or the entire body turned to one side. Don't force any object into the mouth. Contrary to popular belief, you won't prevent tongue biting, but you might push the tongue back, blocking the throat.

• Protect the neck. Anytime a person falls unconscious, a neck injury should be suspected. A neck injury is probable if the head lies at an odd angle. Neck injuries are extremely serious and may cause paralysis. Immediately immobilize the head and neck using whatever is available—rolled-up clothing is often handiest. But *do not move the person's neck,* especially if it appears at all injured. If the head must be turned to one side to clear vomit from the airway, use the "logroll" technique, which takes two people. One person holds the head and neck in a fixed position so there's no neck movement and gently turns them as the other person rolls the torso and legs.

• Protect the person who is having the seizure from self-injury. Use cushions, clothing, or anything handy. Loosen all clothing from around the neck. But you don't have to restrain movements that do not threaten self-injury.

• Look for a MedicAlert bracelet or necklace. It may provide clues to the cause of the seizure.

• After the person wakes, expect confusion for up to an hour. As lucidity returns, ask about previous seizures and whether or not the person takes anticonvulsant medication. Medication lapses can trigger seizures. If the person has been remiss about taking prescribed anticonvulsants, the medication should be taken as soon as the person is fully awake and capable of swallowing without choking.

• Ask if the person is diabetic. Low blood sugar is a frequent seizure trigger in diabetics. If diabetes appears to be the culprit, the person should be given some high-sugar foods as soon as normal swallowing is assured.

• Even those who emerge from grand mal seizures quickly and uneventfully should consult a physician as quickly as possible. This happens automatically if they drive off in an ambulance summoned by calling 911. But if a person has a seizure in an area that is not served by a paramedical service, transport the person to an emergency medical facility or contact the person's doctor.

Anyone with a history of seizures should wear a MedicAlert bracelet or necklace (see RESOURCES at the end of this chapter).

SHOCK

(see BLEEDING in this chapter)

RESOURCES

American Red Cross Standard First Aid and Personal Safety Guide. (American Red Cross, revised periodically, $7.95). Obtain a copy from your local Red Cross chapter.

MedicAlert Foundation. For a $25 lifetime membership, you receive a wrist bracelet or necklace which lists your illness and an emergency phone number. Call the number, and operators provide the name and phone number of the person's physician and a list of any required medications. 1-(800)-344-3226 or 1-(800)-432-5378.

CHAPTER 4

Whole Body

Health Problems

ALLERGIES

Allergies are the result of an overzealous immune system, the body's complex set of defense reactions. Tens of millions of Americans have some type of allergy.

What's Going On?   When germs enter the body, the white blood cells and specialized proteins of the immune system search them out and destroy them. In allergies, the immune system mistakes harmless things— pollens, molds, dusts, animal dander, and certain foods—for germs and, depending on the type of allergy, mounts different defensive reactions. These reactions may cause such symptoms as nasal congestion, runny nose, watery eyes, and possibly eczema, hives, wheezing, swelling of the tongue and throat, and other annoying, and possibly serious, physical changes.

Depending on the type of allergy, symptoms may appear minutes to days after the offending exposure.

Shortly after insect stings or ingestion of some drugs (for example, penicillin) or some foods, about one person in 200 suffers a whole-body ("systemic") allergic reaction, typically hives. But a few people develop a more serious, in fact, life-threatening, allergic reaction, a form of shock called "anaphylaxis." Anaphylactic shock is a medical emergency. It strikes quickly and causes difficulty breathing, collapse, convulsions, and without prompt treatment, quite possibly death.

Allergies are not classically genetic, but they tend to run in families, with some members affected in every generation. Pregnant women often experience changes in their allergies—about one-third suffer more severe allergy symptoms during pregnancy, about one-third suffer less, and the rest experience no change in their allergy symptoms.

Allergies can develop at any age. It all depends on the allergens you're exposed to. People who never had allergies in one place often develop them when they move. Similarly, moving may eliminate others' symptoms.

In addition to pollens and molds, many allergies are caused by reactions to the house dust mite, a microscopic insect that lives in rugs, upholstery, and bedding and feeds on the flakes of dead skin people constantly shed. The typical home contains millions of dust mites, with the greatest number in areas with high humidity.

Before You Call the Doctor.   The best treatment is to avoid the offending allergen(s). In many cases, these self-care strategies help:

• Tree, grass, and weed pollen counts are highest in the morning. Schedule outdoor activities for the afternoon.

• Keep your home, car, and office windows closed.

• Install home and auto air conditioning. The filters in air conditioners can cut pollen counts in half. Set the air conditioner to "recirculate," which decreases exposure to outside allergens. Have all air conditioners serviced regularly to assure good filtration.

• For best filtration, buy a high-efficiency particulate air (HEPA) filter. These appliances, about the size of a window fan, are available from medical supply houses which sell asthma management equipment.

• Pull up your rugs. If you can't live without them, consider replacing shag rugs with short-pile rugs and vacuum them frequently.

• Use washable throw rugs and machine wash them regularly.

• Vacuum your upholstered furniture regularly.

• Dust regularly. If housecleaning aggravates your allergies, hire someone else to do it or wear a dust mask (sold in hardware stores). Recent studies have shown that the exhaust from most vacuum cleaners increases the amount of allergens in the air. Special "allergy-control" vacuums are worthwhile if you're allergic to the common dust mite. Use a silicone-treated dust rag that causes dust to cling to it.

• To keep dust mites from settling on your mattress, enclose your mattress in a zippered plastic case. Change bedding often and wash blankets frequently.

• Treat any rugs with a chemical that kills dust mites. Ask your pharmacist for a recommendation.

• Change bed linens frequently.

• Replace feather pillows and down comforters with foam or fiberfill.

• If your home or office is damp, buy a dehumidifier.

• To kill molds around sinks and bathtubs, wash them with bleach.

• Consider finding a new home for your pet. If you can't live without your pet, keep it out of your bedroom.

• Take an "allergy-free" vacation in an area without the allergens that affect you. Many hayfever sufferers find relief in desert areas.

• Contact the Asthma and Allergy Foundation of America for more information (see RESOURCES at the end of this chapter).

If allergen avoidance does not provide sufficient relief, try over-the-counter antihistamines, such as chlorpheniramine and diphenhydramine. Unfortunately, these antihistamines cause drowsiness and aren't recommended for people who must drive or operate machinery. Alcohol compounds the problem. However, nonsedating antihistamines are available by prescription (see below).

Decongestant nasal sprays can relieve nasal stuffiness associated with some types of allergies. But don't use them for more than three days in a row or you'll develop "rebound congestion," which causes worse stuffiness than you had to begin with.

Oral decongestants, such as pseudoephedrine (Sudafed), can also help. But decongestant pills can raise blood pressure and may cause insomnia and nervousness.

The rough, dry, scaly skin of eczema can be treated with steroid skin creams (see ECZEMA in Chapter 6).

As a first effort in identifying possible food allergies, try eliminating common food allergens one at a time for at least two weeks and monitor how you feel. Common food allergens include milk, wheat, soy, and eggs, among many others. Unfortunately, this informal approach rarely yields useful results, and a true elimination diet may be necessary.

Here's how to organize a true elimination diet:

• For one week, eat *only* the foods indicated in the box. These foods are unlikely to cause allergic reactions. Eat as much of the allowed foods as you wish.

ELIMINATION DIET

Beverages:
Mineral or spring water
Juices from allowed fruits

Fruits:

Apples	Dates	Pears
Apricots	Figs	Persimmons
Bananas	Grapes	Pineapples
Berries	Kiwis	Plums
Cantaloupe	Mangos	Pomegranates
Casaba	Nectarines	Prunes
Cherries	Papayas	Rhubarb
Coconuts	Peaches	

Meat and Fish:

Deer	Lamb	Turkey
Duck	Pheasant	Water-packed
Game hen	Quail	tuna
Goose	Rabbit	

ELIMINATION DIET (Continued)

Nuts and Seeds:

Almonds	Filberts	Pumpkin seeds
Brazil nuts	Hazelnuts	Sesame seeds
Butternuts	Hickory nuts	Sunflower seeds
Cashews	Macadamia nuts	Tahini
Chestnuts	Pistachios	Water chestnuts

Sweeteners:

Clover honey	Date sugar	Maple syrup

Vegetables:

Artichokes	Collard greens	Parsnips
Asparagus	Cucumbers	Pumpkin
Avocados	Jerusalem	Radishes
Beet greens	artichokes	Rutabaga
Beets	Kale	Spinach
Broccoli	Leeks	Squash (all types)
Brussels sprouts	Mustard greens	Sweet potatoes
Cabbage	Okra	Turnips
Carrots	Olives	Watercress
Cauliflower	Other leafy greens	
Celery	Parsley	

Miscellaneous:

Bay leaves	Caraway	Pear or plum
Buckwheat kasha	Celery seed	vinegar
Buckwheat grits	Cumin	Sea salt
Buckwheat groats	Dill	

• Use fresh or frozen vegetables and fruits without sugar.

• Nuts and seeds should be purchased whole in the shell without additives.

• At the end of the elimination week, your symptoms should have cleared up. If they have not cleared, consult a physician.

• Assuming your symptoms have cleared after a week, begin adding foods back into your diet, one item every other day.

• Pay close attention to how you react to each newly introduced item.

Keep a diary and note any symptoms and the food(s) you believe cause them. For example, if your symptoms clear up during the elimination week but recur when you add cheese to your diet, note this in your diary and stop eating cheese.

• Add foods back in their most basic form. For example, when adding wheat, begin with a plain puffed wheat or cream of wheat cereal (without milk) rather than bread. Bread contains other substances, such as yeast, that might contribute to your symptoms.

• When adding eggs, first try them boiled.

• After about two weeks of adding foods to your diet, you should be eating more or less normally again. At that time, decide if your self-care elimination diet has produced sufficient relief from your symptoms. If so, great. You don't have to see a doctor. But even the most rigorous self-administered elimination diet may prove frustrating and misleading because you're experimenting on yourself. Whenever you do that, you have to expect a strong placebo component. In other words, there's about a one-in-three chance that you'll feel better on *any* elimination diet, even if you do not eliminate the foods to which you are truly sensitive. Then, after the diet is over, you'll develop symptoms again, even though you're eating foods the diet supposedly showed were okay for you. When in doubt, consult an allergist familiar with detecting and treating food allergies.

If allergies cause wheezing or other asthma-type symptoms, see ASTHMA in Chapter 11.

When to Call the Doctor.   If self-care measures and over-the-counter drugs don't provide sufficient relief, ask your physician for a referral to an allergist/immunologist. These specialists can administer tests to see what's causing your allergies and prescribe medications and other treatments not available over the counter.

The physician should take a thorough medical and environmental history, including information about pets, diet, bedding, living conditions, family history, seasonal variations in symptoms, and exposure to chemicals, especially through your job and hobbies. The doctor may also take a nasal smear to differentiate between an allergy and an upper respiratory infection and order a pulmonary function test for additional information about your respiratory system.

Before taking any allergy test, be sure to tell the doctor if you're taking any medications, especially antihistamines, which may interfere with test results.

Here are some of the many tests available to identify allergies. (Note:

Most health insurance companies cover allergy tests, but some do not. Check your policy.)

• Skin tests. There are three types: scratch tests, intradermal tests, and patch tests. In scratch tests, the doctor places small amounts of common allergens on your back, then scratches each area with a pin. If you're allergic, a red welt appears within thirty minutes. The patch and intradermal tests are similar except that the allergens are either taped to the skin with a patch or injected under the skin. Positive reactions provide useful information, but they may be uncomfortable, causing itching and swelling. In rare cases they may produce potentially life-threatening anaphylactic reactions. Skin tests cost $200 to $500 depending on where you live.

• RAST. Short for "Radio Allergosorbent Test," this blood test is less sensitive than skin testing and it's expensive—$10 to $30 per allergen for twenty to thirty allergens.

• Advanced Cell Test (ACT). The ACT was developed by a former National Institutes of Health researcher. Its proponents claim it can identify allergies to 186 different foods.

If over-the-counter antihistamines help your symptoms but cause enough drowsiness to bother you, a physician can prescribe powerful— and nonsedating—antihistamines, such as terfenadine (Seldane) or astemizole (Hismanal). Symptoms of hay fever and asthma-associated allergies can often be prevented with the prescription drug cromolyn sodium (Intal), available as an inhalant, nasal spray, or eyedrops. Steroids available as inhalants or nasal sprays may also be used to prevent the inflammation that causes allergy symptoms.

Allergy shots ("immunotherapy") are another alternative. You receive gradually increasing doses of your allergy triggers and, when it works, over time you stop having the allergic reaction. Allergy shots involve considerable commitment. Treatment usually begins with one or two shots a week for several months and over a few years decreases to one shot a month. However, newer "rushed desensitization" programs can get people to one shot a month in less than a year. Allergy shots usually work better for children than adults, but many adults find them effective.

For food allergies, physicians can arrange a more scientific type of elimination diet, called a DBPCFC, a double-blind, placebo-controlled food challenge, in which you do not eat foods but capsules containing carefully controlled food extracts.

▶ **RED FLAGS**   Pregnant women should not take any allergy medication, including over-the-counter drugs, without consulting their physicians. Pregnant women with asthma need special care because untreated asthma can harm the developing fetus.

Anaphylactic shock is a potentially life-threatening allergic reaction. Symptoms typically develop within thirty minutes of the offending exposure and include:

- Agitation.
- Hives.
- Dizziness.
- Wheezing and difficulty breathing.
- Rapid heart rate.
- Abdominal cramps.
- Nausea and vomiting.

The person quickly loses consciousness and may die unless treated immediately. Anaphylaxis may strike anyone, but people at greatest risk include:

- Those with asthma or other respiratory diseases.
- Those with a history of hives, wheezing, or anaphylactic shock from previous insect stings.

If you notice any of these symptoms, call 911 immediately. If necessary, administer CPR.

People who have had previous anaphylactic reactions, especially to insect stings or foods, should *always* carry an "epi kit," a syringe filled with epinephrine (adrenalin), which is injected into the thigh. This first-aid treatment can be a lifesaver. (Epinephrine is not recommended for the elderly or those with heart disease or high blood pressure because it may trigger a stroke or heart attack.) After using an epi kit, someone should call 911 immediately and request assistance, even if the person seems to be feeling better after the injection. Anaphylactic reactions should be evaluated professionally.

ANEMIA

Anemia causes one or more of the following symptoms: paleness, fatigue, weakness, fainting, headaches, breathlessness, and heart palpitations. In children, it can cause behavior and learning problems.

What's Going On?   Anemia is not a disease. Like fever, it's a sign of many possible health problems. Anemia involves a decrease in the number of red blood cells or a decrease in the amount of hemoglobin, the chemical in red blood cells that carries oxygen throughout the body. Without adequate oxygen, no cell in the body can function properly. Several factors can reduce the number of red blood cells or the amount of hemoglobin inside them and cause anemia:

• Vitamin or mineral deficiencies, such as deficiencies of vitamin B_{12} or folic acid.

• Inherited blood defects, such as sickle-cell anemia.

• A blood problem called "hemolytic anemia," in which the red blood cells are destroyed faster than they are produced.

Anemia can also occur as a symptom of certain acute or chronic illnesses, such as hepatitis, tuberculosis, pneumonia, or rheumatoid arthritis.

The most common cause of anemia—and the number one nutritional deficiency in industrialized countries—is iron deficiency. Iron is an essential component of hemoglobin and is important in the production of new red blood cells. As red blood cells die, the body recovers most of their iron and uses it to make new red cells. The body also obtains additional iron from iron-rich foods, such as spinach and beans.

Unfortunately, diet doesn't always supply enough iron to meet the body's needs. Then the body draws on iron stored in the liver, spleen, and bone marrow. When these stores become depleted, red-blood-cell production suffers. New red blood cells become smaller and paler and are unable to carry sufficient oxygen.

Iron-deficiency anemia is a special risk for babies after six months of age. Babies are born with enough iron to last several months, even if the mother is anemic. For the first few months of life, this natural iron supply protects them from anemia. However, at about six months, babies often develop iron-deficiency anemia unless they are fed iron-supplemented formula and cereals. As they begin to eat solid foods, babies should be introduced to iron-rich foods, such as spinach, peas, and meats.

Adolescents may also suffer iron-deficiency anemia. If they eat large amounts of junk foods instead of foods rich in iron and vitamins, they may not ingest enough iron to keep up with the production of new red blood cells during this time of rapid growth.

Women lose iron every month through menstruation. Usually, this iron loss isn't enough to cause anemia. However, women who have heavy menstrual bleeding may be at risk for iron deficiency.

Iron-deficiency anemia can occur with any excessive blood loss. Surgery or everyday accidents that cause bleeding can cause a temporary decline in the number of red blood cells, but surgery and most accidents don't usually cause anemia. The body copes with temporary blood loss by increasing iron storage and red-blood-cell production. But chronic blood loss as a result of stomach or duodenal ulcers or intestinal cancer can cause anemia.

Finally, sometimes digestive problems impair the body's ability to absorb iron from foods.

Before You Call the Doctor. According to the National Research Council, adult men and postmenopausal women need about 10 mg of iron a day. The recommended daily allowance (RDA) for menstruating women is 18 mg. During the latter half of pregnancy, the placenta requires extra iron. Without supplementation, pregnant women are likely to become anemic.

If anemia is caused by an iron-deficient diet, eat more beans, fish, dried fruits, lean meats, and leafy green vegetables.

If anemia persists, consider iron supplementation. For menstruating and nursing women, a Food and Drug Administration (FDA) Advisory Panel recommends daily supplementation with 10 to 30 mg of elemental iron. For pregnant women, the recommendation is 30 to 60 mg a day. (Pregnant women should consult a physician before taking any vitamins, minerals, or drugs.) For growing children, the FDA recommends supplementation with ½ mg of elemental iron per pound of body weight up to 15 mg a day.

The doses above apply to routine supplementation or mild anemia. More severe anemia and replacement of iron stores requires two to three times the doses listed above.

Iron supplements are available in several forms. Ferrous sulfate is the cheapest. A 325 mg tablet contains 65 mg of elemental iron. Ferrous gluconate (325 mg tablet, 36 mg elemental iron) and ferrous fumarate (150 mg tablet, 50 mg elemental iron) are alternatives that may cause less stomach upset.

Take iron supplements with vitamin C or fruits or juices rich in this vitamin to improve iron absorption.

If iron supplements cause indigestion, take them with meals. Iron may cause constipation (see CONSTIPATION in Chapter 13), and it usually turns the stool dark gray.

Liquid iron supplements can leave brown stains on the teeth of young children. Either squirt the liquid into children's mouths behind their teeth or, preferably, if they are older than one year, mix the supplement liquid in citrus fruit juice, which aids mineral absorption.

When to Call the Doctor. Iron-deficient adults should consult physicians. In adults, iron deficiency anemia typically means chronic blood loss, a situation that should be investigated by a physician. In women, the cause of the blood loss is usually, but not always, menstrual. In men, iron deficiency may have many causes, some potentially serious.

For the small proportion of people who cannot tolerate oral iron supplements, iron injections are an option.

▶ **RED FLAGS**   If you take iron supplements, do not exceed FDA recommendations Too much iron can damage the liver, pancreas, and heart. Keep iron supplements out of the reach of children. Iron overdose can cause poisoning.

BODY ODOR

(See also SWEATING EXCESSIVELY in Chapter 6)

Everyone has a characteristic body odor. It becomes a problem only when it's particularly strong.

What's Going On?   Body odor is caused by the interaction of sweat with the bacteria normally present on the skin. Two types of glands produce sweat: "eccrine glands," which regulate temperature and play a relatively modest role in body odor, and "apocrine glands," which respond to emotions and produce sweat rich in organic substances that combine with bacteria to cause body odor. Apocrine glands become activated during puberty, which is why body odor is rarely a problem before then. Apocrine glands are concentrated under the arms, around the nipples, and in the groin.

Before You Call the Doctor.   Americans are obsessed with eliminating body odors. We spend more than $700 million annually on deodorants, antiperspirants, skin creams and lotions, feminine hygiene products, and other concoctions designed to mask or eliminate our natural scents.

There are three ways to mask or diminish body odors—reduce the number of bacteria on the skin, decrease sweating, and/or replace natural body odor with another scent.

Regular washing with soap and water also helps eliminate bacteria on the skin. Some soaps contain antimicrobial agents such as triclocarban (in Coast, Dial, Zest, and Safeguard) and triclosan (Lifebuoy) to further reduce bacteria. However, these chemicals can be absorbed through the skin, raising questions about their safety. Most authorities believe the small amounts absorbed during bathing are safe, but no one has established the safety of using these products over a lifetime.

Antiperspirants reduce sweating while also masking odors with a perfume.

Deodorants contain antimicrobial agents which reduce bacteria and mask natural odor with other fragrances.

For most people, regular washing and use of a deodorant or antiperspirant adequately controls body odor. Those who suffer from sweaty, odorous feet should wash them frequently, wear open shoes whenever possible, and wear hose or socks of cotton or wool rather than silk or synthetic fibers.

So-called "feminine hygiene sprays" are a waste of money. They often cause vaginal irritation and can mask odors arising from vaginal infections, delaying necessary treatment.

The same goes for douches—only more so. A study in the *Journal of the American Medical Association* recently linked regular douching to significant risk of pelvic inflammatory disease (PID), a potentially fatal infection of the reproductive organs, which is a leading cause of infertility in women (see DOUCHING in Chapter 16). The healthy vagina is a self-cleansing organ. For best odor control, wash the area regularly, change underwear frequently, and wear cotton or cotton-lined underwear.

When to Call the Doctor.   If you believe you sweat excessively ("hyperhidrosis"), discuss your condition with your physician or ask for a referral to a dermatologist. Drysol, a potent prescription antiperspirant, may help. Drysol has a higher concentration of aluminum chlorhydrate than over-the-counter antiperspirants, and it's more likely to cause skin irritation.

CHINESE RESTAURANT SYNDROME

(See MONOSODIUM GLUTAMATE (MSG) INTOLERANCE in this chapter)

CHRONIC FATIGUE SYNDROME

(See FATIGUE in this chapter)

DIABETES

An estimated 12 million Americans have diabetes, but only about half know it. Diabetes is one of the nation's most serious chronic diseases, a factor in more than 250,000 deaths each year, according to the Centers for Disease Control. The good news is that diabetics have the power to keep themselves healthy with a few life-style adjustments.

What's Going On?   More than 2,000 years ago, the ancients noticed that some people produced copious amounts of strangely sweet-smelling urine. They named the condition "diabetes mellitus," from the Greek for "fountain" and the Latin for "honey."

Diabetes occurs when the body stops producing the pancreatic hormone insulin or becomes unable to use the insulin it produces. Without insulin, blood sugar ("glucose"), the body's major fuel, cannot enter our cells. It builds up in the bloodstream and eventually turns up in the urine, causing the sweet aroma the ancients noticed. The high sugar content of the urine draws water out of the body, causing increased urination and thirst. For reasons not well understood, diabetes also causes narrowing of the small blood vessels throughout the body. It seems that the higher the blood sugar level, the more narrowing of the small blood vessels. As these blood vessels narrow, they carry less blood, and circulation becomes impaired. Poor circulation in turn leads to the complications of poorly controlled diabetes: kidney disease, poor wound healing, and foot and eye problems. Diabetes also alters fat metabolism, increasing the risk of atherosclerotic plaques in the bigger blood vessels (see ANGINA and HEART ATTACK in Chapter 12), resulting in considerable risk of heart disease in diabetics.

Few people survived very long after developing diabetes until 1921, when scientists discovered that injected insulin could substitute for the body's own. Now diabetics who practice good self-care can avoid the disease's complications and lead normal, active lives.

There are two kinds of diabetes, which used to be called "juvenile" and "adult," but those names were confusing. You can develop "juvenile" diabetes as an adult. What used to be called juvenile diabetes is now called "insulin-dependent" or "Type 1," and "adult" diabetes is now called "non–insulin-dependent" or "Type 2." Insulin-dependent diabetics must inject the hormone daily to control their blood sugar. Non–insulin-dependent diabetics produce their own insulin, but their cells don't respond to it properly. They can usually control their blood sugar through weight loss and diet, sometimes along with oral medication that boosts their own insulin's effect. In some cases, insulin injections are also necessary.

Type 2 is by far the more prevalent form of diabetes, accounting for 85 to 90 percent of cases.

Experts don't know what causes diabetes, but recently researchers demonstrated that the insulin-dependent (Type 1) form is an autoimmune disease. Something goes wrong with the immune system, and the mechanisms that protect us from illness suddenly destroy the pancreatic cells that produce insulin. Type 1 diabetes also has a genetic component. Those

with close relatives who must inject insulin are at increased risk themselves. Finally, Type 1 diabetes appears to have environmental triggers.
Genetically susceptible people often develop the disease shortly after a
viral infection such as chickenpox or the flu.

In Type 2 diabetes, the body continues to produce insulin—sometimes normal amounts—but is unable to use it properly. Type 2 diabetes
is typically associated with obesity. It can usually be controlled through
weight loss, diet, and exercise in conjunction with a physician's care.

Before You Call the Doctor.   Be aware if you have any risk factors for
diabetes:

•Family history. If one parent has diabetes, your risk is 20 to 25
percent. If both parents have it, your risk jumps to about 70 percent. Your
risk also increases if siblings, grandparents, or blood-related aunts and
uncles are diabetic.

• A personal history of diabetes while pregnant ("gestational diabetes"). This temporary diabetes strikes about 3 percent of nondiabetics—
some 60,000 pregnant women a year. Gestational diabetes can cause
severe problems for the mother and fetus. Overweight women over age
thirty-five are at highest risk, but gestational diabetes can develop in
anyone. The American Diabetes Association (ADA) urges all pregnant
women to get tested for gestational diabetes during their twenty-fourth to
twenty-eighth week of pregnancy. Unfortunately, experts estimate that
only about half of pregnant women get screened. If diagnosed, gestational
diabetes can be treated with diet and sometimes with insulin, which
decreases the risk of maternal and fetal harm. After delivery, gestational
diabetes disappears, but the condition is a risk factor for Type 2 diabetes
later in life.

• Age. Type 2 diabetes, the vastly more prevalent form, generally
develops after age forty, though it may develop earlier.

• Ethnicity. Diabetes can develop in anyone, but African Americans,
Hispanics, American Indians, and Asian Indians have unusually high rates.

• Obesity. Being overweight increases risk. But where you carry the
weight is also important. If you have "pear-shaped" obesity, with the extra
weight in your hips and buttocks, you're less likely to develop diabetes
than if you have "apple-shaped" obesity, which is characterized by a big
belly.

When to Call the Doctor.   Consult a physician if you develop diabetes'
initial symptoms, particularly increased thirst and urination and weakness
or listlessness. Be extra alert to these symptoms if you have any diabetes

risk factors, but understand that the disease can develop in anyone. Another symptom that suggests diabetes is numbness in the feet.

In children, diabetes is sometimes mistaken for the flu. If your child appears lethargic, ill, and thirsty, consult a physician.

Once You Get Diagnosed.   Diabetes requires a physician's ongoing care, but there's a tremendous amount diabetics can do for themselves to manage the condition effectively and minimize their risk of developing complications:

• Administer insulin if needed. Type 1 diabetics must inject insulin up to several times a day. Self-injection is unpleasant at first, but it quickly becomes routine and virtually painless. It's important to develop a system for rotating injection sites to prevent the buildup of scar tissue. For example, inject in a line from left to right across the upper abdomen the first and third weeks of each month, and left to right across the lower abdomen the second and fourth weeks.

Diabetic children as young as seven years of age can be taught to inject themselves.

• Monitor your glucose level. Diabetics who keep their blood glucose levels as close to normal as possible are less likely to develop the disease's serious complications. Within the last decade, glucose control has become easier thanks to electronic blood glucose monitors. You prick your finger, place a drop of blood on a special test strip, insert it into your monitor, and bingo—the machine displays your blood glucose level, allowing you to adjust your insulin dosage, exercise, and/or diet for optimal glucose control.

• Manage your diet. If you're overweight it's important to lose weight. And even if you're not, proper dietary management is essential to diabetes self-care. Contact the ADA for diet guides and cookbooks (see RE-SOURCES at the end of this chapter)—or read Chapter 1. A good diabetic diet is exactly the same as the healthy diet recommended in this book.

• Control your risk factors for cardiovascular disease. Diabetics are at increased risk for heart disease and stroke and should do their best to minimize their risk factors. (See EAT AND DRINK RIGHT in Chapter 1 and HEART ATTACK in Chapters 3 and 12).

• Remind your doctor to examine your feet. Nerve damage associated with diabetes ("diabetic neuropathy") causes foot numbness, and quite frequently diabetics don't notice foot infections. These infections can become so serious that amputation is the only alternative. Unfortunately, some doctors neglect to examine diabetics' feet. During every doctor visit, remove your shoes and socks and have your feet examined. And if you ever notice blood on your socks (the blood will be red or rusty brown in color), call your physician.

• Request an ophthalmological referral at least once a year. Eye damage associated with diabetes ("diabetic retinopathy") can cause blindness. Fortunately, if the eyes are examined regularly, the condition can be controlled with laser surgery. Unfortunately, some doctors do not encourage diabetic patients to have regular eye exams. If your doctor doesn't refer you, ask for a referral.

• Don't give up on having children. Diabetic women used to be told they could not have children. Some can't, but more and more women with well-controlled diabetes are having children. Diabetes complicates pregnancy considerably, but if you want children, read the ADA's booklet, "Diabetes and Pregnancy: What to Expect."

• Don't give up on sex. Some—*but not all*—diabetic men suffer erection impairment. Unfortunately, the myth is that all diabetic men lose their erections, and when diabetic men hear this, the news can be so traumatic that their penises call it quits. If you're having any erection difficulty, ask your physician for a referral to a certified sex therapist near you or contact the American Association of Sex Educators, Counselors, and Therapists for a list of sex therapists in your state (see RESOURCES at the end of this chapter). Few physicians are trained in sex therapy, and some even tell diabetic men that nothing can be done to treat diabetic erection loss. Wrong! Studies show that sex therapy helps many diabetic men with this problem regain their ability to maintain an erection. For those who suffer more serious sex problems, implants and other therapies are available (see ERECTION PROBLEMS in Chapter 19).

• Join the ADA. The ADA has fifty-six state affiliates and hundreds of local support groups around the country, to help diabetics and their families cope with the disease. The ADA even sponsors summer camps for diabetic children (see RESOURCES at the end of this chapter).

• Always keep supplies on hand. An excellent source of diabetic supplies—books, test strips, blood glucose monitors, and diabetic foods and snack items—is the Sugar-Free Diabetes Center (see the Resources at the end of this chapter).

• Be prepared for emergencies. Always wear a MedicAlert bracelet or necklace (see RESOURCES at the end of this chapter).

▶ **RED FLAGS** Very high or very low blood sugar levels or acid buildup in the blood can lead to confusion, lethargy, and if not corrected, ultimately coma. Discuss with your physician what to do if these symptoms develop. If they develop and do not improve quickly with the recommended treatment, call your doctor or 911 right away.

EDEMA

(See FLUID RETENTION in this chapter)

FATIGUE

Feelings of fatigue, weariness, or listlessness are among the most common health complaints.

What's Going On?   All of us feel tired at times. People who juggle job, home, and child-rearing responsibilities often feel tired much of the time. Fatigue is the body's way of letting us know we need to rest. But sometimes, fatigue becomes unusually severe and/or chronic. It may be a symptom of other—sometimes serious—health problems, or it may be "chronic fatigue and immune dysfunction syndrome" (CFIDS). This condition is similar to mononucleosis, but the fatigue symptoms last much longer. Unfortunately, because fatigue can have physiologic and psychosocial causes and may be related to life-style as well, it's often difficult to get to the bottom of it.

In recent years, CFIDS has received considerable media attention. This controversial condition was first identified in the early 1980s. It was originally called "chronic Epstein-Barr virus syndrome" because most early sufferers were shown to be infected with the Epstein-Barr virus, which causes mononucleosis. But many people who complain of chronic fatigue or recurring flu-like illness with depression, headaches, muscle and joint pain, swollen lymph nodes, and emotional problems show no trace of Epstein-Barr virus infection. If you think you might have CFIDS and/or want the latest information on it, contact the Chronic Fatigue/ Immune Dysfunction Syndrome Foundation (see RESOURCES at the end of this chapter).

Before You Call the Doctor.   If you think you suffer unusually severe fatigue, take a moment to answer these questions:
   • Within the last six months, have you had surgery, a significant illness or injury, a significant emotional trauma, or the birth of a child? If so, it's likely these events have caused—or at least contributed to—your fatigue.
   • Are you now or have you recently been involved in a stressful or grief-producing situation? Stress and strong emotional upheavals often cause fatigue.

• Have you recently increased your physical activity—either on the job or recreationally? Often, in an effort to "get fit" quickly or prepare for competition, people overtrain. Trainers say most people increase the strenuousness of workouts too quickly.

• Have you started, stopped, or changed medications recently? Fatigue is a side effect of many drugs, including some over-the-counter medications, for example, antihistamines.

• Have you been sleeping less than usual? Do you have difficulty falling or staying asleep? Most people require six to eight hours of sleep every day, and recent research suggests that most of those who think they can get by on six hours actually need seven or eight. Chronic sleep deprivation or changes in sleep patterns associated with jet lag or changes in schedule can scramble the body's natural sleep-rest cycle ("circadian rhythm") and cause fatigue (see INSOMNIA in this chapter).

• Have you recently been exposed to chemicals such as solvents, pesticides, or heavy metals? Toxic chemicals can cause fatigue and other problems.

• Do you feel worthless and hopeless, with loss of interest in previously pleasurable activities? You may be suffering from the kind of depression which is not simply a reaction to a sad occurrence (see DEPRESSION in Chapter 5).

• Have you been drinking more alcohol lately? Have you been using more mood-altering drugs? Alcohol depresses the central nervous system, interferes with sleep patterns, and often causes fatigue. Tranquilizers and sedatives (including Valium and many other drugs) can cause hangover effects that are experienced as fatigue. After using amphetamines and other "uppers," users often "crash" into a state of fatigue.

If you think any of the factors discussed above might be contributing to your fatigue, do what you can to alter, or "ride out," the situation. You may also find relief in some of the suggestions below for CFIDS sufferers.

If you answered "no" to all the questions above, skip to "When to Call the Doctor," below.

If you suffer from CFIDS:

• Acknowledge your situation and make an effort not to feel guilty about it. If you feel tired, rest. Take naps. Reduce your expectations.

• Mobilize support from your friends and family. Many chronic fatigue sufferers complain that their loved ones think they are faking illness or malingering or that they are "neurotic." Assemble some resources from the Chronic Fatigue/Immune Dysfunction Syndrome Foundation, and confront any preconceptions directly. Support from friends and family can be crucial.

•Support groups whose members all have chronic fatigue can also provide perspective and valuable insights. Contact your local mental health agencies or the Chronic Fatigue/Immune Dysfunction Syndrome Foundation for a referral, or start a support group yourself.

•A low-fat, high-fiber diet and supplementation with a multivitamin and mineral "insurance formula" might help.

•Exercise as your energy permits, but don't overdo it.

•A change of scene might help. Try taking a vacation.

•Try to remain optimistic. Many people with chronic fatigue report turning a corner after about twelve to twenty-four months and then slowly (sometimes very slowly) regaining energy, typically with many setbacks along the way. Many feel fatigued for a few years, but most report improvement over time.

When to Call the Doctor.   If you can't identify an obvious fatigue culprit and correct the situation within a month or two, consult a physician. To help your physician pinpoint the cause of your problem, be prepared to answer the following questions:

•When did you first notice feeling fatigued?

•Does anything make it worse? Or better?

•Does your fatigue appear to be related to your job? Relationship? Friends? Family? Personal problems?

•Are you more fatigued in the morning, afternoon, or evening?

•Does physical activity relieve or aggravate the problem?

•Do you have other symptoms in addition to fatigue?

•Has anyone in your family ever complained about chronic fatigue?

•Is your family situation stressful or supportive?

The physician should conduct a thorough physical exam to investigate possible physical causes of your fatigue. If the doctor dismisses your complaints as "all in your head," consult another doctor. Many diseases—diabetes, hypothyroidism, anemia, lupus, rheumatoid arthritis, AIDS, and others—can start out with fatigue. However, when fatigue is the only complaint, the cause is often psychological (stress or depression). The longer the fatigue continues without other symptoms, the more likely it is to be depression.

Don't expect any miracles. Most physicians find complaints of chronic fatigue baffling and difficult to deal with. Get several opinions from mainstream and alternative practitioners. Try the approaches that appeal to you.

FEVER

Fever is an oral temperature of 100° F (38° C) or higher.

What's Going On?   Fever usually means the body is fighting an infection. However, fever may also be caused by simple overheating, or it may be a reaction to immunizations, medications, or injuries.

Fever rarely occurs by itself. Look for other symptoms to guide you to the cause and proper treatment.

Most people consider fever "bad," something to get rid of as quickly as possible. In fact, fever is of considerable value in fighting infection. Most disease-causing microorganisms have difficulty reproducing at temperatures much above normal body temperature. Chemicals released into the blood stream as a result of infection signal the brain to turn up the body's "thermostat," which helps impair the reproduction of germs.

Before You Call the Doctor.   Since fevers contribute to healing, some physicians suggest not treating them unless they reach 102° in children or 101° in adults, or unless they cause significant discomfort and/or insomnia. Decide for yourself when you want to begin treatment.

Whether or not you treat a fever, drink plenty of nonalcoholic liquids to replace fluids lost through the heavy sweating fever causes.

To relieve the feeling of being overheated, try taking a cool bath.

If you must take something, aspirin, acetaminophen, and ibuprofen all help bring down fever. Aspirin and ibuprofen are more likely than acetaminophen to cause upset stomach.

Children often have low-grade fevers without appearing uncomfortable. Even if the child does not seem to notice a low fever, give more liquids. For minor discomfort, give the child a sponge bath with lukewarm water. For higher fevers, give acetaminophen every four to six hours.

When to Call the Doctor.   Consult a physician for:

• Any fever in a pregnant woman.

• Any fever in anyone with heart disease, a chronic respiratory disease, or any serious chronic medical condition.

• Any fever that lasts longer than five days (three days for children).

• Any fever that does not respond to concerted treatment within thirty-six hours.

• Any fever that initially responds to treatment, then suddenly recurs.

▶ **RED FLAGS**   *Never* give aspirin to a child under sixteen years of age whose fever is associated with colds, flu, or chickenpox. It may cause Reye syndrome, a rare but potentially fatal condition affecting the brain.

Consult a physician immediately if fever is accompanied by a rash, severe headache, stiff neck, marked irritability or confusion, cough with brown/green sputum, severe back pain, abdominal pain, or painful urination. Fever and any of these signs may indicate potentially serious illness— pneumonia, meningitis, and others.

Consult a physician if signs of dehydration develop—extreme thirst, light-headedness, infrequent or dark urine, dry mouth, and decreased skin elasticity.

FLUID RETENTION

Fluid retention, medically known as "edema," causes abnormal swelling. It can occur anywhere in the body but frequently affects the hands, ankles, and feet.

What's Going On?   When fluid pressure builds up in the veins, some of the fluid is forced out into the surrounding tissues. It often accumulates in the extremities. Edema is a warning sign. Often, the cause is not serious and the treatment simple, but it may also indicate a serious condition, for example, congestive heart failure.

People who must stand for long periods—dentists, hair stylists, bartenders, etc.—often develop edema because constant standing interferes with the ability of the leg veins to return blood to the heart, and fluid builds up, particularly in the feet, ankles, and lower legs. Other conditions that interfere with blood return and cause edema in the feet include:

• Constrictive clothing, such as garters, girdles, and knee-high stockings.

• Weak calf muscles, especially among inactive older individuals. As the calf muscles contract during daily activities, they help push blood through the leg veins.

• Varicose veins, which are veins that have become so stretched out that the valves no longer keep the blood moving against gravity (see VARICOSE VEINS in Chapter 12).

Some conditions cause edema as a result of sodium and water retention throughout the body:

• Congestive heart failure is a weakening of the heart muscle that leads to sodium and water retention and increased fluid pressure in the veins (see CONGESTIVE HEART FAILURE in Chapter 12).

• Liver cirrhosis also causes fluid retention, leading sometimes to massive edema of the legs and/or abdomen.

• Hormonal changes related to the menstrual cycle cause many women to develop edema of the legs, hands, breasts, and abdomen just before their periods. Hormones are also responsible for edema related to pregnancy and birth control pills, especially those high in estrogen.

• A high-salt diet can also contribute to fluid retention and edema.

Before You Call the Doctor.   Simple self-care measures can often eliminate edema:

• If you must stand for long periods of time, take regular breaks, sit down, and elevate your legs. While standing, stand on tiptoes, then return to normal standing five to ten times every fifteen minutes.

• Exercise more. Regular exercise strengthens calf muscles and keeps the cardiovascular system healthy.

• Restrict your salt (sodium) consumption. The average American consumes much more salt than necessary. Don't automatically salt foods. Instead, try salt substitutes or flavor-enhancers, such as lemon or herbs. Many condiments and additives, such as soy sauce, tamari, and MSG, as well as processed foods contain high levels of sodium. Read labels and try to eat fresh, unprocessed foods (see EAT AND DRINK RIGHT in Chapter 1).

• Try natural diuretics, such as cantaloupe, parsley, watermelon, cucumbers, cabbage, and herb teas made with dandelion or juniper. In addition to eliminating excess water, diuretics may deplete body stores of the mineral potassium. If you use diuretics, be sure to eat foods high in this mineral, for example, bananas and potatoes.

• Don't wear tight-fitting clothing.

• If you suffer ankle and/or leg edema, try support stockings.

• Elevate your legs whenever possible. Try sleeping with pillows under your ankles.

When to Call the Doctor.   Consult a doctor for any edema that lasts for more than a few days or recurs without an obvious cause. Edema can be a symptom of serious illness—infection or kidney, liver, or heart disease. Physicians typically treat edema with prescription diuretics and/or other medications, depending on what causes the problem.

▶ **RED FLAG**   Sudden painful edema that is worse on one side may indicate a blood clot in a vein or blockage of a lymph vessel. See a physician immediately.

HANGOVER

Called "the moaning after" by one wit, hangovers are caused by overindulgence in alcohol. Symptoms include headaches, nausea, vomiting, thirst, and feeling like "death warmed over."

What's Going On?   Alcohol is a powerful drug. For most people, very low doses (one beer, glass of wine, or mixed drink) feel relaxing, but after the second or third drink, giddiness becomes drunkenness, and alcohol becomes toxic. Hangover is a mild version of alcohol withdrawal syndrome, which causes delerium tremens (DTs) in alcoholics. The headache of hangover is caused, in part, by alcohol's relaxing effect on the blood vessels. As they relax, they open up ("dilate") and accommodate more blood, which causes the sensation of warmth people associate with drinking. But if the blood vessels of the head open too much, they trigger nerve activity we experience as pain.

Alcohol is also a diuretic. It increases urination and can lead to moderate dehydration, which causes powerful morning-after thirst and head pain.

The nausea and vomiting are a combination of alcohol's irritating effect on the stomach and its many effects on the central nervous system.

The fatigue and general lousy-all-over feeling result from alcohol's depressant effect and a build-up of acids in the blood ("acidosis").

Additives and impurities in alcohol ("congeners") also contribute to hangovers. The general rule is the darker the alcohol, the worse the hangover. Vodka and white wine contain few congeners, but bourbon, scotch, and red wine are loaded with them.

By-products formed as the body metabolizes alcohol contribute to the morning-after blahs, too. Normally, the liver can metabolize one ounce of alcohol an hour and produce few by-products. Any more and the by-products build up, compounding hangover misery.

Before You Call the Doctor.   You don't have to get sloppy drunk to suffer a hangover the morning after. For people of average weight, the hangover-risk threshold is consumption of more than one drink per hour. If you drink at all, nurse your drinks. Alternate them with water or fruit juice to prevent alcohol-related dehydration.

If you have one too many (or more than one), drink lots of water before you go to bed. It won't prevent a hangover entirely, but it can help minimize the misery of alcohol-induced dehydration. Some studies suggest that regular vitamin C supplementation may help, too, by increasing the rate of alcohol breakdown in the body.

If you develop a full-blown hangover, rest. Take acetaminophen to relieve headache pain. Aspirin and ibuprofen also relieve headache, but they are more likely to cause stomach upset, which only adds to hangover misery. However, if you want to take aspirin or ibuprofen, take an "enteric coated" brand, which dissolves in the intestine, not in the stomach.

Ice packs also help relieve headache pain. Wrap a few ice cubes in a plastic bag, then wrap the bag in a clean cloth and apply the ice pack to the forehead for twenty minutes, then remove it for ten minutes before reapplying. An ice substitute may be used instead of ice cubes. Do not apply ice directly to the skin. This can cause the equivalent of frostbite.

Drink plenty of liquids to replace lost fluids, relieve acidosis, and soothe the stomach until the body eliminates the alcohol. Mint tea is especially soothing to the stomach. Coffee and other stimulants don't help. Neither do Valium and other tranquilizers; in fact, they interfere with the body's ability to eliminate alcohol.

Of course, bartenders the world over are fountainheads of folk hangover remedies. One venerable remedy is honey in hot water. The water certainly helps, and honey soothes the throat and digestive tract. But *never* take "some hair of the dog that bit you," that is, more alcohol. It simply compounds the problem.

INSOMNIA

Insomnia means not getting enough sleep. It also refers to difficulty falling or staying asleep.

What's Going On? Everyone needs "a good night's sleep," but how long is good enough? Most people need seven or eight hours a night to wake up feeling refreshed and perform efficiently. Recent research suggests that those who seem to do fine on just five or six hours a night actually need more sleep. As people age, they often find they need less sleep than they did when they were younger. However, they may also sleep less soundly and more fitfully.

Before You Call the Doctor. Insomnia is a major national health problem, as the enormous sleep-aid industry clearly shows. Chronic insomnia may require professional help, but for most people it's simply a result of daily stresses. Before you start swallowing any sleep medications, and certainly before you call the doctor, try these sleep-enhancing life-style suggestions. Studies show that when used conscientiously, they help eliminate about three-quarters of even chronic sleep problems:

• Limit your caffeine consumption. Everyone knows coffee contains this powerful stimulant, but some people are unaware that tea, colas, cocoa, and chocolate also contain caffeine and/or a similar stimulant called theobromine. So do an astonishing number of over-the-counter drugs. Even coffee ice cream and coffee yogurt contain enough caffeine to disturb sleep in sensitive individuals.

• Beware of other drugs. Widely used over-the-counter decongestants, including pseudoephedrine (Sudafed and many others) and products containing phenylpropanolamine, can be as stimulating as caffeine. If you have a sleep problem and take _any_ medication, ask your pharmacist if it might keep you up and, if so, if another might be substituted.

• Exercise regularly, but not within four hours of retiring. Strenuous physical activity—even housework—contributes to sound sleep, but exercising too late in the day can interfere with falling asleep.

• Establish a regular bedtime. The body's internal clock responds best to a regular schedule. Even on weekends, try going to bed and rising as you do on weekdays.

• Let go of stressors before going to bed. If you're worried about forgetting things, write them down. If you're anxious in general, increase your exercise. If you have interpersonal problems, talk them out with your spouse, friends, or relatives or seek professional counseling.

• Use relaxation techniques. Progressively tighten and relax all the muscles of your body starting with your toes and working up to your face. Or try listening to relaxing music before going to bed.

• Take a warm bath. A good soak soothes tense muscles and helps you become drowsy.

• Try warm milk. Milk contains the amino acid tryptophan, which relaxes muscles and induces sleep. Some authorities say there isn't enough in a glass of milk to have much effect, but many people swear by warm milk. Add a touch of honey, cinnamon, and vanilla for a delicious bedtime treat.

• Try an herbal sleep aid. Teas made with hops, passion flower, valerian, and chamomile have been used as sedatives for centuries, and recent research supports their effectiveness. Health food stores sell sleep-aid teas containing these herbs.

• Make sure your bedroom is dark, quiet, and a comfortable temperature. Even dim light causes unnecessary eye movements which can disturb sleep. If noise is a problem, try foam ear plugs, available at pharmacies, or "white noise" tapes. Most people sleep most soundly in rooms kept at 67° to 70° with plenty of fresh air.

• Sleep on a firm mattress. Mattresses that are too soft or hard disturb sleep. Find a mattress that supports your back. Some people find the warmth and support of a waterbed conducive to sound sleep, as long as it doesn't slosh.

• Use your bed only for sleeping and sex. Read, work, watch TV, and talk on the phone elsewhere.

• Try sex. Lovemaking (and masturbation) are relaxing, and after orgasm, people tend to feel drowsy.

• If you can't sleep, get up. If you are unable to fall asleep within thirty minutes, don't lie there and "try" to fall asleep. Get up and stay up—read, watch TV, or listen to music or the radio—until you feel tired. Then go back to bed. If you still can't fall asleep within thirty minutes, get up again and repeat the process. At first you may bounce in and out of bed several times a night, but using this approach, most people train themselves to fall asleep within thirty minutes after a week or two.

When to Call the Doctor.   Chronic insomnia that does not respond to a month of committed self-care requires professional evaluation. It may be caused by serious anxiety, depression, medications, or other problems.

If your physician can't help you, contact the American Sleep Disorders Association for a referral to a clinic that specializes in sleep problems (see RESOURCES at the end of this chapter).

JET LAG

Jet lag is the fatigue and disorientation experienced after flying across time zones.

What's Going On?   Jet lag, formally known as "circadian desynchronosis," is a disruption of the subtle but powerful internal biological clock that regulates many body functions, such as temperature, kidney output, and normal sleep/wake patterns.

This disruption affects not only business travelers and vacationers but also the growing number of people who work odd-hour shifts, such as pilots, police, and health care workers. Jet lag is more than just a nuisance. Scientists who study the biological clock ("chronobiologists") believe circadian desynchronosis causes reasoning lapses that contribute to hospital medication errors, police shooting incidents, and even airline disasters.

Before You Call the Doctor.   Two methods have been developed to prevent jet lag. The easier one involves determining the number of time zones you'll cross, counting back that number of days, then preadjusting to your destination by going to sleep and getting up one hour a day earlier if you plan to fly east, or one hour later if you're flying west.

The more complicated approach is the Anti–Jet Lag Diet developed by Dr. Charles Ehret of the U.S. Department of Energy's Argonne National Laboratory in Illinois. For travel within continental North America (except Alaska), two days on his diet should suffice. For travel abroad (or between the East Coast and Alaska or Hawaii), allow four days.

To get your body into synch with your destination's time zone, the Anti–Jet Lag Diet alternates feast days with fast days:

Day one: Eat a high-protein breakfast and lunch (eggs, cheese, meats, and high-protein cereals) and a high-carbohydrate supper without high-protein foods (pastas, potatoes, pancakes, rice, and breads).

Day two: Fast by eating light meals of salads, thin soups, fruits, and juices. Keep carbohydrates and fats to a minimum, and do not exceed 800 calories.

Day three (or day one of the two-day program): Feast as on day one.

Departure day (day four or two): Fast, then have a high-protein breakfast during *local breakfast time at your destination*. If no breakfast is scheduled on your flight, bring hard-boiled eggs, cheeses, and high-protein cereals. Do some isometric exercises after this breakfast, and do not sleep again until bedtime at your destination. On arrival, eat the rest of your meals on local time. If you arrive at night, don't break your final fast until breakfast the next day.

Authorities also recommend exercising after arrival. Toronto researchers found that hamsters suffering from circadian desynchronosis recovered more quickly when they exercised.

Caffeine can shift circadian rhythms forward or back, depending on when it is consumed, but between 3:00 and 5:00 P.M., it has little effect on body rhythm. If you use caffeine, consume it only from 3:00 to 5:00, except on the day you travel. Then use it in the morning if traveling west, or in the evening if traveling east.

Don't drink alcohol while flying. Pressurized cabins increase its effects, and it slows the biological clock.

For short-stay trips across only one or two time zones, consider staying on your home schedule while away. While you may be a bit out of synch with the local mealtimes, you can avoid the fatigue, disorientation, and judgment problems caused by jet lag.

MONOSODIUM GLUTAMATE (MSG) INTOLERANCE

Monosodium glutamate is a flavor enhancer that has been used for close to 100 years. But in recent decades it has been blamed for a combination of symptoms, including nausea, dizziness, headaches, depression, joint pains, racing pulse, shortness of breath, and, in children, asthma attacks.

What's Going On?   Back in 1968, the prestigious *New England Journal of Medicine* published a letter from a physician who reported "two hours of numbness, weakness, and heart palpitations" after eating dishes containing large amounts of MSG at Chinese restaurants. The phenomenon has been widely reported since and is often called Chinese restaurant syndrome.

But Chinese restaurants represent just the tip of the MSG iceberg. Some authorities say that up to 20 percent of Americans—some 50 million people—have noticeably bad reactions to the seasoning which has become the world's third most popular spice (after salt and pepper). MSG was first isolated from seaweed in Japan in 1908 and immediately became widely used in Asian cooking. It came to the U.S. after World War II, and today it's as American as Stovetop Americana New England Style Stuffing, which authorities say contains enough MSG to cause problems in those who are sensitive. In fact, more than 250 supermarket items now contain MSG, and you'd be hard pressed to find a soup mix, TV dinner, airplane meal, prepared side dish, or fast-food meal without it.

Unfortunately for those interested in limiting MSG consumption, food labels do not necessarily list it. Instead they might list "hydrolyzed vegetable protein," which contains up to 20 percent MSG, and "natural flavors," which usually contain MSG as well.

Although the Food and Drug Administration includes MSG in its list of food additives "generally regarded as safe," a Harvard researcher concluded that about 30 percent of people develop reactions to five grams of MSG, and 90 percent react to 10 grams. (One teaspoon of Accent seasoning contains six grams.)

Before You Call the Doctor.   If you feel uncomfortable after eating at Asian restaurants or after eating fast-food meals, you may be sensitive to MSG. Reactions depend on the amount ingested. Most people need not eliminate MSG completely to notice a decrease in symptoms. Every little bit helps. Here's how to reduce your exposure:

• Eat the type of diet discussed in EAT AND DRINK RIGHT in Chapter 1, one based on fresh fruits and vegetables and whole grains. If a food is fresh, it doesn't have any MSG added.

• Read food labels carefully. Stay away from anything containing MSG, hydrolyzed vegetable protein, and natural flavors.

• Steer clear of processed and prepared foods, especially anything that comes with a "flavor packet." Flavor packets almost always contain MSG.

When to Call the Doctor. Those who are extremely sensitive to MSG—or any food item—should consult an allergist/immunologist for testing and treatment.

MOTION SICKNESS

It can ruin your pride, your clothes, and possibly your entire vacation. Motion sickness, also called "sea," "car," and "air" sickness, involves nausea, excessive perspiration, dizziness, and rapid breathing and progresses to vomiting and prostration.

What's Going On? Motion sickness results from an upset of the body's balance mechanism, which is controlled by fluid moving in the semicircular canals of the inner ear. As this fluid moves, it changes the position of two flap-like inner ear structures and moves special calcium carbonate crystals ("otoliths") contained in a jelly-like substance in two sacks in the inner ear. The flap and otolith movements stimulate nerves in the area, which we experience as dizziness, nausea, and other motion-sickness symptoms.

Motion sickness can also occur without movement. If you watch a film about riding a roller coaster or driving a race car, the eye sends signals that you're moving while the inner ear sends signals that you're standing still. If your brain favors the visual signals over the inner-ear messages, you may become ill.

Before You Call the Doctor. Prevention is more effective than treatment once motion sickness develops. Here's how the experts recommend preventing it:

• Get plenty of rest before your trip.

• Eat lightly and avoid heavy, fatty foods before or during the trip.

• Don't drink alcohol before or during travel.

• Stay away from cigarette smoke and other unpleasant odors.

• Position yourself in the vehicle where there is the least disorienting movement—in the front seat of a car or bus, or amidships in a boat.

If you begin to feel queasy, take slow deep breaths and fix your eyes on the horizon or on any stationary object in the distance.

Two over-the-counter drugs can be used to prevent motion sickness: Dramamine and Bonine. Take Dramamine thirty to sixty minutes before travel, then every four hours during the journey. Take Bonine thirty to sixty minutes prior to departure, but only one a day. Both drugs can cause drowsiness. You should not drive or operate machinery while taking them. Children under twelve years of age should not take Bonine, but cherry-flavored Dramamine is available in a liquid form for children two years of age and older.

Ginger also helps prevent motion sickness. Chinese sailors began using it more than 1,000 years ago to prevent and treat seasickness. The ancient Greeks adopted the herb as a stomach-soother and ate it wrapped in bread after big meals. Eventually, they began baking the ginger into the bread and invented the world's first cookie, gingerbread. In Elizabethan England, physicians prescribed a ginger drink, ginger beer, for abdominal distress. It evolved into today's ginger ale, still a popular folk remedy for stomach distress and morning sickness of pregnancy. In a 1982 study in the British medical journal *Lancet,* researchers gave confirmed motion sickness sufferers either a standard dose of Dramamine or one gram of ginger, then strapped them into a moving chair programmed to induce motion sickness. Each subject could press a button to stop the chair when they felt queasy. The ginger takers lasted significantly longer than the Dramamine group. Powdered whole ginger root is available at health food stores. Take a gram or two about forty-five minutes before you depart. Ginger is safe, but some people report mild heartburn.

Acupressure has also proven effective. Apply steady pressure with your thumb or finger to a point on the palm side of the forearm, three finger widths above the major crease of the wrist, between the two tendons, in line with the middle finger. The point should feel tender momentarily, but the discomfort should moderate as the motion sickness symptoms begin to subside.

When to Call the Doctor. If modifying your life-style and taking over-the-counter drugs don't provide sufficient relief, a doctor can pre-scribe scopolamine, available in a dime-sized patch (Transderm-V or Transderm-Scōp), which delivers the drug through the skin for up to three days. It should be applied four hours before departure. Although the manufacturer suggests wearing the patch behind the ear, it can be worn on any hairless area. Scopolamine may cause side effects: dry mouth, drowsiness, giddiness, blurred vision, and a dilated pupil on one side when the patch is placed behind the ear.

▶ **RED FLAG**   Scopolamine should not be used by people with glaucoma because it increases pressure within the eye. Those with benign prostatic enlargement should also not use it because the drug affects muscles involved in urination. Also, be sure to wash your hands after handling the scopolamine skin patch since the drug may be rubbed from the fingers into the eyes and cause blurred vision.

OVERWEIGHT AND OBESITY

More than 50 million North Americans carry extra pounds, and about half of them are clinically obese—more than 20 percent heavier than their recommended weight. Obesity is a risk factor for heart disease, several cancers, high blood pressure, stroke, diabetes, arthritis, back pain, and other health problems.

What's Going On?   An extra five pounds isn't a medical problem (though it may be a cosmetic or self-esteem issue), but an extra twenty-five may become a significant health risk. Until recently, weight-control authorities believed that the more calories you ingested, the more weight you'd gain, and they recommended caloric limitation for weight loss. Now we know that weight gain and loss aren't that simple. The body's weight control mechanisms are more complex. Many studies have shown that overweight people don't necessarily eat more than slim people. In fact, many consume fewer calories yet continue to gain weight. Weight, particularly obesity, is under genetic control to a considerable extent. Basal metabolic rate (BMR) also plays an important role. BMR is the number of calories burned while resting. People with high BMRs can eat more and not gain weight. In addition to burning calories, exercise increases BMR, not just during the exercise but for hours after, so you burn more calories even while resting.

Research has clearly demonstrated that quick-loss diets don't work for long-term weight control. People who diet are prone to frustrating "yo-yo" cycles of weight loss and gain. They repeatedly lose a few pounds, then regain them—plus a few more. The problem, according to weight experts, is that the body can't tell the difference between dieting and starvation. When deprived of sufficient calories, the body slows BMR to use calories more slowly. When dieters return to normal eating, their

BMRs remain depressed, and they regain all the weight quickly—plus a few extra pounds for insurance against the next "famine."

In addition, lean tissue (muscle) is metabolically active, that is, it burns calories. Fat does not. People who have more lean tissue naturally burn more calories than those with more fat tissue.

Weight experts also know that people who are overweight behave differently around food than those who are slim. People who are over-weight eat in response to *external* cues, such as time of day or the look and smell of foods, rather than *internal* cues of hunger. Many eat for psycho-logical reasons other than hunger: to relax, celebrate, or console them-selves and/or to relieve feelings of boredom, anxiety, or anger.

Recent evidence also suggests that how much we eat may not be as important as what we eat. Fat in the diet becomes body fat. Protein and carbohydrates are less likely to be stored as fat.

Before You Call the Doctor.   New fad diets seem to pop up every week. Most of them are high-protein, low carbohydrate, low-fiber regi-mens. You *can* lose weight on them—but only temporarily. The path to permanent weight control involves changing life-style habits that contrib-ute to excessive fat storage.

•Eat a low-fat, high-carbohydrate, high-fiber diet based on fresh, whole, unprocessed foods. Despite what your mother may have told you about "starch being fattening," it isn't. High-carbohydrate, high-fiber foods such as potatoes and whole-grain breads contribute to weight control. They fill you up, so you can eat more of them without consuming too many calories. Perhaps more importantly, they stabilize your blood sugar level, which affects appetite, mood, energy level, and mental abilities. Remember, it's not the baked potato that adds the pounds, it's the high-fat butter and sour cream you pile on top of it. Fresh fruits and vegetables are terrific foods for permanent weight control. Like whole-grain breads, they are rich in nutrients and fill you up without filling you out. You can eat more of them without fear of gaining weight so you don't have to feel unsatisfied. And compared with high-fat, weight-gain foods, they're con-siderably less expensive.

•Cut fats. This bears repeating: Fat gets stored as fat. High-fat foods are usually high-calorie. High-fat diets have also been associated with cancer, stroke, and heart disease. The typical American diet contains about 40 percent of calories from fat. Aim to cut your fats to 20 percent or less of your total daily caloric intake. (One gram of fat contains nine calories.)

•Eat breakfast. Surveys show that people who are overweight tend to skip breakfast, eat a light lunch, then pig out on dinner and snacks until bedtime. One key is to start your day with a high-carbohydrate breakfast such as cereal and fruit, then eat a light supper. Eating triggers a rise in BMR that lasts several hours, so the earlier you begin eating, the more calories you burn throughout the day.

• Try grazing. Traditional dieting advice dictated three meals and no snacks between them. But mini-meals of low-fat, high-fiber foods every two or three hours prevent the blood sugar from dropping so low you feel ravenous. Then at mealtimes, you eat less because you feel less hungry.

• Exercise regularly. Research has shown that regular, moderate exercise is essential to both good health and permanent weight control. Even modest exercise programs can make a difference. Brisk walking for as little as twenty minutes a day can burn fat calories, rev up your BMR, and dramatically decrease your health risks. Aerobic exercise is even better. It burns more calories and revs up your BMR for hours longer.

• Be patient. Permanent weight loss is a relatively slow process. Aim for a slow, steady loss of one pound a week.

• Get extra help. For some people, weight and body image are associated with other problems—childhood trauma, fears about sexuality, an inability to express feelings, and other emotional concerns. If these or other issues contribute to your weight problems, seek help from a skilled psychotherapist.

When to Call the Doctor.   An increasing number of intensive professionally-directed programs can help people lose weight and teach them how to keep it off. Pritikin Centers enjoy good success and focus not only on reducing weight but also on reducing the risk of heart disease, stroke, and cancer.

SICK BUILDING SYNDROME

Sick building syndrome causes a group of vague, persistent symptoms including cough, headache, nose and eye irritation, lightheadedness, difficulty concentrating, and in serious cases, severe debilitation and nervous system ("neurological") disorders.

What's Going On?   Sick building syndrome is relatively new. Virtually unheard of until the late 1970s, its symptoms are an ironic result of the Arab Oil Embargo of 1973 and the "energy crisis" it precipitated. As the nation became painfully aware of the need to conserve energy, architects and engineers came up with what appeared to be an important innovation, the energy-efficient "sealed" office building with central heating and air-conditioning systems and windows that did not open.

If sealed buildings' ventilation systems work properly, they provide sufficient fresh air for the occupants. But if they don't, the result is an accumulation of indoor air pollutants that can make office air as dirty as air in steel mills or auto plants.

Experts estimate that millions of office buildings cause sick building syndrome. Here are just a few of the indoor air pollutants that can cause this illness:

• *Tobacco Smoke.* Even if you don't smoke, in a sealed building with faulty ventilation, you can breathe considerable amounts of the smoke cigarette smokers exhale ("second-hand smoke") or smoke given off by their cigarettes between puffs ("sidestream smoke"). Cigarette smoke contains hundreds of potentially hazardous chemicals, and passive smokers may suffer eye and respiratory irritation or asthma symptoms.

• *Formaldehyde.* Formaldehyde is the chemical that makes carpeting, drapes, office furniture, and automobiles smell "new." It's also a key ingredient in particle board, an increasingly ubiquitous building material. The "new" smell means formaldehyde is being released into the air. Even at relatively low concentrations, formaldehyde trapped in sealed buildings can cause headaches, fatigue, nausea, asthma symptoms, and skin, eye, and respiratory irritation.

• *Pesticides.* Ants, roaches, and other bugs are bad, but in sealed buildings, the chemicals often used to control them can be worse. Other potentially hazardous pesticides include those sprayed on potted plants.

• *Ozone, Ammonia, and Methyl Alcohol.* Unless they are properly vented and maintained, copy machines and other office equipment can release these chemicals. So can white-paint correcting fluids and even felt-tipped marking pens. Ammonia, which has a sharp, biting odor, can cause headache, dizziness, asthma symptoms, and eye, nose, and respiratory irritation. Ozone, a sweet-smelling gas formed by electrical sparks, can cause respiratory irritation, asthma symptoms, and in high concentrations, chest pain and lung disease.

• *Carbon Monoxide.* This chemical in automobile exhaust may be sucked into sealed buildings from the outside because of poorly placed air intake vents. Even in low doses, carbon monoxide can cause headache and dizziness.

• *Microorganisms.* In 1976, participants at an American Legion convention at a Philadelphia hotel were stricken with a strange form of pneumonia. Many died. Their illness, now known as "Legionnaire's disease," was caused by bacteria spread by the hotel's air-conditioning system. Molds and fungi can also be spread by poorly maintained ventilation.

Symptoms include fatigue, runny nose, nasal congestion, headaches, cough, fever, and asthma symptoms.

Before You Call the Doctor. If you've been experiencing vague, odd, persistent respiratory symptoms at work and they are not caused by colds, flu, or allergies, you might be suffering from sick building syndrome. Ask yourself these questions:

• Are you the only one? When sick building syndrome strikes, typically several people in an office or on one floor develop similar symptoms.

• Do you feel better on weekends and while on vacation? Some people who notice they feel sick at work but fine off the job blame their symptoms on their own "neurotic" relationship to work. But with sick building syndrome, you feel ill when exposed to trapped pollutants and better when you've been away from them for any period of time.

• Are there any noticeable odors in the building? If anything smells odd, chances are the ventilation system isn't working properly.

• Are symptoms confined to one area, or are they generalized throughout a floor or the entire building?

• Was your office recently renovated with new drapes, carpeting, furniture, partitions, paint, or machinery? All these can produce formaldehyde.

• Did a large number of new people recently begin working in your area? Even if the building's ventilation system is working properly, it may not be powerful enough to provide fresh air to huge numbers of people.

If you answer "yes" to two or more of these questions, next ask your supervisor, building manager, or union representative about the building's ventilation system. Don't feel intimidated. Ventilation systems are simple. Fresh air enters the building through an intake vent. Fans push it around the building through large cylindrical or rectangular ducts. And stale air is eliminated through an exhaust vent.

The fresh air duct should be located on the roof, but sometimes it isn't. If it's located at ground level, you may wind up breathing car and truck exhaust.

But having the fresh air intake on the roof may not guarantee fresh air. If you work in a low-rise building surrounded by taller buildings, your "fresh" air may be contaminated with stale, polluted air exhausted from neighboring buildings.

Next check your office ventilation. Every work area should have supply and exhaust vents. To tell one from the other, hold a hand or tissue near them. The supply vent blows air into the room; the exhaust vent sucks it out. The vents should be across the room from each other to produce good circulation. If they're too close, the fresh air may be sucked out before it has a chance to circulate, leaving you breathing stale air all day long. If the ventilation system is turned off, you won't detect any movement at all at the vents. (Frequently the ventilation system is turned off each weekend, and sometimes, maintenance personnel neglect to turn it back on.)

The American Society of Heating, Refrigeration, and Air Conditioning Engineers (ASHRE) recommends five cubic feet of fresh air per person per minute in nonsmoking work areas and twenty cubic feet in work areas where smoking is permitted.

Even if your ventilation system blows recommended amounts of air, you may still have a sick building if that air is *recirculated*. Many sealed buildings recirculate air to reduce heating and cooling costs. This may be good for the utility bill, but it's bad for those who work in the building.

ASHRE also recommends relative humidity in the "comfort zone" of 20 to 50 percent. Air with a relative humidity below 20 percent feels uncomfortably dry. It dries the eyes, nose, mouth, and throat and increases the risk of colds by opening tiny cracks in the mucus layer that lines the throat (see COLDS in Chapter 11). Relative humidity above 50 percent allows molds to grow, which contributes to sick building syndrome and allergies (see ALLERGIES in this chapter).

Air conditioning tends to dry the air. One way to raise relative humidity into the comfort zone is to use a humidifier or cold-water vaporizer. But don't use ultrasonic models. They atomize the minerals in water, and these minerals should not be breathed. And be sure to clean humidifiers regularly with bleach. Otherwise they might breed microorganisms which contribute to sick building syndrome.

Another way to increase indoor air humidity is to keep broad-leafed houseplants in your office. When properly watered and misted, the leaves give off both water vapor and oxygen.

If your building houses several businesses but uses only one building-wide ventilation system, beware. Businesses that typically use chemicals implicated in sick building syndrome include dry cleaners, hair salons, print shops, copy shops, medical and photo laboratories, and medical and dental offices.

For more information about sick building syndrome, contact the American Lung Association (see RESOURCES at the end of Chapter 11).

For a professional evaluation of the air quality in your building, consult an industrial hygienist (see RESOURCES at the end of this chapter).

When to Call the Doctor.   Most physicians are not well informed about sick building syndrome. Even if they are, treating those made ill by indoor air pollution does not deal with the problem. The building's ventilation system must work efficiently and be properly maintained. If your job or building management does not take your complaints seriously, a doctor should be able to help document changes in respiratory function. For example, your doctor could take pulmonary function tests at the beginning and end of a work week.

SWOLLEN FEET, ANKLES, HANDS

(See FLUID RETENTION in this chapter)

SWOLLEN GLANDS

These "glands" are actually lymph nodes, and doctors call this problem "swollen lymph nodes" or "lymphadenopathy." Swollen glands feel like hard, tender knots under the skin.

What's Going On?   As the body responds to infection, the lymph nodes swell. Nodes are scattered around the body, but swollen glands typically develop under the jaw and arms and in the groin.

Lymph nodes, the lymphatic vessels that connect them, and the spleen make up the lymphatic system, one of the body's defenses against infection. The glands produce special white blood cells ("lymphocytes") that destroy disease-causing microorganisms. They also help keep infections localized by trapping microorganisms.

A swollen node is a signal that something is wrong. Usually, it's a minor infection, but in some cases, swollen lymph nodes may indicate more serious illness.

Before You Call the Doctor.   A swollen node is a message to look for infection in the area near it. If a swollen node is found in the head or neck, check your face, teeth, throat, or scalp. If one is found under the arm, check your arms and breasts. In the groin, check the legs, feet, and genitals. In the elbow, focus on the hands and wrists. Swollen nodes may also indicate whole-body ("systemic") problems.

If you can identify any infection, initiate home treatment:

•For pain and achiness, take aspirin, acetaminophen, or ibuprofen. Aspirin and ibuprofen also relieve inflammation, but acetaminophen does not. Aspirin and ibuprofen cause more stomach upset than acetaminophen. Pregnant women and those with a history of ulcers should not take aspirin and ibuprofen. Pregnant women should consult a physician before taking any medication.

- Drink more fluids.
- Rest.
- Apply warm compresses and antiseptic ointments to any wounds.

When to Call the Doctor. If pain, redness, heat, swelling, or other symptoms increase over a few days despite self-care, consult a physician. Any node that gradually gets bigger should be evaluated by a physician. Minor infections are not the only things that can cause swollen glands. Other possibilities include serious infections, chronic inflammatory diseases, and cancer. Physicians usually diagnose these conditions by sampling the cells of the node with a fine needle ("fine needle aspiration biopsy").

▶ **RED FLAG** A swollen gland at the collarbone or bellybutton may indicate cancer. Consult a physician immediately.

RESOURCES

American Association of Sex Educators, Counselors, and Therapists. 435 North Michigan Ave., Suite 1717, Chicago, IL 60611. Write for a free list of all the certified sex therapists in your state.

American Diabetes Association. P.O. Box 25757, 1660 Duke St., Alexandria, VA 22313; (703) 549-1500 or 1-(800)-232-3472. Provides information, publications, support, and referrals to diabetics, their families, and physicians.

American Industrial Hygiene Association, 475 Wolf Ledges Parkway, Akron, OH 44311; (216) 762-7294. Provides information about workplace air pollution and referrals to industrial hygiene resources around the country.

American Sleep Disorders Association. 604 Second St., S.W., Rochester, MN 55902. Write, don't call, for a list of sleep clinics around the country.

Asthma and Allergy Foundation of America. 1717 Massachusetts Ave., N.W., Suite 305, Washington, D.C. 20036; (202) 265-0265. Provides information, educational programs, and referrals to physicians and the public.

Chronic Fatigue/Immune Dysfunction Syndrome Foundation. 965 Mission St., Suite 425, San Francisco, CA 94103; (415) 882-9986.

Provides education, support, information, and referrals for those with chronic fatigue.

MedicAlert Foundation. For a $25 lifetime membership, you receive a wrist bracelet or necklace which lists your illness and an emergency phone number. Call the number, and operators provide the name and phone number of the person's physician, and a list of any required medications. Call 1-(800)-344-3226 or 1-(800)-432-5378.

Sugar-Free Diabetic Center. Located in Van Nuys, California, this self-help organization run by diabetics sells everything diabetics need to live rich, full, active lives. Call 1-(800)-972-2323 or, in California 1-(800)-336-1222.

C H A P T E R 5

Emotional Health

ANOREXIA NERVOSA

(See EATING DISORDERS in this chapter)

ANXIETY

Depending on its severity, anxiety causes feelings ranging from mild nervousness and vague malaise to dread, doom, or panic.

What's Going On?   Anxiety is our biological alarm. When we perceive danger, we respond by becoming anxious. A certain amount of anxiety is normal and even productive. For example, when parents sense their children have suddenly become too quiet and rush to investigate, their anxiety might prevent a tragedy. We respond to anxiety emotionally with a complex range of feelings including fear, dread, and anger. We respond physically with tensed muscles, racing hearts, shallow breathing, and sweating palms and feet. Intellectually, anxiety often interferes with clear thinking. Behaviorally, we exhibit the "fight-or-flight" response, poising ourselves for self-defense or escape. Unfortunately, the anxiety alarm sometimes goes awry and we misperceive safe situations as dangerous or mildly threatening situations as life-threatening.

Mental health authorities traditionally view anxiety as a reflection of conflicts within the individual. For example, a person who lies might feel anxiety about doing something wrong and about the possibility of getting caught. However, such explanations don't explain other types of anxiety, such as phobias and panic attacks. Scientists now believe our "anxiety alarm system" is influenced by a complex interaction of genetics, illnesses, drugs, and our history of traumatic events.

Heredity plays an important role in certain types of anxiety, particularly panic attacks. However, environmental factors also contribute. People who suffer panic attacks often have histories of early loss or extreme stress.

Physical factors such as anemia, diabetes, menopause, premenstrual syndrome, thyroid disorders, low blood sugar ("hypoglycemia"), pulmonary disease, endocrine tumors, and various heart problems all can cause anxiety symptoms.

Drugs such as cocaine, amphetamines, diet pills, and caffeine also contribute to anxiety.

Anxiety takes many forms. Here we'll deal with its most common manifestations:

• *Generalized Anxiety.* Everyone suffers everyday tensions from ordinary upsets. But people who suffer generalized or "free floating" anxiety experience almost constant worry and apprehension and typically have other problems as well: insomnia, nightmares, stomach upsets, aches and pains, heart palpitations, and/or difficulty concentrating. They are often called "worry warts," always edgy, irritable, and impatient.

• *Phobias.* A phobia is a situational form of anxiety which produces a morbid fear of specific objects, activities, or settings. Common phobias include fears of flying, heights, public speaking, crossing bridges, and closed or open spaces. Some people think the term "phobia" implies severe, morbid fear. It doesn't. An estimated 10 percent of Americans—some 25 million people—are fearful flyers. Some are so phobic they cannot fly at all, but the vast majority are experienced air travelers who simply wish the skies were a bit more friendly. Fearful flyers and people with other mild phobias cope as best they can and somehow muddle through their fearful situations.

• *Post-traumatic Stress Syndrome.* Some people who have lived through extreme stress, such as rape, sexual abuse, war, or natural disasters, don't recover normally. Instead, they may spend months and sometimes years troubled by anxiety, depression, insomnia, flashbacks, mood swings, loss of self-esteem, phobias, and compulsions, including drug and alcohol abuse.

• *Panic Attacks.* Some people suffer severe, spontaneous anxiety attacks. These recurrent, unpredictable episodes involve trembling; heart palpitations; shallow, rapid breathing; dizziness and light-headedness; hot or cold flashes; chest tightness or pain; tingling of the extremities; feelings of terror and doom; and fear of dying or "going crazy." Most panic attacks last only a few minutes, but occasionally they may last several hours.

Not only are panic attacks the most debilitating of the anxiety disorders, they may also be followed by phobias, such as agoraphobia (fear of public places). In extreme cases, agoraphobics become prisoners in their own homes.

Before You Call the Doctor. In a nation where Valium and other tranquilizers are among the most widely used (and abused) prescription medications, many people seek quick fixes for their emotional ills through pills. But nondrug self-care techniques are often a more effective—and less anxiety-producing—approach to mild-to-moderate generalized anxiety, phobias, and post-traumatic stress syndrome. Self-care techniques help you to develop coping skills. In addition, they allow you to replace feelings of loss of control, which are central to anxiety, with new feelings of self-confidence and personal power.

• Stop using caffeine. The powerful, addictive stimulant in coffee, tea, cola soft drinks, cocoa, chocolate, and many over-the-counter drugs is a major—and often overlooked—contributor to anxiety. In fact, in high doses caffeine produces a condition known as caffeinism, with symptoms identical to those of serious anxiety problems.

If you're accustomed to drinking coffee, colas and other forms of caffeine, stopping often causes withdrawal symptoms: headache, sluggishness, and possibly constipation. Withdrawal symptoms typically subside within a few days. When they do, most people are amazed how relaxed and unflappable they feel.

• Exercise. Any exercise helps, but aerobic exercise works best. Get your pulse up to 70 to 80 percent of the maximum recommended heart rate for your age group (220 minus your age, multiplied by .7 or .8) four or five times a week. Aerobic exercise releases endorphins, the body's own pain- and anxiety-relieving "feel good" chemicals. If you already exercise regularly, increase the frequency or duration of your workouts. If not— and you're not physically limited by a chronic illness or disability—start by taking a brisk twenty-minute walk, swim, or bike ride three times a week. After a few weeks, most people notice new feelings of clearheadedness and energy, with decreased tension and anxiety.

• Get adequate rest. If insomnia is a problem, see INSOMNIA in Chapter 4.

• Try relaxation training. A variety of techniques, including meditation, visualization, biofeedback, music therapy, and progressive relaxation, can help people release tension and relieve anxiety (see MANAGE YOUR STRESS LOAD in Chapter 1).

• Call a friend or family member. Talking things out with someone you know well can defuse anxiety and reorder scattered emotions.

• Make love. Many people find sex a powerful anxiety reliever. Even without intercourse, anxiety often melts away simply by holding—and being held by—someone whose intimate company you enjoy.

• Keep a journal. Some people find solace writing down their anxious thoughts and feelings. Instead of simply focusing on how bad you feel, think about possible causes and what you might reasonably do about them. Perhaps your job, family, or other relationships are causing your anxiety. If so, consider alternatives: What can you do to change the situation? To whom can you turn for the help you need?

• Practice cognitive therapy. *Feeling Good* by David Burns, M.D., might help (see RESOURCES at the end of this chapter). It advocates cognitive therapy, which is based on the notion that people often view the problems in their lives inaccurately and create emotional mountains out of molehills. For example, some people "overgeneralize." If one little thing goes wrong, they decide everything has gone to hell. Others engage in "all or nothing thinking," the idea that if they're not the best, they must be the absolute worst. Then there's "jumping to conclusions." If a friend is late for a date with you, those who jump to conclusions assume they've been cruelly stood up rather than considering the more likely possibilities of traffic jams and parking problems. Cognitive therapy doesn't comfort everyone, but many psychotherapists recommend *Feeling Good.* It often helps clarify thinking and reduce anxiety.

• Try a self-help group. Both peer- and professionally-led groups can help people with specific anxiety problems. Call your local mental health agency for referrals. If your problem involves a particular aversion, the Phobia Society of America can refer you to a group in your area (see RESOURCES at the end of this chapter).

• Try a class. Classes are particularly successful in helping people overcome fear of flying (see RESOURCES at the end of this chapter).

When to Call the Doctor.   If self-care approaches don't provide sufficient relief after a few weeks or months or if the problem is panic attacks, consult a physician. Few primary care doctors treat serious anxiety problems. Most refer patients to psychiatrists, psychologists, clinical social workers, or other mental-health therapists whose treatment may include one or more of the following:

• Psychotherapy. Psychotherapy focuses on uncovering and dealing with underlying issues that promote anxiety. It is especially helpful for anxiety caused by losses or post-traumatic stress. In the latter, a key element involves retelling the traumatic events to a skilled listener in an effort to face them and come to terms with the stress they caused.

Some psychotherapists offer specialized group sessions for people suffering from particular anxiety problems. Group therapy is generally less expensive than individual therapy, and group participants can provide support and feedback and share coping strategies.

• Behavioral therapy. Behavior therapy ignores underlying causes and focuses instead on strategies that alter the undesired behavior. It's a particularly effective treatment for phobias. The specific approach is "desensitization." The person is gradually exposed to the dreaded object or situation and trained to react without anxiety. For example, fear-of-flying classes progress from instruction about the principles of flying, to having the group sit in an airport waiting area, then on a parked airplane, then on a plane that taxis without taking off, and finally, on a plane that goes up for a short flight.

• Drug therapy. Psychiatrists may prescribe such mood-altering drugs as imipramine, phenelzine, buspirone, and alprazolam, particularly for agoraphobia and severe anxiety attacks. If you and your doctor opt for drug therapy, discuss potential side effects, including the possibility of addiction or loss of sexual desire.

BAD HABITS, COMPULSIONS, AND ADDICTIONS

Too much of almost anything—from hand washing to cigarette smoking to cocaine—can become a bad habit. And if it isn't controlled early on, it often progresses to a compulsion and ultimately to an addiction, where the person has no real control over the undesired behavior.

What's Going On?   Some authorities, for example drug expert and medical philosopher Andrew Weil, M.D., contend that the desire to alter consciousness is an innate human need. Even if it isn't innate, it's certainly common. These days, it's almost impossible to find an adult (and a teen or even pre-teen) who hasn't gotten drunk, tried smoking, gone on a spending spree, or eaten too much ice cream when upset. Certainly no one should smoke, but for most other human activities with a potential for abuse, the real question is: How can we tell when any behavior changes from a "fling" into a bad habit, and from there to a compulsion, which involves feeling pulled against one's conscious will, or to an uncontrollable addiction, which might ruin our lives?

Psychologists debate the definitions of "bad habit," "compulsion," and "addiction," but for purposes of this discussion, they're all points along a continuum of loss of personal control over our lives. The goal is to regain that control so we no longer feel victimized by irresistible impulses. In this discussion, we use the term "addiction" metaphorically to refer to any bad habit in need of change.

Are you addicted to anything that is harming, or might harm, you or your family or friends? A major stumbling block is that addicts usually deny they have a problem. Consider any behavior you're concerned about. If you answer "yes" to any of the following statements, you may be using that behavior addictively:
- I do it to make me feel okay about myself.
- I forget my problems when I indulge in it.
- Sometimes it interferes with things in my life I consider important.
- I feel ashamed and guilty about it.
- I'm secretive about it.
- I use it to celebrate my accomplishments.

•I use it for comfort when things are going poorly.

•Many of my routines revolve around it.

•I used to enjoy it more than I do now.

•I keep doing it even when it's not pleasurable.

•Friends, family, and/or coworkers have said they think I have a problem.

•I'm afraid to quit because I don't know if I can function without it.

•I'm afraid to quit because I don't know if I can.

Substance abuse is usually easier to identify than abusive relationships. Often, people who are raised in dysfunctional homes, such as those who grow up in alcoholic families, become what substance-abuse experts call "codependent." Psychiatrist Timmen Cermak, M.D., a leader in counseling adult children of alcoholics, defines codependency as neglect of one's own needs because of preoccupation with the needs of another. Put another way, one wit offered this definition of codependence: "When codependent people are drowning, *someone else's* life flashes before them." Women, our culture's primary caretakers, are particularly vulnerable to codependency. Just like other addictions, people often deny codependency. Dr. Cermak says a "yes" answer to any of the following questions suggests a codependent situation:

•Do you often assume responsibility for others' needs, even when you know you're neglecting your own?

•During intimate moments or during times of separation, do you often feel anxious and confused?

•Do you feel happy or depressed based on your ability to control someone else's behavior?

•Do you feel happy or depressed based on your ability to control how the world views someone else's behavior?

•Are you involved with someone you know has a drug, alcohol, or personality problem?

•Do you have difficulty expressing your feelings about that person's problems?

Before You Call the Doctor.   It's not easy to recover from any addiction or codependency. It takes time, commitment, and hard work. Most addiction authorities say that before the destructive behavior can change, two things must happen—unhappiness about it must accumulate, and a "moment of truth" must occur which underscores the person's loss of control over the behavior. For some, the moment of truth comes in a tragedy such as an auto accident or major illness. For others, it comes as an "intervention," in which friends and family confront the person about the problem and present treatment options and a clear ultimatum about the consequences of ignoring their request to begin treatment.

After the moment of truth, experts on breaking bad habits, for example, Patricia Allison, author of *Hooked, But Not Helpless,* suggest applying the twelve-step approach developed by Alcoholics Anonymous (AA) and adopted by other Anonymous groups, everything from Gamblers Anonymous to Sex and Love Addicts Anonymous. Four of the steps are:

• Acknowledge your powerlessness over the addiction and the fact that your life has become unmanageable because of it.

• Recognize that you need help and cannot fight the addiction alone. Alcoholics Anonymous groups advocate turning to God or any higher spiritual authority the addict identifies with for solace and support. However, an increasing number of Anonymous groups are less spiritual and are organized with special sensitivity to certain communities, including atheists, gays, nonsmokers, and older adults. One is SOS, the Secular Organization for Sobriety based in North Hollywood, California.

• Become honest with yourself and with others. In her stop-smoking program, BreatheFree, in Portland, Oregon, Patricia Allison calls addicts' dishonesty "junkie thinking" and says that addicts use dishonesty to rationalize their destructive behavior. AA confronts the honesty issue directly by insisting that everyone who gets up to speak at a meeting begin with: "My name is ———, and I'm an alcoholic."

• Take an honest inventory of your life. Acknowledge both the good and bad you've done, and commit to improving yourself and resolving the harm you've done.

Anonymous groups are always open to offer assistance—consult the white pages of your phone book. They also offer members "buddies" and emergency phone numbers that members can call whenever they feel in danger of slipping back into addictive behaviors. The structure and support of Anonymous organizations may be an effective path to recovery for those who feel ready but unable to change their lives.

Here are some other potentially effective self-care techniques:

• Keep a diary. Diaries help identify the sometimes-hidden "triggers" that prompt addictive behavior. Whenever you feel the urge to indulge in your addiction, stop and pull out your diary. Note the date, time, your feelings, and what just happened that made you want to indulge. Later, add what you did to cope and the consequences of your behavior. Typical triggers include boredom, loneliness, rejection, frustration, difficult interpersonal encounters, and having unstructured time.

• Change your patterns. Once you know what triggers the habit you're committed to breaking, plan ahead to minimize the likelihood you'll slip into a triggering situation. An alcoholic might decide not to join coworkers at the weekly TGIF party. An overeater might decide to catch the bus farther away from that seductive bakery. A smoker might commit to having a cup of herbal tea or taking a walk instead of lighting up after meals. For a codependent in an abusive relationship, a constructive change might involve a refusal to apologize for the other person's behavior.

•Positive thinking. Practice positive statements, such as "I am in charge of my life. I can change." Some people dismiss such personal pep talks as silly, but they're often surprisingly effective. Remember the classic children's story *The Little Engine That Could.* The engine kept repeating, "I think I can. I think I can," which soon became a triumphant "I knew I could."

•Change your self-image. Along with changing your behavior patterns, adopt a new self-image to fit your new healthier reality. Instead of calling yourself "a smoker (or drinker) who's trying to quit," call yourself an "ex-smoker" or a "recovering alcoholic."

•Consult the *Recovery Resource Book,* which lists helpful books and organizations for dealing with addictions to alcohol, cigarettes, cocaine/ crack, marijuana, narcotics, prescription drugs, overeating, sex, gambling, debt, and work (see RESOURCES at the end of this chapter).

When to Call the Doctor.   If you still feel out of control after a few weeks or months of committed self-care, consult a physician. Family doctors can often help people quit smoking. For other addictions, they are likely to provide referrals to therapists who specialize in the problem.

BULIMIA

(See EATING DISORDERS in this chapter)

DEPRESSION

Depression causes persistent feelings of anxiety, listlessness, self-hatred, helplessness, hopelessness, fatigue, and difficulty concentrating and making decisions.

What's Going On?   Feeling "blue" from time to time is a normal part of life. However, the blues become depression when lethargy and listlessness affect a person's ability to function normally.

An estimated thirty million Americans feel so depressed that they are unable to experience pleasure in their lives and are often unable to function. Depression is so prevalent it's called the "common cold of mental health." Most forms of depression share similar symptoms:

• Preoccupation with feelings of guilt, self-blame, worthlessness, helplessness, and hopelessness.

• Loss of interest in usually pleasurable activities.

• Loss of sexual interest.

• Crying spells.

• Insomnia.

• Difficulty concentrating.

• Memory loss.

• Appetite changes, with noticeable weight fluctuations.

• Periods of intense activity followed by inactivity.

• Recurrent thoughts of suicide.

Mental health authorities have identified several types of depression, each requiring its own treatment.

• *Reactive Depression.* This results from an inability to recover normally from stressful life events: the death of a loved one, relationship problems, job loss, a chronic illness, or any personal tragedy. It affects people of all ages and there's usually no family history of depression. Symptoms include pessimism and self-pity, but there is usually little loss of self-esteem. Although reactive depression often causes loss of interest in life, those who suffer it are usually able to continue working and are not usually at risk for suicide.

Of course, intense feelings of unhappiness after a major loss or traumatic event are normal and healthy. They are part of mourning. But healthy grieving involves a gradual change of feelings from bad to better over time. Eventually we come to terms with the loss and begin to experience life's pleasures again.

• *SAD.* "SAD" is an acronym for "seasonal affective disorder," or the winter depression that often occurs from November through March among those who live in northern latitudes. SAD is caused by a lack of exposure to sunlight. It's quite common in Alaska, which remains dark much of the day throughout winter. In addition to the lethargy associated with other forms of depression, SAD symptoms often include irritability, chronic headache, increased appetite, weight gain, and an increased need for sleep. Usually SAD begins in a person's 20s. Episodes may last several weeks. It affects women six times more often than men, and about half of SAD sufferers have relatives with SAD or other emotional problems.

Although mental health experts are unsure of the physiological mechanism that causes SAD, they speculate that increased amounts of the hormone melatonin released by the pineal gland during the longer, darker days of winter may be the culprit.

• **_Physically-based Depression._**   Some cases of depression develop for no apparent reason in mid-life or later. Authorities believe this type of depression results from biochemical problems in the brain, and it is most likely to respond to antidepressant medication. Physically-based depression sufferers often have a family history of depression.

Other physical causes of depression include certain illnesses (AIDS, hepatitis, mononucleosis, stroke, chronic pain, etc.) and many drugs (alcohol, tranquilizers, heart and blood-pressure medications, and withdrawal from amphetamines, cocaine, and other drugs).

• **_Manic Depression._**   Now medically known as "bipolar disorder," this biochemically-based illness involves severe mood swings. Manic depressives have bursts of intense energy and activity followed by periods of severe despair.

• **_Suicide_**   People who suffer depression are at significant risk for suicide. Each year, about 200,000 Americans—most of them depressed—attempt to kill themselves, and about 27,000 succeed. People of all ages consider and attempt suicide, but over the last 20 years, suicide rates among teens and the elderly have risen dramatically. Authorities suggest that increased suicide rates in these age groups reflect an increased incidence of depression. Often a suicide attempt is a cry for help. Friends and loved ones should always take suicidal hints and threats seriously and encourage the person to consult a mental health professional immediately.

Although anyone might attempt suicide, authorities have identified many risk factors for self-destruction in depressed people:

• Previous suicide attempts, even if they appeared to be ineffectual gestures, for example, minor knicking of the wrists.

• Male sex.

• Over forty-five years of age.

• Alcohol abuse or a recent increase in the use of other depressants, such as sedatives or tranquilizers.

• Recent loss of a spouse or child or, for a child, loss of a pet.

• Recent loss of health or diagnosis of a dread disease.

• Having a detailed suicide plan.

• Lack of a social support system.

Before You Call the Doctor.   Mild to moderate depression often responds to self-care:

• Ask yourself: What's making me feel angry and/or frustrated? Depression often involves unacknowledged feelings of anger or frustration turned inward on yourself. If you feel yourself sinking into a depression, look within and explore these feelings.

• Eat a balanced, low-fat, high-fiber diet rich in vitamin B. Deficiencies in vitamins B_6, B_{12}, and folic acid can contribute to depression. Good sources of B_6 include milk, whole grains, and meats, especially liver and kidney. B_{12} can be obtained from milk and meats, especially liver and kidney. (B_{12} is not present in vegetables, so strict "vegan" vegetarians, who eat no meat or dairy products, might become deficient without supplementation.) Good sources of folic acid include raw, dark green leafy vegetables as well as liver and kidney.

• Don't use sugar. A few hours after eating sugary foods, some people feel let down and blue.

• Take a vacation. Sometimes a weekend getaway or longer vacation provides perspective on stressful events and lifts the spirits.

• Exercise regularly. See the discussion of exercise in the ANXIETY section of this chapter. Exercise is among the most powerful self-care tools for relieving depression. Studies have shown that for mild to moderate depression, it's often as effective as antidepressant drugs. Aerobic exercise stimulates the release of endorphins, the body's own pain-relieving, mood-lifting chemicals. It is also a healthy release for anger and other negative emotions.

• Don't use alcohol. It's a powerful depressant.

• Stick to your routines. Routines help anchor us in the world. Particularly in cases of reactive depression, going to school or work and continuing to participate in other regular activities can help relieve depression.

• Reach out. Friends and relatives can often lend a sympathetic ear and help unburden a heavy heart. Crisis intervention and support groups are available for many causes of reactive depression, such as loss of a child or various chronic illnesses. Local mental health agencies can supply referrals.

• See comedies. Laughter is powerful antidepressant medicine. It helps provide perspective. Take in some funny movies or comedy acts.

• Keep a journal. Write down your fears, feelings, and potential options.

• Relax. Use relaxation tools such as music, meditation, biofeedback, and progressive relaxation to help counteract stress and depression.

• Try cognitive therapy. See the discussion in the ANXIETY section of this chapter.

• Sit under high-intensity, full-spectrum lights. About 80 percent of SAD sufferers can eliminate their depression with phototherapy, which consists of daily exposure to intense, full-spectrum lights (or almost-full-spectrum lights, with the ultraviolet wavelengths filtered out to prevent sunburn and reduce the risk of melanoma). The lights are housed in special phototherapy appliances available through psychiatrists and should be used in the context of professional care. Phototherapeutic relief usually begins within a week or so. A trip to the Caribbean also works well. Relief typically lasts a few weeks after returning home.

• If you are reading this section because you feel concerned about a friend or loved one, work to persuade them to try some of these suggestions *even though they don't think they'll work*. Remember, hopelessness is a major feature of depression.

Because anyone who is depressed is at increased risk for suicide, friends and loved ones should become sensitive to this possibility. After a suicide, loved ones often say, "Well, he kind of mentioned that he was thinking about it, but I never thought he was serious." When dealing with possible suicide, it's always best to err on the side of taking hints seriously.

Two-thirds of those who kill themselves communicate their intent in advance by words or deeds, or both. Here's a sampling of remarks which suggest a possible suicide attempt:
• "Life isn't worth living."
• "Maybe things would be better if I weren't around."
• "Sometimes I just want to go to sleep and not wake up."
• "Who do you think would come to my funeral?"
• "I'm thinking about killing myself."
Here's a sampling of pre-suicidal actions:
• Any self-injury.
• Giving away valued personal property.
• Taking drug overdoses "accidentally."
• Saying goodbye in a way that implies you won't see the person again.
• Unusual apathy, lethargy, hopelessness, withdrawal, or loss of appetite.

If you think someone close to you may be considering suicide, don't be afraid to ask. Asking this question doesn't put the idea into a depressed person's head. On the contrary, asking often opens up the issue to discussion. Most people answer honestly and give some indication how serious the risk is.

If you feel the person is at all serious, encourage him or her to get professional help. A call to a suicide hotline is often a good first step. Look in the white pages of your phone book under "Suicide," or call your county department of mental health.

If you fear a suicide attempt may be imminent, get the person to a psychiatric emergency service. Call 911 for the facility nearest you. What if the person refuses to go? Your coaxing may do the trick. If not, your coaxing plus the urgings of other friends and family members might prove persuasive. If all else fails, a 911 operator can send the police to place the person in protective custody. This is clearly a drastic step, but sometimes it's necessary to prevent a tragedy.

When to Call the Doctor. If self-care does not provide sufficient relief, consult a *psychiatrist,* not your family doctor, though you might ask your family physician for a referral. Some studies show that family physicians often under-diagnose depression. Psychiatrists are more likely to recognize the condition and be better informed about treatment.

Several types of depression can be treated with drugs, including tricyclic antidepressants and MAO inhibitors. The highs and lows of manic depression can often be controlled with lithium. Make sure you understand the potential side effects of any drugs you take.

EATING DISORDERS

The two we discuss are "anorexia nervosa" and "bulimia." The former involves a refusal to eat to the point of starvation and a distorted body image which makes the person feel "fat" even when clearly emaciated. Bulimia involves overeating binges followed by purges during which sufferers eat enormous quantities of food, then induce vomiting or use laxatives to get the food out of their systems so they won't gain weight.

What's Going On? Authorities aren't sure what causes anorexia and bulimia, but most believe they stem from disordered family relationships rather than the sufferer's individual psychological problems. Both anorexia and bulimia are characterized by a morbid fear of fat influenced by our culture's obsessions with thinness.

An estimated 1 percent of American women turn dieting into the self-starvation of anorexia, defined by a variety of symptoms: loss of at least 25 percent of body weight with no organic cause, fear of fat, distorted body image, and menstrual irregularity. As dieting progresses to starvation, vital signs grow weak, the extremities become cold, and downy hair may appear on the limbs to help conserve body heat. Anorexia can be fatal. One complication is anorexia-related cardiac arrest, which killed popular singer Karen Carpenter.

Some men also become anorexic, though men are at much lower risk than women.

Recent studies suggest that as many as 13 percent of American teenagers and up to 10 percent of college women practice some sort of bulimic binge-purge eating. Some authorities contend that as many as one in eight women from age nineteen to thirty nine are or have been bulimic. Nancy J. Kolodny, author of *When Food's a Foe,* says eating binges can range from as few as 1,000 calories to an astonishing 55,000.

Because bulimics typically maintain normal weight, they often successfully hide their problem for many years. It frequently comes to light when they begin suffering the pattern of medical complaints peculiar to bulimia:

• Chronic sore or burning throat from exposure to so much stomach acid in vomit.

• Tooth enamel erosion and decay caused by stomach acid from vomiting.

• Swollen salivary glands which cause a "chipmunk" face.

• Hernias.

• Chronic diarrhea or constipation.

• Rectal bleeding and other bowel problems.

• Menstrual irregularities.

• Nutritional deficiencies, particularly potassium deficiency ("hypokalemia"), the symptoms of which include weakness, numbness, muscle fatigue, kidney damage, erratic heart beat, and even paralysis.

If the stomach or esophagus ruptures, the medical complications can be life-threatening. Or if the sodium-potassium balance becomes too abnormal, it can lead to kidney failure or cardiac arrest.

Before You Call the Doctor.   Those with eating disorders often deny the problem so strenuously, it may be up to friends or family members to sound the alarm and call for professional help. Suspect an eating disorder if you or anyone you know has more than three of the following:

• A family history of eating disorders or other similar compulsions, such as alcoholism.

• Any personal history of an eating disorder. Experts estimate that as many as 50 percent of anorexics become bulimic, and at least 20 percent of bulimics become anorexic.

• Unusual weight loss or fluctuations. Advanced anorexics become "skin and bones," but any significant, unusual weight loss should arouse suspicion. Bulimics lose less weight but often exhibit sudden weight fluctuations.

• Chronic dental problems, particularly tooth decay but also gum disease and a series of root canal problems caused by the acids in vomit.

• Calluses or teeth marks on the hands from sticking fingers down the throat to induce vomiting.

• An intense fear of or preoccupation with fat and weight.

• Body image distortion. Despite excessive weight loss, anorexics believe they are fat. Bulimics have a similar belief.

• Scale watching. Some anorexics and bulimics weigh themselves twenty times a day.

• Preoccupation with food. Some eating disorder sufferers develop food fetishes—eating only foods of a particular color or texture or meticulously arranging food or cutting it into tiny pieces.

• Sudden disappearance of food items. If full jars of peanut butter or half-gallons of ice cream keep vanishing, suspect bulimia.

• Chronic use of laxatives, diuretics, emetics, or diet pills.

• Exercise obsession. Some anorexics exercise intensely to achieve their "perfect weight."

• Extra long showers. Some bulimics run the shower for long periods to cover up the noise of vomiting.

• Strange odors in the bathroom. Vomit has a distinctively pungent smell.

• Hair loss, deteriorating hair texture and quality, and nail problems. When starving, the body "lets go" of these nonessentials and directs any nourishment to the vital organs.

• Hypothermia. Anorexics often complain of being cold due to lack of the natural protection of fat. Downy body hair ("lanugo") may develop in an effort to keep the body warm.

• Other problems that might suggest an eating disorder include rashes, dry skin, menstrual irregularity, poor self-esteem, chronic insomnia, preoccupation with preparing and serving food to others, and constipation due to lack of food or overuse of laxatives, diuretics, and emetics.

When to Call the Doctor. If you suspect an eating disorder, consult a physician, mental health professional, or contact Anorexia Nervosa and Related Eating Disorders, Inc. (see RESOURCES at the end of this chapter). The anorexic or bulimic and the person's family may all require therapy.

Treatment options include psychotherapy, which addresses sufferers' underlying emotional conflicts; behavioral therapy, which uses psychological conditioning and behavior modification to change eating patterns; family therapy, a form of group therapy, which seeks to change family dynamics; and hospitalization, a last resort for many anorexics who are in mortal danger. Sometimes drugs, particularly antidepressants or tranquilizers, may be prescribed in addition to one or more of these therapies.

▶ **RED FLAG** People with eating disorders may be at risk for suicide. About one-third of anorexic deaths are suicides. Always take suicide threats seriously. See the discussion of suicidal signals in the DEPRES-SION section of this chapter.

FEARS AND PHOBIAS

(See ANXIETY in this chapter)

MANIC DEPRESSION

(See DEPRESSION in this chapter)

STRESS

(See ANXIETY in this chapter and MANAGE YOUR STRESS LOAD in Chapter 1)

RESOURCES

Feeling Good by David Burns, M.D. (New York: New American Library, 1980, $4.95) An excellent guide to cognitive therapy. Widely recommended by mental health professionals for dealing with anxiety and depression.

Anxiety Disorders Association of America. 6000 Executive Blvd., Suite 513, Rockville MD 20852; (301) 231-9350. Information about phobias and referrals to resources around the country that help overcome them.

Institute for the Psychology of Air Travel (IPAT). Send $2.50 and a self-addressed stamped envelope to 25 Huntington Ave., Suite 300, Boston, MA 02116 for referrals to forty fly-without-fear programs around the world.

Fearless Flying: The Complete Program for Relaxed Air Travel. Produced by the IPAT, this program includes four ninety-minute cassettes and a book on fearless flying. $49.95 postpaid from the address above.

USAir Fearful Flyers Program. Write P.O. Box 100, Glenshaw, PA 15116. The program distributes the book *Fly Without Fear* by Program Director Carole Stauffer, M.S.W., and Frank Petee for $11.95 postpaid.

Anorexia Nervosa and Related Eating Disorders, Inc. P.O. Box 5102, Eugene, OR 97405; (503) 344-1144. Information about anorexia and bulimia, and referrals to resources throughout the U.S.

Recovery Resource Book by Barbara Yoder (New York: Fireside, 1990, $12.95) A "Whole Earth Catalog" of information and other resources for people troubled by almost any bad habit, compulsion, or addiction.

CHAPTER 6

The Skin and Hair

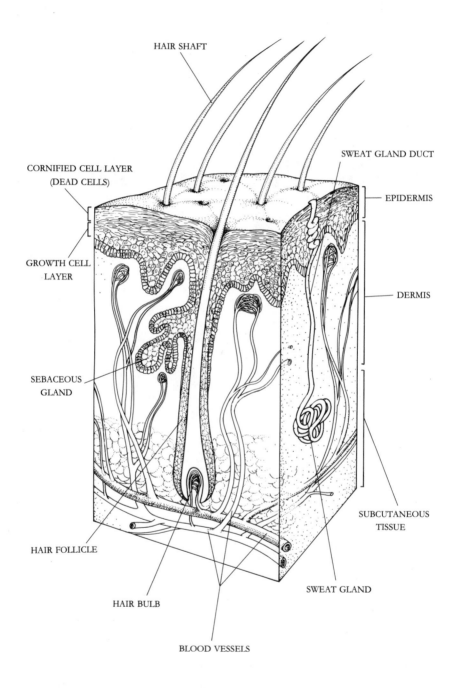

HAIR SHAFT

SWEAT GLAND DUCT

CORNIFIED CELL LAYER
(DEAD CELLS)

EPIDERMIS

GROWTH CELL
LAYER

DERMIS

SEBACEOUS
GLAND

SUBCUTANEOUS
TISSUE

HAIR FOLLICLE

SWEAT GLAND

HAIR BULB

BLOOD VESSELS

Anatomy of the Skin.

ABSCESSES

(See BOILS in this chapter)

ABRASIONS

(See CUTS in this chapter)

ACNE

(See also BOILS and HEAT RASH in this chapter)

Acne can range from a sparse scattering of pimples and blackheads to large cysts and infected nodules.

What's Going On?   An estimated 85 percent of adolescents suffer the heartbreak of "zits," the pimples, blackheads, cysts, and nodules of acne. Acne incidence peaks at around eighteen years of age, but many people suffer pimples on the face, chest, and back well into their forties. Acne tends to run in families.

Acne eruptions are caused by problems with the skin's normal processes. Pimples begin in the skin's hair follicles, which are connected to oil-producing ("sebaceous") glands. Normally, the oil ("sebum") flows out of the hair follicle to the skin's surface, carrying with it dead skin cells from the follicle lining. During puberty, however, male sex hormones ("androgens"), which are produced by both sexes, stimulate increased sebum production. In acne, the excess oil combines with the dead skin cells, hair fragments, and bacteria to form plugs ("comedones") that block the follicle pore. Since men produce more androgens, acne tends to affect more men than women.

Once the plug forms, it may be pushed to the skin surface and protrude slightly to form a blackhead. Contrary to advertising claims, dirt does not cause blackheads. Their dark color comes from skin pigment mixed into the plug debris. Usually, blackheads do not become full-fledged pimples.

If the plug doesn't reach the skin's surface but continues to grow in the follicle, it can rupture the follicle wall, discharging its mixture of oil, bacteria, and dead cells into the surrounding tissue and causing a minor infection. In response, infection-fighting white blood cells rush to the area, and the result of their battle with the bacteria is a white-headed acne pimple.

Acne pimples appear in three forms: "papules," red bumps; "pustules," pimples that come to a whitehead; and "nodules" or "cysts," which look like welts and can cause serious scarring. Dermatologists classify acne into mild ("comedonal"), moderate ("papulopustular"), and severe ("cystic"). Mild acne involves a predominance of blackheads and whiteheads. Moderate acne is characterized by black- and whiteheads with up to fifteen papules and general skin redness. Severe acne resembles the moderate form, but the person also has nodules or cysts.

Experts are still puzzled by what causes acne, but most point to a combination of enlarged oil glands, excess oil, bacteria, and enzymes or hormones.

Contrary to popular belief, teens' favorite foods—soft drinks, French fries, and chocolate—do not cause acne. Diet changes do not affect the condition. However, if you believe certain foods in your diet aggravate your acne, eliminate them and see what happens.

Another common myth is that acne is caused by poor skin hygiene. Ordinary surface skin oil has little to do with pimples. Oil that reaches the skin's surface isn't the problem; it's the oil trapped *below* the surface that causes pimples.

While doctors aren't sure what causes acne, they know certain factors can aggravate it:

•Cosmetics. Anything applied to the face can clog pores and contribute to pimple formation. Some cosmetics actually irritate the cells lining the oil gland pores, encouraging the formation of plugs. Some dermatologists suggest using "hypoallergenic" cosmetics or applying cosmetics only lightly, but if acne is a problem, try to use cosmetics as little as possible. If you must use some cosmetics, unscented, water-based ("noncomedogenic") products are less likely to irritate and clog facial pores than oil-based products.

•Stress, illness, or fatigue. There's little hard evidence here, but some people say their acne flares up when they're under emotional stress or when they're ill or exhausted. Stress stimulates the adrenal glands, which may increase androgen production.

•Sunlight. Some acne conditions improve with sun exposure. Others worsen.

•Hormones. For many women, acne outbreaks coincide with menstruation. Most women experience less acne during pregnancy, but some suffer aggravations. Depending on their estrogen content, some birth control pills improve acne.

•Occupations. Those who must work around grease—service station mechanics, short-order cooks, fast-food workers—are at increased risk for acne because the oil and/or grease on their jobs may block follicle openings. "Chloracne," a particular form of acne, is prevalent among people who work with the chlorinated hydrocarbons found in many pesticides, paints, varnishes, motor oil, and roofing materials.

• Drugs. Some drugs cause acne: lithium, corticosteroids, anti-convulsants, and certain asthma medications. If you take any of these and notice a flare-up, don't stop taking your medication. Consult your physician. It's possible a substitute drug might cause fewer problems.

Before You Call the Doctor.   Experts say only one case in ten requires professional care. If you have severe (cystic) acne—red, hot skin with cysts and nodules—see a dermatologist. But self-care usually minimizes problems from simple black- and whiteheads.

• Keep your skin clean, but don't overdo it. Wash your skin twice daily with a mild soap such as Dove or Neutrogena Extra Mild Liquid Cleanser. So-called "acne soaps" with sulfur aren't particularly effective because the medication washes away with rinsing. Excessive washing and scrubbing with harsh cleansers has little impact on acne and may dry, chap, and irritate the skin. It may also exacerbate the side effects of effective topical treatments. To minimize oiliness, try wiping with astringent witch hazel or mild alcohol-and-water astringents such as Stri-Dex Pads or Clearasil medicated Astringent.

• Don't use cosmetics. See above for the reasons why.

• Over-the-counter products. The Food and Drug Administration (FDA) studied over-the-counter acne remedies and found only three that were effective: sulfur, sulfur/resorcinol, and benzoyl peroxide. Although not part of the FDA's review, most dermatologists also contend that products containing salicylic acid are effective for mild acne. Buy only products that contain at least one of these ingredients. Since individual skin sensitivity varies widely, no one product is effective for everyone. Experiment and see which one(s) work for your acne.

For an occasional pimple, conservative treatment with a salicylic acid preparation such as Stri-Dex Medicated Pads or Clearasil Medicated Cleanser is usually enough. The salicylic acid can help unplug mild lesions and the alcohol removes surface oil.

For more extensive pimples, sulfur or sulfur/resorcinol products such as Postacne, Rezamid, and Acnomel Acne Cream can help hasten healing by drying the skin and promoting healing.

The most effective over-the-counter ingredient is benzoyl peroxide. It is the only one that prevents the formation of new pimples. Several preparations, such as Benoxyl, Loroxide, Oxy-5, Oxy-10, Persadox and

Quinolor, contain benzoyl peroxide in effective concentrations. Benzoyl peroxide dries the skin and causes some peeling, which helps unplug oil ducts and allows excess oil to escape. It may also kill infection-causing bacteria. Gels such as Fostex BPO and Clear By Design are more effective than creams or lotions but may cause more skin irritation. Prescription benzoyl peroxide gels may cause even more irritation.

Start with a 5 percent benzoyl peroxide preparation. Apply a *thin* coat twice a day. Remember, benzoyl peroxide prevents new pimples, so use it all over your face, not just on your pimples. If your skin feels dry and begins to peel, that means the preparation is working. If your acne does not begin to clear up with a 5 percent formulation, try a 10 percent product. Some people can use benzoyl peroxide only once a day. Others can use it more often. Experiment and find the schedule that works for you. If irritation develops, skip a day or two, and don't apply the product immediately after washing—wait about fifteen minutes. Some people develop allergic reactions. If a red, itchy rash appears, stop using the medication.

• Clay masques. Made of kaolin or Fuller's earth (available in most pharmacies or health food stores), clay masques remove oil from the skin. Mix a teaspoon of the clay with enough water to make a paste. Smooth on your face, avoiding the eyes. Allow it to dry ten minutes before rinsing it off.

• Steam. Some people report steam helps unclog their pores. Those who use this approach often add one or two herbs, chamomile or fennel. Boil 2 cups of water with ½ cup of herb. Reduce heat and simmer. Take the pot off the heat and place your face over the steamy liquid (not too close). Drape a towel over your head to form a tent. Steam for five to ten minutes before rinsing with cool water.

When to Call the Doctor.   If cleansing and over-the-counter products don't provide sufficient relief after two months, consult a physician for one of the four prescription acne treatments: benzoyl peroxide gels, antibiotics, Retin-A (also called vitamin A acid, tretinoin, and retinoic acid), and the newest treatment, Accutane (isotretinoin or 13-*cis*-retinoic acid):

• Benzoyl peroxide gels. These are simply stronger formulations of over-the-counter products.

• Antibiotics. Antibiotic gels or lotions have no effect on blackheads, but they help prevent the formation of pimples. They contain erythromycin or clindamycin and are typically as effective as oral antibiotics but have fewer side effects. Applied twice daily, topical antibiotics tend to be slightly drying and less irritating than benzoyl peroxide. In severe cases, dermatologists often prescribe antibiotic–benzoyl peroxide combinations.

In stubborn cases, physicians prescribe oral antibiotics (tetracycline or erythromycin) in combination with a topical treatment. Antibiotics work by eliminating the bacteria in the acne plug. Do not take tetracycline with milk, dairy products, or vitamin/mineral supplements. They interfere with the drug's action. Pregnant women should not take tetracycline because it can discolor the developing fetus's teeth. Avoid exposure to sunlight and/or wear sunblock with SPF 15 or higher when outdoors. Tetracycline can also decrease the effectiveness of oral contraceptives; therefore, other forms of birth control should be used while taking this drug.

Oral antibiotics take several weeks to work and may cause unpleasant side effects: diarrhea, stomach upset, increased sun sensitivity (photosensitivity), and, in women, an increase in the incidence of vaginal infections (antibiotics alter the vagina's natural pH).

• Retin-A interferes with acne plug formation by preventing the dead skin cells from sticking together in the follicle. It works best against blackheads but also reduces pimples. Because it often causes considerable skin irritation, it can usually be used only once a day or every other day. It comes in gels, creams, and liquids. The liquids are strongest and most irritating. During the first few weeks, the medication may aggravate acne and cause redness, peeling, and itching. It may take up to two months to see positive results. Retin-A should be applied thirty minutes after washing and thoroughly drying the skin. Immediate application after washing may aggravate irritation. Don't apply it around sensitive areas, such as the eyes, near the nostrils, or the corners of the mouth.

Dermatologists often prescribe Retin-A in combination with benzoyl peroxide or topical antibiotics. Use the drugs on alternate days or apply one at night and the other in the morning. Mixing drugs can neutralize them.

Retin-A causes photosensitivity. Use sunscreens while outdoors.

• Accutane is another derivative of vitamin A. Most experts believe it reduces oil production as well as sebaceous gland size. It may also decrease inflammation and pore plugging. It is particularly effective against stubborn facial acne and usually clears acne on the back and chest. Unlike other medications, Accutane continues to work for weeks, months, and possibly even years after treatment.

Users take Accutane orally for three to five months. If it is not completely successful, another course may be taken after a two-month rest period. Unfortunately, Accutane is quite expensive and extended use can cost hundreds of dollars.

Numerous side effects are possible. Accutane may increase cholesterol levels and alter liver-function tests. Anyone taking it should have cholesterol and liver-function tests beforehand, then periodically during treatment.

It may also cause skin rash, dry mouth, chapped lips, nose bleeds, eye dryness and irritation, breaking and thinning of hair, and decreased night vision. In addition, it can cause fatigue, headache, and muscle and joint aches. Since many of these side effects resemble those of a vitamin A overdose, don't take vitamin A supplements while taking Accutane. Other drugs may aggravate Accutane side effects, so talk with your physician about any other medications you are taking before beginning Accutane therapy.

▶ **RED FLAGS**   Accutane may cause miscarriage and birth defects in unborn babies. *Pregnant women, or women trying to become pregnant should not take this drug.* Use a reliable form of birth control and have at least one normal menstrual period after discontinuing the drug before becoming pregnant.

ATHLETE'S FOOT

(See also BLISTERS, NAIL PROBLEMS, and RINGWORM in this chapter)

Athlete's foot causes mild to severe itching and burning on the feet, and often blisters and skin cracking between the toes.

What's Going On?   On any given day, more than 4 percent of Americans are afflicted with athlete's foot. It's the most common fungal infection of the skin. Athlete's foot is seven times more prevalent in men than women and more common in hot, humid weather. Those whose socks become sweaty because of poorly ventilated athletic shoes and those who use school or health club locker room showers are particularly susceptible, hence the name. But athlete's foot doesn't just affect athletes or only the feet. The fungal family which causes it can infect anyone and many other places on the skin.

Also known as "tinea pedis," athlete's foot is a skin infection caused by a *Trichophyton* fungus. *Trichophyton* can infect the scalp, causing hair loss and scaly patches. On the body, it causes round, red, scaly, itchy patches (see RINGWORM in this chapter). On the fingers, it appears as itchy scales, or raised itchy bumps. In the groin, it's known as "jock itch" (though it can affect women as well as men) and causes itching and skin thickening. On the feet, this fungus causes mild to severe itching. In severe cases, fissures open between the toes and fluid "weeps" from the openings. The skin becomes soft and painful and may burn and itch. Sometimes secondary bacterial infections complicate the original fungal infection.

Athlete's foot spreads by direct contact with an infected person or with contaminated surfaces such as shower or locker room floors. As a result, athlete's foot spreads easily among family, team, and health club members.

Before You Call the Doctor. Most cases of athlete's foot can be treated easily with hygienic and life-style measures:

• Keep your feet as dry as possible, especially between the toes. Use a blow dryer after bathing and towel drying. Don't wear socks. If you do, wear thick, absorbent socks, which wick perspiration away from the skin, and change them often, airing your feet between changes. Wear well-ventilated shoes. If possible, wear sandals or open-toed shoes. Dust your feet with corn starch to absorb excess moisture. And be sure to wear thongs in showers, bathrooms, and locker rooms so you don't reinfect yourself and spread the infection to others.

• Try an over-the-counter antifungal cream or powder. Creams are more effective than powders, but powders help absorb moisture. Effective antifungals include miconazole nitrate, clotrimazole, undecylenic acid and/ or zinc undecylenate, and tolnaftate. Despite their effectiveness, people respond to these products differently. If one doesn't provide sufficient relief, try another. Or try rotating or combining them. Experiment for yourself.

Wash and dry your feet completely, then apply a thin layer of antifungal cream once or twice a day between the toes and all over the feet—not just where it itches. Your heels can be infected and not itch, but they may keep spreading the infection to your toes. Most products recommend daily use for four weeks. Although symptoms usually begin to resolve within a few days, continue using the product for the recommended time to prevent recurrence.

When to Call the Doctor. If symptoms persist after using an over-the-counter remedy for four weeks, a physician can prescribe a different antifungal cream, such as ketoconazole.

In persistent cases, take a look at your toenails. Do they appear thickened and oddly white or discolored? If so, your athlete's foot may be complicated by a fungal toenail infection, which requires prescription medication for several months (see NAIL PROBLEMS in this chapter).

BITE WOUNDS

(See also INSECT BITES and SPIDER BITES in this chapter)

Dogs inflict about 85 percent of animal bites, cats about 10 percent, and humans, rodents, and other animals, both wild and domestic, account for the rest.

What's Going On?   Contrary to the common myth, most animal bite wounds are not occupational. Dogcatchers, mail carriers, delivery people, and animal handlers are cautious around animals and experienced dealing with them, so they rarely get bitten. Most of these injuries occur to children.

Children also suffer the most human bite wounds; they sometimes bite each other in day-care settings. Day-care personnel may be bitten by the children they work with. And young adult men may suffer these wounds in street fights when they punch adversaries in the mouth.

Animal bite wounds raise three concerns: bleeding; the possibility of bacterial infections, including tetanus; and the possibility of viral infections, including rabies and hepatitis B.

Tetanus is a potentially fatal bacterial infection that can develop in deep wounds, particularly puncture wounds inflicted by fang-like animal teeth. About seventy-five cases develop each year in the U.S. Most people recover with prompt treatment, but some die.

Rabies, a viral infection, is quite rare in the U.S.—only forty-three cases have occurred in the last twenty-five years—but if the disease develops, it's always fatal. Animals carry the rabies virus in their saliva. It may be transmitted not only by biting but also by licking any open wound. Many Americans get bitten or licked abroad, where rabies is much more common. As a result, about 25,000 Americans get rabies shots each year. In general, the risk of rabies is greatest in the U.S. following unprovoked attacks by bats, bobcats, coyotes, foxes, raccoons, or skunks.

Hepatitis B is a possibility if the biter is a person in a high-risk group: a hospital patient, prison inmate, or intravenous drug user.

Before You Call the Doctor.   Stop any bleeding by applying firm pressure with a clean tissue, cloth, or your hand. Then wash the wound thoroughly with soap and water—even if it has not bled. Animal bites are almost always contaminated and should be thoroughly cleaned. Then apply a thin layer of antiseptic ointment (Bacitracin, Neosporin) and consider covering the wound with an adhesive bandage. Some doctors recommend against bandaging minor hand, foot, and puncture bites.

When to Call the Doctor. If an animal bite causes bleeding, consult a physician after appropriate self-care. Animals, including humans, may have an enormous number of microorganisms in their mouths, and bite wounds that break the skin carry a considerable risk of infection. Don't fool yourself into thinking that a nice pet from a good home somehow has an uncontaminated mouth. It doesn't. And human bites are even more likely than animal bites to cause infection. The physician will evaluate the wound and probably prescribe an antibiotic.

If you've never had the basic three-shot tetanus series or it's been longer than five years since your last booster, get a tetanus shot. For clean, minor wounds, physicians recommend a tetanus booster if you haven't had one within the last ten years. For deeper wounds, they advise the shot if you haven't had one in five years.

For most animal bites, you have a few days before rabies shots must begin. During that time, the biting animal should be quarantined to see if it develops the disease. If the animal cannot be located and quarantined, you will be advised to get the series of shots. Rabies shots have a reputation for being quite painful. But that was the old vaccine. A new, less painful vaccine was introduced in the early 1980s, making rabies shots less of an ordeal.

If a bite raises the possibility of hepatitis B infection, you should receive hepatitis B immune globulin and hepatitis vaccination.

BLISTERS

(See also ATHLETE'S FOOT, BURNS, CHICKENPOX, CYSTS, ECZEMA, HEAT RASH, IMPETIGO, IRRITATIONS, PSORIASIS, RASHES, and SPIDER BITES in this chapter, FROSTBITE in Chapter 3, COLD SORES in Chapter 10, and HERPES in Chapter 18)

Blisters are raised areas of skin filled with watery fluid. They may or may not cause pain.

What's Going On? Blisters have many causes—friction, chemical irritations, and many other medical problems, including burns, cold sores, frostbite, shingles, poison oak, or athlete's foot.

Here we'll discuss friction-type blisters, the kind you get from hiking in shoes that rub. Injured by the friction of constant rubbing, the body protects inner skin structures by padding them with fluid, mostly water, under the outer layer of skin ("epidermis"). Eventually, new skin forms beneath the blister and the fluid inside it is gradually reabsorbed.

Before You Call the Doctor. Don't break blisters open or attempt to drain them. Once opened, the sensitive skin under the blister's protective covering can become quite painful and possibly infected.

Simply cut a hole in a strip of molefoam and fit it directly around the blister to cushion it. To relieve pain and inflammation, take aspirin or ibuprofen. Acetaminophen relieves pain but not inflammation. If aspirin or ibuprofen upset your stomach, try an "enteric coated" brand. Pregnant women and those with a history of ulcers should not use aspirin or ibuprofen unless a doctor recommends it.

If molefoam does not provide sufficient cushioning or if a blister breaks, wash the area with soap and water and protect it with a thin layer of antibiotic ointment and an adhesive bandage. Rewash, reapply the ointment, and rebandage the area at least once a day until it heals.

To prevent friction blisters on the feet wear thick dry socks, thin liner socks next to the skin, and well-fitting, well–broken-in shoes. Moisture contributes to blister formation, so wool or cotton socks are better than synthetics. Foot powders help absorb excess foot moisture. To prevent blisters on the hands, wear well-fitting garden or sports gloves.

When to Call the Doctor. Consult a physician if a blister does not improve significantly after two weeks of self-care or if the area becomes infected. Signs of infection include increased pain, redness, swelling, and a yellowish-green pus discharge.

▶ **RED FLAG** Consult a physician promptly if you develop rapidly spreading blisters that are not caused by friction. This may indicate Stevens-Johnson syndrome, a rare, potentially serious inflammatory condition.

BOILS

(See also ACNE and INFLAMED HAIR FOLLICLES in this chapter)

Most boils look like extra-large pimples. They appear red and swollen and feel tender, hot, and painful.

What's Going On? Boils are hair follicle infections caused by the *Staphylococcus* bacteria normally found on the skin. Similar in some ways to acne, they usually occur when a hair follicle becomes plugged and body fluids, oils, and cell debris back up behind the plug and nourish bacteria trapped there. Early in boil development, the body sends the immune system's white blood cells to battle the infection, and a large pimple called a boil or "furuncle" forms. If the boil continues to grow, a pus cavity forms, and the boil becomes an "abscess." If the infection spreads and a group of boils or abscesses become joined together by small tunnels under the skin, the result is a "carbuncle."

When a boil forms, the staphylococcal infection has spread from the hair follicle to the surrounding skin tissue. Local blood vessels expand ("dilate") to carry white blood cells and infection-fighting antibodies to contain the infection. Meanwhile, fiber-making cells ("fibroblasts") lay down filaments of collagen to wall off the infection and keep it from spreading. Boils cause pain because the infection causes local inflammation.

Boils are fairly common. They may occur anywhere on the body but develop most often in areas that experience chronic irritation, such as the neck, armpits, breasts, face, buttocks, and genitals. Scratching boils can spread the bacteria to healthy tissue and cause new boils to develop.

Before You Call the Doctor.   Don't pop boils. Popping them may force bacteria into surrounding tissue and spread the infection. However, boils cannot heal without rupturing because there is no blood supply to the pocket of pus that forms the boil. The key to self-treatment is to encourage the boil to rupture on its own. To do this, use hot, moist compresses. Apply the compress for ten minutes at a time, several times a day, rewarming it as it cools. The heat increases blood flow to the area, which draws more white blood cells to fight the infection. Compresses also soften swollen tissue, encouraging the boil to come to a head naturally, then rupture and drain.

To relieve pain and inflammation, take aspirin or ibuprofen. Acetaminophen relieves pain but not inflammation. If aspirin or ibuprofen upset your stomach, try an "enteric coated" brand. Pregnant women and those with a history of ulcers should not use aspirin or ibuprofen unless a doctor recommends it.

Even without compress treatment, most boils rupture and drain on their own within two weeks. When this happens, wash the area thoroughly with soap and water, apply some antibacterial ointment, and cover the area with a sterile gauze bandage. Change the bandage several times a day, repeating the hot compress treatment described above. After a few days, most of the inflammation should have subsided. Discontinue hot compresses. Change the bandage once a day, washing the wound and applying ointment before rebandaging.

Prevent the spread of boils by avoiding contact with boil sufferers' towels, bedding, and clothing. Keep your skin clean, especially areas like the arm pits where hair follicles can become clogged with deodorants and antiperspirants.

We do not recommend self-lancing, but many people can't resist it. A boil may be lanced if the overlying skin is thin, taut, and obviously straining to contain its fluid ("fluctuant"). Use a sharp knife, not a needle. Needles generally do not make large enough holes for adequate drainage. Be sure to sterilize the knife with alcohol before and *after* lancing—before so you don't introduce additional bacteria into the wound, and after so you don't spread the bacteria in the boil. Then wash the area thoroughly with soap and water. Apply firm pressure for at least five minutes to stop any bleeding, which is often copious. Then apply antibacterial ointment and bandage the wound as discussed above.

When to Call the Doctor.   Consult a physician if the boil does not seem to be healing and signs of further infection develop: pain, tenderness, heat, and swelling. Oral antibiotics and/or professionally assisted drainage may be necessary.

If boils recur, consult a physician for antibiotics and/or antibacterial soap.

If a boil persists longer than two weeks without rupturing, or if it grows larger than half an inch across, have a physician lance it, that is, open it with a scalpel and force it to drain.

▶ **RED FLAGS**   Do not self-lance boils on the breasts or buttocks. They tend to be much deeper than they appear. Don't lance fatty areas in obese people for the same reason.

If you notice a tender red streak near an abscess, it usually indicates a lymph-system infection, which must be treated with antibiotics.

BRUISES

Bruises are red, blue, or purple marks anywhere on the skin caused by a fall or blow. Around the eye, they're called "black eyes."

What's Going On?   Bruises occur when any impact damages the tiny blood vessels beneath the skin ("capillaries"), causing them to leak blood into the surrounding tissue. Initially, they usually look red-purple, but as the body reabsorbs the blood pigments, bruises typically change color to green, yellow, and brown before disappearing completely, usually within ten to fourteen days.

People taking prescription anticoagulants ("blood thinners") may bruise easily if they take too much medication.

Older people often bruise easily because the skin capillaries become more fragile with age.

Before You Call the Doctor.   Wrap some ice cubes in a plastic bag, then wrap the bag in a clean cloth to make an ice pack. Apply it as quickly as possible. Ice packs help reduce the pain and swelling. Ice substitute gels may also be used. Hold the ice pack on the bruise for twenty minutes, then remove it for ten minutes before reapplying. Do not apply ice or ice substitutes directly to the skin. This may cause the equivalent of frostbite.

After twenty-four hours, when the bleeding under the skin has had time to "set," apply warm compresses on the same schedule to help speed blood reabsorption.

To relieve pain, take acetaminophen. Aspirin and ibuprofen interfere with blood clotting and may make the bruise worse.

When to Call the Doctor.   If bruises seem to develop after minor impacts, consult a physician to rule out bleeding disorders.

▶ **RED FLAG**   If you notice bruises appearing without any trauma, consult a physician to check for a bleeding disorder.

BURNS

(See also BLISTERS in this chapter and FIRE in Chapter 3)
Burns are injuries caused by flames, sun, steam, chemicals, electricity, or hot liquids. Minor burns simply turn the skin red and painful. More serious burns cause severe pain and blistering. The most serious burns, which are medical emergencies, char the skin and, ironically, cause no pain.

What's Going On?   Each year, two million Americans are burned seriously enough to require medical attention. Half of them are children.

No matter what causes a burn, the results are the same: skin injuries which vary from mild to potentially fatal. Burns are classified as first-, second-, or third-degree depending on their severity:

• First-degree. These are superficial burns—most sunburns and household accident burns. The damage does not spread below the outer layer of the skin ("epidermis"). First-degree burns cause pain and redness but no blisters. They involve little risk of infection because the protective outer skin does not sustain significant injury.

• Second-degree. These more serious burns damage both the outer and inner skin ("dermis"). Fluid leaking from damaged blood vessels collects near the boundary between the two layers, and the outer skin separates from the inner, forming blisters. Second-degree burns appear moist, mottled, and red with blisters. Although quite painful, these burns are usually not serious unless they are quite large or become infected.

• Third-degree. Always a medical emergency, third-degree burns destroy the outer and inner skin as well as the hair, nerves, blood vessels, glands, fat, and sometimes even muscle and bone. The burned areas appear white or blackened. If extensive, third-degree burns are often fatal because the skin no longer functions as the body's natural barrier to disease-causing microorganisms. Body fluids seep out, blood pressure falls, and bacteria can move in. Third-degree burns usually cause no pain because the injury destroys the nerves that carry pain messages to the brain. When they heal, third-degree burns typically leave scars.

Before You Call the Doctor.   For first-degree burns—sunburns and most household scalds and stove injuries—wrap some ice cubes in a plastic bag and wrap the bag in a clean cloth to make an ice pack. Apply it as quickly as possible. Ice packs help reduce the pain and swelling. Ice-substitute gels may also be used. Hold the ice pack over the burn for twenty minutes, then remove it for ten minutes before reapplying. Repeat until pain subsides. Do not apply ice or ice substitutes directly to the skin. This may cause the equivalent of frostbite.

To relieve pain and inflammation, take aspirin or ibuprofen. Acetaminophen relieves pain but not inflammation. If aspirin or ibuprofen upset your stomach, try an "enteric coated" brand. Pregnant women and those with a history of ulcers should not use aspirin or ibuprofen unless a doctor recommends it.

Once pain and inflammation are under control, apply fresh aloe vera gel from a potted aloe houseplant. Simply snip off a fleshy aloe leaf, slit it open, and scoop out the gel. Studies show aloe vera gel helps speed burn healing. Keep a potted aloe in your kitchen, site of most household burns. That way, it'll be handy when you need it.

Most second-degree burns can be self-treated if the area isn't too large. However, if the burn is extensive or involves the hands, face, or genitals, consult a physician immediately. Treatment is the same as for first-degree burns: ice packs, over-the-counter pain relievers, and aloe gel. Leave all blisters intact to prevent infection unless they are larger than one inch across. In that case, consult a physician. If any blisters rupture spontaneously, wash them thoroughly with soap and water, apply an antibiotic ointment, such as silver sulfadiazene, and cover with a sterile bandage. It's less painful if you apply the ointment to the gauze rather than directly to the burn. Do *not* apply butter, lard, or petroleum jelly. Change the antibiotic dressing and wash the wound once a day. If signs of infection develop—increased pain, swelling, redness, and pus—consult a physician. If the burn itches during healing, over-the-counter antihistamines, such as chlorpheniramine or diphenhydramine, may help. Healing usually takes from three to six weeks.

For chemical burns caused by corrosives, such as drain, oven, and toilet cleaners, or other chemicals, remove any contaminated clothing and jewelry and immediately flush the area with cool water continuously for fifteen to thirty minutes. If the chemical container is available, read and follow the first-aid instructions on the label. For large burns, seek medical attention promptly.

For chemical burns in the eye, immediately flush the eye with water. If only one eye is involved, be careful not to flush the chemical into the unburned eye. Cover the eye with a cool compress and transport the person to emergency medical treatment.

When to Call the Doctor.   Consult a physician if burn blisters are larger than one inch across. The doctor may decide to open ("unroof") the blister under sterile conditions to speed its healing.

Electrical burns are often deeper and more serious than they appear. Consult a physician.

▶ **RED FLAGS**   *All* third-degree burns and any second degree burn involving the hands, genitals, or face (especially the eyes, nose, or mouth) require immediate medical attention. Wrap the burned area in a clean sheet and call for emergency help. Do *not* try to remove burned clothing. Do *not* immerse the person in a cold bath, ice water, or snow pack. Do *not* apply ointments or dressings that may adhere to the burned area. Just get the person to an emergency room as quickly as possible.

CALLUSES

(See also BLISTERS in this chapter)

Calluses are raised bumps of dead skin that develop on the hands, toes, bottoms of the feet, or anywhere the skin is subjected to friction over time. They are usually painless but may hurt if associated with blisters.

What's Going On?   Unusual rubbing first produces blisters (see BLIS-TERS in this Chapter). But over time, the skin in any area subjected to regular rubbing thickens and the body protects sensitive areas by building up a tough layer of dead skin. The feet are heavily callused because they are under such frequent pressure from walking, running, etc. Depending on people's jobs and hobbies, their hands often become callused.

Before You Call the Doctor.   Calluses usually require no treatment. They develop for a reason—to protect the sensitive under-layer of skin ("dermis"), and in general they should not be disturbed.

But sometimes, calluses become unsightly or grow uncomfortably large. You can usually reduce their size by applying an acid paste of 5 crushed, powdered aspirin tablets (acetylsalicylic acid) and 1 tablespoon lemon juice (citric acid) mixed with 1 tablespoon water to form a paste. Apply this paste generously, and cover the area with a bandage or plastic bag for fifteen to thirty minutes. Then use a pumice stone or metal file to remove the outer layer of callus tissue. Repeat two to three times a week until the callus has been reduced to the desired size.

When to Call the Doctor.   Calluses caused by such biomechanical problems as fallen arches should be evaluated by a physician to assess the need for correction (see FLAT FEET in Chapter 15).

CHICKENPOX

Chickenpox causes sudden fever, a usually mild generalized ill feeling ("malaise"), and a characteristic itchy rash ("pox"), which progresses from spots to blisters over about five days.

What's Going On?   Chickenpox is caused by the varicella zoster virus, a member of the herpes virus family. Most people consider chickenpox a childhood disease—and in the vast majority of cases, it is. However, adults who never had it as children can develop it at any age, and those who had chickenpox as children may develop the related disease, shingles, or herpes zoster, later in life (see below).

In children, chickenpox typically develops before age nine. It is highly contagious, passed by contact with an infected person's exhalations. When one child in a family, day-care group, or classroom gets it, the other children who have not already had it usually get it. A child (or adult) with chickenpox is infectious from one day before the rash appears until all the pox have dried up, usually five to seven days after the rash's appearance.

Chickenpox develops eleven to twenty-one days after exposure to a person with the disease ("incubation period"). The fever and malaise develop before the rash erupts. The rash begins as small red bumps and, over several days, changes into fluid-filled blisters on top of red skin patches, described by medical poets as "a dew drop on a rose petal." The blisters eventually break and scab over. The child's lymph glands may also swell (see SWOLLEN GLANDS in Chapter 4). Some children develop only a low-grade fever and a few pox. Others suffer high fevers (up to 105°) and hundreds of pox. The symptoms usually feel worst during the first three or four days from onset of the fever until the rash has erupted. Then the child begins to recover and is usually well again within a week or two.

Chickenpox confers a long, usually lifelong, immunity. Second attacks are possible but rare.

In some people, the chickenpox virus remains dormant in the body for several decades, then reemerges as shingles. Shingles causes a blistery, red rash on one side of the face or in an area supplied by one particular spinal nerve, which results in a strip of blisters on one side of the body. The shingles rash may be preceded by a few days of tingling or prickling sensation on the skin. Shingles usually clears up by itself within a few weeks, but in some people, nerve pain ("postherpetic neuralgia") persists for months or even years. The pain varies from mild to possibly quite severe. Direct contact with shingles rash can give a susceptible person chickenpox (not shingles), but shingles is much less contagious than chickenpox.

As this book goes to press, a chickenpox vaccine is close to approval. Once it becomes available, chickenpox (and shingles) should be less of a problem.

Before You Call the Doctor. *Never* give a child aspirin for the fever caused by suspected chickenpox. The combination of aspirin and chickenpox is associated with an increased risk of Reye syndrome, a rare but potentially fatal condition involving the brain and liver. Give children acetaminophen instead.

Soothing baths can relieve the itching. Use Aveeno powder, available at pharmacies (one to two cups per bath), baking soda (one-half to one cup per bath), or finely ground oatmeal (one to two cups per bath). Either buy pre-ground "colloidal oatmeal" at a pharmacy or grind your own in a coffee grinder.

Over-the-counter Calamine lotion, Caladryl, or antihistamines may also help relieve itching. Antihistamines also cause drowsiness, which helps the sufferer rest.

Trim the child's fingernails short to minimize the risk of infection from scratching the itchy pox. In severe cases, have the child wear mittens. Other infection-preventive strategies include frequent changes of clothing and giving the child frequent baths.

Otherwise, give children plenty of fluids, encourage rest, and keep them comfortable and occupied.

A child who develops chickenpox is contagious from one day before the rash erupts until about five days after it appears. Notify the parents of any children exposed to your child during this contagious period. Contacts are highly likely to develop the disease within eleven to twenty-one days after exposure.

Pregnant women who have never had chickenpox and newborns should stay away from anyone with the disease. Chickenpox is associated with an increased risk of birth defects, and in newborns, it may be quite severe. Fortunately, newborns whose mothers have had chickenpox are usually protected by maternal antibodies.

For shingles, take acetaminophen (not aspirin) to relieve the discomfort. Try warm or cool compresses, whichever work better, but take care not to break the blisters. If the blisters break, the skin under them may become infected.

When to Call the Doctor.   Any adult who develops chickenpox should consult a physician. The disease is often severe in adults, and though complications are rare, they may develop pneumonia or a brain infection ("encephalitis"). Doctors can treat chicken pox with high-dose acyclovir, an antiviral drug. If the treatment is started early, it makes the symptoms milder. In children, patches of pox that don't heal are probably infected with skin bacteria and should be treated with antibiotics.

For persistent shingles pain not relieved by acetaminophen and for postherpetic neuralgia, physicians can prescribe capsaicin (Zostrix) cream.

In people over sixty years of age or those with altered immune function (HIV infection, diabetes, etc.), the risk of severe shingles is greater. Consult a physician as early as possible regarding possible anti-inflammatory or antiviral medication (acyclovir).

▶ **RED FLAG**   Consult a physician immediately if there is a risk of chickenpox in a pregnant woman or newborn. Immune stimulants may prevent the infection if given within four days of exposure.

For chickenpox or shingles involving the eye, consult an ophthalmologist promptly to prevent damage to vision.

CONTACT DERMATITIS

(See IRRITATIONS in this chapter)

CRABS

(See LICE in this chapter)

CUTS

Cuts are narrow slices into the skin. Abrasions are superficial scrapes. Punctures are stabbing wounds.

What's Going On?   Shortly after any of these injuries break the skin, serum, the clear fluid portion of the blood, bathes the wound. Meanwhile the area becomes inflamed, a result of extra blood flooding the area. This blood brings white blood cells and other components of the immune system to prevent infection or fight it if it occurs. In the event of infection, nearby lymph nodes may also swell.

After a few days, pus may form. It's made up of dead bacteria, white blood cells, and other debris. A scab creates a natural Band-Aid to protect the injury while it heals.

Before You Call the Doctor.   Most cuts, scrapes, and puncture wounds respond to self-care. Usually any bleeding from minor wounds stops spontaneously. If not, apply direct pressure with a gauze pad until it does. However, in the case of puncture wounds, allow bleeding for a few minutes to flush out any harmful microorganisms. Clean all wounds carefully with soap and water. Remove any remaining dirt and foreign matter, then disinfect them with hydrogen peroxide. Finally, soak puncture wounds in hot water for fifteen minutes every few hours for several days to prevent infection. Small wounds are best left uncovered, unless they could be better protected from dirt with the help of a bandage. For larger wounds, use butterfly strips to draw the edges together and encourage knitting.

A dab of antibiotic ointment (Neosporin, Bacitracin) may help prevent infection. The ancients covered wounds with honey. Recent research shows they were right. Honey has antibacterial properties and does not cause allergic reactions, which are possible with antibiotics.

For pain and inflammation, take aspirin or ibuprofen. Acetaminophen relieves pain but not inflammation. If aspirin or ibuprofen upset your stomach, try an "enteric coated" brand. Pregnant women and those with a history of ulcers should not use aspirin or ibuprofen unless a doctor recommends it.

Wounds naturally cause pain, tenderness, heat, redness, and swelling. As the wound begins to heal, these should subside. If they persist or become worse, the wound is probably infected. Try scrubbing with a wash cloth and soak the area in soapy water for about ten minutes a few times a day, removing any scab covering the wound.

When to Call the Doctor.   Consult a physician promptly for:
• Any human or animal bites that break the skin.
• Large deep wounds on the face, hands, feet, or genitals.
• Wounds with jagged edges that won't come together.
• Wounds that cause profuse or uncontrollable bleeding, numbness, or an inability to move the affected part.
• Wounds containing dirt or other foreign material you cannot remove.
• Wounds that develop signs of infection: increased pain, swelling, tenderness, redness, red streaks, and/or pus.
• Wounds that don't show significant healing within two weeks.

▶ **RED FLAG**   Deep or contaminated wounds can cause tetanus, a potentially fatal bacterial infection. If you've never had the basic three-shot tetanus series, or if you have a dirty, contaminated wound and it's been longer than five years since your last booster, get a tetanus shot. For clean, minor wounds, have a tetanus shot if you haven't had one within the last ten years. Most of the tetanus deaths in the U.S. occur in older people who did not keep up their boosters.

CYSTS

(See also BLISTERS in this chapter)
Cysts are fluid-filled sacs. Skin cysts are called "epidermal" (formerly "sebaceous") cysts or "wens."

What's Going On?   Not too long ago, doctors thought epidermal cysts were caused by blocked oil glands. Now the consensus is that they arise from pouches that form under the skin independent of oil glands. These skin pouches continue to produce and shed cells and oil ("sebum") into the pocket. Undisturbed epidermal cysts are simply painless bumps under the skin that slide with the skin when you pull it. However, they can become painful and tender if an injury breaks the cyst wall or if you attempt to "pop" the cyst as though it were a pimple. The cyst then releases its contents into the surrounding tissue, which becomes irritated.

Before You Call the Doctor.   Usually, epidermal cysts subside on their own without treatment or remain as permanent harmless bumps. The most important advice is to leave them alone. Even if it's easy to squeeze the contents out, this measure is only temporary because the cyst wall continues to release cells and sebum into the pocket. And the more you fiddle with cysts, the greater the risk of inflammation. Cysts that have previously been inflamed often become more persistent because the cyst wall becomes "scarred into" the surrounding tissue.

When to Call the Doctor.   Occasionally, cysts become infected and require antibiotics. Signs of infection include increased pain, swelling, tenderness, redness, red lines, and/or pus. Also consult a physician for cysts that keep growing or don't begin to resolve within two weeks with a complete "hands-off" policy.

Some doctors cut open ("lance") cysts. This provides only temporary relief, unless the cyst wall can also be removed.

DANDRUFF

(See also SEBORRHEA in this chapter)
Everyone experiences some degree of dandruff—skin scaling and flaking on the scalp.

What's Going On?   The skin sheds millions of flakes of dead skin every hour. But for reasons that remain unclear, the scalp sheds more than other areas, and sometimes the flakes become trapped by oil and hair. Eventually they fall in large, conspicuous lumps called dandruff. An estimated 20 percent of Americans shed scalp flakes conspicuously enough to consider dandruff a problem.

First, let's dispense with the common myths about dandruff:
•Dandruff has nothing to do with cleanliness.
•Dandruff isn't a precurser to baldness.
•Dandruff isn't caused or cured by changes in diet.
•Dandruff is neither a "man's problem" nor a "woman's problem." Both sexes suffer the annoying flakiness equally.

Authorities aren't sure why some people shed scalp flakes so obviously, but one theory blames a microscopic fungus called *Pityrosporum,* which normally lives on the scalp and other oily parts of the skin. People with dandruff seem to have unusually large *Pityrosporum* populations. Other authorities speculate that dandruff sufferers simply shed dead scalp cells faster. Dandruff can't be cured medically, but it can be controlled without much difficulty.

Before You Call the Doctor.   The Food and Drug Administration has identified five effective antidandruff agents: coal-tar extract, selenium sulfide, sulfur preparations, salicylic acid, and zinc pyrithione. Antidandruff shampoos all contain one or more.

Initially, it can take a few weeks of regular shampooing to begin to notice benefits. For best results:

• The antidandruff effect lasts only two or three days, so you have to shampoo every other day until your dandruff is under control. If you shampoo more often, use non-medicated shampoo in between.

• To be effective, the medication must remain in contact with the scalp for several minutes before rinsing. So lather it up, then leave it on for a while.

• Lather and rinse only once. Most dandruff shampoos suggest twice, but dermatologists say there's no need.

• For severe cases that don't improve with routine medicated shampooing, try lathering and covering the shampooed scalp with a plastic shower cap for thirty minutes to a couple of hours before rinsing.

If your dandruff doesn't improve, switch antidandruff shampoos. Depending on the person, some active ingredients work better than others.

When to Call the Doctor.   If you run through all the active ingredients and after a few months still have a significant problem, consult a physician to rule out other possible problems—for example, psoriasis (see PSORIASIS in this chapter), or other scalp inflammations that can mimic dandruff. Physicians can prescribe stronger medication, such as topical steroids and stronger selenium or tar shampoos.

DIAPER RASH

(See also IRRITATIONS in this chapter)

This rash appears as small pimples and patches of rough, red skin on baby's buttocks, thighs, and genitals.

What's Going On?   Most babies develop diaper rash and other rashes from irritants or friction. The problem is rarely serious, but it means the baby's sensitive skin needs extra care. Usually, diaper rash is caused by the ammonia in urine, the bacteria in bowel movements, or by soaps or detergents used to launder diapers and other clothing.

Before You Call the Doctor.   Diaper rash can usually be treated at home:
   • Change diapers frequently. Don't allow urine or feces to remain in contact with baby's skin for long.
   • Allow the rashy area to dry in the air. After changing, allow the baby to remain naked for ten or fifteen minutes. Place the baby on soft towels.
   • At every diaper change, dust the rashy area with baby powder or corn starch to help keep it dry.
   • Don't use packaged wipes containing alcohol, which overdries the skin and makes it susceptible to irritants.
   • Switch diaper methods. If you use disposables, try a diaper service. The superabsorbent materials in today's disposables can irritate young skin. So can the plastic at the waist and legs. Cloth diapers are also cheaper and more ecological.
   • Soaps can contribute to diaper rash. After bathing the child, rinse off all soap thoroughly.
   • Use a blow dryer set on low at diaper changes to dry baby's skin, especially creases, more completely.
   • If the skin seems raw, apply a thin coat of zinc oxide ointment after *thoroughly* air-drying the area.
   • If skin seems chapped without a rash (bumps) or if zinc oxide seems to cause irritation, try petroleum jelly, with or without vitamins A and D.
   • If neither plain zinc oxide nor petroleum jelly helps, try a combination diaper rash ointment containing 40 percent zinc oxide (double the strength of plain zinc oxide). However, the fish oil in these products can stain cloth diapers.
   • Sometimes the rash becomes infected with microorganisms such as the *Candida* fungus, which causes vaginal yeast infections. If *Candida* are present, the rash looks brighter red, usually spreads to the skin deep inside the baby's thigh creases, and may have pinpoint red spots around the edges. Try an over-the-counter antifungal cream—miconazole or clotrimazole.
   • If your baby suffers frequent, recurring diaper rash, consider a diet change. Decrease foods containing yeast (breads and pastas); avoid tomatoes and acidic fruits, whose high acid content tends to make stools more irritating; and try giving the baby some fresh live-culture yogurt. If

the baby has more than one or two bowel movements a day, try rice, bananas, and applesauce to decrease stool frequency.

When to Call the Doctor.   For persistent or particularly severe diaper rash, see a physician for prescription medication.

DISHPAN HANDS

(See also IRRITATIONS in this chapter)
Hands often become dry, cracked, and scaly from exposure to water, soap, cleansers, and detergents.

What's Going On?   This contact dermatitis is common among people whose hands spend a great deal of time in soapy water or other liquids. Homemakers, nurses, cooks, dishwashers, bartenders, and photographers are all at increased risk. The water robs the skin of its protective oils, and without them, it becomes dry and irritated. Eczema, psoriasis, and other rashes may also appear on the hands. Initial home treatment is the same.

Before You Call the Doctor.   Keep the hands dry and out of water as much as possible. If you must immerse them, frequency is more important than duration. Wash one large load of dishes rather than several small ones. Plastic gloves, even those with cotton flocking, don't usually help because the hands sweat inside the gloves, which typically aggravates the problem.
   Don't use commercial lotions and moisturizers, which often contain fragrances and chemicals that may irritate the skin.
   The best approach is to apply a thin layer of mineral oil or petroleum jelly several times a day, especially after exposure to water. During immersion, wear cotton gloves under waterproof gloves, and change them as they become moist. Thin cotton gloves are available at photography supply stores. (Photographers use them when handling slides and negatives.)
   For severely inflamed skin, cortisone creams may help. Over-the-counter brands are weak and unlikely to work on thick hand skin, but try applying some at bedtime and wearing two layers of cotton gloves overnight for a week or two.

When to Call the Doctor.   If over-the-counter cortisone is not strong enough, consult a physician for a prescription cream. These are usually applied two or three times a day for short periods. Sometimes after application, severe rashes must be covered with a plastic glove for a few hours or overnight to help the medication penetrate, soften, and remoisturize the skin.

DRY SKIN

(See also DISHPAN HANDS and ECZEMA in this chapter)

When skin loses too much moisture, it becomes dry, rough, scaly, and itchy.

What's Going On?   Almost everyone suffers the itching, roughness, and scaling of dry skin at some point. The condition is most common in dry, cold climates. Many things rob the skin of moisture—wind, frequent bathing, and low relative humidity in centrally heated and air-conditioned buildings. Dry skin is also a common complaint among older adults, because as we age, the skin produces less moisturizing oil.

Before You Call the Doctor.   Try these tips:

• Take short showers and baths. Water dries the skin, drawing out its natural oils.

• Use soap sparingly. Oilated or superfatted soaps such as Dove and Aveenobar are less drying. For super dry skin, forego soap and use a soap-and-water substitute such as Cetaphil.

• Bath oils are only moderately effective because rinsing largely removes them. They also tend to make the tub dangerously slippery.

• After bathing, pat—don't rub—yourself dry with a soft towel and apply a moisturizer, which helps replace the body's natural oils. Use ointments (Vaseline), creams (Eucerin,) gels (Aqualin), or baby, mineral, or vegetable oil. Ironically, many so-called "moisturizing" lotions do more harm than good. They are mostly water, which contributes to dry skin.

When to Call the Doctor.   If creams, oils, and gels prove ineffective, ask a dermatologist about Lac-Hydrin, a prescription product that acts on skin-cell metabolism and helps remoisturize dry skin.

A dermatologist can also examine you to rule out the medical problems which occasionally cause dry skin (and dry mouth and eyes).

ECZEMA

(See also BLISTERS and DRY SKIN in this chapter)

Eczema is characterized by redness, cracking, and thickening of dry patches on the skin, sometimes accompanied by small, water-filled blisters.

What's Going On?   "Eczema" and "dermatitis" are dermatologists' catch-alls for conditions that cause itching and blistering with red, scaly, thickened skin. Among the many types of eczema, the following three are most common:

• *Chronic Eczema.*   It looks different depending on the individual, but it shares two attributes: Its origin is a mystery, and the side effects from the itch-scratch cycle often prove worse than the eczema itself. Chronic eczema often develops in areas easily scratched—the neck, arms, legs, and genital area. Scratched areas may become dry, red, thick, and leathery. The itching sensation may be continuous or sporadic, but the scratch response becomes automatic.

• *Nummular Eczema.*   This variety causes round, coin-shaped patches which may be red, swollen, blistered, or crusty. They itch and may ooze and often become thickened. The condition often occurs in older people or children with other skin irritations. Nummular eczema has no known cause, though stress and excessively dry or humid climates appear to trigger eruptions. It typically appears on the buttocks, forearms, backs of hands, and lower legs.

• *Atopic Eczema.*   This causes an itchy, localized rash, usually on the backs of the knees or on the inner elbow creases. In severe cases, the rash may extend to the neck, waist, trunk, and eyelids. An inherited condition, atopic eczema may start in early infancy with itching on the normal-looking skin of the cheeks, ears, scalp, and/or forehead and continue sporadically into adulthood. Rubbing or scratching the itchy skin brings out the rash, often initially in the folds of the knees, neck, and elbows. Although not usually triggered by normal allergens such as pollen or other airborne pollutants, atopic eczema is associated with hives, asthma, and hay fever. Eruptions often develop in association with stress, sweating, grease, oils, soaps, detergents, dry climates, hot or cold temperatures, irritating fibers such as wool, and sometimes environmental pollutants. Scratching aggravates and spreads the itchy rash. Most episodes resolve on their own. An important aspect of treatment is identifying and avoiding the "triggers."

Before You Call the Doctor. All forms of eczema have similar home treatments. In addition, follow the suggestions in the DRY SKIN section of this chapter:

• If you live in a dry climate, consider installing a central humidifier in your home. Smaller models and pans of water have little effect.

• If heat and humidity make you itch, install a dehumidifier and air conditioning. In addition, steer clear of greases and oils which plug pores. Wear loose, lightweight cotton or cotton blend clothing. Don't wear wool or polyester.

• Wear plastic gloves (or better yet, cotton gloves covered with plastic gloves) when handling soaps, detergents, or chemicals.

• Try a soothing bath. Use Aveeno powder, available at pharmacies (one or two cups per bath), baking soda, (one-half to one cup per bath), or finely ground oatmeal (one or two cups per bath). Either buy pre-ground "colloidal oatmeal" at a pharmacy or grind your own in a coffee grinder.

• Apply moisturizing creams, oils, or gels immediately after showering.

• Get some sun. Take care not to get burned, but don't use sunscreen all the time. The sun's ultraviolet light (the same light which in excess causes sunburn) helps the rash heal.

• Try to relax. Since episodes of atopic eczema may be triggered by stress, take breaks during the day and incorporate stress management activities into your life (see MANAGE YOUR STRESS LOAD in Chapter 1).

• Try over-the-counter antihistamines. These products often cause drowsiness, so it's best to take them before going to bed.

• Apply one-half percent hydrocortisone cream for the itching. To improve the penetration and effectiveness of weak over-the-counter preparations, wrap the affected area in plastic wrap for a few hours.

When to Call the Doctor. If self-care measures don't provide adequate relief after two weeks, a doctor may prescribe stronger corticosteroid ointments and/or antihistamines. Prescription antihistamines are more expensive, but some cause less drowsiness.

EXCESSIVE HAIR

Unwanted excess hair, known as "hirsutism" or "hypertrichosis," often appears on the face, abdomen, or around the nipples.

What's Going On? "Hirsutism" refers to pigmented hair growing on a woman's body where it is not normally a secondary sex characteristic. In hirsutism, hair growth is stimulated by male hormones ("androgens"), which both men and women produce. In most cases, hirsute women simply produce excess androgens. But sometimes a hormonal imbalance or even hormone-producing tumors may cause hirsutism.

"Hypertrichosis" is excess growth of the peach-fuzz ("vellus") hair that covers most of the body. Most women who complain of hirsutism actually have hypertrichosis. Vellus hair is unpigmented in most women, but among women of Mediterranean and Eastern European descent, vellus hair is typically pigmented.

Hormonal changes due to aging, drugs, or pregnancy may produce excessive hair growth. Many over-the-counter and prescription drugs, for example, corticosteroids and certain high blood pressure medications, can stimulate excessive hair growth.

Before You Call the Doctor. All the self-care methods are temporary and must be repeated often to maintain results, but depending on the extent of your problem, these may be sufficient. Basically you have two choices—disguise it or remove it:

• Shaving is the most popular temporary solution. Contrary to the popular myth, shaving does not cause the growth of more hair or thicker hair. If you shave, shave with the grain of the hair. Unfortunately, for women trying to remove unsightly facial hair, shaving can leave tell-tale stubble.

• Bleaching unwanted hair makes it less noticeable. Although bleaching is painless for small amounts of hair, repeated bleaching may damage hair shafts or cause skin irritation. Home-made bleaching solutions may be too harsh on tender skin. Use commercial preparations. If you develop a rash from any hair bleach, stop using it.

• Plucking or tweezing is an effective, albeit painful, hair removal method. Apply an ice pack to the area beforehand to decrease discomfort, but be forewarned: This technique works well only on small areas. Wash your skin and tweezers beforehand with soap and water to reduce the risk of infection. Do not pluck hairs from moles or warts. This may cause bleeding and infection. Repeated plucking may inflame hair follicles (see INFLAMED HAIR FOLLICLES in this chapter) and cause tiny, pitted scars.

• Chemical depilatories dissolve hairs or break them off just below the skin surface. Available in foams, creams, or liquids, they may cause skin irritation and should never be used on broken or irritated skin. As with any new skin product, apply a small amount first to make sure you aren't allergic. Then after washing and drying the area, apply the depilatory and leave it on for the recommended time (usually ten to fifteen minutes). Rewash the area and pat it dry. Apply a moisturizer to prevent skin drying.

• Waxing involves applying hot wax to the skin, allowing it to harden, then rapidly pulling off the wax sheet, which plucks out the hairs. It's actually mass plucking with the additional risk of burns from the hot wax. As you've probably guessed, waxing is painful and may cause skin irritation and hair follicle inflammation.

When to Call the Doctor.   If the self-care approaches don't provide sufficient peace of mind, consult your physician and ask about electrolysis. Electrolysis is currently the only permanent hair removal method. It must be performed by a physician or certified electrologist, using one of two techniques. The older "galvanic" method involves insertion of a slender needle into the hair follicle and application of a small electric current for thirty seconds to three minutes, which destroys the hair root. Once the root is gone, the hair cannot grow back. The newer "shortwave" technique uses a stronger current, but for less than one second. Some electrologists use a combination of the two, though this takes longer and hasn't proved more effective than the shortwave technique alone.

Even with the most skilled practitioner, electrolysis is expensive, painful, and tedious. Sometimes the electric current isn't strong enough or the needle positioning isn't quite right to destroy the hair root. If the root isn't destroyed, the hair grows back, necessitating repeat treatments. A single hair may have to be zapped several times before it stops regrowing.

Administered by a well-trained professional, electrolysis is relatively safe. (Don't use do-it-yourself electrolysis kits.) Licensing for electrologists varies from state to state. Get a personal recommendation, or look for a practitioner who belongs to national and state professional organizations. Stay away from practitioners who make outrageous claims or guarantee a maximum number of treatments. Needles should always be sterilized before use. Each session usually lasts about fifteen minutes (about $20 per session). Occasionally, temporary darkening of the skin ("hyperpigmentation") occurs and tiny scars and pits may develop, especially on the upper lip.

In addition to cosmetic remedies, hirsutism may be treated with a variety of drugs: birth control pills to offset overproduction of androgens; corticosteroids, such as prednisone or dexamethasone, for nontumor adrenal disorders; and spironolactone, an anti-androgen drug. Success rates of up to 80 percent have been reported using these drugs. But you might not be so fortunate. Be sure to ask your physician about the pros and cons of any drug therapy, including all possible side effects.

▶ **RED FLAG**   In rarer cases, hormonal imbalances and hair growth may be traced to tumors or cysts in the ovaries, thyroid, adrenals, pituitary, or other hormone-producing glands. A physician should rule these out before prescribing treatment. If you notice new male-pattern hair growth on the face and extending up the abdomen and down the thighs from the pubic area and the hair growth is associated with menstrual abnormalities, see a physician immediately.

HAIR LOSS

Everyone loses hair all the time. We shed 50 to 100 hairs each day as part of hair's natural growth and replacement cycle. But sometimes hair loss becomes excessive enough to cause concern.

What's Going On?   Ordinary hair loss is normal and healthy. New hairs grow to replace those lost to everyday shedding. Most excessive hair loss is the result of a hereditary condition called male pattern baldness (MPB or "androgenic alopecia"). But hair loss has many other causes:

• Many prescription drugs cause noticeable hair loss. Chemotherapy drugs are notorious for this, but here are some other common medications that cause the same hair-raising side effect:

　○ The cholesterol-lowering drugs clofibrate and gemfibrozil.
　○ Many arthritis medications: gold salts (auranofin), indomethacin, naproxen, sulindac, and methotrexate.
　○ Beta-blocking drugs used to treat high blood pressure: atenolol (Tenormin), metoprolol (Lopressor), nadolol (Corgard), propranolol (Inderal), and timolol (Blocadren).
　○ And occasionally the commonly prescribed ulcer drugs: cimetidine (Tagamet), ranitidine (Zantac), and famotidine (Pepcid).

• Sudden loss of patchy clumps of hair in men or women is known as "alopecia areata."

• In women, temporary hair loss may be associated with periods of hormonal fluctuation, such as menstruation, pregnancy, menopause, or postmenopausal hormone therapy.

• Patchy hair loss, especially in children, suggests ringworm ("tinea capitis"), a fungal infection which must be treated with antifungal medication (see RINGWORM in this chapter).

• Occasionally, hair loss is symptomatic of serious illnesses, such as thyroid disease or lupus ("systemic lupus erythematosus").

• Hair loss may also be a side effect of surgery, extreme stress, and many other conditions.

Here we'll examine two of the most common types of hair loss: male pattern baldness and alopecia areata.

• *Male Pattern Baldness*   This is an odd hereditary condition. The genetic predisposition may be inherited from either parent, but the actual extent of balding varies greatly within families. Almost all men experience some MPB. About 10 percent of women also experience significant hair loss as they age, but it's typically much less extensive and noticeable.

MPB begins with the hairline receding from the forehead. Then the crown peeks through in a circle at the rear of the top of the head. Next the two bald areas meet and grow until all that remains is a "horseshoe fringe" around the head at ear level.

What's Going On?   Male sex hormones ("androgens") are the culprit. The hair follicles in areas that become bald metabolize androgens differently than those in non-balding areas. This difference causes some hair follicles to shrink, slowing hair growth. Ultimately, the follicles die, causing permanent hair loss.

MPB can begin at any age. Most hair loss follows the "10 percent rule:" about 10 percent of men show obvious balding in their teens, 20 percent in their twenties; 30 percent in their thirties, and so on. The earlier hair loss begins, the more severe it is likely to be.

Before You Call the Doctor.   Until recently, the single most important recommendation was not to waste your money on the many over-the-counter hair restorers advertised in newspaper sports sections and men's magazines. But in 1985, the Food and Drug Administration banned these products, so men aren't likely to get taken anymore.

Don't assume your hair loss is MPB just because you're a man in a susceptible age group. Check your medicine cabinet. Does your hair loss seem at all associated with the use of any drugs? An enormous number of medications can cause temporary hair loss, far more than we listed above, and neither physicians nor drug industry advertising typically mention this possibility. If you suspect a drug cause, ask your pharmacist or physician if your medication is at all associated with hair loss. If so, ask if another drug might be substituted.

If your hair loss is MPB, the only nonmedical approach is a toupée. In recent years, "rugs" have become much more natural looking. Some attach using glue, but others are anchored to existing hair by fine wires. These latter do not shift or fall off, even while swimming, showering, or engaging in strenuous exercise. Depending on their size and their composition of human or artificial hair, toupées cost from $750 to $3,000.

When to Call the Doctor.   If you don't like toupées, two surgical approaches and one prescription drug are available:

• Hair transplantation. This surgical approach takes tiny "plugs" of hair-bearing scalp and inserts them into bald areas. The hair plugs continue to grow hair. Transplants typically cost $30 to $35 per plug, and the average transplant requires 50 to 200 transplanted plugs. Health insurance rarely covers the $1,500 to $5,000 operation. If you opt for hair transplantation, be sure you see your surgeon's "before" and "after" pictures of other patients. In unskilled surgical hands, the new hair may have a disconcerting "corn row" look. Pay special attention to the forehead hairline. A natural look requires transplantation of single hairs. Hair transplants may also leave small scars. Although the operation is relatively safe, there is some risk of infection. Transplanted hair should always come from somewhere else on your body. Don't consent to synthetic hair transplants, which can cause serious infection and scarring.

• Scalp reduction. The scalp is elastic. In this operation, the surgeon removes an oval-shaped piece at the top of the head, then pulls the hair-bearing scalp upward to cover more of the head. To encourage the scalp to stretch better, some surgeons inflate small balloons beneath the skin above the ears for several months prior to surgery. This leaves the man looking rather strange for a while, but the balloon technique works better than simple scalp reduction for covering large areas evenly.

• Minoxidil. A few years ago, the FDA approved minoxidil (Rogaine), the only prescription hair restorer. The catch is that it only works well in about one-third of those who use it, and the new hair falls out when you discontinue it.

Originally a blood pressure medication, researchers stumbled on minoxidil's hair growth properties accidently when people taking it for high blood pressure reported hair growth in previously non-hairy areas. Minoxidil works by increasing blood flow to the scalp and stimulating the follicles to start growing longer hairs. Unfortunately, very few users experience luxuriant hair regrowth, and only a minority report significant benefit.

It takes six months to a year before users know how they'll respond, if at all. Applied twice a day, the drug costs about $50 per month. Because any new hair falls out within a few months of stopping treatment, minoxidil means a lifetime commitment to an expensive drug. The long-term effects of minoxidil are unknown.

The drug works best among those with relatively recent balding, particularly on top of the head. Some users report an irritant-type reaction on the scalp that is characterized by blistering, peeling, and itchiness. Minor heart disturbances have been observed on electrocardiogram in some users, so those with heart disease shouldn't use it. Some users also report dizziness because the drug lowers blood pressure.

• *Alopecia Areata.* This condition causes sudden patchy hair loss in both sexes. In mild cases, the hair usually spontaneously regrows. In severe cases, however, hair loss can be permanent and total. Alopecia areata is poorly understood, but aggressive professional treatment usually controls hair loss and in some cases halts it. Prompt treatment is critical. If you ever pull out a handful of hair, consult a physician immediately. Also contact the National Alopecia Areata Foundation (see RE-SOURCES at the end of this chapter).

HEAT RASH

(See also RASHES in this chapter)

Heat rash or "prickly heat," medically known as "miliaria" is an intensely itchy rash that commonly develops on the chest, waist, back, groin, and armpits in hot, humid climates.

What's Going On? When skin is exposed to excessive heat, sometimes it swells enough to block the sweat gland openings. Sweat trapped under the skin causes irritation, itching, blisters, and sometimes pimples.

Before You Call the Doctor. Prickly heat responds quickly to cooling. Get out of the sun or heat. Replace heavy clothing with lightweight garments. Take a cool shower or use cool compresses. But don't use soaps or anything possibly irritating until the rash resolves. Once you get out of the heat and get cool, heat rash usually clears up quickly.

Heat rash may coexist with "intertrigo," a rash caused by friction between such surfaces as the inner thighs, armpits, or other skinfold areas. It's especially common in people who are overweight. In very mild cases, dusting with corn starch two to three times a day may help, but even moderate sweating quickly causes the powder to cake. Wash the area thoroughly with soap and water, air dry it, and then apply a thin layer of zinc oxide. Unfortunately, the moisture from sweat and the heat caused by friction create the perfect environment for the growth of bacteria and fungi. If the rash appears infected—brighter red with a yeasty or cheesy odor—apply antibacterial and antifungal creams before applying zinc oxide. Although many over-the-counter antifungal preparations are available, miconazole and clotrimazole are the only over-the-counter products effective against yeast.

HERPES ZOSTER

(See CHICKENPOX in this chapter)

HIVES

(See also ALLERGIES in Chapter 4)

Hives, medically known as "urticaria," is a frustrating, often chronic problem. Hives appear as red, itchy, welts, also known as "wheals."

What's Going On?   Hives are an allergic reaction. Something stimulates the release of histamine from special cells, and fluid leaks out of skin capillaries, raising the characteristic welts.

Foods and drugs are common causes: nuts, soy, eggs, milk, fish, shellfish, chocolate, and strawberries; and aspirin, penicillin, and bromides, (as in Bromo-Seltzer). Some people develop hives from ingesting aspirin-like chemicals called salicylates often found in commercial baked goods and mint flavorings. Food dyes, such as sodium benzoate, and vaccines for measles and polio can cause hives in susceptible individuals. In very sensitive people, dusts, molds, animal dander, and even some plants can cause the characteristic welts. Heat, sun exposure, and stress may also be factors.

Before You Call the Doctor.   The key to treatment is to discover what's triggering the hives. Food allergies are often easy to spot because the hives appear soon after eating the offending item. Drug reactions can usually be identified because the hives erupt shortly after taking the drug and disappear when the medication is discontinued.

If hives come and go regularly for more than a few weeks, you have chronic urticaria. Unfortunately, it can be difficult—sometimes impossible—to identify chronic hives triggers. If food or drugs don't seem to be the cause, consider a chronic infection, such as gum disease, athlete's foot, yeast infection, intestinal parasite infection, or more rarely, tuberculosis, a sexually-transmitted disease (STD), or other health problem. The great majority of chronic hives sufferers never find a treatable cause but get along with symptomatic treatment. Many cases resolve on their own after a few months . . . or years.

For itching, try over-the-counter antihistamines. However, they cause drowsiness, so you shouldn't take them if you must drive or operate heavy machinery. If you must drive, consider prescription antihistamines. They cost more, but some don't cause drowsiness.

Soothing baths can also relieve itching. Use Aveeno powder, available at pharmacies (one to two cups per bath), baking soda (one-half to one cup per bath), or finely ground oatmeal (one to two cups per bath). Either buy pre-ground "colloidal oatmeal" at a pharmacy or grind your own in a coffee grinder.

Since stress and hives have been associated, try stress management techniques.

Also contact the Asthma and Allergy Foundation (see RESOURCES at the end of this chapter).

When to Call the Doctor.   If you can't figure out what's causing your hives and the welts do not respond to self-care after a few weeks, consult a physician who can help you look for the cause. Hives may be caused by such serious diseases as hepatitis, mononucleosis, and lupus ("systemic lupus erythematosus"), which require professional care.

▶ **RED FLAG**   If you develop hives after a bee sting, you are at increased risk for the potentially rapidly fatal allergic reaction known as "anaphylactic shock." Contact a physician immediately for an "epi kit," a prescription syringe preloaded with epinephrine (adrenalin). Take the epi kit with you at all times so it will be handy if you develop the symptoms of anaphylactic shock, among them dizziness, difficulty breathing, and nausea.

HUMAN BITES

(See BITE WOUNDS in this chapter)

IMPETIGO

Common in children and newborn babies, impetigo appears as shallow sores that form a crusty surface with a characteristic "honey" color.

What's Going On?   The redness, weepy blisters, and crusty surface of impetigo are the result of a bacterial infection *(Staphylococcus* or *Streptococcus)*. The infection begins with reddening of the skin, then tiny blisters form. When they break, they form the honey-colored crust. The infection then spreads at the edges, forming new blisters. Although it may erupt anywhere on the skin, impetigo is most common around the nose and mouth.

Before You Call the Doctor.   Impetigo rarely becomes serious in adults and most children. However, in babies, it can spread all over and make them quite ill. Treatment involves gently removing the crust with soap and water and an antiseptic agent (hydrogen peroxide). The crusts may need to be softened and soaked off with wet dressings. Apply an antibiotic ointment (Bacitracin, Neosporin). Wash the surrounding skin twice a day to keep it free of bacteria.

When to Call the Doctor.   If extensive areas of the body are infected, or if the infection doesn't improve significantly within three or four days of committed self-care, consult a physician for antibiotics.

▶ **RED FLAGS**   Impetigo is highly contagious. Have the infected person wash hands frequently and quarantine his or her soap and towels. Don't touch the infected area. For impetigo affecting children in school or daycare, consult a physician immediately for antibiotics to prevent contagion. After twenty-four hours on antibiotics the children won't spread the infection.

INFECTIONS

(See ACNE, ATHLETE'S FOOT, BITE WOUNDS, BLISTERS, BOILS, CHICKENPOX, CUTS, DIAPER RASH, IMPETIGO, IN-FLAMED HAIR FOLLICLES, JOCK ITCH, NAIL PROBLEMS, RINGWORM, SCABIES, SCALY PATCH RASH, SEBORRHEA, and WARTS in this chapter)

INFLAMED HAIR FOLLICLES

(See also BOILS in this chapter)

Hair follicle inflammations, medically known as "folliculitis," appear as tiny red bumps around hair follicles, usually on the buttocks, thighs, or upper arms.

What's Going On?   Folliculitis is a superficial *Staphylococcus* bacterial infection of the hair follicles. Both friction and moisture contribute to it. It's common among men who shave frequently and among people like office workers or professional drivers who sit for long periods of time. Most sufferers report the condition worsens in the fall and winter months when they must wear warm, constricting clothing. It usually improves during warm months when the affected area can be exposed more easily to air and sunlight.

Before You Call the Doctor.   Usually, folliculitis responds well to antibacterial soaps (Hibiclens, Betadine Scrub) and to topical antibiotics (Neosporin, Bacitracin). In addition, try these self-care measures:
 • Bathe frequently.
 • Keep fingernails clean and short to avoid a secondary infection from scratching.
 • Before shaving your legs, face, or other affected areas, wash them with antibacterial soap. Afterward, apply alcohol and antibacterial ointment.
 • To keep the infection from spreading, don't share razors or towels. Soak razors in alcohol, and wash and sterilize towels.

When to Call the Doctor.   If self-care does not resolve folliculitis within a few weeks, or if the infection appears to be spreading, consult a physician for oral antibiotics.

INGROWN TOENAILS

(See NAIL PROBLEMS in this chapter)

INSECT BITES AND STINGS

Insect bites and stings cause reactions varying from minor itching and swelling to a potentially fatal form of shock called "anaphylaxis." Here we'll discuss these wounds by the type of insect involved.

 • *Fleas, Gnats, and Mosquitoes.*   The bites of these and other nonvenomous insects are annoying but rarely dangerous—unless they become infected or cause allergic reactions.

What's Going On?   The bite feels like a pinprick. It introduces irritants into the skin, which produce an itchy bump.

Before You Call the Doctor.   Wash the area thoroughly with soap and water. The itching can be relieved with cool compresses; a paste of baking soda and water (one teaspoon of water in three teaspoons baking soda); over-the-counter Calamine lotion or Caladryl; and/or over-the-counter antihistamines.

Of course, prevention is better than treatment. Try to keep pets relatively free from fleas. Eliminate mosquito breeding grounds near your home, basically anyplace where stagnant water can accumulate. If you have a birdbath, introduce fish that eat mosquito larvae. Wear protective clothing, and use insect repellant containing 95 percent DEET (diethyl-toluamide). But on children, don't use DEET at concentrations greater than 15 percent.

If insect bites become infected—red, tender, swollen, and more pain-ful, with possibly a yellowish-green pus discharge—wash them thoroughly with soap and water, soak them in warm water for ten minutes at a time several times a day, and apply an antibiotic ointment (Bacitracin, Neosporin).

When to Call the Doctor.   If infected insect bites don't respond to home treatment, consult a physician.

• *Ticks.*   The bite of this spider relative has become a serious concern in recent years because the deer tick *(Ixodes dammini)* spreads Lyme disease, a potentially serious problem.

What's Going On?   Ticks are parasites which attach themselves to humans and other mammals with sharp, saw-like teeth. They suck blood and can transmit microorganisms that cause three diseases:

•Babesiosis. This rare infection causes high fever, anemia, and possibly kidney failure. Most cases have occurred in the Northeast. No drug treatment is available, but most people recover on their own.

•Rocky Mountain spotted fever. About 1,000 cases are reported in the U.S. each year. Though the name implies this is a disease of the West, it actually occurs throughout the U.S., especially in the Southeast. The infection causes a severe headache, fever, muscle aches, dehydration, and physical collapse. It is sometimes fatal, but antibiotics cure most cases.

•Lyme disease. First identified in Old Lyme, Connecticut, in the

1970s, this disease now occurs throughout the U.S. Lyme disease causes a red-ring ("bull's-eye") rash, chronic arthritis, and problems in the heart and brain. It's potentially fatal, but it can be cured with antibiotics.

Usually, ticks attach to humans around the neck or waistline and can cause no symptoms, but some people experience soreness, itching and local irritation.

Before You Call the Doctor. To prevent tick bites take the same precautions discussed above for flea, gnat, and mosquito bites.

Contrary to conventional wisdom, a recently extinguished match or cigarette does not induce ticks to let go and back out. First, immobilize the tick with petroleum jelly or mineral oil. Then pull it off, ideally with sterilized tweezers or, if tweezers aren't available, with clean fingers. Make sure you remove all of the tick, including its large jaws, which may be firmly embedded. Carefully wash the wound with soap and water.

When to Call the Doctor. Consult a physician promptly if you develop any symptoms of Babesiosis, Rocky Mountain spotted fever, or Lyme disease.

• Bees, Wasps (Hornets), and Yellow Jackets. Though nowhere near as scary as black widow spiders, these flying insects cause more U.S. fatalities than *all other poisonous animals combined.* Honeybees leave their stingers and venom sacs in victims' skin when they sting, but wasps and yellow jackets can sting repeatedly.

What's Going On? Most people experience only a sharp stinging sensation usually followed by localized pain, redness, and swelling. However, some people are seriously allergic to these stings and, if stung, quickly experience potentially-fatal anaphylaxis.

Before You Call the Doctor. For uncomplicated stings, first remove any stingers and venom sacs left in the skin by *scraping* across the sting site with a sterilized knife (or if nothing else is handy, a credit card). Do not try to grasp and pull out the stinger. Pulling inevitably squeezes the attached venom sac, sending more venom into the wound.

Then wash the area with soap and water, and apply a paste of unseasoned meat tenderizer and water, which helps neutralize the venom.

To control pain and swelling, try an ice pack. Wrap a few ice cubes in a plastic bag, then wrap the bag in a clean cloth. Hold it on the sting site for twenty minutes, then remove it for ten minutes before reapplying it. An ice substitute may be used instead of ice cubes. Do not apply ice directly to the skin. This may cause the equivalent of frostbite.

Aspirin and ibuprofen may also be used to control pain and inflammation. Acetaminophen relieves pain but not inflammation. If aspirin and/or ibuprofen upset your stomach, try an "enteric coated" brand. Pregnant women and those with a history of ulcers should not use aspirin or ibuprofen unless a doctor recommends it.

For itching and any hives, try over-the-counter antihistamines (see HIVES and ITCHING in this chapter).

Insect repellants don't work against bees, wasps, and yellow jackets, but common sense does. They don't sting unless threatened. And they may be found on the ground as well as in the air. Don't go barefoot.

▶ **RED FLAG**   *An anaphylactic reaction to an insect sting may be rapidly fatal.* Symptoms typically develop within thirty minutes and include:
- Agitation.
- Hives.
- Dizziness.
- Wheezing and difficulty breathing.
- Rapid heart rate.
- Abdominal cramps.
- Nausea and vomiting.

The person quickly loses consciousness and may die unless treated immediately. Emergency medical help is *vital.*

Anaphylaxis may strike anyone, but people at greatest risk are those with a history of hives, wheezing, or anaphylactic shock from previous insect stings.

Anyone at risk for anaphylaxis should *always* carry an "epi kit," a syringe filled with epinephrine (adrenalin), which is injected into the thigh. This first aid treatment can be a lifesaver. After injection, call 911 immediately. Anyone treated for anaphylaxis should be evaluated professionally.

IRRITATIONS

(See BLISTERS, BURNS, CALLUSES, DISHPAN HANDS, and DRY SKIN in this chapter and ALLERGIES in Chapter 4)

Medically known as "contact dermatitis," these skin problems are caused by substances that come in contact with the skin. Here we'll discuss the two most common types—irritant reactions and allergic irritations.

• *Irritant Reactions.*   These usually appear as red, blistery, raised rashes, which may or may not cause itching, discomfort, and/or pain. In some cases, the skin appears burned, cracked, or peeling.

What's Going On?   Irritant contact dermatitis is an occupational hazard for anyone who works with chemicals: homemakers, laundry, janitorial, agricultural, photographic, chemical, construction, and oil refinery workers, and anyone regularly exposed to detergents, solvents, abrasives, and other chemicals. Common household irritants include soaps, bleaches, laundry detergents, metal cleaners, paint removers, and gasoline, among others. Some irritants require only a few moments of contact to cause a reaction. Others take hours or days.

The underlying tissues may sustain damage depending on the type and concentration of the irritant as well as the extent and length of exposure.

Before You Call the Doctor.   Irritant reactions caused by chemicals should be treated like burns (see BURNS in this chapter).

In mild cases, it may be difficult to pinpoint the irritant, and it may take some detective work on your part to discover the offending substance. The best approach is prevention—wear gloves and other protective clothing to avoid irritant reactions (see DISHPAN HANDS in this chapter).

For alkaline irritations (for example, irritations caused by drain cleaners), immediately flush the area with water for at least fifteen minutes or until it no longer feels soapy, and scrub the skin to remove any particles. Then neutralize the area with a weak acid solution—one part vinegar and four parts water.

For acid contact, wash the area in lukewarm water for fifteen to thirty minutes. Be sure to remove any contaminated clothing or jewelry.

When to Call the Doctor.   If the reaction causes pain that is not relieved quickly by self-care, consult a physician. Irritations caused by acids should generally be seen by a physician, especially if they affect the face, hands, feet, or genitals.

▶ **RED FLAG**   For severely painful irritant reactions, go directly to an emergency medical facility.

• *Allergic Irritations.*   These may cause itching, burning, stinging, and red areas filled with swollen, red dots, which may weep and/or ooze fluid. Crusted or infected areas may fill with pus.

What's Going On?   Most allergic dermatitis reactions are caused by plants, cosmetics, drugs, metals, and/or chemicals. Authorities aren't sure why people develop contact allergies. Some react to new products. Others react to items they've used for years. Allergic reactions occur when the immune system mistakes a harmless substance for a germ and attacks it. On the skin, that usually means itching and inflammation—redness and swelling—with more serious reactions possible.

Like irritant reactions, it may be difficult to identify the offending substance. The rash's distribution can provide clues. If it appears on the ears, neck, or ring finger, check your jewelry. If your face breaks out, check soaps, cosmetics, eyeglass frames, nose drops, or other products you apply. If the eruption develops on the feet or legs, suspect your shoes, socks, or stockings. The only way to be sure is to eliminate possible offenders, then reintroduce them one at a time until you find the culprit.

Although plants such as sagebrush, ragweed, daisies, tulips, and chrysanthemums can cause allergic contact dermatitis, the most hazardous plants by far are poison ivy, oak, and sumac, all of which contain the same oily resin. On contact with the resin, more than 50 percent of Americans develop a red, bumpy, itchy rash, which may persist for weeks.

Poison ivy grows throughout the East, South, Midwest, and Great Plains. Poison oak's territory is the West and Southwest. And poison sumac thrives along the Eastern Seaboard. On first contact, it may take up to a week for the rash to erupt. After that, it typically develops in a few hours or at most a day or two. Some experts claim that washing off the exposed area with soap and water within the first hour of contact prevents the reaction. Most poison-plant reactions occur in spring and summer, but these plants are dangerous year round. During the winter, when stripped of their leaves, the twigs can still cause a powerful reaction. In addition to direct contact with the plant, you can develop a reaction from touching contaminated clothing, equipment, or animals, or from the smoke these plants give off when burned, which can cause severe reactions on the face and eyelids—even in the throat.

Before You Call the Doctor.   Treatment depends on the severity of the rash. Try not to scratch, which can lead to a secondary infection. Itching can be relieved with such home remedies as:

• Over-the-counter Calamine lotion or Caladryl, available at pharmacies.

• Baking soda paste. Add 1 teaspoon of water to 3 teaspoons of baking soda, blend until smooth, and apply.

• A soothing bath. Use Aveeno powder, available at pharmacies (one to two cups per bath), baking soda (one-half to one cup per bath), or finely ground oatmeal (one to two cups per bath). Either buy pre-ground "colloidal oatmeal" at pharmacies, or grind your own in a coffee grinder.

Or try over-the-counter antihistamines, which not only treat the itching but also help suppress the allergic reaction. They also cause drowsiness, which helps the sufferer sleep. Diphenhydramine is somewhat more sedating than chlorpheniramine.

Some people swear by hot showers, which initially intensify the itching but, after a while, provide relief for up to eight hours.

For any blistering and oozing, use cool wet compresses. Apply a wet washcloth for five minutes several times a day until the blisters dry up.

The best way to deal with poison-plant dermatitis is to learn to identify poison ivy, oak, and sumac in every season and avoid them like the plague they are. Some backpackers soap their bodies before venturing into the woods. The soap acts as a barrier to the oil. If you try this method, shower immediately when you return to wash any oil off.

Cosmetics often cause allergic reactions. Some of the biggest offenders are colognes, hair dyes, nail polishes, sunscreens, antibacterial soaps, deodorants, antiperspirants, mascara and eye shadows, and aftershave lotions and creams. So-called "hypoallergenic" cosmetics don't contain the more common reaction-producing ingredients, but they may still cause reactions.

The critical element in treating any contact dermatitis is to discover what causes the reaction and then to avoid all contact with it. If you develop a reaction, first identify any new products you've used recently. Change to mild, unscented soaps and stop using all scented products—a single fragrance may contain as many as 100 chemicals. Discontinue cosmetics for one week, then reintroduce them one at a time and watch for reactions.

Many drugs cause allergic reactions. Any drug may cause problems, but the most common offenders include aspirin, ampicillin, penicillin, sulfa drugs, neomycin, streptomycin, novocaine, and other local anesthetics.

Metal and chemical allergies are especially common in work settings. Some people develop an itchy rash and blisters. Others get hives, itchy blotches, or burning wheals. Some of the most common offenders include chrome, nickel, mercury, and formaldehyde, often used in particle board, furniture, waxes, polishes, carpets, and even permanent-press clothing. Again, the key is to identify the offender and then avoid it.

When to Call the Doctor.   For severe allergic skin reactions, consult a physician. Prescription steroid creams and/or oral or injected steroids can bring quick relief.

If you can't discover the offending substance, consult a dermatologist or allergist for a thorough allergy workup.

▶ **RED FLAG**   Some allergic drug reactions go beyond simple dermatitis and may be life-threatening. If any exposure causes labored breathing, seek emergency medical treatment *immediately*. See the "Red Flag" section of INSECT BITES AND STINGS in this chapter.

If you have serious allergies to drugs, wear a Medic-Alert bracelet which identifies your drug sensitivity (see RESOURCES at the end of Chapter 3).

ITCHING

(See also ATHLETE'S FOOT, CHICKENPOX, DANDRUFF, DRY SKIN, ECZEMA, HEAT RASH, HIVES, INFLAMED HAIR FOLLICLES, INSECT BITES AND STINGS, IRRITATIONS, LICE, PSORIASIS, RASHES, RINGWORM, and SCABIES in this chapter)

Itching is that all-too-familiar crawling, burning, sometimes tickling sensation that triggers the urge to scratch.

What's Going On?   Itching, medically known as "pruritus" has an enormous number of possible causes:
- Mechanical irritants like wool or fiberglass.
- Bites from fleas, lice, and other insects.
- Chemicals, such as those in poison ivy.
- Allergic reactions to foods.
- Prescription and over-the-counter drugs.
- Psychological problems.
- Even excessive bathing because it dries the skin.

Stress often aggravates itching, and itch-producing conditions tend to itch more at night than during the day.

Authorities still don't understand exactly what causes itching, but they agree that nerve endings in the skin pick up itch stimuli and transmit them through "C-fibers," which also carry pain impulses. Certain substances reduce the threshold for itching. Histamine, a chemical certain cells release, plays a significant role in itching.

Scientists also aren't sure how the scratching response relieves itching. Some theorize that it causes pain, which distracts people from itching. Others believe scratching may dissipate histamine, or overwhelm the skin's nerves so they can no longer transmit the itch sensation.

Scratching is a mixed blessing. Sometimes it provides relief. Other times it leads to chronic itching and raises a rash. And vigorous scratching with dirty fingernails can cause infection.

Before You Call the Doctor. The biggest challenge in treating itching is to determine its cause. Consider the following questions:

• Is there a rash? The characteristics of any rash are your best guide to its cause (see RASHES in this chapter. The causes of rashes discussed in this book are listed at the beginning of that section.)

• When did you start itching? Did the problem begin shortly after exposure to any drug, plant, animal, or chemical irritant?

• Where do you itch? The location can provide clues to the cause. An itchy rash around the eyes suggests an allergy to makeup. An itchy rash around the neck or on the ear lobes may mean an allergy to the nickel sulfate found in jewelry. Itching on the back, nape of the neck, or back of the scalp may indicate a skin condition caused by the itch-scratch cycle itself.

• What is the quality of the itching? Does it burn, tickle, or feel crawly? Tickling itching often suggests allergic contact dermatitis. Burning itching may indicate irritant contact dermatitis or shingles (see CHICKENPOX in this chapter). A creepy or crawly feeling may be psychological or suggest infestations such as lice or scabies (see LICE and SCABIES in this chapter).

• Does the itching ever get better or worse? Seasonal itching suggests an allergy or reaction to an environmental factor. Many people suffer from "winter itch," caused by dry skin due to forced air heating, frequent hot baths, and exposure to cold, dry air. If your itching subsides on your days off, suspect some irritant or allergic exposure at work (see SICK BUILD-ING SYNDROME in Chapter 4).

• Do you spend time in wooded areas, work with plants, or have contact with animals? People who work outdoors may develop itching from contact with insecticides, toxic plants, or insect bites. Scabies and fleas can migrate from animals to humans.

• Have you recently changed your diet? Food allergies can cause itchy gums, cheeks, lips, tongue, and/or anus within a few hours of eating the offending food.

• Have you started taking any new vitamins, minerals, or over-the-counter or prescription drugs recently? Reactions to any of these may cause itching.

• Have you tried any new soaps, deodorants, laundry detergents, or hand and body lotions recently? These products can cause itching, usually within a week or two of beginning their use. Even if you're using the same old products, sometimes manufacturers change their formulations and the new one causes allergic reactions.

•What stressors are causing problems in your life? Anxiety, depression, and other psychological problems can cause chronic itching.

Before You Call the Doctor.   Try a soothing bath. Use Aveeno powder, available at pharmacies (one to two cups per bath), baking soda (one-half to one cup per bath), or finely ground oatmeal (one to two cups per bath). Either buy pre-ground "colloidal oatmeal" at a pharmacy, or grind your own oatmeal in a coffee grinder.

The over-the-counter antihistamines chlorpheniramine or diphenhydramine often relieve itching. They may cause drowsiness.

Over-the-counter Calamine lotion, Caladryl, or hydrocortisone cream might also help.

If the problem is caused by dry skin, try moisturizers.

When to Call the Doctor.   If itching does not respond to two weeks of committed self-care, consult a physician. Prescription antihistamines might work.

In some cases, itching is the first sign of more serious health concerns, such as kidney, liver, or thyroid disease. The doctor might order diagnostic tests to determine why you're itching.

JOCK ITCH

(See ATHLETE'S FOOT and RINGWORM in this chapter)

LICE

Today, the term "lousy" means "bad," as in "I'm feeling lousy." But 200 years ago, "feeling lousy" meant that you had lice, a common problem not so long ago. Lice are tiny bugs that cause intensely itchy red dots, deep scratch marks, or pus-filled areas on the scalp, pubic hair, and skin.

What's Going On?   Lice are pinpoint-size, blood-sucking insects that infest hair and clothing. Their saliva is irritating and causes intense itching. A single female louse can lay 50 to 100 eggs. She cements them to hair shafts with a glue-like substance. The eggs ("nits") appear as waxy-looking dots and are often mistaken for dandruff. Lice also attach their nits to clothing fibers. It takes eight to eleven days for an egg to hatch into a baby louse. Within a month, the louse is full grown and begins its reproductive cycle anew.

Head lice are particularly prevalent among school-aged children. More than six million cases of head lice are reported each year. The bugs latch onto young and old alike via close person-to-person contact as well as from sharing hats, combs, and bedding.

In contrast, pubic lice, also known as "crabs," are generally an adult problem transmitted sexually. Pubic lice can survive for up to four days in bed linens, so it's also possible, though not all that common, to become infested by sleeping in contaminated bedding. Occasionally, the eyelashes, trunk hair, and armpit hair also become infested.

In North America, body lice are generally confined to those who are unable to bathe and launder clothing properly. Body lice don't actually live on the body, but rather in clothing. They return to the body periodically to feed.

Before You Call the Doctor.   Lice are difficult to see, but under a magnifying glass, you should be able to discern the rounded nits attached to hair shafts. Once lice have been discovered, everyone in the household or classroom should be treated.

To kill head lice, use a medicated shampoo or lotion (Rid, R&C Nix). Leave the shampoo on for five minutes before rinsing; leave lotion on for fifteen minutes. Avoid contact with the eyes. For pubic lice, apply a shampoo or lotion (A-200 Pyrinate) liberally from waist to knees to ensure adequate coverage (cover the armpit and chest areas too if they are infested). The lice die quickly after contact with the medication, but it may take up to a week for the itching to subside.

You may repeat the treatment *once* after a week, but no more. Repeated treatments irritate the skin and prolong the itching.

Once dead, lice wash off the body, but nits often remain stuck to hair. If the dead nits don't comb out easily, try this approach:

• Soak the hair in equal parts water and white vinegar.

• Wrap the wet scalp in a towel or shower cap for fifteen minutes to soften the glue-like attachments.

• Comb gently with a fine-toothed comb ("lice comb").

• Rinse thoroughly.

• Repeat the process if necessary.

All bedding and clothing must also be thoroughly washed in *hot* water for at least ten minutes and machine dried for at least twenty minutes. Vacuum all carpets, drapes, upholstery, mattresses, and furry toys. Wash and vacuum the inside of the car, especially fabric-covered seats and headrests. Soak combs, brushes, and other hair accessories in hot water or alcohol for ten minutes.

In recurrent cases, consider spraying mattresses, carpeting, and upholstery with pyrethrin spray, Rid, or R&C.

When to Call the Doctor. If lice have infested the eyelashes, see a doctor for a prescription ointment that should be applied thinly with a cotton swab twice a day.

Physicians often prescribe lindane (Kwell) to treat lice, but it is no more effective than over-the-counter products and may be more toxic, especially to children.

LUMPS

A lump is a raised area under the skin without overlying skin changes.

What's Going On? Skin lumps are usually *not* cancer. Cancer rarely shows up as a lump except in the breast and testicles. Most lumps are one of the following:

• Swollen glands. If the lump is in your groin, armpit, or elbow crease or under your jaw, at the base of your skull, or along your collarbone, it's probably a swollen lymph node, generally known as a "gland." Lymph glands store specialized white blood cells called lymphocytes, which help the body defend against disease-causing microorganisms. When the body fights an infection, the lymph nodes often swell and become firm (see SWOLLEN GLANDS in Chapter 4).

• Cysts. Cysts are benign fluid-filled sacs (see CYSTS in this chapter).

• Lipomas. These are benign growths composed of fat cells enclosed by a fibrous capsule. They commonly occur on the neck, back, shoulders, and abdominal wall and vary in size from tiny to huge. If they become a nuisance, they can usually be removed without much difficulty.

• Fibromas. Benign and painless, these growths are similar to lipomas except that they are composed of scar tissue.

▶ **RED FLAGS**   See a doctor *immediately* for:

• Any lump in the breast or testicles.

• Any lumps elsewhere on the body that cause pain or continue to grow.

• Enlarged lymph nodes ("swollen glands") that don't get smaller after two weeks.

MOLES

Moles, medically known as "pigmented nevi," are dark, usually benign growths found anywhere on the skin.

What's Going On?   Darker and usually larger than freckles, moles are groups of special pigment-producing cells which range in color from pink to black. They may be flat, raised, smooth, or hairy. Moles usually appear in early childhood and keep appearing through a person's twenties and thirties. The average adult has about forty moles. For some unknown reason, moles often disappear after age sixty.

Many people erroneously believe that moles are precancerous tissue. The fact is, malignant melanoma, the most serious skin cancer, is as likely to arise from normal-looking skin as from a mole. Moles are normal, healthy tissue that should be of concern only if they change in size or color.

Before You Call the Doctor.   Get to know your moles. That way you'll recognize any changes in them. Examine yourself regularly—or have someone else do it—to spot any possibly suspicious changes. Use a full length mirror and hand mirror under good light. Don't forget your scalp, inner thighs, bottoms of feet, and other hard-to-see areas. Skin self-examination is especially important for those with fair skin and those with any family history of skin cancer or many large, irregular moles ("dysplastic moles").

For more information about moles' relationship to malignant melanoma, contact the Skin Cancer Foundation (see RESOURCES at the end of this chapter).

When to Call the Doctor.   Moles need not be removed unless they undergo significant changes. If you see a mole change size, shape, or color, don't panic. Most mole changes are no cause for alarm. But if any mole changes, consult a physician, just in case.

If a mole is unsightly or in an area where it is frequently irritated, it can be removed with a simple procedure in a doctor's office. The physician numbs the area with a local anesthetic, then removes the mole and a small amount of surrounding tissue for laboratory analysis, and finally sews up the area and covers it with a bandage.

▶ **RED FLAG**   In recent years, malignant melanoma rates have increased faster than any other serious cancer. Fortunately, malignant melanoma has a high rate of long-term survival *if* it's caught and treated early. Consult a physician promptly if any of your moles:

- Start to hurt.
- Itch.
- Bleed.
- Open up like pimples.
- Don't heal if injured.
- Develop blue or black nodules, beaded bumps, or areas of pink or white.
- Have "fuzzy" borders, with color slopping over the margin of a raised mole.
- Crust over.
- Seem to grow larger.
- Develop a surrounding white ring or "halo."
- Or change suddenly in any other way.

NAIL PROBLEMS

The problems include chipping, clubbing, splintering, thickening, pitting, spooning, and color changes; fungal or bacterial infections; and ingrowing.

What's Going On?   The nails protect the delicate nerve-rich tips of the fingers and toes from injury, enhance our sense of touch, and help us pick up small objects.

Nails, like hair, are composed of a protein ("keratin"). Nail structure is amazingly complex: The "matrix" is the collection of cells below and behind the base of the nail from which the nail grows. The "plate" is the nail itself. The "lunula" is the "half-moon" that rises above the cuticle. And the "bed" is the skin on which the nail grows.

- *Fingernail Changes*   (see illustrations). The fingernails can provide windows into problems elsewhere in the body:
  - Beau's lines. The nail plate contains depressed horizontal furrows. This problem may be a symptom of the eating disorder anorexia nervosa (see EATING DISORDERS in Chapter 5). It is caused by malnutrition or several severe illnesses, including measles, mumps, heart attack, or carpal tunnel syndrome (see CARPAL TUNNEL SYNDROME in Chapter 15).
  - Blue lunulae or nail beds. The bluish color suggests poor circulation, possibly a symptom of diabetes, heart disease, or Raynaud's syndrome, a

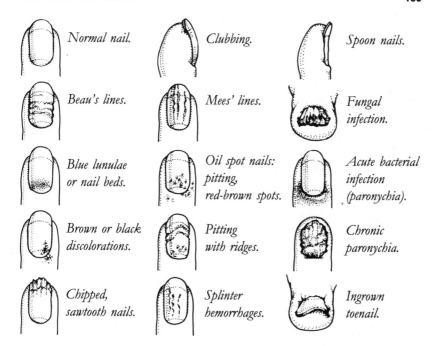

The various types of fingernail changes.

condition in which the fingertips turn blue and white in response to cold (see FINGER PAIN in Chapter 15).

• Brown or black discolorations. Nail injury or infection may cause discoloration. But if it extends from the nail bed to the surrounding tissue and the discolorations appear as spots, the problem may be gastrointestinal polyps. If the discolorations extend to the surrounding tissue and appear as a single large patch or a collection of small freckles, especially on the thumb or big toe, the problem may be malignant melanoma. Consult a physician.

• Chipped, sawtooth nails. These suggest malnutrition, vitamin deficiencies, radiation exposure, or chemical damage.

• Clubbing. The nail plates curve upward and curl around the fingertips. Clubbing may indicate cirrhosis, tuberculosis, emphysema (see EMPHYSEMA in Chapter 11), cardiovascular disease (see Chapter 12), or ulcerative colitis (see COLITIS in Chapter 13).

• Mees' lines. The nails have longitudinal white streaks from the cuticle to the nail end. These lines may indicate heart attack (see HEART ATTACK in Chapters 3 and 12), kidney failure, Hodgkin's disease or sickle-cell anemia or they may develop as a result of cancer chemotherapy.

• Oil spot nails. Pitting accompanied by red-brown spots and nail loss is a common sign of psoriasis (see PSORIASIS in this chapter).

• Pitting with ridges. This is often associated with eczema (see EC-ZEMA in this chapter).

• Splinter hemorrhages. These longitudinal red streaks in the nail bed are caused by bleeding under the nail. This may indicate a variety of conditions, including psoriasis (see PSORIASIS in this chapter), high blood pressure (see HIGH BLOOD PRESSURE in Chapter 12), peptic ulcer (see ULCERS in Chapter 13), rheumatoid arthritis (see ARTHRITIS in Chapter 15), or an infection of the lining of the heart (subacute bacterial endocarditis).

• Spoon nails. The nail plates appear depressed and flat or spoonlike. Possible causes include syphilis (see SYPHILIS in Chapter 18), iron deficiency anemia, thyroid disorders, and rheumatic fever.

• *Fungal Infections.*   Medically known as "onychomycosis," fungal nail infections may be caused by a variety of microorganisms, including *Trichophyton,* the culprit in athlete's foot. Fungal nail infections typically begin as discolorations at the tip of the nail that spread toward the cuticle. Eventually, the nail becomes thickened with irregular ridges. In severe cases, the nail falls off.

Before You Call the Doctor.   Fungal nail infections usually don't respond quickly to self-treatment, but they rarely cause discomfort, so unless appearance is an issue, you might not require treatment. Treat any infections associated athlete's foot and follow the preventive guidelines in the ATHLETE'S FOOT section of this chapter.

When to Call the Doctor.   If you experience pain or discomfort, or if self-care measures don't seem to be working within a month, consult a physician. Doctors usually prescribe topical antifungal drugs, such as clotrimazole, miconazole, ketoconazole, and the oral antibiotic griseofulvin. Treatment can take three to twelve months because the nail must be treated until normal growth entirely replaces the infected nail. In some cases, the nail must be removed.

• *Bacterial Nail Infections.*   Medically called "paronychia," bacterial nail infections are common among those who must keep their hands immersed in water, for example, dishwashers and bartenders. Water causes the cuticle to disintegrate and allows bacteria to penetrate into the nail bed and underlying tissue. Symptoms include pain, redness, tenderness, swelling, pus under the nail, and brown, black, green, or green-black discoloration. Sometimes a crack in the skin results in a blister of pus ("whitlow") alongside the nail. Bacterial nail infections are caused by such common bacteria as *Staphylococcus, Streptococcus, E. coli,* and *Pseudomonas.* Often, a bacterial infection becomes complicated by the *Candida albicans* fungus, leading to chronic paronychia, a slightly tender, red swelling of the skin next to the nail.

Before You Call the Doctor.   If you suffer from chronic paronychia, keep your hands as dry as possible. Wear cotton gloves inside water-tight plastic gloves. Dry the pocket under the damaged cuticle by applying rubbing (isopropyl) alcohol. The alcohol displaces the water, kills the bacteria, and then evaporates quickly. Don't push back the cuticle. You might also try an over-the-counter antifungal cream containing miconazole or clotrimazole.

For acute paronychia, which is characterized by very tender pus pockets next to or under a nail edge, follow the suggestions in the BOILS section of this chapter.

When to Call the Doctor.   If nail infections do not improve significantly within two weeks, consult a physician. For chronic paronychia, you may receive a prescription for Drysol, a potent drying agent, which you apply to the nail margins. The doctor might also prescribe a topical antifungal agent and/or a course of oral antibiotics.

   • *Ingrown Toenails.*   These occur when the edge of a nail grows into the surrounding flesh, causing pain, swelling, inflammation, and sometimes an abscess.

What's Going On?   Ingrown toenails are usually caused by cutting the nail too short on the sides, injury to the toe or nail, or a congenital deformity, such as very curved nails or enlarged nail margins.

Before You Call the Doctor.   Prevent ingrowth by cutting nails *straight across.* Don't round their edges.

If a toenail becomes ingrown but is neither infected nor annoyingly painful, soak the foot in warm water to soften the nail, then raise the edge of the nail away from the nail bed with a clean tweezers and pack a small plug of cotton under the corner to keep it growing away from the skin. Repeat this procedure daily, and you can train the nail not to become ingrown.

When to Call the Doctor.   Severely ingrown nails require professional attention. Under local anesthetic, the doctor cuts away the nail to relieve the pain. If the nail is infected, antibiotics may be necessary. If this treatment proves ineffective, the entire nail may have to be removed.

POISON PLANTS

(See IRRITATIONS in this chapter)

PRICKLY HEAT

(See HEAT RASH in this chapter)

PSORIASIS

Psoriasis consists of red, scaly patches of varying sizes usually covered with gray, white, or silvery thickening ("scale").

What's Going On?   Psoriasis is a rashy skin condition that commonly occurs on the scalp, lower back, and over the elbows, knees, and knuckles. On the toenails and fingernails, it causes pitting and brownish discoloration and sometimes causes the nail to lift and crack. Typically the rash first appears in teens and young adults, and it may continue throughout the person's life, increasing and decreasing in severity, often for no apparent reason. Psoriasis leaves no scars and usually itches only when it appears in body creases. In severe cases, it may cause scales, cracks, and blisters on the soles and palms, pitted, deformed nails, a rash on the genitals, profuse shedding of dead skin flakes, and arthritis involving the spine and large joints.

Authorities aren't sure exactly what psoriasis is. They know it's not an infection or allergic reaction. It doesn't appear to be caused by stress, foods, or vitamin or mineral deficiencies. It's not contagious. And it isn't hereditary, but it sometimes runs in families. Illnesses, scrapes and bruises, and emotional upsets may exacerbate it.

Psoriasis somehow interferes with the normal growth/replacement cycle of skin cells. Normally, the body replaces skin cells every twenty eight days or so. Psoriasis speeds up this process to five to ten times the normal rate, which causes the buildup of scaly patches.

Before You Call the Doctor.   Sunlight often helps. Sunbathing has become unfashionable in recent years because melanoma rates have risen so dramatically, but for psoriasis sufferers, sunlight can be a real boon. Sunlamps are another alternative.

In addition, mild cases may respond to over-the-counter one-half percent hydrocortisone creams. These products are so mild that they usually have no effect on the thickened skin of psoriasis plaques, but you can increase their effectiveness by covering the treated area overnight with plastic wrap.

For additional information and self-care suggestions, contact The Psoriasis Foundation (see RESOURCES at the end of this chapter).

When to Call the Doctor.   Stronger prescription cortisone, tar, and anthralin products are also available. In severe cases, the doctor may prescribe oral methotrexate, a drug that inhibits cell growth. However, this potent drug may also cause quite a few potentially serious side effects.

The newest treatment for psoriasis, PUVA, involves a combination of an oral drug (psoralen) and special-wavelength ultraviolet light. PUVA has potentially serious side effects and should only be administered by psoriasis specialists.

▶ **RED FLAG**   Though it's common in the general population, psoriasis may also be an early manifestation of AIDS or AIDS-related complex (ARC). If you are in a high-risk group and develop psoriasis, consult a physician promptly for an HIV blood test.

PUNCTURE WOUNDS

(See CUTS in this chapter)

RASHES

(See also ACNE, ATHLETE'S FOOT, CHICKENPOX, DIAPER RASH, DRY SKIN, ECZEMA, HEAT RASH, HIVES, IMPETIGO, INFLAMED HAIR FOLLICLES, INSECT BITES AND STINGS, IRRITATIONS, PSORIASIS, RINGWORM, SCABIES, SEBORRHEA,

SCALY PATCH RASH, and SPIDER BITES in this chapter and HERPES and SYPHILIS in Chapter 18)

A rash is any eruption on the skin. Rashes are typically red, often itchy, and may appear as bumps, pimples, or welts.

What's Going On?   There are dozens of types and causes of rashes. Many of the common ones are discussed individually in this chapter. If you are unsure of any rash's cause, first observe it carefully. Doctors ask particular questions to help correctly diagnose the cause of your rash. You can use these same characteristics at home:

• Does it itch? In medical jargon, "pruritic" means that it's itchy, and "nonpruritic" means that it doesn't itch.

• How do the individual spots or bumps look? Carefully examine them and try to identify them using the following descriptions:

  ◦ Flat spots ("macules"). Not raised, but differing in color from the surrounding skin.
  ◦ Small bumps ("papules"). Pimple-like eruptions.
  ◦ Small blisters ("vesicles"). Like papules, but filled with clear or whitish fluid.
  ◦ Large blisters ("bullae"). Similar to friction-induced blisters.
  ◦ Pus blisters ("pustules"). Small bumps filled with yellowish or greenish fluid.
  ◦ Welts ("wheals"). Puffy, pink, flat-topped bumps.
  ◦ Patches ("plaques"). These bumps appear flat and "pasted-on."
  ◦ Flaky ("scaly"). The rash sheds pieces of skin.
  ◦ Crusted. The eruptions are covered with dried fluid ("exudate").

• Where is the rash? How extensive is it?

• Shape/Pattern. Do groups of the spots or bumps form a pattern, such as a ring, a line, or a small cluster?

Before You Call the Doctor.   Regardless of a rash's cause, dermatologists say, "If a rash is dry, wet it; if it's wet, dry it."

A dry rash is typically itchy and scaly. To wet it, use a plain, unscented lubricant such as over-the-counter Eucerin cream or a petroleum jelly (Vaseline). Don't use water, which is mildly drying. Apply the lubricants often, especially after exposure to water.

A wet rash oozes, crusts, or has open blisters. To dry it, apply cool water compresses, then allow the rash to air dry. Don't use ointments or wet dressings.

When to Call the Doctor.   Consult a physician for a rash if you can't determine its cause by reading the suggested sections of this book and:

• The rash does not respond to two weeks of committed self-care.

• The rash becomes more extensive or painful or appears infected (red, painful, swollen, tender, and oozes yellowish-green pus).

• The rash comes and goes over time.

Many potentially serious diseases, for example syphilis and lupus ("systemic lupus erythmatosus"), cause rashes.

▶ **RED FLAG**   If you develop a fever and a rash consisting of flat purplish spots of any size that do not fade when pressed, consult a physician immediately to rule out a blood infection ("meningococcemia").

RINGWORM

(See also ATHLETE'S FOOT and NAIL PROBLEMS in this chapter)

Ringworm has nothing to do with worms. It's a fungal infection that causes a red, itchy, ring-shaped rash.

What's Going On?   Medically known as "tinea," ringworm commonly appears on the trunk ("tinea corporis"), on the scalp ("tinea capitis"), in the crotch ("tinea cruris" or "jock itch"), and on the feet ("tinea pedis" or "athlete's foot"). In addition, it may also appear anywhere else on the skin or nails. The fungi that cause it—*Microsporum, Trichophyton,* or *Epidermophyton*—all grow well in moist areas, such as the groin. On the skin, the lesions spread outward, forming the characteristic ring pattern. On the scalp, especially in young children, the fungus causes hair loss and patchy bald spots.

Before You Call the Doctor.   Ringworm is rarely serious and generally responds to over-the-counter remedies. Miconazole is usually effective for infected feet and groin areas. If it doesn't provide sufficient relief, try undecylenic acid, clotrimazole, or tolnaftate.

When treating warm, moist places like the crotch, keep the area as dry and cool as possible:

• Use cotton underwear, not synthetics, which tend to trap heat.

• Dry well after bathing. Use a blow dryer after toweling.

• Consider wet compresses if the rash "weeps" fluid. Applying wet compresses may sound odd if the goal is to keep the area dry, but water actually dries the skin. Be sure to towel and blow dry the area after the compress treatment.

Ringworm is highly contagious. Avoid direct contact with people or even animals who have it. Don't share sufferers' towels, clothing, bedding, or combs (contaminated hairs are contagious). Children with ringworm of the scalp should be kept home from day care or school until the condition has started to improve with treatment.

When to Call the Doctor.   Over-the-counter antifungal creams do not work on scalp ringworm or severe cases of tinea of the feet or hands, especially those involving the nails. For these infections, the oral prescription drug griseofulvin must be used. Severe nail infections may take many months to clear up.

SCABIES

Scabies are tiny bumps that typically appear in short lines and cause intense itching.

What's Going On?   Scabies' itchy bumps commonly occur on the buttocks, genitals, around the waist, between the fingers, and on the wrists and elbows. They are caused by mites, *Sarcoptes scabiei,* that are too tiny to see. They burrow under the skin, where the females lay eggs. Within five days, the new mites hatch, mate, burrow, and lay more eggs. During the initial infestation, scabies are contagious but don't cause a rash or itching. After two or three weeks, the infected person develops an allergic reaction and the characteristic itchy rash.

Scabies are attracted to moist areas, such as the genitals, skin folds, and the webbing between fingers. Some people develop only a mild reaction with a few bumps and little itching. Others develop hundreds of bumps and intense itching, especially at night. In adults and older children, scabies rarely infect above the neck. In infants, however, the rash is usually more extensive and often occurs with small blisters over the entire body.

Before You Call the Doctor.   For the itching, try over-the-counter antihistamines. Unfortunately, no nonprescription products can get rid of these pesky parasites.

When to Call the Doctor.   Scabies can be easily treated with prescription creams or lotions: 5 percent permethrin (Elimite) or crotamiton (Eurax). Apply to the entire skin surface below the neck at bedtime. Wash it off in the morning. In children under five, wash it off an hour or two after application. One or two treatments usually resolve the problem. You may repeat the treatment once after a week, but no more. Repeated treatments irritate the skin and prolong the itching.

Since scabies spread by skin-to-skin contact, be sure that anyone who has come into direct physical contact with the infestation gets treated simultaneously. Wash clothing and bedding after treatment.

Scabies can only survive off the body for a day or two, so anything that cannot be easily washed may simply be quarantined for two days.

Don't be alarmed if the itching persists for more than a week after treatment. It doesn't mean you still have scabies. It takes a few days for the body's allergic reaction to subside.

If new bumps appear more than twenty four hours after treatment, repeat the treatment.

SCALY PATCH RASH

Medically known as "tinea versicolor," this infection causes the eruption of discolored, slightly scaly, sometimes itchy patches over the upper trunk and arms. The patches may appear red, white, or brown and range in size from one-eighth inch to one-half inch across.

What's Going On?   Surprisingly, there is no common name for this highly prevalent malady. Tinea versicolor means "fungus which changes color." It's caused by an organism which normally lives in small numbers on the skin. For some unknown reason, especially in young adults, it may multiply and cause the scaly discoloring rash. It is not considered contagious.

Before You Call the Doctor.   Washing with regular soap helps stop the scaling temporarily, but over-the-counter dandruff shampoos that contain selenium sulfide (Exsel or Selsun Blue) often cure the problem. These shampoos soften and remove the top layer of dead skin. Apply the shampoo as a lotion to all affected areas and leave it on for several hours or overnight before washing it off. Remove it sooner if it begins to itch. When rinsing it off in the shower, use the shampoo as a cleanser and scrub the skin with a washcloth to remove the fungus and dead skin. Repeat the treatment once a week for six weeks. If the shampoo dries the skin, apply a moisturizing oil or lotion after bathing.

If the rash returns, repeat the process. Don't be alarmed if it takes several months for the skin to return to normal color.

When to Call the Doctor.   Dermatologists treat tinea versicolor with a variety of topical fungicides. Ketoconazole may also be prescribed orally. It's usually effective after just one dose.

SCRAPES

(See CUTS in this chapter)

SEBORRHEA

(See also DANDRUFF in this chapter)

Seborrhea is similar to dandruff, except that the scaling and flaking affect not only the scalp but also other areas: the nose, ears, eyebrows, chest, underarms, anal-genital area, and skin folds. The scaling may include redness, oozing, and crusting.

What's Going On?   Doctors aren't sure what causes seborrhea. Many believe the condition is inherited. Often, it accompanies neurologic disorders such as Parkinson's disease. Stress exacerbates it.

Before You Call the Doctor.   First, try treating the scalp with an over-the-counter dandruff shampoo. The skin rash often resolves on its own once the scalp condition is controlled.

When to Call the Doctor.   In severe cases, physicians prescribe more powerful corticosteroids, administered in pills or by injection, as well as topical tar preparations, sometimes with softening agents for thickened plaques.

SHINGLES

(See CHICKENPOX in this chapter)

SPIDER BITES

Spider bites are usually more frightening than serious, but it's important to be able to recognize the two North American spiders whose bites are venomous.

What's Going On?   Among the 20,000 varieties of spiders in North America, only the black widow and brown recluse (also known as the hobo, wood, or fiddler spider) cause serious problems.

The half-inch long female black widow is shiny black and has a red marking on its abdomen which resembles an hourglass. (The male is smaller, nonvenomous, and brown.) Black widows favor warm dry climates—most bites occur in California and the Southwest. They often live in refuse piles or woodpiles.

The smaller brown recluse has a violin-shaped marking on its upper body and also favors the hidden, dry, dark environments found under porches and in refuse piles and woodpiles.

These spiders, especially the black widow, have terrible reputations as poisonous, and their bites may prove fatal to children and the elderly who remain untreated. However, even without medical attention, most otherwise healthy adults usually recover within a few days.

Black widow bites are usually not very painful, but within about thirty minutes, most people develop a headache, cramps, vomiting, muscle spasms, and sometimes a rash.

The brown recluse delivers a painful, stinging bite which quickly turns red, then becomes blue in the center with a blister. Within twenty four to forty eight hours, the skin around the bite begins to turn black, and the person develops a fever, weakness, malaise, and vomiting.

Before You Call the Doctor. Most people have strong visceral reactions against spiders crawling on them and are much more likely to smash any biting spider beyond recognition than take the time to figure out if it's a black widow or brown recluse. To prevent their bites, take care not to stick your hands into places they might inhabit, particularly refuse piles. Wear gloves when doing yardwork.

If you suspect you've been bitten by either poisonous spider:

• Wash the bite thoroughly with soap and water.

• Place a *loose* lymphatic tourniquet above the bite to limit the spread of the venom. Tie a string around the area just tightly enough to indent the skin, but not so tight that you cut off circulation.

• Apply an ice pack to control swelling and limit the spread of the venom. Wrap a few ice cubes in a plastic bag, then wrap the bag in a clean cloth. Hold it on the area for twenty minutes, then remove it for ten minutes before reapplying it. An ice substitute may also be used. Do not place ice directly on the skin. This may cause the equivalent of frostbite.

• Keep the area immobilized, which also limits venom spread.

When to Call the Doctor. Even though these bites are rarely serious in adults, consult a physician or visit an emergency medical facility if you feel at all panicky or if the victim is younger than one year of age or older than seventy five. Medical treatment for black widow bites usually involves intravenous calcium and muscle relaxants, which relieve the symptoms. In severe cases, an anti-venom drug ("antivenin") may be required.

Treatment for brown recluse bites is more controversial, but current recommendations involve cutting away the dead tissue surrounding the bite, applying ice packs, and giving an antibiotic (Dapsone).

▶ **RED FLAG**   If you've been bitten by a spider you cannot identify and you have extreme pain or any of the symptoms described above, seek medical help promptly.

SUNBURN

(See also BURNS in this chapter)

Sunburn ranges from mild redness to fiery, mottled, swollen skin with weeping blisters.

What's Going On?   Despite recent warnings that sun overexposure causes wrinkles, freckles and roughening of the skin and increases the risk of malignant melanoma skin cancer, many people still strive for a deep bronze tan. Sun exposure sufficient to cause tanning often causes burning. In an effort to protect itself from the sun's ultraviolet radiation, the skin produces more of the brown pigment, melanin. If pigment production can't keep pace with ultraviolet exposure, the result is a painful sunburn. Excessive sun exposure also damages superficial blood vessels, destroys connective tissue in the skin's inner layer ("dermis"), and breaks down the skin's elastic fibers, resulting in older-looking, more wrinkled skin.

Certain chemicals and drugs, including the antibiotic tetracycline and some birth control pills, make the skin more sun-sensitive ("photosensitive"). Fair-skinned people are at greatest risk for sunburn, though those with darker skin are by no means immune.

It's easy to prevent sunburns:

• Limit your sun exposure from 10:00 A.M. to 3:00 P.M., when the sun's rays are most intense. That goes for cloudy as well as sunny days. Clouds scatter sunlight so you don't feel as hot, but you can still wind up with a painful burn.

• Watch your exposure at high altitudes, in the tropics, or around snow or water. The higher the altitude, the thinner—and less sun-filtering—the air. For every 1,000 feet in altitude, ultraviolet radiation increases about 5 percent. The sun also becomes more intense the nearer you approach the equator. Snow and water reflect up to 85 percent of sunlight onto the skin.

• If you take any over-the-counter or prescription medication, ask your physician or pharmacist about photosensitivity reactions.

• Whenever possible, wear a hat and long sleeves in the sun.

• Ultraviolet rays can penetrate wet and white clothing. Wearing a T-shirt while swimming provides little protection.

• Apply a sunscreen with a Sun Protective Factor (SPF) of 15 or greater. Products such as baby oil, olive oil, cocoa butter, and mineral oil do *not* provide protection. Be sure to apply sunscreen under the chin and on and behind the ears. The active ingredient is usually PABA (para-aminobenzoic acid) or a benzoquinone. Some people are allergic to PABA. If you develop itching or a rash, try a PABA-free sunscreen. If that doesn't work, stop using sunscreen and simply cover up and stay out of the sun. Sunscreens with PABA may stain clothing. Reapply sunscreen frequently, especially after swimming.

• Don't use tanning beds, booths, reflectors, and lamps. Although proprietors of artificial tanning salons want you to believe artificial tanning is perfectly safe, authorities insist otherwise.

Before You Call the Doctor.   A sunburn is a real burn and should be treated like one. A first-degree sunburn (mild redness, no blistering) can be treated with cool compresses. Rewet compresses as they warm.

For pain and inflammation, use aspirin or ibuprofen. Acetaminophen relieves pain but not inflammation. If aspirin or ibuprofen upset your stomach, try an "enteric coated" brand, which dissolves in the intestine instead of the stomach. Pregnant women and those with a history of ulcers should not use aspirin or ibuprofen unless a doctor recommends it.

You might also try a cool bath with Aveeno powder, available at pharmacies (one or two cups per bath), baking soda (one-half to one cup per bath) or finely ground oatmeal (one or two cups per bath). Pharmacies sell "colloidal oatmeal," which is finely ground, or you can grind your own in a coffee grinder.

Don't use products with benzocaine or other anesthetic "caines." They may cause allergic reactions and may delay healing. Instead, try aloe vera gel, which helps to cool your hot, swollen tissues. Scoop it fresh from inside the fleshy leaves of the common houseplant. Aloe is also available in various commercial gels and creams, but the plant's active constituents lose some effectiveness in processing.

When to Call the Doctor.   Any sunburn with blisters (a second-degree burn) should be examined by a physician if the blistering is extensive.

Blistered burns carry a risk of infection. The physician may recommend topical lotions and creams as well as a short course of oral or injected corticosteroids to reduce tissue damage and relieve symptoms. If the sunburn causes fever, chills, nausea, and fatigue, doctors recommend going to bed for a day or two to give the body time to recover.

SWEATING EXCESSIVELY

(See also BODY ODOR in Chapter 4)
   "Excessively" means it isn't associated with heat or physical activity.

What's Going On?   Sweating is an integral part of the body's temperature regulation system. When heat or exercise increase body temperature, sweating cools us. However, some people sweat excessively ("hyperhidrosis") in response to conditions other than hot weather or physical activity. Here are a few common causes:
   • Fever. Sweating is a normal cooling response to fever.
   • Synthetic materials. Some people sweat excessively when they wear synthetic fabrics that don't breathe.
   • Obesity. People who are overweight and not physically fit often find themselves sweating with minimal activity.
   • Drugs or alcohol. Large doses of aspirin can cause sweating. The same goes for many other drugs. Alcohol can also increase sweating because it opens the blood vessels (it is a "vasodilator"), causing a temporary warming flush.
   • Emotional stress. Stress and anxiety commonly cause physical reactions, such as shallow breathing, heart pounding, and increased sweating.
   • Hormonal changes. Some women find they sweat in response to menstruation or menopause ("hot flashes"). Teenagers often experience increased sweating due to the hormonal changes of adolescence.

Before You Call the Doctor.   In most cases, excessive sweating is more of a cosmetic problem than a health problem. The cause of the problem often points toward its solution:
   • For relief of fever, see FEVER in Chapter 4. Aspirin, ibuprofen, and acetaminophen all reduce fever. Tepid baths help as well.
   • Wear cotton underwear and cotton or wool clothing. Cotton and wool breathe, allowing moisture to escape. Synthetic fibers usually trap it.
   • Control your weight. The more active your life-style, the less you tend to sweat due to nonstrenuous activities (see EAT AND DRINK RIGHT and EXERCISE REGULARLY in Chapter 1).

• Limit your alcohol consumption.

• Control stress (see MANAGE YOUR STRESS LOAD in Chapter 1).

• If any drug seems to be the culprit, consult a pharmacist and ask if another with equivalent action might be substituted.

In addition, try an over-the-counter antiperspirant (not a deodorant) in a nonsticky cream you can rub in. Unlike deodorants, antiperspirants contain aluminum chlorhydrate, which actually decreases sweating.

When to Call the Doctor.   If self-care does not provide sufficient relief, ask your physician about the prescription antiperspirant Drysol, which contains a higher concentration of aluminum chlorhydrate.

For anxiety-related sweating, talk with your physician about the pros and cons of taking propranolol, an oral beta blocker often prescribed for high blood pressure.

For hot flashes of menopause, ask your physician about the pros and cons of estrogen replacement therapy (see MENOPAUSE in Chapter 16).

▶ **RED FLAGS**   Consult a physician immediately if:

• Excessive sweating is accompanied by weight loss and a persistent cough. This may indicate tuberculosis or Hodgkin's disease.

• Excessive sweating occurs in combination with unexplained weight loss, increased appetite, bulging eyes, and rapid heartbeat. This suggests a thyroid disorder.

TINEA VERSICOLOR

(See SCALY PATCH RASH in this chapter)

WARTS

(See also PLANTAR WARTS in Chapter 15 and VENEREAL WARTS in Chapter 18)

Warts appear as raised, rough-textured, greyish growths that vary in size from a pinhead to large masses.

What's Going On?   Warts are viral infections that usually appear on the skin, but they can also emerge on the genitals or in the rectum, urethra, bladder, or mouth. On the skin, the virus usually enters through a cut, crack, or scratch and incubates a few months before erupting into a wart.

Most warts go away by themselves without treatment (they are "self-limiting"). However, warts on the genitals, around the fingernails, or on the palms or soles of the feet are particularly long-lasting and difficult to treat. In children, warts usually last a few months to a year; in adults, they commonly last months to years. Some people never completely get rid of them and are bothered by recurrences throughout life.

Common skin warts are the most prevalent type. They may grow large and generally erupt on the hands and fingers, though they may appear anywhere. Warts on the soles of the feet, called plantar warts, grow inward rather than outward (see PLANTAR WARTS in Chapter 15).

Common warts are mildly contagious and are often spread on the same person by picking, scratching, shaving, or biting one's nails. They can be passed to others through direct contact. Genital warts are often passed between sexual partners (see VENEREAL WARTS in Chapter 18).

Before You Call the Doctor.   Duo-film, an over-the-counter plaster, is fairly effective at eliminating warts. Follow package directions. The immune system also fights the wart virus, so anything you can do to stay healthy helps.

In addition, the medicinal herb echinacea (eh-kin-AYE-sha) is an immune stimulant. Studies show that when taken orally, it helps fight viral infections by stimulating the release of interferon, the body's own virus-fighting chemical. Echinacea teas, pills, and tinctures (alcohol preparations) are available at health food stores.

When to Call the Doctor.   Treatments abound, but few work all that well. Physicians treat warts with freezing ("cryotherapy"), burning ("cauterization"), chemicals, and scalpel or laser surgery. Freezing, burning, and surgery all leave scars, but freezing causes the least scarring. Freezing involves applying liquid nitrogen for thirty to sixty seconds. A blister forms and may lift the wart off its bed. Several freezing treatments may be necessary.

Unfortunately, all wart treatments are painful and regrowth is common. Repeated treatments may eventually "cure" the wart, but in most cases, the wart disappears on its own.

▶ **RED FLAG**   Venereal warts, fleshy warts around the genitals or anus, should always be evaluated and treated by a physician because they are associated with cervical cancer in women. They are quite contagious (see VENEREAL WARTS in Chapter 18).

RESOURCES

Asthma and Allergy Foundation of America. 1717 Massachusetts Ave., N.W., Suite 305, Washington, D.C. 20036; (202) 265-0265. Provides information, educational programs, and referrals to physicians and the public.

National Alopecia Areata Foundation. 714 C St., San Rafael, CA 94901; (415) 456-4644. Provides information, support, and referrals nationwide.

National Psoriasis Foundation. 6415 S.W. Canyon Ct., Portland, OR 97221; (503) 297-1545. Provides education and support for psoriasis sufferers and their families.

Skin Cancer Foundation. 245 Fifth Ave., Suite 2402, New York, NY 10016; (212) 725-5176. Provides information and referrals to experts in the field.

The Head and

Nervous System

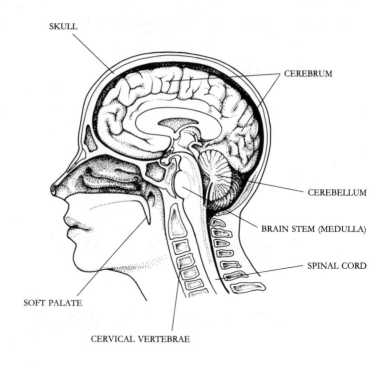

SKULL

CEREBRUM

CEREBELLUM

BRAIN STEM (MEDULLA)

SPINAL CORD

SOFT PALATE

CERVICAL VERTEBRAE

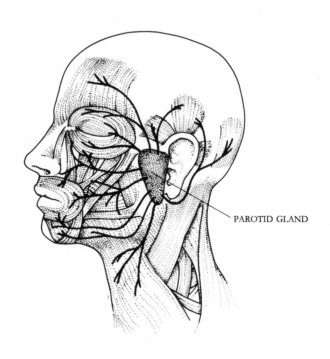

PAROTID GLAND

The Head and Nervous System.

ALZHEIMER'S DISEASE

(See also MEMORY LOSS in this chapter)

Alzheimer's disease causes relentlessly progressive deterioration of brain functions, including loss of memory, reason, language, and ability to care for oneself.

What's Going On?   Alzheimer's is the most common of about a dozen conditions that cause age-related loss of mental function ("senile dementia"). First described by Alois Alzheimer in 1907, it can strike at any age but usually occurs after age sixty. About 10 percent of sixty-five-year-olds and 25 percent of those eighty-five and older suffer some Alzheimer's symptoms. That means as many as four million people nationwide suffer this degenerative brain disorder that first destroys the memory, then cognition, and severely impairs a person's ability to function.

At present, scientists are unsure what causes the mental deterioration of Alzheimer's. Some believe a slow-acting virus or virus-like organism called a "prion" is the culprit. In about 25 percent of cases, the condition appears to be inherited. When this is the case, Alzheimer's may develop early during the person's early fifties. Recent studies have traced the inherited form of the disease to a specific defect on chromosome 21, which causes excess deposition of a protein-rich substance ("amyloid") within the brain.

Other researchers have discovered that the brains of Alzheimer's sufferers are deficient in a certain enzyme (choline acetyltransferase). Pilot experimental drug treatments to correct this have shown some promising results.

Alzheimer's-disabled brains also contain high levels of aluminum, though the significance of this finding remains unclear. Some authorities suggest that the disease somehow allows aluminum to be deposited in the brain. Others speculate that exposure to aluminum—cooking with aluminum cookware and drinking carbonated beverages from aluminum cans— may contribute to Alzheimer's risk. No persuasive cause-and-effect relationship has yet been established.

There is no definitive diagnostic test for Alzheimer's disease in a living person. The disease can be definitively diagnosed only on autopsy. Physicians make the diagnosis based on a thorough personal and family history, the exclusion of other possibilities (see MEMORY LOSS in this chapter), and a battery of psychological tests. The diagnosis is tricky: An estimated 10 percent of those diagnosed as having Alzheimer's disease actually have serious depression (see DEPRESSION in Chapter 5).

Once Alzheimer's Disease Has Been Diagnosed.   At this writing, the disease remains incurable and resistant to treatment. The goal is to control symptoms, provide supportive care, and until they need to be institutionalized, keep those with the disease from injuring themselves and others.

Physicians can prescribe a variety of drugs to help control the disease's various symptoms until impairment becomes severe.

When a loved one is diagnosed with Alzheimer's, families typically feel traumatized, helpless, and confused. It's crucial to investigate all your alternatives before deciding what to do. Talk with your physician, and get referrals to social workers and community agencies that might be able to help. Also, contact The Alzheimer's Disease and Related Disorders Association (see RESOURCES at the end of this chapter).

In the early stages of the disease, the Alzheimer's sufferer can be cared for at home—*if* someone is willing to devote a great deal of time and energy to this challenge. Day-to-day Alzheimer's care takes a tremendous physical and emotional toll on caregivers. Do not ignore your own needs. If you do, you're asking for trouble. Alzheimer's authorities suggest the following:

• Have an ID bracelet or necklace made and make sure the person cannot take it off. This is perhaps the single most important thing to do. Have your name and phone number and the words "Memory impaired" imprinted on it. People with Alzheimer's often wander off and have no idea where they are. This simple precaution can save a tremendous amount of worry.

• Keep reminding yourself that like toddlers, Alzheimer's sufferers are not in control of their actions. Expect them to scream that you're robbing them, poisoning them, and doing all sorts of dreadful things to hurt them. This is simply the nature of the disease.

• Display memory aids prominently all over the house: clocks, calendars, TV schedules, datebooks, etc.

• Label household items so they are easier to identify.

• Develop a daily routine for the person and adhere to it as much as possible.

• Encourage the person to do as much as possible for as long as possible: dress, eat, bathe, and go to the bathroom.

• As impairment progresses, simplify activities so the person can continue to be involved. Break tasks down. A person who no longer understands how to take a bath independently may still be able to respond to simplified directions: "Take off your shoes. Take off your shirt, your pants, your underwear. Now step into the tub."

• Limit the person's choices. Instead of offering thirty-one ice cream flavors, which may be overwhelming, offer two.

• Maintain good nutrition. Make sure the person eats as well-balanced a diet as possible. A multivitamin/mineral insurance formula is also a good idea.

• Eliminate alcohol. It aggravates mental impairment.

• Modify your home. This is similar to childproofing. Place potentially dangerous items out of the person's reach. Install gates at staircases, and install window stops so the person cannot open windows wide enough to fall out.

• Try to accept the progressive nature of this disease. Lost skills are gone for good. A woman who can no longer cook will never relearn how.

• Understand that minor excitements can cause major upsets. Noise, travel, visitors, etc., can aggravate confusion and cause angry outbursts. Stimulating activities should be kept simple—a short walk, a brief visit to one friend.

• Continue to talk to Alzheimer's sufferers. As impossible as they are apt to become, try to value their feelings and human dignity.

• Explore out-of-home day care. Contact local mental health agencies or your local office of The Alzheimer's Association. Senior day care centers are often excellent alternatives for those with early-stage Alzheimer's. They allow the sufferer to get out of the house, remain reasonably active, and spend time socially. They also give family caregivers crucial time off and allow them to get used to the idea of eventually placing the person in a residential facility. Don't feel guilty about enrolling the Alzheimer's sufferer in senior day care. But before doing so, make sure the center is licensed, call the licensing agency and ask about the center's record, and talk with other families whose Alzheimer's-afflicted loved ones are already enrolled.

• Caregivers *must* take time off. This is an absolute necessity. If you martyr yourself and ignore your own needs, you cannot provide effective care. Either rotate caregiving among several family members, or enroll the Alzheimer's sufferer in adult day care.

• Acknowledge your own feelings. It's perfectly normal to feel anger, guilt, sadness, shame, embarrassment, and helplessness and to wish for an early end to the Alzheimer's sufferer's misery—and your own.

• Talk with other people involved in Alzheimer's care. Families of others with the disease can share tips and provide support, perspective, and referrals. Clergy can help, too.

• Try to maintain your sense of humor. Though Alzheimer's is heartbreaking, there are moments of tenderness and laughter as well. Savor them.

• Don't expect to be perfect. You won't be. When you lose your temper with the Alzheimer's sufferer—and you will—forgive yourself. The one mercy of this disease is that its sufferers quickly forget caretakers' outbursts.

At some point—usually by the time incontinence becomes a significant problem—even the most devoted caregiving family must investigate nursing homes. Ambivalence is inevitable, but Alzheimer's authorities agree that good nursing homes provide the best, most comprehensive care for those with advanced disease. Social workers and other mental health professionals can make referrals. Ideally, families should start looking into nursing-home care as soon as possible after the diagnosis. Involve the Alzheimer's sufferer as much as possible when the person can still take part in financial decision-making. Check the person's insurance coverage, savings, and other assets. Consult a financial adviser; nursing homes are very expensive.

Those considering nursing homes should investigate the following issues:

• Is the home currently licensed? Contact the licensing agency and ask if complaints have been filed against the home and the outcomes of the investigations any complaints engendered.

• Is it accredited by the Long-Term Care Council of the Joint Commission on Accreditation of Hospitals?

• Is the staff experienced with Alzheimer's? Are trained nurses on duty at all times? Are physicians and social workers on staff? How often are they on site?

• How long has the average staff member worked at the facility? How much turnover is there?

• Is the home clean and cheerful?

• Are programs available to keep residents as alert and active as possible?

• Are the meals nutritious?

Once a loved one has been institutionalized with Alzheimer's, it's very trying emotionally to watch them mentally waste away and become completely different from the person you once knew. Try to remember the person at his or her best, and continue to seek support and comfort for your own feelings of loss and grief.

BELL'S PALSY

(See FACIAL PARALYSIS in this chapter)

DIZZINESS

(See also FAINTING AND LIGHTHEADEDNESS in this chapter)

The disconcerting sensations of spinning and loss of balance can be a symptom of many health problems, some minor, some more serious. It's important to decide if you're experiencing true dizziness or just the dizzy feeling that accompanies faintness (lightheadedness) because the list of possible causes is quite different.

What's Going On? Dizziness accounts for an estimated fifty million physician visits a year. Most doctors dread these consultations because dizziness has so many potential causes.

The body maintains its equilibrium through constant unconscious adjustments based on information from several sources: visual cues, the inner ear, the muscles of the neck, and feedback supplied by the nerves and muscles that govern posture and movement ("the proprioceptive senses"). When a lack of equilibrium causes dizziness, there's usually a problem in one of those areas, or with the integration of the information coming from them.

Before You Call the Doctor. Dizziness is disconcerting, but many cases have easily identified causes that point toward simple solutions:

• Alcohol. It's notorious for interfering with balance. You don't have to become "stumbling drunk" to have alcohol interfere with your equilibrium.

• Other drugs. If your dizziness began shortly after taking any new medication—either over-the-counter or prescription—suspect that it's drug-related and discuss the possibility with your pharmacist.

• A change in altitude. Air contains less oxygen at altitudes above sea level. Many people report mild, temporary dizziness or lightheadedness with altitude changes of only a few thousand feet.

• Getting up after sitting or lying in one position for a long period. Any sudden change in position after a period of restricted movement can cause dizziness. This is a frequent cause of dizziness on airplanes, where passengers not only sit in unnaturally confining seats but also breathe air pressurized to an altitude of 8,000 feet, which contains less oxygen than air at sea level.

• Motion sickness. Low-level motion sickness may cause dizziness or lightheadedness without the nausea that develops in more serious cases. (see MOTION SICKNESS in Chapter 4).

• Other motion-related problems. Even if you don't become motion-sick, traveling in unfamiliar vehicles, for example, a truck or motorcycle, might cause dizziness. Some people who usually drive themselves everywhere experience dizziness as passengers, especially in the back seat.

•Illness. Many illnesses can affect balance, particularly those that cause ear congestion, such as the common cold.

•Blows to the head. Any head trauma may injure the delicate mechanism in the inner ear that helps govern balance.

In addition to dealing with dizziness by eliminating its cause, some people find relief by taking over-the-counter antihistamines, such as chlorpheniramine or diphenhydramine, or motion sickness drugs (Dramamine or Bonine).

When to Call the Doctor. If dizziness does not clear up quickly, consult a physician because it can be a sign of many serious illnesses. Physicians use the mnemonic SNOOP to classify the potential causes of dizziness:

"S" for *systemic* causes, such as heart disease or sensory failure in the brain ("multisensory deficit syndrome"), which develops in some diabetics and elderly people.

"N" for *neurologic* problems, such as migraine headaches, multiple sclerosis, rare brain tumors, or other degenerative nerve diseases.

"O" for *ophthalmologic* (eye) problems.

"O" for *otolaryngologic* (ear) problems, such as inner-ear trauma or tumors.

And "P" for *psychological* problems, which account for a surprising one-third of chronic dizziness problems.

The doctor will first ask you to explain what you mean by "dizziness" because the condition appears in many forms:

•"True vertigo" is the sensation that the room is spinning around. It suggests an inner ear (or occasionally a brainstem) problem.

•"Lightheadedness" means you feel like you're about to faint. It suggests reduced bloodflow to the brain.

•"Disequilibrium" is the sensation of being unable to keep your balance without actually staggering. It usually indicates a problem with vision or the sense of position.

•"Vague lightheadedness" is the most difficult type of dizziness to diagnose. It may be associated with anxiety, depression, migraine headache, low blood sugar, medication side effects, or even seizures.

Physicians administer various tests similar to the field sobriety test police use to screen motorists for drunk driving. Depending on the primary-care physician's suspicions about the cause of the problem, you might be referred to a neurologist, cardiologist, or other specialist.

Few cases of dizziness are medical emergencies except those caused by a stroke ("cerebral hemorrhage"). In stroke, dizziness is typically accompanied by weakness of one side or a particular part of the body.

To treat vertigo, doctors often prescribe meclizine. In addition to its anti-vertigo effect, meclizine is also sedating, so don't drive or operate machinery while taking it.

▶ **RED FLAG** Recurrent dizziness accompanied by morning headaches, nausea, and vomiting suggests a brain tumor. Seek medical attention promptly.

FACIAL PARALYSIS

This common nervous system disorder, medically known as "Bell's palsy," causes sudden paralysis on one side of the face.

What's Going On? Bell's palsy is frightening but usually temporary. It develops when one or both major facial nerves stops functioning. The paralysis usually develops suddenly, often overnight. The classic symptoms are drooping of one corner of the mouth and loss of the ability to blink or close the eye on the affected side. Sometimes Bell's palsy involves ear or facial pain. In severe cases, speech becomes impaired, and the senses of hearing and taste suffer.

Before You Call the Doctor. Don't panic. Most people recover without treatment within a few weeks, and 80 percent of cases resolve within two months. In some people, the whole cycle recurs months or years later.

The most important aspect of dealing with Bell's palsy is to keep the affected eye protected and lubricated. Wear glasses during the day. At night, a protective patch is a good idea. So is regular treatment with over-the-counter artificial tears (Lacri-Lube, Liquifilm, Refresh, Tears Plus). In serious cases, try Liquifilm Forte, an "enhanced" artificial-tears product. However, don't use products marketed for tired, red, bloodshot eyes. These constrict the blood vessels in the eye and are not good for the eyes under normal circumstances, let alone when you have Bell's palsy.

When to Call the Doctor. It's important to see a physician for a first episode of Bell's palsy to rule out a stroke (see Red Flag). In most cases, physicians simply review the eye-care instructions discussed above. Some prescribe anti-inflammatory steroids or a hormone secreted by the pituitary gland ("corticotropin"). These sometimes hasten recovery but often don't do much.

Bell's palsy is occasionally associated with diabetes or AIDS, so the doctor might suggest testing for them. If you're at risk for either disease, say so (see DIABETES in Chapter 4 and AIDS in Chapter 18).

▶ **RED FLAG**   Bell's palsy causes facial droop *without* numbness and or weakness on that side of the body. However, facial droop *with* numbness or weakness of the arms and/or legs suggests a stroke. If you develop these symptoms, consult a physician immediately, especially if you have a personal history of high blood pressure and/or a family history of stroke.

FAINTING OR LIGHTHEADEDNESS

(See also DIZZINESS in this chapter)

Fainting, medically known as "syncope" (SINK-oh-pee), is a sudden feeling of weakness and unsteadiness that results in temporary loss of consciousness.

What's Going On?   Fainting is a common problem shared equally by men and women. A true faint ("vasovagal syncope") occurs when the blood supply to the brain suddenly drops. Feeling faint may last from ten seconds to a few minutes. Other symptoms may include nausea, weakness, sweating, salivating, blurred vision, and altered heartbeat. The person usually regains consciousness without treatment shortly after collapsing.

Vasovagal syncope is rarely serious. Common causes include:

•Hunger. Few people actually collapse from ordinary hunger, but hunger makes many feel lightheaded.

•Exhaustion. It's not unusual for marathon runners to feel faint after races. Faintness is common among those who push themselves to their physical limits. If you're not in good physical condition, you might feel faint after a brief walk.

•Emotional upsets. In old movies, women often faint or swoon after getting terrible news. Tragedy can literally "floor" anyone. When bad news leads to fainting, the person usually hyperventilates before losing consciousness (see Hyperventilation under CHEST PAIN in Chapter 12).

•Severe pain. Many people pass out after breaking bones or suffering severe injuries. In such cases, fainting protects us from having to consciously bear unbearable pain.

•Hot, stuffy environments. Poorly ventilated rooms filled with cigarette smoke often cause faintness.

• Laughing or urinating. Strange as this may sound, it's a fact that these actions can cause faintness.

Before You Call the Doctor. In most cases, a momentary loss of consciousness is not a cause for concern. In many cases, faintness resolves after having a bite to eat or getting some rest or fresh air.

Anytime you feel faint, lie down with your feet elevated. If this isn't possible, sit with your head between your legs until you feel better.

When to Call the Doctor. Fainting may also be caused by factors which require professional care:

• Drugs. Medications used to control high blood pressure can reduce blood pressure enough to cause temporary loss of consciousness. If this is the problem, ask your physician to adjust your dosage or change your medication.

• Low blood sugar ("hypoglycemia"). Especially among diabetics, this can cause lightheadedness.

• Standing suddenly. Faintness or fainting when arising may mean blood loss or a loss of blood volume from dehydration. Some drugs may also cause this.

• Heart rhythm disturbances ("arrhythmias"). Especially if you have a history of chest pain, heart disease, or heart palpitations, faintness may be caused by arrhythmias.

• Arthritis in the neck. This may cause bony growths ("spurs") that interfere with blood flow to the brain when the head is turned.

• Seizures. Seizures cause temporary loss of consciousness with jerky movements (see SEIZURES in this chapter and in Chapter 3).

▶ **RED FLAG**   Frequent or persistent faintness should be evaluated by a physician, especially if you have a chronic illness: diabetes, heart disease, or a history of stroke.

FEBRILE SEIZURES

(See SEIZURES in this chapter)

FEVER FITS

(See SEIZURES in this chapter)

HEADACHE

Headache means any head pain, from dull throbbing throughout the head to sharp, searing, localized pain.

What's Going On?   Everyone suffers headaches from time to time. In fact, headache is the leading reason people consult doctors. More than 40 million Americans suffer chronic headaches, and for half of them, the pain is frequently so severe it significantly disrupts their lives.

The three most common causes of headache are muscle contractions around the head ("tension headache"), blood-vessel contraction in the head ("vascular" or "migraine headache"), and sinus congestion related to sinus infection or hayfever-type allergies ("sinus headache"). Many headaches aren't strictly one type or another but a mixture. Headache may also be associated with viral infections such as colds or the flu. Contrary to popular belief, high blood pressure rarely causes headache.

• *Tension Headaches.*   The most common type, muscle contraction headaches are caused by persistent tightening of muscles in the head, face, and neck. They cause generalized pain all over the head and a feeling of tightness in the back of the neck or forehead. In addition, the scalp and neck muscles usually feel sore. These headaches tend to be chronic and can last from a few minutes to several years. The traditional theory is that contracted muscles stimulate pain-sensitive nerves. New research suggests that muscle contraction headaches may also involve processes deep inside the brain and brain stem.

• *Vascular or Migraine Headaches.*   Often quite severe, migraines cause intense throbbing pain, usually on one side of the head, and often nausea and vomiting. Some migraine sufferers experience "auras," premonitory symptoms such as flashing lights, vision darkening, or peculiar smells. Most migraines last from eight to twelve hours, but they may be shorter or longer. Although a genetic connection hasn't been firmly established, migraines tend to run in families, and women are affected three times more often than men.

Some people suffer "cluster headaches," migraines which strike several times in rapid succession and tend to localize around or behind one eye. More often suffered by men, these extremely painful headaches typically strike at night and are accompanied by nasal stuffiness and tearing on the affected side.

Many headache specialists believe migraine pain is caused by expansion of blood vessels in the head, which stimulates pain-sensitive nerve endings.

• **Sinus Headaches.**   These headaches cause pain in the face, usually in the forehead, cheeks, behind the eyes, and across the nose. The pain feels dull, constant, usually worse in the mornings, and increases when the head tilts down. Sinus headaches are caused by irritation and inflammation of the membranes lining the spaces in the bones of the face ("sinuses"). Sometimes the culprit is an infection (see SINUS INFECTION in Chapter 11) or hayfever (see ALLERGIES in Chapter 4), often aggravated by individual anatomical peculiarities in the nose that interfere with sinus drainage.

• **Caffeine-Withdrawal Headaches.**   Caffeine is the popular, powerful stimulant found not only in coffee, but also in tea, colas, cocoa, chocolate, coffee- and chocolate-flavored items, and many over-the-counter drugs. Caffeine is addictive, and if "java junkies" don't get their regular "fix," they often develop caffeine-withdrawal headaches, which may last for several days.

Before You Call the Doctor.   Try these home treatments first:

• Aspirin, acetaminophen, and/or ibuprofen. Aspirin and ibuprofen upset the stomach more than acetaminophen. If you suffer this stomach upset but would still like to take aspirin or ibuprofen, try an "enteric coated" brand. Pregnant women and those with a history of ulcers should not take aspirin or ibuprofen unless a doctor recommends it.

• A wet towel placed in the freezer until it's cold but not frozen and applied to the neck and forehead.

• Ice packs. Wrap a few ice cubes in a plastic bag, then wrap the bag in a clean cloth. Apply it across the forehead for twenty minutes, then remove it for ten minutes before reapplying it. Replace the ice as necessary. An ice substitute may also be used. Do not apply ice or ice substitutes directly to the skin. This can cause the equivalent of frostbite.

• Deep massage of the head, neck, and shoulders.

• Acupressure. This needle-free version of acupuncture often relieves headache pain. One effective technique is to press the pads of the thumbs into the hollows on either side of the neck at the base of the skull. Another is to press on the fleshy area on the back of the hand just inside the point where the bones of the forefinger and thumb meet. Press firmly for thirty seconds, then rest thirty seconds, and reapply pressure. Acupressure points should feel tender when pressed. If you don't feel this tenderness, you're not on the point. Poke around until you find it.

People with muscle-contraction headaches often benefit from limiting caffeine and from such relaxation techniques as yoga, progressive relaxation, and biofeedback (see MANAGE YOUR STRESS LOAD in Chapter 1).

Migraine sufferers often experience relief after taking the medicinal herb feverfew, according to recent studies published in such journals as *Lancet*. With fresh feverfew, thoroughly chew two medium-size leaves a day. They taste bitter. Or take the powdered prepackaged herb in capsules—60 mg a day. It usually takes a few weeks to notice improvement.

For sinus headaches, relief of nasal congestion usually helps. Try a hot shower. Or inhale steam from a kettle to liquify nasal mucus. But don't drape a towel over your head and lean over a pan of boiling water or you may end up with a bad facial steam burn. The over-the-counter decongestant pseudoephedrine might also help. Or try tea made from decongestant herbs: ephedra, peppermint, pennyroyal, eucalyptus, and/or thyme. (Don't use ephedra or pseudoephedrine if you have diabetes, glaucoma, high blood pressure, heart disease, or a history of stroke.) If sinus drainage is not completely blocked, you may find relief using salt water nose drops. Mix ¼ teaspoon of salt with 8 ounces of warm water, lie on your back, insert the salt mixture into the nostrils using an eyedropper or a small squeeze bottle, and inhale gently. Salt loosens the mucus and promotes drainage.

Caffeine-withdrawal headaches disappear shortly after the consumption of more caffeine. Even without added caffeine, they eventually resolve themselves on their own.

The real key to headache management, according to pain specialists, is prevention. Recently, multidisciplinary pain centers have begun promoting the idea that life-style and personality have a great deal to do with chronic head pain. Most tension and migraine headaches have "triggers," such as certain foods, poor posture, sleep disturbances, and medications, among others. Foods commonly associated with headaches are chocolate, ice cream, processed meats that contain nitrates, caffeinated beverages, alcohol (especially red wine), aged cheeses, and the food additive monosodium glutamate (MSG). Clenching and grinding the teeth or problems with the jaw joint (temporomandibular joint) may also trigger head pain (see TEMPOROMANDIBULAR JOINT (TMJ) JAW PROBLEMS in this chapter).

One way to begin to identify your headache triggers is to keep a headache diary. Every time you develop a headache, write down the date and time and any psychological, physical, or environmental factors that might have contributed to it. List all the foods and beverages you consumed within the previous twelve hours. Then grade the headache intensity from one (mildest) to ten (most severe). Also note any nondrug therapies that provided relief.

For more information, contact the National Headache Foundation (see RESOURCES at the end of this chapter).

When to Call the Doctor.   If self-care strategies don't provide sufficient relief within seventy-two hours, consult a physician. You may need
a referral to a headache specialist.

For muscle-contraction headaches, doctors often prescribe muscle
relaxants or narcotics, such as codeine. However some muscle relaxants
and all narcotics are habit-forming. Don't use them if headaches are a
chronic problem. Nonnarcotic prescription pain relievers, such as indomethacin or low-dose antidepressants, which block nerve pain, are
alternatives. Be sure you understand these medications' side effects and
how to use them properly.

For migraine sufferers, propranolol or other beta blockers may be
effective in preventing new headaches. A class of drugs called ergotamines
works to stop migraines once they have struck. However, ergotamines
may cause increased blood pressure and rebound withdrawal headaches
when you stop taking them. Before taking any medication, be sure to
discuss all the side effects with your physician and pharmacist.

Sinus headaches due to bacterial infection are treated with antibiotics
(see SINUS INFECTION in Chapter 11).

▶ **RED FLAGS**   See a physician immediately:
   • For any unusually severe headache.
   • If any headache lasts longer than three days.
   • If a sinus headache is accompanied by a fever of 102° or higher, or
if pain increases when you bend your chin to your chest. These symptoms
suggest meningitis.
   • If a headache is accompanied by slurred speech, visual disturbances,
or numbness or weakness in the arms or legs. These symptoms suggest
a stroke.
   • If a headache is associated with a recent head injury. There might be
internal bleeding.
   • If headaches recur frequently.

MEMORY LOSS

(See also ALZHEIMER'S DISEASE in this chapter)

Have you heard the joke about the three signs of aging? Poorer vision,
poorer hearing, and . . . damn, what was that third one, anyway? Everyone
forgets things occasionally, but minor memory lapses have become more
ominous recently because of all the publicity about Alzheimer's disease,
which typically begins with memory losses.

What's Going On?   Most of us suffer some memory loss as we get older. In fact, two-thirds of people over age sixty-five complain about having trouble remembering names and numbers and absorbing new information. Most older people's performance on memory tests is about 30 percent below that of people in their twenties. The fact that the nerve cells involved in memory shrink somewhat and lose some of their connections as we grow older may account for some of what physicians call "senescent memory loss." But recent research strongly suggests that age-related memory loss is *not* inevitable if we continue to exercise our cognitive faculties with mentally challenging activities. Just as the muscles shrink from disuse, so does the brain.

In addition to lack of intellectual stimulation, memory loss may be related to stress, fatigue, poor personal organization, or depression.

In the elderly, depression is an important cause of memory loss. In addition to classic depression symptoms—apathy, lethargy, sleep problems, and loss of appetite and pleasure in life—depressed older adults often stop taking care of themselves and become forgetful. They may appear to be senile, but aren't really ("pseudodementia").

Alcohol and other drugs—even medications available over-the-counter—are major causes of memory impairment, particularly among the elderly. Older adults take more drugs than their younger counterparts. Frequently they take several simultaneously, and their interactions may impair memory. Older adults are frequently overmedicated. As people age, they become more sensitive to drug effects, but many physicians neglect to adjust dosages downward to compensate for this, leaving the elderly taking higher doses than they should. Meanwhile, many older adults assume incorrectly that they should suffer age-related memory loss and don't even suspect drugs might be causing their memory problems.

Before You Call the Doctor.   If you think your memory isn't as sharp as it used to be:

• Cut back on alcohol.

• Make a list of all the drugs you've been taking and your dosages (including alcohol), and bring it to your pharmacist for evaluation. Your dosages may need to be decreased. It's also possible that some of your medications have memory-impairing interactions.

• Take a look at your sleep patterns. Insomnia often interferes with memory (and mental functioning in general). If you have trouble falling or staying asleep, see INSOMNIA in Chapter 4.

• Get into the habit of making lists. If you don't use a date book to remind you of engagements, get one. Note loved ones' birthdays and other special occasions, and make a note *a week before* each one to remind you to send cards or gifts. Make daily "To do" lists. The fact is, no one has a great memory. Those who appear to are usually just well organized.

•Try memory-jogging tricks. Studies show that these tricks can improve recall by as much as 40 percent. One of the best involves simple repetition. Salesmen use this trick all the time. As they speak to you, they keep repeating your name, which makes it easier to remember. Next time you meet someone, repeat the name aloud five times. Then when you part, consciously cement it in your memory by repeating it five more times silently to yourself. You'll be amazed at the improvement in your ability to remember names.

Another useful trick is the "association technique." Simply associate the item you'd like to remember with something already familiar to you. Say you meet a man with bushy eyebrows whose name is Bill. You might associate "Bill" with a dollar "bill," and imagine that its picture of George Washington has bushy eyebrows. The next time you meet Bill, you visualize a bushy-browed Washington on the dollar bill, and it's easier to remember the name, Bill.

Another technique involves a tour through your house to remember items on a list. In each location, you mentally "drop" an item to be remembered. If it's a shopping list, the bread might go on the front door, paper towels in the hallway, etc.

•Exercise your brain. One of the most important keys to retaining memory is intellectual stimulation. As people grow older, they sometimes become less willing to learn new skills or accept new challenges. But experts say the old adage "use it or lose it" applies to memory. Memory authorities suggest reading books, taking classes, doing crossword puzzles and brain teasers, and playing memory-tweaking board games such as Trivial Pursuit.

•Physical exercise is also important for good memory. The brain benefits tremendously from the improved blood flow that comes from regular exercise, particularly aerobic workouts. Just as aerobic exercise can help prevent bone loss, it may also help prevent decline of mental acuity.

•Try ginkgo. This herbal medicine, extracted from the oldest surviving tree on earth, has been shown to help improve memory and overall mental functioning in well-designed human studies. Ginkgo contains chemicals which stimulate blood flow to the brain. It was originally used to help speed recovery from stroke. Those taking it also reported improved memory, presumably as a result of improved cerebral blood flow. Ginkgo is available at health food stores and wherever supplements are sold.

•Diet? It's not clear whether vitamin and mineral supplements aid memory. Recently, lecithin and choline have been touted as memory aids, but most scientists hesitate to endorse them until a great deal more research has been published. However, older people do not absorb nutrients as well as they did when younger. Anyone concerned about maintaining memory should make every effort to eat a nutrient-rich, low-fat, high-fiber diet. It may be a good idea to take as insurance a multi-vitamin/mineral supplement as well.

When to Call the Doctor.   If memory lapses begin to preoccupy you, your doctor may prescribe a memory-boosting medication. More than twenty memory-enhancing drugs are sold in Europe, but only one, ergoloid mesylates (Hydergine), has been approved for use in the United States. But be forewarned: The optimal dosage remains unclear as this book goes to press, and only a small percentage of people respond to it.

Most memories are stored in cells in two banana-shaped areas deep in the center of the brain ("hippocampi"). A neurologist can test for damage to this part of the brain.

Then there's Alzheimer's disease, the reason so many people are so concerned about memory loss. How do physicians tell the difference between Alzheimer's and those with senescent memory loss from lack of brain exercise? Generally, people in the early stages of Alzheimer's tend to deny their problem; people with non-Alzheimer's forgetfulness often worry about their memory loss and complain of memory lapses. Early Alzheimer's sufferers also typically have difficulty with spatial relations and may become confused or lost in even the most familiar surroundings (see ALZHEIMER'S DISEASE in this chapter).

▶ **RED FLAG**   If you seem to suffer recurrent bouts of significant memory loss—particularly an inability to remember the names of those close to you—see a physician promptly.

SEIZURES

(For first-aid procedures, see SEIZURES in Chapter 3)

Seizures can range from small lapses in attention to the "grand mal" variety, which involves loss of consciousness and convulsions.

What's Going On?   "Seizure disorder," formerly called epilepsy, is a problem for an estimated two million Americans. A seizure is an uncontrolled discharge of bioelectrical energy, a kind of short circuit in the brain. Surrounding cells try to contain the discharge. Sometimes they succeed. Other times the discharge becomes overwhelming, and the electrical impulses disrupt normal neurological functioning, causing loss of consciousness and the jerky movements we call a seizure. Where in the brain the seizure begins and where it spreads determine the symptoms and type of seizure.

Just before seizures, people often report warning signs, such as a peculiar anxiety, feelings of impending doom, and/or visual disturbances. Most seizures end by themselves after a few seconds to several minutes, but some may last hours. Afterwards, the person feels confused, disoriented, and unable to recall the seizure.

There are several types of seizures:

• Generalized tonic-clonic or grand mal seizures. These major seizures cause physical collapse and muscle rigidity followed by jerky movements, frothing at the mouth, shallow breathing, bluish skin, and sometimes loss of bladder control. They usually last from two to five minutes.

• Simple partial or sensory seizures. Often a preliminary symptom of a grand mal seizure, the person sees, hears, and senses things not normally detected in the everyday world. Some authorities speculate the "visions" Joan of Arc reported may have been sensory seizures.

• Absence or petit mal seizures. Common among children, this minor type of seizure causes inattention, staring, and loss of awareness of surroundings for a few moments. Most children with this condition grow out of it as they reach their teens.

• Complex partial or temporal lobe seizures. Much like petit mal seizures, sufferers stare blankly and lose conscious contact with their surroundings. In addition, they may act oddly, for example, by making chewing-type motions of the jaw. During these seizures, people may appear normally conscious, but afterward they have no memory of the period.

• Myoclonic seizures. This form of seizure is characterized by brief, massive muscle jerks.

• Atonic or drop attack seizures. In this type of childhood seizure, children lose consciousness for about ten seconds and collapse.

Another type of seizure common among children is the "febrile seizure," also known as a "fever fit." It is *not* epilepsy nor any neurological disorder. It's simply the result of a rapid increase in body temperature, which causes convulsions, rolled-back eyes, and possibly vomiting, urination, or defecation. Some children convulse at temperatures as low as 102°, but most febrile seizures occur at temperatures above 103.5°.

Before You Call the Doctor. Anyone who has ever had a seizure should wear a MedicAlert bracelet or necklace (see RESOURCES at the end of this chapter), so that if they lose consciousness, first-aiders will know they have seizure disorder.

First aid for epileptic seizures is fairly simple (see SEIZURES in Chapter 3).

Febrile seizures rank among the most terrifying experiences of parenthood. However, most resolve on their own, and very few cause any lasting problems. During a febrile seizure, place the child face down in bed, head turned to one side, protected from hitting anything hard. Don't force anything into the child's mouth. Make sure the child can breathe freely and clear the nose and mouth of any vomitus.

In the vast majority of febrile seizures, the child has no problem breathing. Simply protect the head and provide supportive touch. Time the seizure and notice which limbs are flailing and how. Febrile seizures that last more than ten to fifteen minutes or the occurrence of any seizure in the absence of a fever may indicate epileptic-type seizures. Consult the child's physician.

In the rare event that the child stops breathing, call 911 and begin CPR. If you are not trained in CPR, the 911 operator can talk you through it. CPR cannot be taught in a book. To learn it, contact your local American Red Cross or American Heart Association and sign up for a class. Your entire family should learn CPR. In 90 percent of cases, people administer CPR to relatives or close friends.

Febrile seizures typically stop by themselves. Afterward, the child is usually weak and groggy and unable to remember the seizure. When the child is able to swallow, give acetaminophen (*not* aspirin, because in children under 16 with fevers associated with colds, flu, and chickenpox, it has been linked to Reye syndrome, a potentially fatal condition). Then consult the child's physician for a post-seizure evaluation. Children who have had one febrile seizure are at increased risk for another. Discuss treatment options with your child's doctor, and plan to treat fevers early with acetaminophen. After several febrile seizures, parents and physicians may decide to give the child anticonvulsant medication, usually for six to twenty-four months.

Until recently, epileptic seizures were controlled with powerful anticonvulsive drugs. Today, however, many people with seizure disorder have successfully learned to prevent their seizures, or control them, allowing them to keep their medication to a minimum. For a complete discussion of the self-care approach to seizures, consult the book *Epilepsy: A New Approach* by Adrienne Richard and Joel Reiter, M.D. (see RESOURCES at the end of this chapter).

A crucial element in seizure self-care is a positive attitude and willingness to take control of your seizure situation. Like headaches, seizures often have triggers: stress, fatigue, and alcohol or drug consumption. One way to determine your triggers is to develop a seizure diary that tracks your diet, stress, physical activity, and warning signs prior to your seizures. Every time you have one, ask yourself:

• What emotional stress was I under? Work, relationships, financial, etc.?

• What physical stress was I under? Illness, fatigue, menstruation, etc.?

• How balanced was my diet?

Stress, a frequent seizure trigger, can be managed through a program of regular physical exercise and relaxation techniques (see MANAGE YOUR STRESS LOAD in Chapter 1). Any form of gentle, vigorous exercise releases tension and improves mood. One study at the University of Minnesota School of Medicine showed that progressive muscle relaxation reduced seizures 75 percent.

For more information, contact The Epilepsy Foundation of America (see RESOURCES at the end of this chapter).

When to Call the Doctor.   If you suffer seizures, chances are you're already under a physician's care. Discuss the new self-care approach to seizures with your physician, and as you gain more control, consider reducing your medication.

However, medication may still be necessary. Seizures can often be controlled with phenytoin, carbamazepine, valproic acid (Depakene or Depakote), or any of the many brands of phenobarbital. Before you take any of these drugs, make sure you understand all their possible side effects.

▶ **RED FLAG**   After any seizure or suspected seizure, consult a physician.

SINUS HEADACHE

(See HEADACHE in this chapter and SINUS INFECTION in Chapter 11)

STROKE

Stroke results from a sharp reduction in blood flow to a part of the brain and the death of some brain tissue. A related problem, "transitory ischemic attacks" (TIAs) are mini-strokes that cause temporary brain impairment due to a brief disruption of blood flow.

What's Going On?   Stroke is the nation's third leading cause of death (after heart disease and cancer). Strokes typically occur among people over sixty years of age but may strike at any age, even during childhood. Although strokes affect the brain, they are actually a cardiovascular problem, that is, they are related to heart disease. Strokes involve disruption of blood flow to the brain due to one of three causes: bleeding ("cerebral hemorrhage"), a blood clot ("thrombosis"), or an obstruction ("embolism").

In cerebral hemorrhage an artery leaks or bursts, usually because of high blood pressure, and blood floods part of the brain. In thrombotic strokes, clots may form when arteries in the brain become narrowed by the same deposits ("atherosclerotic plaques") that cause heart attacks. Embolic strokes are similar to the thrombotic variety.

Frequently, thrombotic strokes are preceeded by TIAs. TIA symptoms include temporary dizziness, weakness or paralysis on one side, and speech and vision problems. Sometimes the symptoms come and go quickly, and the person pays little or no attention to them. However, TIAs are warnings that should not be ignored. Prompt medical intervention may be able to prevent subsequent stroke or at least reduce the damage.

Before You Call the Doctor.   The best approach to both strokes and TIAs is prevention. All the risk factors for heart attack also apply to stroke: high blood pressure ("hypertension"), high cholesterol ("hypercholesterolemia"), cigarette smoking, family history, alcohol abuse, sedentary life-style, high-fat diet, and poorly managed stress. But uncontrolled high blood pressure is the leading cause of stroke.

For stroke prevention:

• *Control your blood pressure.* This is critical. People with normal blood pressure rarely have strokes. Have your blood pressure checked regularly, and if it's high, work with a physician to bring it under control. Eat a low-fat, high-fiber diet. Limit your caffeine and salt (sodium) intake. Get regular exercise. Get adequate rest. Limit your alcohol consumption. If necessary, take blood-pressure-lowering medications.

• Keep your total blood cholesterol level below 200 by following the life-style suggestions for blood pressure control above. Oat bran and psyllium seed powder can also help reduce cholesterol. If necessary, take cholesterol-lowering medications.

• Don't smoke.

• Take one aspirin tablet a day. Regular low-dose aspirin has been shown to reduce the risk of TIAs and thrombotic strokes. If aspirin upsets your stomach, take an enteric coated brand. But if you bruise easily, have a clotting disorder, are pregnant, or have a history of ulcers and/or allergic reactions to aspirin, consult a physician before taking aspirin regularly.

When to Call the Doctor.   Once a stroke has occurred, doctors can try to limit the extent of damage with drugs that dissolve clots and thin the blood (thrombolytics and anticoagulants). In some cases, surgery can relieve pressure on the brain or be used to bypass damaged blood vessels. Although the nerve cells damaged by strokes cannot regenerate, therapy may be able to restore movement, speech, and other abilities. Recent research suggests that if aggressive physical therapy begins as quickly as possible after a stroke, just about anyone who survives can regain some function. The physician can also recommend treatment to help prevent future strokes.

If you think you or a loved one has had a stroke, see a physician immediately. About one-third of strokes cause death. One-third cause some disability. And about one-third of stroke sufferers make a full recovery. The severity of damage depends on the area of the brain affected and on the extent of damage.

STUTTERING AND STAMMERING

Stuttering means rapid serial repetitions of sounds or syllables. Stammering is similar, except that the person vocally hesitates before speaking.

What's Going On?   No one is sure why some people stutter and stammer. These speech problems often run in families, but they are not considered hereditary. They occur more frequently in men than women and more often in left-handed or ambidextrous people and in lefties who try to become right-handed. Stuttering and stammering are also common among children two to three years of age who are learning to talk. People who stutter or stammer tend to exhibit the problem more when they're excited or under stress.

Before You Call the Doctor.   If your two-year-old stutters, don't rush to your pediatrician. Most children outgrow the problem in a few months. Rather than prompting or correcting a stuttering child, slow down *your own* speech, and allow children to speak at their own pace.

If stuttering or stammering troubles older children or adults, contact The Speech Foundation of America (see RESOURCES at the end of this chapter).

When to Call the Doctor.   Few physicians are equipped to treat these problems, but they may be able to provide referrals to local agencies or speech therapists, who use breathing exercises, relaxation techniques, and speech reeducation training to improve the person's speaking abilities.

TEMPOROMANDIBULAR JOINT (TMJ) JAW PROBLEMS

Malfunctions in the joint that opens and closes the mouth can cause a wide range of confusing symptoms, including headaches, facial pain, jaw clicking, and neck, back, and shoulder pain.

What's Going On?   Recognized only during the last decade, temporomandibular joint (TMJ) dysfunction affects an estimated ten million Americans, according to the American Dental Association. However, some authorities still doubt that the condition exists and charge that some dentists, chiropractors, and physicians are profiting handsomely from treating what they call a "non-malady." Nonetheless, most experts believe TMJ dysfunction is a real problem that can cause a bewildering array of chronic painful symptoms.

TMJ dysfunction is controversial because it has no single cause. Misalignment of the jaw joint can be caused by:
• Postural problems.
• Physical stresses, such as toothgrinding or clenching ("bruxism").
• Cradling the phone between the shoulder and jaw.
• Poorly fitting teeth ("malocclusion").
• A blow to the jaw or chin.
• Whiplash from a rear-end car accident.

The problem involves not only the temporomandibular joint but also the nerves and muscles of the head, neck, and shoulders. TMJ dysfunction is difficult to diagnose, and not all health authorities subscribe to the same diagnostic criteria.

Before You Call the Doctor (or Dentist).   If you answer "yes" to more than one or two of these questions, you may have a TMJ problem:
• Do you have frequent headaches, especially in the morning?
• Do you clench and grind your teeth during the day?
• Have roommates or bedmates ever complained about you grinding your teeth at night?

• Have you noticed any teeth, especially your eye teeth, wearing down?

• Do your jaw muscles feel tender?

• Does your jaw make popping or clicking sounds when you open or close your mouth?

• Do you have difficulty opening or closing your mouth?

• Do you have facial pain? Tooth pain? Neck pain? Shoulder pain?

• Does it hurt to chew, yawn, or open your mouth widely?

• Does your jaw ever get stuck open or closed?

• Do you feel pain in or around your ears?

• Do your ears feel stuffy or itchy?

• Do you suffer earaches without ear infections?

• Do you have ringing, roaring, hissing, or buzzing in the ears?

• Do you often feel dizzy?

If you suspect a TMJ problem, try:

• Over-the-counter pain relievers for chronic pain or soreness: aspirin, acetaminophen, or ibuprofen. If aspirin or ibuprofen upset your stomach, try an "enteric coated" brand, which dissolves in the intestine, not in the stomach. Pregnant women and those with a history of ulcers should not use aspirin or ibuprofen unless a doctor recommends it.

• Reduce your caffeine consumption and stop taking over-the-counter decongestants and other "speedy" drugs, all of which can cause jaw clenching.

• Do not chew gum.

• Consciously relax your jaw. Most people keep their jaws tightly clenched much of the time. Is your jaw clenched right now? If so, part your teeth slightly, keeping your lips closed. Remind yourself to unclench your jaw every few minutes until it becomes second nature.

• Massage your jaw, neck, and shoulders.

• Try hot packs and cold packs for pain and soreness.

When to Call the Doctor (or Dentist). Treatment of TMJ dysfunction can range from simple massage to surgery. Try conservative treatment first: massage and chewing modifications.

If you still have problems, the next step usually involves an acrylic splint custom-fitted to your mouth that prevents your teeth from coming together. Worn twenty-four hours a day for several months, the device allows the jaw muscles to relax into what TMJ specialists call the "neutral" position.

Other approaches include moving teeth ("orthodontics"), shaping and/or moving bony structures ("orthopedics"), or regrinding tooth surfaces ("equilibration").

In a few cases where the TMJ has become severely deteriorated, surgery may be required. However, before you consent to any treatment for TMJ dysfunction, get several opinions. Don't forget to ask about cost. Without dental insurance, treatment may cost more than $1,000, and even with insurance, it may still cost a good deal.

TICS AND TWITCHES

Tics and twitches are brief, rapid, involuntary, nonrhythmic waking movements of the eyelids, facial muscles, hands, shoulders, legs, or other areas.

What's Going On?   Most people experience occasional, temporary tics and twitches such as eyelid flutter, particularly when stressed or fatigued. Tics that last a month or two often occur in childhood or early adolescence, especially among boys. They typically include movements such as eye blinking, facial grimacing, and head turning. Often a child's tics or twitches begin after a particularly stressful event and become more pronounced and frequent or develop into other movements during times of stress.

Before You Call the Doctor.   Most tics usually last only a few weeks and disappear without treatment. Even chronic childhood tics usually disappear during adolescence. Doctors usually take a wait-and-see attitude, and you can do this before you call the doctor. Because stress and muscle tension are usually important factors in tics and twitches, stress reduction and tension relief often help. Try deep breathing, hot baths, massage, or anything else that helps you relax (see MANAGE YOUR STRESS LOAD in Chapter 1).

Parents concerned about childrens' tics and twitches should never embarass or punish them. Instead, experts recommend ignoring the tic/twitch and helping the child learn to manage his or her stress through deep breathing, exercise, emotional support, and creative play.

When to Call the Doctor.   If a tic or twitch lasts more than a month, or if it becomes so annoying that it interferes with sleep or other activities, consult a physician. A muscle relaxant may be prescribed.

In rare cases, tics may indicate Tourette's syndrome, a disorder which causes severe chronic tics and the utterance of involuntary sounds. Tourette's can be treated with a variety of medications.

Other rare but serious causes of persistent twitches are seizures and certain hereditary nerve disorders.

TRANSITORY ISCHEMIC ATTACKS (TIAs)

(See STROKE in this chapter)

TREMORS

Tremor means shaking. The shaking is rhythmic as opposed to jerky, and the affected area—usually the hands—doesn't move up and down very far.

What's Going On?   Hold out your arms, and your hands will shake a tiny bit as a reaction to the beating of the heart. But this "normal tremor" is virtually imperceptible without sensitive instruments. Tremor becomes a problem when shaking becomes visible and interferes with self-esteem or the performance of tasks such as writing.

There are three basic types of tremor. "Rest tremors" occur when the hands are at rest. "Postural tremors" appear when the arms are outstretched. And "kinetic tremors" occur when the hands are in motion.

Tremors have many possible causes:

•Drugs and toxins. Dozens of drugs—legal and illegal, over-the-counter and prescription medications—and toxins can cause tremors. Here is just a partial list: alcohol, caffeine, amphetamines, diet pills, carbon monoxide, monosodium glutamate (MSG), meperidine (Demerol), phenytoin (Dilantin), lithium, haloperidol (Haldol), methyldopa (Aldomet), L-dopa, metoclopramide (Reglan), dozens of brands of the asthma drug theophylline, withdrawal from barbiturates, and use of various illicit so-called "designer drugs."

•Heavy metals. Lead and mercury exposure.

•Stress or anxiety.

•Fatigue, especially after prolonged exercise.

•Low blood sugar ("hypoglycemia").

•Taking too much insulin, a possibility for diabetics.

•Thyroid disorders.

•Multiple sclerosis.

•Psychological problems, particularly anxiety.

•Parkinson's disease. About 75 percent of those with this degenerative disease of the nervous system develop resting and postural tremors which grow worse over time. Parkinsonian tremors are aggravated by stress and alleviated during sleep. The classic movement is called a "pill-rolling" tremor. The thumb and forefinger shake in opposite directions.

Stress markedly aggravates the shaking. The disease has many causes: certain infections, drugs, toxins, tumors, and head injuries. It is considered nongenetic. As the disease progresses, embarrassment becomes a major problem and often causes social withdrawal.

• Essential tremor. More than one million Americans have essential tremor, which usually begins between forty and sixty years of age. It is often misdiagnosed as Parkinson's disease, but it rarely causes resting tremors as Parkinson's does, and oddly, alcohol temporarily eliminates the shaking. About half of cases are hereditary. The tremor comes on gradually, often disappears for a while, then returns. Stress aggravates the shaking. Essential tremor often grows slowly worse, and sometimes affects the voice as well as the hands. But it does not lead to Parkinson's disease. Many people who seek treatment say they've experienced "the shakes" for more than twenty years. Embarrassment can become a major problem and cause social withdrawal.

Before You Call the Doctor.   Most tremors are self-diagnosed, and many can be self-treated:

• Check the list of possible causes and see if any might apply to you.

• Empty your medicine cabinet and take everything in it—over-the-counter and prescription medications—to your pharmacist. Be sure to mention any illicit drugs as well. Ask if anything you take, or interactions among them, might cause tremors. If so, ask if other drugs that don't cause tremors might be substituted.

• Pay special attention to your family history. Tremor at any age is abnormal. If you dimly recall that your father developed tremors after age eighty, don't write them off to "old age." He may have had essential tremor, and you may inherit the condition. Alcoholism in a close relative is another warning sign because alcohol relieves essential tremor, and people may become alcoholic in an effort to self-medicate the condition.

• Contact the International Tremor Foundation (see RESOURCES at the end of this chapter) for more information.

When to Call the Doctor.   Consult a physician if you cannot self-diagnose your tremor, if you suspect a family history of essential tremor, or if you suspect you have any other tremor-causing illness (Parkinson's disease, multiple sclerosis, a thyroid condition, etc.). The doctor will probably order some diagnostic tests and, depending on their results, may refer you to a neurologist or another specialist or start medication. Essential tremor that interferes with functioning can be treated with beta blockers.

VERTIGO

(See DIZZINESS in this chapter)

RESOURCES

The Alzheimer's Disease and Related Disorders Association. 70 East Lake Street, Suite 600, Chicago, IL 60601; (312) 853-3060, or 1-(800)-621-0379 (in Illinois, 1-(800)-572-6037). The national office can supply referrals to local affiliates and other resources around the country.

The National Headache Foundation. 5252 North Western Ave., Chicago, IL 60625; (312) 878-5558. Provides information, publications, and referrals nationwide.

MedicAlert Foundation. For a $25 lifetime membership, you receive a wrist bracelet or necklace which lists your illness and an emergency phone number. Call the number, and operators provide the name and phone number of the person's physician and a list of any required medications. Call 1-(800)-344-3226 or 1-(800)-432-5378.

Epilepsy: A New Approach by Adrienne Richard and Joel Reiter, M.D. (New York: Prentice Hall, 1990, $19.95) The best book on self-care for people with a seizure disorder.

The Epilepsy Foundation of America. 4351 Garden City Dr., Landover, MD 20785; (301) 459-3700. Provides information, support, advocacy, and referrals to eighty-five affiliates around the U.S.

The Speech Foundation of America. P.O. Box 11749, Memphis, TN 38111; (901) 452-0995. Provides referrals to speech specialists around the country who can help those who stutter, stammer, or have other speech problems.

The International Tremor Foundation. 360 West Superior, Chicago, IL 60610. Provides information, support, and referrals.

C H A P T E R 8

The Eyes

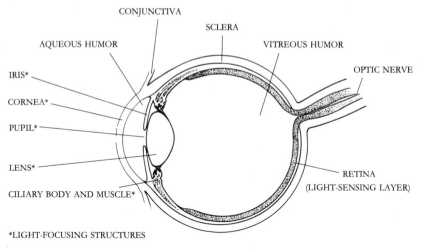

CONJUNCTIVA

SCLERA

AQUEOUS HUMOR

VITREOUS HUMOR

OPTIC NERVE

IRIS*

CORNEA*

PUPIL*

LENS*

CILIARY BODY AND MUSCLE*

RETINA
(LIGHT-SENSING LAYER)

*LIGHT-FOCUSING STRUCTURES

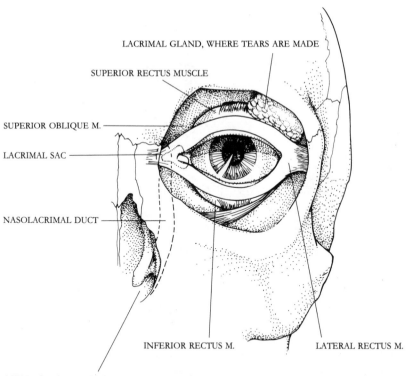

LACRIMAL GLAND, WHERE TEARS ARE MADE

SUPERIOR RECTUS MUSCLE

SUPERIOR OBLIQUE M.

LACRIMAL SAC

NASOLACRIMAL DUCT

INFERIOR RECTUS M.

LATERAL RECTUS M.

OPENING OF TEAR DUCT INTO NASAL CAVITY

The Eye.

BAGS UNDER THE EYES

Some people develop dark semicircular "bags" of folded skin under their eyes, especially when they're tired or as they age.

What's Going On? The skin under the eyes is particularly thin. When fluid accumulates in this area, it pulls the skin into the characteristic semicircular sag pattern.

According to folklore, bags develop when people become tired or lack sleep. That's true. Fatigue attracts fluid to the eye area, and as the extra fluid accumulates, bags develop. Other bag-producing factors include:

• Cigarette smoking, which diminishes the elasticity of skin and contributes not only to bags but also to facial wrinkling.

• Cortisone medications, which can cause fluid retention.

• Allergic reactions, which draw fluid toward the eyes, some of which emerges as the "watery eyes" of hayfever.

• Other ailments that cause fluid retention, such as kidney or thyroid disease.

• Sleep position. When you sleep on your stomach, extra fluid accumulates under the eyes.

• Heredity. Some people are genetically predisposed to pronounced bags.

• Advancing age. As the skin ages, it loses its elasticity and its ability to counteract the skin-sagging of fluid accumulation.

Before You Call the Doctor. An understanding of what causes bags points the way toward self-treatment:

• Get enough rest, at least seven hours a night and preferably eight.

• Don't smoke.

• Sleep on your side or back.

• Control your allergies (see ALLERGIES in Chapter 4).

• If you have any medical condition associated with fluid build-up, discuss diuretics with your physician. Diuretics often deplete potassium. If you take them, be sure to eat plenty of potassium-rich foods, such as bananas or potatoes, but don't take potassium supplements unless your doctor recommends them. In some cases, the kidneys can't handle the extra potassium.

Makeup can hide most bags. If bags become worse or interfere with your self-esteem despite self-care measures, plastic surgery is an option.

BLACK EYE

(See BRUISES in Chapter 6)

BLURRY, DISTORTED, OR DOUBLE VISION

Vision is so important to functioning in the world that any fuzziness, distortion, or multiple imaging is quite frightening.

What's Going On?   Vision is an amazingly complex and delicate photochemical process. Light rays reflected off objects pass through the transparent covering at the front of the eye ("cornea"). The cornea bends or "refracts" the light, which then passes through the circular opening in the eye's colored iris ("pupil") to the curved lens, which focuses it on the nerve-rich back of the eye ("retina"). When light hits the retina, nerve impulses are generated and sent along the optic nerve to the brain, where the image is interpreted and we "see."

Here we'll discuss the most common causes of blurry, distorted, or double vision: refractive errors and muscle problems, cataracts, glaucoma, and macular degeneration.

• **Refractive Errors and Muscle Problems.**   An enormous number of problems can impair the elaborate visual process. Among the most common are refractive errors, which have to do with the way the eye focuses incoming light. The four most common refractive errors are nearsightedness ("myopia"), farsightedness ("hyperopia"), "astigmatism," and "presbyopia."

•Nearsightedness. A person with myopia can see nearby objects clearly, but anything at a distance appears fuzzy. The problem is that the lens is too thick, the cornea too curved, or the eyeball too long. As a result, the light rays do not focus exactly on the retina. About 20 percent of the population is nearsighted. They squint to focus on anything far away from them.

•Farsightedness. A person with hyperopia can see distant objects clearly, but things close by look blurry. In farsightedness, the lens is too thin, the cornea too flat, or the eyeball too short. Farsighted people often complain of headaches, eyestrain, fatigue, and difficulty concentrating on near objects. When reading, they exhibit the "trombone effect," holding books and papers far away from them and focusing by moving them up and back as though playing the trombone.

• Astigmatism. Caused by an uneven curvature of the cornea or lens, astigmatism focuses light rays in a diffuse pattern on the retina, resulting in visual distortions at all distances. Frequently, vertical (but not horizontal) lines appear out of focus or vice versa. Sometimes astigmatism occurs in addition to near- or farsightedness. Headaches, blurred or distorted vision, eye fatigue, and squinting are common.

• Presbyopia. This is an age-related hardening of the lens that affects nearly everyone over fifty years of age to some extent. It results in an inability to focus on nearby objects. Usually progressive, the problem can be corrected with glasses.

• Muscle problems. Sometimes problems with the muscles of the eye are misdiagnosed as refractive errors. Problems with "binocular coordination," how the eyes work together, and "tracking," the ability of the eye to follow an object, cause double vision rather than blurring. These muscular problems can usually be treated with eye exercises rather than corrective lenses.

Before You Call the Doctor.   To distinguish between a refractive error and other possible problems, poke a tiny pinhole in a piece of paper and look through it at a well-lighted object. If looking through the pinhole improves clarity, you probably have a refractive error which can usually be corrected with eyeglasses or contacts. If not, some other problem is probably causing your blurry vision (see the "Red Flags" below).

When to Call the Doctor.   If a refractive error is the problem, either an optometrist or ophthalmologist can provide treatment. Optometrists specialize in refractive problems. Ophthalmologists are doctors who specialize in eye diseases. If the problem is muscular, either of these practitioners can refer you to a specialist in vision exercises ("orthoptics").

Consult an ophthalmologist if:

• Glasses do not fully correct your vision problem.

• You have a chronic condition that can affect the eyes, for example, diabetes, high blood pressure, and/or heart disease.

• You take medication that can affect the eyes, for example, anything with "anticholinergic" effects—antidepressants and strong antihistamines, among others. Ask a pharmacist whether any medication you take—either prescription or over-the-counter—might be affecting your eyes.

• The problem does not seem to be related to either a refractive error or muscular problem.

• *Cataracts.*   Cataracts cause clouding of the normally transparent eye lens and prevent light from reaching the retina. Cataracts cause blurring, double vision, and, in severe cases, blindness. Most cataracts develop in those over sixty as a result of aging. Other causes are also possible: eye injuries, congenital defects, exposure to extreme heat or radiation, or long-term use of some medications, for example, corticosteroids. Diabetics are also at increased risk for developing cataracts.

Before You Call the Doctor.   Do what you can to prevent cataracts. When you're out in the sun, vision experts recommend wearing a hat and sunglasses with good UV protection to prevent overexposure to sunlight. If you're exposed to heat or extremely bright light on your job or recreationally, wear eye protection. There have been some anecdotal reports of unusual clusters of cataracts in people who use video display terminals (VDTs) at work. The jury is still out, but experts urge those who use VDTs to sit at least three feet away from the screens and, ideally, to use a computer with a detachable keyboard, which allows even greater distance between the operator's eyes and the screen.

For more information contact the National Society to Prevent Blindness and the American Society of Cataract and Refractive Surgery (see RESOURCES at the end of this chapter).

When to Call the Doctor.   Treatments for cataracts include drops to open the pupils to let in more light around the cloudy lens, or surgical removal of the lenses and replacement with special cataract glasses, contact lenses, or plastic intraocular lenses. The surgical approach is a thirty-five to forty-five minute outpatient procedure under local anesthesia. Experienced surgeons achieve good to excellent results in about 90 percent of cases, though complete healing sometimes takes months.

• *Glaucoma.*   Glaucoma, one of the nation's four leading causes of blindness, is often called the "sneak thief of sight" because the common "open angle" type progresses so slowly that the person may not notice any problem until vision loss has become significant. Caused by increased fluid pressure within the eye due to either excess fluid production or the breakdown of the eye's natural drainage system, glaucoma eventually destroys the optic nerve. The only symptom of open angle glaucoma is gradual loss of peripheral vision. Glaucoma tends to run in families. It's more prevalent among black people and diabetics. And it may be linked to chronic inflammation, eye trauma, and some blood vessel ("vascular") diseases.

Before You Call the Doctor. Anything that raises fluid pressure else-where in the body also raises it inside the eye and increases the risk of glaucoma. The major cause of increased fluid pressure is high blood pressure. Keep yours within the normal range (see HIGH BLOOD PRESSURE in Chapter 12).

Prevent diabetes by controlling your weight (see DIABETES in Chapter 4). The preventive suggestions for controlling diabetes and blood pressure are similar.

Glaucoma is difficult to detect before considerable vision has been significantly damaged. Authorities urge everyone over forty-five years of age to be tested every five years, or more frequently if they have any risk factors. Physicians can perform the test, which is quick and painless, but vision organizations now also offer testing at malls, county fairs, and other events.

For more information, contact the National Society to Prevent Blind-ness and the Foundation for Glaucoma Research (see RESOURCES at the end of this chapter).

When to Call the Doctor. Glaucoma cannot be cured, but if it's diagnosed early, further vision loss can usually be prevented with medica-tion. Some cases require surgery to drain the fluid from the eye. Laser surgery has improved success rates.

If you have diabetes, establish a relationship with an ophthalmologist and have your eyes checked regularly. Diabetics are at risk not only for glaucoma but also for other forms of eye damage ("retinopathy").

• *Macular Degeneration.* A leading cause of blindness in people over sixty-five years of age, macular degeneration involves abnormal growth of blood vessels and fibrous tissue in the central portion of the retina ("macula"). Peripheral vision is unaffected, but scar tissue in the macula causes the appearance of blind spots in the central portion of the visual field. Symptoms include distortion of central vision, blind spots, and a wavy appearance of straight lines.

When to Call the Doctor. If you experience any symptoms of macular degeneration, consult a physician. Sometimes special low-vision devices help: telescopic and microscopic lenses, magnifying devices, and special reading lenses. If treated in the early stages, some authorities believe laser surgery can be helpful.

• *Other Possible Causes of Vision Impairment.* Distorted vision may also be related to a recent head injury, medications, or a ministroke, known as a "transitory ischemic attack," or TIA (see STROKE in Chapter 7). Temporary vision loss may also be an early symptom of multiple sclerosis.

▶ **RED FLAGS**   Consult a physician immediately if:
• A vision problem is related to a head injury.
• You suddenly lose all or partial vision in one or both eyes, even if it returns quickly.
• Any vision problem causes significant eye pain.
• You are diabetic.
• You develop a vision problem shortly after starting any medications, either over-the-counter or prescription.
• You first notice your vision problem after age fifty.
• Your eyes appear to bulge.
• You see flashing lights or floating black spots.

CATARACTS

(See BLURRY, DISTORTED OR DOUBLE VISION in this chapter)

"COMPUTER SCREEN" EYES

(See EYESTRAIN in this chapter)

CONJUNCTIVITIS

(See also DRY EYES and RED EYES in this chapter)
Commonly known as "pink eye," conjunctivitis causes redness in the eye (hence the name pink eye), swelling, and an uncomfortable feeling of grittiness.

What's Going On?   Usually caused by a virus but also possibly by bacteria, allergies, or chemical irritants, conjunctivitis causes inflammation of the thin membranes ("conjunctiva") that line the inner surface of the eyelid and cover a portion of the eyeball. Viral conjunctivitis, common among children, is sometimes accompanied by a cold or sore throat. In addition to redness and swelling, the infection usually produces a yellow-greenish pus discharge. It is highly contagious, passed by finger contact.

Bacterial conjunctivitis causes similar symptoms, except there's usually more pus and crusting. Middle ear infections may accompany bacterial conjunctivitis in children. Gonorrhea and chlamydia can also cause this infection (see GONORRHEA and CHLAMYDIA in Chapter 18).

Allergies and/or irritating chemicals such as swimming pool chlorine, over-the-counter eye drops, and bacterially contaminated mascara brushes can also cause conjunctivitis.

Before You Call the Doctor. Don't share mascara brushes or eye drops.

If you're around a child with conjunctivitis, wash your hands very frequently with soap and water and consciously refrain from touching or rubbing your eyes. This is harder than it sounds. Most people subconsciously rub or touch their eyes several times an hour.

Also try to keep the child's hands clean. Of course, this may be impossible.

Viral conjunctivitis almost always clears up on its own in a week or so. But it's often impossible to tell the difference between viral and bacterial conjunctivitis, so just in case the infection is bacterial, physicians recommend treating any conjunctivitis with antibiotic eye drops or ointment. Ophthalmic antibiotics are available only by prescription. Over-the-counter antibiotics are not formulated for use in the eyes. However, you can use premixed over-the-counter boric acid solution (Collyrium Eye Lotion), a mild, soothing antiseptic, for mild cases of conjunctivitis. Just make sure it does *not* include any chemical that narrows blood vessels ("vasocontrictors"), for example, tetrahydrozoline.

For allergic conjunctivitis, try over-the-counter antihistamines and allergen avoidance (see ALLERGIES in Chapter 4).

If you wake in the morning with your eyes stuck shut due to accumulated discharge from conjunctivitis, loosen the crust with warm water and wash away as much of the discharge as possible.

When to Call the Doctor. Because it's impossible to tell the difference between viral and bacterial conjunctivitis from symptoms or appearance, it's best to consult a physician for any suspected conjunctivitis. Physicians can prescribe ophthalmic antibiotic drops or ointment.

Other viruses, such as measles, German measles ("rubella"), and chickenpox, can also cause conjunctivitis. Herpes of the eye can also cause pain, redness, and blisters on the eyelid. A physician should rule out these infections.

If antihistamines and allergen avoidance don't provide sufficient relief of allergic conjunctivitis, your doctor may suggest a trial of prescription antihistamines. Severe cases respond to steroid drops, which should only be prescribed by an opthalmologist.

CONTACT LENS PROBLEMS

(See RED EYES in this chapter)

DOUBLE VISION

(See BLURRY, DISTORTED, OR DOUBLE VISION in this chapter)

DRY EYES

(See also RED EYES in this chapter)
   Too few tears can produce red, swollen, gritty eyes.

What's Going On?   Tears keep the eyes moist, but wind, allergies, medications, high altitude, airplane travel, air conditioning, air pollution, and soft contact lenses increase tear evaporation and may contribute to dry, itchy eyes. In addition, the tear glands shrink with age and produce less eye lubrication.

   Women suffer dry eyes more frequently than men. Usually both eyes are affected. Dry eyes tend to be more prone to infection.

Before You Call the Doctor.   If wind seems to be causing the problem, shield your eyes using goggles or glasses with protective side shields.

   For dryness associated with air travel, drink lots of water before flying and drink fruit juices, not alcohol, while in the air. Alcohol is dehydrating. Also, try removing contact lenses before airplane flights.

   If the problem is air conditioning, try a humidifier or leafy houseplants. In automobiles and on airplanes, turn off the air vent or at least turn it away from you.

   Make every effort to limit your exposure to smoke and dust. If necessary, purchase a high-efficiency particulate air (HEPA) filter, available at medical supply houses that sell asthma and allergy devices.

   Consider a new pair of contacts. In low humidity environments, such as air conditioned buildings, try removing your contacts and wearing glasses.

Over-the-counter artificial-tear products are another alternative (Lacri-Lube, Liquifilm). These products contain preservatives which prevent bacterial growth and eye infections. However, they may cause allergic reactions. If so, products without preservatives, such as Refresh, Duolube, or Ocu-Lube, are available. Keep nonpreserved products refrigerated and be sure to check their expiration dates. Wash your hands thoroughly with soap and water before placing drops or ointments into your eyes. Be sure the eye drops contain no extra drugs meant to shrink swollen blood vessels "to get the red out," such as tetrahydrozoline. These may aggravate dryness.

When to Call the Doctor.   If self-care treatments don't provide sufficient relief within two weeks, or if artificial tears become necessary routinely, consult a physician. Long-term tear deficiency can lead to corneal problems, which should be treated by an ophthalmologist. In some cases, dry eyes are associated with rheumatoid arthritis, Sjögren's syndrome, or other diseases.

EYE PAIN

(See also EYESTRAIN and RED EYES in this chapter)
Intermittent or continuous pain in or around the eye may be related to infection, injury, or a more serious eye disease.

What's Going On?   Eye pain is always a cause for concern. Usually it results from infection or some kind of trauma.

Any eye injury can cause pain. The cornea, the clear covering over the colored part of the eye, is the eye's most pain-sensitive area. Even minor injury to a single layer of corneal cells can cause intense, stabbing pain.

Rubbing the eyes because of irritation caused by conjunctivitis, having something in the eye, or other conditions may also injure the cornea and cause pain. Fortunately, corneal cells usually regenerate within twenty four hours.

If eye pain is accompanied by a swollen red bump, it's probably a sty (see STY in this chapter).

Before You Call the Doctor.   First aid for traumatic eye pain involves irrigating the eye with water using an eyedropper. Try not to rub. It's hard not to, but it only makes things worse. Cool compresses also help.

When to Call the Doctor.   If there's something in your eye that does not come out with irrigation, or if you cannot determine the cause of any eye pain and treat it quickly and successfully at home, consult a physician. Your vision may be at stake.

Herpes-related eye infections are a leading cause of blindness among children. If you suspect a herpes eye infection, seek professional care promptly. Treatment usually includes the prescription herpes drug acyclovir.

Some eye infections involve the *inside* of the eye. They typically cause intense pain, light sensitivity, and redness of the white part of the eyeball, especially close to the iris. These infections require immediate treatment by an ophthalmologist.

Any injury that causes severe pain, vision disturbances, or visible damage to the eye requires immediate medical attention. The physician uses a fluorescent dye to examine the cornea and applies a prescription ophthalmic antibiotic ointment to prevent infection. The eye is usually protected with a patch for twelve to twenty-four hours to prevent blinking and rubbing.

One unusual and serious form of glaucoma, acute "angle-closure" glaucoma, causes eye pain and redness brought on by opening ("dilation") of the pupil. See an ophthalmologist immediately. (Also see "Glaucoma" under BLURRY, DISTORTED, OR DOUBLE VISION in this chapter.)

▶ **RED FLAGS**   Consult a physician immediately for:
  • Any visible damage to the eye.
  • Severe eye pain.
  • Any loss of vision.
  • Eye pain accompanied by sensitivity to light.
  • Pain behind the eye accompanied by headache, light sensitivity, pain when you bend the head forward, and/or drowsiness or confusion.
  • Any tenderness in the nose, cheekbone, or temple near a painful eye.

EYESTRAIN

(See also EYE PAIN in this chapter)
Eye fatigue and soreness have become increasingly common occupational complaints now that computer video display terminals (VDTs) dominate so many people's work lives.

What's Going On?   Here's a formula almost guaranteed to produce chronic eyestrain: Require people to sit in front of poorly positioned

VDTs without glare screens for hours on end without breaks under fluorescent lights while keeping their eyes focused on small print. Secretaries, word processors, typesetters, and many employees in today's electronic offices report chronic eyestrain. Studies suggest chronic eyestrain does not cause permanent vision damage, but the condition is certainly annoying and it often interferes with work quality, so employers whose computers cause this problem have a significant interest in eliminating it.

Before You Call the Doctor.   Glare is often the major culprit in eyestrain, particularly VDT-related problems. VDT screens should face away from windows. Replace fluorescent fixtures with desk-type lighting that the VDT operator can adjust. Ideally, the light source should be directed away from the screen. Be sure the office lighting isn't too bright for the VDT. Most experts recommend a workplace light intensity of thirty- to fifty foot-candles for overhead lighting, with computer screens four times brighter than the ambient lighting. Some computers come fitted with antiglare screens. For those that don't, glare screens can be purchased for about $25 at most computer stores.

VDTs should be positioned so that operators look slightly down at their screens. Computers with detachable keyboards are best because they allow the operator the most control over positioning. Operators should sit at least an arm's length (thirty six inches) from screens. Papers should be placed on well-lighted copy stands. VDT operators should get up and take breaks every hour. In addition, every few minutes while working, they should exercise their eyes by focusing at some distant object. Other strain-relieving eye exercises include moving the eyes in circles in both directions and looking up and down several times. A cool compress placed lightly on the eyes can also help them feel refreshed.

GLAUCOMA

(See BLURRY, DISTORTED, OR DOUBLE VISION in this chapter)

MACULAR DEGENERATION

(See BLURRY, DISTORTED, OR DOUBLE VISION in this chapter)

PINKEYE

(See CONJUNCTIVITIS this chapter)

RED EYES

(See also BLURRY, DISTORTED, OR DOUBLE VISION, CON-
JUNCTIVITIS, EYE PAIN, and EYESTRAIN in this chapter and AL-
LERGIES in Chapter 4)

Redness of the whites of the eyes, also known as "bloodshot eyes,"
may or may not be painful, but the redness is usually easily noticed.

What's Going On?   Redness may have many causes, including infection, irritation, allergies, and/or eye disease. For information on these
causes of red eyes, consult the sections listed above.

Another possible cause is problems with contact lenses. Contact
lenses are foreign objects, which may cause irritation and the redness that
results from it. Problems include improper fit, dirty lenses, or wearing
contacts for too long. Redness typically results from either injury to the
extremely sensitive layer of cells that cover the eyeball ("corneal ulceration") or irritation of the conjunctiva, the thin membranes that line the
inner surface of the eyelid and cover a portion of the eyeball.

Conjunctival irritation causes small bumps to develop under the lid.
The bumps itch, burn, swell, and lead to redness. This condition is most
common among those who use extended-wear lenses.

Red eyes may also be caused by a painless blood blister under the
conjunctiva ("subconjunctival hemorrhage"). This problem may result
from high blood pressure (see HIGH BLOOD PRESSURE in Chapter
12), eye rubbing, a blow to the eye, or it may occur spontaneously. A
subconjunctival hemmorrhage looks like a bright red spot or blotch,
which covers part of the white of the eye.

A painless bright red blotch in the white of the eye may also be caused
by a local inflammation that opens ("dilates") the blood vessels in the eye
("episcleritis"). Its cause is unknown.

Corneal ulceration, a more serious problem for contact lens wearers,
can dramatically limit vision and in rare cases possibly even cause permanent vision impairment. Like conjunctival irritation, it's most likely to
strike extended-wear contact users. Symptoms include eye pain, light
sensitivity, redness of the whites of the eyes, distorted or blurry vision, and
a white spot on the front surface of the cornea.

Another problem that commonly causes redness of the eyelids is an infection of the eyelids and their oil glands ("blepharitis"). In blepharitis, redness is typically accompanied by crusting, itching, swelling, grittiness, and inflammation. In cases where the infection extends to the eyelashes, pus may be discharged and crust over at night. The underlying problem is a form of eczema (see ECZEMA in Chapter 6). It's often caused by cosmetic allergies, bacterial infection, or irritants, including wind-borne particles.

Before You Call the Doctor. To avoid both conjunctival irritation and corneal ulceration, clean your contacts frequently with a solution made for your lenses. Do not use saliva for wetting. It contains bacteria which might cause infection. Think twice before using homemade saline solutions. They contain no preservatives and have been associated with a rare but serious eye infection. If you insist on using homemade saline solutions, follow these guidelines from the Food and Drug Administration:

•Use homemade saline solutions only before or during heat disinfection. Never use them after heat disinfection.

•Never use homemade saline solutions with chemical or hydrogen peroxide disinfection.

•Never use homemade saline solutions in the eye or as a wetting solution.

•Prepare fresh homemade saline solution daily.

•Sterilize the solution bottle weekly in boiling water.

In addition, contact-lens wearers should protect their eyes carefully from high-intensity light and wind, which contains many irritating particles.

Subconjunctival hemorrhage and episcleritis may look scary, but they are medically minor and require no treatment. It takes about a week for the former to go away by itself, and two to three weeks for the latter.

For blepharitis, wash the eyelids daily with baby shampoo and a washcloth or cotton swab. If blepharitis is associated with dandruff, use a medicated dandruff shampoo on your hair (see DANDRUFF in Chapter 6). For blepharitis associated with eye cosmetics, discontinue eye makeup until the inflammation resolves, then switch brands or try going without eye cosmetics.

When to Call the Doctor. If red eyes don't return to normal within a week or if pain develops, consult a physician. For conjunctival problems caused by contact lenses, treatment involves prescription eye drops several times a day for up to six weeks.

Corneal ulceration requires immediate contact removal and professional medical care.

If blepharitis doesn't improve after two weeks of self-care, consult a physician for a medicated eyelid ointment.

SOMETHING IN YOUR EYE

Foreign objects in the eye cause pain, redness, irritation, and, in serious cases, permanent vision impairment.

What's Going On?   The tiniest dust particle or grain of sand can cause sharp eye pain. Larger objects, such as eyelashes, woodsplinters, and wood shavings, may be excruciating.

Before You Call the Doctor.   Most foreign objects in the eye can be safely removed at home. However, if the object has penetrated the eyeball or causes bleeding, do not attempt to remove it at home. Instead, cover the eye with a loose patch or have the person cover the eye with a cupped hand and seek medical attention immediately. Don't rub the eye. Rubbing may further damage the cornea, the clear membrane that covers the iris.

The standard object-removal advice is to wash your hands then gently irrigate the eye using an eye dropper or small squeeze bottle filled with cool water—never use a match, toothpick, tweezer, or other hard object. But most people find this method is difficult and often impossible. Instead, fill a basin with cool water, plunge your face in, and open the affected eye underwater. Roll the eye, slowly moving your head back and forth until the object floats away.

If irrigation doesn't remove the object, it may be stuck to the lower lid's inner surface. Have the person look up, then gently pull down on the skin under the lower lid. If you can see the object, try irrigating the eye again. If the object doesn't wash out, use the corner of a clean handkerchief, paper towel, or facial tissue to try to coax it out.

If you can't see anything on the lower lid, use the same procedure on the upper lid with the person looking down. Pull the lid up and turn it inside out by holding onto the lashes and pressing the lid gently with a clean cotton swab. An inside-out lid looks strange but causes no harm or pain. Then irrigate quickly, grasp the lashes, and gently pull them out to restore the lid to its normal position.

When to Call the Doctor.   Consult a physician promptly if:
•You cannot remove the object.

• Pain remains even after the object has been removed.
• The eye bleeds.
• The foreign object sticks to the eye.
• The object causes redness, warmth, swelling, increased pain, or a yellow/green pus discharge.

STY

A sty is a boil-like swelling on the eyelid. It may be very painful, especially if touched.

What's Going On?   A sty, medically known as a "hordeolum," is a bacterial infection of an eyelash follicle that causes a red, painful, swollen boil on the lid. A few days after the swelling forms a pimple-like white head, it bursts, discharging cell debris from the infection and relieving the pain. The affected eyelash also falls out. Sometimes additional styes develop due to the spread of the bacteria.

Before You Call the Doctor.   You can speed the sty's draining by applying hot compresses frequently. Don't squeeze the pus sack. This may spread the infection deeper into eyelid tissue. Instead, gently pull out the eyelash, which releases the pus. After the sty bursts, wash the eyelid carefully to remove all the pus. Finally, apply a thin layer of antibacterial ointment (Neosporin, Bacitracin).

When to Call the Doctor.   For recurring sties, consult a physician for antibiotics to clear up the bacterial infection.

TEARING OR EXCESSIVE WATERING

Those with this problem seem to "cry" for no reason.

What's Going On?   Excessive watering has several possible causes, most commonly blocked tear-drainage ducts, sinus infection ("sinusitis"), and/or aging. If the tear-drainage ducts become blocked, the tears normally produced to clean and lubricate the eye roll down the cheeks instead.

Excessive tearing is a common symptom of sinusitis, inflammation of the mucous membranes of the air spaces of the bones behind and above the nose. Other symptoms include runny nose and headache with pain across the bridge of the nose and under the eyes (see HEADACHE in Chapter 7 and SINUS INFECTION in Chapter 11).

With age, some people become increasingly sensitive to light, wind, or temperature changes and their eyes tear excessively. Another age-related problem is ingrown eyelash ("entropion"), which irritates the eyeball and causes tearing.

Before You Call the Doctor.   Blocked tear ducts can sometimes be treated by pressing warm compresses into the inner corners of the eye. Direct the pressure toward the nose, not the eyeball. This treatment is usually more effective in infants than adults.

If tearing is caused by sinusitis, it may be possible to obtain relief by the use of saunas, hot, steamy showers or baths, or a humidifier or vaporizer. Also, drink plenty of fluids, and sleep with your head elevated on extra pillows (see SINUS INFECTION in Chapter 11). The over-the-counter decongestant pseudoephedrine might also help. For sinus headache pain, take aspirin, acetaminophen, or ibuprofen. Aspirin and ibuprofen may cause stomach upset. If so, try "enteric coated" preparations. Pregnant women and those with a history of ulcers should not take aspirin or ibuprofen.

If watery eyes are caused by aging-related sensitivity to wind, light, and temperature, sunglasses with side protectors usually help.

When to Call the Doctor.   Blocked tear ducts that don't respond to the compress treatment should be treated medically. Oral antibiotics or eye drops are prescribed if the area is infected. Severe blockage may require surgical correction.

If sinusitis does not respond to self-care within a week or so, consult a physician for antibiotics, prescription decongestants, and/or nose drops or sprays.

For ingrown eyelashes, consult a physician. You may need minor surgery to correct the problem.

RESOURCES

American Society of Cataract and Refractive Surgery. 3702 Pender Dr., Suite 250, Fairfax, VA 22030; (703) 591-2220. The AMSCRS is primarily an ophthalmological organization, but it also sponsors public information programs on eye care and cataract prevention and care.

Foundation for Glaucoma Research. 490 Post St., Suite 830, San
Francisco, CA 94102; (415) 986-3162. Promotes awareness of glaucoma by distributing educational materials, including "Understanding
and Living with Glaucoma."

National Society to Prevent Blindness. 500 East Remington Rd.,
Schaumberg, IL 60173; (708) 843-2020. Publishes and distributes
information on eye care and prevention of eye diseases.

CHAPTER 9

The Ears

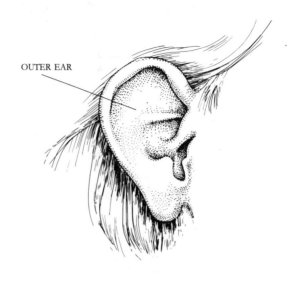

OUTER EAR

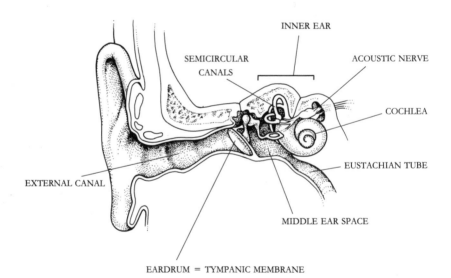

INNER EAR

SEMICIRCULAR
CANALS

ACOUSTIC NERVE

COCHLEA

EUSTACHIAN TUBE

EXTERNAL CANAL

MIDDLE EAR SPACE

EARDRUM = TYMPANIC MEMBRANE

Structures of the Ear.

AIRPLANE EARS

(See "Barotitis" in EAR PAIN in this chapter)

EAR INFECTIONS

(See EAR PAIN in this chapter)

EAR PAIN

Pain in the ear can be mild or excruciating, constant or intermittent, and feel sharp, dull, throbbing, stabbing, or burning.

What's Going On?   In most cases, ear pain is not serious and is not likely to cause permanent impairment of hearing. Causes of ear pain include problems in the outer, middle, or inner ear. Ear pain may also be "referred" pain that originates elsewhere in the head, neck, mouth, or teeth.

• *Outer Ear Infections.*   These usually minor infections typically develop in the area behind the ear, particularly in those whose ears are dry and itchy from eczema or seborrhea (see ECZEMA and SEBORRHEA in Chapter 6). Dry-skin problems cause scratching, which in turn can lead to bacterial infection.

Before You Call the Doctor.   If you treat outer ear eczema or seborrhea early, the irritation rarely becomes infected. But if infection develops, wash the area with soap and water and treat it with hydrogen peroxide and an over-the-counter antibiotic ointment (Neosporin, Bacitracin).

When to Call the Doctor.   Consult a physician if outer ear infections don't clear up after a week of home treatment. Infected insect bites or deep scratches that don't respond to home treatment can lead to more serious infection of the connective tissue beneath the skin ("cellulitis"), which must be treated with antibiotics.

• *Ear Canal Problems.*   The ear ("auditory") canal is a narrow tunnel leading from the outer ear to the ear drum. Though only about an inch long, it's loaded with nerve endings, and even the slightest touch or pressure causes immediate discomfort. The ear canal is lined with a brown or yellowish wax ("cerumen") that protects the ear, particularly from water. This wax may build up, blocking the canal and causing pain, ringing, and hearing loss.

Ear pain, itching, swelling, inflammation, and hearing loss may also be caused by an ear canal infection ("otitis externa"). This common complaint, also known as "swimmer's ear," is often caused by frequent immersion in water and/or an accumulation of water in the ear. However, otitis externa can also be caused by trauma from cotton-tipped swabs (usually in an overzealous attempt to clean out ear wax) or by an allergic reaction to perfumes or hair sprays. If pain increases when you move the external ear or push the little button of flesh near the ear opening, suspect an external ear infection.

Before You Call the Doctor.   If the problem is caused by wax impacted in the ear canal, it can usually be removed at home with warm water and a bulb syringe. *Don't use cotton swabs, which tend to push the wax further into the canal and aggravate the problem.* If the wax is hard and dry, soften it for a day or two with an over-the-counter ear-wax–removal preparation or a few drops of hydrogen peroxide. Then, using a bulb syringe, wash out the ear with a gentle stream of warm water. If the wax plug does not emerge quickly, be patient. Keep irrigating the ear canal with warm water and, in the vast majority of cases, it eventually comes out.

To prevent swimmer's ear, use ear plugs while swimming or afterwards place a few drops of a solution consisting of half white vinegar (acetic acid) and half rubbing (isopropyl) alcohol in each ear canal. However, don't use this solution if the eardrum may be ruptured or in a child who has had ear tubes ("tympanostomy tubes") inserted. After swimming or bathing, dry the ears thoroughly, but don't use cotton-tipped swabs, which can traumatize water-irritated ear canals and contribute to infection. Instead, twist the end of a disposable facial tissue and use that.

Swimmer's ear infections can usually be treated at home with straight white vinegar. Use an eyedropper to insert it several times day. Take aspirin or ibuprofen for the pain and inflammation. Acetaminophen relieves pain but has no anti-inflammatory effect. If aspirin or ibuprofen upset your stomach, try an "enteric coated" brand. Pregnant women and those with a history of ulcers should not take aspirin or ibuprofen unless a doctor recommends it.

When to Call the Doctor. If home irrigation is not successful in removing impacted wax, see a doctor for professional irrigation, suction, or mechanical removal with an ear "loop."

If swimmer's ear does not respond to home treatment within a few days, consult a physician for eardrops containing acetic acid stronger than vinegar or a prescription antibiotic-corticosteroid liquid. The antibiotic treats the infection. The corticosteroid relieves the swelling and inflammation.

• *Fluid in the Middle Ear.* Medically known as "serous otitis media," the ears feel stuffy, sensitive, or crackly, with mild hearing loss.

Normally, the middle ear, the space behind the eardrum, is filled with air and lubricated with fluid secreted by the cells lining the area. The only opening to the outside is a tiny tube ("eustachian tube"), which runs from the middle ear to the back of the throat. When this tube becomes blocked, the air in the middle ear gets absorbed into the bloodstream and fluid fills the middle ear cavity.

Sometimes the blockage becomes chronic. The longer the fluid remains undrained in the ear, the thicker it becomes. In extreme cases ("glue ear"), there can be significant hearing loss.

Before You Call the Doctor. Blockage of the eustachian tube is a plumbing problem, not an infection, so antibiotics are ineffective. The oral decongestant pseudoephedrine may provide relief. If the blockage is associated with allergies, antihistamines may help. Chewing gum, swallowing, or even blowing with your thumb in your mouth as if you were blowing balloons can also help open the tube. Most cases of serous otitis media clear up within a week.

When to Call the Doctor. If serous otitis media does not clear up in a week or if pain or fever develop, consult a physician. Examination will confirm that there is no infection and that no abnormal growth is blocking the eustachian tube. The physician may prescribe a higher dose of decongestant or use a special device to force air into the eustachian tube and middle ear. In children, chronic serous otitis that interferes with hearing may need to be treated with tubes placed surgically through the eardrums ("tympanostomy tubes").

• *Middle Ear Infection.* Caused by bacteria or viruses, these painful infections, medically known as "otitis media," can strike anyone but tend to occur in infants and young children in association with colds.

Middle ear infections often torture young children and their parents. They are one of the leading reasons children visit physicians, and the intense pain they cause—and the uncontrollable screaming that results—sends many a frightened, harried parent to the nearest emergency room in the dead of night.

Most middle ear infections develop as a complication of colds. The cold causes congestion, which interferes with middle ear drainage. Stagnant fluid, trapped in the warm, dark environment of the middle ear, is a good growth medium for bacteria and viruses. As the infection develops, it causes intense pain—and screaming children.

Before You Call the Doctor.   Middle ear infections cause redness of the eardrum with bulging from the accumulated fluid and pus. Parents can keep from having their childrens' ear infections drive them crazy by taking a few common-sense steps:

First, get to know what your childrens' ear drums look like *when they are healthy.* Buy an otoscope, the device physicians use to examine ears, from a surgical supply house. Relatively inexpensive models are available for parents. Ask your child's physician or local parents' resources center if there's a "Pediatrics for Parents" class in your area. If so, we'd recommend it; they always devote a good deal of attention to ear infections. If not, you can still learn to examine your childrens' ears. Before you attempt to use your otoscope, however, it's crucial to understand that children's ear canals are quite narrow and that anything inserted in them is likely to cause flinching, squirming, and possibly pain. To keep things as mellow as possible, make a game of ear examinations. Show your children the otoscope. Let them play with it. Let them look in *your* ears before you look in theirs. When you examine them, pull the outer ear down and back to straighten the ear canal and give you the best view. You need not insert the otoscope tip very far or for very long. Practice taking quick looks.

The healthy eardrum looks translucent pink or gray with a bright triangular "light reflex" area at the bottom.

Serous otitis media makes the eardrum look yellowish or dull gray-red.

Incipient ear infections change eardrum appearance to red with distortion of the light reflex.

And full-blown ear infections make the eardrum look brighter red with bulging outward.

Now that you've read how eardrums are supposed to look under various circumstances, don't be surprised if you feel totally at sea and unable to distinguish *any* landmarks in your children's ears. Inexperienced physicians have the same problem. Ear exams are quite challenging. Just be patient, and keep plugging away at it. As you practice, you're not only becoming more skilled at ear exams, but also your children are getting more used to being examined. This mutual familiarity definitely helps when a child has ear pain.

Studies show that parents who practice home ear examination wind up spending fewer nights in emergency rooms with screaming children. They don't panic over ear pain. They can assess their childrens' ears during the course of any colds and, if the ears start to redden, they can simply consult the child's physician by phone or, if necessary, in the office.

Ear infections are rarely medically serious, but they must be treated fully and carefully. Fortunately for parents, the typical ear infection need not be treated the moment the child wakes up screaming at night. In other words, you don't have to do what many parents do for this problem in the wee hours—rush the child to an emergency room. The antibiotic prescription can usually wait till the next morning.

Otitis media actually involves two problems: the pain and the infection. The former is what makes children howl. To deal with it, give the child acetaminophen for the pain (*not* aspirin, because in rare cases, it may cause Reye syndrome, a potentially fatal condition). Then have the child lie down on a heating pad, and for additional comfort place a few drops of warm vegetable oil in the affected ear. If necessary, give the child more acetaminophen.

The next morning, call the child's physician and discuss the need for antibiotics.

Some parents also become concerned that repeated or chronic ear infections may impair the child's hearing and become a learning disability. Permanent hearing impairment is possible but not all that common. If you become concerned, have your child's hearing checked professionally.

When to Call the Doctor. The standard treatment for middle ear infections is a ten-day course of oral antibiotics. Make sure the child takes all the medication; otherwise you may wind up breeding antibiotic-resistant bacteria. Some children suffer from recurrent otitis media, and some physicians prescribe antibiotics preventively. Others believe this is unnecessary. For chronic ear infections, some physicians recommend surgical insertion of special tubes through the eardrum ("tympanostomy tubes"). This, too, is controversial.

• *Ruptured Eardrum.* Infections, explosions, blows to the ear, or sharp objects can all rupture the thin, delicate eardrum ("tympanic membrane"). A ruptured eardrum usually causes mild ear pain, partial temporary hearing loss, and a slight discharge or bleeding from the ear. Symptoms usually last a few hours.

Before You Call the Doctor.   Ruptured ear drums usually heal without treatment within a week or two. Any pain can usually be relieved by using a heating pad and taking aspirin, acetaminophen, or ibuprofen. Acetaminophen is least likely to cause stomach upset. Pregnant women and those with a history of ulcers should not take aspirin or ibuprofen.

As the eardrum heals, hearing almost always returns to normal.

The biggest problem with a ruptured eardrum is increased susceptibility to infection because the break in the eardrum may allow potentially harmful microorganisms into the usually-sterile middle ear. Take reasonable precautions:

•Keep the ear clean and dry.

•Don't use cotton swabs except to clean the outer ear (the part you can see).

•When in doubt, cover the ear with a plastic patch.

•For bathing, place a wad of cotton covered with petroleum jelly in the outer ear canal. Don't push it in too far.

When to Call the Doctor.   Any fever, swelling, increase in pain, feeling of heat, or additional hearing impairment suggests infection. Consult a physician for antibiotics. Occasionally, ruptured eardrums don't heal after several months; minor surgery may be required to close the opening.

• **Barotitis.**   Also known as "airplane ears," barotitis is middle-ear pain caused by the rapid changes in barometric pressure that occur when driving in the mountains or as aircraft cabin pressure changes. Normally, the barometric pressure inside the ears is the same as the pressure outside. But when the outside pressure changes rapidly, the two pressures may differ enough to cause tension on the eardrum and pain.

Before You Call the Doctor.   Adults can usually alleviate the problem by swallowing, yawning, chewing gum, or by gently attempting to exhale while holding the nose with the mouth closed ("blowing"). Gum or blowing usually work for older children as well. Infants should be given a breast or bottle to suck.

However, among those with colds or middle-ear infections, these techniques may not work. An over-the-counter decongestant, for example, pseudoephedrine, may become necessary. Take the decongestant about an hour before take-off to give it time to work. On long flights, take more before landing. Decongestants often cause insomnia, which may aggravate jet lag.

When to Call the Doctor. If barotitis symptoms don't dissipate after a day or two of taking decongestants, consult a physician. Initial treatment usually involves stronger prescription decongestants.

• *Temporomandibular Joint (TMJ) Jaw Problems.* Sometimes ear pain is referred from problems in other areas in the head, neck, or mouth, such as dental problems or misalignment of the jaw joint (see TEMPOROMANDIBULAR JOINT (TMJ) JAW PROBLEMS in Chapter 7).

HEARING LOSS

(See also EAR PAIN and SOMETHING IN YOUR EAR in this chapter)
Temporary hearing loss usually occurs fairly suddenly. Permanent hearing loss is typically a gradual process.

What's Going On? There are two basic types of hearing loss: conductive and sensorineural. Conductive hearing loss involves mechanical problems that keep sound from reaching the inner ear. The most common cause of conductive hearing impairment is impacted ear wax, but fluid behind the eardrum is another common cause (see "Fluid in the Middle Ear" and "Middle Ear Infection" in the EAR PAIN section of this chapter).

Sensorineural hearing loss involves damage to the nerves that detect sound and transmit it through the inner ear to the brain. Noise is the main cause of sensorineural hearing loss. Noises above 90 decibels—jackhammers, sirens, aircraft, live rock music and other sources—cause nerve damage. This damage is cumulative. Many rock musicians suffer significant hearing loss after a few years.

Age is also a factor in hearing problems. As adults grow older, the wax-producing glands in the ear work less efficiently and the wax they produce becomes drier and more prone to impaction. The ear drum may thicken or become less elastic, interfering with sound transmission. Inner-ear nerves may atrophy. And key inner-ear structures, for example, the snail-shaped cochlea, may deteriorate. Currently, about one-quarter of those from sixty-five to seventy-four years of age have hearing problems.

Among those age seventy-five and older, the figure increases to 40 percent.

Experts predict that sensorineural hearing problems will become much more prevalent in coming decades. Life is noisier than ever. Many people in the post–World War II generations have literally "blown their ears out" with loud music, not only at concerts but through the use of personal stereos with headphones. And the nation as a whole is growing older.

• **Sudden Hearing Loss.**   This common, anxiety-provoking complaint can strike at any age, but it tends to occur among those forty years of age or older. Some people waken with noticeably diminished hearing. Others experience growing difficulties over a few days or a week.

Before You Call the Doctor.   Sudden hearing loss is often caused by impacted ear wax, infection, trauma, or drugs.

To deal with impacted ear wax, see "Ear Canal Problems" in the EAR PAIN section of this chapter. For ear infections, see the "Fluid" and "Middle Ear Infection" discussions in EAR PAIN.

If you suspect trauma, see the "Ruptured Ear Drum" discussion in EAR PAIN.

If the problem started after pressure changes due to flying or diving, see the "Barotitis" discussion in EAR PAIN. When problems with impacted wax, infection, or trauma are resolved, hearing returns to normal.

If the problem occurred shortly after you started taking a new drug, new drug combination, or new dose of an old drug, ask your pharmacist if your medication regimen might contribute to hearing loss. If so, ask if a different drug or different regimen might be substituted.

When to Call the Doctor.   If you can't resolve the problem on your own within two weeks, consult a physician. In rare cases, neurological disorders or acoustic tumors may cause sudden hearing loss.

• **Gradual Hearing Loss.**   Recurrent infections, barotitis, or trauma might cause this problem (see the relevant sections in EAR PAIN in this chapter). But most gradual hearing loss results from a combination of noise exposure and aging.

Before You Call the Doctor.   We can't stop the clock of life, but we *can* protect our hearing from noise. First, take the noise problem seriously.

Every loud noise you hear adds to cumulative hearing damage and gradual hearing loss. Keep TVs, radios, and stereos at low volume. If a truck or airplane roars by or if you pass jackhammers on the street, roll up your windows and/or cover your ears. If you know you're going to be exposed to loud noise for an extended period of time, use ear plugs or other forms of ear protection.

A major problem with gradual hearing loss is that people often deny the problem and endure increasing social isolation without seeking professional help. If you think you or someone you know may suffer from a hearing problem, have them answer the following questions adapted from the American College of Otolaryngology:

• Do you frequently ask people to repeat themselves?

• Do you frequently complain that people don't speak loudly or clearly enough?

• Do you misunderstand what others say and make inappropriate responses?

• Do you have problems hearing over the phone?

• Have you recently turned your phone volume up?

• Have visitors remarked that your phone or TV are too loud?

• Do you have trouble following conversation when two or more people are talking at the same time?

• Do you have to position yourself carefully to understand conversations?

• Does background noise interfere with your ability to understand conversations?

• Do you become confused about where sounds are coming from?

• Have you ever worked in a noisy environment?

• Do you avoid social activities because you cannot hear well and fear you'll reply inappropriately?

If you answered "yes" to two or more of these questions, you may have a hearing problem and should see an ear specialist.

Sometimes hearing problems are congenital. It's very important to catch childhood hearing problems early. Babies have the following expected responses to noises:

• Birth to five months. Babies should be startled by loud noises. They should blink, make grabbing motions ("Moro reflex"), and wake up if asleep.

• Five to ten months. Babies should turn their heads to the side where the noise originates.

• Ten to fourteen months. Babies should become more skilled at discerning where sounds come from: side to side, and up and down.

• Eighteen months. By this age, toddlers should look directly at hidden sound sources.

To help you evaluate a child's hearing, ask yourself:

• Do you worry about the child's hearing?

• While sleeping in a quiet room, does the child move and begin to wake up when there's a loud sound?

• Does the child try to turn toward an interesting sound or when his or her name is called?

• Does the child enjoy ringing a bell or shaking a rattle?

• Does the child try to imitate sounds you or others make?

If you become concerned about your own hearing or anyone else's, contact the National Association for Hearing and Speech Action (see RESOURCES at the end of this chapter).

When to Call the Doctor.   If you suspect that you or your child might have a hearing problem, seek professional help immediately. Often early detection and prompt treatment can prevent permanent hearing loss. After age fifty, hearing evaluations every few years can spot developing problems early.

PIERCED EAR INFECTIONS

Piercing the earlobes can cause infection: redness, pain, swelling, crusting, oozing, inflammation, and discharge.

What's Going On?   Pierced-ear earrings don't fall off and get lost as easily as clip-ons do. But piercing sometimes causes earlobe infection. Most of these infections are minor, but they can be painful and their redness may cause temporary cosmetic problems. Inflammation usually precedes any infection. A common cause of problems is an allergic reaction to posts or wires made from nonprecious metals such as nickel. Any allergic inflammation weakens the lobe's ability to resist microorganisms, and the inflammation may progress to infection.

Before You Call the Doctor.   Stop wearing earrings until the inflammation has resolved or until the infection is completely healed. Wash away any crusty material or discharge with soap and water, and apply rubbing (isopropyl) alcohol two or three times a day as a disinfectant.

If you've just had your ears pierced and don't want the holes to close back up, try treating the earlobes with the soap/water/alcohol treatment with earrings in place, but *wear posts made only of surgical steel or solid gold (not gold fill)*. Cleanse three or four times a day, including the earring post (pull the post at least part way out as you cleanse). Twirl the post after applying the alcohol.

When to Call the Doctor. With old or new piercing, if you see no improvement within two days or if the swelling and pain spreads to the firm (cartilage) part of the ear, consult a physician.

PIERCED EAR CUTS AND TEARS

Occasionally, something catches an earring and pulls it hard enough to rip the earlobe.

What's Going On? A ripped earlobe is simply a cut ("laceration"). However, due to its visibility, such injuries may raise significant cosmetic and self-esteem issues.

Before You Call the Doctor. Stop the bleeding by applying firm pressure.

Numb the pain with an ice pack. Wrap a few ice cubes in a plastic bag and wrap the bag in a clean cloth. Apply the ice pack to the earlobe for twenty minutes, then remove it for ten minutes before reapplying. An ice substitute may be used as well. Do not apply ice directly to the skin. This may cause the equivalent of frostbite.

Then examine the wound. Small rips heal on their own. Wash them with rubbing (isopropyl) alcohol, then apply an antibiotic ointment (Bacitracin, Neosporin) to prevent infection. Finally, use adhesive bandages to cover the wound and hold the ripped tissue together.

When to Call the Doctor. If signs of infection develop—redness, warmth, swelling, increased pain, and yellowish-green discharge—consult a physician.

Large earlobe tears heal with the best cosmetic results if the wound is stitched ("sutured") closed by a physician.

▶ **RED FLAG** If the bottom of the lobe has been entirely ripped away, make every effort to retrieve the severed piece. Store it in a clean wet cloth. Touch it as little as possible. Seek medical attention immediately.

RINGING IN THE EARS

Medically known as "tinnitus," some people hear persistent ringing, buzzing, clicking, and other noises in their ears. For some the problem is intermittent. For others, it's continuous.

What's Going On?   Tinnitus is quite common. It can be caused by aspirin and other drugs, wax in the ear, rapid changes in barometric pressure (for example, when flying or riding a ski lift), or a number of diseases, including thyroid conditions and heart disease. The majority of cases are associated with sensorineural hearing loss (see HEARING LOSS in this chapter). In many cases, the cause remains a mystery.

Before You Call the Doctor.   Aspirin is a leading cause of temporary tinnitus. Ringing in the ears is one of the first signs of aspirin overdose. If you take aspirin regularly for arthritis or any painful inflammatory condition, try taking less, or ask your pharmacist about switching to another pain relieving anti-inflammatory.

For impacted ear wax, see the "Canal Problems" discussion in the EAR PAIN section of this chapter.

For tinnitus due to flying or rapid changes in altitude, follow the suggestions in the "Barotitis" discussion of the EAR PAIN section of this chapter.

For those with persistent tinnitus, tiny "white noise" generating devices similar to hearing aids can help mask internal sounds and make the condition more tolerable.

For support and information about this annoying condition, contact the American Tinnitus Association (see RESOURCES at the end of this chapter).

When to Call the Doctor.   If tinnitus becomes persistent or interferes with daily activities, consult a physician for a thorough evaluation. Tinnitus accompanied by hearing loss and/or vertigo could be a chronic but treatable condition known as Ménière's syndrome, or it could result from other conditions that should be evaluated professionally.

RUPTURED EARDRUM

(See EAR PAIN in this chapter)

SOMETHING IN YOUR EAR

(See also EAR PAIN in this chapter)
Foreign objects in the ear can cause pain, hearing loss, and infection.

What's Going On?   The ear evolved its structure to limit this problem, but children in particular seem to have a talent for jamming tiny objects into their ears: beans, buttons, bugs, popcorn kernels, etc. Improper removal may damage the delicate ear canal and eardrum.

Before You Call the Doctor.   Never try to remove foreign objects with matchsticks, bobby pins, knives, needles, or cotton swabs. Usually, all they do is push the object further into the ear, raising the specter of painful damage to the ear canal or puncture of the eardrum. First, try tilting and shaking the head. Next try floating the object out by irrigating the ear canal with warm water or vegetable oil from an eyedropper. This usually works well for insects. Pull the earlobe gently backward, then pull it upward to straighten the canal when you introduce the fluid. If irrigation doesn't work and the object is soft and easily visible, try gently removing it with tweezers.

When to Call the Doctor.   If the self-care approaches above don't work, consult a physician.

SWIMMER'S EAR

(See EAR PAIN in this chapter)

WAX IN THE EAR

(See EAR PAIN, HEARING LOSS, and RINGING IN THE EARS in this chapter)

RESOURCES

American Tinnitus Association. P.O. Box 5, Portland, OR 97207; (503) 248-9985. Provides information and support for people with this problem.

National Association for Hearing and Speech Action. 10801 Rockville Pike, Rockville, MD 20852; (301) 897-8682. Advocates on behalf of the hearing-impaired. Provides information on a wide range of hearing problems and their treatment, including hearing-assistance devices.

CHAPTER 10

The Mouth, Nose, and Throat

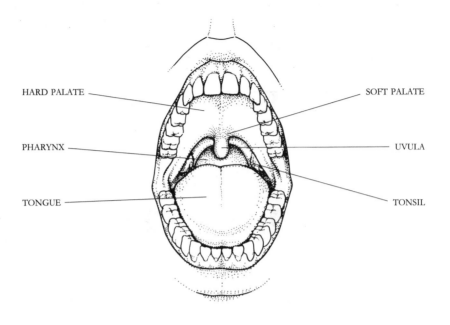

HARD PALATE

SOFT PALATE

PHARYNX

UVULA

TONGUE

TONSIL

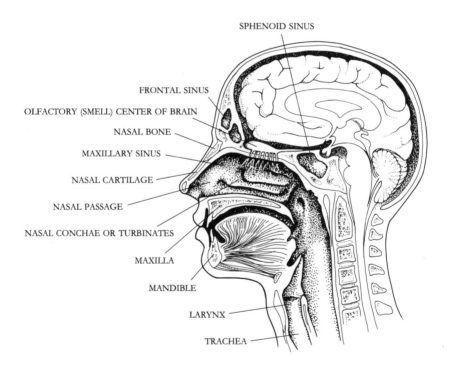

SPHENOID SINUS

FRONTAL SINUS

OLFACTORY (SMELL) CENTER OF BRAIN

NASAL BONE

MAXILLARY SINUS

NASAL CARTILAGE

NASAL PASSAGE

NASAL CONCHAE OR TURBINATES

MAXILLA

MANDIBLE

LARYNX

TRACHEA

The Mouth, Nose, and Throat.

BAD BREATH

Bad breath, medically known as "fetor oris," lives up to its derivation from the Latin for "smelly mouth."

What's Going On?   Most bad breath is caused by bacteria that live in the mouth. Oral bacteria feed on food residues and form "plaque," soft, sticky deposits that cling to teeth. In children, oral bacteria cause tooth decay. In adults, they cause gum disease ("gingivitis"). If plaque isn't regularly brushed and flossed away, oral bacteria produce gum-irritating toxins which eventually cause the gums to pull away from the teeth. Without adequate support, the teeth become undermined and eventually fall out or must be extracted.

In addition, as oral bacteria digest their food, they produce sulfur compounds with foul odors, causing bad breath. And when the gums pull away from the teeth, large spaces open up which are perfect for bacterial colonization—and aggravation of bad breath. If infection develops, pus pockets form, which smell even worse.

"Morning mouth," the furry-tongued, foul smelling breath first thing in the morning, is a natural by-product of sleeping for several hours. During waking hours, we chew and talk, which keeps the tongue moving and saliva flowing. This action continually cleans and rinses the mouth. When we sleep, this activity stops and mouth odors accumulate.

Certain foods also cause bad breath. These often contain sulfur compounds. The odor originates not just in the mouth but also in the lungs. Onions, garlic, coffee, certain cheeses, and alcohol may leave unpleasant odors behind in the mouth. As these and other foods, such as meats, fish, broccoli, cabbage, bean sprouts, and curries, are digested, their sulfur compounds enter the bloodstream and travel to the lungs, where some malodorous sulfur is exhaled. Even exemplary oral hygiene can't prevent bad breath that originates in the lungs. These odors usually disappear within twelve to twenty-four hours as the body metabolizes odor-producing foods.

Finally, certain medications, particularly those that dry the mouth, can upset the area's odor-controlling self-lubrication system and contribute to bad breath. Common odor-producers include diuretics, tranquilizers, antihistamines, and some medications for cancer, high blood pressure ("hypertension"), and chronic severe chest pain ("angina").

Before You Call the Doctor (or Dentist).   In most cases, treating bad breath is simply a matter of good oral hygiene. Plaque forms within twelve to twenty-four hours of brushing and flossing. To prevent odor-causing buildup, brush and floss twice a day. Brush the tongue too as it also harbors bacteria. Use a soft, rounded-bristle toothbrush, stroking it five or six times over each tooth. Floss with unwaxed or lightly waxed dental floss. And have your teeth professionally cleaned once or twice a year, depending on your rate of plaque build-up and your level of concern about bad breath.

Drink plenty of water throughout the day. Water helps prevent dehydration of mouth tissues and washes odor-causing food residues out of the mouth. Or drink citrus fruit juices. In addition to washing food residues away, they also stimulate the secretion of saliva, which helps cleanse and deodorize the mouth.

One of the best natural breath fresheners is parsley. That sprig of parsley on restaurant plates is a distant echo of the ancient Roman practice of chewing parsley after meals to freshen the breath. Modern science has shown that parsley contains large amounts of the green plant pigment chlorophyll. Chlorophyll is the "Clor" in Clorettes breath mints and one of the active ingredients in Certs.

Other herbs also freshen the breath: peppermint, ginger, and cloves. In ancient China, anyone wishing an audience with the emperor was required to chew cloves to eliminate the possibility of bad breath offending the Son of Heaven.

Then there are the dozens of commercial mouthwashes, breath sprays, and breath-freshening candies. These mask bad breath for an hour or two but don't eliminate odor-causing plaque. The American Dental Association recognizes only one nonprescription mouthwash as a plaque fighter—Listerine, which contains thymol, extracted from thyme oil.

If you use breath mints, use only sugarless brands. Sugar is counterproductive because it provides food for odor-causing bacteria.

Oral irrigation devices such as the Water Pik do not remove plaque, but they help eliminate its gum-destroying and odor-causing by-products beneath the gumline.

When to Call the Doctor (or Dentist). If persistent bad breath doesn't clear up after a few weeks of aggressive oral hygiene and dietary adjustments, consult a physician.

About one person in 100 suffers from chronic bad breath ("halitosis"). Cases not caused by poor oral hygiene and a high-sulfur diet may be caused by chronic postnasal drip, tonsillitis (see POSTNASAL DRIP and TONSILLITIS in this chapter), or sinus infection (see SINUS INFECTION in Chapter 11). If the odor gets worse when you exhale through your nose only, consult an ear, nose, and throat (ENT) specialist. Chronic bad breath may also signal lung disease or liver or kidney disorders.

BLEEDING GUMS

Bleeding gums usually signal gum disease ("gingivitis").

What's Going On?   If oral bacteria are not brushed and flossed away at least once a day, they accumulate in the spaces between the teeth and gums and weaken gum tissue. Weakened gums bleed easily during brushing, flossing, or eating. If oral bacteria deposits ("plaque") are allowed to build up on teeth, they cause gum irritation, swelling, and gingivitis. If left untreated, gingivitis progresses to a more serious condition ("periodontitis"), which may necessitate tooth extraction.

Pregnancy sometimes triggers bleeding gums. The problem usually disappears soon after delivery.

Bleeding gums may also be caused by diabetes, thyroid disorders, vitamin C deficiency, blood-clotting disorders, tooth-grinding ("bruxism") or teeth that don't fit together properly ("malocclusion").

Before You Call the Dentist.   Brush and floss twice a day. Initially, this stimulates gum bleeding, but over a few weeks, it eliminates oral bacteria, and as the gums heal, they stop bleeding. Other helpful home treatments include rinsing the mouth with salt water, Listerine, or a solution of baking soda and water.

When to Call the Dentist.   Have a professional dental examination and cleaning annually. Professional cleaning is the only way to remove hardened ("calcified") plaque, also called "tartar" or "calculus."

If bleeding gums are the result of a systemic bleeding disorder, there are usually additional signs: easy bruising, prolonged bleeding from minor cuts, and nosebleeds without trauma. If you have such symptoms, see a physician for diagnostic tests.

BROKEN NOSE

Sharp blows can break the bone that forms the bridge of the nose. The blow often causes a snapping sound and sharp, intense pain, bleeding, and black eyes.

What's Going On?   The hard upper portion of the nose is bone. The softer, lower part is cartilage. It takes a powerful blow to break the large bones in the arms or legs, but lesser blows can break the nose.

Before You Call the Doctor.   Stop the bleeding by pinching the nose just above the nostrils.

To control pain and swelling, apply an ice pack. Wrap a few ice cubes in a plastic bag, then wrap the bag in a clean cloth. Apply the ice pack for twenty minutes, then remove it for ten minutes before reapplying. Ice substitutes may be used as well. Do not apply ice directly to the skin. This may cause the equivalent of frostbite.

For pain control, take acetaminophen. Aspirin and ibuprofen interfere with blood clotting.

As the swelling subsides, consider "the two F's," form and function. How does the nose look? If it's still straight, chances are it will heal straight and not affect breathing or cosmetic acceptability. A doctor visit may not be necessary. Healing usually takes about six weeks.

When to Call the Doctor.   But if you're concerned that a broken nose is not straight ("displaced"), or if it becomes very swollen, consult a doctor for an x-ray. If necessary, doctors fit the nose with a small metal splint to prevent displacement. If displacement has occurred, the broken bones can be realigned.

▶ **RED FLAG**   See a doctor immediately to rule out serious damage if:
- Bleeding cannot be easily controlled. The nose may require packing.
- The pain and tenderness extend into the cheeks or eyes.

BRUXISM

(See TOOTHGRINDING in this chapter)

CANKER SORES

Small, painful flat sores ("ulcerations") inside the mouth are usually canker sores.

What's Going On?   Canker sores, called "aphthous ulcers" by physicians, are red, crater-like erosions an eighth of an inch to an inch in diameter that usually appear on the sides of the mouth or on the gums. They usually occur singly but sometimes appear in clusters. They're painful and may make talking and eating difficult.

Doctors don't know what causes canker sores, but people who develop them often link their appearance to such resistance-lowering phenomena as stress, menstruation, wounds inside the mouth, and deficiencies in iron, folic acid, zinc, and vitamin B_{12}.

Before You Call the Doctor.   Canker sores clear up by themselves within ten days to two weeks. Over-the-counter oral anesthetic gels (Anbesol and others) may be useful.

Or try pain relievers: aspirin, acetaminophen, or ibuprofen. Aspirin and ibuprofen may cause stomach upset. If so, try an "enteric coated" brand. Pregnant women and those with a history of ulcers should not take aspirin or ibuprofen unless a doctor recommends it.

If you suspect a nutritional deficiency, try taking a multi-vitamin/mineral supplement.

When to Call the Doctor.   Consult a physician if a canker sore doesn't heal within three weeks. Many conditions—from oral yeast infection ("thrush") to mouth cancer—may look like canker sores.

CHAPPED LIPS

Dry, cracked, irritated lips are quite common, especially in cold, dry climates.

What's Going On?   Normally, the lips moisturize themselves, but cold, dry, windy conditions or mucus-drying drugs, such as antihistamines, can interfere with this process and cause the lips to become chapped. People who habitually lick their lips may suffer chronic chapping. Some women may find that certain brands of lipstick also contribute to this problem.

Sometimes inflamed, painful cracks develop in the corners of the mouth ("perleche"). Frequently they don't heal because they become infected with yeast fungi.

Before You Call the Doctor.   A variety of effective, over-the-counter products treat this annoyance. They all prevent moisture loss from the lips. Plain petroleum jelly is inexpensive, goes on easily, and provides instant relief. Wax-based products also help (Chapstick, Blistik). Other products contain lanolin, the moisturizer obtained from fleece.

To prevent chapped lips, avoid prolonged exposure to sun and wind and try not to lick your lips. If you must be in dry, cold, windy, or sunny conditions, use chapped-lip treatments preventively, before the condition starts.

For perleche, apply an over-the-counter antifungal cream (miconazole or clotrimazole) two or three times a day, and dab on zinc oxide ointment at night. Wipe the zinc oxide off in the morning.

COLD SORES

(See also HERPES in Chapter 18)

Cold sores are red, painful blisters that appear around the nose and mouth, usually in association with colds—hence the name.

What's Going On?   Cold sores (and genital herpes) are caused by either of two closely related viruses, herpes simplex Type 1 or Type 2. Highly contagious, the blisters first appear one to three days after the virus particles enter the body through a break in the skin, and they usually last one to three weeks. Eventually, the blisters crust over, dry up, and heal.

The first outbreak can be quite painful and usually begins with a day or two of tenderness, followed by the appearance of one or more small blisters. Lymph nodes under the jaw may become swollen and tender. Sometimes the initial outbreak is accompanied by a fever.

Some people suffer only one outbreak. Their immune systems successfully fight off recurrences. But others experience subsequent eruptions when colds or other infections have reduced their resistance. Recurrent cold sores are usually less painful than initial outbreaks and don't last as long (a week to ten days) thanks to the immune system's ability to fight the infection. People who develop recurrent cold sores often report an itching or tingling sensation and tenderness a few hours before their outbreaks; these early symptoms are known medically as a "prodrome."

After healing, the virus remains dormant in the body, raising the possibility of recurrences. However, recurrent cold sores in otherwise healthy people tend to tail off and eventually cease over time. Many people experience only one or two recurrences. Others suffer periodic recurrences for a few years, then stop having them.

Before You Call the Doctor.   Cold sores are highly contagious, even during the prodrome before the blisters appear. Avoid skin-to-skin contact with anyone with a cold sore or prodrome.

Try not to catch colds and flu (see COMMON COLD and FLU in Chapter 11) and stay as healthy as possible (see Chapter 1).

When ill or stressed, take the immune-stimulating herb echinacea (eh-kin-AYE-sha). Studies have shown it helps the body defend against viral infections. Echinacea is available at health food stores in teas, tinctures, and tablets. Follow package directions.

Some people who suffer recurrent cold sores report success preventing outbreaks, reducing severity, and speeding healing by taking 500 mg a day of L-lysine, an amino acid available in health food stores.

If cold sores erupt, aspirin or ibuprofen can relieve the pain and minimize the inflammation. Acetaminophen has no anti-inflammatory action. Aspirin and ibuprofen may cause stomach upset. If gastrointestinal distress is a concern try "enteric coated" brands. Pregnant women and those with a history of ulcers should not take aspirin or ibuprofen unless a doctor recommends it.

In addition, several over-the-counter cold sore remedies are available (Blistex, Carmex, Anbesol). However, they don't prevent cold sores or reduce their healing time. They simply relieve discomfort.

When to Call the Doctor. The prescription herpes drug acyclovir can be used to treat cold sores, but it's not as effective as it is against genital herpes. It speeds healing on average by about one day, but it's fairly expensive.

▶ **RED FLAG**   Herpes infections can be extremely dangerous to newborn babies within the first few weeks of life. Newborns should not be exposed to anyone with active cold sores or cold-sore prodromes.

HOARSENESS AND LARYNGITIS

Hoarseness and laryngitis range from a mild huskiness to total loss of voice.

What's Going On?   The voice box ("larynx") has two flaps of tissue, the vocal cords, which vibrate as air passes over them. Laryngitis occurs when the vocal cords become inflamed and swollen and cannot move freely. Frequently the laryngitis sufferer experiences no discomfort other than hoarseness or loss of voice. Hoarseness is often caused by viral infections, usually colds or flu. Occasionally, bacterial infections damage the larynx, causing hoarseness. People who use their voices a great deal—

singers and teachers—often suffer chronic laryngitis due to overuse or misuse of the voice. Those who smoke cigarettes, abuse alcohol, or work around paints, solvents, and other chemicals may also suffer chronic laryngitis.

Hoarseness may also result from problems with the nerve that controls the vocal cords or from callus-like growths ("nodules" or "polyps") on the cords typically caused by overuse.

Before You Call the Doctor.   The following self-care suggestions usually relieve hoarseness:

• Quit smoking.

• Minimize alcohol consumption.

• Use a respirator to control throat irritation from occupational chemicals.

• Rest your voice. This not only means talk as little as possible, but also try not to *whisper*. Recent studies suggest whispering strains the vocal cords as much as talking.

• Drink lots of warm liquids.

• Use a steam vaporizer for five minutes four times a day.

• Throat lozenges, hard candies, and chewing gum often help by keeping saliva flowing, but steer clear of mint flavors, which may dry throat tissues.

• Don't use mouthwashes, most of which contain alcohol and phenol, which is irritating.

• Don't gargle or clear your throat.

If hoarseness is caused by a viral infection, it usually clears up without specific treatment.

When to Call the Doctor.   Consult a physician if hoarseness lasts more than a week or for laryngitis that does not appear to be related to irritation or infection. Bacterial laryngitis is treated with antibiotics. If hoarseness is accompanied by fatigue, dry skin, dry hair, sudden weight gain, and/or feeling cold much of the time, the problem may be related to an underactive thyroid gland ("hypothyroidism").

In some cases, nodules on the vocal cords must be surgically removed. Speech therapy can teach a person to change speaking technique to prevent recurrences.

Rarely, hoarseness is the first sign of cancer of the larynx. Smoking is the major risk factor.

LOSS OF SMELL

(See also LOSS OF TASTE in this chapter and HAYFEVER in Chapter 11)

Loss of smell may occur suddenly or gradually. The sense of taste depends to a large extent on the sense of smell, so any problem with smell usually results in taste impairment as well.

What's Going On?   Sudden loss of smell is usually caused by colds, flu, or allergies because increased mucus production and nasal congestion temporarily impair the olfactory receptors in the nose. Occasionally, sudden loss of smell is the result of a neurological disorder or a blow to the head which damages the odor-detecting ("olfactory") nerves.

Gradual loss of smell is usually associated with smoking or occupational or hobby exposure to volatile chemicals or solvents.

Before You Call the Doctor.   Quit smoking. Around chemicals, improve ventilation and use a respirator.

When to Call the Doctor.   If loss of smell persists or does not return after recovery from colds, flu, or allergies, consult a physician.

In many cases, loss of smell results from nasal polyps, the growth of fleshy bumps inside the nose. Nasal polyps are harmless, but they can block the nasal passages and cause loss of smell. Polyps are removed surgically. If loss of smell is not caused by polyps, a neurological examination is indicated.

Serious loss of the sense of smell ("anosmia") is a problem for several hundred thousand Americans. It interferes significantly with quality of life and often leads to chronic depression. Using new "scratch-and-sniff" tests, the level of impairment can now be quantified, which aids diagnosis and treatment.

LOSS OF TASTE

(See also LOSS OF SMELL in this chapter)

Researchers estimate that about two million Americans suffer taste or smell disorders. The two are often related because aroma is a key part of the sense of taste.

What's Going On?   A number of drugs, diseases, and nutritional deficiencies can cause taste disturbances. We taste food when nerves on the
tongue ("taste buds") and/or in the nose become chemically stimulated.
The senses of taste and smell in combination with reactions to temperature and texture allow us to perceive an enormous number of flavors.

Taste bud cells are constantly replaced every ten days. The most
common cause of the loss of taste is disruption in this renewal process.
Problems include loss of the sense of taste altogether ("ageusia"), impaired taste sensation ("hypogeusia"), or distorted sense of taste ("dysgeu-
sia").

Taste impairment is a normal consequence of aging. Older people
often complain food doesn't taste as good as it used to—and with good
reason. Some taste buds and aroma receptors stop functioning as people
age. The average seventy-five-year-old has only about half as many functioning taste buds and olfactory receptors as the average twenty year old.

A diet high in processed and junk foods often lacks the essential trace
mineral zinc. Zinc deficiency impairs the sense of taste. Other symptoms
of zinc deficiency include skin eruptions, loss of sexual desire, slow wound
healing, diarrhea, visual problems, and emotional changes. In children,
lack of adequate zinc levels can retard growth.

An enormous number of illnesses and life-style factors can interfere
with the sense of taste. Here's just a partial list:

•In the mouth: smoking, gum disease, oral radiation treatments.

•Allergies: chronic nasal congestion.

•Infections: colds, flu, sinusitis, hepatitis, mononucleosis, food poisoning.

•Gastrointestinal: colitis, malabsorption.

•Nutritional: alcoholism, cirrhosis, anorexia nervosa, the general
wasting associated with chronic disease ("cachexia").

•Rheumatic: chronic dry mouth ("Sjögren's syndrome").

•Kidney: treatment for kidney failure ("dialysis"), the accumulation of
urine components in the blood ("uremia").

•Cancer: chemotherapy drugs.

•Trauma: major burns, major surgery.

•Hormonal: pregnancy, oral contraceptives, thyroid disorders.

•Nervous system: head injury, cranial nerve injury.

Many drugs can also impair the sense of taste:

•Acetazolamide (Diamox) for glaucoma.

•Captopril for high blood pressure ("hypertension").

•Carbamazepine (Tegretol) for epileptic seizures.

•Clofibrate (Atromid) to reduce elevated cholesterol.

• Griseofulvin for ringworm and other fungal infections.
• Impiramine for depression.
• Iron for mineral deficiency.
• Lithium carbonate for manic depression.
• Metronidazole for protozoan infections, such as trichomoniasis and giardiasis.
• Nifedipine for angina and high blood pressure.
• Phenytoin (Dilantin) for epileptic seizures.
• Tetracycline for bacterial infections.
• Trifluoperazine (Stelazine) for psychiatric problems.

Before You Call the Doctor.   Stop smoking. Reduce alcohol consumption. Eat more whole grains and fresh fruits and vegetables to eliminate any zinc deficiency, or take a supplement (but do not exceed package directions—overdose is possible).

If loss of taste appears to be the result of age, food can be made more tasty by adding more herbs and spices: garlic, basil, dill, fennel, thyme, pepper, red pepper, etc. Other flavor extracts also help: soy sauce, vanilla extract, Worcestershire sauce, etc.

If you have any of the manageable illnesses which may impair sense of taste—colds, allergies, etc.—then take heart. Your sense of taste should return as your condition clears up.

If you take any drug which may impair your sense of taste, ask your pharmacist or physician if another may be substituted.

When to Call the Doctor.   If home treatment does not improve your ability to taste food within two weeks, consult a physician. Loss of taste may be a symptom of significant illness.

If you have a chronic condition which may cause this problem, ask your physician if your sense of taste might be improved despite it.

NOSEBLEEDS

A nosebleed, as defined here, is any nasal bleeding that is not caused by a punch or blow to the nose.

What's Going On?   Most nosebleeds are caused by picking the nose or blowing it frequently due to colds or allergies. The dry air in air-conditioned buildings and airplanes increases the likelihood of nosebleeds because the low relative humidity dries out the protective layer of nasal mucus that covers the tiny blood vessels in the nose ("capillaries"), increasing the risk of bleeding from the minor trauma of picking and blowing.

Nosebleeding is common among alcoholics because alcohol enlarges ("dilates") the blood vessels, including those in the nose, and dilated blood vessels bleed more easily. Heavy alcohol use can also lead to problems with blood clotting because of toxic effects on the liver and bone marrow.

People who take anticoagulant drugs, such as aspirin, may also suffer from nosebleeding.

Before You Call the Doctor.   If blood is coming only from one nostril, press against the nostril firmly. If both nostrils are bleeding, pinch the fleshy part of the nose together. In either event, maintain pressure for five to ten minutes to allow time for the blood to clot. Do not stop pinching before five minutes. The vast majority of recurrences are the result of impatience. Just keep applying pressure for five to ten minutes. If bleeding continues, apply pressure for another ten minutes.

If bleeding persists, rub an over-the-counter antiseptic ointment (Bacitracin, Neosporin) in sterile half-inch or one-inch roll gauze and pack the affected nostril(s) by pushing the gauze in gently with your little finger. The ointment helps prevent infection and keeps the gauze from sticking to the inside of the nostril and causing renewed bleeding when removed. Because the nose opens into the back of the throat, it can hold a surprisingly large amount of gauze. Insert gauze by pushing toward the back of the head, *not* up toward the bridge of the nose. Leave it in for thirty to sixty minutes, then gently remove it.

Don't blow your nose for a while after the bleeding has stopped. Broken capillaries may take up to twenty-four hours to heal completely, especially in dry conditions. Recurrences are common for up to a week. Simply repeat the instructions above.

When to Call the Doctor.   Consult a physician if bleeding cannot be stopped by pinching or packing. Occasionally, nosebleeds may also be caused by chronic high blood pressure ("hypertension"), if the pressure is elevated enough to rupture the nasal capillary walls (see HIGH BLOOD PRESSURE in Chapter 12). Nosebleeds associated with spontaneous bruising and/or cuts that bleed for a long time may indicate a clotting disorder. Consult a physician for testing.

POSTNASAL DRIP

(See also RUNNY NOSE and SORE THROAT in this chapter and COUGH in Chapter 11)

Postnasal drip can cause sensations of dripping or drainage behind the nose ("postnasally") and in the back of the throat, with throat irritation, cough, and a frequent urge to clear the throat.

What's Going On?   Mucus flows constantly from the back of the nose down into the throat where it is swallowed, but we're unaware of it unless some infection or abnormality alters the process. Two changes can produce postnasal drip: mucus overproduction and abnormally low mucus production with impaired flow and postnasal accumulation.

Mucus overproduction increases the amount that drains down into the throat. Causes include:

• Upper respiratory infections (see STREP THROAT and TONSILLITIS in this chapter and COMMON COLD, FLU, and SINUS INFECTION in Chapter 11).

• Hayfever-type inhalant allergies (see HAYFEVER in Chapter 11).

• Respiratory irritants (see COUGH in Chapter 11 and SICK BUILDING SYNDROME in Chapter 4).

• Air pollution. Two major components of smog, nitrogen dioxide and sulfur dioxide, can increase mucus production.

• Foreign bodies in the nose (see SOMETHING IN YOUR NOSE in this chapter).

• Nasal or sinus polyps.

• Anatomical abnormalities—for example, deviated nasal septum, the tissue between the nostrils.

Mucus underproduction results in thicker, more viscous mucus, which does not flow normally. It accumulates postnasally and eventually flows down, but abnormally slowly, creating the subjective sensations of postnasal drip. Causes include:

• Aging. As people grow older, they produce less nasal mucus, and the mucus is more viscous with lower water content.

• Inhalation of cold dry air. This tends to occur in winter or in buildings with forced-air heating, though it may also occur in air-conditioned settings.

• "Drying" medications. Any drug that dries the mouth and/or eyes can dry out nasal mucus: antihistamines, tranquilizers, and diuretics, among others.

• Exposure to smoke or dusts.

Before You Call the Doctor.   Try to determine the cause, then eliminate it:

• For upper respiratory infections, irritations, and hayfever, follow the suggestions in the appropriate section(s) of this book. However, don't take antihistamines. Because they are drying and may impair mucus drainage, they may cause postnasal drip.

·For postnasal drip caused by smog, check the newspaper for air quality data and limit outdoor activities on smoggy days. Air-conditioning, which filters the air, might help, but refrigerated air tends to be quite dry, which may contribute to impaired mucus drainage and aggravate the problem.

·For dry mucus, limit exposure to smoke and dusts, drink more nonalcoholic fluids, and humidify the air with a humidifier or leafy houseplants. You might also try a salt water ("saline") nasal spray. And ask your pharmacist if any drugs you take might contribute to the problem, and if so, whether others might be substituted. For allergies, cromolyn sodium might be substituted for antihistamines.

When to Call the Doctor.   If you believe your drip is caused by a bacterial or fungal infection, by nasal or sinus polyps, by a foreign body, or by an anatomical abnormality, consult a physician for testing and treatment. Also ask a doctor about switching from antihistamines to cromolyn sodium or steroidal allergy medication.

RUNNY NOSE

(See also ALLERGIES in Chapter 4 and COMMON COLD and FLU in Chapter 11)

A discharge drips from the nose. It may be thin and watery or thick and gunky. Typically the nose also becomes congested.

What's Going On?   Runny nose is usually caused by one of the following: allergies, an upper respiratory infection (cold or flu), overuse of nasal sprays, or a foreign body trapped in the nose.

• *Allergies*   (see also ALLERGIES in Chapter 4). Also known as hayfever or medically as "allergic rhinitis," allergies usually involve a combination of runny nose, sneezing, and watery, itchy eyes. Inhaled allergy-triggers ("allergens"), such as ragweed pollen, stimulate throat cells to release a chemical called histamine, which causes runny nose and the other hayfever symptoms. A variation ("vasomotor rhinitis") consists of congestion and runny nose brought on by eating or a sudden change in temperature or humidity.

Before You Call the Doctor.   If you smoke, stop. Smoking irritates the nasal passages. Allergy attacks present excellent opportunities to quit. For help quitting, see RESOURCES at the end of Chapter 11.

Blow your nose *gently* with disposable tissues. Blowing too hard may contribute to congestion, cause nosebleeds, and damage the eardrums.

Try the over-the-counter antihistamines chlorpheniramine and diphenhydramine. These drugs often cause drowsiness and dryness of the mouth and throat. Because of possible sedation, don't drive or operate machinery while using them. Unfortunately, recent surveys show that a majority of Americans ignore this advice and drive anyway, placing themselves—and others—at risk of injury in auto accidents. Take antihistamine side effects seriously. If you must drive, consult a physician for nonsedating antihistamines. Alcohol greatly increases antihistamine sedation. *Never* drive after drinking while taking antihistamines.

Over-the-counter decongestants can also provide quick, temporary relief of allergy-induced runny nose and nasal congestion. Decongestants come in pills, nasal sprays, or nose drops. Pills may cause restlessness and insomnia and raise blood pressure, a potential hazard for those with chronic high blood pressure ("hypertension"), diabetes, glaucoma, heart disease, or a history of stroke. Anyone with these conditions should use decongestant nasal sprays or nose drops. But sprays and drops have their own downside. After three days, they cause "rebound congestion," or worse stuffiness and runny nose than you had to begin with. Don't use decongestant sprays or drops for more than a day or two.

When to Call the Doctor.   Recently, nonsedating antihistamines have become available by prescription (Seldane, Hismanal). They're stronger than their over-the-counter counterparts, and they don't interfere with driving. Physicians may also prescribe other allergy medications, such as cromolyn sodium. For severe allergies, skin tests can pinpoint worst-offender allergens, and allergy shots ("immunotherapy") may minimize their ability to trigger reactions. Initially, allergy shots require once- or twice-weekly physician visits, with visits tapering off to once a month over two or three years. Children generally benefit most from allergy shots.

• *Upper Respiratory Infections*   (see also COMMON COLD and FLU in Chapter 11). The runny nose of colds and flu typically occurs with cough, sore throat, and in the case of flu, sudden fever and body aches. The mechanism is different from that of hayfever. Histamine plays little or no role. Instead, cold-infected nose and throat cells release interferon, the body's own antiviral chemical, and bradykinin, a poorly understood product of the infection, which draw extra blood to the area. This additional blood contains white blood cells and other components of the immune system, which fight the infection. Some of the fluid portion of the extra blood diffuses out of the tiny blood vessels ("capillaries") in the nose and mixes with extra nasal mucous secreted because of the infection, causing congestion and runny nose.

Before You Call the Doctor.   If you smoke, stop. Colds and flu present excellent opportunities to quit.

Blow your nose *gently* with disposable tissues. Blowing too hard may contribute to congestion, cause nosebleeds, and damage the eardrums.

Like grandma always said, drink hot liquids. They help unclog the nose and promote mucus clearance. Among hot liquids, a now famous 1978 study showed that chicken soup, sometimes called "Jewish penicillin," works best, but hot water and tea work well, too. In addition to combatting runny nose and nasal congestion, hot liquids warm the throat, impairing the ability of cold and flu viruses to replicate.

Moist heat from hot showers, warm facial cloths, and vaporizers also help liquify congested mucus, making it easier to blow out.

Over-the-counter decongestants also help. See the discussion of their side effects—including possible runny nose—in the section on "Allergies" above.

Antihistamines do not help relieve cold symptoms. For decades, physicians thought they did, and antihistamines are still standard ingredients in multi-symptom cold formulas. They're not a total waste because their sedative action can help combat the jitters and insomnia caused by decongestants. But the latest research shows that histamine, the body chemical that causes allergy symptoms, plays little or no role in the runny nose of colds and flu. Over-the-counter antihistamines may cause sedation and increase the risk of auto accidents.

When to Call the Doctor.   Physicians can't do anything more for the common cold than you can do yourself at home, so there's no point consulting them for colds.

However, flu is another story. Many people call any bad cold "the flu," but flu ("influenza") is actually a separate disease that strikes in annual epidemics from around Thanksgiving to Easter. The most serious form of flu, influenza A, may cause a fatal pneumonia in people over sixty-five years of age and in anyone with a chronic respiratory disease (asthma, cystic fibrosis, etc.). Flu-associated pneumonia contributes to tens of thousands of deaths a year in the U.S. Those over age sixty-five and anyone with a chronic respiratory disease should get the annual flu shot every autumn. And if the news media report flu in your area and you develop a sudden high fever and muscle aches that send you to bed, call your doctor immediately for the flu drug amantadine (Symmetrel). Even for those not at high risk of pneumonia, amantadine can shorten a bout of flu and reduce its severity. In the elderly and those with chronic diseases who don't get flu shots, amantadine may also be used to help *prevent* flu in the event of a local outbreak.

• *Runny Nose On Just One Side.*   This fairly common childhood problem usually means the child has inserted a small object—a bead or bean—up the nose and it has become stuck in the nostril. Or, at the end of a cold, a one-sided runny nose could signal a sinus infection (see SINUS INFECTION in Chapter 11).

Before You Call the Doctor.   Gentle nose-blowing usually ejects the object. The discharge should stop within a day or two if all of the foreign body has been removed.

When to Call the Doctor.   If the object will not come out, consult a physician.

▶ **RED FLAGS**   Call a physician for a runny nose if:
• Fever rises to 102° or higher.
• Nasal discharge that is not associated with a cold appears reddish or bloody.
• You experience significant pain and tenderness in the forehead, cheeks, and upper teeth.
• The problem lasts longer than three weeks.

SNORING

Snoring, or "sleeping out loud," has been recorded as loud as eighty decibels, the volume of an electric alarm clock buzzer.

What's Going On?   Any room- or bedmate of someone who snores knows how irritating this common problem can be. Researchers estimate that at age thirty, about 20 percent of men and 5 percent of women snore. The figures rise dramatically with age. By age sixty, nearly two-thirds of men and 40 percent of women sleep aloud.

Snoring occurs when a partial obstruction in the back of the throat restricts airflow during inhalation. Colds and flu cause general swelling of throat tissues, which explains why people often snore when they have upper respiratory infections. Allergies, tonsillitis, swollen glands or adenoids, and various infections may also inflame tissues in the back of the throat enough to cause snoring. In children, chronic snoring that is not related to upper respiratory infection is usually caused by enlarged tonsils or adenoids.

Chronic snoring typically results from:

• Loss of tone in the muscles which line the throat and support the rear part of the roof of the mouth ("soft palate") and the punching–bag-shaped flap of tissue that hangs from the soft palate down into the throat ("uvula").

• Obesity. Extra weight aggravates loss of throat muscle tone because it packs the throat with so much extra tissue.

• Drugs. Alcohol, tranquilizers, and/or sedatives all relax the muscles in the throat, making snoring more likely. Some allergy sufferers find that their snoring is related to antihistamines.

• Anatomical abnormalities. Some snorers have unusually fleshy soft palates or nasal obstructions such as polyps. A small proportion of snorers have cysts on their tonsils or adenoids. A few have receding chins that alter the position of the tongue, narrowing the airways and promoting noisy inhalation.

Before You Call the Doctor.   Most snoring occurs when people sleep on their backs. Rolling over, which changes the position of structures in the back of the throat, usually opens the airway and stops the noise. That's why exasperated spouses give snorers a swift kick to make them roll over. But why wake up enough to kick? Try these alternatives:

• The ball-in-the-back solution. Sew a golf or ping pong ball into a special pocket on the back of the snorer's pajamas. This prevents sleeping on the back—and the snoring associated with it.

• Weight loss. As excess tissue disappears from the throat, so do the blockages which cause snoring.

• Don't drink alcoholic beverages within four hours of retiring.

• Quit smoking to relieve chronic swelling of throat tissues and the mucus buildup it causes. For help quitting, see RESOURCES at the end of Chapter 11.

• Don't eat big meals close to bedtime.

• Stay away from antihistamines, tranquilizers, and sedatives before bed. If these drugs have been prescribed, discuss possible alternatives with your physician.

• Try a nasal decongestant spray. If congestion-related blockage of the nasal passages is the problem, sprays such as Afrin may provide relief. But if sprays help, don't keep using them. After about three days, they cause "rebound congestion," or worse congestion than you had to begin with. Some people experience rebound congestion even when they only use sprays once at bedtime. Instead, switch to a low-dose decongestant pill (pseudoephedrine, 30 mg) before bedtime to help maintain throat muscle tone during sleep. Unfortunately, decongestant pills have a stimulant effect, which cause insomnia. That's why it's important to use a low dose.

• Try special head-cradling anti-snoring pillows, available at department stores, or a soft, wrap-around neck pillow ("cervical whiplash collar"), available at medical supply stores. But stay away from thick pillows that kink the neck.

• Try elevating your head. This usually helps relieve cold- and flu-related snoring and sometimes helps relieve chronic snoring as well. Sleep with extra pillows under the entire upper body, not just the head, or raise the head of the bed with bricks or blocks.

• Try air filtration. An air filter or air conditioner reduces allergy-triggers in the air and helps control allergy-related snoring. In addition, eliminate feather pillows, pull up bedroom rugs, place mattresses in zippered plastic cases, and banish all pets from the bedroom.

When to Call the Doctor.   If snoring sounds unusually loud and the snorer thrashes in bed, consult a physician. The problem may be caused by such severe throat obstruction that the snorer actually stops breathing for periods of up to one minute ("sleep apnea"). Obesity is the major risk factor. In addition to loud volume and thrashing, apnea-related snorers are usually drowsy during the day and may exhibit personality changes. Apnea is also associated with elevated blood pressure ("hypertension") and heart-rhythm disturbances ("arrhythmias"). Chronic sleep apnea may trigger heart failure. Weight loss is the treatment of choice. Electronic apnea alarms can be used to wake apnea sufferers if they stop breathing. Surgery may be necessary to correct anatomical problems.

Chronic snoring in children should be evaluated by a physician. It interferes with sleep and increases the risk of behavior and learning problems.

SOMETHING IN YOUR NOSE

Anything stuck up the nose feels uncomfortable and may interfere with breathing.

What's Going On?   Children often insert objects—from beans to but- tons—up their noses. And during efforts to stop nosebleeds, adults some- times get bits of cotton, gauze, or other materials stuck in there. In addition to causing discomfort and possibly interfering with breathing, the object may contribute to infection or be inhaled ("aspirated") into the lungs.

Before You Call the Doctor.   Do not attempt to remove the object with a toothpick, swab, knife, or any sharp instrument. Usually this just drives it further into the nose. Instead, have the person inhale through the mouth to prevent moving it further up the nasal passage, then gently blow the nose to try to dislodge the object. If that doesn't work and you can see the object near the nostril entrance, use tweezers *gently* to try to pull it out. After removal, bleeding is common and rarely serious (see NOSE- BLEEDS in this chapter).

When to Call the Doctor.   If these efforts don't succeed quickly, consult a physician.

▶ **RED FLAG**   If grasping the object causes pain, especially in a person with allergies, it may be a nasal polyp (see LOSS OF SMELL in this chapter). Stop attempting to extract it, and consult a physician.

SORE THROAT

(See also STREP THROAT in this chapter)
    A red, irritated throat can make swallowing and talking difficult.

What's Going On?   The most common causes of sore throat are viral or bacterial infections, allergies, or irritants such as cigarette smoke. Often, sore throats are accompanied by hoarseness. The lymph nodes under the jaw may become swollen and tender. Allergy-related sore throats are usually accompanied by runny nose and watery, itchy eyes.
    When bacteria or viruses attack, throat tissues fight back. Blood vessels open up, attracting more blood to the area. The increased blood supply and the infection-fighting substances it carries cause throat tissues to redden, swell, and hurt.
    It's important—though often difficult—to distinguish between viral and bacterial infections. Untreated strep throat, caused by *Streptococcus* bacteria, can cause rheumatic heart disease or kidney damage. "Classic" strep throat causes sudden fever, sore throat, and swollen glands, with

whitish pus spots on the tonsils. But not all cases of strep throat cause the classic symptoms, and other infections can mimic strep symptoms. The only way to get an accurate diagnosis is to have a physician take a throat culture (see STREP THROAT in this chapter.)

Allergies or chronic sinus infections can cause sore throat because of irritation due to nasal mucus dripping down the throat (see POSTNASAL DRIP in this chapter). During cold weather, dry air in offices or the home can also cause sore throats.

Before You Call the Doctor.   Most sore throats unaccompanied by fever can be effectively treated at home. Try these self-care remedies:

• Stop smoking. For help quitting, see RESOURCES at the end of Chapter 11.

• Drink at least six glasses of water a day. If your sore throat is caused by an infection, stick to hot drinks, for example, tea or chicken soup. Cold beverages lower throat temperature, which contributes to viral replication.

• Gargle with warm salt water (¼ teaspoon per 4 ounces of water).

• Suck on sore throat lozenges, cough drops, or hard candy to keep the throat lubricated.

• Adults may take aspirin or ibuprofen for relief of pain and inflammation. Acetaminophen relieves pain but not inflammation. However, children who need relief should *always* be given acetaminophen. Children under eighteen who take aspirin for some viral infections (colds, flu, and chickenpox) are at risk for Reye syndrome, a rare but potentially fatal condition. Aspirin and ibuprofen may cause stomach upset. Pregnant women and those with a history of ulcers should not use aspirin or ibuprofen unless a doctor recommends it.

When to Call the Doctor.   For sore throat with any fever, consult a physician for a strep culture, especially if you've been exposed to someone with this infection. Physicians treat strep throat with a ten-day course of penicillin (or, for those allergic to penicillin, erythromycin). Symptoms usually clear up in a few days, but be sure to take all the medicine to eradicate the infection.

▶ **RED FLAGS**   Consult a physician if:

• Your temperature rises above 101° with no other cold symptoms.
• You have significant difficulty swallowing or any trouble breathing.
• You develop a rash.
• You develop hoarseness or enlarged lymph nodes which last longer than three weeks.

SORES IN THE MOUTH

(See CANKER SORES and THRUSH in this chapter)

STREP THROAT

(See also SORE THROAT in this chapter)

Classic strep throat infection causes a sudden fever, a red sore throat, white spots of pus on and/or around the tonsils, and swollen glands, but not all cases exhibit all these symptoms.

What's Going On?   Strep throat is an infection caused by *Streptococcus* bacteria. The bacteria are transmitted on respiratory droplets that are exhaled, coughed, or sneezed by people who carry them in their throats. These "carriers" may have strep throat infections, but studies show strep bacteria live in 5 to 20 percent of children's throats without causing infection. Strep throat infection is most common during the winter months. An estimated seven to twenty million Americans develop the infection each year. Anyone can get strep throat, but most infections occur in children five to fifteen years of age.

Strep almost always goes away by itself as the immune system gains the upper hand against the bacteria ("self-limited infection"). But if strep is not treated, one to three weeks after strep throat has cleared up, the person may develop rheumatic fever, a serious illness that can cause permanent damage to the valves in the heart, sometimes necessitating open-heart surgery.

Before You Call the Doctor.   Use common sense. Many children suffer several colds each winter involving sore throat and fever. It's impossible for most parents to rush off for a throat culture every time. But if a child's class- or playmates have strep, and the child develops a sudden fever and sore throat without the runny nose and congestion of a cold, then strep is more likely and the physician visit becomes worth the trouble.

Check the child's throat. The whitish pus spots of classic strep look like small globs of cheesy material, and the throat looks quite red.

When to Call the Doctor.   Physicians treat strep throat with penicillin (or, if the person is allergic, erythromycin). For classic strep symptoms, they typically prescribe antibiotics immediately. If the diagnosis is questionable, they take a throat culture, or administer a rapid strep test, which is not quite as accurate but gives immediate results and costs less. For both tests, the physician uses a cotton swab to remove some fluid from the throat. If the test shows strep, they prescribe antibiotics. Most physicians perform throat cultures or rapid strep tests on all suspected strep throats—even those with classic symptoms—just to be sure.

Have a throat culture or rapid strep test taken if you have any one of the following:
- Sore throat without cold symptoms (cough, sneezing, runny nose).
- Fever higher than 101°.
- Whitish spots on the tonsils or back of the throat.
- Tender, swollen glands in the neck.
- Recent exposure to someone with strep.
- A history of rheumatic fever.

If you're given an antibiotic prescription, it's important to take the complete course of treatment, even if you start to feel better within a few days. Remember, the full ten-day course is necessary to prevent rheumatic fever.

STUFFED NOSE

(See RUNNY NOSE and SOMETHING IN YOUR NOSE in this chapter)

TEMPOROMANDIBULAR JOINT (TMJ) JAW PROBLEMS

(See the discussion in Chapter 7)

THRUSH

White patches with inflamed red borders in the mouth suggest thrush.

What's Going On?   Thrush is caused by the fungus *Candida albicans,* the same organism that causes vaginal yeast infections ("yeast vaginitis") (see YEAST INFECTION in Chapter 16). This fungus is one of the many organisms normally present in the mouth. However, if an illness or anything else upsets the normal balance of oral microbes, *Candida* can overgrow and cause thrush sores.

Thrush is particularly common among young children, the elderly, or those with chronic health problems, such as diabetes or HIV infection. Iron deficiency and recent use of antibiotics increase the risk of this infection.

Before You Call the Doctor.   Thrush often develops when resistance is low as a secondary result of some other health problem. Try to stay as healthy as possible by following the advice in Chapter 1.

Yeast feed on sugar. Eliminate sugar from your diet until the sores have cleared up. That means fruit, milk, dairy products, and the hidden sugar in processed foods in addition to table sugar. Read food labels carefully.

When to Call the Doctor.   Physicians may touch the sores with a swab ("take a smear") and analyze it to confirm thrush and rule out other problems. Once confirmed, they treat it with an antifungal medication, typically nystatin or clotrimazole. Most cases respond to treatment, but recurrences are common if the underlying condition remains.

▶ **RED FLAG**   If you are neither very young nor elderly, have no known reason to have thrush (no recent illness or use of antibiotics), and you are in a high risk group for AIDS, thrush may be a symptom of infection by the human immunodeficiency virus (HIV) which causes AIDS. Consult a physician immediately.

TONGUE BITE

Wherever there's chewing, there's inevitably tongue biting.

What's Going On?   The teeth are sharp enough to cause deep, painful, bloody bites of the tongue.

Before You Call the Doctor.   Despite their sudden sharp pain, most tongue bites are minor, and any bleeding stops in a minute or two without treatment. If it doesn't, stick out your tongue and press firmly on the bleeding area with a clean handkerchief or washcloth. Maintain the pressure until the bleeding stops, usually no more than five or ten minutes.

When to Call the Doctor.   In the rare event that the bite continues to bleed despite firm pressure, or if bleeding stops then starts again, you may need stitches ("suturing") and possibly antibiotics.

TONSILLITIS

(See also SORE THROAT and STREP THROAT in this chapter)
Infection can cause the tonsils to become inflamed and swollen.

What's Going On? The tonsils, a first line of defense against bacterial
invasion through the nose and mouth, are lymph nodes that can easily be
seen on both sides at the back of the throat. Upper respiratory infections
(see COMMON COLD in Chapter 11) frequently enlarge and inflame
children's tonsils and reduce resistance, allowing tonsillitis to develop.
Streptococci, the bacteria that cause strep throat (see STREP THROAT in
this chapter) and viruses such as the one that causes infectious mononucleosis can also cause tonsillitis.

Tonsillitis typically causes symptoms similar to strep throat—sore
throat and fever. The tonsils become enlarged and inflamed and sometimes whitish material ("pus") sticks to them. Tonsillitis is so similar to
strep throat because in about one-third of cases, strep bacteria cause the
problem. About two-thirds of the time, tonsillitis has viral origins. Bacterial tonsillitis tends to produce redder, more swollen, more coated tonsils,
with foul-smelling breath. Lymph nodes in the neck typically swell and
become tender, and fever and headache are common.

Before You Call the Doctor. Most tonsillitis is viral and, as with the
common cold, in otherwise healthy people, the body heals itself. Rest.
Gargle with salt water (½ teaspoon of salt in 8 ounces of warm water) and
drink plenty of hot fluids. To relieve pain and inflammation, adults may
take aspirin or ibuprofen. Acetaminophen relieves pain but not inflammation. However, *always* use acetaminophen for children to avoid any risk
of Reye syndrome, a rare but potentially fatal condition that can occur
when children take aspirin for certain viral infections, including colds and
flu. Aspirin and ibuprofen may cause stomach upset. An "enteric coated"
brand may be easier on the stomach. Pregnant women and those with a
history of ulcers should not use aspirin or ibuprofen unless a doctor
recommends it.

You might also take echinacea (eh-kin-AYE-sha), an herbal medicine
which boosts the immune system's ability to fight viral infections.
Echinacea is available at health food stores and herb outlets in teas,
tinctures, and tablets. Follow package directions.

When to Call the Doctor. Consult a physician if a week of home
treatment does not provide significant relief or if you've been exposed to

anyone with a strep infection. The physician takes a throat culture or rapid strep test, and if the diagnosis is strep tonsillitis, the treatment is a ten-day course of penicillin. Symptoms usually subside in a day or two, but it's important to take the full course of medication to completely eradicate the infection. Untreated strep tonsillitis can cause serious complications, primarily rheumatic fever, a form of heart disease.

Surgical removal of the tonsils ("tonsillectomy") used to be routinely performed on children who developed tonsillitis. Today, few doctors recommend it unless a child has recurrent strep infections (three or more per year), chronic tonsillitis, or tonsillar abscesses. If your child's physician recommends tonsillectomy, get several opinions before consenting.

▶ **RED FLAGS**   Consult a physician immediately if:
- Your temperature rises above 101° with no other cold symptoms.
- You have difficulty swallowing or any trouble breathing.
- You develop a rash.
- You develop hoarseness or enlarged lymph nodes that last longer than three weeks.

TOOTH DECAY

(See also BLEEDING GUMS and TOOTHACHE in this chapter)
Tooth decay causes toothache and possibly tooth loss.

What's Going On?   Tooth decay is generally caused by a combination of too much dietary sugar and inadequate oral hygiene. The hard outer surface of teeth is composed of enamel. When we chew foods, a sticky combination of mucus, bacteria, and food particles forms on the tooth surfaces, particularly between the teeth and at the gum line. Bacteria in the mouth quickly convert the food particles, especially refined sugars ("sucrose"), into acid. The acid breaks down tooth enamel, forming a small pit or "cavity," which is the beginning of tooth decay.

If left untreated, the decay can progress down into the tooth's next layer ("dentin"). Acid may reach the dentin's nerve endings and cause pain. Dentin contains minute canals that lead to the tooth's blood and nerve supply ("pulp"). If decay reaches the pulp, the result is severe pain.

Before You Call the Dentist.   Plaque develops roughly every twelve hours, so brush teeth at least twice a day, particularly after meals. Food particles collect between teeth, so floss daily. In addition, the low-fat, high fiber diet we recommend for optimal health minimizes consumption of refined sugars, which tend to stick to teeth and spur tooth decay (see EAT AND DRINK RIGHT in Chapter 1). Make a special effort not to eat sweet foods that stick to the teeth. Instead of a caramel, for example, have a piece of fruit.

When to Call the Dentist. Have your teeth professionally cleaned at least once a year. It's the only way to remove calcified plaque. Ask your dentist about "fissure sealing," a method of closing off the areas where food and bacteria tend to collect.

For children, "sealing" teeth inside a thin plastic coating has become popular in recent years. Once sealed, the teeth are protected from decay for several years. Dentists seal children's teeth as their permanent teeth come in.

Once tooth decay begins, it must be treated by a dentist or it can destroy the teeth and gums. In the early stages of decay, the dentist can simply drill out the decayed area and fill it. When performed properly, this treatment halts the progression of decay. Sometimes old fillings must be replaced.

If the decay involves pulp damage, it may require more elaborate dentistry ("root canal"). The dentist or dental specialist ("endodontist") can usually clean out the infected pulp, disinfect the pulp canal, and fill it with an inert material. Although the tooth is no longer alive, it can usually continue to function for a lifetime.

In recent years, some critics of dentistry have charged that the material used to fill cavities ("amalgam") may be harmful because it is about 50 percent mercury, a toxic metal. The American Dental Association insists that the mercury in amalgam remains completely contained within the tooth and poses no hazard. However, recent studies have raised troubling questions about this claim and about amalgam safety in general. Fortunately, amalgam is not the only filling material available. If you are concerned about amalgam's possible hazards, practice good oral hygiene, have your children's teeth sealed, and if any teeth become decayed, ask your dentist about using an alternative filling material.

TOOTH KNOCKED OUT

Sports are the leading cause of this painful problem, followed by automobile accidents and assaults.

What's Going On? More than two million teeth are knocked out every year. When a tooth is knocked out, the periodontal ligament that holds the tooth in its bony socket becomes severed. Part of the ligament remains in the socket, and part of it stays attached to the lost tooth. The good news is that almost any knocked-out tooth can be replanted—*if* you can keep the ligament alive.

Before You Call the Doctor.   The half of the ligament left in the bony socket stays alive because it is bathed in blood after the injury. The trick is to save the part of the ligament still attached to the tooth. The best way to do this is to immediately place the tooth back into its socket. If the tooth is replanted within fifteen to thirty minutes of the accident, it has a 90 percent chance of surviving. Of course, this takes tremendous presence of mind in the immediate aftermath of the tooth-loss injury. If you replant the tooth yourself, you should still consult a dentist as quickly as possible to make sure it was replaced properly.

If the tooth is not replaced back in its socket, it may still be able to be replanted if you store it properly until the person and the tooth get to a dentist. Do not use gauze or tissue, which dries out the ligament. The tooth may be carried under the tongue for a short period of time. But saliva damages the ligament cells after about an hour, and this method carries the risk of swallowing the tooth. A better medium is cold, whole milk (not skim or powdered), which can be used to store the tooth for short periods. The best approach is a pH-balanced, cell-culture fluid, such as Hank's solution or Eagle's medium, which can keep the tooth alive for four to twelve hours. If you or your children participate in organized sports activities, encourage the coach to obtain a supply of a tooth-preserving solution through a physician or dentist. Pop the tooth into the solution, and transport it in a clean plastic container. Do not touch the root end of the tooth when handling it. Do not attempt to clean, sterilize or scrape the tooth in any way. Get the person and the tooth to a dentist as quickly as possible. Your best bet is a hospital emergency room. They have dentists on call trained to handle dental emergencies.

TOOTHACHE

(See also TOOTH DECAY in this chapter and TEMPOROMANDIBU-LAR JOINT (TMJ) JAW PROBLEMS in Chapter 7)

Toothache pain may be dull or sharp, intermittent or constant. Usually it's impossible to ignore for long.

What's Going On?   Pain in the teeth or gums usually indicates tooth decay or a problem in the jaw joint. In the early stages of tooth decay, there may be no symptoms. As the decay progresses, you may feel mild pain when you eat something sweet, sour, hot, or cold. If left untreated, the decay progresses down into the tooth's nerve and blood supply ("pulp"), and the pain may become more persistent and spread over more than one tooth. Extreme sensitivity to hot or cold suggests pulp involvement.

Cracked teeth can hurt, too. Cracks are usually the result of trauma, often biting down unexpectedly on something extra-hard or toothgrinding ("bruxism") (see TOOTHGRINDING in this chapter).

Sometimes tooth pain isn't related to dental disease but to misalignment of the jaw joint (see TEMPORMANDIBULAR JOINT (TMJ) JAW PROBLEMS in Chapter 7). The misaligned joint stresses the head and neck nerves and muscles. In addition to pain in the teeth, TMJ dysfunction often causes headaches, ear or jaw popping, facial pain, and neck and shoulder pain.

Before You Call the Dentist. Most tooth decay can be prevented with regular brushing and flossing and the use of fluoride in areas where water is not fluoridated. In addition, the low-fat, high fiber diet we recommend for optimal health minimizes consumption of refined sugars, which tend to stick to teeth and spur tooth decay (see EAT AND DRINK RIGHT in Chapter 1).

If decay has progressed to the toothache stage, there's little you can do except control the pain until you can get a dental appointment. Try Anbesol, a topical anesthetic for the teeth and gums. In addition, aspirin, ibuprofen, or acetaminophen all help. Aspirin and ibuprofen may cause stomach upset. Pregnant women and those with a history of ulcers should not use aspirin or ibuprofen unless a doctor recommends it.

TMJ pain can usually be managed with a combination of aspirin, massage, and warm facial packs until you can be evaluated and treated by a dentist.

When to Call the Dentist. If a toothache lasts more than a day or two or gets worse, consult a dentist.

▶ **RED FLAGS** Request an emergency dental appointment if a toothache:
- Causes constant pain.
- Keeps you awake at night.
- Is accompanied by facial or gum swelling or any fever.

TOOTHGRINDING

(See also TEMPOROMANDIBULAR JOINT (TMJ) JAW PROBLEMS in Chapter 7)

Toothgrinding causes significant noise at night, worn teeth, headaches, and jaw and facial pain.

What's Going On?   Toothgrinding, medically known as "bruxism," means any nonfunctional movement of the jaw. It includes not only grinding but also tapping the teeth together ("clicking") and biting down with continual pressure ("clenching"). Chances are your teeth are clenched right now. Consciously relax your jaw muscles and read on.

Who hasn't reacted to life's irritations by "gritting their teeth?" Or sat in a traffic jam "chomping at the bit" to get moving? Authorities estimate that 98 percent of adults clench their teeth for emotional reasons at one time or another. Women are four times more likely than men to grind their teeth. And 20 percent of adults develop some of the symptoms listed above.

Clenching and grinding do the most damage. They break tiny enamel chips ("prisms") off the teeth. Prisms act like sandpaper and speed tooth wear. Even a seemingly innocuous habit like pencil-chewing can cause considerable damage to teeth over time.

Dentists use a bite-force measuring device to rate the severity of bruxism. Chewing food normally involves 25 to 50 pounds of bite force. Some toothgrinders bite and clench with a force of 500 pounds.

Toothgrinding is usually related to stress. People who are physically active, do precise work, or work under pressure are particularly prone to this problem. And bite force increases when toothgrinders experience unusually stressful life events.

Since people clench and grind their teeth subconsciously, the condition is often difficult to diagnose. Are you a toothgrinder? Ask yourself:

• During stressful times, do you clench your jaw?
• Do your face and jaw muscles often feel tight?
• On waking, do your teeth feel loose and sore?
• Does your jaw ever throb, even slightly?
• Are your teeth chronically sensitive to heat and/or cold?

If you answer "yes" to any of these questions, you might be a toothgrinder. To be sure, ask your dentist, who can usually diagnose the problem based on the wear patterns on your teeth.

Before You Call the Dentist. Daytime clenching is easier to control than nighttime grinding:

• Concentrate on keeping your jaw relaxed and teeth slightly apart. Jaw awareness is often enough to control daytime clenching. When you feel yourself tensing, take a moment to relax your jaw.

• Substitute teethgrinding with another habit—for example, balling up your fists, wriggling your toes, or even pacing to relieve stress.

• Don't chew gum, pencils, tobacco, or anything but food.

• Maintain good posture. Hunching over a computer terminal, cradling a phone between your ear and shoulder, or tightening back and neck muscles while slouching can trigger clenching.

• Cut back on caffeine in coffee, tea, colas, cocoa, chocolate, and over-the-counter drugs. Minimize your use of over-the-counter decongestants, which have stimulating effects similar to caffeine's.

• Engage in regular moderate exercise, and practice other forms of stress management (see EXERCISE REGULARLY and MANAGE YOUR STRESS LOAD in Chapter 1).

• Relax before bed. Take a hot bath, listen to music, make love, or have a glass of warm milk. Don't think about stressful subjects in bed.

• Train your subconscious as you retire for the night by repeating to yourself: "Lips closed, jaw apart and relaxed."

When to Call the Dentist. If self-care approaches don't provide sufficient relief within a month or so, consult a dentist who specializes in bruxism. Ask your regular dentist for a referral if necessary.

The standard treatment is to fit you for a custom-made acrylic mouthguard ("bite splint" or "nightguard") that slips over your teeth while you sleep. It won't cure grinding and clenching, but it absorbs much of the pressure and prevents tooth damage. Replace your splint as you grind through it. Don't use one-size-fits-all athletic mouthguards. Most people find they don't work. Some say they aggravate the problem. Get a bite splint custom made for your mouth.

CHAPTER 11

The Respiratory System

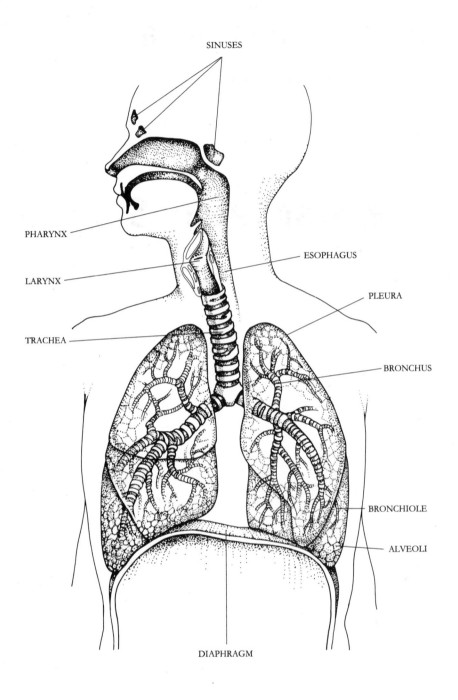

SINUSES

PHARYNX

LARYNX

TRACHEA

ESOPHAGUS

PLEURA

BRONCHUS

BRONCHIOLE

ALVEOLI

DIAPHRAGM

The Respiratory System.

ASTHMA

Asthma causes difficulty breathing, which usually means wheezing but may include coughing, shortness of breath, and chest tightness. Episodes ("attacks") occur periodically. Some cases are little more than a nuisance, but others may require hospitalization.

What's Going On?   Asthma involves the narrowing of the small airways in the lungs ("bronchioles"). During asthma attacks, the muscles around the bronchioles tighten ("bronchospasm"), restricting the flow of air and making breathing difficult. In addition, the bronchioles become inflamed and secrete extra mucus, adding to breathing problems. In asthma, exhaling is more difficult than inhaling, so stale air remains in the lungs. In severe attacks, this retained air can cause asthma sufferers to feel like they're suffocating.

Asthma can develop at any age, but most cases are diagnosed in childhood. Asthma often runs in families, but it is not considered an inherited condition. Parental smoking greatly increases children's susceptibility. Among adults, risk factors include smoking or occupational exposure to inhaled irritants.

Asthma bears some similarities to hayfever-type allergies (see ALLERGIES in Chapter 4). Attacks may be triggered by pollens, mold spores, dust mites, and animal dander. In addition, just about any inhaled irritant may cause some asthmatics' bronchioles to constrict: tobacco smoke, air pollutants, chemical fumes, insecticides, sawdust, and literally hundreds of occupational dust-producers. Certain food items can also trigger asthma attacks, particularly milk and eggs. Colds and flu may aggravate asthma symptoms. One form of this condition, "exercise-induced asthma," is triggered by strenuous physical activity. Emotional stress also plays a role in asthma attacks, and once attacks begin, sufferers—and if they're children, their parents—often panic, which aggravates the problem.

Before You Call the Doctor.   Asthma need not limit anyone's life or physical activities. Many Olympic athletes have had asthma. This condition can be controlled, and most asthma attacks can be prevented:

•No one in an asthmatic's family should smoke. For help quitting, see RESOURCES at the end of this chapter.

•Everyone in the asthmatic's family should become well-informed about the condition. Education corrects the many myths about asthma being a debilitating disease and reduces the panic that asthma attacks typically cause (see RESOURCES at the end of this chapter).

• Learn your asthma triggers (or your child's). Try to discern a pattern that precedes attacks, and then break the pattern.

• Follow the environmental-control suggestions in the ALLERGIES discussion of Chapter 4. Get skin tests to identify any allergies specifically.

• Install air conditioning in your home and car, and consider purchasing a high-efficiency particulate air (HEPA) filter.

• Stay away from smoke and smokers.

• Work to prevent colds and flu (see COMMON COLD and FLU in this chapter). Everyone in the family should get a flu shot every autumn.

• Watch out for fumes. Paint fumes are notorious for provoking asthma attacks. Fumes from household cleaning products can also cause bronchospasm. Some asthmatics react badly to perfumes and the fragrances in deodorants and personal care products.

• Try to avoid sudden temperature changes. In summer, going in and out of air-conditioned environments can trigger asthma attacks. In winter, going in and out of cold weather can do the same.

• Engage in moderate exercise daily. The myth is that asthma limits physical abilities. It doesn't. In fact, studies show that as part of a professionally guided program of asthma management, regular moderate exercise helps prevent asthma attacks. Don't overexert yourself, but daily, moderate exercise helps manage stress and encourages asthmatics to view their lungs as friends, not just problems. Walking, swimming, and cycling, can be quite helpful. Yoga teachers can suggest special postures and breathing exercises asthmatics often find quite helpful. Your local office of the American Lung Association may offer classes on breathing and exercise (see RESOURCES at the end of this chapter).

• Use a peak-flow meter twice a day. These simple tube devices can make a tremendous difference in controlling asthma. Peak flow meters measure exhalation force, which becomes restricted during asthma attacks. Peak flow typically declines considerably *before* asthma attacks, the way the barometer falls before a storm. By charting your peak flow twice a day, you learn your baseline exhalation force. Then, if you see it declining, you can take quick self-care steps to prevent an asthma attack. Physicians who specialize in childhood asthma say that peak flow meters cut way down on asthma attacks and often eliminate emergency room visits.

• Drink plenty of fluids. Asthma authorities recommend six to eight glasses of liquids a day to help keep bronchial secretions thin and easy to cough up.

• Use over-the-counter drugs cautiously. Aspirin and ibuprofen trigger asthma attacks in some people. Antihistamines and decongestants may dry bronchial secretions and make them harder to cough up. If you have asthma, make a list of all the over-the-counter medicines you take and ask your pharmacist if any might contribute to bronchospasm. If so, ask if other drugs might be substituted.

• Learn the signs of impending asthma attacks. Different people have individual signs, including wheezing, coughing, congestion, chest tightness, and rapid breathing. If a peak-flow meter reading confirms airway constriction:

  ° Try not to panic.
  ° Take bronchodilators immediately to prevent or minimize the attack.
  ° Practice yoga-style breathing exercises.

• Don't use sleeping pills. Sleep aids tend to slow breathing. If coffee, colas, or tea keep you awake, don't take them in the late afternoon or evening. If coughing or other symptoms keep you awake at night, elevate the head of your bed with bricks or prop your head up on extra pillows.

• Control heartburn. This may sound odd, but recent studies show that asthma predisposes people to chronic heartburn and that heartburn aggravates asthma symptoms (see HEARTBURN in Chapter 13). If heartburn is a problem for you, limit your use of theophylline (an asthma medication) and caffeine. Use other bronchodilators instead.

For more information, contact the American Lung Association and the Asthma and Allergy Foundation of America (see RESOURCES at the end of this chapter).

When to Call the Doctor. Good asthma self-care requires professional back-up. Look for a physician who supports self-care and home asthma management. But don't hesitate to consult your doctor if the situation calls for professional care. Always update your doctor on all the home asthma treatments you use because prescription medicines may interact with over-the-counter products. In some cases, you may experience greater relief with fewer side effects by discontinuing home treatments and using prescription drugs instead.

Physicians treat asthma with cromolyn sodium (Intal), which blocks the allergic reaction leading to bronchospasm; ipratropium (Atrovent), which prevents mucus accumulation in the respiratory tract; and two kinds of prescription bronchodilators: beta-adrenergics and theophylline. Corticosteroids, which block inflammation, have recently been promoted from third-line asthma medications to first- or second-line medicines. Many of these drugs are now available in oral inhalers, which deliver a burst of aerosolized medication at the touch of a button. Asthma medications are also available in pill and liquid form. Some may also be taken using inhaler-style appliances ("nebulizers").

Be sure you get detailed instructions from your doctor or pharmacist on proper inhaler use. Compared with misuse, proper use provides two to five times greater effectiveness.

▶ **RED FLAGS**   Uncontrolled asthma can cause serious complications. Consult a physician for any fever during an asthma attack or for persistent coughing, labored breathing, shortness of breath, or chest pain.

BRONCHIOLITIS

(See also BRONCHITIS (ACUTE) in this chapter)

Adults and older children get bronchitis. Infants get bronchiolitis.

What's Going On?   The small airways in infants' lungs ("bronchioles") are much narrower than those in older children and adults. If they become infected with certain viruses, the result is bronchiolitis. About 90 percent of cases occur in children less than one year old, and it's more likely to strike infants born prematurely, whose respiratory systems are not fully developed at birth. Symptoms include rapid breathing with prolonged, labored exhalations, and fever is often present. It's often difficult to distinguish bronchiolitis from asthma. Most physicians presume that bronchiolitis is present if infants are wheezing, especially if the child had a cold before the wheezing began. Although bronchiolitis is not asthma, about half of infants who develop bronchiolitis develop asthma later in childhood.

Before You Call the Doctor.   To prevent bronchiolitis, parents should not smoke. For help quitting, see RESOURCES at the end of this chapter. In addition, treat colds in infants aggressively with rest, plenty of fluids, a vaporizer, and lots of cuddling. If wheezing develops, continue these treatments. Bronchiolitis typically lasts from four to ten days. It rarely becomes serious, except in children with other chronic conditions, especially respiratory diseases.

When to Call the Doctor.   Bronchiolitis is a viral infection, so antibiotics do not help. However, antibiotics may be prescribed if bronchiolitis progresses to become bacterial pneumonia, a potentially life-threatening condition. Recently a new prescription drug called ribavirin (Virazole) was approved for the treatment of bronchiolitis. It's administered as an aerosol. Infants with severe bronchiolitis need to be hospitalized and placed in oxygen tents.

▶ **RED FLAG**   In some cases, bronchiolitis causes death in infants or progresses to bacterial pneumonia, also potentially fatal. If your baby begins wheezing, consult a physician promptly. Contact a physician immediately if an infant develops symptoms of pneumonia: fever, cough, and rapid breathing.

BRONCHITIS (ACUTE)

(See also BRONCHIOLITIS, COMMON COLD, and FLU in this chapter)

Acute bronchitis causes the annoying cough that often lingers for a week or two after colds and flu. In some cases the cough is dry and hacking. In others the person brings up grayish or yellowish phlegm.

What's Going On?   Bronchitis is an inflammation of the major airways ("bronchi"), which branch off from the windpipe ("trachea") and lead into the lungs. The inflammation is typically caused by a virus and aggravated by cigarette smoke, dusts, chemical vapors, and air pollution. Occasionally bacteria cause this condition.

The bronchi are lined with tiny hairs ("cilia"), which sweep mucus and other cellular debris out of the respiratory tract. During bronchitis, the cilia stop working. The only way the body can keep the bronchi clear is to cough, which is the major symptom of this illness. Severe cases may also cause chest pain and/or painful breathing.

Before You Call the Doctor.   The best way to prevent bronchitis is to prevent colds and flu (see COMMON COLD and FLU in this chapter). In addition, don't smoke. For help quitting, see RESOURCES at the end of this chapter. And stay away from dusts, paints, smoke, chemical vapors, and other respiratory irritants.

If bronchitis develops, the vast majority of cases can be managed with self-care.

• Redouble your efforts to steer clear of respiratory irritants.

• Drink plenty of nonalcoholic fluids. Authorities recommend six to eight glasses a day. Don't hesitate to drink more. Fluids help liquify bronchial secretions, making them easier to cough up. Warm fluids work better than cold.

• Humidify the air. Use a humidifier or vaporizer, or take hot, steamy showers.

• Try to stay out of buildings heated by forced air. Forced air is dry, irritating air. Air conditioning also dries the air.

• For a dry cough, take an over-the-counter cough suppressant containing dextromethorphan. Don't try to suppress "productive" coughs that bring up phlegm. During the day, cough drops or hard candies can help keep saliva flowing, which soothes a hacking cough.

• For phlegm that feels thick and stuck inside your airways, drink plenty of nonalcoholic fluids and take an over-the-counter cough preparation containing the expectorant guaifenesin. Don't take multi-ingredient cold formulas containing antihistamines or decongestants. These medicines dry bronchial secretions, making them more difficult to cough up.

When to Call the Doctor.   Consult a physician if coughing lasts longer than two weeks. A bacterial infection may have developed, which might require antibiotics. Bacterial infections usually cause heavier yellowish or greenish phlegm. The physician should also consider other possible causes for the cough, for example, asthma or sinus infection (see ASTHMA and SINUS INFECTION in this chapter).

▶ **RED FLAGS**   Consult a physician immediately if fever develops during bronchitis or if coughing brings up bloody, brown, or greenish-yellow phlegm. These symptoms suggest pneumonia. However, they may also be caused by bacterial bronchitis—less of an emergency, but usually requiring treatment with a prescription antibiotic.

BRONCHITIS (CHRONIC)

(see also BRONCHITIS (ACUTE), COPD, and COUGH in this chapter)
Chronic bronchitis, often called "smoker's cough," is similar to acute bronchitis except that the coughing persists over time and gets worse.

What's Going On?   Chronic bronchitis typically begins with extended bouts of acute bronchitis, but over time it becomes constant and the cough grows deeper. Coughing continues all day and at night, though it's usually worst first thing in the morning, and it may cause breathlessness and some wheezing. The cough is "productive," that is, it brings up thick phlegm.

Chronic bronchitis is the result of respiratory irritation over time. It's almost always caused by smoking, though dusts, air pollutants, chemical vapors, and other occupational irritants may also play a role. The tiny hairs ("cilia") that line the lungs' major branches ("bronchi") stop clearing mucus from the airways, and the bronchi and the smaller airways ("bronchioles") become permanently inflamed and constricted due to secretion of thick mucus. Chronic bronchitis increases the risk of other respiratory infections, particularly pneumonia.

Before You Call the Doctor. There's a good reason why chronic bronchitis is called "smoker's cough." It's quite common among smokers and rare among nonsmokers.

• If you smoke, quit. For help quitting, see RESOURCES at the end of this chapter.

• If you work around respiratory irritants, use a respirator or other protective gear.

• If you live in an area with considerable air pollution, install home and auto air-conditioning for its filtering action.

• Consider obtaining a high-efficiency particulate air (HEPA) filter, available through medical supply houses.

• Stay away from people with colds, flu, and other communicable respiratory illnesses.

• Follow the other suggestions under BRONCHITIS (ACUTE) in this chapter. But be aware that smoking cessation is the only real way to treat this condition.

When to Call the Doctor. Physicians can prescribe the kind of bronchodilators used to treat asthma (see ASTHMA in this chapter), but again, these provide only temporary relief. The key to treating chronic bronchitis is to quit smoking.

If chronic bronchitis symptoms grow suddenly worse—increased cough, shortness of breath, or increased production of unusually dark phlegm—doctors prescribe antibiotics and sometimes extra bronchodilators.

▶ **RED FLAG** In addition to the risk of chronic bronchitis (and emphysema and lung cancer), parental smoking significantly increases the risk of acute bronchitis, bronchiolitis, and pneumonia in infants and children.

COMMON COLD

(See also BRONCHITIS (ACUTE), COUGH, CROUP, and FLU in this chapter)

Colds cause variable symptoms, but the classic cold begins with a sore throat, then progresses to nasal congestion and runny nose and finally a dry cough, which may linger for a week to ten days.

What's Going On?   The common cold is humanity's most prevalent illness. Expert says that over a lifetime the average American spends more time sick with colds than with *all other illnesses combined.* Medically known as an "upper respiratory infection," colds are caused by any of more than 200 viruses. Technically, each individual virus produces a "different" cold, but because they all cause similar symptoms, we consider the common cold a single illness.

Cold viruses reproduce best in relatively dry air at around 90° F. The nose defends the body by warming and moistening incoming air. In addition, the mucus that lines the nose and throat ("nasopharynx") traps virus particles like flypaper, and microscopic hairs in the throat ("cilia") push this virus-laden mucus down into the stomach, where it's destroyed.

But two to four times a year for the average adult, and up to twelve times a year for young children, a few virus particles penetrate the protective mucus and infect throat cells. Infection kills the cells, but before they die, they release chemicals that trigger inflammation and attract virus-eating white blood cells, which arrive on a wave of extra blood fluid ("plasma"). The plasma warms the area, impairing viral replication, and swells nasopharyngeal tissues. Infected nasopharyngeal cells also release other substances—histamine, interferon, and bradykinin—which increase mucus production to trap and carry away new virus particles and the cellular debris of the "cold war."

It may come as a surprise, but those all-too-familiar cold symptoms are caused not by the virus itself, but rather by the body's war against it. About a day after infection, the developing inflammation triggers sore throat, and the cold sufferer feels a "cold coming on." As the days pass, successive waves of white blood cells flow into the area, and fluid and mucus accumulate, causing swelling, which the cold sufferer experiences as nasal congestion, runny nose, and eventually the dry, hacking cough (see also POSTNASAL DRIP in Chapter 10).

Young children catch the most colds because their immune systems are not fully developed and because they are lax in personal hygiene (see below). In addition, recovery from every cold confers an estimated three-to five-year immunity—and possibly longer—to that specific virus and its close relatives, and children have not lived long enough to have developed much virus-induced immunity.

Contrary to what your mother told you, *chilling and dampness have nothing to do with susceptibility to the common cold.* Researchers have had people stand naked in frigid meat lockers and drafty gyms wearing wet socks for hours on end, and in no experiment have those in the "chill/damp" group caught more colds, or worse colds, than people who spent the same amount of time happily ensconced in warm cozy rooms.

The contemporary twist on the "chill" myth is that people who live in centrally air-conditioned homes or work in modern office buildings often blame their colds on over-active air conditioners. The problem is not the air's low temperature, but rather its *low relative humidity.* Air conditioning dries air, often to the point where it may dehydrate the protective mucus in the nasopharynx and allow cold viruses to do their worst.

Colds are transmitted by either the "aerosol route" or "direct contact." Aerosol means through the air. Someone with a cold (with or without symptoms) exhales, coughs, or sneezes cold virus particles into the air, and those about to become infected inhale them. Or people with colds touch their noses—most people touch their noses unconsciously several times an hour—and contaminate their fingers with virus particles. Then they deposit the virus on other peoples' hands or on hard, nonporous surfaces, such as countertops, doorknobs, and telephones, where others literally pick it up on their fingertips. Those with infected fingers then touch their noses and get infected. They might also rub their eyes. The tear ducts in the inner corners of the eyes are connected by a tube to the nasopharynx, so eye-rubbing with cold-contaminated fingertips can also transmit the common cold.

But one way colds *don't* spread is by kissing. In a famous experiment, a leading cold researcher had cold sufferers engage in extended kissing of healthy volunteers. The result: No significant transmission. The mouth remains remarkably virus-free during colds. Most live virus is concentrated in the nose. So feel free to kiss cold sufferers—just don't rub noses with them.

Smoking has not been shown to increase susceptibility to colds, but smokers typically suffer longer and worse coughs at the end of their colds.

Before You Call the Doctor. Most people are fatalistic about colds. But the fact is, you *don't* have to catch that next one, and you *don't* have to feel miserable if you do. To prevent cold transmission:

• Humidify your air to keep the mucus layer lining your nose and throat intact. In one Canadian study, children whose schools had unusually low relative humidity suffered more cold-related absences than children whose classrooms had relative humidity in the "comfort zone" of around 50 percent. To humidify your air, install a humidifying appliance. Introduce leafy houseplants and mist them frequently. Or consider an aquarium or fountain. These precautions are extra important in buildings with forced-air heating, which dries the air.

• Limit your exposure to people with colds. Authorities say close encounters of up to an hour don't pose significant risk of infection by the aerosol route, but longer visits do.

• Don't touch things cold sufferers have touched. You don't want to pick up virus on your fingers. It's especially risky to shake hands, because cold sufferers' hands are highly likely to be contaminated with live virus.

• Wash your hands frequently. Hand-washing with soap and water removes any cold virus particles you pick up.

• Make a conscious effort not to touch your nose or eyes. If you can't help contaminating your fingers, this prevents self-inoculation.

• Wipe countertops, doorknobs, telephones, and other hard, nonporous objects with Lysol. In one experiment, washing countertops with Lysol reduced cold transmission 20 percent.

• When you have a cold, blow your nose into paper tissues—not cloth handkerchiefs. Most people throw paper tissues away after using them, so they don't contaminate their fingers with more virus. But cloth hankies get used again and again. Each time people touch cloth handkerchiefs, they recontaminate their fingers, increasing the likelihood of spreading their colds. Encourage those close to you to use paper tissues as well.

When you feel a cold coming on, remember, you've already been infected for at least twenty-four hours. But you may still be able to nip your cold in the bud with concerted self-care efforts:

• Remember grandmotherly advice. The more scientists learn about the common cold, the more they have come to appreciate folk medical wisdom—particularly the importance of drinking hot fluids. Heating the throat impairs viral replication. Hot liquids also have decongestant, throat-soothing, and cough-suppressive action. Among hot liquids, one famous study showed the best is none other than chicken soup ("Jewish penicillin"), a folk cold remedy since the twelfth century.

• Take at least 2,000 mg of vitamin C a day. Since 1970, when Nobel Prize–winner Linus Pauling, Ph.D., first recommended large doses of vitamin C to treat the common cold, he has been hailed as a visionary and dismissed as a buffoon. Opinion is so divided because vitamin C research results are so divided. Since World War II, more than two dozen studies have tested the vitamin as a cold treatment. About half have shown no effect. The other half have shown 30- to 50-percent decreases in symptom severity and duration. What gives? All the studies showing no effect used low doses (250 mg or so) for short periods of time (a day or two). All the studies showing significant benefit used high doses (2,000 mg and up) from the moment the first tickle appeared in the throat until symptoms completely cleared up. Conclusion: There's a threshold dose below which vitamin C has no effect. Above the threshold, vitamin C boosts the immune system's ability to fight the virus. Pauling recommends 20,000 mg/day, but studies show significant benefit at doses of 2,000 to 6,000 mg/day. Two notes of caution: High doses of vitamin C may cause diarrhea. If it develops, reduce your dose. And people with kidney problems should consult their physicians before taking vitamin C supplements.

• Try zinc gluconate lozenges. A few studies show that sucking on zinc lozenges can stop colds in the throat. Zinc apparently boosts the immune system's ability to fight cold viruses. But the lozenges must dissolve completely in the mouth, and zinc gluconate tastes disgusting—so bad, in fact, that many people would rather endure a cold for a week than gag on this mineral. But supplement manufacturers have risen to the occasion with several new brands of candied zinc lozenges, which mask the awful taste with plenty of sweetener and fruit flavor. Take 23 mg of zinc every two waking hours from the moment you feel the throat tickle until symptoms have disappeared. High doses of zinc can cause problems; if nausea develops stop taking it.

• Try echinacea (eh-kin-AY-sha). Echinacea is a medicinal herb native to the Great Plains. Studies have shown that it stimulates the immune system to fight viral infections with action similar to interferon, the body's own antiviral chemical. Echinacea teas, tablets, and tinctures are available at health food stores. Follow package directions.

• Give yourself a pep talk. Colds usually trigger the blues—depressed thoughts of miserable days, sleepless nights, and wasted weekends. But many studies show that negativity depresses the immune system, causing longer, more severe colds. Other studies agree that people who adopt an optimistic, combative, I-can-beat-this-cold attitude enjoy greater immune-system vigor and shorter, milder colds.

But if you can't nip your cold in the bud:

• Keep taking hot liquids, vitamin C, zinc, and echinacea. They can still help minimize the duration and severity of your cold.

• Use single-action over-the-counter drugs. At the first sign of a cold, most people reach for one of the heavily advertised, multi-symptom cold formulas. Shotgun cold formulas provide relief from cold symptoms, but cold authorities recommend against them for two reasons—unnecessary expense and overmedication. The commercials never tire of saying that multi-symptom cold preparations "treat every major cold symptom."

That's true, but cold symptoms occur serially, not all at once. Why pay for cough medicine if all you have is a sore throat? And why risk side effects from decongestants and antihistamines if you don't need them? (Antihistamines have only a placebo effect on cold symptoms, anyhow—see "runny nose" below.)

· To relieve a sore throat, drink hot liquids, suck on hard candies, or try medicated sore-throat lozenges, which contain mild throat-numbing anesthetics. Hot liquids also impair viral replication and help relieve nasal congestion and cough.

· To relieve nasal congestion, try hot showers or inhale steam from a pot of boiled water after you've removed it from the heat. Don't put your face into steam from actively boiling water or you might get scalded. Let the water cool off a bit, then inhale the vapors. Or use over-the-counter decongestant sprays (oxymetazoline) or pills (pseudoephedrine). Sprays should not be used for more than three days or you might develop "rebound congestion," even worse congestion than you had to begin with. Decongestant pills don't cause rebound congestion, but they are stimulating and might cause insomnia, restlessness, irritability, anxiety, and "speediness." Those with high blood pressure, diabetes, glaucoma, heart disease, or a history of stroke should not use decongestant pills.

· If you have a runny nose, use paper tissues. Many people reach for an antihistamine. But authorities now agree that antihistamines have only a placebo effect on cold symptoms. Antihistamines work fine for allergies. They suppress the release of histamine, which causes the itchy eyes, nasal congestion, and runny nose of hay fever. Colds trigger some histamine release, but the major causes of cold-related runny nose appear to be interferon and bradykinin, against which antihistamines have no effect. Antihistamines also cause drowsiness. Don't drive while taking them.

· If you have a cough, don't smoke. For help quitting, see RESOURCES at the end of this chapter. In addition, suck on hard candies or cough drops or take an over-the-counter cough syrup containing the safe, nonnarcotic cough suppressant dextromethorphan (see COUGH in this chapter).

· To relieve headache, fever, and/or achiness, adults may take aspirin, ibuprofen, or acetaminophen. But *never* give a child under eighteen years of age aspirin for any fever associated with the common cold (or flu or chickenpox) because it has been associated with Reye syndrome, a rare but potentially fatal condition affecting the brain and liver. Instead, give children acetaminophen.

· Forget antibiotics. Antibiotics kill bacteria, not cold viruses, so they're ineffective in treating the common cold. However, antibiotics may be prescribed if you develop a bacterial complication, for example, pneumonia.

• Hot toddies. Centuries before cold sufferers reached for bottles of cold formulas, they grabbed bottles of something else—hard liquor. A popular eighteenth-century prescription was to place a hat on a bedpost, then get into bed and drink whiskey. When two hats appeared, you were supposedly on your way to recovery. Alcohol itself does nothing to attack the cold virus, spur the immune system, or suppress cold symptoms. It does, however, promote rest, which helps the body focus its energy on fighting the cold. The traditional way to imbibe medicinal alcohol is in a hot toddy, a combination of tea, lemon, honey, and your choice of distilled spirits. Hot toddies provide some vitamin C (in the lemon) and help soothe and decongest the nasopharynx and raise its temperature, which helps impair viral replication. Never drive after drinking a hot toddy. And one is enough. Overindulgence in alcohol suppresses the immune system.

When to Call the Doctor. Physicians can't do any more for the common cold than repeat the self-care advice above. But consult a doctor if a post-cold cough lasts longer than two weeks.

▶ **RED FLAGS** Consult a physician immediately if any of the following situations arise:

• Any fever that develops toward the end of a cold. This might indicate pneumonia, especially in anyone with a bad cough, shortness of breath, difficulty breathing, and bloody, brownish, or greenish phlegm.

• Any fever plus sore throat and swollen glands under the jaw joint, which may indicate strep throat.

• Any fever plus sore throat, a bright red tongue, and a sandpapery rash, which might be scarlet fever.

• Fever with rash, stiff neck, severe headache, marked irritability, or confusion, which may indicate meningitis, infection of the fluid surrounding the brain and spinal cord.

• Great difficulty swallowing, breathing, or opening your mouth fully.

• Any sore throat that lasts longer than a week.

• Nasal congestion that lasts longer than three weeks or causes severe ear pain or sudden hearing loss.

• Nasal congestion with a severe headache and pain in the nose, cheeks, or upper teeth. This may be a sinus infection ("sinusitis").

• Any cough accompanied by a fever over 102°, or coughs that produce bloody, brown, or greenish mucus, chest pain, wheezing, or shortness of breath. Such coughs may indicate asthma, bronchitis, or pneumonia.

• Coughs that last longer than two weeks.

• Any diarrhea in an infant (more than five watery stools a day), or childhood diarrhea with stomach distress or bloody stools, or diarrhea that lasts longer than three days. These symptoms suggest a bacterial infection or another problem requiring professional treatment.

COPD

(See also BRONCHITIS (Chronic) and EMPHYSEMA in this chapter)
COPD is an acronym for "chronic obstructive pulmonary disease." It's a combination of chronic bronchitis and emphysema.

What's Going On?   People with COPD suffer *both* the narrowed airways, productive cough, and cilial paralysis of chronic bronchitis and the damaged alveoli of emphysema. Like the two conditions which comprise it, COPD's major cause is smoking, though chronic exposure to respiratory irritants—dusts, air pollutants, chemical vapors, etc.—may also play a role.

Before You Call the Doctor.   If you smoke, quit smoking. For help quitting, see RESOURCES at the end of this chapter. Depending on how much damage the lungs have suffered, quitting may reduce or eventually eliminate symptoms of chronic bronchitis. Quitting also stops the progression of emphysema but does not reverse the process. Alveolar damage is permanent, and emphysema symptoms remain. In addition, see the suggestions under BRONCHITIS (CHRONIC) and EMPHYSEMA in this chapter.

When to Call the Doctor.   Physicians can prescribe the kind of bronchodilators used to treat asthma (see ASTHMA in this chapter), but these provide only temporary relief. The key to treating COPD is to quit smoking.

Even if you quit smoking, COPD increases susceptibility to bronchitis and pneumonia. Your doctor should provide pneumococcus and influenza vaccinations and be available to treat acute infections.

If chronic bronchitis symptoms grow suddenly worse—increased cough, shortness of breath, or increased production of unusually dark phlegm—doctors prescribe antibiotics and sometimes extra bronchodilators.

COUGH

(See also ASTHMA, BRONCHIOLITIS, BRONCHITIS (ACUTE and CHRONIC), COMMON COLD, COPD, CROUP, EMPHYSEMA, and FLU in this chapter, SICK BUILDING SYNDROME in Chapter 4, and POSTNASAL DRIP in Chapter 10)

A cough can be a symptom of an enormous number of illnesses, from the common cold to lung cancer. It can be dry and hacking, or it can be "productive," meaning it brings up phlegm, which doctors call "sputum."

What's Going On?   Coughs are always annoying, but they aren't necessarily bad. Coughing is the respiratory tract's reflex response to irritation. You cough if some food or drink goes down the wrong tube or if you inhale smoke, dusts, chemical vapors, or other irritants. Coughing also clears phlegm.

However, a cough can also be a sign of trouble. The lungs have only two ways to signal that something is wrong with them—coughing and shortness of breath. Everyone gets short of breath after strenuous exercise, but if everyday activities leave you winded, it's time to see a doctor. And if a cough persists beyond two weeks—especially if you have a fever, wheezing, chest pain, or yellow, green, brown, or red sputum—consult a physician.

Coughing has dozens of causes, but smoking tops the list. Smoking increases bronchial mucus production, so you have more phlegm that needs to be cleared. It also paralyzes the microscopic hairs in the respiratory tract ("cilia"), which move sputum up and out of the respiratory tract. Passive smoking, that is, exposure to other people's cigarettes and exhaled smoke, can also cause coughing, especially if you have a tendency toward asthma.

Irritants can cause coughing. People with allergies, chronic sinus infections ("sinusitis"), or occupational exposure to dusts, paints, chemical vapors and other inhalable particles often produce extra mucus, some of which trickles down the throat and irritates the respiratory tract enough to cause coughing (see POSTNASAL DRIP in Chapter 10).

If a cough is productive, the color of the sputum provides important clues to its cause. Clear, thin, watery sputum is usually associated with allergies, upper respiratory infection, asthma, or irritants like cigarette smoke. Thicker yellow or greenish sputum often indicates bronchitis, sinus infection, or pneumonia. And brown or reddish sputum usually contains blood and suggests either severe irritation, pneumonia, tuberculosis, or even lung cancer.

Before You Call the Doctor.   Try to figure out what's causing your cough. Sometimes the cause is obvious, as in coughs associated with colds, flu, or smoke from a burning building. But if the cause is not self-evident, ask yourself:

•Do you smoke? If so, see BRONCHITIS (CHRONIC) in this chapter. Quit smoking. For help quitting, see RESOURCES at the end of this chapter.

• Have there been any changes recently in your work or home environment? If you've recently moved to a new community or acquired a furry pet, see ASTHMA in this chapter and ALLERGIES in Chapter 4. If you've recently been exposed to new furniture, drapes, carpeting, paint, floor finishes, chemicals, or air conditioning in your home, office, or car, see SICK BUILDING SYNDROME in Chapter 4.

•Do you have heartburn? Untreated heartburn, caused by stomach acids washing up the esophagus, can cause chronic cough when small amounts of acid are inhaled and cause lung irritation (see HEARTBURN in Chapter 13).

• If you have a family history of asthma or allergies, see the ASTHMA section of this chapter or the ALLERGY discussion in Chapter 4. Children with mild asthma may cough, especially at night, without audible wheezing or shortness of breath.

• If anyone in your home smokes, your cough may be the result of passive smoking. Encourage everyone you know to quit smoking—or at least not do it around you.

• Miminize your exposure to lung irritants. If your work or hobbies expose you to dusts, smoke, or chemical vapors, make sure your workspace is well ventilated. If necessary, wear a respirator.

• Make sure all gas appliances are properly vented, and if you cook with gas, make sure all flames are blue. Any orange flame means your range or oven is polluting the air with carbon monoxide. If necessary, call your gas company for an adjustment.

• Exercise carefully outdoors. Air pollution is lowest during mornings and evenings. Try not to exercise near congested streets where auto and truck exhaust can reach hazardous levels. Ozone smog tends to be worst during the May-to-September "smog season." Take smog alerts seriously. If you live in a high-pollution area, consider an indoor exercise program.

• Consider an air filter. A good air filter or air conditioner can help if you have allergies or asthma.

• Consider your asbestos risk. Asbestos, a fibrous mineral used in an enormous number of materials and industries, can cause severe lung disease and contribute to lung cancer. Many schools, homes, and worksites are contaminated. Call your local American Lung Association office for information and a referral to an asbestos inspector in your area (see RESOURCES at the end of this chapter.)

•Consider your radon risk. Depending where you live, radon gas from deep within the earth may be accumulating in your basement. Radon increases lung cancer risk. It's not clear exactly how much lung cancer radon causes. Estimates range from 5,000 to 30,000 of the 155,000 new diagnoses each year. Find out if you live in a high-radon area, and if so, make sure your home—particularly your basement—is well ventilated.

Here's how to treat a dry cough:

•Drink hot liquids. Any will do, but a traditional cough remedy consists of hot water, lemon, and honey.

•Suck on hard candies.

•Suck on cough drops. Many contain menthol or eucalyptus oil, which are mild anesthetics. They cool and numb the throat, counteracting the irritation that often causes dry coughs.

•Elevate your head at night. Use extra pillows, or place bricks under the head side of your bed.

•Increase the moisture content of the air with a humidifier or vaporizer, or take hot steamy showers.

•For dry coughs, take dextromethorphan, the nonnarcotic, cough-suppressing ingredient in dozens of over-the-counter cough remedies. Dextromethorphan often means the difference between a restful and sleepless night.

•Don't suppress a productive cough. Productive coughs have a purpose: to expel phlegm from the respiratory tract. Trapped phlegm increases the risk of bronchitis and pneumonia. If you have trouble coughing up phlegm, don't take any over-the-counter product with dextromethorphan. Instead, take an expectorant cough medicine with guaifenesin, and drink plenty of nonalcoholic fluids.

Coughing may place considerable strain on the ribcage and back. It's not unusual for people to strain a chest muscle or throw their backs out during intense coughing episodes (see BACK PAIN (LOWER and UPPER) and RIB INJURY in Chapter 15).

When to Call the Doctor. Consult a physician if strenuous exercise causes coughing. This may be exercise-induced asthma. Consult a doctor for any cough that lasts longer than two weeks. It may indicate a serious disease, possibly tuberculosis, emphysema, or lung cancer.

For a short-term cough, physicians can prescribe codeine, a narcotic cough suppressant which is more powerful than dextromethorphan.

If you take the type of heart or blood pressure medicine called an ACE inhibitor (captopril, enalapril, lisinopril), substituting another medication might improve your cough. Discuss this possibility with your physician.

▶ **RED FLAG**   Call your doctor immediately if you have a cough plus fever with chest pain, wheezing, shortness of breath, or any other unusual symptoms. This might be pneumonia or a blood clot in the lung.

CROUP

Croup is a childhood respiratory problem which usually occurs late at night and causes a combination of shrill wheezing on inhalation ("stridor") and a harsh barking ("croupy") cough.

What's Going On?   Croup is frightening for both children and parents, but it's rarely serious and almost always responds rapidly to self-care. The symptoms are caused by a sudden spasm or swelling in the windpipe ("trachea") or voice box ("larynx"), usually as a result of a cold or flu. The child typically awakens in the middle of the night with breathing that sounds like crowing on inhalation and barking on exhalation. These terms might not describe exactly how croup sounds in *your* child, but the wheezing and cough are distinctive, and parents immediately realize the situation is unusual. The child becomes anxious, and the parents often panic, thinking the child can't breathe.

Before You Call the Doctor.   Croup sends many parents rushing to the nearest emergency room—almost always unnecessarily. Here's what to do:

• Try not to panic. Parental anxiety increases the child's anxiety, which aggravates croup symptoms. Panic also clouds your judgment.

• Soothe the child's throat with hot vapor mist. Take the child into the bathroom, turn on all the hot water taps full blast, and hold, comfort, and reassure the child as he or she breathes the warm, misty air. Some physicians and home medical guides suggest exposing the child to steam from a tea kettle, but this is not a good idea. Steam can scald parents and children. Sitting in a steamy bathroom is quicker, easier, and safer.

• If warm mist doesn't provide significant relief within about a half-hour, open a window and allow the child to breath cool air while continuing to provide parental reassurance.

• Be prepared for croup to improve in the daytime and return at night for up to several days. Use the steam and/or cold air treatment along with plenty of reassurance whenever breathing and coughing become croupy.

When to Call the Doctor. Consult a physician if symptoms do not clear up within a few hours. Most physicians simply reassure the parents, observe the child, and encourage the parents to continue holding and comforting the child.

Occasionally, croup symptoms are caused by an inflammation of the valve that separates the trachea and the food tube to the stomach ("esophagus"). This valve is the "epiglottis," and the inflammation is "epiglottitis." Epiglottitis is a different, more serious infection which can cause sudden airway obstruction. Children with epiglottitis appear very sick and typically have fevers over 102°. They often do not want to lie down or even swallow saliva. Physicians treat the condition with antibiotics.

But even when children are hospitalized for severe croup, antibiotics are not routinely prescribed. Instead, the child is placed in a mist tent, and parents are encouraged to remain at the bedside as much as possible to provide comfort and reassurance.

▶ **RED FLAGS** Consult a physician immediately or call 911 if:
•Fever rises above 102°.
•The child seems exhausted or has blue lips.
•The child is not swallowing saliva.

EMPHYSEMA

(See also COPD in this chapter)
Emphysema is slow suffocation. The lungs become less efficient. The person becomes short of breath, wheezes, coughs, and develops a characteristic barrel-shaped chest.

What's Going On? In emphysema, the tiny air sacs in the lungs ("alveoli") become damaged and lose their ability to transfer oxygen into the blood and carbon dioxide out of it. Healthy alveoli are tiny, numerous, spongy, and elastic. Emphysemic alveoli are larger, less numerous, and comparatively stiff.

Emphysema results from chronic respiratory irritation, almost always because of smoking, though dusts, air pollutants, chemical vapors, other occupational irritants, and certain hereditary conditions may also play a role. The main symptom is shortness of breath, which becomes worse as the condition progresses. As the person struggles to breathe, the chest becomes barrel-shaped. In advanced emphysema, the person may require supplemental oxygen and be unable to tolerate even minor physical activity. Emphysema can be fatal.

Before You Call the Doctor. Quit smoking. For help quitting, see RESOURCES at the end of this chapter. Quitting stops the progression of emphysema but does not reverse the process. Alveolar damage is permanent, and emphysema symptoms remain. In addition, see the suggestions under BRONCHITIS (CHRONIC) in this chapter.

People with emphysema typically become exhausted performing activities of daily living which require only minimal effort. In order to live as normally as possible despite this chronic condition, adopt "pursed-lip" breathing:

•Take a breath before any exertion.

•Do the actual work while exhaling.

•Use pursed-lip breathing. Keep your lips shut tight except for a tiny opening at the center. Inhale in through your nose. Exhale slowly, with steady pressure, through your nose and the small opening in your lips for twice as long as you inhale.

•Stop and rest whenever you feel short of breath.

•Use supplemental oxygen whenever necessary.

Here are other suggestions for adjusting to life with emphysema:

•Plan ahead. Figure out the most efficient, least strenuous ways to do what you need to accomplish.

•Prioritize. You can't accomplish as much as you used to. Decide what must get done, then delay or let go of the rest.

•Pace yourself. Maintain a slow, steady level of exertion instead of bursts of activity.

•Schedule rest periods frequently during the day.

•When bathing, use an exhaust fan or leave the door open to decrease bathroom humidity. Run your oxygen tubing over the shower rod to keep it out of your way. Instead of exerting yourself to get dry, simply slip on a thick terry cloth robe and let it dry you.

•While dressing, shaving, or applying makeup, sit on a stool.

•Wear jogging suits whenever possible. They're easy to get on and off. Use suspenders instead of a belt. Wear open-neck shirts.

•If you're overweight, make every effort to lose weight. It takes a great deal of effort to carry extra weight. Eat the low-fat, high-fiber, nutrient-rich diet described in Chapter 1, but steam or blanche vegetables to soften them for easier chewing. Rearrange your kitchen for maximum efficiency. Eat slowly. If you wear dentures, make sure they fit properly in order to minimize the effort it takes to chew. Use an exhaust fan, a portable fan, or open windows to keep the kitchen from becoming too warm.

•For lovemaking, learn to savor non-intercourse caresses: talking, holding, kissing, cuddling. Plan to make love at your most energetic time of day. Don't attempt sex when you're tired or after a big meal. Use medication to open your airways ("bronchodilators") and oxygen. Increase the time you spend in foreplay. Encourage your partner to be more active. If you become short of breath, take a break, but keep kissing, caressing, and cuddling. Rest before and after intercourse with relaxing music.

• For daily tasks, use a small utility cart for doing chores. Break tasks into parts. Do one part, rest, then do another. Do as much as possible while seated. Consider a microwave oven, remote-controlled TV, a cordless phone, electric automobile windows and doorlocks, ramps instead of stairs, and home lifts, small elevator chairs that eliminate the need to climb stairs.

• For other suggestions, consult the American Lung Association (see RESOURCES at the end of this chapter).

When to Call the Doctor.   Physicians can prescribe the kind of bronchodilators used to treat asthma (see ASTHMA in this chapter), but these provide only temporary relief. The key to treating emphysema is to quit smoking.

Even if you quit smoking, emphysema increases susceptibility to bronchitis and pneumonia. Your doctor should provide pneumococcus and influenza vaccinations and be available to treat acute infections.

FLU

(See also COMMON COLD and COUGH in this chapter)

One minute you feel fine, then the next it's like a truck ran over you. You've suddenly got a high fever, and all you can do is drag yourself to bed. Your muscles begin to ache, especially your back and the backs of your legs. Then, a day or two later, the fever breaks, and you experience more cold-like symptoms—cough, congestion, headache, and runny nose. But you still have no energy, and you may have to stay in bed for several days. And even after you're up and around again, you might feel tired and lethargic for another week or two.

What's Going On?   Most people call any bad cold "the flu." Like the common cold, influenza is an upper respiratory infection, but that's where the similarity ends. Flu, medically known as "influenza," is a much more severe illness. In fact, in the elderly or those weakened by chronic diseases, flu and the pneumonia it often causes can be fatal. Flu-related pneumonia is the nation's leading cause of death from an infectious disease, accounting for about 50,000 fatalities every winter, and in some years many more.

Flu is caused by three viruses, designated A, B, and C. Type A flu (also known as influenza A) causes the worst symptoms and the most deaths. Type B flu can cause symptoms as severe as Type A, but it's usually not as bad. Type C flu is hardly even an illness. When public health officials say "flu," they mean Type A and B.

Type A flu is much worse than your worst cold. Few adults get fevers and muscle aches ("myalgia") from colds, and most can still function and go to work even when they have bad colds. Not so when you develop influenza A. Suddenly you've got a high fever. And your body really aches badly. In addition, you develop cold-like symptoms, but you know from the start that what you've got is not a cold.

Flu spreads much faster than the common cold. A person with the virus exhales, coughs, or sneezes it into the air, and other people inhale it and become infected. Many colds spread the same way, but not as quickly. If a person with a bad cold spends a few hours in a crowded room, several people might catch the cold. But if a person with influenza A spends the same amount of time in the same room, chances are most will develop flu. One famous study of flu transmission involved a commercial jetliner carrying fifty-four passengers. One passenger boarded the five-hour flight infected with Type A flu, and within three days, 72 percent of the other passengers came down with the disease. Another involved a Navy ship where one infected crew member transmitted flu to most of his shipmates.

Flu viruses change constantly. Scientists at the federal Centers for Disease Control carefully track flu outbreaks around the world and analyze which viral strains cause them. Then they direct vaccine manufacturers to produce vaccines against the Type A and B flu strains they consider most likely to strike the U.S. each winter during the annual "flu season" from around Thanksgiving through about Easter.

Flu is not only a serious, often fatal illness, it's also an American medical tragedy because the tens of thousands of deaths it causes every year can be *prevented* with the annual flu vaccine. Unfortunately, less than half of those who should be vaccinated get immunized, and physicians are often remiss about encouraging flu shots.

Before You Call the Doctor. Anyone can get flu vaccine, but the estimated thirty million Americans at high risk for developing flu-related pneumonia *definitely should:*

• Everyone sixty-five years of age or older.

• Everyone—including children—with heart disease, diabetes, kidney disease, asthma, or any chronic lung diseases, for example, emphysema or cystic fibrosis.

• Everyone living in a nursing home.

In addition, flu authorities now urge vaccination for many people outside the traditional risk groups:

• Health care personnel. Flu-infected health workers can spread the disease to large numbers of people, many of whom already have other serious health problems that put them at risk for the potentially fatal pneumonia.

• Everyone in regular contact with people in any risk group. If your parents are over age sixty-five and you see them during flu season, you could give them the flu if you and they are not immunized. If you're a teacher, chances are there are asthmatic children in your school. You could infect them if you and they are not immunized.

• Everyone living in close institutional quarters. Flu can sweep through college dormitories, boarding schools, and military bases like wildfire.

Flu vaccine is good, but it's not perfect. It provides healthy young people with about 90 percent protection, but the figure is closer to 70 percent for the elderly, whose immune systems don't work as well. If you get the flu after you've had a flu shot, it's usually a mild case.

Flu shot side effects, if any, are usually mild—some people feel a little achy, and children sometimes develop a brief low-grade fever.

It takes about two weeks after vaccination to develop effective immunity. Authorities recommend getting immunized in late October or early November.

Adults receive a vaccine made from deactivated whole flu virus. Children under twelve years of age get a vaccine made from only part of the virus ("split-virus"), which causes fewer side effects in young people.

Pregnant women can get flu shots, but only after their first trimester. If you're pregnant, discuss flu vaccination with your physician.

The only people who should not receive flu shots are those with serious allergies to eggs, which are used to manufacture the vaccine.

If you catch the flu, treat its symptoms like the common cold (see COMMON COLD and COUGH in this chapter), with the following additions:

• Headaches, body aches, fever. Colds don't usually cause fever in adults, but flu does. Half-hour sponge baths with water at room temperature can help reduce fever and the discomfort it causes. Nonpregnant adults may also take aspirin, acetaminophen, or ibuprofen according to package directions. Aspirin and ibuprofen may cause stomach upset. Pregnant women and those with a history of ulcers should not take aspirin or ibuprofen unless a doctor recommends it. Children under eighteen years of age should *never* be given aspirin for flu (or colds or chickenpox) because it is associated with Reye syndrome, a rare but potentially fatal condition that affects the brain and liver. Children should *only* be given acetaminophen.

Fever increases perspiration and may cause serious loss of body fluids ("dehydration"). That's why it's so important for flu sufferers to increase their nonalcoholic fluid intake. Serious dehydration causes thirst, decreased urination, darkening of any urine produced, and lightheadedness.

• Diarrhea. This flu symptom is rare in adults but may occur in children. The major risk is dehydration, so make sure the child drinks plenty of liquids—water, half-strength apple juice, chicken broth (bouillon), ginger ale, etc. Infants should drink specially formulated rehydration solutions (Lytren, Pedialyte) available over-the-counter at pharmacies. To treat diarrhea at home, use the BRAT diet, an acronym for bananas, rice, applesauce, and toast—all binding foods. Kaopectate, available over-the-counter, may help add bulk to watery stools and ease discomfort.

• Be patient. Influenza is considerably more severe than a bad cold. It can last two weeks, and post-flu fatigue and cough can linger for another week and possibly longer.

When to Call the Doctor.   If you neglect to get a flu shot, then learn through the media of a Type A flu outbreak in your community, you might still be able to prevent it by taking the prescription antiviral drug amantadine (Symmetrel), which prevents Type A flu (but not Type B flu or the common cold). Anyone can request amantadine, but it's used preventively mostly in nursing homes and respiratory disease wards of hospitals among people who are at high risk for flu-related pneumonia. The dose is one 100 mg pill a day for up to three months during flu season.

Amantadine also treats Type A flu. It doesn't instantly cure it, but it usually helps a good deal. Instead of a week to ten days of feeling really miserable, you're sick for only three or four days.

For flu treatment, those ten to sixty-five years of age should take 100 mg of amantadine twice a day for up to a week. Those over age sixty-five should take the same dose, but only once a day. Consult your pediatrician about dosages for children under ten years of age.

Amantadine typically causes side effects in up to 10 percent of those who use it: insomnia, irritability, anxiety, lightheadedness, or difficulty concentrating. Side effects are most likely in the elderly.

▶ **RED FLAGS**   Consult a physician if any of the following situations arise:

• Any fever if you're pregnant.

• A fever higher than 103° in an adult, or 102° if over age sixty, or 100° in children younger than three months.

• Any fever over 100° that lasts longer than five days.

• Any fever plus sore throat and swollen glands under the jaw joint, which may indicate strep throat.

• Any fever plus sore throat, a bright red tongue, and a sandpapery rash, which might be scarlet fever.

• Fever accompanied by rash, stiff neck, severe headache, marked irritability, or confusion, which may indicate meningitis, infection of the fluid surrounding the brain and spinal cord.

• Great difficulty swallowing, breathing, or opening your mouth fully.

• Any sore throat that lasts longer than a week.

• Nasal congestion that lasts longer than three weeks or causes severe ear pain or sudden hearing loss.

• Nasal congestion with a severe headache and pain in the nose, cheeks, or upper teeth. This may be a sinus infection ("sinusitis").

• Any cough with a fever over 102°, or coughs that produce bloody, brown, or greenish mucus, chest pain, wheezing, or shortness of breath. Such coughs may indicate asthma, bronchitis, or pneumonia.

• Any cough that lasts longer than two weeks.

• Any diarrhea in an infant (more than five watery stools a day), or childhood diarrhea with stomach distress or bloody stools, or diarrhea that lasts longer than three days. These symptoms suggest a bacterial infection or another problem requiring professional treatment.

FORMALDEHYDE POISONING

(See SICK BUILDING SYNDROME in Chapter 4)

HAYFEVER

(See ALLERGIES in Chapter 4 and RUNNY NOSE in Chapter 10)

HICCUPS

Hiccups are jerky ("spasmodic") inhalations. Most cases are brief, but hiccups can become chronic and last years, even decades.

What's Going On?   Hiccups occur when the flap of tissue that serves as the gateway to the lungs ("glottis") closes suddenly and unexpectedly at the same time as the abdominal muscle that controls breathing ("diaphragm") contracts. The glottis' spasmodic closure stops the column of air being drawn into the lungs and produces the characteristic hiccup sound.

Scientists aren't sure what causes hiccups. Most folk remedies either distract people from the problem or stimulate the nerves in the back of the throat.

Before You Call the Doctor.   The world abounds with folk hiccup remedies. Here are several:
- Ignore them. Most hiccup attacks last only a few minutes.
- Hold your breath.
- Swallow a teaspoon of granulated sugar, breadcrumbs, or crushed ice.
- Bend over and drink water from the far side of a glass.
- Suck on a lemon wedge.
- Breathe repeatedly into a paper bag.
- Gargle water.
- Pull on your tongue to induce a gag reaction.
- Tickle the roof of your mouth with a cotton swab.
- Using a teaspoon, lift the little punching-bag flap of tissue that hangs down in the back of the throat ("uvula").
- Pull your knees up to your chest and lean forward.

When to Call the Doctor.   Consult a physician for hiccups that last longer than twenty-four hours, especially if they interfere with sleep. Chronic hiccups usually require a neurological workup.

INFLUENZA

(See FLU in this chapter)

PAINFUL BREATHING

Pain on inhalation or exhalation may be mild or severe and indicate problems ranging from minor to life-threatening.

What's Going On?   Painful breathing has a large number of possible causes.

Before You Call the Doctor. Read the following sections:
• ASTHMA, BRONCHITIS (ACUTE and CHRONIC), COPD, COUGH, CROUP, and EMPHYSEMA in this chapter.
• CHEST PAIN in Chapter 12.
• HEARTBURN in Chapter 13.
• MUSCLE STRAINS and RIB INJURY in Chapter 15.

When to Call the Doctor. Other possible causes of painful breathing include a blood clot in the lungs ("pulmonary embolism"); an inflammation of the membrane surrounding the lungs ("pleurisy" or "pleuritis"), collapsed lung ("pneumothorax"), and other potentially serious problems. When in doubt consult a physician.

▶ **RED FLAGS** Consult a physician immediately for painful breathing accompanied by fever, shortness of breath, difficulty breathing, or brown, bloody, or greenish phlegm. These symptoms might indicate pneumonia or another potentially serious respiratory disease.

SHORTNESS OF BREATH

(See ASTHMA, BRONCHITIS (CHRONIC), COPD, EMPHYSEMA, and PAINFUL BREATHING in this chapter, and ANGINA, the discussion of hyperventilation in CHEST PAIN, CONGESTIVE HEART FAILURE, and HEART ATTACK in Chapter 12)

SINUS INFECTION

(See also COMMON COLD and COUGH in this chapter, ALLERGIES in Chapter 4, and POSTNASAL DRIP in Chapter 10)
Sinus infection, medically known as "sinusitis," causes nasal congestion, fullness and pressure throughout the sinus area, headache, runny nose, pain on one side or both sides of the face, and possibly, sore throat, cough, and laryngitis.

What's Going On? Which body structure causes the largest number of people the most pain and discomfort? Most people would say the lower back, but many authorities insist that the eight nasal sinuses, air pockets in the bones around the nose, cheeks, and eyes, cause more misery. According to the National Center for Health Statistics, more than thirty-two million Americans suffer chronic sinus problems. Many cases are caused by hayfever (see ALLERGIES in Chapter 4), but millions of Americans who do not have allergies suffer chronic sinusitis.

The sinuses give the voice resonance and decrease the weight of the skull, making it easier to hold up. They are lined with glands that produce moist mucus—about a quart a day—which moistens, warms, and humidifies the air we inhale. This warming, moistening action helps prevent humanity's most prevalent illness, the common cold (see COMMON COLD in this chapter).

In sinusitis, something disrupts normal sinus drainage. Trouble often develops when allergies, asthma, colds, chronic bronchitis, flu, sick building syndrome, an irritant, or a structural abnormality in the nose or bones of the face causes the sinuses' drainage openings to swell or become obstructed. Fluid accumulates and microorganisms infect it. Bacteria account for about 80 percent of cases, viruses for about 20 percent, and occasionally, fungi may also cause this problem. In the classic case, a cold leads to bacterial sinusitis.

Those who suffer chronic sinusitis often find the problem associated with sudden changes in barometric pressure, for example, flying, swimming, downhill skiing, or scuba diving.

Before You Call the Doctor.   The best way to steer clear of sinusitis is to prevent the conditions that typically precede it: allergies, colds, flu, and sick building syndrome (see ALLERGIES and SICK BUILDING SYNDROME in Chapter 4 and COMMON COLD and FLU in this chapter).

If allergies, colds, flu, or sick building syndrome strike despite your best preventive efforts, treat them aggressively.

If the facial pain and greenish nasal discharge of sinus infection develop:

• Keep using decongestants but stop taking antihistamines, which dry sinus mucus and interfere with its drainage.

• Drink plenty of nonalcoholic fluids.

• Hot water vapor helps moisten dry nasal mucus and promotes drainage. Try a vaporizer, or breathe steam from an open pan of boiled water after it's been removed from the heat.

• Try salt-water nose drops (NaSal, Salinex), or mix your own: ¼ teaspoon of salt in 8 ounces of water. Lie down, apply a few drops at the nasal opening, and sniff gently.

• Try an expectorant cough medicine containing guaifenesin.

When To Call the Doctor.   Consult a physician if sinus infections do not respond to self-care within a few days, or if they are accompanied by a fever of over 100°. Physicians treat sinusitis with antibiotics. Ask for at least a two-week supply. The latest evidence suggests that inadequate treatment of sinusitis contributes to the risk of chronic sinusitis.

For chronic sinusitis caused by anatomical abnormalities, surgery may be recommended.

UPPER RESPIRATORY INFECTION

(See COMMON COLD and FLU in this chapter)

WHEEZING

(See ASTHMA, BRONCHIOLITIS, BRONCHITIS (CHRONIC), COPD, CROUP, and EMPHYSEMA in this chapter and CONGESTIVE HEART FAILURE in Chapter 12)

Wheezing may also be caused by inhalation of a foreign body. This requires professional medical treatment.

RESOURCES

American Lung Association. 1740 Broadway, New York, NY 10019; (212) 315-8700. An excellent source of stop-smoking information and classes. Also provides information about respiratory diseases and referrals to local affiliates.

Asthma and Allergy Foundation of America. 1717 Massachusetts Ave., N.W., Suite 305, Washington, D.C., 20036; (202) 265-0265. Provides information and education programs about asthma and allergies.

The No-Nag, No-Guilt, Do-It-Your-Own-Way Guide to Quitting Smoking by Tom Ferguson, M.D. (New York: Ballantine, 1989, $4.95) This is the best self-help book for aspiring ex-smokers.

CHAPTER 12

The Cardiovascular System: The Heart and Blood Vessels

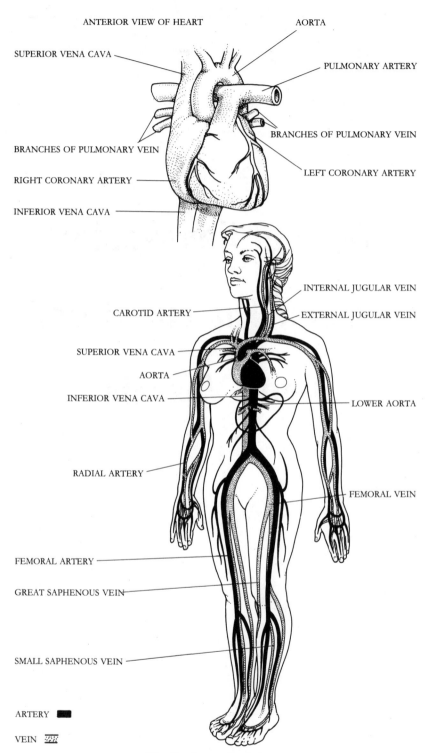

ANTERIOR VIEW OF HEART

AORTA

SUPERIOR VENA CAVA

PULMONARY ARTERY

BRANCHES OF PULMONARY VEIN

BRANCHES OF PULMONARY VEIN

LEFT CORONARY ARTERY

RIGHT CORONARY ARTERY

INFERIOR VENA CAVA

INTERNAL JUGULAR VEIN

CAROTID ARTERY

EXTERNAL JUGULAR VEIN

SUPERIOR VENA CAVA

AORTA

INFERIOR VENA CAVA

LOWER AORTA

RADIAL ARTERY

FEMORAL VEIN

FEMORAL ARTERY

GREAT SAPHENOUS VEIN

SMALL SAPHENOUS VEIN

ARTERY

VEIN

The Cardiovascular System.

ANGINA

Angina, medically known as "angina pectoris," causes recurrent chest pain or discomfort, which typically becomes more severe during physical activity.

What's Going On?   Angina is caused by a narrowing of the arteries that supply blood to the heart. The pain is a sign that the heart is being undernourished. Angina symptoms usually become more severe during exercise and subside during rest. However, some types of angina ("variant," "mixed," and "unstable") can cause severe pain when the person is at rest or even asleep.

Angina pain can be aggravated by emotional stress, a full stomach, and exposure to cold. The pain may spread to the jaw or left arm. Angina is a potentially life-threatening condition which requires professional care. But self-care plays a key role in controlling it.

Before You Call the Doctor.   Review Chapter 1. To summarize it briefly:

• If you smoke, quit. Smoking forces the heart to work harder. Recent studies suggest that smoking often triggers angina attacks. For help quitting, see RESOURCES at the end of Chapter 11.

• If you're overweight, lose those extra pounds. But don't get sucked in by the latest fad diet. Fad diets and crash diets don't work. Lose weight gradually by switching to a low-fat, low-cholesterol, high-fiber diet. Heart-healthy foods can be quite delicious and filling. We recommend *Eater's Choice: A Food Lover's Guide to Lower Cholesterol* by Ron Goor, M.D., and Nancy Goor as an excellent introduction to the wonderful world of tasty, heart-healthy foods (see RESOURCES at the end of this chapter).

• Exercise regularly. But don't simply jump into a fitness program. If you have chest pain, have a physical exam and discuss sensible exercise with your physician. Almost anyone can take walks or swim. You may have to work up to other fitness activities while your physician monitors your cardiovascular condition.

• Manage your stress load. Complete the StressMap™ questionnaire to see where your strengths and problems lie (see RESOURCES at the end of Chapter 1). Then incorporate stress-reducing activities you enjoy into your life, among them: yoga, meditation, exercise, gardening, a hobby, prayer, talking with friends, volunteer work, and/or playing with a pet.

• Control your blood pressure. All the strategies above help. In addition, a low-salt diet may help. So might increasing your potassium and calcium intake. Bananas and potatoes are high in potassium. Low-fat dairy products, for example, yogurt and skim milk, are high in calcium. Supplements are also available. Do not exceed package dose recommendations. Anyone taking these supplements should have normal kidney function.

• Don't drink alcohol to excess. Don't have more than two drinks a day. "Two drinks" means two one-ounce shots of liquor, two four-ounce servings of wine, or two standard bottles or cans of beer.

• Eat small meals. Try having four or five light meals instead of three big ones.

• Rest for thirty to forty-five minutes after eating.

• Avoid extremely cold and windy weather.

• Don't wait until you "really need" your angina medication to take it. Take medications prescribed "as needed," such as nitroglycerin, as soon as symptoms strike. You may even want to take your as-needed medication *before* a strenuous activity. The earlier in an attack you take your angina medication, the more effective it is likely to be.

For more information, contact the American Heart Association (see RESOURCES at the end of this chapter).

When to Call the Doctor.   Anyone with angina should establish a relationship with a physician and schedule regular visits.

If you have trouble quitting smoking on your own, your doctor can refer you to stop-smoking programs in your area and/or prescribe a nicotine substitute (chewing gum or patch) that helps smokers wean themselves from the addictive drug in cigarettes.

Some people with angina require medications, including:

• Aspirin.

• Nitrates: isosorbide dinitrate, nitroglycerin, or others.

• Beta blockers: propranolol, atenolol, or others.

• Calcium-channel blockers: verapamil, diltiazem, nifedipine, or others. Surgical approaches include coronary artery bypass surgery or angioplasty, inflating a balloon inside the narrowed coronary arteries to expand them.

CHEST PAIN

(See also ANGINA and HEART ATTACK in this chapter, HEART ATTACK in Chapter 3, ANXIETY in Chapter 5, COUGH in Chapter 11, HEARTBURN in Chapter 13, and MUSCLE STRAINS and RIB INJURY in Chapter 15)

Chest pain varies from a feeling of mild pressure or squeezing to stabbing, crushing, knock-you-off-your-feet agony. It may occur intermittently or strike and not stop.

What's Going On? Chest pain should never be ignored. It may signal a heart attack (see HEART ATTACK in this chapter and Chapter 3) or angina, another form of heart disease (see ANGINA in this chapter).

But, in many cases, chest pain has nothing to do with the heart. It is often caused by heartburn or indigestion (see HEARTBURN in Chapter 13) and may also be caused by infections, chronic cough (see COUGH in Chapter 11), anxiety or stress (see ANXIETY in Chapter 5), or muscle and/or rib injuries (see MUSCLE STRAINS and RIB INJURY in Chapter 15).

Chest pain may also be caused by a musculoskeletal problem: a rib injury, muscle strain, or the arthritis-like condition which may develop when a rib attaches to the breastbone ("costochondritis"). Musculoskeletal pain is typically well localized. You can point to the spot, and it hurts when you either press on it or move around. Angina, heartburn, anxiety, and some heat attacks cause more diffuse pain, a pain that doesn't become worse when you press on the chest.

A frequent cause of chest pain not discussed elsewhere in this book is rapid breathing ("hyperventilation"). Also known as overbreathing, this practice, associated with anxiety, removes carbon dioxide too rapidly from the blood and alters the delicate balance of blood gasses. In addition to causing squeezing chest pain, hyperventilation may cause faintness, numbness, headaches, visual disturbances, and tingling sensations in the hands and lips. Paradoxically, it also causes a feeling of breathlessness.

Before You Call the Doctor. Breathe into a lunch-size paper bag so that some exhaled carbon dioxide can be reinhaled and reabsorbed into your bloodstream.

Consciously try to slow your breathing to one normal (not deep) breath every four or five seconds. Also see the suggestions in the ANXIETY section of Chapter 5.

When to Call the Doctor. If the self-care suggestions here and in Chapter 5 do not relieve your chest pain in ten minutes, consult a physician. The problem might be angina, a chest-area injury, or another problem.

▶ **RED FLAGS** Chest pain is a potentially life-threatening danger sign. If the problem appears to be caused by anything other than coughing, heartburn, hyperventilation, or a muscle or rib injury, consult a physician immediately. In addition to angina and heart attack, several other problems might cause chest pain, including pneumonia, inflammation of the lung lining ("pleurisy"), or lung cancer. When in doubt, consult a doctor without delay.

CONGESTIVE HEART FAILURE

Heart failure is a serious medical problem, but the word "failure" makes this condition sound more frightening than it often is. A better term would be heart *fatigue*. Congestive heart failure causes shortness of breath, rapid heartbeat, and fluid retention ("edema").

What's Going On?   The heart beats about three *billion* times during the average lifetime. Normally, the heart responds to the increased energy demands of exercise by pumping faster, and afterward, its pumping action returns to normal. But if extra energy demands become the rule, over time the heart becomes fatigued and weakened. Eventually it loses some of its pumping ability and can't keep the blood circulating properly.

An early sign of heart failure is shortness of breath ("dyspnea") during minor exertion, such as walking up a slight grade. Another is rapid heartbeat, because the heart tries to compensate for its weakened pumping action. A third is edema in the feet and ankles, because the weakened heart does not have the power to force all of the blood fluid back up to the central body from those distant extremities. People with congestive heart failure often gain as much as fifteen pounds because of edema. Initially puffy, swollen feet and ankles return to normal size after sleeping or sitting with the feet up. But as heart failure becomes more severe, the swelling increases, the feet and ankles remain swollen, and the hands may swell as well.

Congestive heart failure has several causes:

• High blood pressure ("hypertension"). The heart must beat extra-forcefully to keep blood under abnormally high pressure flowing.

• Atherosclerosis. The heart must work harder to force blood through arteries clogged with plaque deposits.

• Previous heart attacks. Heart attacks cause the death of part of the heart, forcing the muscle that remains to work extra hard to keep blood flowing.

• Heart valve damage from rheumatic fever or other heart infections.

• Obesity. The heart becomes fatigued by having to move blood through so much excess tissue.

• Conditions not directly related to the heart, such as severe anemia, an overactive thyroid, or a chronic infection.

In advanced congestive heart failure, the person may have trouble breathing when lying down due to edema in the lungs. Some people wake up coughing, choking, or feeling suffocated.

Before You Call the Doctor.   Weight loss is essential to relieving stress on the heart. It eliminates the blood needs of the excess tissue, and it reduces blood pressure, which also relieves heart fatigue. A low-salt diet often helps eliminate edema. Diuretic foods help as well, for example, cucumbers, grapefruit, and parsley. Diuretics may deplete potassium stores. If you eat diuretic foods frequently or take diuretic drugs, be sure to include high-potassium foods in your diet as well, for example, bananas and potatoes. Regular exercise is also a good idea, but it should be nonaerobic, nondemanding exercise—for example, leisurely walking or swimming (see Chapter 1). Pushing yourself to aerobic levels may overtax the heart and is *not* recommended.

For more information, contact the American Heart Association (see RESOURCES at the end of this chapter).

When to Call the Doctor.   Congestive heart failure is a serious condition. It requires professional care in addition to self-care. Physicians treat it by encouraging weight loss and a low-salt diet. In addition, they prescribe diuretics to control edema, vasodilators and other antihypertensive medication to reduce blood pressure, and heart stimulants, such as digitalis, to stimulate the heart's pumping action.

HEART ATTACK

(See also CHEST PAIN, CONGESTIVE HEART FAILURE, HIGH BLOOD PRESSURE, and HIGH CHOLESTEROL in this chapter. For first-aid intervention, see HEART ATTACK in Chapter 3)

When people have heart attacks in the movies, they clutch their chests in agony and keel over. Massive heart attacks do, in fact, cause such reactions. But many heart attacks cause considerably less severe pain. Frequently, people suffering heart attacks dismiss them as "heartburn."

What's Going On?   A heart attack, medically known as a "myocardial infarction" or "MI," represents the culmination of a complex series of developments over many years, but for our purposes here, it's essentially a two-step process. First, the coronary arteries, which nourish the heart, become clogged ("occluded") with cholesterol-rich atherosclerotic plaques. Then a bit of plaque breaks off, or a blood clot ("thrombus") forms inside an occluded coronary artery, completely blocking blood flow and causing serious damage to part of the heart.

Pain from a heart attack differs from the chest pain of angina (see ANGINA in this chapter) in that it doesn't subside with rest. It generally lasts thirty minutes or longer and often radiates up to the jaw or down an arm. Other heart attack symptoms include sweating, nausea, vomiting, dizziness, and fainting. Some people say they experience premonitions of doom beforehand.

A heart attack can come on gradually, preceded by a few weeks of angina, or strike without warning. About one-third of those who have heart attacks don't survive them. Most deaths occur within two hours.

Before You Call the Doctor. Heart attacks are often preventable. See Chapter 1 or the brief summary in the ANGINA section of this chapter for information on prevention.

For first-aid information, see HEART ATTACK in Chapter 3.

Heart attack first-aid requires familiarity with CPR ("cardiopulmonary resuscitation"). *Everyone* should invest the few hours it takes to learn CPR. Don't wait for tragedy to strike someone you love. In about 90 percent of cases, people use CPR on relatives or close friends. CPR courses are available through local chapters of the American Red Cross and the American Heart Association (see RESOURCES at the end of this chapter and at the end of Chapter 3).

When to Call the Doctor. A heart attack is a medical emergency that requires immediate professional help. If you are having the attack, do not try to drive yourself to the hospital, even if you have only minimal pain. Call 911 for an ambulance and do what the operator tells you.

If you are with someone who has a heart attack, call 911, and while waiting for the ambulance, keep the person warm and as calm as possible. Do not give the person anything to eat or drink except for aspirin, unless instructed by a medical professional. If the person loses consciousness, check for breathing and a pulse. If you detect no breathing or pulse, begin CPR immediately, and keep doing it until help arrives.

At the hospital, the staff attempts to determine the severity of heart damage using a battery of diagnostic tests including an ECG ("electrocardiogram"). If treated early, the person may be given new clot-dissolving ("thrombolytic") drugs. The length of hospital stay depends on the person's overall health, the extent of coronary artery disease, and the damage suffered by the heart. These factors also influence recovery time.

Mental attitude is key to recovering from a heart attack. The good news is that once heart attack survivors have adopted a healthy life-style, most can return to work, engage in normal sexual relations, and enjoy old hobbies and interests, with only minor modifications.

▶ **RED FLAGS**   Consult a physician immediately if you experience unexplained chest pain—even if it feels like heartburn—and shortness of breath, rapid heartbeat, nocturnal breathlessness, foot and ankle swelling, or unexplained weight gain.

HIGH BLOOD PRESSURE

High blood pressure, medically known as "hypertension," is a major risk factor for stroke, heart disease, kidney damage, glaucoma, and many other health problems.

What's Going On?   Every time the heart pumps, it forces blood through the arteries under "systolic" pressure. When the heart rests between beats, a certain residual "diastolic" pressure remains. "Blood pressure" measures both of these pressures, which is why it's expressed as a fraction of two numbers—for example, 120/80 millimeters of mercury (mm Hg). The first number represents systolic pressure, the second, diastolic.

Textbook "normal" blood pressure is 120/80, but that's misleading. Blood pressure varies during the day. In the morning and when you're at rest, it's often lower. When you have to run to catch a bus, it rises dramatically. Normal blood pressure for adults under sixty and children older than four years ranges from 85/60 to about 135/90. For those older than sixty, normal systolic may be as high as 160.

Because blood pressure varies so much, "high" blood pressure means *chronically* high readings. One high reading may be meaningless, especially if it shows up during a doctor visit. A doctor's appointment makes many people anxious—and can raise their blood pressure significantly. Many studies have documented "white coat hypertension," the tendency for blood pressure readings to be temporarily high during encounters with health professionals.

In general, physicians diagnose hypertension when blood pressure is consistently greater than 140/90 for several readings over a month or two.

More than sixty million Americans have high blood pressure. It causes no symptoms, yet it's a key risk factor for many serious health conditions:

heart attack, stroke, glaucoma, and kidney disease. As a result it's often called the "silent killer."

In a small proportion of cases, hypertension is a symptom of another health problem, such as kidney disease or a hormonal imbalance. But in the vast majority of cases, high blood pressure is "idiopathic," the term doctors use for "cause unknown." However, several factors increase risk:

• Sex. Men are at higher risk of high blood pressure than women.

• Race. African-Americans are more likely to have hypertension than whites.

• Diet. High-salt intake is associated with hypertension among the estimated one-third to one-half of the population who are "salt-sensitive."

• Obesity. People who carry excess weight are more likely to have high blood pressure. In most people, as weight falls, so does blood pressure.

• Smoking. Cigarette smoking increases blood pressure.

• Alcohol. Those who drink excessively often develop high blood pressure.

• Family history. Doctors aren't certain about the role of heredity in hypertension, but a family history of stroke or high blood pressure increases the risk of elevated blood pressure.

Before You Call the Doctor.   Physicians are often quick to prescribe antihypertensive medication, but many studies show that if blood pressure is mildly elevated (up to 105 diastolic), diet and life-style modifications are often effective. All of the following have been shown to reduce elevated blood pressure:

• Quit smoking.

• Lose weight. If those who are overweight lose to within 15 percent of their recommended weight, this is the single most effective life-style approach to blood pressure control.

• Limit alcohol consumption.

• Adopt a regular, moderate exercise program.

• Manage your stress load.

See Chapter 1 or the brief summary of self-care recommendations in the ANGINA section of this chapter for additional information on healthy living.

Pay special attention to your salt intake. Salt is chemically known as sodium chloride, and it's the sodium that raises blood pressure. Not every person with high blood pressure is "salt sensitive," but many are. Never salt food before tasting it. If you decide it needs salt, add just a little, then taste it again. But for most people, the salt shaker used in cooking or added at the table is *not* the problem. It's the salt and other sodium compounds for example, monosodium glutamate (MSG), added to foods during processing. Fast foods, junk foods, canned soups, TV dinners, frozen pizzas, and most other manufactured food items are saturated with sodium. Read food labels carefully, and watch out for added salt or sodium. One reason the diet in Chapter 1 is based on fresh foods—whole grains and fresh fruits and vegetables—is that they're low in sodium.

Salt is an acquired taste. If you are used to salting everything, stopping cold turkey may make food seem unacceptably bland. Here are two suggestions. Switch to a nonsodium salt substitute, for example, NoSalt. When the commercials say, "There's no salt in NoSalt," they mean no *sodium.* Salt substitutes usually contain potassium chloride. They taste salty but contain no sodium. In addition to limiting sodium intake, the potassium in salt substitutes may help replace losses due to diuretic high blood pressure medications. On the other hand, potassium-based salt substitutes may be hazardous when used in combination with certain other medicines. Check with your physician or pharmacist before using salt substitutes. Also, try weaning yourself off salt by experimenting with herbs and spices. Some herbs, for example, garlic, have been shown to help control blood pressure.

If your physician says you have hypertension, discuss any exercise program you plan to adopt before starting it.

Fish oil has also been touted for its blood pressure lowering capabilities. However, supplementation with the omega-3 fatty acids (the beneficial ingredients in fish oil) may interfere with the ability of blood to clot and may cause excessive bleeding in some individuals. Instead of popping fish oil supplements, eat salmon and other cold-water fish two or three times a week.

Everyone with hypertension should have a home blood pressure cuff ("sphygmomanometer"). Take your blood pressure regularly, and chart your progress as you reduce it. Both digital and mercury models are available at pharmacies, medical supply houses, some department stores, or from mail-order catalogs. Take your blood pressure cuff in to your doctor annually to have its calibration checked.

For more information, contact the American Heart Association (see RESOURCES at the end of this chapter).

When to Call the Doctor.   Hypertension that does not respond to self-care approaches or does not come down sufficiently with self-care alone requires professional treatment. Many different kinds of medication are available:

•Diuretics: hydrochlorothiazide and others work by flushing out sodium through the kidneys.

•Alpha-blockers: clonidine, methyl-dopa, and prazosin work by opening up ("dilating") blood vessels and by affecting how the brain controls blood pressure.

• Beta-blockers: propranolol and others work by reducing the heart's pumping force.

• Calcium-channel blockers: nifedipine, verapamil, and diltiazem work by dilating blood vessels.

• Vasodilators: hydralazine and others also open blood vessels.

• ACE inhibitors: captopril, enalapril, and lisinopril also dilate blood vessels.

Those who use self-care approaches to blood pressure control usually require less medication. Drugs can control hypertension, but they don't cure it. Usually these drugs must be taken for life. If you stop taking them, blood pressure often soars to previous hypertensive levels. The various antihypertensive medications produce a variety of side effects, such as fatigue, dizziness, faintness, or increased urination, especially early in the treatment course. Discuss these side effects with your physician and pharmacist.

In men, several blood pressure medications can interfere with the ability to get or maintain an erection and other aspects of sexual function (see ERECTION PROBLEMS in Chapter 19). Ask for medication with a low risk of erection impairment, and if you experience any difficulty, discuss possible substitute medications with your physician and pharmacist.

▶ **RED FLAG**   Anyone with elevated blood pressure should be thoroughly evaluated by a physician to rule out other health problems that might contribute to, or result from, the condition.

HIGH CHOLESTEROL

Total blood cholesterol higher than 200 milligrams per deciliter (mg/dl) is a significant risk factor for heart disease. Many cardiovascular authorities urge people to reduce their total cholesterol to around 160.

What's Going On?   Cholesterol is a waxy substance essential to good health. It plays an important role in making bile, cell membranes, and several hormones. But too much of a good thing becomes a major risk factor for the nation's leading cause of death.

Most discussions of cholesterol focus on the total amount in the blood. But the cholesterol story is actually a bit more complex. Cholesterol comes in three "packages":

- LDL, low density lipoprotein.
- HDL, high density lipoprotein.
- VLDL, very low density lipoprotein.

LDL accounts for about 75 percent of total cholesterol in the blood. High levels of LDL, also known as "bad" cholesterol, are associated with atherosclerosis or "hardening of the arteries," the plaque deposits on artery walls that narrow ("occlude") them and restrict blood flow. Plaques on the coronary arteries, which nourish the heart, can lead to angina and heart attack (see ANGINA and HEART ATTACK in this chapter). A high-fat, high-cholesterol diet is the major culprit in high LDL levels, though some hereditary conditions can cause it as well.

In contrast, HDL, "good" cholesterol, protects against plaque formation. Unlike LDL, the more HDL, the better. Authorities believe that HDL levels rise with increased exercise and loss of body fat. On the other hand, HDL levels are depressed by obesity, cigarette smoking, sedentary life-style, and certain medications, for example, beta blockers.

At present, scientists are unsure of the role VLDL plays in atherosclerosis.

Most authorities say that a total cholesterol level of 200 or higher significantly increases the risk of heart disease. The risk rises steadily with total cholesterol levels between 150 and 200. After 200, the risk rises sharply. Ideally, total cholesterol should be less than 160 and LDL should be no more than 100. However, most doctors consider these ideals unrealistic and follow the guidelines of the National Cholesterol Education Project, which call for life-style modifications if total cholesterol is over 200 or LDL is over 130.

Before You Call the Doctor.   If your total cholesterol is higher than 200 and/or your LDL is higher than 130, you need to take steps to lower them—and your risk of heart disease. In most people, elevated cholesterol does come down through diet and life-style modifications. See ANGINA in this chapter and, for a more thorough discussion of heart-healthy lifestyle recommendations, see Chapter 1.

Many people with elevated cholesterol become upset when their physicians tell them they must change their diet. They feel like they must give up everything they enjoy eating. You may have to cut back on high-fat, high-cholesterol foods in general, but with careful planning, you can still enjoy an occasional cheeseburger, ice cream cone, pizza, or piece of chocolate fudge cake. Here are several suggestions to help reduce cholesterol without taking the joy out of living:

- Eat more salmon and other cold-water fish. These fish are high in omega-3 fatty acids, which help cut cholesterol.

• Eat more oatmeal and beans. Their soluble fiber helps reduce cholesterol.

• Eat more apples. An apple a day keeps heart disease at bay. Apples contain pectin, a soluble fiber which helps cut cholesterol.

• Use more garlic and ginger in cooking. Both of these herbs have been shown to reduce cholesterol.

• Snack on fruit. Every time you reach for a sweet, succulent, piece of fruit instead of potato chips, pork rinds, or some cheesy junk snack, you're doing your heart a big favor.

Regular aerobic exercise boosts the proportion of cholesterol carried as HDL, good cholesterol. But if you have elevated cholesterol or other risk factors for heart disease, check with your physician before jumping into an exercise program.

If these measure do not reduce cholesterol to an acceptable level, two over-the-counter products might help:

• Metamucil and other products made from psyllium. Psyllium is a tiny powdery seed traditionally used as a bulk-forming laxative (see CONSTIPATION in Chapter 13). Recent studies show that it also reduces total cholesterol and LDL. Take one teaspoon three times a day with plenty of water.

• Niacin ("nicotinic acid"). In doses of 1,500 to 3,000 mg a day, this vitamin cuts total cholesterol and LDL and raises HDL. However, at cholesterol-lowering doses, it also causes an unpleasant but harmless flush reaction in most people. To minimize flushing, start with 50 mg three times a day and gradually increase your dose. Take the pills after eating to slow absorption. It also helps to take a sustained-release niacin formulation or to take one-quarter tablet of aspirin (one baby aspirin) thirty minutes before taking the vitamin. But don't use niacin if you have diabetes or gout. It may aggravate these conditions.

For more information, contact the American Heart Association (see RESOURCES at the end of this chapter).

When to Call the Doctor.   If self-care measures don't reduce elevated cholesterol significantly within three months, or if an inherited high-cholesterol condition ("hypercholesterolemia") runs in your family, your physician can prescribe cholesterol-lowering drugs.

HYPERTENSION

(See HIGH BLOOD PRESSURE in this chapter)

PALPITATIONS

Most people occasionally experience the fluttery feeling of the heart "skipping a beat." Most skipped beats are not serious, though sometimes this condition suggests potentially serious heart problems.

What's Going On? Palpitations, medically known as "arrhythmias," are disturbances in normal heart rhythm. The normal resting heart rate is from 60 to 100 beats per minute. The heart's two smaller chambers ("atria") contract together, then the two larger chambers ("ventricles") contract together, producing the heart's two-stroke "lub-dub" beat. Exercise or emotional stress can increase heart rate to 200 beats per minute or more. In people with normal hearts, when demand on the heart returns to normal, so does heart rate.

Sometimes, however, the heart suffers arrhythmias for extended periods of time. It may beat too slowly ("bradycardia") or too rapidly ("tachycardia"). In most cases, arrhythmias occur briefly, resolve themselves without intervention, and pose no health risks. But persistent fast rhythm may be a symptom of congestive heart failure (see CONGESTIVE HEART FAILURE in this chapter). And serious arrhythmias occur during many heart attacks.

Caffeine, tobacco, alcohol, and other stimulant drugs (both legal and illicit) can trigger extra beats of both the atria and ventricles. Any arrhythmias usually disappear when the person stops using the offending stimulant(s). But if extra beats occur with rapid or very slow heartbeat, dizziness, and shortness of breath, the problem may be heart disease.

A common—and potentially life-threatening—cardiac arrhythmia called "fibrillation" occurs when the atria or ventricles contract in an erratic, uncoordinated fashion. People with atherosclerosis may experience this along with chest pain (see CHEST PAIN in this chapter), which sometimes precedes a heart attack.

Before You Call the Doctor. If you experience irregular, rapid, or extra heartbeats and have no history of heart disease, the problem may be caused by caffeine, cigarettes, emotional stress, and/or over-the-counter or prescription medications. Cut back on coffee, tea, colas, and other soft drinks that contain caffeine. Stop smoking. Review Chapter 1 for stress-management suggestions. And talk with your doctor or pharmacist about the possibility that your medication(s) may be causing your arrhythmias.

When to Call the Doctor.   If you have a personal or strong family history of heart disease and/or if your arrhythmias are not associated with drugs, alcohol, tobacco, or stress, the problem may be heart disease. Consult a physician promptly. Doctors use several tests to evaluate this problem: a history and physical, electrocardiogram, a twenty-four-hour electrocardiogram (Holter monitor), sometimes a treadmill exercise test, and possibly even a direct examination of the heart ("cardiac catheterization") to pinpoint the cause of the arrhythmias and suggest the best treatment.

Arrhythmias are treated with a variety of drugs. In some cases, pacemakers are surgically implanted in the chest to regulate heartbeat.

If you're nervous, sweaty, and hot all the time, your arrhythmia may be associated with an overactive thyroid gland ("hyperthyroidism"). Consult a physician.

▶ **RED FLAG**   Palpitations associated with pressure-like or crushing chest pain or with loss of consciousness are a medical emergency. Call 911.

VARICOSE VEINS

People who must stand for long periods, for example, beauticians, teachers, and bartenders, often suffer the leg pain, swelling, and visible bluish/ purplish lines of varicose veins.

What's Going On?   Varicose veins are enlarged, twisted blood vessels (see illustrations). The leg veins, which return blood to the heart after it has been distributed around the lower extremities, contain many valves that keep blood from being drawn back down into the feet by gravity. Sometimes, however, these valves don't work efficiently and blood pools in the legs, distending the superficial leg veins and causing them to twist and swell.

Varicose veins usually develop along the backs of the calves or on the insides of the legs. The veins appear bluish/purplish and swollen. The skin covering them often itches and feels sensitive to the touch. The legs may ache, and standing for even short periods may become painful, with swelling of the ankles and feet. Women may experience worse symptoms at certain times during their menstrual cycles.

More serious cases involve the deep veins of the leg as well as the superficial veins. This condition, called "venous insufficiency," often causes ankle edema, reddish-brown skin discoloration, and skin ulcers.

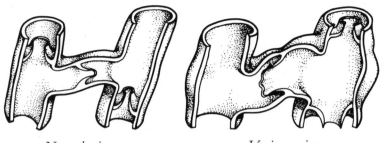

Normal veins.   *Varicose veins.*

Before You Call the Doctor.   Varicose veins are rarely a serious health problem, but they *are* painful and unsightly. For mild to moderate varicose veins:

• Stay off your feet as much as possible. Try not to stand in one place for long. If you must be on your feet, keep moving. As you move, the muscles in your legs help keep the blood moving and prevent pooling.

• When seated, sit with your legs raised above your heart to help blood return to the central body from the ankles and feet.

• Invest in support socks and stockings manufactured specifically to help relieve this condition. Some users report that donning support leg-wear before rising from bed works best. Elastic bandages may also help, but they tend to be hot and difficult to put on.

• Walk as much as possible to promote good circulation. Walking is one of the most effective strategies for preventing varicose veins.

If you cut a varicose vein, it can bleed profusely. Lie down immediately and raise the affected leg above the level of the heart. Apply firm pressure with a clean cloth or towel until the bleeding stops. Then clean and dress the wound.

When to Call the Doctor.   For persistent intense pain, consult a physician, who can diagnose superficial varicose veins simply by looking at them when you are standing. The physician may use a tourniquet test to evaluate the problem and may also want to observe the leg's circulation with a special x-ray ("venography") or heat map of the leg ("thermography").

The most popular treatment is surgical removal of the affected veins ("stripping"). The surgeon makes several incisions, inserts a wire hook, pulls out the affected veins, and then wraps the leg(s) in tight bandages. This procedure takes only about thirty minutes per leg, but you may have to remain hospitalized for up to a week. Afterwards, home recovery may take another few weeks.

For varicosities in the superficial veins, some physicians inject a chemical that collapses the veins so they no longer carry blood. Complete vein closure typically requires two or three injections. This treatment cannot be used on varicosities in deep veins.

With both treatments, doctors recommend walking several miles per day to stimulate circulation and the growth of new healthy blood vessels.

▶ **RED FLAG**   Varicose veins predispose people to phlebitis, painful vein inflammation, which in turn can lead to blood clots in the affected vein ("thrombophlebitis"). When the clot is in a deep vein, a piece may break off and travel to the lung, causing serious damage and possibly even death. If you experience any painful swelling in one or both legs that doesn't go away after elevation, consult a physician immediately.

RESOURCES

Eater's Choice: A Food Lover's Guide to Lower Cholesterol by Ron
   Goor, M.D., and Nancy Goor. (Boston: Houghton, Mifflin, 1992,
   $11.95) Contains hundreds of delicious, easy-to-prepare recipes that
   contain no more than 20 percent of calories from fat.
The American Heart Association. 7320 Greenville Ave., Dallas, TX
   75231; (214) 373-6300. Or, consult the white pages of your phone
   book for your local affiliate. Provides information and programs
   which encourage cardiovascular self-care and control of cholesterol,
   blood pressure, and other risk factors for heart disease and stroke.

CHAPTER 13

The Digestive System

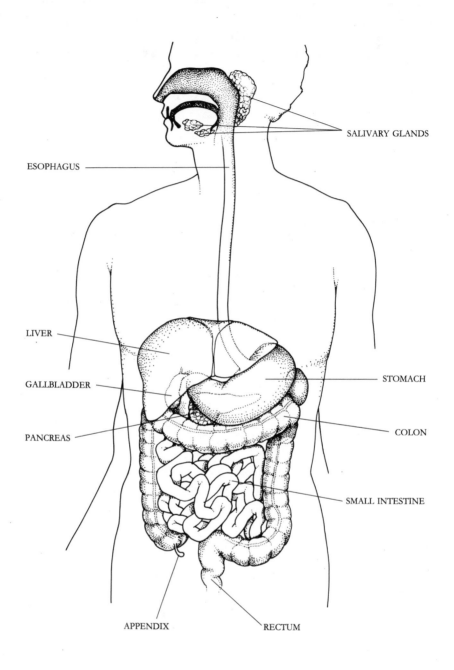

SALIVARY GLANDS

ESOPHAGUS

LIVER

GALLBLADDER

PANCREAS

STOMACH

COLON

SMALL INTESTINE

APPENDIX

RECTUM

The Digestive System.

ABDOMINAL CRAMPS, DISTRESS, PAIN, AND UPSET

(See STOMACHACHE in this chapter)

AMEBIASIS

(See DIARRHEA and STOMACHACHE in this chapter)

ANAL BLEEDING

(See also ANAL DISCHARGE, COLITIS, CONSTIPATION, DIAR-
RHEA, DIVERTICULAR DISEASE, HEMORRHOIDS, and ULCERS
in this chapter and CHLAMYDIA, HERPES, GONORRHEA, and VE-
NEREAL WARTS in Chapter 19)

Bleeding can range in severity from barely noticeable pink streaks on
toilet paper to significant blood loss that turns toilet water bright red.

What's Going On?   The digestive tract is one continuous tube from the
mouth to the anus. Bleeding anywhere along it may introduce blood into
the stool or cause anal bleeding. However, the rule of thumb is: The
redder the blood, the lower down the problem. Bleeding in the mouth,
throat, and stomach is more likely to cause bloody vomit than bloody
stools or anal bleeding. Bleeding in the upper intestine, often from severe
ulcers, may also cause bloody vomit, but black or bloody stools (the dark
color may be due to the fact that the blood has dried) are also possible.
Anal bleeding not mixed with stools suggests bleeding in the lower gastrointestinal tract; the bleeding may be a result of anal fissures, colitis,
diverticular disease, or hemorrhoids.

Before You Call the Doctor.   Anal bleeding can be frightening, but
quite frequently the cause is not serious:
  • For anal bleeding associated with hard stools and constipation, see
HEMORRHOIDS in this chapter or "Anal Fissures" in the ANAL PAIN
section of this chapter.
  • Review the healthy diet suggestions in EAT AND DRINK RIGHT
in Chapter 1 and the CONSTIPATION discussion in this chapter. Eat a

high-fiber diet. Snack on fresh fruits and vegetables and popcorn. Drink plenty of nonalcoholic liquids. Get adequate rest and exercise.

• Review the HEMORRHOIDS section of this chapter. Don't strain on the toilet. Don't sit on the toilet too long.

• Carefully categorize any other symptoms you experience, particularly abdominal pain or cramping, so you can discuss your situation thoroughly with your physician.

When to Call the Doctor.   Consult a physician for any sudden or persistent anal bleeding. Doctors perform a number of examinations and diagnostic tests to discover the cause. The most common cause is hemorrhoids, but many others are possible. After age fifty, anal bleeding might be colorectal cancer (earlier if you have a family history). Review the screening guidelines for this cancer in the REDUCE YOUR RISK section of Chapter 1.

▶ **RED FLAG**   Consult a physician promptly for anal bleeding with burning or any other unusual symptoms.

ANAL BURNING

(See also CHLAMYDIA, HERPES, GONORRHEA, and VENEREAL WARTS in Chapter 18)

Burning typically occurs during and shortly after defecation.

What's Going On?   Anal burning is usually caused by extremely hot spices in food, particularly Texas-style chili and Mexican, Indian, and Hunan Chinese cuisines.

Before You Call the Doctor.   Stop eating highly spiced foods for a few days and see if the problem clears up. If so, you can reasonably assume it was diet-related.

When to Call the Doctor.   Consult a physician if anal burning does not resolve after a few days on a bland diet. Symptoms may be caused by more serious conditions.

▶ **RED FLAGS**   Consult a physician promptly for anal burning:
• With bleeding.
• Not associated with defecation.
• With pain or other unusual symptoms.

ANAL DISCHARGE

(See also ANAL BLEEDING, COLITIS, and HEMORRHOIDS in this chapter and CHLAMYDIA, HERPES, GONORRHEA, and VENE-REAL WARTS in Chapter 18)

The typical discharge is watery, or it may contain pus ("purulent") and/or blood. It may or may not be accompanied by pain.

What's Going On?   The most common causes of anal discharge are hemorrhoids (see HEMORRHOIDS in this chapter), anal abcesses, anal tissue tears ("fissures") (see ANAL PAIN in this chapter), other openings in anal tissue ("fistulas"), or any inflammation of the anorectal area ("proctitis"). Here we'll discuss anal fistulas and proctitis.

- *Anal Fistulas.*   A "fistula" is an abnormal tissue opening. In anal fistula, the opening typically occurs in the intestine and tracks extend from it and reach the skin around the anus, causing a watery pus discharge and possibly anal itching. Sometimes a fistula is caused by rectal infection, diverticular disease (see DIVERTICULAR DISEASE in this chapter), or inflammatory conditions, such as Crohn's disease or ulcerative colitis (see COLITIS in this chapter).

Before You Call the Doctor.   See the self-care suggestions in the ANAL PAIN section of this chapter.

When to Call the Doctor.   The doctor may want to examine the colon ("sigmoidoscopy" or "colonoscopy"). If sigmoidoscopy is indicated, make sure the physician uses a flexible sigmoidoscope, not a rigid one. A flexible instrument causes less discomfort. Infections may require antibiotics. Inflammatory conditions may require steroids and other medication. In some cases, surgery might be necessary.

- *Proctitis.*   In addition to an anal discharge, anorectal inflammation may cause pain, bleeding, a feeling of rectal fullness and lower abdominal pain and/or cramps. Causes include ulcerative colitis (see CO-LITIS in this chapter) and several sexually transmitted diseases (see CHLAMYDIA, GONORRHEA, HERPES, and VENEREAL WARTS in Chapter 18). In addition, some parasitic infections—including those associated with AIDS—can cause proctitis.

Before You Call the Doctor.   See the sections of this book mentioned above.

When to Call the Doctor.   Consult a physician if you suspect proctitis.

ANAL ITCHING

See also ANAL DISCHARGE in this chapter)
Anal itching may be continuous, or it may occur only with defecation.

What's Going On?   Anal itching has many possible causes. Chronic diarrhea—and the frequent wiping associated with it—can irritate the anal area. The hard stools associated with chronic constipation can irritate the anal area when they pass. Poor anal hygiene can leave fecal material around the anal area which causes irritation and itching. In addition, overzealous anal hygiene can also cause significant irritation and itching. In some cases, certain foods may be responsible.

Before You Call the Doctor.   Anal itching is usually medically minor:
   • Review the DIARRHEA section of this chapter and implement its suggestions to reduce the irritation of frequent, watery stools and frequent wiping.
   • Try dusting the area with corn starch or talcum powder.
   • Try zinc oxide ointment to decrease chafing and absorb excess moisture.
   • Review the CONSTIPATION section of this chapter and implement its suggestions to soften hard stools.
   • Review the HEMORRHOIDS section of this chapter to minimize the itching and pain of this common problem.
   • Always wipe thoroughly, but no more than three times per bowel movement.
   • If you require additional wiping, use tissues moistened with vegetable or mineral oil.
   • Use only white, unscented tissues. Color dyes and perfumes can cause irritation.
   • Don't apply alcohol. It's drying and can cause irritation.
   • Try warm baths, then pat—don't rub—the area dry.
   • Over-the-counter anesthetic anal ointments (any hemorrhoid product with benzocaine) may help relieve itching. However, benzocaine causes allergic reactions in some people, which may increase itching.
   • Keep the anal area well ventilated so it remains relatively dry. Wear

breathable underwear—cotton, not synthetic fabrics. If you sit for long periods on plastic seats, try a woven seat cushion.

• Try changing your laundry detergent.

• In some cases, certain foods may contribute to this problem including acidic or highly spiced foods and chocolate. Experiment for yourself.

When to Call the Doctor.   Consult a physician if anal itching persists for more than two weeks despite concerted self-care. Symptoms may be caused by a parasitic infection, for example, pinworms.

▶ **RED FLAGS**   Consult a physician promptly if anal itching occurs:
• With bleeding.
• Not associated with diarrhea, constipation, hygiene, or diet.
• With pain or other unusual symptoms.

ANAL PAIN

(See also ANAL BLEEDING, ANAL DISCHARGE, ANAL ITCH-ING, COLITIS, CONSTIPATION, and HEMORRHOIDS in this chap-ter and CHLAMYDIA, HERPES, and GONORRHEA and VENEREAL WARTS in Chapter 18)

Anal pain may be caused by several sexually transmitted diseases (see Chapter 18), anal abscesses or fissures, colitis, hardened or clotted ("thrombosed") hemorrhoids, an injury of the tailbone ("coccyx"), or a muscle spasm in the rectum ("proctalgia fugax"). Here we'll discuss causes not covered elsewhere in this book:

• *Anal Abscesses.*   Abscesses are pus pockets caused by bacterial infection (see BOILS in Chapter 6). Infections in the anorectal area can cause an anal pus ("purulent") discharge, usually with anal tenderness and throbbing pain. Anal abscesses often begin as anal fissures or as fistulas (see ANAL DISCHARGE in this chapter), which become infected by bacteria that normally live in the digestive tract.

Before You Call the Doctor.   Aspirin and ibuprofen may provide temporary relief from pain and inflammation. Acetaminophen treats pain but not inflammation. If aspirin or ibuprofen upset your stomach, try an "enteric coated" brand. Pregnant women and those with a his-tory of ulcers should not take aspirin or ibuprofen unless a doctor recommends it.

Warm sitz baths—sitting in warm water for five to ten minutes three times a day—may also help. But home treatments rarely cure the underlying infection.

When to Call the Doctor.   Consult a physician if there is any anal pus discharge or a tender red bump that does not improve after a day of aspirin and sitz baths. Anal abscesses must be opened ("lanced") and drained by a physician. Antibiotics are usually prescribed to prevent reinfection.

• *Anal Fissures.*   "Fissure" means a tissue tear. Anal fissures may be caused by hard stools or trauma from vigorous wiping or anal intercourse. Sharp pain occurs during bowel movements and for about a half hour afterward.

Before You Call the Doctor.   Self-care for anal fissures parallels self-care for hemorrhoids, particularly stool softeners (see HEMORRHOIDS in this chapter). In addition:
   • Take sitz baths. Sit in warm water for five to ten minutes three times a day.
   • Apply zinc oxide to soothe the area.
   • Use aspirin, acetaminophen, or ibuprofen to relieve pain. If aspirin or ibuprofen upset your stomach, try an "enteric coated" brand or use acetaminophen. Pregnant women and those with a history of ulcers should not take aspirin or ibuprofen unless a doctor recommends it.

When to Call the Doctor.   Consult a physician if the pain gets worse despite self-care, or if it lasts longer than a week.

• *Tailbone Injury.*   Injury to the "coccyx" or tailbone is almost always caused by trauma—a fall, automobile or bicycle accident, or some other blow. The pain may become chronic, and the injury hurts more when the area is pressed.

Before You Call the Doctor.   Be patient. Coccyx injuries often take a surprisingly long time to stop hurting. In the meantime:
   • Take aspirin, acetaminophen, or ibuprofen for any pain. If aspirin or ibuprofen upset your stomach, try an "enteric coated" brand or use acetaminophen. Pregnant women and those with a history of ulcers should not take aspirin or ibuprofen unless a doctor recommends it.

• Apply heat: hot packs, hot baths, heating pads.
• Try sitting on firm surfaces. Get a hard cushion to place on chairs, sofas, and car seats.
• Try sitting on an inflatable U-shaped or doughnut-shaped cushion.

When to Call the Doctor. Consult a physician if pain becomes more severe, or if you experience no improvement within two weeks.

• ***Proctalgia Fugax.*** This condition causes sudden, searing pain not associated with bowel movements that lasts from a few seconds to several minutes. It is caused by muscle spasms.

Before You Call the Doctor. Stretch and massage the muscles around the rectum with a lubricated finger inserted into the anus.

When to Call the Doctor. If pain recurs or becomes chronic, consult a physician to rule out more serious possibilities. A doctor may also prescribe muscle relaxants to minimize spasms.

BELCHING

(See also "Giardiasis" in the DIARRHEA section of this chapter and HEARTBURN and IRRITABLE BOWEL SYNDROME in this chapter)
    Belching or burping occurs when gas is expelled from the stomach through the mouth, often with a characteristic low-pitched sound.

What's Going On? Belching is caused by the escape of swallowed air or carbon dioxide, the gas that makes carbonated beverages fizz. People naturally swallow some air when eating. They swallow more air when they swallow saliva, so anything which increases salivation contributes to belching, for example, chewing gum and sucking on hard candies. Most belching isn't a medical problem, but it can be a social faux pas.

Before You Call the Doctor. If you feel you belch excessively:
    • Don't drink soda, beer, champagne, sparkling wines, and hard ciders.
    • Eat slowly, chew thoroughly, and don't wolf your food.
    • Don't chew gum or suck on hard candies.
    If belching causes burning and brings up stomach acids, see HEART-BURN in this chapter.
    If you experience a sudden increase in belching along with diarrhea

and abdominal distress, see "Giardiasis" in the DIARRHEA section of this chapter.

When to Call the Doctor. Belching may also be a symptom of ulcer. If you experience burning abdominal pain between meals and at night, consult a physician.

BLOOD IN THE STOOL

(See ANAL BLEEDING in this chapter)

COLIC

All babies cry—that's how they express themselves. But when otherwise healthy babies seem to cry incessantly, usually after their evening feeding, from 6:00 to 10:00 P.M., they often have colic.

What's Going On? Colic is painful for babies and often frightening for parents, but fortunately, it's almost always a short-lived malady. Colic causes abdominal pain, which typically starts from age two to six weeks, and usually ends by four months of age. Crying, which may be quite piercing, lasts from a few hours a day to most of the day in severe cases. Other symptoms include flatulence, a swollen-looking stomach ("abdominal distention") after feedings, and altered posture, often alternating between curling up into a ball and stretching out and stiffening. Sometimes the infant passes greenish, mucus-rich stools.

Colic occurs in an estimated 25 percent of all infants, but it does not interfere with normal or even above-average weight gain and development. The cause is usually a mystery, but it may be a transient food allergy, with cow's milk protein the major culprit. This protein occurs in many infant formulas and can be transmitted through breast milk. Another possibility is a baby version of lactose intolerance (see "Lactose Intolerance" in the DIARRHEA section of this chapter). Colic may also result from excessive amounts of air swallowed during sucking and crying. Spontaneous gastrointestinal spasms may also be a factor.

Before You Call the Doctor. Parents can often comfort colicky babies—and themselves:

• Breast-feeding mothers should stop drinking milk. Take a calcium supplement instead. For formula-fed babies, eliminate the cow's milk and switch to a soy-milk/hydrolyzed-protein formula. Studies show this eliminates colic in about 30 percent of infants and reduces symptoms in another 10 percent.

• If the mother continues to drink milk, add Lactaid to expressed breast milk to deal with any lactose intolerance.

• Be sure to burp the baby after each feeding and also after prolonged crying spells (unless, of course, the baby is asleep).

• Offer a pacifier. Most colicky babies take them for short periods.

• Stomach-soothing drugs ("antispasmodics") are not recommended for infants, but a traditional herbal approach, dilute mint tea, might help.

• Keep the baby moving in your arms or in a cradle, swing, rocking chair, stroller, infant carrier, or car.

• Colicky babies are usually more comfortable on their stomachs.

• Keep the baby warm. A warm-water bottle on the tummy sometimes helps.

• Colic seems to last forever, but in fact, it rarely lasts longer than a few months.

When to Call the Doctor.   Few parents of persistently crying babies can restrain themselves from calling the doctor. It's important to feel reassured that your baby is physically healthy. Beyond that, most pediatricians recommend the self-care strategies discussed above.

▶ **RED FLAGS**   Colic should not cause diarrhea, vomiting, or persistent abdominal distention. If any of these occur, consult a physician.

COLITIS

(See also DIARRHEA and IRRITABLE BOWEL SYNDROME in this chapter)

Colitis means inflammation of the colon. "Colitis" actually indicates either of two diseases: Crohn's disease (regional enteritis) or ulcerative colitis. Symptoms typically occur episodically in "attacks" and include pain in the lower abdomen and diarrhea, which may be bloody. Other symptoms may include fatigue and anxiety during attacks.

What's Going On?   It's not clear what causes colitis. Heredity seems to play a role because the condition tends to run in families, though it's not strictly genetic. Certain diets, alcohol, and stress aggravate symptoms.

Colitis typically develops in young adults, and in its early stages it is often difficult to distinguish from irritable bowel syndrome (IBS) (see

IRRITABLE BOWEL SYNDROME in this chapter). However, there are important differences. Colitis tends to flare up, then subside, whereas IBS tends to be an ongoing problem. In colitis, the abdominal pain tends to be more severe and more localized on the left side (the descending colon). In colitis, the main other symptom is diarrhea, whereas in IBS, often both diarrhea and constipation occur. And IBS often causes increased belching and bloating, which are rare in colitis.

In severe cases, wounds ("ulcers") develop in the colon wall, and the condition becomes marked by more severe abdominal pain and bloody diarrhea. A history of ulcerative colitis is a significant risk factor for colon cancer, the leading cause of cancer death in nonsmokers.

Before You Call the Doctor.   Review the IRRITABLE BOWEL SYNDROME section of this chapter. Colitis and IBS are treated with the same basic self-care program.

When to Call the Doctor.   Most physicians treat colitis aggressively with anti-inflammatory drugs. In serious cases, the colon is removed surgically.

▶ **RED FLAGS**   Consult a physician promptly if:
- Abdominal pain becomes severe.
- Attacks increase in frequency.
- Blood appears in your stool.
- Other unusual symptoms develop.

CONSTIPATION

(See also IRRITABLE BOWEL SYNDROME in this chapter)

The commercials call it "irregularity" or "feeling sluggish" or "out of sorts." Euphemisms aside, constipation is one of America's leading health annoyances. It affects an estimated 25 percent of the population—some 65 million people—and laxative sales now top $400 million a year.

What's Going On?   On TV, "regularity" means one bowel movement a day. But studies show that this frequency is completely unnecessary. The Food and Drug Administration's (FDA) Advisory Review Panel on over-the-counter laxatives judged anything in the range of three bowel movements a day to three a week as normal. The FDA's magazine, *FDA Consumer,* states: "Much of the public fears health-endangering consequences if the bowel is not evacuated daily. Such fears are unfounded and lead to unnecessary use of laxatives."

Most constipation is caused by a combination of too little exercise and too little fiber and fluid in the diet. Exercise stimulates the natural wavelike colon contractions ("peristalsis") we recognize as "the urge." Fiber adds bulk to the stool, which also helps stimulate peristalsis.

However, constipation has other possible causes:

• Travel, which alters people's regular toilet rhythms.

• Pregnancy, which places pressure on the colon and decreases peristalsis.

• Various drugs which interfere with colonic peristalsis: codeine and other narcotics, antidepressants, antihistamines, antispasmodics, antiparkinsonism drugs, decongestants, nonsteroidal anti-inflammatory agents, and tranquilizers.

• Certain minerals, particularly, iron, calcium, and aluminum.

• And more serious medical problems (see "Red Flags" below).

Constipation also becomes increasingly common with advancing age because natural peristalsis loses some of its power.

Finally, overuse of chemical-stimulant laxatives can actually *cause* a form of constipation known as "lazy bowel syndrome," in which peristalsis ceases without chemical stimulation. Lazy bowel syndrome is one reason why physicians recommend limiting laxative use to no more than once or twice a month.

Before You Call the Doctor. When the going gets tough, the tough can usually get going by practicing self-care:

• Eat more fiber. Enjoy fresh fruits, vegetables, and whole grain products at every meal and when snacking. Wheat bran, a leading constipation preventive, is available in dozens of cereals, crackers, and muffins, as well as in an unprocessed powder form. Popcorn makes a satisfying snack that helps get things moving as well. Prunes and prune juice often help. Raisins, broccoli, beans, dried apricots, and sweet potatoes also contain generous helpings of fiber. But don't overdo the fruits because you may develop gas (see FLATULENCE in this chapter).

• Limit your consumption of constipating ("binding") foods: bananas, cheeses, white rice, applesauce, and white flour products.

• Drink plenty of nonalcoholic liquids. Liquids are natural stool softeners. Soft stools pass more easily than hard ones. Many people find that caffeine-containing beverages (coffee, tea, cocoa, and colas) have a laxative effect. The downside is that it doesn't take much caffeine to cause nervousness and irritability, and caffeine gives many people insomnia.

•Eat at regular hours without rushing so that coordinated bowel activity after eating becomes part of your body's daily routine.

•Exercise daily. No need to run a marathon. Walking for a half-hour or so a day is usually sufficient.

•Never ignore the urge.

•Establish a regular toilet time. Most authorities recommend after breakfast. Sit, but don't strain. Straining might contribute to hemorrhoids. Some authorities suggest using a small footstool to bring you to more of a squatting position.

•If these approaches don't provide sufficient relief within a few days, try an over-the-counter laxative in the following order: first, bulk formers, then lubricants and stool softeners, and finally chemical stimulants and enemas.

•Bulk formers are the most natural type of laxative. They increase stool volume. Larger stools press on the colon wall and stimulate peristalsis. Bulk formers usually work within twelve to seventy-two hours. Bran and dietary fibers are bulk formers, so it should come as no surprise that commercial bulk-forming laxatives also use plant fibers, in particular psyllium (Metamucil, Correctol, Fiberall, and others). However, bulk formers don't work by themselves. They need water. If you use psyllium laxatives, take them with lots of liquids. Psyllium has also been shown to help reduce blood cholesterol levels (see HIGH CHOLESTEROL in Chapter 12).

•Lubricants coat the stool to promote easier passage. Mineral oil is the only FDA-approved ingredient. This petroleum distillate works in six to eight hours, but if used routinely, it may deplete the body of fat-soluble vitamins (A, D, E, and K). If you take other medications, mineral oil may interfere with their absorption. Wait at least two hours after taking mineral oil to take other medications, and vice versa. The very young and very ill should not use mineral oil because accidental inhalation can cause lung damage.

•Stool softeners do what the name implies. They work by pulling more water into the stool, so drink plenty of nonalcoholic liquids for best results. Docusate sodium (Colace) or docusate potassium (Dialose) should produce results within twelve to seventy-two hours. The typical dose is 100 mg two or three times a day. Stool softeners are safe for extended use. But if you are salt-sensitive or have a history of high blood pressure, heart disease, stroke, diabetes, or glaucoma, stay away from sodium. Use docusate potassium in consultation with your physician and pharmacist. Milk of magnesia is another stool softener which usually works in one to six hours. The recommended dose depends on one's age: two to four tablespoons for adults, one to two tablespoons for children six to twelve years of age, and one to three teaspoons for children two to five years of age. If one dose of milk of magnesia does not provide relief, it may be taken a second time, but it should not be used more than twice in twelve hours and should not be used for extended periods.

• Enemas irrigate the bowel and act as lubricants and stimulants. But frequent enemas contribute to lazy bowel syndrome. Enemas are most useful for the occasional "crisis" but should not be used routinely.

• Chemical stimulants, which work in six to twelve hours, are the most potent laxatives—and the most toxic if abused. The gentlest ones contain the plant extract cascara sagrada (Stimulax, Comfolax) or the chemical phenolphthalein (Ex-Lax, Feen-a-Mint). More potentially cathartic ones contain bisacodyl (Dulcolax), extract of buckthorn (Movicol), or senna (Perdiem). Chemical-stimulant laxatives may cause abdominal cramping and diarrhea.

Do not take laxatives more than once or twice a month without consulting a physician.

When to Call the Doctor.   Consult a physician if you find yourself using chemical stimulants regularly more than once or twice a month or if constipation recurs despite the diet and life-style suggestions above. Be sure to bring a list of all the medications you take—both over-the-counter and prescription. If the problem is drug-linked, other medications may be able to be substituted. Constipation may also contribute to anal fissures, tiny tears in the tissue in the anal area that are usually the result of hard stools (see ANAL PAIN in this chapter).

▶ **RED FLAGS**   Although the vast majority of constipation is medically minor and can be self-treated effectively, the condition may be caused by such potentially serious health problems as prostate enlargement, uterine fibroids, or uterine or colorectal cancer. If constipation does not improve after a week of committed self-care, consult a physician.

DIARRHEA

(See also COLITIS, "Chemical Stimulants" in the CONSTIPATION section of this chapter, and FLATULENCE, GASTROENTERITIS, IRRITABLE BOWEL SYNDROME, and STOMACHACHE in this chapter)

Diarrhea means loose, watery stools and significantly increased frequency of defecation.

What's Going On?   Most cases of diarrhea are caused by:

• Viral or bacterial infections—including food poisoning, viral gastroenteritis, traveler's diarrhea (also called tourista or Montezuma's revenge), as well as *Salmonella* and other forms of dysentery.

• Intestinal parasites—amebiasis or giardiasis.

• Drug side effects—from some antibiotics; high doses of vitamin C; some prescription heart and cancer drugs, for example, propranolol (Inderal); magnesium-based antacids (Maalox, Mylanta, and Di-Gel); and laxative abuse (accidental use by children or intentional purging by bulimic adults).

• Lactose intolerance, the inability of some adults to digest the milk sugar found in dairy products ("lactose").

• Sorbitol intolerance, the inability to digest this widely used artificial sweetner.

• Motility disorders (see IRRITABLE BOWEL SYNDROME in this chapter).

The only real complication of everyday diarrhea is water loss ("dehydration"). The body is more than 75 percent water. The function of the colon is to reabsorb two to four quarts of water a day from solid wastes. Diarrhea disrupts this process, resulting in excessive fluid loss in watery stools and eventual impairment of every system in the body. Otherwise healthy adults can still function when moderately dehydrated, but the condition can become serious more quickly in infants, children, and the elderly. Symptoms of dehydration include dry mouth, cracked lips, lethargy, confusion, and decreased urination. Dehydration also depletes body stores of two essential minerals, sodium and potassium ("electrolytes").

Some forms of diarrhea are discussed elsewhere (see COLITIS, GASTROENTERITIS, and IRRITABLE BOWEL SYNDROME in this chapter.) The following varieties of diarrhea are discussed below: common everyday diarrhea, infectious diarrhea, traveler's diarrhea, amebiasis, giardiasis, and lactose intolerance.

• ***Common Everyday Diarrhea.***   This illness typically has only one symptom—loose, watery stools. For diarrhea with other symptoms, see the other types of diarrhea that follow.

What's Going On?   The cause of this malady may be difficult to identify. Many cases are viral, particularly in children. Sometimes combinations of foods, drugs, and stress precipitate it, for example, too much pizza and coffee the night before final exams. Sometimes it's related to travel—not a full-blown case of tourista, but frequently when people travel, even within the United States, they react poorly to the new local water supply.

Before You Call the Doctor. At the first sign of diarrhea, increase your fluid intake. Drink eight to ten large glasses of water a day for as long as the diarrhea lasts. But water does not replace lost electrolytes, so authorities now recommend Gatorade or other rehydration fluids which contain both sodium and potassium. (Those with high blood pressure, heart disease, diabetes, glaucoma, or a history of stroke should consult their physicians before self-treating with electrolyte-replacement beverages because the sodium may elevate their blood pressure.) Bouillon and other clear broths are also helpful. Gatorade is not recommended for infants. Instead, for infants and children, use other electrolyte-rich—but less concentrated—rehydration fluids: Pedialyte, Infalyte, and Lytren. Sip rehydration fluids, don't gulp them. Gulping can overstimulate the gastrointestinal tract and contribute to cramping. Flat soft drinks or dilute apple juice can also be used, but authorities say fluids like Pedialyte are preferable. Recently, a growing number of pediatricians have also recommended thin watery rice cereals.

Don't stop eating. People with diarrhea typically associate food with stomach distress and reduce their food intake. This is a mistake. It aggravates dehydration and does not supply the nourishment necessary for the body to resolve the diarrhea. Instead, change your diet to BRAT foods, an acronym for bananas, rice, applesauce, and toast, all of which are binding. Bananas are also rich in potassium, so they help replenish electrolytes. Some people say tea also helps. But stay away from coffee, milk, fruit juices, and spicy, fried, and junk foods, which usually aggravate the problem, as well as alcohol, which is dehydrating. As symptoms begin to improve, gradually reintroduce other foods: crackers, cooked vegetables, skinless chicken, fish, etc., but stay away from high-fat items like pizza, burgers, ice cream, and french fries until stools return to normal again.

Read food labels carefully. Many people develop diarrhea from the artificial sweetener sorbitol. Eliminate it from your diet and see what happens.

If diarrhea does not respond to fluids and the BRAT diet within a day or two, try over-the-counter Kaopectate. (The antidiarrheal fiber in applesauce is pectin. It's also the "pectate" in Kaopectate.) Adults should take four to eight tablespoons after each watery bowel movement. Children three to twelve years of age should be given one to four tablespoons. For diarrhea in children under three that doesn't respond to BRAT within a day or two, consult the child's physician.

Another approach is to take a bulk-forming over-the-counter laxative, for example, Metamucil. It may sound crazy to take a laxative for diarrhea, but bulk formers do not chemically stimulate defecation as other laxatives do. Instead, they contain fiber which absorbs water and adds mass to watery stools.

When to Call the Doctor.   See the "Red Flags" at the end of this section.

• *Infectious Diarrhea.*   Common in children, this type of diarrhea causes a variety of additional symptoms, including abdominal cramping, fever, and fatigue, with severity ranging from hardly noticeable to severe.

What's Going On?   Infectious diarrhea is caused by a large number of viruses and bacteria, including *Rotavirus, Campylobacter, Shigella, Yersinia,* some strains of *E. coli,* and *Salmonella,* which is also a cause of food poisoning. It's quite common among day-care center children. These microorganisms spread on little hands that touch contaminated fecal material, then touch food or go into their own, or other children's, mouths. Children are unconscious of good hygiene—and often quite resistant to it—so infectious diarrhea is difficult for day-care staff to prevent and control.

Before You Call the Doctor.   Infectious diarrhea can be prevented. Here are some guidelines childcare centers should follow:
   • Children should always wash hands with soap and water before eating meals or snacks.
   • Children who are toilet trained should be taught to wash with soap and water after using the bathroom.
   • During outbreaks of infectious diarrhea, children in diapers should have their hands washed after they're changed.
   • Staff should wash hands after changing children and before beginning any food preparation.
   If diarrhea strikes, follow the self-care suggestions listed under "Common Everyday Diarrhea" above.

When to Call the Doctor.   See the "Red Flags" at the end of this section.

• *Traveler's Diarrhea (Tourista, Montezuma's Revenge).*
This illness is another name for infectious diarrhea.

What's Going On?   Adults in the U.S. rarely catch infectious diarrhea from their children, though this is possible. But campers can develop it if they drink from streams—even pristine looking wilderness streams far from human habitation—without boiling the water first (see "Amebiasis" and "Giardiasis" below). And world travelers often suffer sudden attacks after eating contaminated foods or drinking contaminated water.

Tourista causes urgency, liquid stools, abdominal cramping, loss of energy and appetite, occasionally fever, and gastrointestinal discomfort that may linger for a week or so after the acute symptoms have cleared up. Traveler's diarrhea is most likely to occur in the Third World, where the hygiene standards of the industrialized world may not be maintained, but it also strikes Americans who travel in Europe—and increasingly even in the U.S. and Canada because of deteriorating water quality.

Before You Call the Doctor.   The best way to deal with tourista is to prevent it by scrupulously adhering to the following guidelines:
- Always wash your hands with soap and water before eating.
- Eat only well-cooked foods served *hot*.
- Don't buy foods from sidewalk vendors even if they are served hot.
- Don't eat salads, no matter how delectable the fresh vegetables look.
- Stay away from raw fish (ceviche, sushi).
- Don't drink unpasteurized milk or dairy products made from it. Of course, it's often difficult to learn about pasteurization. If you have a sensitive stomach, steer clear of dairy products.
- Peel all fruits before eating them.
- Don't drink tap water. Drink only mineral water and soft drinks from containers you open yourself.
- If you must drink tap water, sterilize it with chlorine tablets (Halazone)—two and a half tablets per quart for at least thirty minutes—or iodine tablets (Globaline)—one tablet per quart for thirty minutes. Pregnant women and people with thyroid disease or iodine allergy should not use iodine.
- Don't use ice. The ice you pop into your mineral water may have been made with contaminated water.

The only effective over-the-counter preventive for travelers' diarrhea is a bottle a day of Pepto-Bismol—yes, a bottle a day. This works, but it means you have to lug around a suitcase full of the stuff and drink a bottle a day, which is none too appetizing. The tablet form is more convenient, but the recommended dose is still quite high—two tablets four times a day starting one day before travel. Pepto-Bismol can turn stools black, so don't become alarmed. People who develop upset stomach or other side effects from aspirin should not use Pepto-Bismol.

Unfortunately, even those who eat very carefully often succumb to traveler's diarrhea. If it happens to you:

• Immediately increase your fluid intake—drink safe, uncontaminated, nonalcoholic liquids—to prevent dehydration.

• Travel with loperamide (Imodium), until recently a prescription antidiarrheal drug but now available over-the-counter. Loperamide does not treat the infection that causes tourista, but it slows the passage of food through the intestines, which minimizes abdominal cramping and feelings of urgency. Do not take loperamide if you have fever or blood in the stool. Loperamide is available in capsules or liquid. Follow package dosage directions.

• Don't leave home without a supply of the combination antibiotic trimethoprim/sulfamethoxazole or one of the new quinolones (ciprofloxacin, norfloxacin, ofloxacin). These antibiotics cure the bacterial infection that causes traveler's diarrhea. Before you go, tell your physician you're about to go abroad. Most are happy to write the prescription and tell you how to take the drug in the event that the unfortunate occurs.

When to Call the Doctor.   Tourista often clears up by itself after a few days without antibiotic treatment. But if you have fever or blood in the stool, or you feel particularly uncomfortable or debilitated, consult a physician. Doctors treat tourista with the antibiotics mentioned above. If they don't work, the doctor takes a stool culture, grows the microorganism causing the problem, determines which antibiotic kills it, and prescribes that drug.

• *Amebiasis (Amebic Dysentery).*   This illness causes a range of symptoms from none at all, to mild stomach upset and flatulence, to fever, abdominal cramping, and frequent, debilitating, liquid stools tinged with blood.

What's Going On?   Amebic dysentery is caused by a one-celled animal, the protozoan *Entamoeba histolytica,* which enters the gastrointestinal tract in contaminated food or water. Once encountered only in the tropics, this disease is becoming more prevalent in temperate climes. When camping, never drink water directly from streams even at high elevations, no matter how pristine they seem. Always boil stream water before drinking it.

Before You Call the Doctor.   For prevention and self-care treatments, see "Infectious Diarrhea" and "Traveler's Diarrhea" above.

When to Call the Doctor. Physicians diagnose amebiasis by stool examination for "O&P" (ova and parasites), which shows the protozoan. They treat it depending on symptoms, but in most cases they prescribe metronidazole. Do not drink alcohol while taking metronidazole or you'll get very sick. Persistent cases are treated with metronidazole plus other antibiotics.

• *Giardiasis (Giardia).* This infection causes a range of symptoms from mild stomach upset to persistent diarrhea or mushy stools, with abdominal distress, belching, bloating, headache, and fatigue.

What's Going On? Caused by the protozoan *Giardia lamblia* and commonly called "giardia," this infection spreads through contaminated feces and into the digestive tract through the mouth in contaminated food and water. It may also be transmitted sexually among those lax in sexual hygiene. Giardia has become widespread among rodents and other small mammals throughout North America. Their contaminated wastes have introduced it into virtually all water sources (with increasingly rare exceptions in remote parts of Alaska and Northern Canada). As a result, it has become a significant health problem for backpackers who drink from streams without boiling their water first. Always boil your water no matter how pristine the source appears.

Before You Call the Doctor. For prevention and self-care treatments, see "Infectious Diarrhea" and "Traveler's Diarrhea" above.

When to Call the Doctor. Physicians diagnose giardiasis using a test which detects the protozoan. Unfortunately, the test is not very good, and many cases are misdiagnosed as "irritable bowel syndrome." If you've been diagnosed with an irritable bowel—especially if you're a camper or world traveler—and you're not responding to irritable bowel syndrome treatment, ask your physician to retest you for giardia. Physicians treat giardia with metronidazole or quinacrine (Atabrine). Persistent cases are treated with quinacrine plus other antibiotics.

• *Lactose Intolerance.* Lactose is milk sugar and is found in all dairy products. "Intolerance" means an inability to digest it, which causes a variety of symptoms, including stomach upset, diarrhea, gas, and abdominal cramps.

What's Going On?   Nursing mammals produce an enzyme ("lactase") which allows them to digest the milk their mothers feed them. After weaning, most mammals never drink milk again and lose the ability to produce lactase. But most humans continue to drink milk and consume dairy products throughout life. Like our evolutionary cousins, many people lose the ability to produce lactase and suffer lactose intolerance. This condition is most common among African-Americans and Asians, but authorities estimate that up to 75 percent of adults suffer some degree of this problem, which usually remains unsuspected, undiagnosed, and untreated. No wonder so many people complain of chronic stomach upset and gas.

Before You Call the Doctor.   Pay close attention to how you feel for several hours after eating dairy products. Then eliminate all dairy products from your diet for a few days and see how you feel. If you feel noticeably better, chances are you're lactose intolerant.

If so, you have a few choices. You can simply refrain from eating dairy foods, though that can be rather challenging (no ice cream). Most people with lactose intolerance can consume cultured milk products without difficulty: yogurt, buttermilk, and hard cheeses. If you eliminate most dairy products, be sure to increase your calcium intake by eating lots of cultured-milk dairy products and by consuming other foods rich in calcium, such as salmon, green leafy vegetables, and tofu. You might also take a calcium supplement.

Or you can buy milk and dairy products with added lactase, which are becoming more widely available as this condition receives increased media attention.

Or you can add your own lactase to milk using an over-the-counter lactase supplement, Lactaid, available in caplets or drops at pharmacies. Free information on Lactaid can be obtained by calling 1-(800)-257-8650.

Finally, you can use milk substitutes: soy and soy-milk products and Mocha Mix.

Don't substitute goat's milk for cow's milk. Goat's milk also contains lactose, so it won't help the problem.

Some infants develop lactose intolerance. Those prone to the condition have a family history of it. They are typically removed from the breast and fed formula based on soy milk.

When to Call the Doctor.   If you think you're lactose intolerant and want to be sure, consult a physician. Doctors can test for it. If tests show lactose intolerance, doctors recommend the self-care approaches discussed above.

▶ **RED FLAGS**   Diarrhea may be an early symptom of serious illness: gastrointestinal ulcers and bleeding, several cancers (pancreatic and endocrine), diseases causing nutrient malabsorption (pancreatitis, scleroderma, and several other relatively rare disorders), and even AIDS. Consult a doctor promptly if:

• Diarrhea does not respond to self-care within a week.

• Diarrhea in a child under three does not respond within forty-eight hours.

• Stools appear black or red, which indicate blood.

• Stools appear bulky but greasy, an indication of nutrient malabsorption.

DIVERTICULAR DISEASE (DIVERTICULOSIS, DIVERTICULITIS)

More than half of those over sixty years of age have diverticulosis, the early, usually symptomless form of this condition. Most are unaware of it, but some develop diverticulitis, which causes lower-left abdominal pain and fever.

What's Going On?   The cause of diverticulosis is unknown, but it seems that increased pressure in the large bowel plays a role. A common cause of increased pressure is lack of bulk-forming foods (fiber) in the diet. The increased pressure causes small outpouchings ("diverticula") in the bowel wall (see illustrations). Diverticulosis simply means the presence of diverticula. Sometimes diverticula become plugged with feces, leading to inflammation and swelling of the colon in that area ("diverticulitis"). This inflammation causes pain and fever and may cause a blockage of the colon. Sometimes diverticulum bleed, causing painless bloody stools.

Before You Call the Doctor.   Diverticular disease is closely linked to low-fiber diets. The best way to prevent and treat this condition is to eat the type of diet recommended in EAT AND DRINK RIGHT in Chapter 1 and to follow the diet suggestions in the CONSTIPATION section of this chapter:

• Increase your consumption of liquids, whole grains and fresh fruits and vegetables.

• Avoid constipating foods—bananas, rice, applesauce.

• Eat at regular hours.

• Consider taking a bulk-forming supplement (psyllium).

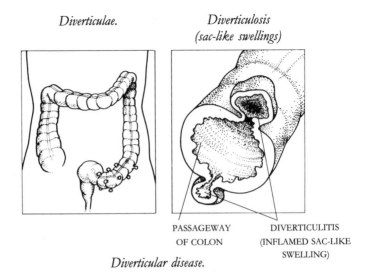

Diverticulae.   *Diverticulosis*
                        (sac-like swellings)

PASSAGEWAY   DIVERTICULITIS
OF COLON   (INFLAMED SAC-LIKE
                       SWELLING)
Diverticular disease.

• Also, don't eat small indigestible seeds—poppy, sesame, raspberry, strawberry, etc.—which can plug diverticula and lead to diverticulitis.

When to Call the Doctor.   Diverticulosis rarely requires professional treatment, but diverticulitis usually does. Consult a physician if diverticulitis symptoms develop. Some cases require hospitalization.

▶ **RED FLAGS**   Consult a physician promptly if:
• You experience dull, aching, intermittent, abdominal tenderness or pain on the lower left side, or if you experience severe, constant abdominal pain.
• Abdominal pain occurs with fever, nausea, or vomiting.
• You pass black or bloody stools.

FLATULENCE

(See also BELCHING and IRRITABLE BOWEL SYNDROME in this chapter)
Intestinal gas can feel quite uncomfortable. But for most people, the real issue is the social discomfort engendered by passing it rectally, commonly known as "farting" and medically known as "flatulence."

What's Going On?   Gas leaves the digestive tract either orally as belching or anally as flatus. Some swallowed air does not exit upward. It enters the small intestine and is eventually expelled anally.

But most flatus is produced in the intestine by undigested carbohydrate. Instead of being broken down in the stomach, some complex carbohydrate enters the small intestine intact. The intestine does not produce the enzymes necessary to digest it, so the carbohydrate just sits there. Eventually bacteria which normally reside in the bowel ferment it, a process which releases gas.

If you think you're producing more gas than you did a few years ago, you may be right. The healthy diet discussed in EAT AND DRINK RIGHT in Chapter 1 is low in fat but high in fiber, which means high in carbohydrate. If you've evolved your diet in a healthier direction recently, chances are you've been eating more of the foods most likely to produce gas.

On the other hand, most people who complain of "excessive gas" actually produce amounts gastroenterologists would call perfectly normal. Studies show that the average adult passes gas from eight to twenty times every waking day. In other words, there's nothing unusual about releasing gas more than once an hour.

But just because something is normal doesn't mean it's socially welcome. Flatus cannot be banished from the body, but it's likelihood can be significantly reduced.

Before You Call the Doctor.   Diet is the key:

• As most people know, legumes, that is, beans, peas, lentils, and soy products, are major gas offenders. They're high in nonabsorbable carbohydrate, so they're prone to fermentation in the intestine. On the other hand, they're also inexpensive sources of high-quality protein, fiber, and other nutrients. Instead of eliminating legumes, you can remove some of the carbohydrate that makes them gas producers by purchasing dry beans and soaking them in water overnight before cooking. Then discard that water and cook your beans in fresh water. Cook beans thoroughly. Uncooked starch increases gas production. Soybeans are among the most gas-producing legumes, but tofu, a fermented soy product, doesn't cause as many problems. Most of its indigestible carbohydrate is washed out during manufacturing.

• Lactose intolerance (see DIARRHEA in this chapter) is another major cause of flatulence.

• Some people notice an increase in flatulence when they eat foods sweetened with fruit sugar (fructose) or the artificial sweetener sorbitol. Read food labels carefully. Fructose is now used in many products, and many sugarless gums and diet items contain sorbitol.

• Some authorities claim cruciferous vegetables—cabbage, broccoli, cauliflower, and brussels sprouts—are gas producers. Others disagree, saying that these healthful vegetables, which are recommended by the American Cancer Society to help prevent several cancers, have been maligned unjustly. Experiment for yourself and see how they affect you.

• Eat more slowly. Chew food thoroughly. Make meals as relaxed as possible. If you eat quickly and wolf your food down, you swallow larger, harder-to-digest lumps, which are more likely to enter the intestine undigested.

• Eat a high-fiber diet with plenty of fluids. This is standard advice for preventing constipation (see CONSTIPATION in this chapter), and there's good reason to repeat it here. Constipation slows the passage of food through the lower digestive tract, increasing the likelihood of fermentation.

• Other foods possibly associated with gas include onions, radishes, celery, turnips, eggplant, and wheat germ. Some people also react to such white-flour products as bagels, pasta, pretzels, and pizza.

• Don't expect much relief from over-the-counter gas remedies. The much-touted antifoaming agent, simethicone, does not reduce gas production. It simply changes large gas bubbles into smaller ones. This may help reduce gas pains, but it won't do much for flatulence. Products containing activated charcoal don't do much either except interfere with the absorption of some nutrients and medications.

When to Call the Doctor.   Few physicians consider flatulence a medical problem. Those who do might recommend a mild laxative to reduce the time undigested carbohydrates sit in the colon.

FOOD POISONING

(See GASTROENTERITIS in this chapter)

GALLSTONES

Gallstones are solid pellets which form in the gallbladder in the upper right portion of the abdomen under the rib cage. Many cause no symptoms, but some cause severe pain in the upper right abdomen or between the shoulder blades. The pain typically starts a half hour after eating, builds to an intense peak, then subsides in an hour or so. Fever and vomiting are also possible.

What's Going On? About twenty million Americans have gallstones, and one million new cases are diagnosed each year. Only about 5 percent of men develop this illness, but it afflicts about 20 percent of women. Until recently, more than 300,000 Americans had gallbladder surgery each year to remove gallstones, and about 6,000 died from surgical complications. Now new stone-dissolving drugs and nonsurgical shock-wave treatments are becoming more popular, but gallbladder surgery continues to be performed, placing people at risk for its sometimes severe complications. Fortunately, most gallstones can be prevented with self-care.

The gallbladder is a small organ located under the liver. It stores bile, a liver secretion which helps digest fats. When food enters the small intestine, the gallbladder contracts, expelling some bile to help digest it. Bile is a mixture of many substances, but the one most likely to form gallstones is cholesterol, which accounts for about 75 percent of all cases.

Some gallstones simply sit in the gallbladder and cause no symptoms. Other stones, however, get stuck in the bile ducts, blocking the flow of bile into the intestine. The obstruction causes gallstone symptoms, also known as "biliary colic." The pain attacks continue as long as the stone remains in a bile duct. However, many stones either fall back into the gallbladder or get pushed into the intestine. When this happens, the attacks subside.

Many things can alter the composition of bile and trigger gallstone formation. The cholesterol concentration of bile increases in the presence of estrogen, the female sex hormone, which is why women develop gallstones so much more often than men. Anything that increases a woman's estrogen level—pregnancy, birth control pills, or post-menopausal estrogen replacement therapy—increases her risk of gallstones.

Other factors also increase the risk of gallstones:

• A high-fat diet, which increases cholesterol.

• Sedentary life-style, which increases LDL or "bad cholesterol" and decreases HDL or "good cholesterol."

• Diabetes.

• Obesity.

• High blood pressure ("hypertension").

• Smoking.

Before You Call the Doctor. Reduce your risk:

• Eat the high-fiber, low-fat diet recommended in EAT AND DRINK RIGHT in Chapter 1. Stay away from fatty foods. They raise cholesterol.

• Work to maintain your recommended weight. This keeps cholesterol under control and helps prevent both diabetes and hypertension.

• Quit smoking. For help quitting, see RESOURCES at the end of Chapter 11.

• If you have a family history of gallstones, think twice before using birth control pills or taking postmenopausal estrogen replacement therapy.

When to Call the Doctor.   Consult a physician if gallstone symptoms develop. Gallstones may be treated with stone-dissolving drugs, shock-wave therapy, or surgery.

▶ **RED FLAGS**   Consult a physician promptly for any intense pain in the upper right abdomen, particularly if it's associated with fever, nausea, or vomiting.

GAS

(See FLATULENCE in this chapter)

GASTRITIS

(See also GASTROENTERITIS, HEARTBURN, and ULCERS in this chapter)

Gastritis means inflammation of the stomach lining. Symptoms include upper abdominal burning pain under the rib cage and possibly nausea and vomiting. Heartburn and ulcer symptoms are also possible (see HEARTBURN and ULCERS in this chapter).

What's Going On?   Ask the average person to place a hand over his or her stomach, and the hand typically covers the navel. But the stomach sits higher up in the chest, under the ribcage, which is why this condition causes upper-abdominal distress.

Gastritis is a form of indigestion related to heartburn and ulcers. Physicians group all three of these conditions together as "acid peptic disorders." They are all associated with overproduction of stomach acids ("peptic" means digestive). Possible causes of gastritis include:

• Eating foods which disagree with you.

• Stomach irritation caused by aspirin, ibuprofen, or other drugs, particularly arthritis medications and caffeine.

• Smoking, which stimulates acid production.

• Excessive alcohol intake, which breaks down the stomach's natural barrier to acid damage.

• Food allergies.

• Infection with *Heliobacter pylori,* the bacteria now thought to cause many, if not most, ulcers.

• Infection by any of the viruses or bacteria that cause gastroenteritis.

• Anxiety, which stimulates acid production.

Before You Call the Doctor.   Gastritis responds well to self-care and rarely lasts longer than a day or two when treated properly:

• Don't drink coffee, colas with caffeine, or other carbonated beverages during an attack.

• If you smoke, quit. For help quitting, see RESOURCES at the end of Chapter 11.

• Stop drinking alcohol as long as symptoms persist. If you find yourself making excuses not to do this, you may have a drinking problem. Consult your physician for help.

• Follow the eating and life-style suggestions discussed in the HEARTBURN section of this chapter.

• Keep a food diary, and if you can determine whether certain foods trigger this problem, stop eating or cut back on them.

• Take over-the-counter antacids (see HEARTBURN, in this chapter).

When to Call the Doctor.   Physicians can prescribe stronger antacids and help you quit smoking and/or drinking. In persistent cases, they can also check for infection with the bacteria now believed to cause most ulcers, and if it's present in your stomach, they can prescribe antibiotics.

▶ **RED FLAGS**   Consult a physician promptly if you experience abdominal distress with fever and/or nausea or vomiting which does not respond to self-care within twenty-four hours, or if there is any blood in the vomitus.

GASTROENTERITIS

(See also DIARRHEA and VOMITING in this chapter)

Gastroenteritis is commonly called "stomach flu" or "food poisoning." Though symptoms may vary, the classic case involves the sudden onset of "explosions from both ends," vomiting and diarrhea, with fever and abdominal cramping also common.

What's Going On?   Gastroenteritis resembles infectious or traveler's diarrhea (see "Infectious Diarrhea" and "Traveler's Diarrhea" in the DI-ARRHEA section of this chapter), only it's worse. It can be caused by an enormous range of viruses, bacteria, protozoans, and toxins, for example, *Vibrio cholerae* (cholera) bacteria, *Clostridium* bacteria, which may contaminate meats; *Staphylococcus* bacteria, which can contaminate many foods; and *Salmonella* bacteria, which have become notorious in recent years because of news reports that they contaminate a good deal of the poultry supply. But the usual cause of infectious gastroenteritis in developed countries is a virus transmitted from hand to mouth from contaminated objects or people (see "Infectious Diarrhea" in the DIARRHEA section of this chapter).

The typical case of food-borne gastroenteritis is a group phenomenon. Someone brings potato or chicken salad to a picnic. It sits outside unrefrigerated for too long and any microorganisms in it multiply enough to cause food poisoning. Then, within a day or two, just about everyone who ate the contaminated food develops the same horrible symptoms. The best way to determine which food is responsible for food poisoning outbreaks is to catalogue what everyone ate and focus on what those who escaped the illness *didn't* eat.

Food-borne gastroenteritis appears to have become more prevalent in recent years because of *Salmonella* contamination of commercial chicken and other kinds of poultry. In recent years, Americans have cut down on red meat and have increased their consumption of chicken, some of which has been contaminated with *Salmonella* bacteria. Hence, there has been an increased incidence of this infection.

The majority of gastroenteritis cases clear up on their own within a week with bed rest and rehydration. The major risk is dehydration.

Before You Call the Doctor.   Be sure to drink plenty of fluids (see the discussion of rehydration and the "BRAT" diet in the DIARRHEA section of this chapter). In addition:

• Keep all picnic foods cool. Invest in a good cooler and pack it with ice.

• Beware of any picnic item made with mayonnaise. Many outbreaks of gastroenteritis are traced to potato salad, macaroni salad, tuna salad, and other mayonnaise-rich dishes.

• Bacteria thrive best in high-protein, high-moisture foods. Be especially careful to refrigerate poultry, fish, meats, milk, eggs, custards, and gravies.

• Follow the 2-40-140 rule. *Salmonella* and other microorganisms implicated in gastroenteritis grow best in the temperature range of 40° to 140°.

Don't keep foods in this temperature range for more than two hours. Temperatures reached during boiling, baking, frying, and roasting usually destroy *Salmonella*. And once clear of this pesky germ, refrigeration keeps food uncontaminated—as long as your refrigerator is set at less than 40°. Check it periodically with a thermometer.

• Eggs have also been found to be contaminated with *Salmonella*. Steer clear of recipes that call for uncooked eggs—for example, hollandaise sauce, mousse, and some frostings.

• A little *Salmonella* goes a long way. A contaminated chicken can contaminate your hands as well as the cutting board, marinade dish, counters, dish towels, and any other food items they contact. So, during cooking:

  ◦ Refrigerate foods quickly after purchasing them.
  ◦ Cool hot foods in shallow containers in the refrigerator, not by leaving them on the counter.
  ◦ Defrost foods in the microwave or refrigerator, not on the kitchen counter.
  ◦ Marinate foods in the refrigerator.
  ◦ Rinse all raw poultry, meats, and fish before beginning to prepare them.
  ◦ Wash your hands frequently with soap and water while preparing food.
  ◦ Don't use wooden cutting boards for poultry, meats, and fish. They're porous and give *Salmonella* a place to hide and grow. Use acrylic instead.
  ◦ Wash cutting boards after food preparation with soap and water, or in a dishwasher.
  ◦ Wash countertops as well.

• Cook red meat until most of the pink is gone, cook poultry until there is no red in the joints, and cook fish until it's flaky.

• Don't place cooked meat, fowl, or fish on the same plates that held them before they were cooked.

• Store stuffing separately from the poultry it's cooked in.

• Serve small quantities. Keep the rest safely refrigerated.

• Use leftovers quickly, or else divide them and freeze some for later use.

If gastroenteritis causes fever, think twice before taking aspirin or ibuprofen, which may further upset the stomach. Use acetaminophen or cool baths to relieve the fever.

Viral gastroenteritis and many other varieties of this disease usually clear up on their own within a week.

When to Call the Doctor.　Consult a physician if gastroenteritis does not clear up within a week. Doctors culture stool to see if they can grow any microorganisms. If so, they determine what kills them and prescribe that. Persistent gastroenteritis may be caused by the protozoans responsible for amebiasis and giardiasis (see "Amebiasis" and "Giardiasis" in the DIARRHEA section of this chapter).

GIARDIASIS

(See DIARRHEA and STOMACHACHE in this chapter)

HEARTBURN

(See also HEART ATTACK in Chapter 3 and CHEST PAIN and HEART ATTACK in Chapter 12)

An estimated 10 to 20 percent of Americans—some 25 to 50 million people—regularly suffer the burning, belching, discomfort when swallowing, and regurgitation of bitter gastric juices popularly known as heartburn and medically called "reflux," "esophageal reflux," or "gastroesophageal reflux." In addition to burning in the chest and throat, symptoms may include chest pain that is so severe that people think they're having a heart attack.

What's Going On?　Heartburn ranks among our most common ailments. It's also one of the most misunderstood because of its name. Heartburn has nothing to do with the heart. Heartburn is usually the result of a weakening of the opening ("sphincter") at the lower end of the esophagus, the food tube that runs from the throat to the stomach. This opening is called the lower esophageal sphincter, or LES. As food moves down the esophagus, the muscle tissue around the LES relaxes and the sphincter opens, allowing the food into the stomach. After eating, the LES closes to keep food-digesting stomach acids from splashing ("refluxing") up into the esophagus. Sometimes the muscles surrounding the LES lose their tone, and the sphincter remains open when it should be closed. Acid reflux occurs, which causes the pain and burning we recognize as heartburn. Over time, chronic inflammation of the lower esophagus develops ("esophagitis"), leading to scarring and narrowing in severe cases.

Heartburn typically strikes after meals because that's when the stomach secrets the acidic gastric juices that reflux up the esophagus. And when the stomach is full, the pressure inside it builds, so the contents are more likely to get pushed up through the LES. Unlike angina, which also causes chest pain, heartburn symptoms are not associated with physical activity and often become worse when the person lies down. Factors that contribute to LES problems and heartburn include:

- Smoking.
- Large meals.
- Hurried eating.
- Inadequate chewing.
- Emotional stress.
- Certain foods: chocolate, tea, coffee, alcohol, and mint, which is surprising because mint generally soothes the stomach.
- Obesity. All that extra tissue stresses the LES.
- Swallowing air along with food and/or drink—for example, carbonated beverages.
- Pregnancy. The growing fetus pushes other organs out of place and increases stomach pressure. Hormonal effects also relax the LES.
- Certain drugs: alcohol, aspirin, sedatives, tetracycline, asthma medications, calcium-channel blockers, vitamin C, and many others.
- Tight pants and belts. Anything that increases pressure on the abdomen may contribute to heartburn.
- Squatting, bending, or heavy lifting, especially with a full stomach.
- Naps after meals. Lying down after eating encourages reflux.
- Or a congenital LES problem.

Before You Call the Doctor. An understanding of heartburn's causes points the way to prevention strategies:

- Don't smoke (see RESOURCES at the end of Chapter 11).
- Eat smaller meals.
- Eat more slowly.
- Chew your food thoroughly.
- Make mealtime a time of relaxation, not stress.
- Sit when you eat, don't stand or lie down.
- Don't stoop or bend over after eating.
- Never wolf your food.
- Lose weight.
- Drink liquids between meals instead of with meals. Thicker stomach contents are less likely to reflux.
- Don't wear clothes that fit tightly around the abdomen.
- Drink less alcohol.
- Substitute another pain reliever/anti-inflammatory for aspirin, and ask your pharmacist about other possible drug substitutions.

• Chew gum or suck hard candies. These stimulate secretion of saliva, which can soothe the irritated esophagus.

• Cut back on chocolate, tea, coffee, and alcohol, all of which are often associated with heartburn. In addition, keep a food/heartburn diary. See if you can correlate specific foods with the onset of heartburn a few hours later. If so, cut back on the offending foods. In addition, many people find that fatty foods cause heartburn.

• If nighttime attacks are a problem, don't eat within a few hours of retiring, and elevate your upper body while sleeping. Use an upper-body-wedge pillow and/or raise the head of your bed with bricks.

• Over-the-counter antacids can provide temporary relief. Alka-Seltzer and Bromo-Seltzer are powerful and act quickly, but they contain a great deal of sodium and should not be used by people who must restrict their salt intake including those with high blood pressure, heart disease, diabetes, glaucoma, or a history of stroke. Tums and Rolaids are high in calcium and are now advertised as calcium supplements, but they should not be used by people with kidney disease. Also, calcium antacids tend to cause rebound acid overproduction. Milk of magnesia contains magnesium hydroxide. It may cause diarrhea. Maalox, Mylanta, and Di-Gel are combinations of magnesium hydroxide and aluminum hydroxide. Used according to directions, they have the best acid-neutralizing power without rebound acid overproduction.

When to Call the Doctor.   Consult a physician if you experience little or no improvement after two weeks of concerted self-care measures. Diagnosis typically requires x-rays and other tests. Prescription drugs which might help include:

• H2 blockers: cimetidine (Tagamet), ranitidine (Zantac), and famotidine (Pepcid). These are special antihistamines which decrease acid production.

• Sucralfate (Carafate) creates a physical barrier between the esophagus or stomach and its contents.

• Metoclopramide (Reglan) increases LES tone and hastens stomach emptying.

Severe cases with complications, such as narrowing of the esophagus, may require surgery.

Persistent heartburn may be caused by ulcers, gallbladder disease, or other gastrointestinal problems.

▶ **RED FLAGS**   The esophagus can suffer significant injury if exposed frequently over time to stomach acid. Chronic heartburn can actually burn holes in the esophagus ("esophageal ulcers"). Some heartburn symptoms, especially difficult or painful swallowing, may be caused by esophageal cancer. Consult a physician if symptoms resist self-care for more than two weeks.

Some heart attacks feel like heartburn. If you experience "heartburn" with pain that radiates up to the jaw or out to an arm, or if it is accompanied by sweating, nausea, dizziness, shortness of breath, or feelings of impending doom, chances are you're having a heart attack. Call 911 immediately, or have someone take you to an emergency medical facility immediately (see also HEART ATTACK in Chapter 3).

HEMORRHOIDS

(See also ANAL BLEEDING, ANAL ITCHING, ANAL PAIN, and CONSTIPATION in this chapter)

Authorities estimate that hemorrhoids affect one-third of Americans—some seventy-five million people. They cause rectal pain, itching, and bleeding and, in severe cases, make sitting, walking, sneezing, laughing, and defecating extremely painful.

What's Going On? Hemorrhoids are varicose veins of the anus (see VARICOSE VEINS in Chapter 12). Three veins drain blood away from the anal area. They expand ("dilate") during bowel movements and shrink back to normal size afterward. However, repeated straining during defecation—either from constipation or as a result of hard stools—can interfere with these veins' normal functioning. They may drain poorly and remain permanently swollen. As swelling occurs, the enlarged veins trigger nerves in the area, and the sufferer feels itching and fullness. In addition, defecation can rupture the swollen blood vessels, causing bleeding. Bleeding can range from faint pink streaks on toilet paper to bright red blood on underwear or in the toilet. Hemorrhoidal blood is usually not mixed with the stool.

Hemorrhoids can develop either inside or outside the anus (see illustration). Internal hemorrhoids tend to cause more severe symptoms, but external hemorrhoids may also feel quite painful.

Hemorrhoids are quite common during pregnancy because the developing fetus places pressure on all the veins of the lower abdomen.

As with varicose veins of the legs, there is a genetic component to hemorrhoids. Some people inherit more fragile, varicose-prone veins than others. However, if your parents or siblings have this problem, you are not necessarily doomed to it. Use your possible genetic predisposition as a message to practice good bowel habits and the prevention strategies

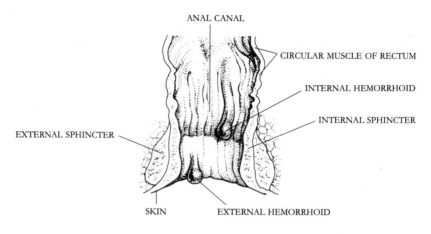

ANAL CANAL

CIRCULAR MUSCLE OF RECTUM

INTERNAL HEMORRHOID

INTERNAL SPHINCTER

EXTERNAL SPHINCTER

SKIN   EXTERNAL HEMORRHOID

Rectum.

discussed below. Meanwhile, if hemorrhoids don't run in your family, you're by no means home free. Tens of millions of North Americans develop this annoying problem—and unless you're careful, you might, too.

Before You Call the Doctor.   Hemorrhoids can usually be prevented with a combination of diet modifications and good bowel habits:

•Work to prevent constipation. Review the CONSTIPATION section of this Chapter. Eat a high-fiber diet. Snack on popcorn and fresh fruits. Drink plenty of nonalcoholic fluids. Get adequate rest and exercise. Never ignore the urge.

•When sitting on the toilet, don't bear down. Try to relax. Straining places considerable pressure on tender anal veins.

•Don't sit on the toilet any longer than necessary. Don't read, work, or watch TV in the bathroom. Even without bearing down, sitting on the toilet stresses anal veins.

•Adopt more of a squatting position on the toilet. Raise your feet on a small stool. This helps many people.

•If your job or other activities require you to sit for long periods, be sure to get up and walk around every hour or so to improve your circulation.

•Warm, twenty-minute sitz baths can help relieve hemorrhoidal discomfort and speed healing.

•For swollen and inflamed hemorrhoids, try ice packs. Their cooling can be soothing, and they help shrink swollen tissue. Wrap a few ice cubes in a plastic bag and wrap the bag in a clean cloth. Apply the ice pack for twenty minutes, then remove it for ten minutes before reapplying it. You may also use an ice substitute. Do not place ice directly on the skin. This can cause the equivalent of frostbite.

• Try wiping with witch hazel. This over-the-counter astringent cools and comforts and may help shrink swollen tissue. Tucks Premoistened Pads are 50 percent witch hazel.

• Try over-the-counter ointments and suppositories (Preparation H, Tucks, Anusol, Medicone, or zinc oxide). These products are popular but controversial. Some authorities say there's no proof they provide real benefit, but many people say they help. Be aware that benzocaine, the topical anesthetic, may cause allergic skin reactions.

When to Call the Doctor.   Severe hemorrhoids can be treated with a variety of surgical procedures.

▶ **RED FLAG**   Consult a physician promptly if you have any anal bleeding to rule out other, more serious problems.

HERNIA

(See also MUSCLE STRAINS in Chapter 15)

Hernias, also popularly known as "ruptures," cause bulging in the groin area and abdominal pain.

What's Going On?   The abdominal organs are encased inside a protective, supportive layer of muscle and connective tissue ("fascia"). If these layers become weakened or tear ("rupture"), the abdominal organs can protrude, causing a hernia.

There are many different kinds of hernia, all named for their location. Protrusions near the bottom of the rib cage are "epigastric hernias." Around the navel, they're "umbilical" or "paraumbilical hernias." And in the lower abdomen, they're "inguinal hernias." Hernias can also develop with no external signs at all (see HIATAL HERNIA in this Chapter). But when people say "hernia," they usually mean the inguinal variety, a protrusion of abdominal contents through an opening in the abdominal case in the area of the groin.

Small hernias may cause no symptoms other than a bulge or swelling. But over time, if the opening in the muscle layer grows larger, the person feels aching which may come and go or become persistent. Hernia pain also tends to become aggravated by activities that place pressure on the lower abdomen, for example, coughing, laughing, lifting, straining to defecate, and prolonged standing. The bulge of an inguinal hernia in a man may eventually extend into his scrotum.

One characteristic of hernias is that they come and go. Intestinal tissue may protrude through the tear for a while, then return to its normal position for a while before protruding again.

Sometimes hernias become obstructed, causing intense pain, nausea, and vomiting. Sometimes they become strangulated, cutting off blood supply to the loop of intestine that protrudes, also causing intense pain. This is a medical emergency because the tissue in the strangled loop can die and become gangrenous.

Before You Call the Doctor.   The myth is that if you feel sudden lower abdominal pain after lifting something heavy, you have a hernia. But the vast majority of people who self-diagnose hernia do not have one. They have lower abdominal muscle strains. It's not a hernia if there's no lump-like bulge in the abdomen or scrotum. For self-care of muscle problems, see MUSCLE STRAINS in Chapter 15.

When to Call the Doctor.   If you have a bulge in your abdomen, consult a physician. Most hernias are repaired surgically.

▶ **RED FLAGS**   Consult a doctor immediately if you have a hernia with intense pain, fever, nausea, or vomiting.

HIATAL HERNIA

(See also HEARTBURN in this chapter)

Hiatal hernia sometimes causes the painful burning in the chest known as heartburn. It may also cause belching and regurgitation of stomach acid up into the throat, causing a feeling similar to vomiting.

What's Going On?   Review the discussion of HEARTBURN in this chapter. The muscular lower esophageal sphincter (LES) opens to allow food to pass into the stomach, then closes to prevent stomach acids from washing back up ("refluxing") into the esophagus. When the LES weakens and reflux happens, the result is heartburn.

The esophagus also passes through the muscle layer known as the "diaphragm" on its way to the stomach. Sometimes part of the stomach protrudes up through the diaphragm, forming a bell-shaped pocket at the base of the esophagus. The protrusion is a hiatal hernia. Hiatal hernia is quite common, especially among the elderly and people who are over-weight. Many people with this condition are not bothered by it, but in some, the hernia interferes with the LES and contributes to heartburn.

Before You Call the Doctor.   Follow the self-care suggestions discussed in the HEARTBURN section. All of them also help relieve hiatal hernia. If you're overweight, try to lose weight.

When to Call the Doctor.   If self-care does not provide sufficient relief within a week or two, consult a physician. Doctors can prescribe antacids stronger than those available over the counter. In severe cases, hiatal hernia can be repaired surgically.

▶ **RED FLAGS**   The esophagus can suffer significant injury if exposed frequently over time to stomach acid. Chronic heartburn due to hiatal hernia can burn holes in the esophagus ("esophageal ulcers") or cause inflammation of the esophageal lining ("esophagitis"). If heartburn persists, consult a physician.

INDIGESTION

(See also GALLSTONES, GASTRITIS, HEARTBURN, HIATAL HERNIA, IRRITABLE BOWEL SYNDROME, STOMACHACHE, and ULCERS in this chapter)
     Indigestion, medically known as "dyspepsia," is a catch-all term for a large number of gastrointestinal problems associated with eating. In common parlance, it means abdominal pain or bloating.

Before You Call the Doctor.   To deal with your indigestion, start by reading the STOMACHACHE section of this chapter to locate the problem specifically. Recurrent upper abdominal pain relieved by eating suggests gastritis, ulcer, or possibly heartburn. Upper abdominal pain aggravated by eating suggests gallstones or heartburn. Midabdominal pain suggests gastroenteritis or irritable bowel syndrome. Lower abdominal distress suggests colitis, irritable bowel syndrome, or, in women, possibly a pelvic problem (see Chapter 16). Indigestion might also be amebiasis or giardiasis (see DIARRHEA in this chapter).

When to Call the Doctor.   Of course, there are many other possible causes of abdominal pain. A single episode that clears up with simple self-care, for example, with antacids or diet changes, is nothing to worry about. But if indigestion persists longer than a week or two despite committed self-care, consult a physician.

▶ **RED FLAGS**   Consult a physician promptly if indigestion is accompanied by fever, vomiting, black or bloody stools, or any other unusual symptoms.

IRRITABLE BOWEL SYNDROME

(See also COLITIS, CONSTIPATION, DIARRHEA, DIVERTICU-LAR DISEASE, and FLATULENCE in this chapter)

Also known as "IBS," "irritable colon," "spastic colon," and "functional bowel disorder," this illness causes pain or cramping in the middle and lower abdomen (often on the left side) and diarrhea. Sometimes there are periods of constipation. Other possible symptoms include belching, bloating, flatulence, and occasionally, fatigue, anxiety, and headache.

What's Going On?   Irritable bowel syndrome isn't really a disease. It's a collection of gastrointestinal symptoms that cause discomfort and abdominal distress. Irritable bowel syndrome is one of the most frequent reasons people consult physicians for gastrointestinal problems. An estimated one American in six—some forty million people—have this problem to some degree. Gastroenterologists estimate that half their patients have it.

IBS usually appears in late adolescence or early adulthood. Women develop it more often than men. Many people with irritable bowel syndrome never do anything about it. They simply live with a "nervous stomach."

IBS is a problem with how the colon works. The colons of people with the condition appear normal, with no ulcers, polyps, tumors, blockages, or other structural problems. However, in severe cases, IBS symptoms may resemble those of more serious colon problems.

After food has been digested, what remains passes in liquid form into the large intestine, also known as the colon or large bowel. The colon removes most of the water from it, leaving semi-solid stools. These move through the colon, into the rectum, and out the anus because of wavelike contractions called "peristalsis." Peristalsis should be a gentle, hardly noticeable process. But in irritable bowel syndrome, for reasons that usually remain a mystery, the contractions become irregular, poorly coordinated, and at times unusually forceful or lethargic. The result is the pain, diarrhea, constipation, and other symptoms of IBS.

Before You Call the Doctor. IBS usually responds to self-care, though it may take a while to resolve:

• Steer clear of high-fat foods: butter, heavy cream, hot dogs, sausage, other fatty meats, pizza, and fast foods. Eat the low-fat, high-fiber diet recommended in EAT AND DRINK RIGHT in Chapter 1.

• If diarrhea is a problem after eating, review the DIARRHEA section of this Chapter—particularly the "Lactose Intolerance" discussion—and beware of foods that have a laxative effect, including fruits and coffee and other caffeine-containing beverages. Dairy products may also be a problem for those with any lactose intolerance. Increase your fluid intake to prevent dehydration.

• If constipation is a problem, review the CONSTIPATION section of this chapter. Increase your fiber intake, exercise, and beware of binding foods, such as bananas, rice, applesauce, toast, and tea.

• Review the FLATULENCE section of this chapter, and limit your consumption of gas-producing foods: beans, other legumes, and carbonated beverages.

• Keep a food diary, and see if you can correlate your symptoms with specific food items. If so, limit their consumption.

• Work at managing stress. Stress, per se, does not cause IBS, but it often aggravates symptoms, and the condition itself can be anxiety-provoking (see MANAGE YOUR STRESS LOAD in Chapter 1). Exercise often helps relieve psychological tensions as well as any constipation.

• Get plenty of sleep. If getting enough sleep is a problem, see INSOMNIA in Chapter 4.

• Limit your consumption of coffee and alcohol.

• Quit smoking. For help, see RESOURCES at the end of Chapter 11.

• Follow the dining suggestions in the HEARTBURN section of this chapter. Eat slowly. Chew thoroughly. Make mealtimes as relaxed as possible. Stick to a regular three-meal-a-day schedule.

• To relieve abdominal pain, try taking a hot bath or apply a heating pad to the lower abdomen.

• When you feel the urge to defecate, do so. Delay may contribute to constipation later.

• Don't eat foods sweetened with the diet sweetener sorbitol.

When to Call the Doctor. Physicians increasingly recommend self-care for IBS, but they can also treat its symptoms with various drugs:

antidiarrheals, antispasmodics, laxatives, and muscle relaxants. In persistent cases, tests should be performed to rule out diverticular disease,
intestinal parasites, and other more serious problems. Ask to be tested for
giardiasis. This parasite is difficult to detect, and giardiasis may be misdiagnosed as "irritable bowel."

▶ **RED FLAGS**   Consult a physician if:
  • You pass black or bloody stools.
  • Abdominal pain becomes more severe or changes from periodic to
constant.
  • Vomiting occurs in addition to abdominal symptoms.
  • Fever occurs in addition to abdominal symptoms.
  • Symptoms do not improve noticeably after two weeks of concerted
self-care.

LACTOSE INTOLERANCE

(See DIARRHEA in this chapter)

NAUSEA

(See VOMITING in this chapter)

NERVOUS STOMACH

(See COLITIS, GALLSTONES, GASTRITIS, HEARTBURN, HIATAL
HERNIA, INDIGESTION, IRRITABLE BOWEL SYNDROME,
STOMACHACHE, and ULCERS in this chapter)

RUPTURE

(See HERNIA in this chapter)

STOMACH FLU

(See GASTROENTERITIS in this chapter)
  "Stomach flu" is a misnomer. "Flu" is short for influenza, a respira-

tory tract infection (see FLU in Chapter 11). Stomach flu is actually gastroenteritis.

STOMACHACHE

(See also COLIC, COLITIS, CONSTIPATION, DIVERTICULAR DIS-EASE, GALLSTONES, GASTRITIS, HEARTBURN, HIATAL HER-NIA, INDIGESTION, IRRITABLE BOWEL SYNDROME, and ULCERS in this chapter)

Ask people the location of the stomach, and most place a hand over the navel. That's not the stomach. It's the intestine. The stomach is located beneath the ribcage slightly to the left of the sternum. As a result of this widespread misconception, when people say they have a "stomachache," the problem may or may not have anything to do with the stomach. For our purposes, we'll equate "stomachache" and "abdominal distress."

What's Going On?   Pain is not a disease. It's a symptom. Abdominal pain can be a symptom of dozens of health problems. To narrow things down a bit, consider abdominal pain in the context of the following issues:

• How is it? Is it acute, coming on fiercely and suddenly? Or chronic, a dull pain that's there all the time? Or recurrent, sharp pains that come and go intermittently? Acute pain might be gas, a perforated ulcer, or many other problems ranging from medically minor to quite serious. Chronic pain might be anything from simple constipation to bowel cancer. Recurrent pain might be heartburn, hernia, or an ulcer.

• Where is it? Think of the abdomen as divided into three zones: an upper area under the ribs, a middle area around the navel, and a lower area below the navel. Pain in the upper area probably comes from the stomach, gallbladder, and upper intestine. It might be heartburn, gastritis, gallstones, or an ulcer. Pain in the middle area probably involves the small and/or large intestine and might be appendicitis, colitis, gas, gastroenteritis, irritable bowel syndrome, or the emotionally caused "pain in the pit of the stomach" associated with stressful life events. Pain in the lower area usually comes from the lower colon and pelvic organs. It might indicate late appendicitis, colitis, gas, irritable bowel syndrome, or problems with the bladder (see URINARY TRACT INFECTION in Chapter 14), uterus, fallopian tubes, or ovaries (see PELVIC PAIN in Chapter 16).

• When and how did it begin? If the pain began suddenly moments after you discovered your priceless Stradivarius violin stolen, chances are the cause is emotional, what doctors call "psychogenic." If the pain recurs in the upper area after meals, it's probably heartburn or gallstones. If it recurs between meals in the upper or middle area, it might be an ulcer. If the pain began as dull, generalized abdominal distress, then localized in the lower right area after a few hours, it might be acute appendicitis, and you should consult a physician immediately. If you gradually become aware of a constant vague pain that doesn't change during the course of the day, especially if you can feel a lump, this could be cancer, and you should be examined by a physician without delay.

• Are there any other symptoms? Upper abdominal pain that recurs after meals and also causes belching and burning chest pain is probably heartburn. Middle and/or lower abdominal pain with diarrhea and bloating might be lactose intolerance or irritable bowel syndrome. The occurrence of these symptoms with fatigue and possibly fever suggest tourista, amebiasis, giardiasis, or some other form of infectious diarrhea. Middle and/or lower abdominal pain with vomiting may be gastroenteritis. Burning pain above the navel between meals and at night suggests an ulcer. And so on.

Before You Call the Doctor.   Ask yourself the questions above and try to develop a portrait of your stomachache that's as precise as possible. Then read the sections of this and other chapters that seem to apply, and follow the self-care suggestions for a week or two.

When to Call the Doctor.   If the pain persists or grows worse, consult a physician. Describe the pain as precisely as possible. Describe what you did, and if anything helped or aggravated the condition. Also take along a list of all the drugs you're taking, both over-the-counter and prescription products. Many widely used drugs can cause abdominal distress.

▶ **RED FLAGS**   Consult a physician immediately if:
• Abdominal pain begins as dull and generalized in the middle area then, over a few hours, becomes sharper and more localized on the right side in the lower middle area. This might be appendicitis.
• Abdominal pain keeps getting worse and is accompanied by vomiting. This might also be appendicitis or an intestinal blockage.
• Abdominal pain is accompanied by black, blood-tinged, or bloody stools. This might be an ulcer or colitis.
• Abdominal pain occurs with fever and vaginal discharge. This might be pelvic inflammatory disease.
• Any abdominal pain does not respond significantly to self-care treatments after two weeks.

TOURISTA

(See DIARRHEA in this chapter)

TROUBLE SWALLOWING

(See also HEARTBURN and HIATAL HERNIA in this chapter)

If difficulty swallowing does not seem to be related to heartburn or hiatal hernia, consult your physician to rule out other possible causes: esophageal cancer, Sjögren's syndrome, esophageal yeast infection ("thrush"), or other serious conditions.

▶ **RED FLAGS** If trouble swallowing doesn't clear up after two weeks of self-care, see a physician to rule out cancer or permanent scarring of the esophagus ("stricture").

ULCERATIVE COLITIS

(See COLITIS in this chapter)

ULCERS

"Ulcers" mean open wounds. You can have skin ulcers, colonic ulcers ("ulcerative colitis"), and ulceration of other parts of the body. But when people say "ulcers," they almost always mean open—sometimes bleeding—sores in the stomach ("gastric ulcers") or at the junction of the stomach and small intestine ("duodenal ulcers").

What's Going On? Gastric and duodenal ulcers are collectively known as "peptic ulcers," because "peptic" means digestive. Stomach acid, mostly hydrochloric acid, is quite powerful. It would burn right through most body tissues. But the stomach lining resists its action, and in the normal healthy stomach, the acid digests only food and not the stomach wall. But when an ulcer forms, the wound destroys the stomach lining's integrity. When stomach acids come in contact with the ulcer, the result is burning pain. Pain is worst when the stomach is empty. During and shortly after meals, the acids work on food, but between meals, the acids irritate the ulcer. Peptic ulcers generally cause burning pain between meals in the small area between the breastbone and navel. Pain also frequently occurs at night, especially if a bedtime snack has stimulated acid secretion.

Ulcers were one of the first serious diseases blamed on stress. The stereotype was that they afflicted primarily hard-driving executives. The theory was that stress stimulated excess acid secretion, which eventually ate holes in the stomach wall and duodenal lining. Then epidemiological studies showed that ulcers were not confined to the executive suite but cut a wide demographic swath across America, in all racial, ethnic, and occupational groups, from children to the elderly. Nonetheless, the stress theory remained entrenched. Anyone can suffer significant stress, so anyone could get an ulcer. And stress does, in fact, increase acid production along with numerous other effects on the body.

But recently the stress theory has come under strong attack from a new view which holds that ulcers are the result of bacterial infection by an organism called *Campylobacter* or *Helicobacter pylori.* This microorganism, until recently quite difficult to detect, has been found in the stomach linings of the vast majority of people with peptic ulcers, and eradicating the bacteria has been shown to heal the disease.

However, there is still a place for self-care in ulcer prevention and treatment. Many people are infected with *C./H. pylori* without having ulcers. The organism seems to run in families, as ulcers do. The current theory is that the bacteria and other cofactors combine to produce the ulceration.

Before You Call the Doctor.   Here's a list of things that contribute to ulcer formation and pain. If ulcers run in your family, or if you have a sensitive stomach, beware of:

- Aspirin and ibuprofen.
- Smoking.
- Alcohol.
- Coffee.
- Stress (see MANAGE YOUR STRESS LOAD in Chapter 1).

To relieve ulcer pain, try the over-the-counter antacids discussed in the HEARTBURN section of this chapter.

Twenty years ago, most doctors recommended a bland, low-spice, low-fiber diet, sometimes with extra milk. Now we know that spicy and high-fiber diets have no significant effect on ulcer healing one way or the other, and that milk has a mild initial antacid effect but then stimulates a rebound increase in stomach acidity.

When to Call the Doctor.   Until the new research on *C./H. pylori,* physicians treated ulcers with high-dose antacids—cimetidine (Tagamet), ranitidine (Zantac), sucralfate (Carafate), and omeprazole (Prilosec)—and, in severe cases, surgery. In the future, however, authorities say they'll be more likely to treat this disease with antibiotics.

▶ **RED FLAGS**   Consult a physician immediately if there is any:
• Vomiting of blood, a sign of gastrointestinal bleeding.
• Black, red, or bloody stools, another sign of GI bleeding.
• Or sudden onset of intense unrelenting abdominal pain, a sign of perforation, which involves the spilling of stomach contents into the abdominal cavity. This is a medical emergency which requires surgery as quickly as possible.

VOMITING

(See also DIVERTICULAR DISEASE, GALLSTONES, GASTRITIS, GASTROENTERITIS, STOMACHACHE, and ULCERS in this chapter)
     Vomiting involves strong gastrointestinal muscle contractions, which expel stomach contents out of the mouth. It's usually preceded by the abdominal distress and queasiness of nausea.

What's Going On?   Vomiting is not a disease but a sign of a problem in the gastrointestinal tract. It may be related to diverticular disease, gallstones, gastritis, gastroenteritis, stomachache, and ulcers. Vomiting may also be caused by pregnancy, hepatitis, or kidney stones (see KIDNEY STONES in Chapter 14). In some cases vomiting may reflect more serious problems, such as intestinal blockage, appendicitis, or peritonitis.

Before You Call the Doctor.   If vomiting appears to be related to one of the gastrointestinal conditions listed above and the situation does not appear to be an emergency (see "Red Flags" below), implement the self-care suggestions in that section of this chapter. In addition, to relieve morning sickness or to relieve the abdominal distress vomiting causes:
• Eat crackers.
• Drink water or bouillon.
• Try ginger ale.
• Try mint tea.
• Temporarily stay away from fatty foods, spicy foods, and milk and dairy products.
     Babies younger than six months often vomit ("spit up") small amounts of breast milk or formula after feeding. This is normal and no

cause for concern. If it occurs, take breaks during feedings to allow the child to burp and digest.

When to Call the Doctor.   However, if food shoots from a baby's mouth forcefully ("projectile vomiting"), or if vomiting in an adult does not respond to self-care within two days, consult a physician for diagnostic testing. Vomiting can be a symptom of many illnesses, some potentially serious.

▶ **RED FLAGS**   Consult a physician immediately if any of the following situations arise:
  • Vomiting blood or brown grainy material.
  • Vomiting and diarrhea in an infant.
  • Vomiting in an infant who cries inconsolably.
  • Vomiting everything you ingest, including sips of water.
  • Vomiting associated with diarrhea in frail people, such as the very old or those with severe heart disease. Dehydration and shock can occur much faster in these groups.

CHAPTER 14

The Urinary Tract

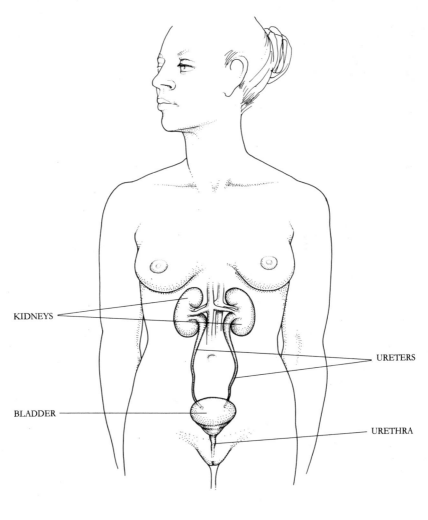

KIDNEYS

URETERS

BLADDER

URETHRA

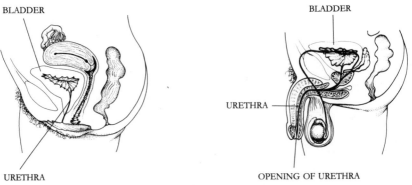

BLADDER

URETHRA

BLADDER

URETHRA

OPENING OF URETHRA

The Urinary Tract.

BEDWETTING

(See also URINARY INCONTINENCE and URINARY TRACT IN-
FECTION in this chapter)

The keys to handling this common and sleep-robbing problem of
preschool children are empathy and patience.

What's Going On?   Bedwetting, medically known as "enuresis," (en-
yure-EE-sis), is largely a childhood problem, though disease and aging can
cause loss of bladder control among adults (see URINARY INCONTI-
NENCE in this chapter). By four years of age, about 75 percent of
children are able to stay dry all night. But by age five, 10 to 15 percent still
regularly wet their beds, and many more have occasional nighttime "accidents." For reasons that remain unclear, boys are almost twice as likely as
girls to wet their beds. No clear hereditary connection has ever been
discovered, but children of parents who were bedwetters appear to be
more likely to suffer the problem.

According to many pediatricians, bedwetting children often have
unusually small bladder capacities. They need to urinate during the day
more frequently than other children and can only hold a small amount of
urine at night. This doesn't mean their bladders are any smaller than those
of non-bedwetters, only that they feel full with less urine.

In the vast majority of cases of chronic childhood bedwetting, the
problem is not caused by any disease or physical abnormality. It's simply
the nighttime version of the problem all children have becoming toilet
trained during the day. Nighttime bladder control is not an easy skill to
master, and parents who berate or punish children for their accidents need
to change their tactics to help their children develop nighttime control.

In cases where bedwetting begins after a dry period of six to twelve
months, the cause is often emotional distress—divorce, starting school, or
the arrival of another child in the family. But in 1 to 3 percent of cases,
there is a physical cause, usually bladder infection, but possibly other
problems as well: diabetes, sickle cell disease, or a neurological disorder.

Before You Call the Doctor.   To deal with the problem constructively,
the first thing parents need to do is let go of the anger and recriminations
this problem often engenders. Children who wet their beds *want* to stop
and may fear they wet because they are bad, stupid, or lazy. Parents who
accuse their children of these traits simply compound the problem. Instead of accusations, parents need to instill confidence that the child can
and will overcome the problem in due course. This supports the child's

desire to stay dry. Some parents also blame themselves for their children's bedwetting. This is equally incorrect and unproductive. Helping children learn to stay dry at night is no different from teaching them the thousands of other skills they must learn as they grow. However, this one is especially challenging because children must learn to rouse themselves from sleep to urinate—and because parents awakened by nocturnal accidents may not be in the best of moods at 3:00 A.M.

Here are the self-care suggestions specialists recommend:

• Never scold, embarrass, or punish children for bedwetting. When you hear that plaintive cry in the middle of the night, take several deep breaths to compose yourself before going into the child's bedroom. Tell yourself what pediatricians know to be true: Getting angry only compounds the problem.

• Be prepared. If your child is having trouble learning nighttime bladder control, place a rubberized pad under the child's bed linens to keep the mattress from becoming soaked with urine. Get ready for accidents before you go to bed. Have a change of pajamas ready. There's no need to change the linen in the middle of the night. Simply place a folded bath towel over the wet spot, and deal with the linen in the morning.

• Listen. Enuresis is sometimes initiated or perpetuated by emotional trauma. Talk calmly with children and ask if anything is bothering them.

• Limit liquids after supper. Reward children for not drinking water when they brush their teeth before bed.

• Take the child to the bathroom at bedtime. Don't demand urination. And never punish them for not urinating. Simply take them into the bathroom and suggest that they "empty the tank" before bed.

• Teach your children "kiddie Kegels." Kegels are bladder-control exercises named after the physician who popularized them. They involve strengthening the muscles which control urine flow by learning to stop urination in midstream, then starting again. Have children practice starting and stopping their urine stream. Make it a game. Offer a reward—for example, an extra bedtime story. As general bladder and urine control improve, greater nighttime bladder control usually follows.

• Transfer responsibility. Bedwetting can become a power struggle between children and parents. Tell children gently but firmly that they are in charge of changing their pajamas and cleaning up after their accidents.

• Lavish praise for dry nights. In addition to hugs and verbal praise, place stars on a calendar, and offer rewards: healthy treats, small toys, or special videos the child enjoys.

• If the child's room or pajamas begin to smell of stale urine, have the child drink cranberry juice for snacks. Cranberry juice helps deodorize urine.

• If the problem persists after age five, discuss it with the child's doctor, who will probably perform simple screening tests. Continue the measures listed above and prepare to wait another year before trying the next two suggestions.

• If children are still having problems after age six and you're at your wits' end, get a bedwetting alarm. These nifty devices sound an alarm at the first sign of wetness. The noise conditions children to wake up when they need to urinate. Studies have shown them very effective in eliminating chronic bedwetting after age seven. Enuresis alarms are available at medical supply houses, or ask your pharmacist or physician where you can obtain one. They cost $50 to $75. But before investing in an enuresis alarm, see the child's doctor for tests to rule out infection.

• After age six, bladder-stretching exercises have been shown to help about one-third of children with bladder capacity problems. When they have to go, ask children to hold their urine for a little while, like five minutes. Gently explain that this isn't a punishment, but rather a way to help them increase the size of the "pee holder" inside them, so they can stay dry at night. Make a game of it, with praise and rewards. Monitor their urine volume on a chart by timing how long it takes them to void.

When to Call the Doctor. Sometimes, particularly among girls, bedwetting may be caused by a urinary tract infection (see URINARY TRACT INFECTION in this chapter). If a bedwetting child complains of abdominal pain, pain on urination, or if you notice any increase in frequency of daytime urination, consult a physician.

Several diseases can increase urinary output and cause bedwetting, including diabetes and sickle-cell disease. See a physician if the bedwetting is associated with unusual daytime thirst and urination. Neurologic problems can also cause bedwetting. Clues include loss of bowel as well as bladder control, or decreased strength, sensation, or coordination of the legs.

If your child takes any medication frequently—even over-the-counter drugs—ask your physician or pharmacist if they might contribute to the problem.

Whenever bedwetting persists after age six, consult a physician to rule out any serious health problems. The doctor will likely do a urine analysis ("urinalysis") and may recommend other tests.

Although nondrug methods usually work, anti-enuretic drugs, such as imipramine and DDAVP, or bladder antispasmodic drugs, such as oxybutynin, may help too.

▶ **RED FLAG**   Sweet-smelling urine with increased thirst, urination, and bedwetting strongly suggests diabetes, a potentially life-threatening disease. Consult a physician immediately.

BLADDER INFECTION

(See URINARY TRACT INFECTION in this chapter)

BLOOD IN URINE

(See also COLOR CHANGE IN URINE, DIFFICULT URINATION, PAINFUL URINATION, and URINARY TRACT INFECTION in this chapter)

This condition is medically known as "hematuria." Bright red blood in urine or on toilet paper requires prompt professional attention, but a little blood, which shows up on a chemical dipstick test, though potentially alarming, may simply be the result of eating certain vegetables or exercising especially vigorously.

What's Going On?   The urinary tract begins with the kidneys, which filter liquid wastes from the blood, creating urine. Urine is stored in the bladder and released through the urine tube ("urethra"). Trauma, infection, or irritation anywhere along the urinary tract can introduce blood into the urine.

Before You Call the Doctor.   If you suspect blood in your urine, first review your diet. That "blood" may not be blood at all. Foods such as beets, rhubarb, and blackberries can stain urine red.

In infants, "blood" may be urate crystals. Urates cause reddish discoloration of diapers. They are harmless. Urates are normally present in urine. But if they cool to room temperature, the reddish crystals form.

Another harmless infant condition that might be mistaken for "blood" is "red diaper syndrome." The predominant bacteria in newborns' intestinal tracts is *Serratia marcescens,* which produce a red pigment that may stain diapers. Actual blood in infants' urine is rare, but when in doubt, consult a physician.

Drugs can also alter the color of the urine. Such drugs include rifampin, an antibiotic, and phenazopyridine (Pyridium), a urinary anesthetic used to reduce the discomfort of urinary tract infections.

Once you're fairly sure the blood in your urine really is blood, then review your exercise program and recent medical history. The cumulative pounding of long-distance running can traumatize the bladder and urinary tract enough to rupture some tiny capillaries, resulting in blood-tinged urine. This is a common experience among marathon runners, but you don't have to race twenty-six miles to suffer it. Exercise-related minor urinary bleeding is usually harmless and disappears within a day or so. Increase your nonalcoholic fluid intake to flush the urinary tract, which helps prevent infection.

Everyday traumas such as falls, minor auto and bicycle accidents, or any sharp blow to the kidney area on either side of the mid-back can introduce blood into the urine.

Finally, ask your parents and other close relatives if they have blood in their urine. Some people have a hereditary condition called "benign familial hematuria," which is usually discovered microscopically during a routine urinalysis. The small amount of blood introduced into the urine by this condition doesn't harm these people, who typically have normal bladder function and no symptoms of urinary disorders. If you have benign familial hematuria, be sure to mention it anytime you see a physician. If you don't and the doctor discovers blood, you may be subjected to unnecessary medical tests.

When to Call the Doctor.   Visible blood in the urine should always be checked by a physician. If you have no history of familial hematuria, your treatment will depend on the results of a physical exam, urinalysis, kidney ("renal") function testing, and quite possibly other tests.

Blood in the urine may also be caused by a variety of more serious health problems, including kidney and urinary tract infection, prostate problems, kidney stones, some tumors, or other diseases.

COLOR CHANGE IN URINE

(See also BLOOD IN URINE in this chapter)

Normal-looking urine is usually yellowish to yellow-gold and clear. Any other color or any loss of clarity may mean trouble.

What's Going On?   Brightly-colored foods, for example, beets and rhubarb pie, can darken urine. Food dyes may also affect urine color.

Certain drugs can turn urine bright orange. Such drugs include rifampin, an antibiotic, and phenazopyridine (Pyridium), a urinary anesthetic used to reduce the discomfort of urinary tract infections.

Blood and certain foods make urine appear pinkish or red (see BLOOD IN URINE in this chapter).

Vomiting and/or diarrhea can cause dehydration, which darkens urine (see VOMITING and DIARRHEA in Chapter 13).

Many factors that decrease the amount of water in the urine can turn it an unusually deep yellow or orange: a fever above 100°, physical exertion in hot weather, laxative overuse, and other causes of dehydration.

If urine turns dark brown, stools appear pale, and skin or the whites of the eyes appear yellow ("jaundice"), the problem may be a liver disorder.

Before You Call the Doctor.   Review the list above and see if there's a simple explanation for the color change. For darkened urine caused by dehydration resulting from fever, vomiting, diarrhea, or exercise, increase your nonalcoholic fluid intake. Drink eight ounces of water, juices, or soup every two hours.

When to Call the Doctor.   Consult a physician if the color change does not resolve within a few days.

▶ **RED FLAGS**   See a physician promptly if:
• Fever associated with a urine color change lasts longer than twenty-four to forty-eight hours or rises higher than 102°, especially if increased fluid intake doesn't help.
• Vomiting associated with any urine color change lasts longer than twenty-four hours without improvement.
• Diarrhea associated with any urine color change lasts longer than forty-eight hours without improvement.
• You develop yellowing of the eyes or skin, which suggests jaundice, a sign of a liver disorder.
• Or if your urine suddenly turns pink, red, or smoky-brown for no obvious reason.

CYSTITIS

(See URINARY TRACT INFECTION in this chapter)

DIFFICULT URINATION

(See also EXCESSIVELY FREQUENT URINATION and PAINFUL URINATION in this chapter and PROSTATE ENLARGEMENT in Chapter 17)

"Difficulty" here means trouble getting started, medically known as "urinary hesitancy." This problem usually includes a decrease in the force of the urinary stream. Primarily a problem in men, difficult urination usually feels as though something is obstructing the urinary tract—which may or may not be the case.

What's Going On?   The most common cause of urinary hesitancy in young men is "bashful bladder," an inability to urinate around others. This problem has nothing to do with heterosexuals' fear of homosexual encounters. It's simply the result of feeling uncomfortable about a lack of privacy at urinals.

The typical cause of this problem in men over fifty years of age is prostate enlargement, usually the result of a noncancerous condition medically known as "benign prostatic hypertrophy" or BPH (see PROSTATE ENLARGEMENT in Chapter 17). The urine tube ("urethra") passes through the prostate gland, like a hose through a doughnut. When the prostate becomes enlarged the doughnut hole grows smaller and squeezes the urethra, narrowing the space through which urine must pass. BPH is often accompanied by one or more of the following:

• The need to get up one or more times at night to urinate.

• Decreased urinary force.

• Dribbling after voiding.

• Incomplete emptying, which may also result in a need to urinate frequently and adds to the need to get up at night.

Once BPH symptoms begin, they do not come and go. If you have intermittent symptoms, you may have another problem, "prostate syndrome" (see PROSTATITIS in Chapter 17).

Before You Call the Doctor.   Here's a simple, surprisingly effective cure for bashful bladder. At the urinal, count down from 100 by sevens: 100, 93, 86, 79, etc. Concentrating on mental arithmetic takes the mind off the minor embarrassment of public urination and allows constricted muscles to relax, which frees urine flow.

If this doesn't work, use a stall.

If BPH is the problem, do not limit your fluid intake. This may increase your risk of bladder and/or prostate infection.

When to Call the Doctor.   As BPH develops, most men don't mind getting up once a night. But when they have to get up two to four times, most say "Enough!" and consult a urologist about treatment. (See PROS-TATE ENLARGEMENT in Chapter 17.)

Difficult urination can also be caused by bladder stones, anatomic abnormalities, the development of narrow areas ("strictures") in the urinary tract, infections that interfere with bladder function, and nerve damage to the bladder from diseases such as diabetes. These require professional care.

▶ **RED FLAG**   Inability to urinate at all is a medical emergency. Consult a physician immediately.

EXCESSIVELY FREQUENT URINATION

No frequency is automatically "too frequent," but any sudden increase in urinary frequency may be cause for concern.

What's Going On?   Frequent urination can signal a variety of changes in the body—some minor, others serious.

Pregnant women often complain of the need to urinate more frequently. This is normal and no cause for concern. The expanding uterus puts pressure on the bladder, decreasing its capacity and increasing the urge to void. The increased blood supply of pregnancy also boosts urine production.

Caffeine and alcohol are both mild diuretics. If your consumption of either or both increases, so will your need to urinate.

Most first-line medications for high blood pressure ("hypertension") and congestive heart failure are diuretics, which lower blood pressure by reducing blood volume. Anyone taking diuretics will spend more time in the bathroom (see HIGH BLOOD PRESSURE and CONGESTIVE HEART FAILURE in Chapter 12).

Some people react to cold weather, emotional excitement, or anxiety with increased urinary frequency.

When increased frequency is associated with fatigue, weight loss, increased thirst, and sweet-smelling urine, the cause is probably diabetes.

In women, frequent and/or painful urination with white or greenish-yellow discharge and/or itching around the genital area may indicate a vaginal yeast infection or trichomonas (see YEAST INFECTION in Chapter 16 and TRICHOMONAS in Chapter 18).

In sexually active men, the need to urinate unusually frequently may be a symptom of genital infection, possibly chlamydia, gonorrhea or venereal warts inside the urethra (see CHLAMYDIA, GONORRHEA, and VENEREAL WARTS in Chapter 18). In men over fifty years of age, frequent urination—especially getting up several times at night—combined with difficulty starting to urinate, a weak stream, and dribbling after voiding indicates a prostate problem (see PROSTATE ENLARGE-MENT in Chapter 17).

Bladder infection and irritable bladder, which causes the bladder to contract uncontrollably, can also increase the frequency of urination. When accompanied by pain in the back at waist-level, frequent urination may indicate a kidney infection (see PAINFUL URINATION in this chapter).

Before You Call the Doctor.   Regardless of the cause, don't stop drinking nonalcoholic fluids or you risk dehydration. On the other hand, limit alcohol, caffeinated beverages (coffee, tea, cocoa), foods with caffeine (chocolate), and such foods as watermelon and parsley, which are diuretic.

When to Call the Doctor.   If you cannot discover an obvious and self-treatable cause for any marked increase in urinary frequency, consult a physician. If you're taking any medications, talk with your doctor about possible urinary side effects. Frequent urination caused by infection can usually be quickly treated with antibiotics. Irritable bladder conditions can usually be alleviated with urine retention exercises designed to help strengthen the bladder muscles or with antispasmodic medication. Prostate enlargement may require surgery.

KIDNEY STONES

(See also BLOOD IN URINE in this chapter)

Kidney stones cause rapid onset of intense, crampy, mid-back pain so excruciating it makes people feel nauseous. Many kidney-stone veterans say the pain was the worst they have ever experienced.

What's Going On?   Most kidney stones are composed of calcium. For some reason, a tiny speck of material gets deposited in a kidney, and over time calcium in the urine forming in that kidney clings to the speck, eventually forming a stone. Tiny stones don't irritate the kidney, and because of their small size they have no difficulty painlessly traveling down the tube ("ureter") that connects the kidney to the bladder and leaving the body in urine. But larger stones can get stuck in the kidney, causing intense pain ("renal colic") just to the side of the backbone at waist level. The pain may be constant, but it usually comes and goes in waves. As the stone travels down the ureter, the pain moves from back to front and down into the groin. After up to forty-eight hours, the pain usually ends when the stone enters the bladder. But as it washes out of the body, you may feel some pain and/or burning on urination.

Kidney stones tend to run in families, though they are not hereditary.

They tend to be more common in hot climates because people sweat more, which means they tend to produce less urine—and more concentrated urine from which calcium is more likely to precipitate out.

Men develop kidney stones more frequently than women. Most stones affect people over thirty years of age.

Before You Call the Doctor.   Kidney stone pain can feel so excruciating some people double over, panic, and call 911 or race for the nearest emergency room. But if you can keep your wits about you, self-care shortens the painful period:

•Drink lots of water—at least one ten-ounce glass an hour—to flush the stone out. This may be difficult if the pain causes nausea, but drink as much as you possibly can.

•Take asprin, ibuprofen, or acetaminophen. Aspirin and ibuprofen may cause stomach upset. Pregnant women and those with a history of ulcers should not take aspirin or ibuprofen unless a doctor recommends it.

•Urinate into a strainer to catch the stone. Though most stones are composed of calcium, some are made of uric acid, which indicates a treatable metabolic disorder.

Kidney stones often introduce a small amount of blood into the urine. Any blood usually clears up in a day or two.

After a stone has passed, you can prevent recurrences by drinking lots of nonalcoholic fluids to keep your urine volume up and its calcium concentration down.

When to Call the Doctor.   Kidney stones are a frequent reason for hospital admission. Physicians prescribe fluids and prescription pain relievers. Usually, doctors simply allow the stone to pass. But recently, researchers have had good success pulverizing kidney stones into powder using ultrasound shock waves ("lithotripsy"). Authorities expect lithotripsy to become more common in the future. Some kidney stones must be removed surgically.

▶ **RED FLAGS**   Consult a physician promptly if:
• Intense back or abdominal pain does not improve after an hour or two. If you have never had a kidney stone, the diagnosis should be confirmed by a physician.
• You can't stand the pain.
• Bleeding on urination grows worse.
• You vomit or develop fever and chills.

PAINFUL URINATION

(See also KIDNEY STONES and URINARY TRACT INFECTION in this chapter, YEAST INFECTION in Chapter 16, PROSTATITIS in Chapter 17, and CHLAMYDIA, GONORRHEA, NONSPECIFIC URETHRITIS, and TRICHOMONAS in Chapter 18)

Pain on urination, medically known as "dysuria," usually feels like a burning sensation. It begins as urination commences and may linger a while after you've finished. After a few episodes of painful urination, most people also experience some difficulty getting started ("urinary hesitancy") because of the painful burning they know they're about to experience.

What's Going On?   Pain on urination indicates an inflammation— usually an infection—somewhere in the urinary tract. Possible causes include gonorrhea, chlamydia, trichomonas, prostatitis, yeast infection, kidney infection or stones, urinary tract infection (UTI, cystitis, or bladder infection), and nonspecific or nongonococcal urethritis (NSU or NGU).

Another common cause is irritation of the urethra from bubble bath, dyed or scented toilet tissue, or friction from sexual intercourse.

Urinary tract infection and kidney stones are discussed under their own headings in this chapter.

Yeast infection is discussed in Chapter 16.

Prostatitis is discussed in Chapter 17.

Gonorrhea, chlamydia, NSU, and trichomonas are discussed in Chapter 18.

Before You Call the Doctor.   Regardless of the cause, painful urination often discourages people from drinking fluids. Keep drinking nonalcoholic fluids. In fact, drink more—eight to ten eight-ounce glasses a day.

Fluids help flush out infection-causing microorganisms and may help alleviate pain.

Stop using bubble bath, scented or colored toilet tissue, and alcoholic and caffeinated beverages, all of which irritate the urinary tract.

When to Call the Doctor.   If pain persists after twenty-four hours, consult a physician for a urine exam ("urinalysis"). Be prepared to answer questions about your sexual activities. Men typically have a urethral smear in addition to a urinalysis. Women with recurring pain on urination who test negative for infections should ask their doctors about the possibility of "interstitial cystitis," a condition often missed because it is hard to diagnose.

▶ **RED FLAGS**   The most serious possible cause of painful urination is kidney infection ("acute pyelonephritis"). Most cases start with a urinary tract infection (see URINARY TRACT INFECTION in this chapter), followed by pain on one or both sides of the mid-back, where the kidneys are located. The pain may spread into the groin. As the infection progresses, other symptoms include fever, chills, nausea and vomiting, and difficult and painful urination. If these symptoms occur, consult a physician immediately. Kidney infections are treated with antibiotics and often require hospitalization.

URINARY INCONTINENCE

(See also BEDWETTING in this chapter)

Involuntary loss of bladder control is an embarrassing problem for an estimated five to ten million Americans.

What's Going On?   Urinary incontinence is usually associated with the elderly—it affects an estimated 20 percent of those over sixty-five years of age and half of nursing home residents. But it can be a problem for people of all ages. Incontinence is not only a physical disorder. The urine odor can be terribly embarrassing and cause social withdrawal and loss of self-esteem.

Bladder control requires a complex set of physical and intellectual processes. Physical or emotional stress at any age can cause some urinary leakage. Children who are toilet trained and completely dry at night may wet their pants because of the stress of extreme fear or hysterical laughter. The same is true for adults.

"Stress incontinence" describes leakage that occurs with increased abdominal pressure—for example, during sneezing, coughing, or heavy lifting. It is the result of weakness of the muscle in the pelvic floor which forms part of the bladder sphincter ("pubococcygeus" or PC muscle). Stress incontinence is often a problem in women whose PC muscles have been weakened by having had babies.

"Urge incontinence" refers to leakage that occurs because of inability to hold back urine flow once the bladder feels full. It may be due to PC muscle weakness, bladder irritation (see EXCESSIVELY FREQUENT URINATION in this chapter), or nerve ("neurological") problems, such as stroke or Alzheimer's disease.

Urine leakage without physical stress or any sensation of urge usually indicates a neurological problem and should be evaluated medically.

Urinary incontinence is associated with aging for several reasons. As people grow older, bladder capacity decreases, and the bladder becomes less elastic, which means it becomes progressively less able to hold urine for long periods. Aging also results in a loss of tone in the lower abdominal and pelvic muscles which play an important role in urinary control. In addition, in some women, menopause contributes to the problem (see MENOPAUSE in Chapter 16), and in many men, prostate enlargement is a factor (see PROSTATE ENLARGEMENT in Chapter 17). Finally, many older people take blood pressure medications, which are often diuretics.

Before You Call the Doctor.   Get past embarrassment. Authorities say nine out of ten people with bladder-control problems can be helped:
- Contact Help for Incontinent People (HIP) (see RESOURCES at the end of this chapter).
- Read *Staying Dry: A Practical Guide to Bladder Control* by Kathryn L. Burgio, M.D., and K. Lynette Pearce, R.N. (see RESOURCES at the end of this chapter).
- Limit your consumption of alcohol and of beverages containing caffeine (coffee, tea, cocoa, colas). They have diuretic action.
- Never hold urine. If you feel any urge, go.
- Strengthen your PC muscle by doing Kegel exercises, named for the physician who developed them. Kegels are easy and no one needs to know you're doing them:
- To locate the PC, begin to urinate, and then stop the flow by squeezing. The muscle that stops the flow is the PC.
- Practice stopping urination a few times to become familiar with your PC.
- The first Kegel exercise involves squeezing the PC muscle for three seconds, then relaxing it for three seconds. Initially, do

ten three-second squeezes three times a day. Over time build up to three sets of twenty squeezes.

° Another Kegel exercise, the "flutter," goes like this: Squeeze the PC as before and then release it as quickly as possible. Repeat this quick squeeze-and-release routine ten times three times a day.

° A third Kegel exercise for women entails imagining a tampon in the vagina and "sucking" it in deeper using the PC muscle. Each "suck" should last three seconds. Do ten repetitions three times a day.

° A fourth exercise for women consists of bearing down as during a bowel movement with the emphasis on the vagina rather than on the anus. Bear down for three seconds then relax. Do ten repetitions three times a day.

° Don't do too many Kegels too quickly or you'll wind up overexerting the muscle and feeling sore.

° Kegel exercises not only help restore urinary control, they also increase the pleasure of orgasm. The PC muscle contracts during orgasm, and as it grows stronger, so do the pleasurable sensations of sexual climax.

° Follow a bathroom schedule. Don't wait for the urge to urinate. Go every couple of hours during the day.

° Try tissues or sanitary napkins. People who suffer mild urinary incontinence usually place tissues in their underwear to catch any urine. This is all some people need. But odor can become a problem, so . . .

° Deodorize your urine. Cranberry juice is an effective urinary deodorant. Drink it throughout the day to minimize odor problems.

° For those with more severe incontinence, the manufacturers of disposable diapers now make many products for incontinent adults. Don't think of them as "adult diapers." Many brands are not bulky and neither swish nor rustle under clothing. Ask your pharmacist about the various brands. Most products work best with loose-fitting clothing.

If you are caring for an incontinent person at home:

° Provide quick bedside access to a portable urinal or commode. These are available for rent or purchase at medical supply houses.

° Make sure clothing is easy to remove so the person can easily use the toilet.

∘Take good care of the skin in the "underwear area" to prevent sores and rashes (see DIAPER RASH in Chapter 6).

When to Call the Doctor. Don't hesitate to consult a physician if incontinence becomes enough of a problem to interfere with your daily activities and/or self-esteem. The good news is that about 90 percent of people can be helped, and more than one-third of chronic cases can be cured. Sometimes a family doctor can treat the problem. For example, you may be able to switch from a diuretic blood pressure medication to a different drug which has no effect on urination. Or an irritable bladder may be treated with antispasmodic bladder-relaxing drugs. In some cases, you may have to consult a urologist, for example, if you need sophisticated tests or surgery.

▶ **RED FLAG** Sudden worsening of incontinence for no apparent reason may indicate infection. Consult a physician promptly.

URINARY TRACT INFECTION

(See also PAINFUL URINATION in this chapter)
Infection or inflammation of the bladder is a common and painful problem mostly among women. Symptoms include fever, back and groin pain, and painful, frequent, or bloody urination.

What's Going On? Urinary tract infections, also known as UTIs, cystitis, or bladder infections, are usually caused by intestinal bacteria necessary for digestion. These bacteria, *Escherichia coli (E. coli),* and others become incorporated into stool. If somehow they move from the anal area into the urethra, they can work their way up to the bladder and cause infection. However, some recurrent bladder infections involve other microorganisms, for example, *Chlamydia trachomatis* (see CHLAMYDIA in Chapter 18).

Both men and women can develop UTI, but the problem is particularly prevalent in women for two reasons. Women's urethral and anal openings are located closer together than men's, so it's easier for anal bacteria to travel from the one to the other. And women's urethras are considerably shorter than men's, which means that once they've been introduced into the urethra, they don't have far to travel to infect the female bladder.

In men and in children, most UTIs are caused by obstructions or structural abnormalities in the urinary tract. In men over fifty years of age, the problem is often an enlarged prostate gland which impedes the out-flow of urine. The trapped urine collects in the bladder and encourages bacterial growth (see PROSTATE ENLARGEMENT in Chapter 17).

Interstitial cystitis is a baffling, apparently noninfectious urinary tract problem. It strikes women and feels like recurrent UTI, but no bacteria can be cultured.

Before You Call the Doctor.   It's easy to recognize the beginnings of a bladder infection: an urgent need to urinate ("urinary urgency"), burn-ing, and scant urine production. If you feel a UTI coming on, here are several tips that might nip it in the bud:

• Immediately start drinking lots of water, and keep drinking it. You may be able to flush the bacteria out of your bladder before they can become established firmly enough to cause a full-blown infection. Some women experience greater relief if they add a teaspoon of baking soda (sodium bicarbonate or bicarbonate of soda) to counteract the irritating acidity of urine. (Do not use baking soda if you're on a salt- or sodium-restricted diet, and do not use it for extended periods of time.)

• Try drinking lots of cranberry juice. Cranberry juice has a long history as a folk remedy for UTI. Medically it's been controversial, with some studies supporting it as a treatment and others showing no effect. Try it yourself and see how it affects your UTIs. (The cranberry juice available commercially is not pure juice because it's too sour to be palat-able. It's "cranberry juice cocktail," with added sugar to make it drinkable.) Cranberry juice apparently works by making the bladder less hospitable to infection-causing bacteria. Do not use cranberry juice if you're taking baking soda for pain relief because their chemical effects cancel each other.

• Urinate frequently. Studies of women with recurrent UTIs show they have a tendency to hold their urine for extended periods. If you feel any urge, go. Even if you don't feel the urge, go anyway.

• Keep some phenazopyridine (Pyridium) on hand. It's a urinary anes-thetic, which can minimize the burning of UTIs. Pyridium requires a prescription, but ask your doctor for enough to see you though several UTIs. Keeping some Pyridium in your medicine chest may save you a future doctor visit, but it should never be taken for more than a day without a test to see if you need antibiotics. Note: Pyridium dyes urine bright orange. Don't be alarmed.

• Take hot baths or use a heating pad on the lower abdomen. Heat helps relieve UTI discomfort.

Most UTIs can be prevented. Here's how:

• Practice good hygiene. Keep the vaginal and anal areas clean. Use a mild soap, such as Ivory, and avoid perfumed, deodorant soaps, which can be irritating.

•*Always wipe from front to back, away from the urethra.*

•Drink plenty of fluids. We recommend at least eight to ten eight-ounce glasses of water a day.

•Try drinking two to four glasses of cranberry juice a day. The latest research suggests it works best preventively. Besides acidifying urine, cranberry juice apparently interferes with the bacteria's ability to attach to the bladder wall.

•Urinate frequently. Go every two or three hours. Go after intercourse. And, if recurrent UTIs are a problem, go once or twice at night.

•Wear cotton underwear, which is less irritating and less allergy-provoking than synthetics.

•Stay away from restrictive, tight-fitting clothing, for example, leotards, which tend to trap heat and moisture and promote bacterial growth.

•After intercourse, empty your bladder and wipe off moisture front to back. This is so important, we're saying it twice. Making love is the number one precipitating event for UTIs—hence the name "honeymoon cystitis."

•Take stress management seriously (see MANAGE YOUR STRESS LOAD in Chapter 1).

•If you use a diaphragm for contraception and suffer recurrent UTIs, talk with your clinician about switching to a smaller size, or another brand, or trying another form of birth control. Some diaphragm rims press against the urethra, irritating it, which increases the risk of infection.

•During your period, change tampons or sanitary napkins often. Blood is an excellent bacterial growth medium.

•Limit your consumption of alcohol, spicy foods, coffee, tea, and other foods and drugs that contain caffeine, which tend to irritate the urinary tract.

When to Call the Doctor.   Many UTIs require professional medical care. Typically, antibiotics are prescribed. Be sure to take the entire course of the drug, which often means continuing the medication even after your symptoms have cleared up.

Antibiotics kill infection-causing bacteria in your urinary tract as well as the helpful bacteria in your intestines, so it's a good idea to replenish the helpful bacteria by eating live-culture yogurt.

If you tend to develop vaginal yeast infections after taking antibiotics, ask your physician to prescribe a yeast medication, such as miconazole, just in case.

If you suspect you might have interstitial cystitis, consult a urologist.

Definitive diagnosis requires special tests most primary care doctors do not perform. If the tests confirm that you have this difficult-to-treat condition, contact the Interstitial Cystitis Association (see RESOURCES at the end of this chapter).

▶ **RED FLAGS**   African-Americans should not take sulfa antibiotics, which are frequently used to treat UTIs, until they've been tested for G6PD deficiency. About 10 percent have a hereditary deficiency of an enzyme called G6PD and should not take sulfa drugs.

Untreated bladder infections can spread up into the kidneys, causing kidney infection ("acute pyelonephritis"). In most cases, the first symptom is pain on one or both sides of the mid-back, where the kidneys are located. The pain may spread into the groin. As the infection progresses, other symptoms include fever, chills, nausea and vomiting, and difficult and painful urination. If these symptoms occur, consult a physician immediately. Kidney infections are treated with antibiotics and often require hospitalization.

RESOURCES

Help for Incontinent People (HIP). For a free sample of the organization's newsletter and publications, send a self-addressed stamped envelope to HIP, P.O. Box 544, Union, SC 29379.

Staying Dry: A Practical Guide to Bladder Control by Kathryn L. Burgio, M.D., and K. Lynette Pearce, R.N. (Baltimore: Johns Hopkins Press, 1990, $12.95.)

Interstitial Cystitis Association. P.O. Box 1553, Madison Square Station, New York, NY 10159; (212) 674-1454. Provides support and information for those with this puzzling ailment.

CHAPTER 15

The Bones, Joints, and Muscles

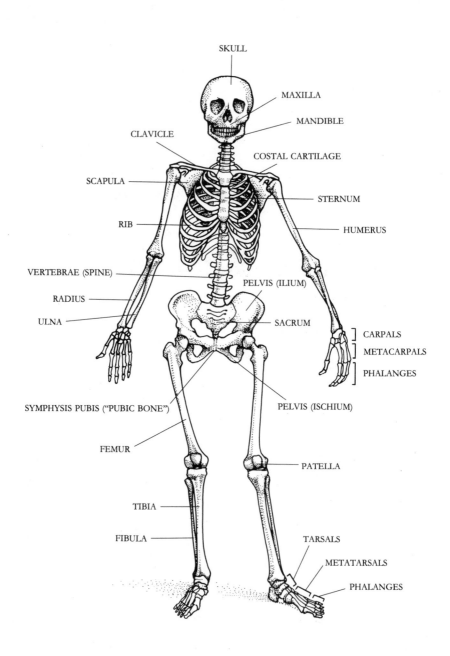

SKULL
MAXILLA
MANDIBLE
CLAVICLE
COSTAL CARTILAGE
SCAPULA
STERNUM
RIB
HUMERUS
VERTEBRAE (SPINE)
PELVIS (ILIUM)
RADIUS
ULNA
SACRUM
CARPALS
METACARPALS
PHALANGES
SYMPHYSIS PUBIS ("PUBIC BONE")
PELVIS (ISCHIUM)
FEMUR
PATELLA
TIBIA
FIBULA
TARSALS
METATARSALS
PHALANGES

The Skeletal System.

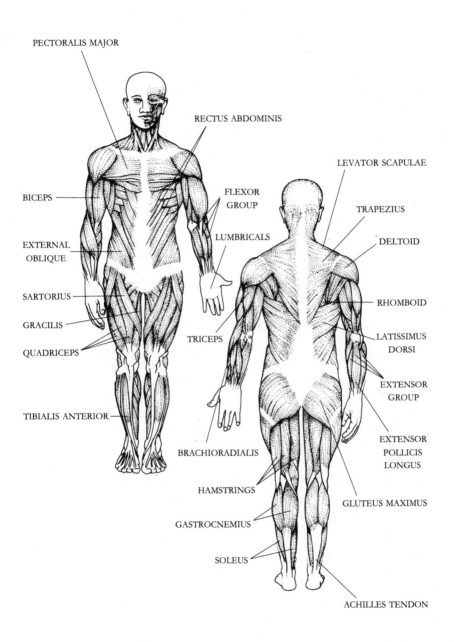

PECTORALIS MAJOR

RECTUS ABDOMINIS

LEVATOR SCAPULAE

TRAPEZIUS

BICEPS

FLEXOR
GROUP

DELTOID

LUMBRICALS

EXTERNAL
OBLIQUE

RHOMBOID

SARTORIUS

LATISSIMUS
DORSI

GRACILIS

TRICEPS

QUADRICEPS

EXTENSOR
GROUP

TIBIALIS ANTERIOR

EXTENSOR
POLLICIS
LONGUS

BRACHIORADIALIS

HAMSTRINGS

GLUTEUS MAXIMUS

GASTROCNEMIUS

SOLEUS

ACHILLES TENDON

The Muscular System.

ACHILLES TENDINITIS

(See ANKLE PAIN and TENDINITIS in this chapter)

ANKLE PAIN

(See also ARTHRITIS, BURSITIS, GOUT, SPRAINS, and TENDINI-TIS in this Chapter)

Ankle pain, often associated with athletic injuries, can range in severity from a dull aching to agony that makes walking and standing impossible.

What's Going On?   Anyone can twist an ankle. More painful and serious ankle injuries are particularly common among runners and those who play basketball, baseball, football, and volleyball, though anyone can develop them.

Ankle problems generally fall into two categories: overuse injuries, particularly among amateur athletes whose ambitions eclipse their abilities, and traumatic injuries, for example, turning an ankle while wearing high-heeled shoes. Ankle pain may also be "referred," which means the pain originates elsewhere. For example, a runner who plants on the foot's inside edge ("pronates") might feel pain in the ankle, knee, and/or leg.

A sprained ankle is one of the most common sources of ankle pain. Many people call any painful injury a "sprain," but the term actually means an injury to the fibrous bands of tissue that hold joints together and attach one bone to another ("ligaments"). The ligaments around any joint can be sprained, but the ankles, knees, and finger joints are the most common sprain locations (see SPRAINS in this chapter).

Mild sprains cause only pain and do not interfere much with use of the joint. Severe sprains cause pain, swelling, tenderness, skin discoloration, and inability to move or use the affected area. Some severe sprains leave the joint looking deformed as well as swollen and discolored.

Ankle bones may also break ("fracture"). A "hairline," "greenstick," or "incomplete" fracture cracks the bone but does not break it. A "simple" fracture breaks the bone but does not do much damage to the surrounding tissue, and the bone does not protrude through the skin. A "compound" fracture damages surrounding tissue and the bone protrudes through the skin. Older people, whose bones are more brittle, or those who suffer from the bone-thinning disease osteoporosis often suffer fractures without much stress on the bone (see OSTEOPOROSIS in this chapter).

Hairline ankle fractures might be mistaken for sprains. Complete fractures often produce audible snapping or cracking sounds when the bone breaks. Symptoms include: severe pain, swelling, discoloration, deformity, and inability to use the area.

Ankle pain may also be caused by arthritis or bursitis (see ARTHRITIS and BURSITIS in this chapter). Arthritis of the ankle is often a result of previous ankle sprains or fractures. It might be caused by obesity because the extra weight places chronic stress on the joint. Ankle bursitis occurs just above the heel under the Achilles tendon, the large fibrous band that forms the back of the foot.

In athletes, particularly runners, problems may develop in the Achilles tendon. Possible problems include inflammation (Achilles tendinitis) or rupture. Achilles tendon injuries are often a major problem for athletes over thirty-five years of age because their tendons have lost some natural elasticity. Achilles tendinitis causes pain in the back of the leg and also possibly ankle pain. Risk factors include overtraining, poorly fitted shoes, running on uneven terrain, dramatic changes in a training schedule, or participation in a sport that demands quick pivoting, for example, racquet sports and basketball.

Before You Call the Doctor.   Twisted ankles and minor ankle sprains can be managed at home with R.I.C.E., an acronym for rest, ice, compression, and elevation (see MUSCLE STRAINS in this chapter).

In addition to R.I.C.E. treatment, take aspirin or ibuprofen for pain and inflammation. Acetaminophen helps relieve pain but offers no antiinflammatory benefits. If aspirin or ibuprofen upset your stomach, try an "enteric coated" brand. Pregnant women and those with a history of ulcers or other gastrointestinal problems should not take aspirin or ibuprofen unless a doctor recommends it.

After a few days, begin gently exercising an injured ankle without forcing it to bear much weight. When not exercising it, keep your ankle elevated to help drain the fluids that promote swelling. Soaking the area in warm water several times a day can also help relieve pain and stiffness. If pain and swelling persist for more than two or three days, you may have a fracture and should consult a physician. Most sprains heal within a few weeks.

Here are some exercises rehabilitation authorities recommend:

• Achilles tendon stretch. Stand facing a wall, but far enough away so that you can step forward with one foot. Lean toward the wall, placing your hands and forearms against the wall. Make sure both feet point directly toward the wall. Lock your back knee. Bend your front knee. Then press forward until you feel a moderate stretch along the back of your straight leg. Hold the stretch for fifteen seconds. Then bend the knee of your straight leg until you feel a moderate stretch in your Achilles tendon. Hold the stretch fifteen seconds. Repeat five times on each side.

• Heel raise. Stand on one foot, holding a chair or table to help keep your balance. Slowly rise to your toes, and just as slowly, lower your heel back to the floor. Repeat five times on each side. Progress to doing this exercise on the edge of a step so you can lower your heel below floor level.

• Ankle extension. Lie on your back. Point your feet and toes down as far as possible. Then bring your toes and feet back up as far as possible. Repeat five times.

• The alphabet. Sitting comfortably with your legs stretched out in front of you, draw the alphabet in the air with each big toe, moving only the foot at the ankle.

Do these exercises two or three times a day. If you feel any pain while doing them, exercise more gently.

• For an additional ankle workout, try swimming with fins or riding a bicycle or stationary bike.

For ankle arthritis or bursitis, see the ARTHRITIS and BURSITIS sections of this chapter.

For Achilles tendon problems, see TENDINITIS in this chapter.

When to Call the Doctor.   Consult a physician promptly for any suspected ankle fracture or Achilles tendon rupture. If you suffer chronic or periodic ankle pain, particularly if the pain occurs during exercise, have a biomechanical evaluation by a health professional experienced in sports medicine.

Ankle injuries usually require x-rays. Some minor fractures simply require splinting. More severe fractures often require the doctor to realign the bones into proper position. Depending on the severity of the break, bone realignment ("reduction") may require surgery under general anesthesia to reach the injured bones. In severe fractures, pins or metal plates may have to be implanted to hold the bones together.

Ankle fracture healing time depends on the severity of the break and the age and general health of the injured person. A child's fracture may take only a few weeks to heal, while an older adult's might take several months. After the cast comes off, physical therapy is often necessary to rebuild atrophied muscles.

Achilles tendon stretch.   *Heel raise.*

Ankle extension.

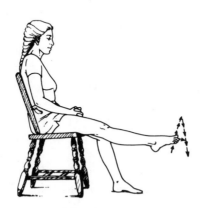

The alphabet.

Ankle exercises.

ARM PAIN

(See also ARTHRITIS, BURSITIS, CARPAL TUNNEL SYNDROME, ELBOW PAIN, MUSCLE STRAINS, SHOULDER PAIN, TENDINI-TIS, and WRIST PAIN in this chapter, HEART ATTACK in Chapter 3, and ANGINA and HEART ATTACK in Chapter 12)

Arm pain may reflect something as minor as sore muscles or be a symptom of a life-threatening heart attack.

What's Going On?   Arm pain can have a variety of causes and the key is to determine whether or not you need professional help. Arm pain may be "referred," meaning it originates somewhere else in the body but shows up in the arm. That's why some angina attacks and heart attacks cause arm pain. Arm pain centered in a joint may be caused by arthritis, bursitis, carpal tunnel syndrome, gout, sprains, or tendinitis.

Before You Call the Doctor.   First, consider the possibility of a heart attack. Many heart attacks do not cause crushing chest pain and physical collapse. Quite a few feel more like heartburn. If you have arm pain with pressure-like chest pain or pain radiating up under your jaw, call 911 immediately (see HEART ATTACK in Chapters 3 and 12). Heart attacks are more likely in those who smoke, have high cholesterol, high blood pressure, or a family history of heart disease.

Next consider the possibility of angina, another form of heart disease caused by inadequate blood flow to the heart. Angina causes chest pain— and sometimes arm pain—during exertion. If squeezing or pressure-like pain begins during exercise and stops after you rest, call your physician immediately (see ANGINA in Chapter 12.)

Once you've ruled out heart attack and angina, consider the following questions:

• Have you recently used your arm in work or play in ways you're not used to? If so, see MUSCLE STRAINS and TENDINITIS in this chapter.

• Does the pain affect the hand and extend up the forearm? If so, you may have carpal tunnel syndrome, a disorder that affects the nerves in the wrist (see CARPAL TUNNEL SYNDROME in this chapter.)

• Do you also have a stiff neck? If so, you may have arthritis of the neck ("cervical osteoarthritis") (see ARTHRITIS and NECK PAIN in this chapter).

• Is the pain localized around your elbow? If so, see ELBOW PAIN in this chapter.

• Is the pain localized around your shoulder? If so, see SHOULDER PAIN in this chapter.

• Is the pain localized in your wrist, elbow, or finger joints and accompanied by redness and swelling? If so, you may have arthritis, bursitis, or tendinitis (see ARTHRITIS, BURSITIS, and TENDINITIS in this chapter).

When to Call the Doctor. If you can't diagnose your arm pain from the questions above, or if your pain is accompanied by a fever or general ill feeling ("malaise"), consult a physician. You may have an infection or some other disorder that requires professional treatment.

When you call your physician, be prepared to answer these questions:

• When did the pain begin? How?

• Is it sharp and stabbing or dull and throbbing?

• Is it constant or intermittent?

• Does it occur or recur at particular times of the day, for example, when you first get up in the morning?

• Do you perform any kind of repetitive motion with your hands or arms?

• Do you have a family history of heart disease, arthritis, or bursitis?

▶ **RED FLAG** Call a physician immediately for any arm pain associated with chest pain. This combination suggests heart disease.

ARTHRITIS

Arthritis symptoms range from mild, occasional joint stiffness and achiness when rising in the morning, to severe constant pain and crippling joint deformity.

What's Going On? Arthritis means "inflammation of the joint." One of the nation's most prevalent debilitating diseases, it affects an estimated thirty-seven million Americans of all ages. It is not just a problem for older adults, though its incidence increases with age.

Doctors don't know what causes the most common form of arthritis ("osteoarthritis"), but they know what happens. The tough, flexible, shock-absorbing cartilage in the joints, which keep the bones from grinding into one another, breaks down or becomes inflamed, causing stiffness, achiness, pain, warmth, movement restrictions, and sometimes physical deformity. There is currently no cure for most kinds of arthritis, but with some planning, imagination, life-style adjustments, and medication, most cases can be managed well enough to allow arthritis sufferers to lead normal, active, productive lives.

Here, we'll discuss the two most common types of arthritis.

• *Osteoarthritis.* Also known as degenerative joint disease (DJD), osteoarthritis is by far the most prevalent form of joint inflammation. More than half of adults over age thirty suffer some form of it. The condition results from a breakdown of the cartilage between the bony surfaces that form affected joints. The degeneration often leads to bony growths ("spurs") next to affected joints. Any joint can develop osteoarthritis, with overuse and previous injury often preceding development of the condition.

People who perform repetitive tasks are particularly prone to osteoarthritis. Typists often develop it in their fingers. Carpenters often develop it in the elbow of their dominant arm. And anyone who has ever been athletic—especially those who have any history of ankle, knee, hip, back, finger, wrist, elbow, shoulder, or neck injuries—are at considerable risk. Frequently, youthful sports injuries return as osteoarthritis years, even decades, later. And as increasing numbers of adults engage in strenuous physical activities into their forties, fifties, and sixties—and subject their joints to the pounding of running, basketball, volleyball, racquet sports, and other sports—they greatly increase their risk.

The main symptoms of oseoarthritis are pain and stiffness. Usually the pain is an aching associated with movement of the affected joint(s). The pain typically subsides when the aching joint is rested. Some osteoarthritis sufferers experience morning stiffness, which usually subsides as they engage in activities of daily living (ADLs).

• *Rheumatoid Arthritis.* This is the second most common form of arthritis, and a more debilitating condition. Unlike osteoarthritis, which generally develops among older adults, rheumatoid arthritis can strike at any age, even during infancy, though it's most likely to occur between the ages of thirty and forty.

The cause of rheumatoid arthritis remains unclear, but researchers suspect it's an autoimmune condition. In autoimmune diseases, the immune system mistakes a person's own tissues for disease-causing germs and attacks them. In this case, the theory is that the immune system attacks the joints and causes the pain and inflammation of rheumatoid arthritis.

The major symptoms are joint pain, stiffness, swelling, and redness. The joints most commonly affected are the hands and feet, which often become severely deformed. But rheumatoid arthritis can strike any joint. The pain is often excruciating and, unlike in osteoarthritis, does not subside with rest. Morning stiffness can be severe and last several hours.

Sufferers may also feel generally ill, with lethargy and low-grade fever. Eventually, the disease may affect the heart and lungs as well as the joints, causing difficulty breathing and further loss of energy.

Before You Call the Doctor.   Any suspected arthritis requires professional evaluation because many potentially serious diseases have arthritis as a symptom. Examples include Lyme disease, the new national epidemic transmitted by ticks; scleroderma, a progressive build-up of fibrous connective tissue; systemic lupus erythematosus (SLE), an unpredictable and potentially life-threatening condition that usually affects women; and ankylosing spondylitis, which causes intense back pain and other symptoms.

However, once other problems have been ruled out and you've been diagnosed with uncomplicated arthritis, there is plenty you can do to manage the condition. The two key concepts are education and adaptation. Studies show that arthritis sufferers who learn about the condition and adapt their life-styles to it lead more normal, fulfilling lives and require less pain medication than those who remain uninformed or give in to despair. The Arthritis Foundation is a good place to start learning about joint disease (see RESOURCES at the end of this chapter).

Once you have a basic understanding of arthritis, take a look at your life, and try to make your daily tasks easier. Use your imagination, and give yourself permission to pamper yourself. If your hands are the problem, junk your old manual can opener and invest in an electric model. If reaching up causes shoulder pain, place commonly used items on lower shelves. If ankle and knee pain bother you when you get up to change television channels, invest in a remote control. Today, literally hundreds of joint-sparing household, automobile, work, and hobby devices are available to make life with arthritis a little easier. Arthritis Foundation publications can make recommendations. Several consumer product catalogs, such as, Comfortably Yours, Bodyline, and the Self-Care Catalog also offer items that help take the pain out of living with arthritis (see RESOURCES at the end of this chapter).

Here are some general suggestions for minimizing arthritis pain and disability:

• Rest the joint until the pain of osteoarthritis subsides. (Rest may not help rheumatoid arthritis).

• Apply heat to soothe dull, throbbing pain and stiffness. Use a heating pad, hot water bottle, hot bath or shower, hot tub, sauna, and/or over-the-counter heating ointments.

• Cold packs may relieve more severe pain. Wrap ice cubes in a plastic bag, then wrap the ice bag in a clean cloth. Apply the cold pack for twenty minutes, then remove it for ten minutes before reapplying it. Commercial gel-filled cold packs are equally effective and often more convenient. When using cold packs, always wrap the frozen element in cloth. Don't apply ice or ice substitutes directly to the skin or you may suffer the equivalent of frostbite.

•Take aspirin or ibuprofen to relieve pain and inflammation. Acetaminophen relieves pain *but not inflammation.* However, acetaminophen can be very useful in treating everyday arthritis, which may not cause much inflammation. If aspirin and/or ibuprofen upset your stomach, try an "enteric coated" brand, or talk with your doctor about prescription nonsteroidal anti-inflammatory drugs. Pregnant women and those with a history of ulcers should not use aspirin or ibuprofen unless a doctor recommends it.

Many arthritis sufferers take more than the standard aspirin recommendation of two tablets every four hours. Within reasonable limits, this is fine as long as the aspirin does not cause stomach upset or gastrointestinal bleeding, which may appear as black, tarry stools. High doses of aspirin cause ringing in the ears, which is a useful way to tell when you've reached your maximum tolerable dose. The pain-relieving ("analgesic") effects of aspirin or ibuprofen taken in combination with acetaminophen are additive. They may be used together.

•Avoid overexertion. Don't stop moving, but learn your limits and don't push yourself beyond them. Some people try to fight arthritis by overdoing things, especially athletes schooled in the old—and completely ridiculous—"no pain, no gain" philosophy. Pain means stop what you're doing, especially if you have arthritis. Overexertion often tempts those with rheumatoid arthritis, which tends to flare up and subside periodically. When it's not causing pain, sufferers often overexert themselves. This is a mistake.

•Try not to hold objects in a tight grip for extended periods. When holding phones, steering wheels, golf clubs, tennis racquets, etc., flex your fingers periodically.

•Use the largest joint possible to accomplish any task. Carry a shoulder bag rather than a clutch purse—the shoulder joint is larger than the finger joints. Push open heavy doors with your whole body, not just your elbow and wrist. Always lift with your legs, not your back.

•If you're overweight, lose weight. Excess weight stresses all the weight-bearing joints.

•When necessary, don't hesitate to ask for help from family and friends. Asking for help is very difficult for some people, who see it as an admission of defeat and disability. Some well-meaning friends and relatives compound the problem by "helping" when their assistance is unnecessary, which often makes arthritis sufferers feel more disabled than they actually are. The best way to handle this issue is to sit your family and friends down and tell them gently but firmly that you intend to do as much as you possibly can for yourself. Tell them they can help you best by rendering assistance only when you specifically ask for it, and then by helping you accomplish only the specific tasks which cause problems. Training family and friends may take a little time, but it helps arthritis sufferers retain their dignity and independence.

• Use good posture. It places the least stress on the joints.

• Try not to stay in one position for long periods of time. Shift. Get up and move around. If you have to, stand up while eating, watching television, reading, and doing things like playing board games.

• When standing for long periods, place one foot on a box or stool to take stress off your back.

• Try to keep joints extended rather than bent ("flexed").

Years ago, doctors encouraged arthritis sufferers to minimize physical activity and adopt a sedentary lifestyle. Today we know that arthritis sufferers *must remain as physically active as their condition allows*. The key phrase is: "Use it or lose it." Without exercise, the joints grow stiffer, the bones become brittle, cartilage receives less nourishment and breaks down more easily, and muscles grow weak and shrink. The Arthritis Foundation has produced several exercise videotapes specifically designed for arthritis sufferers. The goal is to gently move stiff joints through their full range of motion. Don't push beyond what you can do without pain, but over time, range-of-motion exercises produce increased flexibility and range of motion. Many yoga instructors also tailor their stretches and postures to the special needs of arthritis sufferers. Walking, swimming, and gardening all offer excellent low-impact, joint-helping exercise. Get some exercise every day. Stay as physically active as possible.

• About alternative treatments: Because arthritis can be severely painful and debilitating, some sufferers fall victim to fraudulent, expensive "cures." According to the Food and Drug Administration, arthritis products are a leading area of medical fraud. Some people claim genuine relief using such controversial and, according to the FDA, useless approaches as copper bracelets, special diets, vitamin supplements, and various salves and tonics. A low-fat diet, which helps arthritis sufferers lose weight, takes the stress of extra weight off inflamed joints, but beyond weight loss, no specific foods or diet have been shown conclusively to affect arthritis. We've also been impressed with yoga as a way for arthritis sufferers to control their pain and minimize their movement restrictions. If you'd like to try other alternative approaches, fine. Just beware of anyone who claims to have discovered a "medical miracle" that "cures" arthritis. Check with the Arthritis Foundation or other authorities before you invest in any product or treatment that seems too out of the ordinary. Things that sound too good to be true usually are.

When to Call the Doctor.   Your first concern is an accurate diagnosis. Many diseases have arthritis as a symptom. The doctor should take a detailed personal and family history, examine you, and perhaps order tests aimed at ruling out the many diseases which cause joint pain and inflammation. You may need a referral to an arthritis specialist.

For pain which cannot be adequately controlled with over-the-counter drugs, doctors can prescribe stronger pain and anti-inflammatory medications, including nonsteroidal anti-inflammatory drugs (NSAIDs) and corticosteroids. Several other drugs may be prescribed depending on your individual condition.

In some cases, the doctor may recommend splints or other joint-protection devices to prevent or reduce joint stress and deformity. Some devices may need to be worn only a few hours a day; others may be necessary much of the time.

Don't hesitate to ask your doctor for a referral to a physical therapist or a physiatrist, a physician who specializes in rehabilitation medicine. In addition, an occupational therapist may be able to suggest helpful assisting devices and less stressful ways to accomplish necessary tasks of daily living.

In a few cases, surgery may be required to correct joint deformities when the arthritis doesn't respond to other forms of therapy.

▶ **RED FLAG**   If you develop a single warm, swollen, painful joint, consult a physician immediately to rule out infection ("septic arthritis").

BACK PAIN (LOWER)

(See also ARTHRITIS, MUSCLE STRAIN, SCIATICA, and SLIPPED DISC in this chapter, KIDNEY STONES in Chapter 14, FIBROIDS and PELVIC PAIN in Chapter 16, and PROSTATITIS in Chapter 17)

A famous philosopher once said, "I think, therefore I am." He would have been equally correct to say, "My lower back hurts, therefore I am." Studies show that at some point in life, 80 percent of Americans suffer lower back pain severe enough to take medication or consult a health professional. Sometimes, lower back pain strikes once and resolves, never occurring again. But millions of Americans suffer chronic lower back pain for years, sometimes decades.

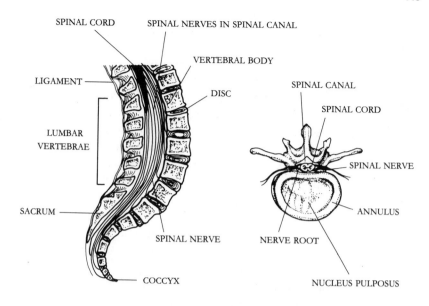

SPINAL CORD   SPINAL NERVES IN SPINAL CANAL

VERTEBRAL BODY

LIGAMENT

DISC

SPINAL CANAL

SPINAL CORD

LUMBAR
VERTEBRAE

SPINAL NERVE

SACRUM

ANNULUS

SPINAL NERVE   NERVE ROOT

COCCYX   NUCLEUS PULPOSUS

The lower back.   *Intervertebral disc.*

What's Going On? When it comes to pain complaints, lower back pain is second only to headache. Lower back pain is the nation's number two cause of lost school and work days (after colds and flu). And a billion-dollar industry has developed to help back-pain sufferers treat the condition and adjust to life with it.

The reason the lower back is so vulnerable to injury has to do with the back's structure. The "backbone" is not a single bone. It's actually thirty-three bones, or "vertebrae," irregular donut-like structures, most of which are separated by flexible cartilage rings or "discs" that act like shock absorbers. The vertebrae are divided into five groups. From top to bottom, the neck contains the seven "cervical" vertebrae. The upper back is composed of the twelve "thoracic" vertebrae. The lower back is made up of the five "lumbar" vertebrae. Running through the buttocks, another five vertebrae are fused together to form the "sacrum." And the lowest four vertebrae are fused to form the tailbone ("coccyx"). (See illustration.)

The back has several functions. It supports the body and all the internal organs from the neck to the genitals. It houses and protects the spinal cord, which runs through the tunnel formed by the donut holes in the vertebrae. And its bone-and-cartilage arrangement is amazingly flexible, which allows us to bend, stretch, twist, and turn. But the back's flexibility comes at considerable cost—vulnerability to injury, whose roots reach deep into our evolutionary past.

The vertebrae-disc arrangement evolved to support animals that walked on all fours. When our ancestors began standing on two legs, they gained a tremendous evolutionary advantage—the separation of the hands from the feet, and the beginning of the ability to manipulate tools. But two-legged walking also placed enormous strain on their back vertebrae because in the upright position, they are not at the center of the body, but toward the rear, and constantly being pulled forward—and out of alignment—by the body's unequal weight distribution around them. In addition, gravity, falls, and other injuries made the vertebrae-disc structure even more suceptible to sliding out of alignment, vulnerabilities we have struggled with ever since. The back's most vulnerable area is just above the hips in the lumbar vertabrae of the lower back. These vertebrae are not the only ones that develop problems, but they are so much more vulnerable to injury than the back's other areas that many people consider "back pain" and "lower back pain" synonymous.

The back-pain problem is further complicated by the back's natural curvature. The vertebrae are not stacked on top of one another like a flagpole. They weave back and forth in a series of curves. There is no such thing as ideal back curvature. Everyone's back is different, just like everyone's feet are different. Just as no pair of shoes feels comfortable to everyone, no single approach to back care eliminates everyone's back pain.

Lower back pain has several possible causes:

•Muscle problems. Injury, usually sudden twisting, can strain or tear the muscles that run up and down the back. Muscle weakness or other problems can also squeeze ("pinch") the spinal nerves or the network of nerves that emanate from them.

•Obesity, particularly a "beer belly," or pregnancy can pull the entire lower back forward out of alignment, which triggers pain nerves in the area.

•Traumatic injury or years of abuse, for example, improper lifting, can wear down the back's discs, also causing alignment problems.

•In severe cases, a disc may rupture, spilling its jelly-like center into surrounding tissue. Disc rupture, also called disc herniation and "slipped disc," produces pressure on a major nerve and usually severe pain.

•Arthritis, abscesses, other infections, or tumors around the back may cause back pain.

•Finally, back pain may not originate in the back itself. It may be "referred" from other areas, particularly the pelvic organs or gastrointestinal tract. Prostate problems in men, pelvic infections and other reproductive problems in women, and kidney and gastrointestinal disorders in both sexes can cause pain experienced as "back pain."

Despite lower back pain's enormous number of possible causes, the fact is that relatively few cases are caused by slipped discs, arthritis, infections, or tumors. Most back pain is caused by back-destructive life-style habits. Here are some of the most common causes:

• Obesity. The more weight your back has to support, the more likely it is to protest.

• Poor muscle tone. If the abdominal and/or lower back muscles become weakened for any reason, the vertebrae may shift out of alignment from healthy curvature into a configuration that causes pain. Strengthening these muscles is one key to back self-care.

• Lack of exercise. Sedentary life-style contributes to loss of muscle tone and obesity.

• Poor posture. Remember all those times your mother told you to stand up straight? Good posture not only looks best, it's essential for a pain-free back. Poor posture places pain-producing stresses on the entire back,—its muscles, ligaments, tendons, discs, and bony structures. Good posture means both standing and *sitting* properly. For many people, sitting hunched up in back-abusing furniture is a one-way ticket to lower back pain.

• Improper lifting. The back has enough trouble holding the body erect. Its muscles simply are not meant to lift heavy objects.

• Improper rising. Rising from a bent position is a form of lifting. For a back already weakened by misuse or a history of previous injury, rising from a bent position may become the straw that . . . well, you know the rest, but we're not talking about camels.

• High heels. Women's high heeled shoes were designed by men centuries ago to accent women's sex appeal. High heels highlight women's breasts and buttocks and interfere with their gait, making them appear frail and vulnerable. High heels also push the pelvis forward, placing considerable strain on the lower back.

Before You Call the Doctor. The vast majority of lower back problems not only can be managed with self-care, they *must be*. In some cases, orthodox physicians and/or alternative practitioners can help, but only you can keep your back pain-free:

• Don't let anyone talk you into anything. Lower back pain is so common, it's become practically a national obsession. Everyone has a story about what worked for them or someone they know. There is no single path to a pain-free back. Sure, listen to your friends. Some of their ideas may apply to you. But don't assume that what works for them will work for you. Focus on your own back pain, and follow the course that brings you relief, even if your friends and relatives dismiss your approach as worthless.

• Lifting. Always lift with your legs using your thigh muscles. Never lift with your back. It doesn't matter how light or heavy the object is. Always lift with your legs, never with your back. Lift straight up. Never twist as you lift. Be sure of your footing. And when you set the object down, again, always lower it with your legs, never with your back. When lifting, hold the object as close to your body as possible.

• Exercise. Many people with lower back problems stop exercising for fear of aggravating their pain. But avoiding exercise is one of the worst things you can do for your back. Exercise is crucial to keeping lower backs pain-free. But you've got to engage in back-friendly exercise. Anything that pounds, jars, or twists the back is out, so forget running, high-impact aerobics, racquet sports, and most team ball games. Begin with walking. Work your way up to at least three thirty-minute walks a week. Walk in comfortable, supportive walking shoes. Ideally, walk on a surface that "gives" a little—grass instead of concrete. In winter, try cross-country skiing. Swimming is also excellent exercise for back pain sufferers, but stay away from the breaststroke and butterfly because these strokes over-arch the back. Cycling, rowing, gardening, and low-impact aerobics help some back-pain sufferers but aggravate pain in others.

Yoga is remarkably effective in eliminating lower back pain, preventing its return, building back strength, and promoting flexibility. In fact, in a national survey of people with chronic lower back pain, yoga turned out to be the most helpful and least harmful treatment program in a list that included care by physicians, chiropractors, physical therapists, and orthopedic surgeons (see Box, p. 456). Yoga helped the greatest proportion of back pain sufferers, and it was the only treatment program that did not aggravate anyone's pain. Yoga classes are available throughout the United States, Canada, and abroad. Among the various forms of yoga, instructors who are certified to teach Iyengar yoga have been trained to adapt the postures to provide maximum benefit and minimum harm to people with lower back problems. Be sure you mention your back problem to any instructor before the class begins. And if any stretch or posture causes *any* pain, stop doing it.

Chronic back pain treatment always includes exercises to stretch the back muscles and strengthen the abdominal muscles, which provide the major support for the back. Here is a standard set of beginning lower back exercises. When doing them, inhale through your nose, then exhale through your mouth during the "work" part of the exercise. Never hold your breath while exercising:

• Pelvic tilt. Lie on the floor on your back and pull in your stomach so that the small of your back is flat on the floor. Then, tightening your buttocks, raise your hips, pressing your waist into the floor. Hold this position for a count of ten, then relax, and repeat, eventually building up to twenty repetitions.

• Bent-leg sit-ups. Lie on the floor on your back with your legs bent and feet flat on the floor. With your arms extended over your knees, use your stomach muscles to gently raise your trunk slightly off the floor. Start by lifting your head, then your shoulders, and finally your upper back, but keep your lower back pressed into the floor. Then slowly relax back down. Repeat, and eventually build up to twenty sit-ups.

• Lower back stretch. Lying on your back with your legs out straight, bring one knee as close to your chest as possible. Return it slowly. Relax and work up to ten repetitions per leg.

• Knee-to-forehead. Lying on your back, with your knees bent and your feet starting flat on the floor, grasp one knee with both hands and bring it to your chest. At the same time, raise your shoulders off the floor and touch your forehead to the knee (or come as close as you can without causing pain). Slowly return to the starting position. Repeat, alternating legs, and work up to ten repetitions per leg.

• Leg raises. Lying on your back, with your knees bent and feet flat on the floor, bring one knee to your chest. Then extend the leg up, and lower

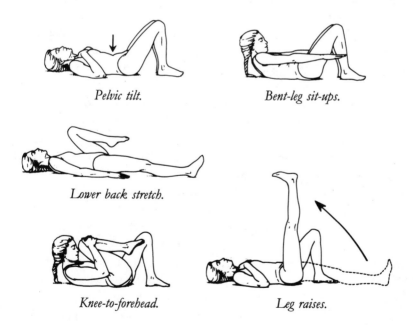

Pelvic tilt.

Bent-leg sit-ups.

Lower back stretch.

Knee-to-forehead.

Leg raises.

Lower back exercises.

it slowly, keeping the small of your back pressed into the floor. Bend your knee and repeat, working up to ten repetitions per leg. For a more advanced exercise, keep your moving leg straight the whole time.

For a more comprehensive, back-strengthening exercise program, try "Say Goodbye to Back Pain," a ninety-six-minute exercise video developed by Alexander Melleby, M.S., national director of the YMCA Back Program. A study published in 1983 in the medical journal *American Family Physician* showed that 81 percent of 12,000 surveyed users reported significant benefit (see RESOURCES at the end of this chapter).

• Maintain your recommended weight. You don't have to be "obese," that is, weigh at least 20 percent more than your recommended weight, to have extra pounds aggravate lower back pain. Even if you're only a few pounds overweight, losing weight can provide dramatic relief from back pain.

• Practice good posture. Try to stand with your weight evenly distributed on both legs, your knees slightly bent, your shoulders down and back, and your buttocks tucked in. Never slouch. Use good posture when sitting as well as standing.

• Drive with your seat pulled close enough so that your knees are slightly bent. Try a rolled up towel behind your lower back. Some people find greater relief at slightly higher cost by investing in a "lumbar pillow." Many newer cars have highly adjustable seats, with built-in, inflatable lumbar supports.

• Take breaks. If you have to sit or stand for long periods, take a break every half hour or so to walk, stretch, or do a few back exercises.

• Try heat. Heating pads, hot baths, saunas, and heat lamps all might help.

• Check your sleep position. Many back authorities recommend sleeping on your back with a pillow under your knees, or on your side with a pillow between your knees. They say that sleeping on your stomach can place stress on your back. But if you're used to sleeping on your stomach, how do you stop? Simple. Sew a tennis or ping-pong ball into a pocket on the front of your pajamas. That usually makes stomach-sleeping uncomfortable enough to train you to roll onto your back or side.

• Check your bed. Mattresses should be neither too firm nor too soft. Some people place plywood boards under their mattresses to make them firmer. Others opt for waterbeds, now called "flotation sleep systems." Waterbeds were invented by hippies of the late 1960s, who claimed they enhanced lovemaking. For some, they do. But waterbeds went mainstream in the 1970s because so many people with back problems reported that they helped control lower back pain. Today, an estimated 10 percent of American homes have waterbeds.

• Practice breathing deeply. Deep, diaphragmatic breathing helps support the spine and relax tensed muscles.

• Practice stress management. Everyday stresses, tensions, and anxieties give some people headaches, others stomachaches, and still others backaches (see MANAGE YOUR STRESS LOAD in Chapter 1).

• Check your bra. Poorly fitted bras can aggravate back pain. If you've never been professionally fitted, or if your bra size has changed recently, have a fitting. Wider back and shoulder straps are more backsparing because they distribute breast weight over a larger area.

• Check your shoes. Wear high heels as little as possible. There's a good reason why "sensible shoes" got that name. If you must wear heels, the lower the better. Take your high heels to work or social events in a bag and change into them there, wearing more back-sparing shoes on the way there and back.

• Wrap your back in pillows. Make yourself as comfortable as possible. Sit, sleep, and even stand with the help of back cushions and pillows. Many consumer catalogs such as Comfortably Yours, Bodyline, and the Self-Care Catalog, sell pillows that can help control back pain (see RE-SOURCES at the end of this chapter).

• Visit a "back store." Today there are an estimated 400 stores around the country that specialize in furniture and other products to make life easier for people with back problems. But before you jump for the back chair your best friend swears by, remember, no two backs are exactly alike, so no back chair works for everyone. Try them all, and see what works best for you. One back store, Back Designs, of Oakland, California, publishes a catalog of 150 back-sparing products, including furniture, desks, mattresses, bent-handle rakes and snow shovels, back books, and other items (see RESOURCES at the end of this chapter).

• Hang in there. Chronic lower back pain often takes quite a while to resolve. Chart your progress and celebrate small victories. Try to remain optimistic. The vast majority of even serious back problems get better if you adopt a committed, consistent back-healing life-style.

When to Call the Doctor.   Medicine has not been particularly successful in healing lower back pain (see Box, p. 456), but for persistent or increasingly severe pain, it's important to consult a doctor to rule out other more serious health conditions that might cause it: kidney disease, bowel or bladder problems, neurological disorders, gynecological problems in women, prostate problems in men, or tumors. After a thorough history and physical examination the doctor will probably order x-rays and possibly a CT scan and an MRI study. Depending on the physician's initial findings, you might also be referred to one or more specialists.

For back pain uncomplicated by other medical problems, doctors traditionally recommended pain medication, extended bedrest, and for chronic problems, surgery. Today, that's all changed. Nowadays doctors recommend pain medication, possibly muscle relaxants, a short period of bedrest until severe pain subsides, and back strengthening exercise, with surgery reserved for special cases. As a result, the number of back operations has plummeted during the past decade, and referrals to yoga classes, physical therapists, osteopaths, chiropractors, physiatrists, and other back-care practitioners have soared. Physiatrists are doctors who practice a little-known medical specialty focused on musculoskeletal rehabilitation, a kind of medical version of chiropractic.

And speaking of chiropractic, this healing art based on spinal manipulation was scorned as absurd by physicians a mere twenty years ago, but today doctors increasingly accept its ability to treat back problems. The American Medical Association used to forbid referrals to chiropractors, but in the late 1970s the AMA removed all objections to physicians referring to chiropractors. (Ironically, although chiropractic made its reputation in the area of back care, the survey of back-pain sufferers showed chiropractors to provide long-term relief in fewer than one-third of cases.)

If any physician recommends back surgery, get several opinions from a variety of back-care practitioners before consenting. Back surgery is traumatic and requires an extended recovery period. It works best for those who have clear symptoms of nerve root compression—numbness, tingling, or weakness down one side—and worst for those with chronic central-back pain. Back surgery's overall success rate is modest at best.

Because so many different kinds of practitioners claim to be "back-care experts," consulting professionals for lower back pain often feels like stepping through the looking glass into an Alice-in-Wonderland world where one practitioner says your spine needs realignment, another insists your posture is atrocious, and a third says your *chi* (Chinese for "life energy") is blocked. When consulting back-care professionals, talk to several and keep an open mind. The survey of back-pain sufferers showed that every form of professional intervention helped some people. But steer clear of practitioners who insist that they have "the answer" and dismiss all other approaches as useless. The survey showed that no single approach helped everyone, and that eight of nine treatments aggravated some people's pain. We recommend a team approach: Select the group of practitioners whose approaches seem to help you. Let them know you're consulting several other professionals. And combine their recommendations with your own committed, consistent self-care.

▶ **RED FLAGS**   Consult a physician immediately if you develop unrelenting back pain which intereferes with sleep or pain that is unresponsive to self-care and accompanied by any of the following: leg weakness, bladder or bowel problems, deep pain in the abdomen, a history of cancer, or any recent abdominal surgery or anticoagulation therapy.

WHAT WORKS FOR CHRONIC LOWER BACK PAIN?

Here's how a national sample of chronic lower-back pain sufferers rated the long-term relief they received from various professionals. The participants were self-selected from advertisements in national magazines, so the survey results should be considered impressionistic and not definitive. However, this survey represents the only attempt published to date comparing back-care practitioners, and the results are intriguing.

Practitioners	Moderate to dramatic long-term relief	Temporary relief only	No relief	More pain
Yoga class	96%	4%	0%	0%
Physiatrists	86	0	7	7
Physical therapists	75	8	17	10
Acupuncturists	36	32	28	4
Chiropractors	28	28	33	11
Orthopedists	23	9	71	7
Neurosurgeons	26	8	51	15
Primary care doctors	20	14	54	12
Neurologists	4	4	76	16

(Source: *Medical Self-Care,* July–Aug. 1987, p. 56, adapted from *Backache Relief* by Arthur Klein and Dava Sobel, New American Library, 1985)

BACK PAIN (UPPER)

(See also BACK PAIN (LOWER), NECK PAIN, and SHOULDER PAIN in this chapter)

Upper-back pain is neither as common nor generally as chronic as lower back pain. But when it strikes, it's no less painful.

What's Going On?   Read BACK PAIN (LOWER), NECK PAIN, and SHOULDER PAIN in this chapter.

Upper back exercises.

Shoulder shrugs.

Upper back stretch.

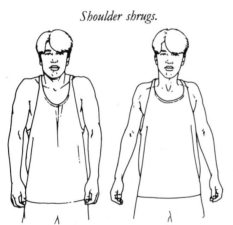

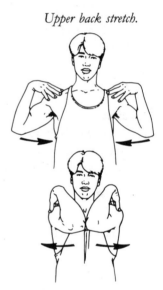

Step 1. Shoulders up and forward (shrugged).   *Step 2. Shoulders pressed back and moving down.*

Head roll.

Upper back strengthener.

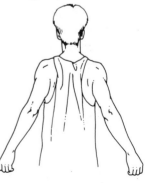

Step 1. Chin down.   *Step 2. Head tilted to one side.*

Before You Call the Doctor. Try the following upper-back stretches:

• Shoulder shrugs. Stand erect, arms held loosely at your sides. Breathe deeply as you make circles with your shoulders up and back toward your ears. Work up to twenty circles twice a day.

• Upper-back stretch. Sit with your back straight and place your hands on your shoulders. Try to touch your elbows together. Bring them together until you feel a stretch across your upper back. Work up to ten repetitions.

• Head roll. In either a standing or sitting position, push your chin down toward your chest. With your head hanging forward, gently rotate your chin from side to side. Return to the starting position. Next, tilt your head to the left, then to the right, feeling your neck stretch each time. Work up to five repetitions of the entire sequence.

• Upper back strengthener. With shoulders down, swing your elbows back and press your shoulder blades toward each other. Work up to ten repetitions.

When to Call the Doctor. If self-care does not provide sufficient relief within two weeks, consult a physician to rule out other problems, for example, heartburn ("esophageal reflux").

▶ **RED FLAG** One possible casue of upper back pain is aortic dissection, a rupture of the aorta (the major artery that leads from the heart) that produces "tearing" pain and usually strikes suddenly, without associated muscle soreness. This is a medical emergency.

BUNIONS

Bunions make the feet hurt and look deformed.

What's Going On? Bunions, medically known as *hallux valgus*, Latin for "turning outward of the first toe," are bony protrusions at the outside edge of the big toe. Once bunions develop, the big toe is often forced to overlap one or more other toes.

Bunions may be caused by a congenital problem that causes the inner foot bone to turn inward ("metatarsus varus"), but more often, they develop as a result of fallen arches ("flat feet"). Pointed and high-heeled shoes don't cause bunions, but they may aggravate the condition. Bunions may also be caused by arthritis, cerebral palsy, or other diseases that cause joint destruction.

Before You Call the Doctor.   If you have a personal or family history of bunions, wear loose shoes that don't place undue pressure on your big toe. Be sure to maintain effective arch support. If necessary, use arch supporting inserts. If you have flat feet, consider investing in custom shoe inserts ("orthotics") fitted by a podiatrist (foot doctor). If bunions develop, sandals or foot pads may help relieve discomfort.

When to Call the Doctor.   Your doctor will probably refer you to a podiatrist or an orthopedist. Depending on bunion severity, treatment may be nonsurgical or surgical. Nonsurgical strategies attempt to relieve the pressure on the area with orthotics or custom shoes with extra large toe areas ("toe boxes").

Surgical treatment removes the bunion and often realigns or makes other structural changes in the big toe and the foot. After bunion surgery, you may have to wear a cast for up to several months.

BURSITIS

Bursitis means inflammation of the bursae (singular: bursa), small fluid-filled sacs that help lubricate the sliding action between bones and tendons, the fibrous, elastic tissues which connect the muscles to bones. Symptoms include pain, inflammation, and possibly movement restriction.

What's Going On?   As we move, our bones and tendons constantly rub against each other. Bone is harder than tendon, so the friction between them would quickly wear out our tendons if it weren't for the protection afforded by the bursae. Most bursae are located near joints, where tendons attach to bones. Injury, usually from strain or overuse, can cause these small sacs to become inflamed and filled with fluid. Repetitive motions, especially such jarring movements as running, can also cause bursitis, for example, Achilles bursitis behind the Achilles tendon near the heel. Bursitis usually occurs in the shoulder, elbow, knee, hip, or ankle. Usually, episodes affect only one area.

Before You Call the Doctor.   Most cases of bursitis clear up within a week or two:

  • Rest the affected area as much as possible.
  • Wrap it in an Ace bandage. The compression helps.
  • Take aspirin or ibuprofen to relieve pain and inflammation. If either one upsets your stomach, try an "enteric coated" brand, which dissolves

in the intestine, not in the stomach. Pregnant women and those with a history of ulcers should not take aspirin or ibuprofen unless a doctor recommends it.

• Try heat or cold (see the heat/cold discussion in the ARTHRITIS section of this chapter).

• To prevent recurrences, try to figure out the activity that led to the episode and stop overdoing it.

• Do exercises to stretch and strengthen the muscles and tendons around the affected area (see SHOULDER PAIN, ELBOW PAIN, HIP PAIN, KNEE PAIN, or ANKLE PAIN in this chapter). You might want to consult an athletic trainer or physical therapist for suggestions.

When to Call the Doctor.   Consult a physician if bursitis pain does not clear up within two weeks. After an exam to rule out other possible problems, the doctor will probably recommend a pain-relieving, anti-inflammatory drug to reduce the discomfort and swelling. You may hear the famous words, "Take two aspirin and call me in the morning," or you may receive a prescription for a more potent medication. In severe cases, corticosteroids may be injected into the inflamed area, or the doctor may draw off the excess fluid in the affected bursa(e) with a syringe to reduce swelling and then bandage the area.

If bursitis in any area becomes chronic and severely painful, your doctor may recommend having the bursa(e) surgically removed. The surgery can be done with local or general anesthetic and usually requires no more than a one-day hospital stay.

▶ **RED FLAG**   If pain, heat, redness, and swelling near a joint seem associated with any break in the skin, the cause is probably not bursitis but an infection. Consult a physician for treatment.

CARPAL TUNNEL SYNDROME

The "carpal tunnel" is an opening inside the wrist through which nerves pass (see illustration). If swelling of the tissues around the carpal tunnel pinches the nerves that pass through it, the result is carpal tunnel syndrome (CTS), a collection of symptoms, which can range from mild tingling and numbness in the fingers to crippling muscle-wasting in the thumbs.

What's Going On?   The hand ("median") nerve travels through a narrow opening formed by the wrist bones ("carpals") and the tough

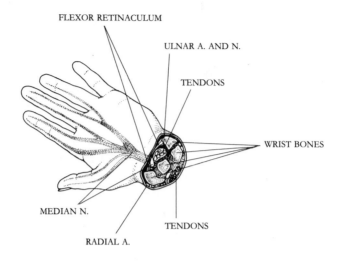

The carpal tunnel.

membrane that holds them together. If tissues around the carpal tunnel swell, the tunnel narrows, and the median nerve becomes compressed, causing CTS symptoms.

Carpal tunnel syndrome is usually caused by a "repetitive motion injury," cumulative trauma associated with constant rapid use of the fingers (low-intensity, high-frequency finger work). CTS has been around for decades, the occupational hazard of bookkeepers and supermarket checkout clerks who punched buttons all day long. But it did not become a household word until the 1980s when personal computers came to dominate so many workplaces. Suddenly millions of people's jobs required the kind of steady, rapid finger movements that cause repetitive motion injuries and CTS. Today, CTS has become common among people who make a living using word processors and other computerized keyboards. It is also a problem for some musicians, factory workers, and others who must constantly use their hands.

CTS can also be caused by strong, steady vibrations that shake the wrist, for example, chain saw work, or by any other condition which causes the wrist to swell such as pregnancy, rheumatoid arthritis, obesity, and many other conditions.

Diabetics and those with low thyroid function ("hypothyroidism") have a higher-than-average risk of carpal tunnel syndrome.

Women are particularly vulnerable to CTS because the hormonal changes involved in pregnancy, menopause, and menstruation can trigger swelling of tissues around the carpal tunnel.

CTS typically begins with feelings of burning, tingling, or "pins and needles" in the thumb, index, or middle finger or the inner side of the ring finger. (The little finger is spared because its nerve supply bypasses the carpal tunnel.) In some cases, the problem affects only the dominant hand, but about half the time, it involves both hands. Symptoms may progress to include pain and numbness or a sensation of cold. Sometimes the pain gets referred to the forearm or shoulder. The hand typically becomes weak and clumsy, and simple tasks, for instance, opening jars, can become difficult, sometimes impossible.

Before You Call the Doctor.   It may be difficult to distinguish hand and arm symptoms caused by CTS from symptoms caused by arthritis in the neck. Try this simple test: Place the backs of your hands together, with your fingers pointing straight down and your wrists at a 90° angle so that your elbows point straight out to the sides. If holding this position brings on your symptoms within one minute, you have CTS.

If your job or hobby involves constant, rapid-fire movements of the fingers and you develop finger burning, tingling, or clumsiness, chances are it's CTS. Try the following:

• If possible, stop your repetitive finger movements for several days and see if you feel better. If so, try to rearrange your time so you don't spend so much time in CTS-stimulating activities. Now that CTS has received so much publicity and has been so clearly associated with computer work, some employers have become more sensitive to the problem and more willing to reassign people who develop it, or at least allow them to alternate computer tasks with other work that does not stress the carpal tunnel.

• Lose weight. CTS is associated with being overweight, because the excess tissue presses on the carpal tunnel.

• Try aspirin or ibruprofen to reduce pain and inflammation. If these drugs upset your stomach, try an "enteric coated" brand, which dissolves in the intestine, not in the stomach. Pregnant women and those with a history of ulcers should not take aspirin or ibuprofen unless a doctor recommends it.

• Try a wrist splint. Available at medical supply houses and many pharmacies, splints consist of cloth-covered metal braces attached to the forearm with velcro straps. Splints should hold the wrist cocked slightly back with the thumb parallel to the forearm, in approximately the same position used to hold a pen loosely. This position keeps the tunnel as open as possible. Activities that require keeping the wrist bent, for example, holding a baby, compress the tunnel. Splints may be worn during the day, at night, or all the time. The extra support they provide often helps control CTS symptoms. Splints may also be custom made.

·Try 100 mg of vitamin B$_6$ (pyridoxine) twice a day. In one study, two-thirds of CTS sufferers reported improvement. But don't take more than 200 mg a day because of possible nerve damage.

·CTS associated with pregnancy usually clears up after the baby arrives.

When to Call the Doctor.   Consult a physician if CTS symptoms progress from initial tingling or burning to actual pain and numbness. Doctors diagnose CTS based on your history and a series of wrist tests, including the nerve conduction velocity test, which measures the time it takes an electrical impulse to travel between various points on the arm and fingers, and electromyography (EMG), which measures electrical activity in the muscles of the thumb.

Physicians treat CTS with anti-inflammatory medications, including steroids, and possibly diuretics. They also prescribe splints and recommend avoiding aggravating activities.

If conservative treatment proves ineffective, surgery may be recommended to open the carpal tunnel. However, surgical treatment is controversial, and many physicians believe it is often performed unnecessarily. The surgery involves cutting the transverse carpal ligament, the thick, fibrous band that forms one side of the tunnel. Performed under local anesthetic on an outpatient basis, the surgeon may make a small incision or a large one. The small incision has the advantage of minimal scarring, but it provides only a limited-area view for the surgeon, raising the risk of damage to other important wrist structures. The large incision means less risk of damage to the inner wrist, but it leaves a more prominent scar.

Pain and numbness usually subside within a few days after surgery; however, some people take as long as two years for symptoms to completely resolve. A splint must be worn for two to three weeks following CTS surgery.

CHARLEY HORSE

(See MUSCLE CRAMPS in this chapter)

ELBOW PAIN

(See also ARTHRITIS, BURSITIS, GOUT, and TENDINITIS in this chapter)

Elbow pain is the bane of many carpenters, golfers, tennis players, and others who tax this joint.

What's Going On? The elbow consists of three separate and interdependent joints. It transmits power from the shoulder to the hand and allows us to flex, extend, or turn the hand and forearm inward and outward. Unfortunately, this amazing body part is also particularly vulnerable to injury.

Elbow pain may be caused by arthritis or gout, especially in construction workers or professional tennis players (see ARTHRITIS and GOUT in this chapter), but most people's elbow pain is caused by muscle strains or such tendon problems as "tennis elbow" or "golfer's elbow" (see MUSCLE STRAINS and TENDINITIS in this chapter).

Probably the most common cause of elbow pain is tennis elbow, an overuse injury medically known as "lateral epicondylitis." An enormous number of people develop tennis elbow, but only a small proportion get it playing tennis. Tennis elbow is generally caused by hammering or other construction work or by the various racquet sports. Golfer's elbow ("medial epicondylitis") is a similar condition. In tennis elbow, the pain occurs on the outside of the elbow; in golfer's elbow, it strikes on the inside. Both types of tendinitis can be identified by tenderness of the "trigger point" just below the bony knob ("epicondyle") on the affected side. Tennis and golfer's elbow occur most commonly from age thirty-five to fifty-five.

Tennis elbow can be caused by a blow, but it's usually a repetitive motion injury. The forearm muscles are not strong enough to sustain the repetitive motions, and eventually the elbow tendons tear, causing the characteristic sharp pain.

Elbow pain may also be caused by bursitis. If you develop a soft, fluid-filled, swollen area directly over the point of your elbow, see BURSITIS in this chapter.

Before You Call the Doctor. When tennis or golfer's elbow strikes, immediately stop whatever activity precipitated it and begin first-aid treatment.

• Use R.I.C.E.—rest, ice, compression, and elevation. For a complete discussion of R.I.C.E. treatment, see MUSCLE STRAINS in this chapter.

• For pain and inflammation, take aspirin or ibuprofen. Acetaminophen relieves pain but not inflammation. If aspirin and/or ibuprofen upset your stomach, try "enteric coated" brands. Pregnant women and those with a history of ulcers should not take aspirin or ibuprofen unless a doctor recommends it.

• Depending on the cause of your pain, follow the general self-care suggestions in the ARTHRITIS or TENDINITIS sections of this chapter.

• Assuming you have tendinitis, as soon as the sharp pain has subsided to a dull aching, begin an exercise program to increase strength and flexibility of your forearm muscles:

  ◦During the first few days after elbow pain strikes, squeeze a rubber ball repeatedly to begin building forearm strength.

  ◦Then move on to weight-lifting exercises. Grasp a small, three- to five-pound weight. Hold your arm out straight. Moving only the hand at the wrist joint, lift the weight repeatedly (see illustration). Work up to five sets of thirty lifts twice a day. This exercise strengthens the forearm muscle group involved in tennis elbow ("wrist extensors").

  ◦Next, hold the weight down at your side, and lift it toward your back moving only the hand at the wrist joint ("reverse curls") (see illustration). Work up to five sets of thirty curls twice a day. This exercise strengthens the forearm muscle group involved in golfer's elbow ("wrist flexors").

 •Do all these exercises, even if your problem is in only one muscle group. Keep doing the exercises even after you feel completely healed to prevent reinjury.

 •If racquet sports caused your tennis elbow, talk with an athletic equipment professional about your racquet. Changing the grip size and loosening the strings may help.

When to Call the Doctor.   When professional athletes suffer tennis elbow, they often have anesthetics and/or the anti-inflammatory drug

Wrist extensor exercise (palm down).

Wrist flexor exercise (palm toward back).

Elbow exercises. It's important for the elbow to be straight (but not rigid) during these exercises.

cortisone injected directly into the painful area. As a result, many weekend athletes and carpenters seek similar treatment. In general, this is not a good idea. Steroids weaken the tendon and make it more prone to reinjury. For lasting relief, follow the steps outlined above and in the TENDINITIS section of this chapter.

However, if your elbow pain was caused by a blow or sudden forceful movement, and the pain and swelling don't resolve within a couple of days despite R.I.C.E. treatment, consult a physician for x-rays to rule out fractures, infection, or other problems. And if the elbow pain is accompanied by pain in other joints, you may have arthritis and need medical treatment.

FIBROMYALGIA

Fibromyalgia causes muscle aches, pain, and stiffness which often begins in the neck and shoulders, then spreads around the body over a period of months. The muscle symptoms are often accompanied by a strange collection of other complaints:

- Swollen joints.
- Headaches.
- Anxiety.
- Depression.
- Irritable bowel syndrome.
- Bladder trouble.
- Tingling, prickling, and/or numbness.
- Fatigue.
- Insomnia or other sleep disturbances.
- Dry eyes and mouth.
- Raynaud's syndrome, in which the tips of the fingers become white and numb in cold weather.

What's Going On?   An estimated six million Americans suffer the often baffling symptoms of fibromyalgia. Doctors aren't sure what causes this condition. Some researchers believe it may be a "pain amplification syndrome," in which minor discomforts become magnified because of some mechanism which remains a mystery. Others believe it may be related to chronic fatigue syndrome, or that it may be triggered by traumas, such as a whiplash injury in an automobile accident. Fortunately, fibromyalgia is neither progressive nor degenerative.

The key to fibromyalgia diagnosis is identification of characteristic tender points. Locations include the sides of the neck, sides of the breastbone, top of the shoulder blade, outside of the upper buttock, outside of the hip joint, and inside of the knee (see illustrations).

Before You Call the Doctor.   Because of the dozens of possible symptom permutations, fibromyalgia can be mistaken for an enormous number of more serious diseases, including lupus (also known as "systemic lupus erythematosus" or SLE), osteoarthritis, hypothyroidism, and malignancies, among others. It's important to seek professional diagnosis and treatment. Don't be surprised if it takes consultations with several specialists to arrive at a definitive diagnosis.

Once fibromyalgia has been diagnosed, self-care definitely helps:

• Treat your symptoms. Take aspirin, ibuprofen, or acetaminophen for muscle pain and achiness. If aspirin or ibuprofen upset your stomach, try an "enteric coated" brand, which dissolves in the intestine, not in the stomach. Pregnant women and those with a history of ulcers should not take aspirin or ibuprofen unless a doctor recommends it.

• Try regular moderate exercise to relieve anxiety and depression (see ANXIETY and DEPRESSION in Chapter 5).

• Make every effort to get a good night's sleep. Identify and eliminate any possible sleep disturbers: light, noise, or a sagging mattress, see the INSOMNIA discussion in Chapter 4.

• Try sleeping with a neck support pillow and using a horseshoe-collar pillow when sitting in high-backed chairs, for instance, airplane seats.

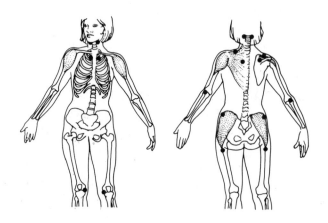

Fibromyalgia tender points.

Neck-supporting pillows are available at some department stores, medical supply houses, and pharmacies and through several consumer catalogs, such as Comfortably Yours, Bodyline, and the Self-Care Catalog (see RESOURCES at the end of this chapter).

• Reduce stress on your lower back by strengthening the abdominal muscles with regular abdominal exercises (see BACK PAIN (LOWER) in this chapter).

• Engage in a supervised, gradually progressing program of aerobic exercise to maintain muscle tone and improve mental health.

• Make physical adjustments in your home or work environment, for example, change the height of desks or chairs to make work more comfortable.

• Be kind to yourself. You're not crazy. This condition is not all in your head. Don't overdo work or play. Enlist the support of friends and family. Take breaks when you feel you need to.

• Consider psychological counseling to deal with stress and/or other factors that may contribute to the condition.

When to Call the Doctor. Fibromyalgia can be treated medically, but so far results have been only partially successful. Symptoms disappear completely in only 25 percent of cases. Doctors typically prescribe pain relievers, and such medications as amitriptyline, a sedative/antidepressant; cyclobenzaprine (Flexeril), a muscle relaxant; or Valium-like tranquilizers (benzodiazepines) to improve sleep.

Some doctors also administer local injections of lidocaine, an anesthetic, or steroidal anti-inflammatories to painful locations. However, such therapies are largely unproven. Deep massage, hot and cold applications, topical anesthetics, stretching, acupuncture, and chiropractic may also help minimize symptoms.

FIBROSITIS

(See FIBROMYALGIA in this chapter)

FINGER INJURY

(See also FINGER PAIN and SPRAINS in this chapter)

Our fingers are so central to how we operate in the world, it's no wonder they often end up pinched, mashed, crunched, smashed, and jammed by hammers, doors, windows, and dozens of other everyday objects.

What's Going On?   Because of their many joints, fingers are particularly prone to ligament injuries ("sprains"). If a twisting or bending force causes sudden pain at a finger joint, see SPRAINS in this chapter.

In a crushing injury, all the tissues in the finger swell and bleed to some extent. But if the skin of a smashed finger remains intact and the injury involes only the fingertip, medical assistance usually isn't necessary.

Before You Call the Doctor.   As quickly as possible, run cold water over the affected finger to numb it.

Then make an ice pack by wrapping an ice cube or two in a plastic bag and then in a clean cloth, and apply it to the injury. An ice substitute frozen gel pack may also be used. Leave the ice pack in place twenty minutes, then remove it for ten minutes before reapplying it. Keep doing this as long as the finger hurts or remains swollen. Do not apply ice directly to the skin. This may cause the equivalent of frostbite.

In addition, to relieve pain and inflammation, take aspirin or ibuprofen according to package directions. Acetaminophen relieves pain but not inflammation. If aspirin and/or ibuprofen upset your stomach, try an "enteric coated" brand, which dissolves in the intestine, not in the stomach. Pregnant women and those with a history of ulcers should not take aspirin or ibuprofen unless a doctor recommends it.

The most potentially frightening aspect of a smashed fingertip is bleeding under the fingernail ("subungual hematoma"). The blood looks black, and the fingertip may become swollen and throb with pain. Ice packs and pain relievers may help, but if they don't, or if the hematoma covers a good deal of the fingernail, the painful pressure can usually be relieved using a hot wire paper clip. This treatment sounds more drastic than it is:

• Bend a paper clip open, and grasping it with a pair of pliers, hold the end over a gas burner or candle until it glows red hot.

• Then touch the glowing end to a spot on the nail over the hematoma. If the paper clip is hot enough, it melts the nail, producing a small hole through which the accumulated blood escapes. This procedure is usually painless. As soon as red blood appears, remove the paper clip, soak up the blood with a clean cloth or tissues, then bandage the fingertip.

• If the paper clip cools before melting through the nail, reheat it and try again.

If a finger injury breaks or otherwise deforms your nail, don't try to remove it. Simply trim off the detached part, cutting off any sharp edges, and bandage it for a few days to prevent further injury. The nail should grow back within a few weeks to several months.

For treatment of common wounds, for example, cuts and splinters, see FOOT PAIN in this chapter and CUTS in Chapter 6.

Fingers may also be "jammed" ("stoved" or "baseball finger"). Simple jams can usually be treated at home with ice packs and over-the-counter pain relievers. You can also immobilize an injured finger by taping it to an adjacent one. When initial pain and swelling subside, use your other hand to begin moving the finger through its full range of motion to prevent later arthritis in the affected joint.

When to Call the Doctor. Consult a physician if you're in doubt about the severity of any finger injury. Don't risk permanent disability to these crucial appendages.

Intense pain, marked swelling, bruising away from the area of impact, and/or visible finger deformity suggest a broken bone ("fracture"), which requires professional care. If a crush injury causes a break in the skin deep enough to bleed, consult a doctor to rule out a fracture. Open ("compound") fractures require special care to prevent infection.

It's especially important to seek professional help for children's finger injuries, because untreated injuries may impair normal growth.

A finger exam involves a history of the injury and an x-ray to determine the extent of damage. Beyond pain medication, finger injuries are usually not treated unless they involve the joints or are fractures, in which case they're usually splinted. However, splinting is controversial among physicians. Some believe that while splinting helps control pain, it encourages arthritis. Others contend that if an injured finger joint isn't splinted, pain may persist, healing may not proceed as rapidly, and you may end up with arthritis anyway. Discuss the pros and cons of splinting with your doctor. Ultimately you must decide whether or not you want a splint.

Splinted fingers are often bandaged to an adjacent finger. Depending on the severity of the injury, the splint remains in place for one to three weeks. Tenderness should begin to diminish within a week or so.

▶ **RED FLAG** If finger pain, swelling, or tenderness increase, despite home and/or professional treatment, consult a physician promptly.

FINGER PAIN

(See also ARTHRITIS, CARPAL TUNNEL SYNDROME, FINGER INJURY, GOUT, and SPRAINS in this chapter and NAIL PROBLEMS in Chapter 6)

Finger pain may be sharp or dull, constant or intermittent, and piercing or throbbing. It also may have many causes.

What's Going On? Pain in a single finger suggests a problem in that finger's joints, tendons, or ligaments (see ARTHRITIS, FINGER INJURY, GOUT, and SPRAINS in this chapter).

If your problem is in more than one finger, but only in one hand, it's probably a joint or nerve problem (see ARTHRITIS and CARPAL TUNNEL SYNDROME in this chapter).

If pain strikes both hands, it may be a systemic, nerve, or circulation problem. Nerve problems—such as carpal tunnel syndrome or arthritis in the neck, which may pinch nerves to the arm or reduce the blood supply to a nerve—tend to cause tingling and/or numbness. Certain vitamin deficiencies as well as alcohol, heavy metal exposure, or a high blood sugar level in diabetes can also cause the numbness and tingling of nerve damage.

Circulation problems usually cause color changes. In cold weather, do your fingers (and possibly your toes and nose) blanch and turn blue, then deep red as they warm? If so, you may have Raynaud's syndrome, which is characterized by circulation impairment of the fingers. The fingers of people who suffer from Raynaud's can react with numbing and blanching even with mild temperature drops—for example, from 70° to 50°. When the hands rewarm, the person usually feels tingling and pulsing pain. For unknown reasons, women develop Raynaud's symptoms more often than men, but men who use vibratory tools or suffer carpal tunnel syndrome may also develop it. Symptoms may become more severe with age. Sometimes Raynaud's symptoms occur without any others. However, the condition may be a side effect of medication, or one symptom of a more serious disease, such as lupus ("systemic lupus erythematosus"), scleroderma, or rheumatoid arthritis.

Another annoying—though usually not very painful—finger condition causes a joint to lock ("trigger finger"). This occurs because a tendon gets caught on the fibrous tissue that holds the tendons close to the finger bone. Trigger finger is an overuse injury. Repetitive motion causes roughening of the tendon, which increases its likelihood of getting stuck.

Before You Call the Doctor. Begin evaluating and treating your finger pain by referring to the appropriate section of this chapter.

Home treatment often can control the discomfort of Raynaud's syndrome:

• Stay away from situations that expose your hands and fingers to cold, such as gripping a cold steering wheel or working in a refrigerator without gloves. Whenever necessary, wear gloves, mittens, or battery-heated gloves and/or footwear available through some consumer catalogs, such as Comfortably Yours (see RESOURCES at the end of this chapter).

If you smoke, stop (see RESOURCES at the end of Chapter 11). Smoking narrows the blood vessels in the hands.

One cold weather specialist reports that the following regimen can relieve Raynaud's symptoms for up to several years. The idea is to condition the hands to stay warm when the rest of the body gets chilled:

• Take two containers large enough to accommodate both hands. Fill them with hot water at about 120°. Place one in a cool area (outdoors or in your basement) and the other in a warm area (your kitchen or bathroom).

• In the warm room, immerse both hands in the 120° water for two to five minutes.

• Wrap your warmed hands in a towel, go to the cool area, and again place your hands in the hot water for ten minutes.

• Return to the warm area, and place both hands in the water for two to five minutes.

• Repeat this procedure three to six times a day every day for a total of about fifty times.

For trigger finger, eliminate or modify the activity that causes it. You may want to splint the finger for a few days by taping it to the next finger, but this won't help if you've had the condition for some time. A one- to two-week course of aspirin or ibuprofen taken four times a day may also help by reducing tendon inflammation. If aspirin or ibuprofen upset your stomach, try an "enteric coated" brand, which dissolves in the intestine, not in the stomach. Pregnant women and those with a history of ulcers should not take aspirin or ibuprofen unless a doctor recommends it.

When to Call the Doctor.　　Consult a physician promptly if you have:
• Severe finger pain.
• Pain that does not respond to self-care within a few days.
• Fingers that feel cold and turn blue.
• Or finger pain with swelling, warmth, tenderness, and pus, which suggests infection.

The physician will attempt to determine the cause of the pain and treat it. X-rays and other tests may be necessary.

FLAT FEET

(See FOOT PAIN in this chapter)

FOOT PAIN

(See also ANKLE PAIN, ARTHRITIS, GOUT, MUSCLE CRAMPS, TOE INJURY, and TOE PAIN in this chapter and ATHLETE'S FOOT in Chapter 6)

Foot pain is so common that 80 percent of Americans suffer from it at one time or another, and an entire medical specialty, podiatry, is devoted to the feet.

What's Going On?   Thousand-page medical texts have been written about foot problems. Here we'll look at some of the common causes of foot pain.

• *Going Barefoot or Wearing the Wrong Shoes.*   Even though the bottoms of the feet contain the most callused skin on the body, it doesn't take much of a pebble, glass shard, nail, splinter, or other object to cut into the foot. Even if you're wearing shoes, tacks, nails, or pieces of broken glass can penetrate the soles and cause pain.

What's Going On?   Wake up, you warm-weather romantics and slaves of fashion. If you go barefoot, you're almost certain to cut your feet. And the feet were not meant to be encased in tight shoes with high heels, pointy toes, platform soles, straps between the toes, or any of the other oddities that pass for "style." Shoes should feel comfortable and hold the feet gently but firmly. Anything else is a one-way ticket to foot pain.

Before You Call the Doctor.   Don't walk barefoot or in shoes with thin soles that provide poor foot protection.

Most foot cuts, scrapes, and bruises are not serious and can be treated effectively at home. If the problem is a splinter, remove it with tweezers sterilized in alcohol or a match flame. Don't forget to let flame-sterilized tweezers cool before touching them to your skin. Never use knives, needles, or razors to remove splinters, but if you can see the entire splinter, it's safe to use a sterilized needle. If you can't remove the splinter within fifteen minutes, consult a physician. More probing may cause greater injury. Once the object has been removed, thoroughly wash the area with soap and water.

If the injury is a puncture wound from a dirty object like a rusty nail, soak the wound for thirty minutes in a solution of half Betadine and half water to disinfect it. Keep the wound clean with an adhesive bandage.

For pain and inflammation, take aspirin or ibuprofen according to package directions. Acetaminophen relieves pain but not inflammation. If aspirin and/or ibuprofen upset your stomach, try an "enteric coated" brand, which dissolves in the intestine and not in the stomach. Pregnant women and those with a history of ulcers should not take aspirin or ibuprofen unless a doctor recommends it.

If your shoes hurt your feet, change them. If you must wear foot-abusing shoes—for example, high heels—wear them as little as possible, and pad them as much as possible for comfort. Most pharmacies carry a wide assortment of self-adhesive foam foot pads.

Check for sharp objects embedded in your shoes and remove them.

When to Call the Doctor.   Even for minor splinters and puncture wounds, see a physician for a tetanus shot if it's been ten years since your last shot. For deeper penetrating wounds from dirty objects, get a tetanus shot if it's been five years since your last booster.

See a physician if any foot injury produces signs of infection: increased pain, swelling, redness, tenderness, or whitish or yellow-green pus discharge.

▶ **RED FLAGS**   Consult a physician immediately if jaw pain or stiffness develop. This is the classic symptom of tetanus, also known as "lockjaw." Mild tetanus is treatable. Severe cases are almost always fatal. Most deaths occur in older adults who neglect to get tetanus boosters every ten years. Be sure to maintain your immunity by getting periodic tetanus shots.

Foot infections can become quite serious for people with diabetes. Diabetics should routinely examine their shoes for tacks and their socks for red or brown stains, which indicate blood. Diabetics who develop any foot problem should consult a physician immediately (see DIABETES in Chapter 4).

• *Corns.*   Corns usually look yellow but can become red when irritated and inflamed.

What's Going On?   Corns are callus-like, hard, thickened areas that appear on the toes due to pressure and rubbing from shoes.

Before You Call the Doctor.   Most corns can be treated at home. The goal is to remove the source of pressure and then remove the corn itself. Immediately start wearing shoes with a larger toe area ("toe box") that doesn't place pressure on the corn. Cushion the area with an adhesive foot pad.

To remove corns you need to soften the hard, dead skin. First, soak the foot in Epsom salts for fifteen minutes and apply a moisturizing cream. Then cover the corn with a moist gauze pad, and wrap the foot in plastic for fifteen minutes. Remove the plastic and rub the area in a side-to-side motion with a clean, abrasive nail file or pumice stone available at pharmacies. Repeat this process daily until the corn disappears.

When to Call the Doctor.   If corns become severe or if your problem is caused by hammertoes, a foot deformity which causes a toe to occupy an unnatural position, see a physician or podiatrist.

• Athlete's Foot.   This fungal infection usually causes itching but sometimes causes burning pain of the toes and soles (see ATHLETE'S FOOT in Chapter 6).

• Flat Feet.   Flat feet may cause no problems, but in some people they cause persistent foot pain.

What's Going On?   The foot's inside edge should be raised in an arch. If the arch is inadequate ("fallen arches"), the feet flatten out, which may cause pain.

Before You Call the Doctor.   If you have painful flat feet, try arch supporting inserts available at pharmacies or some shoe stores.

Here are some exercises that might help:

• Towel curl. Place a towel flat on the floor. Holding your heel in the air, place only your toes on the towel, and by curling your toes, move the towel toward you. Repeat this five times. When it becomes too easy, place a book or other weight on the towel.

• Shin curl. Sitting in a chair, curl your toes as though gripping a pencil and run the arch of your foot up and down the shin of your other leg. Repeat this five times.

• Calf and arch exercise. Standing on the balls of your feet, squat down with your knees together, your arms outside of your legs, and your palms flat on the floor. Rock back gently as far as you can, bringing your heels toward the floor until you feel tension in the bottoms of your feet. Hold this for thirty seconds and repeat it five times. Don't bounce.

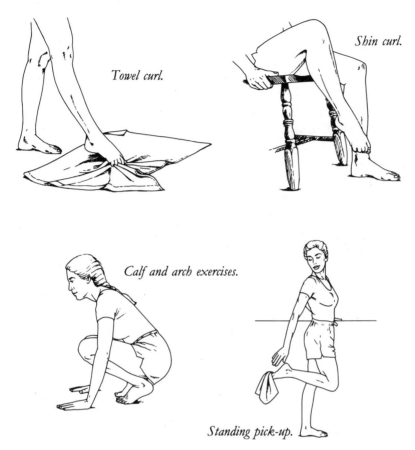

Towel curl.

Shin curl.

Calf and arch exercises.

Standing pick-up.

Flat feet exercises.

• Standing pick-up. Lean with one hand against a table and drop a washcloth at your feet. Pick it up with your toes, and bending your knee, transfer it to your free hand. Do this ten times on both legs.

When to Call the Doctor.   If pain persists longer than two weeks after fitting your shoes with arch supports, consult a podiatrist. You may need orthotics, custom shoe inserts.

• ***Gout.***   The joint most frequently affected by gout is the one at the base of the big toe, but the swelling, redness, and intense pain may also appear on top of the foot (see GOUT in this chapter).

• *Heel Spur Syndrome*   (see also "Plantar Fasciitis" below). Heel spurs cause pain in the heel when you place weight on the foot. Usually the pain occurs on rising in the morning or after resting.

What's Going On?   If the fascia, the tough sheet of connective tissue that runs from the ball of the foot to the heel, becomes stretched excessively, calcified cartilage splinters or "spurs" may develop in the heel area and cause heel spur symptoms. This condition is common among runners and other athletes.

Before You Call the Doctor.   Take a break from any activity that causes foot pounding. Stop running, and switch to swimming, cycling, or another nonimpact sport.

For pain and inflammation, take aspirin or ibuprofen. Acetaminophen relieves pain but not inflammation. If aspirin and/or ibuprofen upset your stomach, try an "enteric coated" brand, which dissolves in the intestine, not in the stomach. Pregnant women and those with a history of ulcers should not take aspirin or ibuprofen unless a doctor recommends it.

Wear shoes with a slightly elevated heel (one-half to one inch) and/or add foam heel pads inside your shoes to shift your weight forward and cushion the painful spot.

To help prevent heel spurs, do the exercises described in the "Flat Feet" discussion above.

When to Call the Doctor.   Heel spurs often require a visit to a podiatrist. The usual treatment involves taping, pain medication, and orthotics, custom-made shoe inserts to correct structural foot problems. Some doctors also inject corticosteriods to treat the inflammation. Surgery is the treatment of last resort, but it does not always work.

• *Ingrown Toenails.*   (See NAIL PROBLEMS in Chapter 6)

• *Plantar Fasciitis.*   Plantar fasciitis causes points of tenderness along the side of the sole, either just behind the ball of the foot or just in front of the heel.

What's Going On?   The plantar fascia is a sheet of connective tissue that runs from the ball of the foot to the heel. It acts like a bowstring to help maintain the arch of the foot. If it becomes overstretched, which commonly occurs in runners and other athletes, small tears can develop and cause pain on the bottom of the foot. Often such problems as flat feet or very high arches can stress the fascia and cause plantar fasciitis.

Before You Call the Doctor.   Treat this condition following the self-care suggestions in the "Heel Spur Syndrome" discussion above.

When to Call the Doctor.   See the "Heel Spur Syndrome" discussion above.

• *Plantar Warts.*   These warts, which appear on the bottoms of the feet, make you feel like you're walking with a pebble in your shoe.

What's Going On?   Unlike warts on other areas of the body (see WARTS in Chapter 6), plantar warts grow inward. For unknown reasons, children appear to be more susceptible than adults.

Before You Call the Doctor.   In addition to the suggestions in the WARTS discussion in Chapter 6, some plantar warts can be treated at home. Soak your foot for ten minutes in two tablespoons of mild household detergent mixed with a half gallon of warm water. Cut out a square of 40 percent salicylic-acid plaster, available over-the-counter at pharmacies, about the size of the wart. Remove the sticky side and apply it directly to the wart. Cover it with tape or a bandage. Remove the plaster in two days. Brush the wart vigorously with a toothbrush moistened with soap and water. Repeat this process for two weeks until the wart is gone.

When to Call the Doctor.   Severe warts or warts that interfere with walking may require professional removal. Options include freezing ("cryosurgery") and burning ("electrocautery" or with chemicals). See a podiatrist experienced with plantar warts and expect to return several times. Slower treatment works best. Quick radical treatments may lead to the growth of permanent, painful scar tissue.

• *Stress Fractures.*   Stress fractures are breaks and cracks in bones caused by trauma. Symptoms include swelling and pain. The area involved along the top of the foot between the ankle and the toes usually feels tender.

What's Going On?   Athletes are particularly susceptible to stress fractures because their feet often take a tremendous pounding. Anyone can develop stress fractures, but people with decreased bone density, such as postmenopausal women with osteoporosis, women who have infrequent or absent periods, or people taking steroids or hormones, are at greatest risk.

Before You Call the Doctor.   If you've had a stress fracture, consider changing your workout from impact aerobics, running, or other bone-pounding activities to nonimpact sports like swimming, rowing, or cycling. Better yet, try weight-bearing but nontraumatic exercise like nonimpact aerobics or walking. Weight-bearing exercise is particularly important for postmenopausal women because it helps prevent osteoporosis.

Wearing well-padded athletic shoes may also help, but the research is inconclusive.

To help prevent stress fractures, do the exercises described in "Flat Feet" on pages 475–76.

When to Call the Doctor.   If foot pain and swelling persist despite two weeks of nonimpact workouts and over-the-counter pain relievers, consult a physician.

Unfortunately, stress fractures often don't show up on x-ray for two to six weeks after the pain and swelling develop.

Foot stress fractures are treated like other fractures: rest, pain relievers, and immobilization in a cast or special shoe. Some foot fractures require casting for up to four weeks. After cast removal, exercise should be resumed gradually. Orthotics or additional cushioning help prevent reinjury.

GANGLION

A ganglion (plural: "ganglia") is a swelling under the skin. The wrist is one of the most common sites. Ganglia may feel soft or hard and are usually painless, though they might become mildly annoying.

What's Going On?   Ganglia are cysts that generally appear on the wrist, but may also develop on the feet. Usually no larger than a pea, but possibly as large as a grape, these cysts form when a jelly-like substance accumulates in a joint or a tendon sheath, causing the area to bulge outward.

Before You Call the Doctor.   Ganglia are usually more bothersome than serious. They often disappear without treatment. Pressing firmly on the ganglion may burst it. When this happens, the jelly-like filling is reabsorbed by the body and the bulge disappears. However, ganglia frequently recur.

When to Call the Doctor.   Unless you're sure that what you have is a ganglion, any unusual swelling should be checked by a physician to rule out more serious problems like tumors, which are also often painless. Some physicians remove painless ganglia contents with a needle and syringe, perhaps injecting a steroid to counteract inflammation. But after such treatment, ganglia may recur. Others recommend no treatment. If ganglia become painful, they can be surgically removed.

GOLFER'S ELBOW

(See TENDINITIS in this chapter)

GOUT

(See also ARTHRITIS in this chapter)

Gout is a form of arthritis. It causes inflammation and often intense pain in one or more joints, most commonly the big toe.

What's Going On?   Gout is caused by the buildup of uric acid, a metabolic waste product which is a component of urine. Normally, uric acid is filtered out of the blood by the kidneys, the organ which creates urine. But in people with gout, some uric acid gets deposited as crystals in the joints or other tissues. A gout attack occurs when crystals in joints irritate the joint lining, causing inflammation. Although the most common gout site is the big toe, the condition can also strike any other joint, though usually only one at a time.

Doctors aren't sure why gout develops. Many people have excess uric acid in their blood ("hyperuricemia"), but only a small proportion of them develop gout. Gout is strongly associated with a rich diet high in alcohol and low in other liquids, which results in overly concentrated urine. Sometimes hyperuricemia is caused by taking diuretics, which eliminate some body fluid and increase the concentration of urine. For reasons that remain a mystery, 80 to 90 percent of gout sufferers are men. Usually the first attack occurs between age forty and fifty.

Acute attacks cause intense pain. Swelling may cause the affected joint to appear red or purple and cause sensitivity to pressure that may make even the weight of a bedsheet intolerable. Initial attacks usually last a few days. Recurrences are possible but infrequent for most gout sufferers. However, without proper treatment, attacks can become longer and more frequent.

Ironically, gout attacks can be triggered by any sudden change in uric acid level either up *or down,* so successful reduction of a high uric acid level can cause an attack unless the person takes recommended precautions—drinking lots of fluids and taking antigout medication.

Sometimes uric acid deposits appear as lumps just under the skin near affected areas. If untreated, these lumps may interfere with joint movement.

In some cases, gout can lead to stones in the kidneys or bladder.

Before You Call the Doctor.   Gout sometimes runs in families, though it's not considered hereditary. If you've ever experienced it, or if close relatives have, you can prevent most attacks by following these suggestions:

• Don't eat foods that contain large amounts of purines, chemical building blocks for DNA whose breakdown product is uric acid. Such foods include organ meats (liver, brains, sweetbreads, etc.), sardines, anchovies, herring, beer, and wine. The Arthritis Foundation can provide additional information on foods high in purines (see RESOURCES at the end of this chapter).

• Limit your alcohol consumption. When it comes to preventing gout, the less alcohol, the better.

• Drink plenty of nonalcoholic fluids, ideally eight ounces with each meal, and at least eight ounces between meals and after supper.

• If you're overweight, lose weight. But *don't* go on fad or crash diets. Crash diets may involve liberal use of diuretics, which eliminate some water weight but increase the concentration of urine, thus boosting risk of gout attacks. Eat the high-fiber, low-fat diet recommended in EAT AND DRINK RIGHT in Chapter 1, and get regular moderate exercise. If you have trouble controlling your weight, consult a nutritionist, and increase your exercise.

When to Call the Doctor.   Consult a physician for any first-time gout attack, and later if gout pain becomes severe. After a thorough history, the physician should order a blood test to check your level of uric acid. Sometimes a needle must be used to withdraw fluid from the affected joint, which is examined for uric acid crystals.

Physicians treat gout with the dietary changes recommended above and with four types of medication:

• Nonsteroidal anti-inflammatory drugs (NSAIDs) are the most common choice. They alleviate pain and swelling.

• Colchicine, an anti-inflammatory that only works for gout, not other forms of arthritis.

• Probenecid (Benemid) and other "uricosuric" drugs, which increase uric acid excretion.

• Allopurinol (Zyloprim), a drug that decreases uric acid production.

These are powerful drugs with many side effects. If your physician prescribes any of them, make sure you're fully informed about all their possible side effects.

HAND PAIN

(See FINGER PAIN and WRIST PAIN in this chapter)

HEEL PAIN

(See FOOT PAIN in this chapter)

HIP PAIN

(See also ARTHRITIS, BURSITIS, FIBROMYALGIA, MUSCLE STRAIN, OSTEOPOROSIS, and SCIATICA in this chapter)

Pain in the hip usually suggests an overuse injury, but in post-menopausal women, it may signal a serious consequence of osteoporosis (see OSTEOPOROSIS in this chapter).

What's Going On? Hip pain is a common complaint of athletes, especially gymnasts, ballet dancers, and runners who train on sloped tracks. Hip pain due to athletic overuse can be felt as far down as the ankles or in the groin, lower back, and buttocks.

You don't have to be an athlete to suffer overuse hip pain. Chronic hip pain is common in people who are not in good physical condition, particularly older women. Often, the cause is arthritis or bursitis (see ARTHRITIS and BURSITIS in this chapter.) While the pain may originate in the hip, it can extend to the ankle and up through the buttocks. Hip pain due to degenerative joint disease usually follows a pattern: stiffness after disuse (on rising in the morning or after sitting), and an increase in pain during or following overuse. Other types of arthritis, such as gout and rheumatoid, can also cause hip pain (see GOUT in this chapter). Hip bursitis is usually due to activities that cause the pelvis to tilt abnormally. The pain and tenderness are located right over the bony prominence brought out by lying on your side and bending your upper hip.

Hip pain may be due to muscle strain ("iliotibial band syndrome"). The pain usually radiates from the buttocks to the knee along the outer thigh. This kind of strain often results from running downhill (see MUS-CLE STRAIN in this chapter).

Hip pain may also be "referred" from other areas, for example, the feet or back (see BACK PAIN in this chapter). Pain in the buttocks may indicate sciatica (see SCIATICA in this chapter).

Hip pain may also result from having one leg longer than the other. This condition is quite common. If the difference in leg length is significant, the hips can become quite stressed. A simple test to see if a leg length difference may contribute to your hip and/or back pain is to stand with one foot on one or more magazines for a minute. If your legs are different lengths, the correction feels right.

Before You Call the Doctor.   Hip pain can often be relieved by:

•Weight loss. If you're overweight, those extra pounds produce hip stress with every step you take. See EAT AND DRINK RIGHT in Chapter 1 for sensible dieting strategies. A regular walking program can help shed extra pounds and strengthen the muscles that surround the hip.

•If your hip pain seems to be caused by your athletic workout, discontinue running or other hip-pounding activities and opt for hip-sparing exercise, for example, swimming. You may also want to discuss your exercise program with an athletic trainer.

•Muscle strains can often be treated with rest, heat, and exercises to improve the strength and flexibility of the muscles surrounding the hip area. For pain and inflammation, take aspirin or ibuprofen. Acetaminophen relieves pain but not inflammation. If aspirin and/or ibuprofen upset your stomach, try an "enteric coated" brand, which dissolves in the intestine, not in the stomach. Pregnant women and those with a history of ulcers should not take aspirin or ibuprofen unless a doctor recommends it.

•No matter what causes your hip pain, weak muscles around the joint increase your risk of hip injury and pain. Exercises to increase the hip's range of motion can help both the athlete and nonathlete heal and avoid recurrence of hip pain. Exercises for specific hip problems vary, but the following stretches often help strengthen painful muscles:

　　　◦Iliotibial stretch. Stand with your left foot slightly forward, and put most of your weight on that leg. Tilt your pelvis down on the right side to stretch the muscles on the left. Repeat the stretch several times for both hips.

　　　◦Leaning stretch. Stand with your side to the wall, an arm's length away. Extend your arm against the wall, cross the foot closer to the wall over your other foot. Let your pelvis sag toward the wall. Hold this pose for fifteen seconds and straighten slowly. Repeat five times, then switch sides.

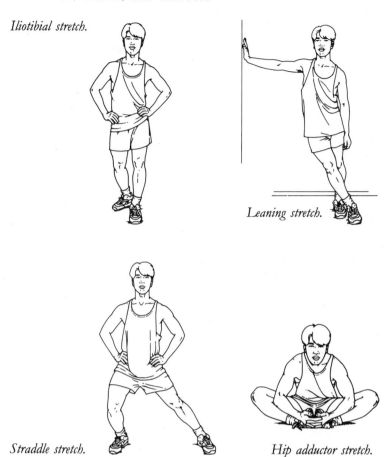

Iliotibial stretch.

Leaning stretch.

Straddle stretch.

Hip adductor stretch.

Hip exercises/stretches.

- ○Straddle stretch. Stand with your legs apart and let your left knee bend slightly. Lean your weight into the leg while keeping your pelvis straight. Straighten slowly. Repeat five times, switch sides, and repeat.
- ○Hip adductor stretch. Sit on the floor and place the soles of your feet together. With your hands, pull your heels toward your groin, and lean forward. Hold this pose for thirty to sixty seconds, then release, and repeat the stretch five times.
- ○Thigh exercises. Perform the hamstring strengthener, quadriceps strengthener, and hamstring stretch described in the KNEE PAIN section of this chapter.

When To Call the Doctor.   Hip pain that persists longer than two weeks despite self-care efforts should be investigated by a physician to rule out serious problems, such as hip diseases, arthritis, and osteoporosis-related hip problems.

For bursitis of the hip, most doctors recommend rest and injections of steroids and anesthetics to deal with the pain and swelling.

If the examination shows one leg is more than one-half inch longer than the other, an orthotic shoe insert often helps.

▶ **RED FLAG**   If buttocks pain occurs with exercise and is relieved within seconds or minutes with rest, suspect an artery blockage and see a doctor without delay.

INGROWN TOENAIL

(See TOE PAIN in this chapter and NAIL PROBLEMS in Chapter 6)

KNEE PAIN

(See also ARTHRITIS, BURSITIS, GOUT, SCIATICA, and TENDINITIS in this chapter)

Painful knee problems are the number one injury treated by sports medicine specialists.

What's Going On?   The knee is both an engineering marvel—and a disaster area. It's a great deal more than merely a simple hinge. It supports most of the body's weight and, at the same time, allows the body to twist and pivot. (See illustration.) It is also quite delicate and injures easily with even minor abuse.

More than half of all runners who log more than thirty miles a week sustain knee injuries each year. Pain in the knee cap ("patella") and tears in the crescent-shaped cartilage within the knee joint ("meniscus") are the most common pain-causing knee injuries. Torn cartilage injuries usually start with a twisting motion, like those demanded by tennis, basketball, or soccer. Kneecap problems are most often caused by overuse: increasing training too quickly, not alternating between easy and challenging training days, running on banked roads in only one direction, running in worn-out shoes, or changing from flat to hill running.

Of course, you don't have to be an athlete to sustain knee injuries. Direct blows to the knee as in falls or auto accidents can cause just as

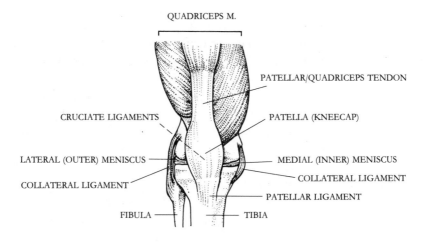

The knee.

much damage as being tackled by a 300-pound lineman. Nonetheless, most knee injuries have athletic origins.

Runner's knee ("patellofemoral dysfunction") accounts for more than 50 percent of all knee problems. It involves misalignment of the kneecap in the groove in which it slides back and forth as the knee flexes and extends. In runner's knee, the kneecap becomes displaced to one side. As the knee moves, it can cause extreme pain and wear down the joint's cartilage, eventually causing further injury.

Softening of the knee cartilage ("chondromalacia of the patella") is a variation of runner's knee, most common in teenage girls. It develops spontaneously rather than from overuse, but it's treated the same way.

Runner's knee can cause chronic pain in one or both knees. The pain is easily aggravated by movement. It may be difficult to walk up or down stairs or sit for long periods of time. The pain usually localizes around and behind the kneecap and the knee may "click" when flexed or extended.

Cartilage tears usually cause pain in the middle or on the sides of the knee. The knee may feel stiff on rising in the morning, and it may "catch" or "freeze" at times. Any twisting motion feels painful.

Jumper's knee ("patellar tendinitis") is caused by inflammation of the quadriceps tendon. When overstressed, tiny tears, degeneration, or inflammation can develop. The pain occurs in the front of the knee and above it, especially with stair climbing or rising from a chair. This type of injury usually occurs after jumping, kicking, climbing, or running (see TENDINITIS in this chapter).

Housemaid's knee ("prepatellar bursitis") develops from prolonged direct pressure on the kneecap, as in kneeling for long periods to wash floors as maids used to do. The sac between the patellar tendon (quadriceps tendon) and the patella directly in front of the kneecap swells with fluid and usually becomes warm, red, and tender.

Knee pain can also be caused by various forms of arthritis (see ARTHRITIS and GOUT in this chapter). If the pain occurs behind the knee, sciatica may be the cause (see SCIATICA in this chapter). Knee pain may also be "referred" from biomechanical problems in the foot.

Before You Call the Doctor.   When knee pain strikes, immediately stop doing whatever is causing it. As quickly as possible, apply R.I.C.E. treatment—rest, ice, compression, and elevation (see MUSCLE STRAINS in this chapter for a complete discussion of R.I.C.E.)

For pain and inflammation, take aspirin or ibuprofen. Acetaminophen relieves pain but not inflammation. If aspirin and/or ibuprofen upset your stomach, try an "enteric coated" brand, which dissolves in the intestine, not in the stomach. Pregnant women and those with a history of ulcers should not take aspirin or ibuprofen unless a doctor recommends it.

Then begin exercising to strengthen the muscles and stretch the tendons and ligaments around the knee. Knee injuries vary, but the following exercises are generally recommended:

• Quadriceps press. Sit on the floor, legs straight out in front of you. Press the backs of your knees into the floor. Hold this for ten seconds, then relax. Work up to three sets of ten presses.

• Quadriceps strengthener. Sit on the floor, legs straight out in front of you. Point your toes and write each letter of the alphabet in the air with them, moving the entire leg as a unit. Work up to two sets of the entire alphabet. For the second set, flex your ankle keeping your knee straight, and write the alphabet with your heel.

• Inner thigh strengthener. Lie on your side, with your lower leg out straight, and your upper leg bent with your knee pointing up and your foot on the floor in front of your lower leg's knee. Raise the lower leg as high as you can, keeping your knee turned forward. Then lower it. Work up to three sets of fifteen lifts, alternately pointing then flexing the foot.

• Quadriceps stretch. Lie face down. Bend one knee and hold your ankle. Slowly pull your heel toward your buttocks. Release and repeat, working up to three sets of ten.

• Hamstring strengthener. Lie face down with your feet pressed into the floor. Bend one knee so that your foot sticks straight up, then lift your foot toward the ceiling from the bent position. Your thigh and knee will come off the floor. Then slowly lower your foot back down. Work up to

Knee exercises.   *Quadriceps press.*

Quadriceps strengthener.

Inner thigh strengthener.

Quadriceps stretch.

Hamstring stretch.

Hamstring strengthener.

three sets of ten lifts, alternating legs. To increase the work, use ankle weights.

•Hamstring stretch. Sit on the floor, both legs straight out in front of you. Slowly reach forward and tuck your hands under your knees or thighs depending on your flexibility. Then gently pull your chest toward your legs until the backs of your thighs (the hamstrings) feel stretched. Work up to three sets of ten stretches. Don't bounce.

When to Call the Doctor. If knee pain persists or becomes more severe despite two weeks of self-care, consult a physician. If the problem is an athletic injury, it's best to see a doctor familiar with sports medicine. After taking a history and possibly ordering x-rays and other diagnostic tests, your physician may prescribe pain relievers and anti-inflammatory drugs not available over-the-counter. Your doctor may also recommend whirlpool therapy and physical therapy. Sometimes surgery may be necessary.

▶ **RED FLAGS**   Consult a physician immediately if:
•You can't move your knee.
•It becomes deformed.
•In addition to knee pain, you have a temperature of 101° or higher, which could mean a local or systemic infection, or a flare-up of a connective tissue disease such as lupus.

LEG PAIN

(See also ANKLE PAIN, ARTHRITIS, FIBROMYALGIA, HIP PAIN, KNEE PAIN, MUSCLE CRAMP, MUSCLE STRAIN, and SCIATICA in this chapter and VARICOSE VEINS in Chapter 12)

Some leg pains are as simple and nonthreatening as a muscle cramp. Others can indicate serious problems, such as a blood clot ("thrombophlebitis").

What's Going On?   One of the more common athletic leg complaints is "shin splints," pain in the front of the lower leg. This problem often develops among runners who wear improper shoes or who run on hard, uneven surfaces, such as banked tracks. Tight Achilles tendons also contribute to the problem. Shin splints result when the leg muscles become strained from overwork and pull slightly away from the lower leg bone ("tibia"), causing irritation and inflammation. Over time, shin splints can cause bony growths on the tibia. Shin splints can also occur in the back of the leg when an imbalance develops between the muscle strength of the muscles in the front and back of the legs.

Pain at the outside of the upper thigh is probably due to a problem around the hip joint (see HIP PAIN in this chapter). If the pain is associated with a numb feeling in the side and front of the upper thigh, it is probably caused by pressure on a sensory nerve in the groin area, a condition known medically as "meralgia paresthetica," which results from obesity or pregnancy.

Another common sports injury that causes leg pain in the narrow area just above the back of the ankle is Achilles tendinitis (see TENDINITIS in this chapter).

Sudden leg pain that feels like a knotting of the muscle is usually a cramp (see MUSCLE CRAMPS in this chapter).

Sudden leg pain associated with a quick pivoting move may be a knee injury, muscle strain, or muscle tear (see KNEE PAIN, MUSCLE STRAINS and MUSCLE TEARS in this chapter).

Leg pains may be "referred" from the back. Leg pain that originates in the buttock and radiates down the leg and hurts more when you cough is often sciatica (see SCIATICA in this chapter).

If both of your legs ache, particularly after standing for long periods of time, and you notice that your leg veins bulge, you may have varicose veins, a circulatory problem (see VARICOSE VEINS in Chapter 12).

Leg pain, especially around the joints, may be caused by various forms of arthritis (See ARTHRITIS in this chapter).

In children, leg pains in the calves or thighs that occur at the end of the day or at night may be "growing pains." Growing pains are an authentic phenomenon, though their cause is unknown. The pain can be severe enough to wake a child from sleep. Growing pains usually occur periodically for a year or two sometime from three to twelve years of age. Growing pains are harmless.

Before You Call the Doctor.   For shin splints:

• Wrap a few ice cubes in a plastic bag, then in a clean cloth and apply the ice pack to the front of the lower leg. Hold it there for twenty minutes, then remove it for ten minutes before reapplying. Do not apply ice directly to the skin. This may cause the equivalent of frostbite.

• Rest or change your exercise regimen. Stop engaging in leg-pounding sports. Switch to low-impact activities: swimming, walking, or cycling.

• If you return to high-impact activities, add cushioning to your shoes, and work out on softer surfaces—grass or wood instead of concrete.

• Do Achilles tendon stretches four times a day (see ANKLE PAIN in this chapter).

•Strengthen your front leg muscles with this exercise: Stand facing a kitchen counter, with your hands on the countertop and your toes in the kickspace under the cabinet. Then raise one leg by bending your knee until your foot is stopped by the cabinet. Push upward against the cabinet for a count of ten. Work up to three sets of ten.

For meralgia paresthetica:

•Lose weight if you're overweight. See the diet and exercise suggestions in EAT AND DRINK RIGHT and EXERCISE REGULARLY in Chapter 1.

•Don't wear tight-fitting pants that place pressure across the upper thigh groin crease.

•Don't sit for prolonged periods.

For growing pains:

•Reassure the child that the pains are not dangerous and will eventually stop.

•Have the child perform the following stretches twice a day: Achilles stretch (see ANKLE PAIN in this chapter), quadriceps stretch, and hamstring stretch (see KNEE PAIN in this chapter).

•During nighttime wake-ups, offer only a brief massage, warm compresses, or acetaminophen, but don't spend more than fifteen minutes with the child in the middle of the night. Don't let the child feel rewarded for nighttime wake-ups.

For other problems, consult the section of this chapter that deals with the cause of your leg pain, and try the self-care suggestions for two weeks.

When to Call the Doctor.   If the source of your leg pain isn't obviously harmless, or the pain does not improve significantly within two weeks, it's important to see a physician for proper diagnosis and treatment. Leg pain may be caused by serious medical problems, for example, a narrowing of the arteries in the legs ("intermittent claudication"), or by fractures.

▶ **RED FLAG**   Consult a physician immediately for painful leg swelling which does not respond to elevation. This might be thrombophlebitis, inflammation of a vein due to an internal blood clot, which is a medical emergency.

MUSCLE CRAMPS

(See also FIBROMYALGIA, MUSCLE STRAINS, and MUSCLE TEARS in this chapter)

Muscle cramps, sometimes called "charley horses," are not serious, but they may be quite painful and frightening.

What's Going On?   Muscle cramps are caused by sudden, painful shortening of a muscle, usually accompanied by knotting you can feel if you press on the area. Muscle cramps can occur at any time, but some people suffer recurring cramps at night.

This problem has a variety of causes: drugs, vigorous exercise in hot weather, and electrolyte (sodium/potassium) imbalances. In some cases, muscle cramping can be traced to a deficiency in potassium, often associated with medications such as diuretics that flush this mineral from the body. Less commonly, cramping may be caused by deficiencies in calcium and magnesium.

Before You Call the Doctor.   The best way to prevent muscle cramps is to drink plenty of fluids when you exercise vigorously, especially in hot weather. There was a time when athletes and coaches believed fluids *caused* cramps, but now we know better. Drink before you begin warming up. Don't drink so much that you feel bloated, just enough to prevent thirst. Drink either water or one of the electrolyte-replacing sports drinks if you engage in extremely demanding exercise, such as running marathons. Drink a little more during breaks, and some more after you complete your workout.

For night cramps in the calf (by far the most common muscle cramp), don't point your toes in bed. Don't lie on your stomach, and if you lie on your back, take care that the weight of the blankets doesn't press your toes into a pointing position. If a cramp strikes, immediately flex your foot—point your toes up toward your head—as you sit up and massage the muscle. Then as soon as you can, stand up and do an Achilles stretch (see ANKLE PAIN in this chapter). Afterward, do some Achilles stretches every night before you go to bed.

If you seem prone to cramps, you may have a potassium deficiency. Try eating potassium-rich foods, such as bananas, potatoes, oranges, and tomatoes. Usually potassium supplementation isn't necessary unless you're taking diuretics.

Some people with chronic nighttime leg cramps obtain relief from quinine sulfate (65 to 325 mg) and/or vitamin E (200 to 400 units) at bedtime. Both are available over the counter. Pregnant women should not take quinine, but may take vitamin E in consultation with their physicians.

When to Call the Doctor.   If cramping continues despite self-care, consult a physician. Muscle cramping can be a symptom of serious neurological illnesses, which require professional treatment.

MUSCLE STRAINS

(See also FIBROMYALGIA in this chapter)

Also known as a "pulled muscle," muscle strains occur when muscles stretch beyond their normal limits. Muscle strains usually cause sharp pain with movement, but some strains may cause dull throbbing pain. Any swelling usually subsides within a week, but depending on the location and severity of the strain, the pain may last several weeks.

What's Going On?   When a muscle becomes overextended ("hyperextended"), some of its cellular fibers get injured, causing the muscle to contract, bleed, and swell. In the most serious strains, the muscle actually rips in two (see MUSCLE TEARS in this chapter).

Before You Call the Doctor.   Pre-exercise stretching increases muscle, tendon, and ligament flexibility so it helps prevent sprains (see SPRAINS in this chapter). Stretch gently. If any stretch hurts, you're going too far. Authorities recommend holding stretches and breathing deeply for about thirty seconds, then relaxing. Don't do "bounce stretches." Bobbing provides considerably less benefit than holding, and it may actually strain muscles.

In most cases, sore, stiff, painful muscles are strained, not ruptured, and can be handled at home with R.I.C.E., an acronym for rest, ice, compression, and elevation:

• Rest. Try to use the injured part as little as possible for several days. If necessary, rent crutches or use a sling. But be careful not to overdo rest. As the initial sharp pain subsides, start using the injured part again. If you don't, you may suffer loss of strength and flexibility. Many sports medicine authorities now recommend starting gentle rehabilitation exercises almost immediately for most injuries.

• Ice. Ice reduces swelling and is especially beneficial immediately after the injury, before the area has swelled. Wrap some ice cubes in a plastic bag, or use an ice-substitute gel. Wrap the ice in cloth and apply it to the injured area for twenty minutes, then remove it for ten minutes before reapplying. Do not apply ice or ice substitutes directly to the skin. This may cause the equivalent of frostbite.

• Compression. After you've thoroughly iced the injury, wrap the area in an elastic bandage, and continue using the bandage for several days. Compression helps keep swelling down and minimizes discomfort as the injury heals.

• Elevation. Extra blood flows into injured areas, but too much blood adds to the pain of joint and muscle injuries. The rule of thumb is: Raise the injured area above the level of your heart. For ankle injuries, put your feet up. For hand or wrist injuries, place the injured arm in a sling. Some injuries, for example, groin pulls, are difficult to raise above the heart. In such cases, lie down as much as possible.

• After twenty-four hours, substitute heat for ice to increase circulation and speed healing of the injured muscle. Use a heating pad, hot compresses, or a hot bath.

• In addition to R.I.C.E. treatment, take aspirin or ibuprofen to relieve pain and inflammation. Acetaminophen helps relieve pain but offers no anti-inflammatory benefits. If aspirin or ibuprofen upset your stomach, try an "enteric coated" brand. Pregnant women and those with a history of ulcers or other gastrointestinal problems should not take aspirin or ibuprofen unless a doctor recommends it.

When to Call the Doctor. If you are in great pain or if the area becomes badly swollen and discolored, consult a physician. Depending on the extent of your injury, the doctor may wrap the area in a larger bandage or recommend a sling or crutches until the muscle heals. Physical therapy may be necessary to strengthen muscles that have become strained several times.

MUSCLE TEARS

Muscle tears or ruptures are the most serious form of muscle strains (see MUSCLE STRAINS in this chapter). They cause intense pain and swelling, which may last many weeks.

What's Going On? Review the section on MUSCLE STRAINS. If a muscle becomes so hyperextended that all of its fibers rupture, then you have a torn muscle. Muscle tears are serious injuries. Unfortunately, many people use the term "torn muscle" rather loosely to describe muscle strains that are not medically "torn."

Before You Call the Doctor. If hyperextension causes sharp pain, follow the suggestions listed under MUSCLE STRAINS.

When to Call the Doctor. For severe or persistent pain, with significant swelling or loss of movement, consult a physician. Some muscle tears respond to conservative treatment, but some require surgery.

NECK PAIN

(See also ARTHRITIS, BACK PAIN (UPPER), FIBROMYALGIA, and SHOULDER PAIN in this chapter)

The neck accounts for only about 3 percent of total body weight, but it supports a head that's considerably heavier. The stress of the load the neck carries makes it vulnerable to injury.

What's Going On?   Sometimes, neck pain is the result of strained muscles from overwork or from sleeping or working in an awkward position, for example, craddling a phone between your ear and shoulder for long periods. This kind of neck stiffness and pain isn't serious and usually resolves within a day or so.

A more serious cause of neck pain and stiffness is whiplash, a sprain-like injury caused by wrenching the neck quickly and violently beyond its normal range of motion. Rear-end car accidents are common culprits in whiplash. This type of injury can cause a myriad of seemingly unrelated symptoms: headaches, loss of balance, a dazed feeling, ringing in the ears, nausea and vomiting, numbness in the fingers, discomfort holding the head up, and inability to turn the head (see SPRAINS in this chapter).

If you have both shoulder and neck pain, you may have a "frozen shoulder" or chronic strain of the muscles connecting the neck and shoulder (see SHOULDER PAIN and BACK PAIN (UPPER) in this chapter).

If your neck pain is severe and you have shooting pains in your shoulder or arms when you move your head, you may have "slipped a disc" (see SLIPPED DISC in this chapter).

For people over fifty years of age, progressive neck pain and/or stiffness that seems to get worse as time passes may indicate degeneration of the bones or discs in the neck (see ARTHRITIS in this chapter.)

Before You Call the Doctor.   When neck pain strikes, take aspirin, ibuprofen, or acetaminophen. If aspirin or ibuprofen upset your stomach, try an "enteric coated" brand, which dissolves in the intestine, not in the stomach. Pregnant women and those with a history of ulcers should not take aspirin or ibuprofen unless a doctor recommends it.

The key to healing sore necks—and preventing neck pain—is good posture, which places the least strain on the neck:

• Good neck posture means your head should be up, your neck drawn somewhat back, your chin somewhat tucked, and your ears in line with your shoulders.

•Don't slouch. Stand up straight. Sit up straight. Don't lean over desks. If you have a tendency to lean over desks, invest in a slant board to hold reading material up so you can sit straight.

•Never cradle a telephone between your ear and shoulder. Don't even use those cradling devices that attach to the handset. You still wind up straining your neck ("telephone neck"). Grasp the handset in one hand and hold it up to your ear. If you'd like to keep your hands free, invest in the kind of no-hands headset professional operators use. They are available at electronics and telephone equipment stores.

•Don't sleep with more pillows than necessary. Feather or polyester fiberfill are preferable to foam and other materials. Or invest in a special neck ("cervical") pillow, available through catalogs, such as Comfortably Yours, Bodyline, and the Self-Care Catalog (see RESOURCES at the end of this chapter).

•Don't sleep on your stomach. This position twists the neck.

•When driving, don't lean forward in your seat. Pull your seat up and use pillows or seat inserts to enable you to sit up and maintain good posture.

•When carrying a heavy shoulder bag or luggage, carry equal weight on each side. If that's not possible, use a backpack.

•Try not to reach for things way up over your head. If you have to get something above your head, use a stool.

•Try not to look up for long periods.

In addition, strengthen your neck muscles with these isometric exercises. Repeat each exercise ten times at least twice a day.

•Chin press. Stand or sit straight. Place both fists side-by-side under your chin. Press your chin down and your fists up without moving your head. Hold for a count of ten.

•Head push. Stand or sit straight. Clasp your hands behind your head—not your neck. Push your head back and pull your hands forward without moving your head. Hold for a count of ten.

•Ear push. Stand or sit straight. Place the palm of your left hand against the left side of your head just above your ear. Push your head against your hand and vice versa without moving your head. Hold for a count of ten. Repeat this exercise using your right hand.

•Finger clasp. Stand or sit straight. With fingers bent, hook your hands together in front of your chest. Pull your hands against each other without moving them. Hold for a count of ten.

•Chair pull. Sitting straight, hook your fingers under the front of your chair. Pull up against the chair without moving your hands. Hold for a count of ten.

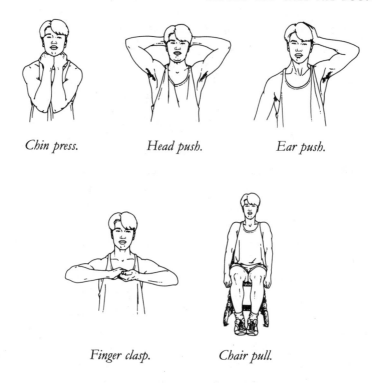

Chin press.   *Head push.*   *Ear push.*

Finger clasp.   *Chair pull.*

Neck exercises.

For other neck problems except whiplash, consult the appropriate section of this Chapter.

When to Call the Doctor.   If you've been involved in an automobile accident, however slight, and suffer any whiplash symptoms, consult a physician experienced in treating musculoskeletal injuries. Whiplash should not be self-treated. Many different health practitioners treat whiplash, including general and family practioners, internists, orthopedists, osteopaths, chiropractors, physiatrists, and physical therapists. The doctor will probably order x-rays of the neck and head. The recommended treatment for whiplash is some combination of hot and cold packs, a neck brace ("cervical collar"), massage, traction, and manipulation. Ice packs and analgesics usually help whiplash-related headaches. For neck and shoulder pain, try lying on a moist heating pad on a bolster pillow. Keep in mind that with injuries such as whiplash, movement is ultimately more healing than rest, but the exercises should be professionally supervised. It's important to stretch and limber up traumatized muscles and ligaments with "passive exercise" such as massage, ultrasound, and traction with heat. Once pain has subsided, you should begin clinician-prescribed stretching and rotating exercises. Do them slowly and gently after applying moist heat or while under a hot shower. If your doctor offers only tranquilizers, neck braces, and traction for a whiplash injury, consult another physician.

▶ **RED FLAGS**   Consult a physician immediately if a whiplash-related painful and/or stiff neck is accompanied by severe headaches, nausea or vomiting, sensitivity to bright light, or drowsiness or confusion; or if you've been injured and have difficulty controlling your arm or leg muscles. These symptoms suggest possible brain or spinal cord injury.

Severe stiff neck—inability to look down—with fever could be an infection of the fluid surrounding the brain and spinal cord ("meningitis"). Consult a physician immediately.

OSTEOPOROSIS

(See also MENOPAUSE in Chapter 16)

Osteoporosis is an age-related condition that causes loss of bone mass, increased bone brittleness, and increased risk of fractures and certain deformities. It occurs in both men and women but is much more common and severe in postmenopausal women.

What's Going On?   One postmenopausal woman in four suffers the bone thinning of osteoporosis and faces the potentially life-threatening risk of fractures, particularly hip fractures.

Bone is living tissue. Like other tissue, the body constantly creates new bone to replace the old bone as it wears out. The process is called "remodeling," and in those under thirty-five years of age, the body draws on calcium dissolved in the blood to replace the entire skeleton about once every ten years. However, after age thirty-five, we begin to lose more bone than we replace. Bone loss begins slowly but accelerates over time.

Osteoporosis affects nine times as many women as men. In women, the bones' ability to absorb calcium from the blood depends on the hormone estrogen. As women pass through menopause, they produce less estrogen, and as a result, their bones absorb considerably less calcium, not enough to replace the lost bone. However, some women are more likely to develop osteoporosis than others. Those at highest risk are thin women who are fair-haired and light-skinned (see MENOPAUSE in Chapter 16). Younger women who have had their ovaries surgically removed or women who diet or exercise to the point of loss of menstruation ("amenorrhea") can also develop osteoporosis.

Osteoporosis weakens the back vertebrae, and they become compressed under the body's weight. This compression can cause pain, a noticeably curved spine ("dowager's hump"), permanent height loss of up to several inches, and vertebral fractures. The most serious effect of osteoporosis is an increased risk of hip fractures, the twelfth leading cause of death in the United States and a major killer in women over seventy-five years of age. (Older men also become shorter due to vertebral compression but are less likely to develop the other symptoms of osteoporosis.)

Life-style factors can also promote osteoporosis, particularly a lack of exercise and poor diet, with inadequate consumption of vitamin D, calcium, and protein.

Before You Call the Doctor.   Because bone loss begins many years before the first signs of osteoporosis appear, osteoporosis prevention should begin in your thirties—ideally even earlier. According to the latest studies, the most important factors in osteoporosis prevention include:

• Exercise. Regular, moderate, weight-bearing exercise has been shown to increase bone mass and density. "Weight-bearing" means putting weight on the major joints, like the hips, in such activities as walking, aerobics, gardening, jogging, and dancing. Once osteoporosis develops, weight-bearing exercise can help slow the rate of bone loss. But extremely strenuous weight-bearing exercise, for example, training for marathons, may be counterproductive because it can interfere with estrogen production and increase the risk of fractures.

• Calcium. Does increasing calcium intake after age thirty-five add the mineral to bone and prevent osteoporosis? This question was very controversial throughout the 1980s. Some authorities insisted calcium supplementation had no bone-strengthening effect, while others maintained that every woman over age thirty-five should consume 1,200 mg of calcium a day instead of the government's recommended daily allowance of 800. The latest research clearly favors the supplementation approach. Calcium intake of up to 2,500 mg a day is considered safe, but most authorities recommend 1,500 mg. Supplementation at a level of 1,000 mg a day is usually adequate because those who eat the type of diet we recommend in Chapter 1 get a good deal of calcium in the food they eat. (Calcium also helps control blood pressure.) Calcium-rich foods include low-fat or nonfat milk and dairy products, tofu (soybean curd), oysters, sardines, and salmon (see Box, p. 500). Chewable calcium carbonate antacids (Rolaids, Tums) are an easy way to supplement your calcium

CALCIUM CONTENT OF SELECTED FOOD ITEMS

Food	Calcium (mg)	Calories
Almonds (3.5 oz.)	235	600
Beans, garbanzo (3.5 oz. dry)	150	360
red or black (3.5 oz. dry)	135	340
Broccoli (6 oz. cooked)	160	45
Cheese, cheddar (3.5 oz.)	750	400
Parmesan (1 oz.)	325	112
Swiss (3.5 oz.)	925	370
nonfat cottage (3.5 oz.)	90	86
Collard greens (3.5 oz. cooked)	152	29
Kale (3.5 oz. raw)	179	80
Milk, lowfat (2%, 8 oz.)	320	130
nonfat (8 oz.)	271	80
Parsley (1 oz.)	57	12
Peanuts and peanut butter (3.5 oz.)	400	585
Salmon, canned (3.5 oz.)	250	200
Sardines (3.5 oz.)	437	203
Sesame seeds (0.5 oz.)	162	80
Spinach (3.5 oz.)	100	23
Tofu (3.5 oz.)	128	72
Wheat flour (self-rising, 3.5 oz.)	265	352
Yogurt (lowfat, 8 oz.)	270	112

intake. Each Rolaids tablet contains 220 mg of calcium and fewer than ten calories.

• Cigarettes and alcohol. Osteoporosis is associated with cigarette smoking and regular consumption of alcohol. Don't smoke, and limit your drinking. For help quitting smoking, see RESOURCES at the end of Chapter 11.

When to Call the Doctor. Once it has reached a certain stage, osteoporosis is irreversible, but treatment can slow bone loss, and possibly stop it. The doctor should take a family history because the condition has a genetic component. Then various painless but fairly expensive tests can be used to determine your bone density. If the tests shows significant bone loss, physicians typically recommend exercise, calcium supplements, and possibly physical therapy, and they prescribe estrogen replacement therapy. However, some women cannot take estrogen, particularly those with a history of estrogen-dependent breast cancer. In addition, estrogen replacement therapy increases the risk of uterine ("endometrial") cancer unless another hormone, progesterone, is also prescribed. As this book goes to press, innovative treatments involving other minerals and bone-strengthening hormones are an exciting area of research.

PLANTAR FASCIITIS

(See FOOT PAIN in this chapter)

RIB INJURY

Rib injuries cause sharp chest pain that lasts a lot longer than you think it should. Rib pain can turn coughing, laughing, sneezing, rolling over in bed, and even ordinary breathing into an ordeal.

What's Going On? Rib injuries fall into three painful categories: bruises ("contusions"), inflammations ("costochondritis"), and broken ribs ("fractures"). Contusions and fractures are typically caused by blows to the chest: falls, auto accidents, kicks, etc. The main symptom is pain, which increases with touch or ordinary chest movement. Although fractures are more serious than contusions, the two injuries are often indistinguishable based on the pain they cause. And sometimes x-rays can't pick up rib fractures, so the difference between the two may be unclear. However, in serious cases, the broken rib penetrates the lung, which can cause air and fluid to flow into the cavity surrounding the lung. With lung complications, the person may have difficulty breathing and possibly have a bluish skin tone. If enough air escapes from the lung into the surrounding cavity, it can result in a collapsed lung ("pneumothorax"). Blood produced by the rib scraping against the lung and damaging the tissue may also congest the chest.

In costochondritis, also known as "Tietze's syndrome," the cartilage of the ribs becomes inflamed. Most commonly, this occurs in the second and third ribs in the mid-chest. Doctors aren't sure what causes this condition. It can occur at any age but strikes most frequently in young adults. It may follow a severe blow to the chest. The chest area feels painful to touch, particularly at the junction of the affected rib(s) and the sternum, and any movement of the chest, even bending and lying down, usually increases the pain.

Rib injuries can also occur without any blow to the chest, for example, as a result of violent coughing.

Before You Call the Doctor.   Many rib injuries can be handled at home. Bruises and muscle strains can be treated with R.I.C.E.—rest, ice, compression, and elevation. See MUSCLE STRAINS in this chapter for a complete discussion of R.I.C.E. treatment. However, in rib injuries, "elevation" is not possible, and "compression," or taping, is no longer used because it may restrict deep breathing, which helps prevent pneumonia.

Take aspirin or ibuprofen to relieve pain and inflammation. Acetaminophen relieves pain but does not treat inflammation. If aspirin and/or ibuprofen upset your stomach, try an "enteric coated" brand, which dissolves in the intestine, not in the stomach. Pregnant women and those with a history of ulcers should not take aspirin or ibuprofen unless a doctor recommends it. Adequate pain relief is important to prevent shallow breathing and cough suppression, which can interfere with the body's defense against bronchitis or pneumonia.

Within twenty-four to forty-eight hours after the injury, consider hot baths or applying heat.

Be patient. Rib injuries can take months to heal. And once injured, the ribs become more susceptible to reinjury.

When to Call the Doctor.   Consult a physician promptly if you have any trouble breathing after a rib injury. You may have a collapsed lung, which requires hospitalization. Doctors extract the air from the chest cavity using a hollow needle or tube.

Consider consulting a physician if rib pain has not improved significantly within three weeks or if it is severe enough to prevent coughing and deep breathing. If x-rays reveal a fracture, the doctor may bind or strap the chest, though rib fractures are usually left unbandaged. But prescription pain medication may be very helpful.

Though rarely serious, rib pain should be checked by a doctor if it causes persistent pain to rule out heart disease or other possibly serious conditions.

Doctors treat costochondritis with aspirin or ibuprofen and, in some cases, a short course of corticosteriod injections.

▶ **RED FLAGS**   See a physician immediately if a rib injury causes obvious damage to the chest or difficulty breathing.

SCIATICA

(See also BACK PAIN (LOWER), HIP PAIN, KNEE PAIN, LEG PAIN, and SLIPPED DISC in this chapter)

Sciatica can cause pain in the buttocks, hip, and back of the leg all the way down to the foot. Usually, the pain occurs only on one side.

What's Going On?   Sciatica is a type of lower back problem. On each side of the lower back, a series of six nerves branch off to different parts of the lower body. The largest, the "sciatic nerve," runs down each leg. When back problems place pressure on this nerve, the result is pain from the lower back to the toes. The sciatic nerve typically becomes irritated when the pulpy inner part of the shock-absorbing discs between the back vertebrae bulge out into the space where the nerve originates. However, other causes are also possible.

Men suffer sciatica more often than women. This may be due to the fact that many men carry their wallets in a hip pocket, the exact spot where the sciatic nerve emerges in the large buttocks muscle ("gluteus"). Sitting on the wallet can cause pressure on the nerve and sciatic pain.

When sciatic pain is caused by a bulging disc in the lower back, it is often aggravated by bending, straining, coughing, or sneezing. The lower part of the back feels stiff and loses its natural contour, and the muscles along each side of the spine may go into painful spasm.

Before You Call the Doctor.   Many cases of sciatica can be effectively managed with self-care:

• Follow the suggestions in BACK PAIN (LOWER) in this chapter to prevent sciatica and relieve it if symptoms develop. Sciatica can become a chronic condition, so you may have to make permanent life-style adjustments to remain pain-free.

• Take aspirin, acetaminophen, or ibuprofen for the pain. If aspirin or ibuprofen upset your stomach, try an "enteric coated" brand, which dissolves in the intestine, not in the stomach. Pregnant women and those with a history of ulcers should not take aspirin or ibuprofen unless a doctor recommends it.

• Try applying heat to the lower back and the affected buttock. Use a heating pad, hot baths or showers, or a sauna.

• Or try ice packs for fifteen minutes once or twice a day. Wrap a few ice cubes in a plastic bag, then wrap than in a clean cloth and apply it. Do not apply ice directly to the skin. This can cause the equivalent of frostbite.

•Try bedrest. Use a firm mattress and lie on your unaffected side with your unaffected leg slightly bent and your affected leg straight and supported by one or more pillows. Comfortably Yours, Bodyline, the Self-Care Catalog, and other consumer catalogs carry many pillows that might help (see RESOURCES at the end of this chapter).

•Men should eliminate unnecessary items from their wallets and/or carry them in places other than hip pockets.

When to Call the Doctor.   If sciatica does not respond significantly to self-care within two weeks, consult a physician. Call sooner if numbness grows worse despite home treatment or if the foot becomes weak or clumsy.

Occasionally, sciatica can be caused by arthritis or various infections. The doctor may order screening tests to investigate these possibilities.

Back pain can be difficult to diagnose and treat. You can help your physician provide the best care by being prepared to answer the following questions:

•When and how did the pain begin?

•Did it follow an injury or any unusual activity?

•Is the pain localized in a particular spot or does it hurt all over?

•Does bending, straining, coughing, sneezing, walking or lifting aggravate it?

•Does standing make you feel better?

Since sciatica is not a disease, the treatment goal is pain relief and disc healing. Most doctors recommend bed rest, limiting leg movement, heat, and pain relievers. Some prescribe physical therapy and special exercises.

If medical treatment does not provide sufficient relief, consider consulting a chiropractor, osteopath, acupuncturist, or yoga instructor.

In a small proportion of cases, surgery may be required to correct an underlying spinal condition. However, back surgery is controversial. Success is by no means assured. Before consenting to back surgery, get several medical opinions, and satisfy yourself that it's your last resort.

▶ **RED FLAGS**   Consult a physician immediately for any loss of bowel or bladder function.

SHOULDER PAIN

(See also ARM PAIN, ARTHRITIS, BURSITIS, BACK PAIN (UPPER), CARPAL TUNNEL SYNDROME, FIBROMYALGIA, GOUT, MUS-

CLE STRAINS, NECK PAIN, and TENDINITIS in this chapter, HEART ATTACK in Chapter 3, and ANGINA and HEART ATTACK in Chapter 12)

Shoulder pain can be caused by a variety of conditions ranging from simple muscle strain to more serious problems, such as arthritis and heart disease.

What's Going On?   The shoulder is a complex joint with many muscles, tendons, and ligaments. It has a wide range of mobility, but we use our shoulders so frequently that we often abuse them and cause injury.

Shoulder pain may also be "referred" from elsewhere in the body, including the abdomen or the heart. Both angina and heart attack may result in shoulder pain as well as chest pain.

Before You Call the Doctor.   First, consider the possibility of a heart attack. Many heart attacks do not cause crushing chest pain and physical collapse. Quite a few feel more like shoulder pain with heartburn. If you have shoulder pain with any chest pain or pain radiating up under your jaw, call 911 immediately (see HEART ATTACK in Chapter 3).

Next consider the possibility of angina, chest pain caused by inadequate blood flow to the heart. Angina also sometimes causes shoulder pain during physical exertion. If you have squeezing or pressure-like pain that begins during exercise and stops after you rest, call your physician immediately (see ANGINA in Chapter 12).

Shoulder pain is usually caused by overuse injuries. Baseball players, football quarterbacks, golfers, tennis players, and carpenters who hammer a great deal are at high risk. But shoulder injuries can strike anyone and may not be traceable to overuse. The most common shoulder injury is an inflammation of the tendons around the shoulder, what doctors call "rotator cuff tendinitis." It typically occurs in young athletes—in swimmers, kayakers, weight trainers, and tennis and racquetball players—but it's also fairly common among nonathletes starting around age forty-five. Symptoms include sharp or dull pain in and around the shoulder joint and difficulty moving the arm through its full range of motion. The pain often becomes more severe at night and may interfere with sleep (see TENDINITIS in this chapter).

If you have other joints that are red, painful, and swollen and your shoulder problem has developed slowly, you may have rheumatoid arthritis (see ARTHRITIS in this chapter).

Shoulder pain that begins suddenly without any injury or obvious overuse may be bursitis, an inflammation of the fluid-filled sacs around the joint, or gout, a form of arthritis (see BURSITIS and GOUT in this chapter).

Shoulder muscles may also be strained or torn (see MUSCLE STRAINS and MUSCLE TEARS in this chapter).

Untreated shoulder injuries can result in "frozen shoulder," also known as "adhesive bursitis" or "adhesive tendinitis." This condition usually starts with a minor shoulder injury that limits shoulder movement. With disuse, the shoulder becomes stiffer and more painful until it hardly moves at all. The pain may remain localized in the shoulder, but it often spreads into the neck and upper arm.

When shoulder pain strikes, stop doing whatever seems to have triggered it and take aspirin or ibuprofen. Acetaminophen relieves pain but not the inflammation that often causes shoulder pain. If aspirin and/or ibuprofen upset your stomach, try an "enteric coated" brand, which dissolves in the intestine, not in the stomach. Pregnant women and those with a history of ulcers should not take aspirin or ibuprofen unless a doctor recommends it.

Next, try R.I.C.E.—an acronym for rest, ice, compression, and elevation. For a complete discussion of R.I.C.E. treatment, see MUSCLE STRAINS in this chapter.

Heat might also help. Try a heating pad or hot baths.

Shoulder tendinitis and many other shoulder problems usually respond to weight-lifting exercises preceded by gentle range-of-motion exercises and followed by muscle stretches. Try the following exercises two or three times a day and see if they help:

• Pendulum swing. Let your injured arm hang from your side. Grasp a small weight (one to five pounds) or a can of beans. Swing your arm back and forth. Start with small swings, then over time gradually swing your arm higher.

• Circle swing. Stand leaning forward toward your injured side. Holding the small weight swing your injured arm in small circles. Over time make larger circles.

• Wall climb. Stand with the injured shoulder toward a wall and extend your injured arm until your hand touches the wall. Keeping your elbow straight, "walk" your fingers up the wall until you feel your shoulder stretch. Hold for ten seconds. Walk your fingers back to the starting position. Repeat ten times, trying each time to stretch a little further.

• Weight resistance. Stand holding a weight in each hand with your elbows straight, thumbs turned toward the floor and arms about thirty degrees forward. Slowly raise your arms out from your sides to just below your shoulder level (avoid hunching your shoulders toward your ears). Slowly lower your arms. Repeat five times. Then repeat the same exercise

Shoulder exercises.

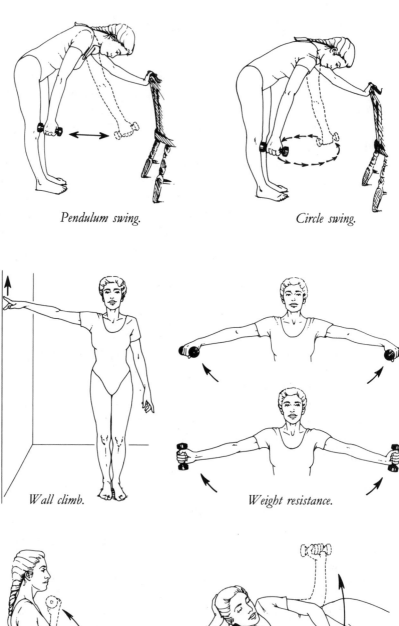

Pendulum swing.   *Circle swing.*

Wall climb.   *Weight resistance.*

Curls.

Strong shoulders.

Shoulder stretches.

 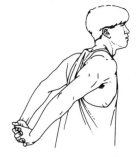 

1. Arm across chest.   *2. Arm behind back.*   *3. Arm over head.*

with the thumbs pointing toward the ceiling. Over time, progress to holding your arms straight and raising them forward up to shoulder height for a set, backward for a set, and out to your side for a set. Work up to two sets of thirty lifts with palms forward, and two sets with palms backward.

• Curling. Grasping the weight, hold your injured arm straight down at your side, palm forward. Bending your elbow, bring the weight up to your shoulder. Work up to two sets of thirty curls twice a day.

• Strong shoulders. Lie on your good side with your injured shoulder up and hold a weight in its hand. Bend your arm, keeping the elbow close to your ribs. Start with the weight on the floor in front of you, then slowly raise your forearm until it points to the ceiling. Slowly return to the starting position. Repeat five times.

After exercising with weight, do these shoulder stretches. Hold each stretch for a count of ten, and do each one five times twice a day:

• Place your injured arm across your chest with the elbow bent slightly in front of your sternum. With your other hand, press the elbow into your chest until you feel your shoulder stretch.

• Interlock your fingers behind your back holding your arms straight. Raise your arms upward until you feel your shoulders stretch. Hold for a count of ten.

• Place one arm over your head with your elbow bent over your ear. Using the other hand, gently pull on the bent arm until you feel your shoulder stretch. Hold for a count of ten. Do both sides.

When to Call the Doctor.   Consult a physician if shoulder pain becomes severe, interferes with sleep, or does not improve significantly after two weeks of committed self-care. The doctor may order x-rays and other tests and inject cortisone into the affected area to reduce the inflammation. Then you'll probably get a referral to a physical therapist or other practitioner who will prescribe range-of-motion and strengthening exercises.

▶ **RED FLAGS**   Consult a doctor immediately for:
    •Shoulder pain that comes on suddenly accompanied by fever and/or a general ill feeling. This may be a systemic illness, such as rheumatic fever.
    •Shoulder pain accompanied by chest pain or heartburn. This may be a heart attack.

SLIPPED DISC

(See also BACK PAIN (LOWER and UPPER), NECK PAIN, and SCIATICA in this chapter)

Discs can slip anywhere from the neck to lower back. The pain can begin suddenly or evolve slowly, depending on what causes the disc problem. But in most cases, the pain quickly becomes severe and interferes with movement. A slipped disc in the neck often makes turning the head impossible. A slipped disc in the lower back can make sitting impossible.

What's Going On?   "Slipped disc" is a misnomer. Nothing slips. Actually, something breaks open ("ruptures" or "herniates")—the cartilaginous discs between the back vertebrae. The back is composed of bony vertebrae separated by discs that act as cushions which absorb the shock of everyday movements. The discs' outer layer is fibrous, but inside is a soft, jelly-like substance which provides shock-absorption. Aging or injury can cause disc degeneration, and eventually a disc may rupture. When this occurs, the soft, pulpy filling oozes out, placing pressure on the nerves that run along the spinal column. This pressure causes the pain and disability.

Any disc may rupture, but the ones most likely to herniate are in the lower back, the same discs involved in lower-back pain and sciatica (see BACK PAIN (LOWER) and SCIATICA in this chapter).

Before You Call the Doctor.   The severe pain of a ruptured disc sends the vast majority of people right to the doctor. This is a good idea because if not properly evaluated and managed, disc problems may damage the spinal nerves, possibly causing paralysis. Ruptured disc symptoms may also indicate other problems: arthritis, syphilis, lead or arsenic poisoning, bacterial infection leading to internal abscesses, or tumors.

However, once nerve damage and other possibilities have been ruled out, recovery depends on self-care. Review the BACK PAIN sections in this chapter. Work with a physical therapist, chiropractor, osteopath, acupuncturist, or yoga instructor. Once a disc has ruptured, it is prone to reinjury. Healing yourself and preventing reinjury takes time, energy, and usually some life-style modifications. But the reward is a healthy, pain-free back.

When to Call the Doctor. After taking a history and conducting a physical exam, the doctor may order x-rays and possibly a CT or MRI scan to confirm a herniated disc.

Orthodox doctors may advise a variety of treatments ranging from pain medications and supportive braces to physical therapy and surgery. Alternative practitioners, such as chiropractors and acupuncturists, may offer manipulation and other therapies. Regardless of the therapy or clinician you choose, exhaust your nonsurgical options before consenting to surgery. Surgical disc repair is by no means assured. Back surgery should be a last resort.

SPRAINS

A sprain causes sharp pain and swelling around the affected joint. The swelling usually subsides within a week, but the pain may last a few weeks, followed by up to several months of stiffness and movement restriction. Some sprains cause joint discoloration. Severe sprains can result in joint deformity.

What's Going On? People commonly use the term "sprain" to describe any painful joint injury. But a true sprain is actually a torn ligament. Ligaments are the fibrous, elastic connective tissue bands that attach bone to bone. (Tendons connect muscle to bone.) The ligaments around any joint can become sprained, but the most vulnerable sites are the ankle, knees, wrist, and fingers.

The severity of a sprain depends on how much of the affected ligament tears. Mild sprains (Type I) involve fewer than 25 percent of ligament fibers. Moderate sprains (Type II) affect 25 to 75 percent of ligament fibers. And severe sprains (Type III) tear more than three-quarters of the ligament.

Before You Call the Doctor.   Pre-workout stretching and strengthening the muscles around the joint can help prevent sprains. Stretching increases ligament flexibility, which increases range of motion. See MUSCLE STRAINS in this chapter and the sections dealing with pain in the various joints for stretching and strengthening suggestions. However, stretching and strengthening cannot prevent all sprains.

Type I sprains can be treated at home:

• For pain and swelling, take aspirin or ibuprofen. Acetaminophen can help relieve pain, but unlike aspirin and ibuprofen, it has no anti-inflammatory action, so it can't help control swelling. If aspirin or ibuprofen upset your stomach, try an "enteric coated" brand, which dissolves in the intestine, not in the stomach. Pregnant women and those with a history of ulcers should not take aspirin or ibuprofen unless a doctor recommends it.

• Use R.I.C.E.: rest, ice, compression, and elevation. For a complete discussion of R.I.C.E. treatment, see MUSCLE STRAINS in this chapter. Ice packs and elevation are especially important during the first twenty-four hours to minimize swelling. To make an ice pack, place a few ice cubes in a plastic bag and wrap the bag in a clean cloth. Ice substitutes may also be used. Apply the ice pack to the affected joint for twenty minutes, then remove it for ten minutes before reapplying. Do not apply ice directly to the skin. This can cause the equivalent of frostbite.

• After swelling has begun to subside, warm or hot water soaks may feel helpful.

• Within a day or so, it's important to begin gently exercising the joint. But don't force it to bear weight while it still hurts. See the section of this chapter dealing with pain in the affected joint for specific exercises.

When to Call the Doctor.   If the joint remains stubbornly swollen and pain persists for more than two or three days, or if you notice any joint discoloration or deformity, suspect a Type II or III sprain, and consult a physician. The symptoms of moderate and severe sprains mimic those of bone fractures, so the doctor will probably x-ray the joint to rule out a broken bone. For severe sprains, the physician may recommend a cast. In some cases, surgical ligament repair may be necessary. Sprains requiring casts and/or surgery usually need physical therapy as well.

STRESS FRACTURES

(See FOOT PAIN in this chapter)

SWOLLEN JOINTS

If swollen joints feel warm, stiff, or painful and appear red, the problem is probably an infection or inflammation (see ARTHRITIS, GOUT, and TENDINITIS in this chapter). A soft, noninflamed swelling over the knee or elbow is probably mild bursitis (see BURSITIS in this chapter).

If the symptoms listed above aren't present and the swelling affects the feet and ankles (and sometimes the hands), the problem may be a fluid build-up ("edema") (see EDEMA in Chapter 4).

TENDINITIS

Tendinitis causes sharp or achy, often burning, pain in the affected joint area. The limb may feel weak, and if not treated, the pain may become chronic.

What's Going On?   The tendons, composed of fibrous, elastic tissue, connect muscles to bones, and most attach to the bones in the general area of the major joints. If a joint/muscle/tendon combination suffers injury or the stress of overuse, the tendon may tear, resulting in inflammation and the sharp pain of tendinitis. Tendinitis generally occurs not because the tendon itself is weak or abnormal, but because the muscles around it are not strong enough to handle the demands placed on them, and the body tries to compensate by calling on the tendon, which tears.

Tendinitis may begin suddenly or gradually, up to a day after over-using the affected joint. Tendinitis can strike any joint, but it's most common in the shoulder ("rotator cuff tendinitis"), the heel ("Achilles tendinitis"), the knee ("jumper's knee" or "patellar tendinitis"), the inside of the elbow ("golfer's elbow"), and the outside of the elbow ("tennis elbow"). You need not play golf to develop golfer's elbow or tennis to get tennis elbow. Other swinging motions can produce the former, and the latter can strike anyone who plays a racquet sport as well as carpenters who hammer a lot.

The pain of tendinitis usually subsides within a few weeks, but some people, particularly older adults, suffer chronic soreness and susceptibility to reinjury.

Before You Call the Doctor.   When tendinitis pain strikes, stop doing whatever caused the injury and immediately take aspirin or ibuprofen to relieve the pain and inflammation. Acetaminopen treats pain but has no anti-inflammatory action. If aspirin or ibuprofen upset your stomach take an "enteric coated" brand, which dissolves in the intestine, not in the stomach. Pregnant women and those with a history of ulcers should not take aspirin or ibuprofen unless a doctor recommends it.

Then apply R.I.C.E.—rest, ice, elevation, and compression. For a complete discussion of R.I.C.E. treatment, see MUSCLE STRAINS in this chapter.

After a few days—or immediately if the pain is mild—start exercising the area to strengthen the muscles around the affected joint. The stronger the muscles, the less stress gets placed on the tendon. The recommended exercises usually require three- to five-pound weights, which can be purchased at most sporting goods stores. Before doing the exercises, warm up the joint by gently moving it around or back and forth through its range of motion. After exercising, stretch the muscles, taking care not to bounce or jerk. After your tendinitis has healed, keep doing the exercises to prevent reinjury.

For shoulder tendinitis, the arm and chest muscles need to be stretched and strengthened. For specific exercises, see SHOULDER PAIN in this chapter.

For tennis and golfer's elbow, the forearm muscles need to be stretched and strengthened (see ELBOW PAIN in this chapter).

For patellar tendinitis, the muscles around the knee need to be stretched and strengthened (see KNEE PAIN in this chapter). Concentrate on the quadriceps and hamstrings.

Achilles tendinitis often resolves with rest. If you're a runner, decrease your mileage, sprints, and hill training. Most sports medicine clinicians recommend reducing training by 25 percent for those who experience pain only after exercising. If pain occurs during and after exercise, reduce training by at least 50 percent. Those who experience pain during and after activity which restricts performance should stop training altogether. Swimming, bicycling, or other nonweight-bearing exercise can be substituted. Achilles pain sufferers should be sure to stretch the area before and after exercising. An ice pack afterward also helps. For specific exercises, see ANKLE PAIN in this chapter.

When to Call the Doctor.   If pain persists after two weeks of self-care consult a physician. Also call the doctor if the tendon or joint area appears discolored or deformed, or if pain and disability increase. The physician will probably provide prescription pain and anti-inflammatory medication and refer you to a physical therapist.

TENNIS ELBOW

(See ELBOW PAIN and TENDINITIS in this chapter)

TOE INJURY

(See also SPRAINS and TOE PAIN in this chapter)

We pinch our toes in shoes, stub them against doors, and drop heavy objects on them. Because they're often in harm's way and contain so many bones, tendons, ligaments, and joints, the toes are particularly prone to all sorts of injuries.

What's Going On?   We usually take our toes for granted, but without them, we couldn't stand or walk. We're not conscious of their major function, but the toes constantly regulate balance. Press them down, and you fall backward. Lift them and you fall forward. Take them for granted, and they're likely to get injured.

Before You Call the Doctor.   As quickly as possible, run cold water over the affected toe to numb it.

Then make an ice pack by placing an ice cube or two in a plastic bag and wrapping the bag in a clean cloth. An ice substitute may also be used. Apply the ice pack for twenty minutes, then remove it for ten minutes before reapplying it. Keep doing this as long as the toe hurts or remains swollen. Do not apply ice directly to the skin. This may cause the equivalent of frostbite.

In addition, to relieve pain and inflammation, take aspirin or ibuprofen. Acetaminophen relieves pain but not inflammation. If aspirin or ibuprofen upsets your stomach, try an "enteric coated" brand, which dissolves in the intestine and not in the stomach. Pregnant women and those with a history of ulcers should not take aspirin or ibuprofen unless a doctor recommends it.

Trauma may also sprain the toes (see SPRAINS in this chapter).

If a toe injury breaks or otherwise deforms a toe nail, don't try to remove it. Simply trim off the detached part, cutting off any sharp edges, and bandage it for a few days to prevent further injury. The nail should grow back within a few weeks to several months.

When to Call the Doctor.   Consult a physician if you're in doubt about the severity of any toe injury. Don't risk permanent disability to these crucial appendages. Intense pain, marked swelling, bruising away from the area of impact, and/or visible toe deformity suggest fracture, which requires professional care. Depending on the toe and the injury, broken toes may or may not be casted or splinted.

TOE PAIN

(See also ARTHRITIS, FOOT PAIN, GOUT, SPRAINS, TENDINITIS, and TOE INJURY in this chapter and NAIL PROBLEMS in Chapter 6)

Toe pain may be sharp or dull, constant or intermittent, and piercing or throbbing.

What's Going On?   Toe pain may have many causes. The most common is a stubbed toe (see TOE INJURY in this chapter).

Before You Call the Doctor.   Check your shoes. Have the soles been punctured by a tack, nail, or piece of glass?

Pain in a single toe suggests a problem in its joints, tendons, or ligaments (see ARTHRITIS, GOUT, SPRAINS, TENDINITIS, and TOE INJURY in this chapter).

A common cause of toe pain is an ingrown toenail (see NAIL PROBLEMS in Chapter 6).

If you experience problems in more than one toe, but only in one foot, it's probably a joint or nerve problem (see ARTHRITIS, BACK PAIN (LOWER), and SCIATICA in this chapter).

If pain strikes both feet, it may be a systemic, nerve, or circulation problem. Nerve problems tend to cause tingling and/or numbness. Other causes of numbness and tingling include alcohol, heavy metal exposure, certain vitamin deficiencies, or a high blood sugar level in anyone with diabetes.

Circulation problems usually cause color changes. In cold weather, do your toes (and fingers) blanch and turn blue, then deep red as they warm? If so, you may have Raynaud's syndrome, which is characterized by circulation impairment of the extremities (see FINGER PAIN in this chapter).

If you have both toe pain and discolored toenails, chances are you have a toenail infection (see NAIL PROBLEMS in Chapter 6).

If your pain is localized on the bottom of the foot at the base of the toes or between them, and there is no obvious corn, callus, or wart, the pain may be caused by neuroma, a painful growth of nerve tissue caused by unusual pressure. It is treated by padding and changing shoes or wearing custom-fitted shoe inserts ("orthotics") available from podiatrists to redistribute the pressure.

When to Call the Doctor. Consult a doctor for severe toe pain that interferes with standing or movement, pain that does not respond to self-care within a few days, or pain with swelling, warmth, tenderness, and any discharge, which suggests infection.

TORN LIGAMENT

(See SPRAINS in this chapter)

WRIST PAIN

(See also ARM PAIN, ARTHRITIS, CARPAL TUNNEL SYNDROME, GANGLION, and TENDINITIS in this chapter)

Wrist pain may be sharp or dull, constant or intermittent, and localized in the wrist or associated with problems in the arm or fingers.

Before You Call the Doctor. Probably the leading cause of wrist pain is carpal tunnel syndrome, which causes pain on the palm side of the wrist extending into the hand or up the arm. The pain is often worse at night. If you spend several hours a day working at a computer keyboard, wrist pain probably means carpal tunnel syndrome (see CARPAL TUNNEL SYNDROME in this chapter).

If it's associated with athletics or holding a baby for long periods, chances are it's caused by tendinitis or a sprain (see SPRAINS and TENDINITIS in this chapter). Wrist tendinitis usually involves the tendons attached to the thumb and causes pain during thumb movement. Treatment consists of wearing a wrist splint (see CARPAL TUNNEL SYNDROME in this chapter) in addition to the general suggestions provided for tendinitis (see TENDINITIS in this chapter).

Ganglion cysts can become large enough to impair wrist movement and cause pain (see GANGLION in this chapter).

In addition, arthritis, may cause wrist pain, particularly among people over forty-five years of age or those with a history of wrist sprains or fractures (see ARTHRITIS in this chapter).

When to Call the Doctor.   Consult a physician for severe wrist pain after any traumatic injury—the wrist might be broken—or for any wrist pain that does not respond to two weeks of committed self-care.

RESOURCES

The Arthritis Foundation. 1314 Spring St., N.W., Atlanta, GA 30309; (404) 872-7100. Publishes an enormous amount of information on coping with arthritis. Sponsors local groups around the country. For the one nearest you, contact the national office or consult your phone book.

Comfortably Yours. 61 West Hunter Ave., Maywood, NJ 07607; (201) 368-0400. This catalogue offers more than 300 products that make life easier for those with mobility impairments.

Bodyline. 3730 Kori Rd., Jacksonville, FL 32257; 1-(800)-874-7715. A good source of pillows for those with painful muscles and joints.

Back Designs, Inc. 614 Grand Ave., Oakland, CA 94610; (415) 451-6600. This store, owned and operated by physical therapists, specializes in back-sparing furniture, desks, mattresses, home and garden tools, and books about back self-care. For a catalog which lists 150 items, send $10.00.

"Say Goodbye to Back Pain." This ninety-six-minute video features the exercise program developed by Alexander Melleby, M.S., national director of the YMCA Back Program. $45.00. To purchase a copy, contact your local YMCA.

Self-Care Catalog. 5850 Shellmound Ave. #390, Emeryville, CA 94608; 1-(800)-345-3371. This excellent consumer products catalog carries many items for people with back pain, including pillows, a yoga video, car seat inserts, and back-supporting chairs.

C H A P T E R   1 6

Women's Health

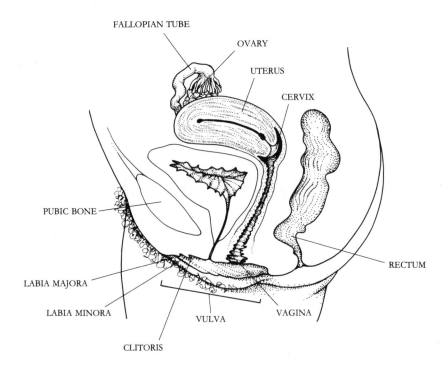

FALLOPIAN TUBE

OVARY

UTERUS

CERVIX

PUBIC BONE

RECTUM

LABIA MAJORA

LABIA MINORA

VAGINA

VULVA

CLITORIS

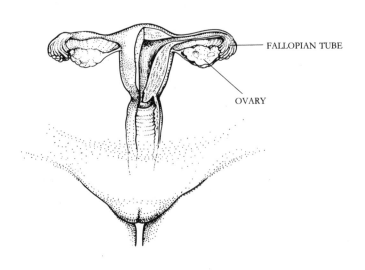

FALLOPIAN TUBE

OVARY

The Female Reproductive System.

ATROPHIC VAGINITIS

(See also MENOPAUSE and VAGINAL DISCHARGE in this chapter)

This vaginal inflammation develops after menopause. Symptoms include abnormal discharge and burning, itching, and vaginal pain or soreness during intercourse.

What's Going On? With menopause, women produce less of the female sex hormone estrogen. As estrogen production decreases, the vaginal walls become thinner and drier, which sometimes leads to inflammation and the symptoms mentioned above.

Before You Call the Doctor. Many women find relief by using vaginal lubricants during intercourse and when the vagina feels irritated. First try vegetable oil, unscented cold cream, or water-based lubricants available over the counter at pharmacies, usually in the family planning section (KY Jelly or Surgilube). Do not use Vaseline or other petroleum-based products. If lubricants help but not enough, two newer products may work better—Astroglide, a longer-lasting water-based lubricant, and Replens, a very-long-lasting moisturizer that adheres to vaginal cells.

When to Call the Doctor. If additional lubrication doesn't eliminate symptoms, consult a physician. The standard treatment is conjugated estrogen (Premarin), either orally or in a vaginal cream daily for two to three weeks, followed by a maintenance schedule to prevent recurrence. If a woman chooses estrogen cream instead of pills, she can use very small amounts (one-eighth of an applicator) two to three times per week. In such small doses, there's less risk of systemic absorption and side effects.

Women who don't want to use estrogen or can't use it, for example, those with a history of estrogen-dependent breast cancer, can try a one-percent testosterone cream. Apply a small amount three times a week. Most women don't use testosterone indefinitely because of its long-term side effects: unwanted hair growth, voice deepening, and acne. Testosterone may also increase libido in some women.

▶ **RED FLAGS** If you notice any vaginal discharge tinged with blood, consult a physician promptly for a cancer test. See MENOPAUSE in this chapter for the many conditions that rule out use of estrogen.

BACTERIAL VAGINOSIS

Bacterial vaginosis ("BV" or "Gardnerella") causes a foul or fishy-smelling discharge and gray or yellowish vaginal secretions. Some women also suffer vaginal itching, low back pain, pain on urination, cramping, and irritation with intercourse.

What's Going On?   Bacterial vaginosis is a catch-all term for vaginal infections caused by organisms other than yeast fungi (see YEAST IN-FECTION in this chapter) or trichomonads (see TRICHOMONAS in Chapter 18). One common cause is *Gardnerella* bacteria, hence the term gardnerella for this infection.

Some physicians consider BV a sexually transmitted disease, but usually it isn't. The infection may be associated with sexual activity, but it often occurs without sexual contact. Most physicians consider it an overgrowth of the various bacteria normally found in the vagina.

Bacterial vaginosis remains localized in the vagina and does not spread up into the uterus or fallopian tubes, so it does not threaten a woman's fertility or lead to potentially life-threatening infection of the reproductive organs ("pelvic inflammatory disease" or "PID").

Before You Call the Doctor.   Bacterial vaginosis requires professional diagnosis and treatment. Douching with Betadine or with *Lactobacillus acidophilus* yogurt have proven ineffective. And douching increases the risk of PID (see DOUCHING in this chapter).

When to Call the Doctor.   For best treatment results:

• Don't douche before the examination, which can interfere with accurate diagnosis. In fact, don't douche at all (see DOUCHING in this chapter).

• Don't visit the doctor during the bleeding phase of your menstrual cycle. Menstrual blood can interfere with an accurate diagnosis.

• Don't use "feminine hygiene" sprays, which can cloud important diagnostic indicators.

• Mention any drug allergies.

• Take all the medication prescribed, even if symptoms clear up before the end of the treatment course.

• Ask whether or not a follow-up visit is necessary.

Bacterial vaginosis can be effectively treated with metronidazole (Fla-gyl). Pregnant women can take clindamycin instead. Some physicians continue to prescribe amoxicillin and vaginal sulfa creams, but authorities no longer recommend these treatments.

BV often recurs after treatment. It can be retreated with the same medication. Many physicians recommend treating partners of women with recurrent infections, but there is no compelling evidence that this helps.

BREAST PAIN, TENDERNESS, OR SORENESS

Breast pain is usually *not* cancer. Breast tumors are usually painless.

What's Going On?   Four of the most common sources of breast discomfort are: hormone therapy, premenstrual syndrome (PMS), fibrocystic breast condition, and pregnancy/breastfeeding.

• *Hormone Therapy.*   The estrogen in hormone replacement therapy or birth control pills may cause breast swelling and/or tenderness as well as nipple soreness.

• *Premenstrual Syndrome.*   If your breasts become painful, tender, or sore (but not lumpy) around your menstrual period and your symptoms improve or disappear with the beginning of menstrual flow, chances are the cause is premenstrual syndrome (see PREMENSTRUAL SYNDROME (PMS) in this chapter). Experts estimate that 85 to 90 percent of all women suffer at least some of its many symptoms, and breast tenderness is one of the most common.

• *Fibrocystic (Lumpy) Breasts.*   Another common cause of breast pain is lumpy ("fibrocystic") breasts. This condition used to be called fibrocystic breast *disease,* but it's so prevalent, it can't be considered a disease. It's a normal variation in breast tissue. In fact, an estimated 60 percent of women have some degree of breast lumpiness, and many suffer the tenderness and pain of moderate-to-severe fibrocystic condition. The cause of fibrocystic breasts is unknown, but women with the condition tend to experience exaggerated monthly breast swelling, tenderness, and lumpiness during the week or two before each period.

There was a time when fibrocystic breasts were considered a risk factor for breast cancer. One subtype of the condition is associated with an increased cancer risk ("duct hyperplasia"), but most women with lumpy breasts need not fear an increased risk of breast tumors.

There are three types of fibrocystic breast condition: fibrosis, cysts, and duct hyperplasia:

• In fibrosis, the connective tissue supporting the milk glands thickens and becomes unusually fibrous. Fibrosis may or may not be painful, and it is not always accompanied by cysts.

• With cysts, the milk ducts become blocked by overgrowth of the surrounding tissue and don't drain properly. Blocked ducts swell into tender, fluid-filled cysts, which can range in size from pinpoints to sacs holding a quarter-cup of fluid.

• Duct hyperplasia means overgrowth of the lining of the ducts which carry milk from the milk glands to the nipple. It is the *only* fibrocystic condition which increases the risk of breast cancer. Duct hyperplasia can be diagnosed only through a biopsy of a suspicious breast lump.

• *Pregnancy/Breastfeeding.*   Sore breasts and nipples are a problem for many childbearing women, often beginning early in pregnancy and continuing until weaning.

Before You Call the Doctor.   Start by giving yourself a thorough breast self-exam. Although breast cancer rarely causes breast pain, tenderness, or soreness, if you suddenly develop this symptom, it never hurts to check for lumps (See BREAST LUMPS in this chapter).

Next, rule out pregnancy. Breast tenderness is often an early sign of pregnancy. If you've had unprotected intercourse within the previous month, either take a home pregnancy test or call your physician or clinic about arranging an office test.

If your breast symptoms appear to be related to PMS try these self-care strategies:

• Eat a healthful diet (see EAT AND DRINK RIGHT in Chapter 1). Steer clear of foods high in sugar, fats, additives, and artificial colors. Eliminate or cut back on caffeine in coffee, tea, colas and other soft drinks, and in many over-the-counter drugs, for example, cold formulas. Limit alcohol to no more than one drink per day (one glass of wine, one can or bottle of beer, or one shot of distilled spirits). Limit salt intake, which increases water retention. Try eating natural diuretics, such as watermelon, parsley, cucumbers, and cabbage, and drinking diuretic herbal teas: dandelion, juniper, nettle, or sarsaparilla.

• Exercise regularly. Aerobic exercise can help release endorphins, the body's own pain relieving chemicals.

• Try heat. A warm bath, heating pad, or hot water bottle may help reduce breast pain.

• Try vitamin and mineral supplements. Many companies offer "PMS formulas" which contain the supplements that some women say help them: vitamin B_6, magnesium, B-complex, vitamin C, and vitamin E.

Keep in mind that vitamin B_6 can be toxic at high doses. Take no more than 200 mg a day.

If monthly breast pain, soreness, or tenderness during the week or so before your period point to fibrocystic breasts, this condition can also be managed with self-care:

•Eliminate caffeine. Several studies have shown that eliminating caffeine can reduce or eliminate breast lumps. However, other studies have shown no effect. Advocates say you must eliminate caffeine *completely,* that is, no coffee (including coffee-flavored items and decaf, which contains a small amount of caffeine), tea, cocoa, chocolate, colas or other soft drinks, or over-the-counter medicines containing the stimulant.

•Decrease saturated fat. Several studies have shown that saturated fat, the kind found in meats, butter, lard, and some oils, for example, coconut and palm oils, promote the secretion of hormones that stimulate breast tissue growth. Eat a low-fat diet based on whole grains and fresh fruits and vegetables.

•Try vitamin supplements. Some women say that vitamins, especially A, B_6, and E, help minimize the discomfort of fibrocystic breasts. Although vitamin A (beta-carotene) may help relieve fibrocystic breast symptoms, don't take more than 5,000 International Units (IU) a day. Some megavitamin enthusiasts recommend much higher doses, but too much of this vitamin can cause headaches, dizziness, hair loss, nausea, and other problems. The recommended dose of vitamin E is 800 to 1,200 mg a day. Don't take more because higher doses may interfere with the absorption of vitamin A. Vitamin B_6, a natural diuretic, is safe in doses of 200 mg per day, but higher doses may cause nerve ("neurological") problems.

•Don't smoke. Nicotine stimulates fibrous tissue growth and the buildup of cyst-causing estrogen.

•Limit sweets. Breast tissue abnormalities are often associated with excessive sugar intake.

•Control your weight. Excess fat predisposes a woman to fibrocystic breasts. If you're overweight, combine the diet outlined in Chapter 1 with regular moderate exercise.

If breast symptoms lead to the discovery that you're pregnant and you intend to keep the pregnancy, consult a physician promptly to begin prenatal care. If you intend to breastfeed, you can minimize nipple problems during nursing by "toughening" them before the baby arrives. Massage your nipples with your thumb and forefinger or rub them with a rough towel after bathing. Massage your nipples with lanolin cream and briefly expose them to fresh air and sunlight.

For women who develop sore nipples while pregnant or breastfeeding:

• Rub them with vegetable oil or cocoa butter after each feeding. Neither of these needs to be washed off before the baby feeds.

• Apply tea bags dipped in boiling water then cooled. Certain chemicals in tea ("tannins") help toughen nipple skin.

• Limit the amount of soap you use to wash your nipples. Soaps are drying and promote cracking.

• Keep lactating breasts clean with warm water.

• Wear a good support bra with convenient flaps you can leave open when you're relaxing. Some models have plastic liners to prevent leakage, but they can cause irritation and even nipple infection. Most women prefer disposable paper or washable liners.

• If one lactating nipple becomes cracked and sore, discontinue nursing on that side if possible. Offer the less sore side first when the baby is hungriest. On the sore side, nurse only five to ten minutes. If you must temporarily stop breastfeeding on one side, be sure to pump or manually express milk from that side after feeding from the other, while the milk let-down reflex is operating.

• If you're breast-feeding and your breasts become engorged and painfully swollen, tender, hard, or congested, feed your infant or pump or express milk. Use a hot washcloth or take a hot shower beforehand to spur milk flow.

• Nonnursing mothers must wait until their breast milk dries up for engorgement to subside. In the meantime wear a tight bra and apply ice packs. To make an ice pack, wrap a few ice cubes in a plastic bag and wrap the bag in a clean cloth and apply it for twenty minutes, then remove the ice pack for ten minutes before reapplying it. An ice substitute may also be used. Do not place ice directly on the skin. This can cause the equivalent of frostbite.

• Over-the-counter pain relievers are a last resort. These drugs can be passed to the infant through your milk. Consult your physician before taking drugs for the discomforts of nursing.

When to Call the Doctor.   Consult a doctor anytime you can't readily identify the cause of any breast problem, especially if you feel a lump.

If nipple or breast soreness seem related to hormone therapy, consult a physician about adjusting your dosage.

If you consult a physician for PMS symptoms, you may be offered a variety of medications, including aspirin, prostaglandin inhibitors, or female sex hormones. We recommend you try self-care life-style changes before resorting to drugs.

One controversial treatment for PMS is the female sex hormone progesterone. Some studies have shown complete elimination of symptoms; others have shown no effect. The hormone is administered using vaginal or rectal suppositories or by intramuscular injection. Possible side effects, particularly for women who have never had children, include uterine cramping, restlessness, and euphoria. The long-term effects are still unknown.

Medical treatment for fibrocystic breasts is usually the same as self-care: eliminate caffeine, go on a low-fat diet, and take vitamin supplements. Some doctors also prescribe diuretics to reduce fluid retention or nonsteroidal anti-inflammatory drugs to minimize discomfort. Finally, some physicians suggest a four-to-six-month course of danazol (Danocrine), a synthetic male sex hormone. This drug is very expensive, and it may cause masculinizing side effects, such as unwanted hair growth and voice deepening. It may also decrease breast size, cause acne and oily hair and skin, and promote weight gain, vaginal dryness, and sweating.

Your doctor may also suggest a breast x-ray ("mammogram") and possibly a breast biopsy, a surgical sampling of breast tissue, to determine if your fibrocystic condition involves duct hyperplasia or if your lumps are benign or cancerous. Some breast biopsies are performed under local anesthesia by inserting a thin needle ("needle aspiration") and withdrawing fluid, which is examined microscopically. Other biopsies require tissue removal under local or general anesthesia.

BREAST LUMPS

(See also BREAST PAIN, TENDERNESS, OR SORENESS in this chapter)

Although an estimated 85 percent of breasts lumps are *not* cancerous, breast cancer is still extremely common—in fact, an epidemic. About 10 percent of American women develop it at some point in their lives. More than 150,000 women in the U.S. are diagnosed with breast cancer each year, and the disease kills about 45,000 annually.

Risk factors for breast cancer include:

• Personal history of breast cancer.

• Family history of breast cancer, especially if your sisters or mother developed it before menopause. About 25 percent of women who develop breast cancer have it in their families.

• Aging. Risk increases with age.

• High-fat diet. Countries with high-fat diets, for example, the U.S., have high rates of breast cancers. Countries with low-fat diets, for example, Japan, have low rates. When Japanese women move to the United States and adopt a more Western diet, their breast cancer rate increases dramatically. Fats raise the estrogen level in the body, and prolonged exposure to estrogen seems to increase breast cancer risk.

• Alcohol. Heavy drinkers have higher rates of breast cancer, and recent research suggests that as few as two drinks a week may increase risk somewhat.

• Childlessness or first child after age thirty.

• Bottle-feeding. Breastfeeding appears to reduce risk.

• First period before age twelve.

• Menopause after age fifty-five.

• Duct hyperplasia, a form of fibrocystic breast condition (see BREAST PAIN, TENDERNESS, OR SORENESS in this chapter).

Before You Call the Doctor.   Conduct a monthly breast self-exam so that any tumors will be detected early when they are most treatable. Unfortunately, most women don't examine their breasts once a month as recommended. If you value your life, do it.

The best time is during the week after your period. In front of a mirror, visually inspect your breasts. Look for any lumps, irregularities, or puckering by standing with your arms at your sides. Then examine yourself with arms raised over your head. And finally, bend at the waist and look again. Do you see any unusual changes in breast shape, size, contour, or skin or nipple color and texture?

Next lie down with a pillow supporting the shoulder on the side being examined. Moving the pads of your fingers in small circles, press both lightly and deeply over the entire breast. Don't forget the area above the breast by your collar bone and the area under your arm. Examine each breast with that side's arm at your side and up over your head. If you find a lump or have any questions about the condition of your breasts, consult a clinician immediately.

Fibrocystic breasts (see BREAST PAIN, TENDERNESS, OR SORENESS in this chapter) don't generally increase the risk of breast cancer, but lumpiness makes breast self-exam more difficult. In general, fibrocystic lumps feel tender and spongy and can be moved about the breast, whereas most breast tumors feel painless and hard and may seem anchored in the breast.

If you'd like to improve your breast-self-exam skill, call your local American Cancer Society (ACS) office. The ACS provides breast self-exam brochures, and many offices offer classes as well. Another option is to learn the MammaCare method of self-exam (see RESOURCES at the end of this chapter). Studies show that the MammaCare method is the

Breast Self-Exam (BSE).

Visual inspection.

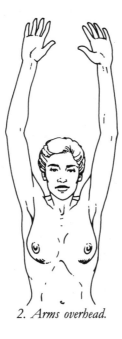

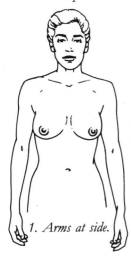

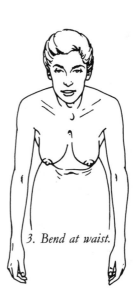

1. Arms at side.   2. Arms overhead.   3. Bend at waist.

Proper hand position for BSE.

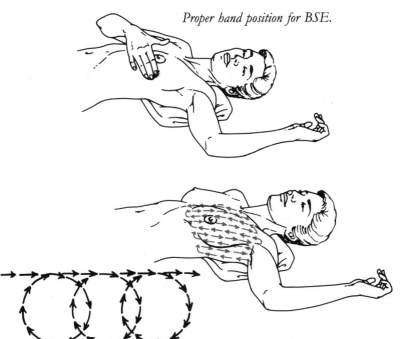

Pattern of search for BSE. Starting in the armpit, do not lift your fingers, but maintain pressure as you slide along, making dime-sized circular massaging motions.

best breast self-exam method, empowering women to detect the smallest breast tumors that can be felt.

When to Call the Doctor.   You'll need to see a physician to follow the American Cancer Society guidelines for breast x-rays ("mammography"):
- A baseline mammogram at age thirty-five.
- A mammogram every two years from age forty to forty-nine.
- An annual mammogram after age fifty.

Women whose mothers or sisters developed breast cancer before menopause should consider themselves genetically predisposed to this disease. They should have their baseline mammogram earlier and all subsequent mammograms more frequently than the ACS guidelines call for. If you may be genetically predisposed to this cancer, be sure to tell your physician.

Unfortunately, a 1989 ACS survey showed that only 37 percent of doctors follow the ACS mammography guidelines by referring women appropriately to radiologists or mammography facilities. Women must take responsibility for their own mammography. When was *your* last mammogram?

If a breast lump, is discovered, either through a self-exam or mammography, consult a physician without delay. The doctor's job is to determine if the lump is a benign fibrocyst or a cancerous tumor. The doctor should ask how long you've been aware of the lump, if it waxes and wanes with your menstrual cycle, and if it is tender during particular times of the month.

If you discovered the lump yourself, the doctor typically orders a mammogram. If it was discovered during a routine mammogram, the doctor may order another as a check.

However, a normal mammogram cannot rule out cancer if the physician believes the lump is suspicious, which is why the physician may also want to perform a breast biopsy, which involves surgical sampling of breast tissue—and sometimes removal of the lump—to determine if it is benign or cancerous. Some breast biopsies are performed under local anesthesia by inserting a thin needle ("needle aspiration") and withdrawing fluid, which is examined microscopically. Other biopsies require tissue removal under local or general anesthesia.

BREAST SWELLING

(See also BREAST PAIN, TENDERNESS, OR SORENESS; MENO-PAUSE; and PREMENSTRUAL SYNDROME in this chapter)

Breast swelling without pain is common among newborns, adolescent girls and boys, adult women, and even men.

What's Going On?   Newborns often experience breast swelling due to the hormones present in the mother's blood before birth and in mother's milk shortly after delivery. Any swelling usually subsides within a few weeks as the hormonal situation changes.

All adolescents, both boys and girls, experience breast development. Boys—and their parents—are often alarmed when young men experience breast swelling and tenderness, but as puberty continues and boys develop a more male physique, the swelling and tenderness subside.

Girls—and their parents—often become concerned about asymmetric breast development. Sometimes one breast grows a full cup size larger than the other. This, too, is normal. Eventually the smaller breast grows to approximately match the larger one, though some minor size difference may remain.

Before You Call the Doctor.   Breast swelling in women is usually associated with hormone therapy, premenstrual syndrome, fibrocystic breast condition, or pregnancy. For self-care suggestions, see BREAST PAIN, TENDERNESS OR SORENESS; MENOPAUSE; and PREMENSTRUAL SYNDROME in this chapter.

When to Call the Doctor.   Women who experience significant discomfort from breast swelling due to birth control pills or postmenopausal estrogen replacement therapy should discuss the situation with a physician. Dose adjustment or a change in medication might help.

Breast swelling in infants that does not subside in a month or two should be evaluated by the child's doctor and followed at regular checkups. In rare cases, the swelling may indicate a hormonal abnormality. The same may be true for prepubertal children with swollen breasts.

Any swelling of only one breast in an adult woman should be checked by a physician. Small differences in breast size are normal, but significant swelling of one side requires professional evaluation.

DOUCHING

Don't douche as a regular part of personal hygiene. It's associated with a significantly increased risk of pelvic inflammatory disease (PID), an infection of the reproductive organs that can cause infertility or even be fatal.

What's Going On? An estimated one-third of American women douche regularly—and spend more than $100 million a year in the process. But in a recent compelling study, University of Washington researchers discovered that compared with women who douched less than once a month, those who douched three or more times a month had 3.6 times the risk of developing PID.

It's not clear why douching is associated with PID. Researchers speculate that the physical action of douching may push PID-causing microorganisms in the vagina up into the uterus. Or douching might change the chemical environment of the vagina so that more microorganisms grow there, allowing some to find their way up into the uterus. It's also possible that both factors play a role.

In the Seattle study, no particular type of douche was more strongly associated with PID. Commercial douches and home-made vinegar-water solutions both increased PID risk significantly.

Women who douche generally were brought up to do so by mothers who persuaded them that it's an important part of personal hygiene. This message is constantly reinforced by douche ads on television and in women's magazines. However, the vagina is a self-cleansing organ. Douching is not necessary.

Before You Call the Doctor. Women interested in improving their vaginal health and minimizing any unpleasant odors should:
• Wear breathable cotton panties.
• Wear stockings or breathable panty hose with cotton crotch panels.
• Always wipe from front to back to keep from introducing anal-area bacteria into the vagina (see URINARY TRACT INFECTION in Chapter 14).
• Wipe the vaginal area dry after lovemaking. Wipe front to back.
• Eat yogurt with live *Lactobacillus acidophilus* culture. A recent study showed that one cup a day reduced vaginitis risk by more than 60 percent. Unfortunately, few yogurts contain live *Lactobacillus*. Those that do say so on the label. Look in health food stores. If you can't find live-culture yogurt, you can make your own from *acidophilus* milk.
• Don't use superabsorbent tampons (see TOXIC SHOCK SYNDROME in this chapter).
• Use diaphragms and contraceptive sponges properly. If left in too long, these birth control devices can interfere with normal vaginal self-cleansing.
• Reconsider your intrauterine device (IUD). IUDs are associated with an increased risk of PID.

When to Call the Doctor.   The only reason to douche is to help treat vaginal infections (see YEAST INFECTION in this chapter). If you develop a yeast infection, discuss the advisability of douching with your physician. If you decide to douche, don't squirt the liquid or hang the bag higher than three feet above you. You may push potentially PID-causing microorganisms into the uterus. Simply let the douche flow in.

▶ **RED FLAG**   Consult a physician immediately for pelvic pain and fever. This might be PID. But PID may not cause fever. Consult a physician promptly for any persistent pelvic pain, especially if you douche frequently or have an IUD.

ENDOMETRIOSIS

More than 10 percent of American women suffer endometriosis, which causes pain, nausea, heavy menstrual bleeding, pain on intercourse, and in some cases, infertility.

What's Going On?   Doctors have been studying endometriosis for more than sixty years but still can't agree on exactly what it is or what causes it. The most popular theory is that "renegade" cells from the uterine lining ("endometrial cells") spill into the abdominal cavity when menstrual blood backs up in the tubes which connect the ovaries and uterus ("fallopian tubes"). These cells attach to structures outside the uterus—the ovaries, uterine ligaments, fallopian tubes, bladder, rectum, etc.

Other theories suggest that pelvic tissues spontaneously convert to endometrial tissue, possibly due to irritation or hormonal activity. Some doctors suggest that endometrial cells enter the pelvic cavity during gynecological procedures, such as abortions or cesarean sections. A few, most notably Dr. David Redwine of Bend, Oregon, suggest that endometriosis is a disease of the cellophane-lining ("peritoneum") that covers the internal organs.

Whatever it is and wherever it comes from, the tissues involved in endometriosis grow and bleed cyclically as if they were still inside the uterus, or they cause the surrounding area to bleed. But this blood has no outlet, so the body reacts with inflammation, pain, cyst formation, and scarring.

Before You Call the Doctor.   Aspirin, acetaminopohen, and ibuprofen may help relieve the pain of mild endometriosis, but the condition cannot be self-treated or prevented. Any persistent pelvic pain or heavy menstrual bleeding should be checked by a clinician. Pregnant women, women who suspect they might be pregnant, and those with a history of ulcers or other gastrointestinal diseases should not take aspirin or ibuprofen unless a doctor recommends it.

When to Call the Doctor.   Endometriosis can be difficult to diagnose because the disease can mimic many other health problems. Doctors usually make a presumptive diagnosis based on a woman's history and pelvic exam. The history typically reveals chronic pelvic pain that is worse during menstruation and often worse during intercourse, with possible infertility. The pelvic exam is normal, with possible bumpiness or thickening around the pelvic organs. Ultrasound may help rule out other conditions, such as uterine fibroids (see FIBROIDS in this chapter) or endometriosis cysts ("endometriomas").

If a history and pelvic exam suggest mild endometriosis, the doctor may suggest a wait-and-see approach along with mild pain relievers and frequent pelvic exams.

To diagnose endometriosis definitively, the physician must perform a laparoscopic exam to examine the entire pelvic area. Laparoscopy, or "belly button" surgery, is performed in a hospital under general anesthesia. It involves a half-inch incision at the naval with another at the bikini line and insertion of a telescope-like viewing instrument ("laparascope"). A woman can usually leave the hospital the same day and complications are rare, although postoperative pain is possible for up to thirty-six hours and full recovery may take several days.

Medical treatment for endometriosis has produced mixed results. Depending on the woman's age, her family history, the location and severity of her endometriosis, her desire for children, and her past experiences with hormone therapy, treatment usually begins with prostaglandin-inhibiting drugs, such as ibuprofen, naproxen, or indomethacin. If these are ineffective, stronger pain relievers may be prescribed. These medications only mask the pain and do not prevent the spread or growth of the lesions.

One hormonal approach to endometriosis treatments involves taking birth control pills, which alters the woman's body chemistry in a way that may minimize pain and prevent the development of new lesions. Some women with mild endometriosis achieve relief from taking birth control pills in the usual manner, stopping every fourth week for a menstrual period. However, some women should not take birth control pills, including those who smoke or have liver disease, high blood pressure, migraine headaches, or a history of internal blood clots. See BIRTH CONTROL PILLS in Chapter 19 for a more complete list.

Women who cannot take regular birth control pills might find relief with progesterone-only birth control pills ("mini-pills").

Another hormonal approach is to become pregnant, which alters hormone levels significantly, and then after delivery, to breastfeed the child, which maintains the altered hormone levels awhile longer. Pregnancy may offer some relief from endometriosis, but it is no guarantee that the disease will not return, not to mention that pregnancy is neither an available nor necessarily desirable alternative for many endometriosis sufferers. In addition, women with endometriosis who decide to opt for pregnancy may have difficulty becoming pregnant because of the disease.

A third hormonal alternative is the drug danazol (Danocrine), a synthetic male hormone. It induces a "pseudomenopause" and may cause masculinizing side effects such as unwanted hair growth and voice deepening. It may also decrease breast size and cause acne, weight gain, vaginal dryness, sweating, and oily hair and skin.

Traditional surgical treatments have also drawn mixed reviews. Most clinicians favor conservative surgery, which removes identified lesions and scar tissue while leaving the female reproductive organs intact. Radical surgery, often recommended for women with advanced endometriosis, removes all endometriosis lesions as well as the uterus and ovaries.

A newer and still-controversial surgical approach has been developed by Oregon's Dr. Redwine. He removes the clear cellophane-like wrapping around the abdominal organs but leaves the reproductive organs intact. Healthy peritoneal tissue begins to regenerate soon after surgery and as this book goes to press, recurrence of endometriosis treated in this manner has been rare.

FIBROCYSTIC BREASTS

(See BREAST PAIN, TENDERNESS, OR SORENESS in this chapter)

FIBROIDS

These benign overgrowths of uterine muscle and connective tissue may cause heavy and/or erratic menstrual periods, bowel or bladder problems, and occasionally, severe pain. Fibroids can also contribute to infertility.

What's Going On? Medically known as "leiomyomas" or "fibromyomas," fibroids are noncancerous growths in the uterine wall. They are often estrogen-dependent, meaning that extra estrogen encourages their growth. This is why fibroids can grow rapidly during pregnancy, when estrogen levels rise, and usually shrink after menopause, when estrogen levels decline. Birth control pills containing estrogen and postmenopausal estrogen replacement therapy can also spur fibroid growth.

Fibroids are often so small they cannot be detected, but they may grow to the size of a cantaloupe. In most cases, they produce no symptoms, and women who have fibroids are often unaware of them until they're discovered during a physician's exam. However, fibroids can grow so large or numerous that they can place significant pressure on the bowel or bladder or bulge into the uterine cavity, causing the symptoms described above. Fibroids are one of the main reasons for removal of the uterus ("hysterectomy").

Before You Call the Doctor. If your physician discovers fibroids that cause no symptoms, they need not be treated. If they cause heavy periods, drink lots of fluids, take iron supplements daily, and get tested for anemia every six months.

To discourage fibroid growth, consider using a birth control method other than the Pill. If you continue to take oral contraceptives, use only the low-dose variety.

If you are past menopause and have fibroids, estrogen replacement therapy will probably stimulate their growth.

When to Call the Doctor. Most women with fibroids consult physicians because of pain, heavy menstrual flow, bowel and bladder problems, and/or infertility. Physicians assess fibroid size by ultrasound examination, an imaging technique that does not carry the hazards of x-rays.

If your physician suggests a hysterectomy for large, painful fibroids, ask about having the growths removed without removing the uterus ("myomectomy"). Myomectomy allows women to retain their fertility. However, hysterectomy is usually the treatment of choice for postmenopausal women with large, rapidly growing fibroids.

GARDNERELLA

(See BACTERIAL VAGINOSIS in this chapter)

LUMPY BREASTS

(See BREAST PAIN, TENDERNESS, OR SORENESS in this chapter)

MENOPAUSE

(See also ATROPHIC VAGINITIS in this chapter and OSTEOPORO-SIS in Chapter 15)

Menopause, also called "the climacteric" or "change of life," is a period of a few months to several years that marks the end of menstrual periods and the possibility of having children. For many women, it also launches a new era of productivity, fulfillment, and enjoyment of life.

What's Going On?   Menopause is a natural event and not an illness, though some physicians treat it that way. During women's fertile years, the ovaries produce hormones and an egg each month at ovulation. Around age fifty, as menopause approaches, egg production and menstrual periods become less regular and eventually cease.

The physical changes that herald menopause actually begin during women's late thirties with a drop in estrogen production by the ovaries. This decrease is subtle and often goes unnoticed. For most women, the noticeable changes of menopause occur from age forty-five to fifty-five—decreased menstrual bleeding or brief heavy periods, skipped periods, insomnia, and "hot flashes," sudden sensations of flushing and sweating. Ovulation becomes sporadic but may still occur, and contraception is still necessary. At the conclusion of menopause, menstrual bleeding stops entirely, signaling the end of fertility, though doctors usually recommend continued use of birth control until one year after a woman's last period.

Women who have their uteruses removed ("hysterectomy") but retain one or more ovaries stop menstruating but still go through the hormonal changes of menopause as gradually as women who have all their reproductive organs. Women who have their ovaries surgically removed along with their uteruses during hysterectomy experience "surgical menopause," which tends to cause more severe symptoms.

Changes in hormone levels, especially the decline of estrogen, cause the hot flashes and night sweats associated with menopause.

Hot flashes occur without warning. Suddenly, a feeling of heat radiates throughout the face, neck, and chest. This sensation of heat is followed by perspiration and a chill. For some women, hot flashes feel quite uncomfortable; for others, they cause little or no discomfort. If hot flashes occur, they usually stop after a year or two.

Another common menopausal symptom which persists afterward is vaginal dryness and soreness (see ATROPHIC VAGINITIS in this chapter). As estrogen production declines, the vaginal mucous membranes become thin and secrete less moisture, which can lead to itching, inflammation, and discomfort, especially during intercourse.

Osteoporosis, bone thinning which can lead to serious fractures, is an unfortunate consequence of menopause for about 25 percent of women. Estrogen plays an important role in maintaining women's bone integrity. As estrogen production declines with menopause, women's bones lose calcium at an increasing rate. Osteoporosis often becomes evident in a woman's sixties or seventies with compressed vertebrae, which can lead to back pain, the hunched-over look of "Dowager's hump" in the upper back, vertebral fractures, and loss of height (up to several inches). There is also an increased risk of bone fractures, particularly of the wrists and hips. Both men and women experience bone loss with advancing age, but osteoporosis is far more common and debilitating in women. Those at highest risk are:
• White and Asian women.
• Thin-framed women of any race.
• Smokers.
• Women with sedentary life-styles.
• Women with a family history of osteoporosis.

Before You Call the Doctor.   There's plenty a woman can do to manage the symptoms of menopause.

For hot flashes, try the following:
• Wear loose, lightweight, natural-fabric clothing that can be easily removed.
• Limit consumption of caffeine and alcohol, which trigger hot flashes in some women.
• Don't overeat. Instead of large meals, eat several small meals throughout the day.
• Drink plenty of water and juices.
• Keep room temperature at 68° or below.
• Use a fan in your home and/or workplace.
• When you feel a hot flash coming on, try sitting quietly and visualizing a cool wave or breeze washing over you.

Other helpful self-care measures include:
• Exercise regularly to improve your mood and your sleep quality.

• Practice daily stress management techniques (see MANAGE YOUR STRESS LOAD in Chapter 1).

• Every day, take 1,000 mg of supplemental calcium, up to 400 International Units (IU) of vitamin E, and vitamin B complex.

• If you experience heavy menstrual flow, consider an iron supplement daily to prevent anemia. (Iron tends to cause constipation, so eat a high-fiber diet, drink plenty of fluids, and get regular exercise to keep things moving.)

• For vaginal dryness and soreness, see ATROPHIC VAGINITIS in this chapter.

• To help prevent osteoporosis, be sure you get an adequate supply of calcium (1,200 to 1,500 mg daily) and exercise regularly to strengthen your bones. Supplemental calcium helps prevent bone loss, and many authorities recommend calcium supplements starting at age thirty-five. Calcium also helps prevent high blood pressure. See OSTEOPOROSIS in Chapter 15 for a list of the calcium content of various foods.

• Regular exercise also helps prevent osteoporosis—but only if it's the right kind of exercise. You must work the weight-bearing joints. Fitness walking and aerobic dance qualify, but swimming and biking do not.

• Don't smoke cigarettes. Women who smoke are more likely to develop osteoporosis. (For help quitting, see Resources at the end of Chapter 11.)

• Don't be too thin. A moderate amount of body fat helps protect against osteoporosis. The healthiest postmenopausal figure is one that's "pleasantly plump."

When to Call the Doctor.   When you begin to experience menstrual irregularity, it's a good idea to see your clinician to be sure that the changes you're noticing are menopause-related and not caused by some health problem. If you're experiencing heavy menstrual bleeding, have a blood test to see if you're becoming anemic. These tests may need to be repeated several times a year until your menstrual bleeding becomes scant.

If you have any of the risk factors for osteoporosis (see above), ask your physician about a bone density study to assess your risk of fractures.

One of the biggest controversies surrounding medical treatment of menopause is the advisability of hormone replacement therapy (HRT), also known as estrogen replacement therapy (ERT). Estrogen replacement or a combination of estrogen and progestin, a hormone similar to progesterone, can help relieve hot flashes, night sweats, insomnia, and vaginal soreness and reduce the risk of osteoporosis and heart disease, the leading killer of women over fifty years of age. Women who receive hormone therapy also report less fatigue and depression. Osteoporosis prevention is a life-and-death issue because the hip fractures that often result from bone deterioration prove fatal for many older women.

But hormone therapy may increase the risk of breast cancer and gallbladder disease. Regarding breast cancer, the studies remain inconclusive. Many experts believe that estrogen promotes the growth of tumors already present but may have no effect on the large proportion of tumors that are not hormone sensitive. Authorities agree that unless post-menopausal women take progestin in addition to estrogen, they face an increased risk of uterine ("endometrial") cancer. Discuss the pros and cons of hormone replacement therapy with your clinician. If you opt for hormone therapy, be sure your physician offers a combination of estrogen and progestin (unless you have had a hysterectomy), and take the smallest hormone dosage possible.

▶ **RED FLAGS**   Don't take estrogen replacement therapy if you have a history of:
- Cancer of the breast or uterus.
- Estrogen-dependent ovarian cancer.
- A history of blood clots in the legs, pelvis, or lungs.
- Uncontrolled high blood pressure.
- Gallstones or gallbladder disease (unless your gallbladder has been removed).
- Large uterine fibroids.

MENSTRUAL CRAMPS

(See also ENDOMETRIOSIS, FIBROIDS, MENSTRUAL DISORDERS, and PELVIC PAIN in this chapter)
It's normal to have menstrual cramping, especially during the first few days of the menstrual cycle. Cramps vary in severity from mild to severe.

What's Going On?   Male doctors used to believe that menstrual cramps, medically known as "dysmenorrhea," were "all in a woman's head." But now they know what women have known all along—that cramps have a clear physiological basis. Much like labor pains, menstrual cramps are caused by contractions of the uterus, which temporarily cut off the organ's blood supply. Recently, researchers have found that prostaglandins, chemicals produced by various parts of the body, especially by the uterine lining after ovulation, cause the uterine contractions, cramping, nausea, vomiting, hot and cold sensations, headaches, diarrhea, backaches, dizziness, and even fainting that women have reported during their menstrual periods. For some women, menstrual cramping is worst before age thirty and tends to decrease with age or after childbearing. Others notice no age-related changes.

Menstrual cramps may also be caused by health problems, such as endometriosis, uterine fibroids, and the scars left from pelvic infections (see ENDOMETRIOSIS, FIBROIDS, and PELVIC PAIN in this chapter).

Before You Call the Doctor. Menstrual cramps that are not related to other health problems can often be self-treated effectively. Try these suggestions:

• Exercise regularly. In addition to improving your overall health, regular moderate exercise releases endorphins, the body's own pain relieving chemicals (see EXERCISE REGULARLY in Chapter 1).

• Drink lots of nonalcoholic fluids. When the body becomes dehydrated, the brain produces a hormone ("vasopressin") that helps conserve water, but it also contributes to uterine contractions. Drinking fluids helps some women minimize cramps.

• Keep warm. Studies have shown that women who work in cold environments generally suffer more severe menstrual cramping.

• Apply heat. Heating pads, hot water bottles, or hot baths can work wonders for a painful lower abdomen.

• Try prostaglandin inhibitors. This class of nonsteroidal anti-inflammatory drugs blocks the synthesis of prostaglandins, which play a key role in menstrual cramping. Aspirin is a prostaglandin inhibitor. So is ibuprofen. Follow package directions. Stronger prostaglandin inhibitors are available by prescription. Note that some women experience harmless changes in menstrual flow patterns when taking these drugs. Women with a history of ulcers should not take aspirin or ibuprofen.

• Switch to menstrual pads. In some women, tampons contribute to menstrual cramping. Consider switching to sanitary napkins.

• Try raspberry leaf tea. Studies show that this traditional herbal remedy for menstrual cramps does, indeed, help relax the uterus.

• Try switching your contraceptive. Some women find that intrauterine devices (IUDs) contribute to menstrual cramping. If you have an IUD, consider having it removed and switching to a barrier method or birth control pills. By eliminating ovulation, oral contraceptives decrease production of prostaglandins. Many women find that the Pill helps minimize cramps.

When to Call the Doctor. If self-care doesn't provide sufficient relief, cramping may be caused by endometriosis, fibroids, a narrowing of the cervix ("cervical stenosis"), or other causes. These conditions should be evaluated by a physician who takes a thorough history and performs a pelvic examination and Pap smear.

▶ **RED FLAG**   Sudden severe cramping may be a potentially fertility- and life-threatening infection of the reproductive organs ("pelvic inflammatory disease"). Consult a physician immediately.

MENSTRUAL DISORDERS

Heavy bleeding, medically known as "menorrhagia," excessively short cycles ("polymenorrhea"), and bleeding between periods ("metrorrhagia"), rank among the most prevalent problems gynecologists treat.

What's Going On?   Normal menstrual cycles vary from twenty-one to forty days from the first day of one period to the first day of the next. Normal periods typically span less than seven days. Usually, the heaviest flow occurs on day one or two. Some perfectly healthy women experience heavy bleeding, particularly women approaching menopause and young teens who have not begun to ovulate consistently. However, any woman who has periods that last more than seven days, especially with large clots or a day or more of soaking more than one pad or tampon every two hours ("flooding"), should consult a physician.

Abnormal menstrual bleeding may also be caused by abortion, pregnancy, and complications of pregnancy, such as tubal ("ectopic") pregnancy. Polyps, intrauterine devices, pelvic infections, endometriosis, thyroid problems, hormone abnormalities, and tumors may also alter menstrual bleeding patterns. Anemia is a common result of heavy bleeding, but surprisingly, anemia may also *cause* heavy menstrual flow.

Keep in mind that changes in menstrual bleeding, especially changes related to age, may be normal. For example, as women approach menopause, three heavy days followed by two light days may evolve into one heavy day followed by seven lighter days.

Lack of menstruation ("amenorrhea") may be the result of pregnancy, stress, excessive exercise, oral contraceptives, dramatic weight loss, hormone imbalances, menopause, or some medications. Anytime your period is more than two weeks late, consult a clinician if you have had sexual intercourse (even with birth control) since your last normal period. If you haven't and you feel well otherwise, most doctors would wait three to six months before looking for a cause other than a temporary hormone imbalance.

Before You Call the Doctor.   If you become concerned about changes in your menstrual pattern, start a menstruation diary, and keep it for a few months. A diary is a good way to see if anything unusual is really happening. If so, take it to your physician and point to specific concerns rather than making vague statements that "something doesn't seem quite right."

When to Call the Doctor.   Consult a physician if:
   • Your period is more than two weeks late and you've been sexually active, even with birth control.
   • Your period lasts longer than seven days.
   • You experience flooding.
   • A menstruation diary confirms significant unexplainable changes in your menstrual pattern.

   The physician should take a thorough history and perform a physical examination that includes a vaginal exam and possibly a rectal exam to feel structures around the uterus through the rectal wall. In some cases, diagnostic and laboratory tests might be necessary to determine the proper diagnosis and treatment.

NIPPLE DISCHARGE

Nipple discharges are common and usually not serious, despite the fact that one of the American Cancer Society's "Seven Warning Signs of Cancer" is "any unusual nipple discharge." Most nipple discharges are not cancer.

What's Going On?   Often during breast self-exam a woman notices a small amount of fluid discharge from one or both of her nipples. This sends many women into panic thinking they have breast cancer. Quite often, the cause of the discharge is simply stimulation from the breast exam itself.

   Such "pseudodischarges" can also be caused by eczema of the breast, glandular infections, inverted nipples that have not been kept clean, or even a blow to the breast. Any infection should be treated, but the other causes typically clear up on their own within a week or two.

   Nipple discharge may be related to pregnancy or breastfeeding. Many women mistakenly believe the breasts dry up soon after weaning. But some women continue to produce tiny milky discharges for up to several years afterward.

   Drugs taken after weaning a child can also cause nipple discharge. Oral contraceptives, high blood pressure medications ("antihypertensives"), and other drugs can cause the milk ducts to continue producing milk ("galactorrhea"). Even recreational drugs, such as marijuana, have been known to cause nipple discharge.

Many more serious health problems may cause nipple discharge, including thyroid or pituitary disorders, milk duct problems ("duct ectasia"), breast infections or abscesses, and breast cancer, among others. Since nipple discharge can be a sign of breast cancer, it's important to have any discharge evaluated by your physician.

Before You Call the Doctor.   Unless your discharge is obviously a pseudodischarge, plan to consult a physician. Be prepared to answer these questions:

- When did you first notice the discharge?
- Is it a new or recurring problem?
- How much discharge is there?
- What is its color and consistency?
- Does it appear at all bloody?
- Does it come from one or both sides?
- Is it associated with a lump, or breast skin abrasion?
- Is the nipple or breast sore, tender, painful, or inflamed?
- Does anything make it better or worse?
- Does it appear to be related to your menstrual cycle?

When to Call the Doctor.   After taking a thorough history, which should include a careful assessment of your breast cancer risk (see BREAST PAIN, TENDERNESS, OR SORENESS in this chapter), the physician should perform a breast exam and test the discharge for blood, which raises suspicion of cancer. But even if blood is present, only about 10 percent of spontaneous, bloody nipple discharges turn out to be cancer. Most bloody discharges are caused by *benign* breast tumors ("intraductal papillomas"). The doctor may order a mammogram, biopsy, and other tests to determine the cause of the discharge.

▶ **RED FLAG**   Consult a physician promptly for any nipple discharge unrelated to pregnancy or breastfeeding which emerges spontaneously from only one side.

NIPPLE PAIN, TENDERNESS, OR SORENESS

(See BREAST PAIN, TENDERNESS, OR SORENESS in this chapter)

OSTEOPOROSIS

(See MENOPAUSE in this chapter, and OSTEOPOROSIS in Chapter 15)

PAIN OR SORENESS DURING INTERCOURSE

(See PAINFUL INTERCOURSE in Chapter 19)

PELVIC PAIN

(See also ENDOMETRIOSIS, MENSTRUAL CRAMPS, MEN-STRUAL DISORDERS, and PREMENSTRUAL SYNDROME in this chapter and STOMACHACHE in Chapter 13)

Pelvic pain is often associated with the menstrual cycle, but it may have many other causes.

What's Going On?   Some women experience considerable pelvic pain due to menstrual cramping (see MENSTRUAL CRAMPS in this chapter). Even if you don't usually suffer cramps, they may be caused by stress, medications, or a recent IUD insertion. If your pain begins shortly before or during your period, it's probably related to your menstrual cycle (see MENSTRUAL DISORDERS in this chapter.) However, pelvic pain may also indicate more serious health problems that should be evaluated by a physician.

Before You Call the Doctor.   Try the self-care suggestions listed under MENSTRUAL CRAMPS in this chapter. If they don't help, you'll proba-bly need to consult a physician. Because pelvic pain has many sources, the key is to provide your doctor with specific information that can help diagnose your problem. Be prepared to answer these questions:

• Do you have any of the following: a heavy or foul-smelling vaginal discharge, and/or a temperature of 100° or higher? If so, you probably have a pelvic infection ("pelvic inflammatory disease" or "PID"). These infections should *never* be ignored. PID is a potentially life-threatening infection of the reproductive organs and a major contributor to fertility problems. PID can also cause chronic pelvic pain.

• How many sex partners do you have? The more partners, the greater the risk of all the sexually transmitted diseases (STDs), some of which can progress to PID.

• Does your pain grow more severe as your period progresses? If so, you may have endometriosis (see ENDOMETRIOSIS in this Chapter).

• Have you recently started using an IUD? IUDs often increase menstrual pain, and IUD problems may cause pelvic pain unrelated to your menstrual cycle.

• Have you recently stopped taking oral contraceptives? Some women experience an increase in menstrual pain when they stop taking the Pill.

• Does the pain occur on one side or the other for one day about halfway between periods? If so, the pain is probably associated with ovulation ("mittelschmerz"), which is normal and harmless.

• In addition to pelvic pain, have you noticed any irregular vaginal bleeding? If so, see MENSTRUAL DISORDERS in this chapter. The most serious possible cause of this combination is tubal ("ectopic") pregnancy, a potential medical emergency.

• Is your urination painful and/or are you urinating more frequently than usual? If so, you may have a urinary tract infection (see PAINFUL URINATION and URINARY TRACT INFECTION in Chapter 14).

• Are you constipated? Do you have gas? Sometimes a change in diet or severe emotional stress can cause gastrointestinal distress which women experience as pelvic pain. (See CONSTIPATION and FLATULENCE in Chapter 13.)

When to Call the Doctor.   Unless you can trace the cause of your pelvic pain to something which is obviously not a cause for concern, for example, constipation or stopping birth control pills, don't wait longer than two days to consult a physician for pelvic pain.

▶ **RED FLAGS**   If you develop pelvic pain and any fever, consult a physician immediately to rule out pelvic inflammatory disease. Pelvic pain with spotting or a missed period also requires immediate medical evaluation to check for ectopic pregnancy.

PREMENSTRUAL SYNDROME (PMS)

(See also BREAST PAIN, TENDERNESS, OR SORENESS in this chapter)

Symptoms of premenstrual syndrome include bloating, breast swelling and tenderness, fatigue, weight gain, headaches, food cravings, back and muscle aches, diarrhea and/or constipation, lack of coordination, emotional upsets, and many other possible complaints.

What's Going On? Experts estimate that 85 to 95 percent of women suffer at least some of the physical, behavioral, and emotional symptoms of PMS. Until the 1970s, doctors (the vast majority of whom were men) believed that premenstrual complaints were psychological—"all in a woman's head." But now researchers recognize the biological nature of PMS symptoms.

Authorities still aren't exactly sure what causes PMS, but they suspect that cyclic changes in sex hormone levels, particularly estrogen, play a key role. Some researchers also believe that the mood swings of PMS— anxiety, irritability, anger, and "spaciness"—may be related to hormonal changes or certain nutritional deficiencies, particularly deficiencies of magnesium or Vitamin B_6. Others think some women may be genetically more sensitive to the effects of changing hormone levels because PMS symptoms tend to run in families.

PMS symptoms vary from mild to almost disabling. Their severity may change from month to month as a result of illnesses and changing stress loads, but most women experience similar symptoms every month.

Before You Call the Doctor. Timing is the key to determining whether your symptoms are PMS. PMS symptoms occur seven to ten days before menstrual periods and improve with the onset of bleeding. To determine whether your problem is PMS, ask yourself these questions:

• Do the same or similar symptoms occur each month?

• Do you suffer other health problems, for example, backaches or headaches, right before your period?

• Do symptoms improve or disappear with the onset of menstrual bleeding?

• Do you have at least one symptom-free week each month? This is crucial. If you don't have at least one symptom-free week each month, consult a physician. You may have endometriosis, a vaginal or pelvic infection, fibroids, or an emotional problem, such as depression. These conditions require professional evaluation and care.

Once you're sure your problem is PMS, plenty of self-care strategies can help. In addition to the diet, exercise, and supplementation programs outlined in the PMS section under BREAST PAIN, TENDERNESS, OR SORENESS in this chapter, try these:

• Talk about it. Support from family, friends, and other PMS sufferers can be helpful. Discussing your situation can help those you care about take your condition seriously. In some communities, PMS support groups offer help.

•Manage stress. As much as possible during your premenstrual days, steer clear of stressful situations and try to take care of yourself—get a massage, read a good book, go to the moves, listen to music you love, take long hot baths, increase your consumption of soothing herb teas, call or write old friends (see MANAGE YOUR STRESS LOAD in Chapter 1).

•Eliminate caffeine completely. Even small amounts of caffeine have been shown to trigger PMS symptoms. Caffeine is found not only in coffee but also in tea, cocoa, chocolate, colas and other soft drinks, coffee-flavored items, and many over-the-counter drugs.

•Eat small meals every three to four hours.

•Adopt the diet recommended in Chapter 1. It is based on whole grains and fresh fruits and vegetables with a minimum of fats.

•Stay away from junk food snacks. Instead, snack on fruit or whole-grain bread products.

•Try mild over-the-counter PMS medications (Sunril Premenstrual Capsules or Trendar Premenstrual Tablets, among others). These usually combine a pain reliever with a mild diuretic.

•Contact Premenstrual Syndrome Action (see RESOURCES at the end of this chapter).

When to Call the Doctor.   Some women's PMS symptoms are severe enough to require professional care. Doctors differ on PMS treatments, but most offer a variety of medications, including:

•Progesterone in the form of suppositories, injections, or birth control pills to treat mood swings and some physical symptoms. Studies differ on progesterone's effectiveness. Some women's symptoms even get worse, especially those on combination birth control pills.

•Prescription prostaglandin inhibitors, for example, extra-strength ibuprofen or naproxyn.

•Drugs to reduce bloating, such as spironolactone (Aldactone).

•Danazol (Danocrine) for breast pain and mood swings.

•Calcium supplements for water retention, cramps, and back pain.

•Thyroid replacement therapy for any deficiency.

•Alprazolam (Xanax) and other Valium-type drugs ("benzodiaze-pines") for anxiety, and antidepressants for depression.

If you feel dissatisfied with any physician's approach to PMS, shop around until you find a doctor whose approach suits you.

TOXIC SHOCK SYNDROME

Toxic shock syndrome is a recently identified, potentially rapidly fatal bacterial infection that causes shock-like symptoms: sudden high fever, vomiting, diarrhea, rash, and a big drop in blood pressure which may cause liver and kidney failure, coma, and death.

What's Going On?   In the early 1980s, newspaper headlines sizzled with reports of several deaths among seemingly healthy women in the prime of life. For no apparent reason, they simply went into shock and died, sometimes within hours. Experts called the bizarre disease toxic shock syndrome (TSS) and began looking for anything that linked its victims. It didn't take long for authorities to discover that many women had been using a new superabsorbent tampon called Rely when they developed TSS. But even after the manufacturer withdrew the product, TSS cases and fatalities continued to mount, mostly in women who used other brands of superabsorbent tampons.

The tampon connection eventually led scientists to the cause of TSS, *Staphylococcus aureus,* a type of bacteria commonly found on the skin and in about 10 percent of women's vaginas. This microorganism produces a powerful toxin which causes severe shock-like symptoms when absorbed into the bloodstream through a cut or other wound or through the vaginal wall.

Researchers determined that in TSS the bacterial toxin enters the bloodstream via minute cracks in the vaginal wall caused by the drying effect of superabsorbent tampons or by the minor vaginal trauma caused by tampon insertion. Contraceptive sponges left in for longer than the manufacturer recommends have also been implicated in a few cases of TSS.

Most people with TSS have been menstruating women, but the syndrome can also strike nonmenstruating women, men, and children, usually after surgery or serious burns.

Before You Call the Doctor.   The best way to deal with TSS is to prevent it:
   • Use sanitary napkins instead of tampons.
   • If you use tampons, change them often—at least every four to six hours—and alternate with pads to allow for more natural vaginal drainage.
   • If you use tampons, don't use the superabsorbent variety. Use the lowest absorbency tampons that work for you. Selecting low-absorbency tampons should become easier because the Food and Drug Administra-

tion recently announced new regulations which require tampon makers to label their products' absorbency.

• Insert tampons carefully. Take care not to scratch the vaginal lining. If necessary, use a water-soluble vaginal lubricant (KY Jelly or Surgilube) and a nonapplicator-style or cardboard-applicator tampon.

• If you use a contraceptive sponge, follow the manufacturer's instructions carefully. Never leave it in for longer than twenty-four hours.

• If you've had TSS or have developed any TSS-like symptoms during your period, stop using tampons until your physician has taken a culture to determine whether or not you carry *Staphyloccus aureus* in your vagina.

▶ **RED FLAG**   If you develop a high fever with vomiting, diarrhea, and rash during your period, call your doctor *immediately*. TSS is a life-threatening medical emergency that requires immediate treatment to restore fallen blood pressure and prevent death.

Once diagnosed, TSS is treated with intravenous fluids and cortisone. Antibiotics help prevent recurrence, but even with antibiotics, recurrence rates as high as 30 percent have been documented.

UTERINE FIBROIDS

(See FIBROIDS in this chapter)

VAGINAL BURNING

(See also ATROPHIC VAGINITIS and YEAST INFECTION in this chapter, TRICHOMONAS and VENEREAL WARTS in Chapter 18, and PAINFUL INTERCOURSE in Chapter 19)

In addition to the causes mentioned above, vaginal burning may be caused by sensitivity to bubble bath, douching, or certain contraceptives: condoms, sponges, and spermicidal foam, cream, jelly, and suppositories. Stop using these items and see if your burning subides. If you douche regularly, stop (see DOUCHING in this chapter).

VAGINAL DISCHARGE

(See also ATROPHIC VAGINITIS, BACTERIAL VAGINOSIS, PEL-VIC PAIN, and YEAST INFECTIONS in this chapter and CHLA-MYDIA, GONORRHEA, and TRICHOMONAS in Chapter 18)

A certain amount of vaginal discharge is normal and healthy. But various vaginal discharges may also indicate disease.

What's Going On?   The amount of normal vaginal discharge varies from woman to woman, and in the same woman depending on her menstrual cycle and her stage of life. The normal discharge is composed of secretions and dead cells from the vaginal wall and of mucus produced by the cervix, the neck of the uterus which opens into the vagina. After menstrual flow ceases, this discharge is thick and clear or milky, but starting around the time of ovulation (about halfway between periods), it becomes thinner, more copious, and gooey and stretchy. As a woman's period approaches, the discharge becomes less copious and tacky. Women can use these cyclic changes in normal vaginal discharge as indicators of their monthly fertile and infertile days. In fact, these changes play a major role in the "fertility awareness" method of birth control (see FERTILITY AWARENESS in Chapter 19).

Many microorganisms normally grow in this warm moist environment, particularly *Lactobacillus* bacteria and yeast fungi. The *Lactobacillus* and the healthy vagina's slightly acid chemical environment prevent overgrowth of yeast and other bacteria, for example, *Gardnerella,* which cause bacterial vaginosis, and *E. coli,* which cause urinary tract infection.

Before You Call the Doctor.   Increased or altered discharge may indicate infection:

• A thick, curdy, white or yellow discharge with itching or burning is probably a yeast infection (see YEAST INFECTION in this chapter).

• A heavy gray or yellow discharge that smells fishy but is not accompanied by pain or itching usually indicates bacterial vaginosis (see BACTERIAL VAGINOSIS in this chapter).

• A slightly foamy or thick yellow or greenish discharge with vaginal burning or itching could be trichomonas (see TRICHOMONAS in Chapter 18).

• A greenish or brownish discharge, especially one associated with pelvic pain, could be a sexually transmitted infection (see PELVIC PAIN in this chapter and CHLAMYDIA and GONORRHEA in Chapter 18).

• A greenish or brownish discharge in a postmenopausal woman could be atrophic vaginitis (see ATROPHIC VAGINITIS in this chapter).

• A white or yellow discharge after intercourse that is not due to infection suggests sensitivity to rubber or spermicide.

• Several other conditions that require medical attention also cause unusual vaginal discharges—for example, inflammation of the cervix ("cervicitis").

When to Call the Doctor.   If you are unable to treat an abnormal discharge successfully using the information supplied here and elsewhere in this book within a week, consult a physician.

▶ **RED FLAGS**   If any vaginal discharge is accompanied by pelvic pain and fever, consult a physician immediately to rule out pelvic inflammatory disease (PID). A combination of unusual vaginal discharge and persistent pelvic pain—even without fever—should also be checked by a doctor. That, too, could be PID.

VAGINAL DRYNESS

(See also ATROPHIC VAGINITIS in this chapter)
Vaginal dryness makes intercourse uncomfortable and often painful.

What's Going On?   Dryness results from a decrease in vaginal secretions and natural lubrication during lovemaking. Sometimes "dryness" is illusory. Men, particularly young men, often become fully sexually aroused much more quickly than women. A man may feel ready and eager for intercourse before a woman has become sufficiently aroused to self-lubricate. Once she becomes sufficiently aroused, she self-lubricates normally and may enjoy intercourse without discomfort. Unfortunately, some men are unaware that women often need extra time and whole-body caresses to become fully aroused, and they may make unkind remarks or push their penises into vaginas not sufficiently lubricated to welcome them.

Vaginal dryness may also be caused by decreased estrogen production. This may occur if women take low-dose birth control pills, when they breastfeed, or after menopause (see ATROPHIC VAGINITIS in this chapter).

Before You Call the Doctor.   For dryness associated with rushed, nonsensual lovemaking, slow down and cultivate whole-body sensuality, which allows time for women (and men) to fully self-lubricate. Good sex requires good lubrication and pain-free intercourse. If slowing down and engaging in whole-body, massage-oriented lovemaking do not produce sufficient lubrication, try vegetable oil or a water-based commercial lubricant (KY Jelly, Surgilube, Astroglide).

For dryness caused by lactation, menopause, or birth control pills, see the self-care suggestions in the ATROPHIC VAGINITIS section of this chapter.

When to Call the Doctor.   See the discussion in the ATROPHIC VAGINITIS section of this chapter.

VAGINAL ITCHING

(See also ATROPHIC VAGINITIS, BACTERIAL VAGINOSIS, VAGINAL DISCHARGE, and YEAST INFECTION in this chapter and TRICHOMONAS in Chapter 18)
   Vaginal itching may occur externally, internally, or both.

What's Going On?   Vaginal itching is usually caused by infection (see ATROPHIC VAGINITIS, BACTERIAL VAGINOSIS, VAGINAL DISCHARGE, and YEAST INFECTION in this chapter and TRICHO-MONAS in Chapter 18). But if external itching occurs without the discharge and internal itching of the various kinds of vaginitis, the cause is usually a local reaction to detergents, synthetic-fabric underwear, soaps, or vaginal deodorant sprays. Also, after menopause some women develop an inflamed itchy condition with thinning and shrinkage of the external genitals ("lichen sclerosis et atrophicus"). In most cases, this condition is merely annoying and no threat to health. But it may eventually contribute to painful intercourse.

Before You Call the Doctor.   Change your soaps and detergents. Unscented brands are less likely to cause reactions.
   Stop using vaginal deodorants. They are unnecessary.
   Wear cotton underwear, and wear stockings or panty hose with a breathable cotton crotch panel.
   Itching can be temporarily relieved with cool baths or cold, wet compresses. It also helps to use ½ percent hydrocortisone cream, available over-the-counter (Cortaid and others). Apply it sparingly twice a day. Do not continue hydrocortisone indefinitely because of potentially permanent thinning of the skin in the area, which is more sensitive to steroid creams than the skin elsewhere around the body.

When to Call the Doctor.   If itching continues for more than two weeks, consult a physician. Simple inflammations may be treated temporarily with stronger steroid cream. After a history and physical examination, diagnostic tests may be necessary to determine the cause.

▶ **RED FLAG**   In a few cases of lichen sclerosis et atrophicus, white patches develop that may be precancerous. If you notice white patches on your inner or outer vaginal lips, consult a physician.

VAGINITIS

(See ATROPHIC VAGINITIS, BACTERIAL VAGINOSIS, VAGI-
NAL BURNING, VAGINAL DISCHARGE, VAGINAL ITCHING,
and YEAST INFECTION in this chapter and TRICHOMONAS in
Chapter 18)

YEAST INFECTION

Vaginal yeast infections, medically known as "monilia" or "candida vaginitis," develop when vaginal chemistry falls out of balance, allowing the
overgrowth of yeast fungi normally present in the vagina.

What's Going On?   At some point in life, the vast majority of women
suffer the thick, whitish discharge, labial redness, mild to severe itching,
and baking-bread odor of a yeast infection, caused by the common fungus
Candida albicans. Several factors can change vaginal chemistry, promoting
yeast overgrowth:

• Pregnancy. Hormonal changes during pregnancy alter vaginal acidity
and increase carbohydrate ("glycogen") production, which provides food
for yeast organisms. Approximately one-third of all pregnant women test
positive for *Candida*. Recurrent attacks are common among pregnant
women and may become increasingly frequent as the pregnancy progresses.

• Menstruation. Some women are particularly suceptible to yeast infections after their periods because cyclic hormonal changes and menstrual
flow alter the vaginal environment.

• Oral contraceptives. Birth control pills change the body's estrogen/
progesterone balance, increasing production of glycogen, a simple starch.
Studies show the Pill increases vaginal glycogen by 50 to 80 percent.
Although researchers haven't established a clear cause-and-effect relationship between birth control pills and yeast infections, the two are associated.

• IUDs. Intrauterine devices apparently decrease vaginal secretions,
creating a more favorable environment for fungal growth.

• Contraceptive sponge. This relatively new birth control method may
alter the vaginal environment, making some women more susceptible to
yeast infections.

• Antibiotics. Tetracycline, ampicillin, and other common antibiotics kill the vagina's *Lactobacillus* bacteria, allowing the *Candida* there to multiply. Tetracycline may actually stimulate yeast growth.

• High blood sugar. Sugar-rich blood promotes yeast growth, a possible problem for people with diabetes.

• High sugar diet. Dairy products and sugar may contribute to yeast infections. A high-sugar diet can alter the vaginal pH and provide food for yeast organisms.

• Tight clothing and tampons. Pantyhose, leotards, and other tight-fitting clothing that restricts air flow and contributes to heat and moisture buildup in the vaginal area encourage yeast growth. Feminine hygiene sprays, deodorant toilet paper, and commercial douches may irritate vaginal tissue and predispose women to yeast infections. Although no studies have directly linked tampon use and yeast infections, they tend to dry out vaginal tissues and may irritate the vagina.

Before You Call the Doctor. Although few studies confirm these reports, some women say they cure yeast infections with the following home treatments:

• Vinegar douche. At the first sign of infection, try douching with a mild solution of one to three tablespoons vinegar to one quart of water. However, don't douche routinely. Douching increases the risk of serious, potentially fertility- and life-threatening infection of the reproductive organs ("pelvic inflammatory disease") (see DOUCHING in this chapter).

• Eat one cup of plain yogurt with live *Lactobacillus acidophilus* culture daily. One recent study shows that this traditional folk approach does, indeed, help prevent recurrent yeast infections. Unfortunately, few yogurt brands contain live cultures; those that do say so on the label. These brands are usually available at health food stores.

• *Lactobacillus* capsules or granules. Some women find relief by inserting one or two into the vagina daily. Increasing the population of these good vaginal bacteria may normalize the vaginal ecology and control *Candida* overgrowth. *Lactobacillus* tablets are available over-the-counter. A similar approach recommends douching with a dilute mixture of plain yogurt and warm water. If the yogurt contains "live culture" *Lactobacillus* bacteria, it would provide the same benefit as *Lactobacillus* tablets. But we recommend against yogurt douches. The yogurt provides food for the yeast, which may cancel out any benefit, and douching is potentially hazardous, as explained above. Stick to *Lactobacillus* capsules or granules. They may also be taken orally to repopulate the intestinal tract and, thereby, the vagina.

• Antifungal mouthwash. Once the infection has cleared up, women who have frequent oral sex and suffer from recurrent yeast infections may find relief by having their partners use an antifungal mouthwash. Others suggest an antifungal cream around the anus and between the anus and vagina to eliminate any spread to the vagina.

• Antifungal vaginal creams. Miconazole (Monistat) and clotrimazole (GyneLotrimin), formerly prescription drugs, recently became available over-the-counter. If you've had yeast infections before and recognize the typical itch and discharge, you'll be relieved to know that you can start treatment without the hassle of another doctor visit. Be sure to use the full course to minimize the risk of recurrence.

Several self-care strategies can also help prevent yeast infection recurrences:

• Decrease your sugar intake.

• Adjust your contraception. If you're using oral contraceptives, try a barrier method. Consider having your IUD removed. Replace your diaphragm or cervical cap during a course of anti-yeast treatment because of the possibility of yeast spores remaining on the device.

• Microwave your cotton underwear. Get them wet, wring them out well, and place them in a microwave oven on high for thirty seconds. This kills any yeasts in them.

• Alternatively, wash all your underwear with chlorine bleach. Follow package directions.

When to Call the Doctor.   Physicians usually treat yeast infections with any of three medications: nystatin, miconazole, or clotrimazole. Newer anti-yeast medications, such as terconazole and butoconazole, don't offer any advantages over the older medications, except that the treatment course is shorter.

Male sex partners may reinfect some women. Even men who have no symptoms may harbor yeast organisms, especially in the foreskin of an uncircumsized penis. They should be encouraged to wash thoroughly and use an antifungal cream on their genitals. Condoms also help prevent transmission. If you feel embarrassed asking a partner to use a condom, listen to the excellent audio tape "How to Talk to a Partner About Smart Sex" (see RESOURCES at the end of Chapter 19). It includes witty comebacks to prospective lovers who don't want to use them.

For persistent or recurrent yeast infections, try these suggestions:

• Use prescription medication for a longer period of time, even during menstruation. Ask your physician for an open prescription for vaginal cream or suppositories.

• Use an antifungal cream or suppositories for a few days before and/or after your period.

• Use vaginal antifungal medications during and for several days after taking antibiotics.

• Discontinue oral contraceptives.

• Apply antifungal cream to your vulva and your partner's genitals twice daily for ten days.

▶ **RED FLAG**   Women who suffer from recurrent yeast infections may have high blood sugar and not know it. High blood sugar often means diabetes or a prediabetic condition. Women with recurrent yeast infections should be tested for diabetes.

RESOURCES

The MammaCare Method of Breast Self-Exam. Contact the Mammatech Corporation, 900 N.W. 8th Ave., Gainesville, FL 32601; 1-(800)-MAM-CARE. MammaCare is a new-and-improved approach to breast self-exam. It's easy to learn and gives women new confidence in their ability to self-detect breast abnormalities. Studies show that those trained in the MammaCare method can identify small, early-stage breast tumors significantly better than those trained in other methods of breast self-exam. As a result, MammaCare is now widely used to train physicians in breast examination. A home training kit includes an instruction video and lifelike breast models.

Premenstrual Syndrome Action. P.O. Box 16292 Irvine, CA 92713; (714) 854-4407. Provides information and publications to both physicians and the public.

CHAPTER 17

Men's Health

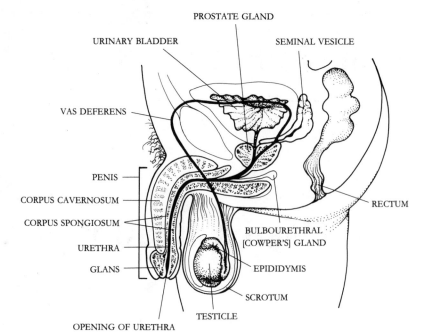

PROSTATE GLAND

URINARY BLADDER

SEMINAL VESICLE

VAS DEFERENS

PENIS

CORPUS CAVERNOSUM

CORPUS SPONGIOSUM

URETHRA

GLANS

RECTUM

BULBOURETHRAL
[COWPER'S] GLAND

EPIDIDYMIS

SCROTUM

TESTICLE

OPENING OF URETHRA

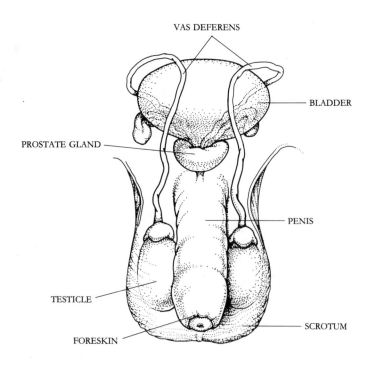

VAS DEFERENS

BLADDER

PROSTATE GLAND

PENIS

TESTICLE

SCROTUM

FORESKIN

The Male Reproductive System.

BLOOD IN SEMEN

(See also DISCHARGE FROM THE PENIS, PAIN IN THE GROIN OR TESTICLES, and PROSTATITIS in this chapter and NONSPECIFIC URETHRITIS in Chapter 18)

Blood in semen usually appears as brown or red dots. It may occur without pain, with pain on ejaculation, or with pain or swelling in the testicles.

What's Going On?   The male genital tract is one continuous tube from the testicles, where sperm are produced, to the opening at the tip of the penis, where semen and urine leave the body. Irritation or infection anywhere along this tube can introduce blood into semen.

Before You Call the Doctor.   Many men notice small amounts of blood in their semen from time to time. If this occurs without pain—including low-back pain, which might indicate a prostate problem—it's usually no cause for concern. Most minor irritations clear up on their own. Some men develop swollen veins in the structures that produce some of the fluid in semen ("seminal vesicles"), which bleed harmlessly once in a while.

Increase your fluid intake to flush your urinary system.

When to Call the Doctor.   Consult a physician if bleeding increases, or if you develop pain on ejaculation or pain or difficulty urinating. The cause is usually a prostate or urinary tract infection, which are treated with antibiotics.

BLUE BALLS

(See PAIN IN THE GROIN OR TESTICLES in this chapter)

BREAST SWELLING

Men don't pay much attention to their breasts, but they have breast tissue, and sometimes it causes problems.

What's Going On?   Some breast swelling in adolescent boys, with possible tenderness, is a normal part of puberty.

Breast swelling in adult men ("gynecomastia") is usually a side effect of prescription medication, but it may also be caused by liver disease, hormonal disorders, occupational exposure to female sex hormones, or even possibly breast cancer, which each year strikes about 900 men, usually those over age sixty.

When to Call the Doctor.   Men should consult a physician for any breast swelling.

CIRCUMCISION

Circumcision means surgical removal of the foreskin, the flap of tissue that covers the head ("glans") of the soft ("flaccid") penis.

What's Going On?   Circumcision has been practiced for thousands of years by many cultures around the world. Today it's the most frequently performed surgical procedure in the United States. It's also among the most controversial.

Advocates claim the operation helps prevent urinary tract infections, penile cancer, and sexually transmitted diseases while causing only minor side effects—easily treatable bleeding and minor infections. They also say it has no effect on the sexual sensitivity of the head of the penis. Opponents counter that proper washing of the foreskin confers the same medical benefits, that side effects can be more serious—copious bleeding, significant infection, and injury to the head of the penis—and that the head of the circumcised penis loses some sexual sensitivity as a result of the operation.

Authorities estimate that about one-quarter of the world's men are circumcised, but in recent decades, the practice has fallen from fashion in Europe and been attacked as unnecessary in the United States. Before 1975, the vast majority of U.S. pediatricians endorsed circumcision as beneficial to men's health. But in that year the American Academy of Pediatrics (AAP) issued a position paper arguing that the procedure was medically unnecessary, and the professional pendulum began to swing against it. Research continued, and in 1989, the AAP backed off from official opposition to circumcision based on studies suggesting that it may, indeed, have the medical benefits its supporters had long cited. On the other hand, the Academy still does not recommend routine circumcision.

No doubt, the authorities will continue to debate circumcision's medical pros and cons, but the fact is, most parents' circumcision decisions have nothing to do with their sons' risk of penile cancer and urinary tract infections. Jews and Muslims circumcise for religious reasons, which have nothing to do with its possible health benefits and side effects. And most other people who choose to have newborn boys circumcised do so because the father is circumcised and they want the son's penis to look like his father's.

The latest research on circumcision is that uncircumcised boys are somewhat more likely to suffer urinary tract infections, kidney infections ("pyelonephritis"), sexually transmitted diseases, and penile cancer, which affects about 1,000 American men a year and causes 275 deaths annually. Most of these problems can be prevented by careful penile hygiene, but the current consensus is that some risk remains:

Circumcision can be performed at any age, but the older the man, the more expensive the procedure. Newborn circumcision costs about $200. In teens and adults, it can cost more than $2,000.

U.S. circumcision rates have fallen since the 1975 report. It's still too early to tell what effect, if any, the AAP's 1989 reconsideration will have. As this book goes to press, the majority of newborn American boys continue to be circumcised.

In uncircumcised infants, the foreskin typically does not retract. But by age three it usually becomes retractable.

Before You Call the Doctor.   Pregnant couples should discuss this issue before their babies are born. In the final analysis, circumcision is a personal decision.

If you opt to leave the foreskin intact, teach your sons to retract it when they bathe and wash the inside of the foreskin and the head of the penis. This helps prevent infection and unpleasant odor and, when men become sexually active, the spread of sexually transmitted diseases.

When to Call the Doctor.   For more information about circumcision, ask your pediatrician.

▶ **RED FLAG**   Sometimes the foreskin in uncircumcised boys remains tightly constricted and does not retract over the head of the penis ("phimosis"). If phimosis persists after age five, erection can be painful and proper hygiene becomes impossible. Phimosis may also develop in adult men with chronic inflammation of the head of the penis ("balanitis") due to yeast or bacterial infection. Physicians relieve phimosis by circumcision.

DISCHARGE FROM THE PENIS

(See also BLOOD IN SEMEN and PROSTATITIS in this chapter and CHLAMYDIA, GONORRHEA, and NONSPECIFIC URETHRITIS in Chapter 18)

Any liquid—other than urine, semen, and pre-ejaculatory fluid—which comes out of the penis is a discharge. Discharges may occur with or without pain and be clear, greenish-yellow (pus), or bloody.

What's Going On?   The normal healthy penis produces no discharges, so any discharge means something is wrong somewhere in the genitourinary tract.

Before You Call the Doctor.   A slippery, clear fluid discharge which emerges during sexual arousal and causes no pain is probably pre-ejaculatory fluid or possibly semen. It's no cause for concern. Occasionally, a small amount of pre-ejaculatory fluid or semen may be discharged independent of sexual arousal. This, too, is normal.

When to Call the Doctor.   Consult a physician for:
• Painless discharge of any semen-like fluid which persists longer than one week.
• Any discharge of pus, whether or not it causes pain. Pus means infection—typically either prostatitis or a sexually transmitted disease.
• Any discharge of blood, whether or not it causes pain. Blood may be a sign of infection, an injury, or other problems.
• Any unusual discharge that doesn't clear up by itself in a day or two.

▶ **RED FLAG**   Consult a physician promptly for any painful discharge of pus or blood with fever, low back pain, malaise, or other unusual symptoms.

FORESKIN THAT WON'T RETRACT

(See CIRCUMCISION in this chapter)

LUMP IN THE TESTICLES

Any lump in the testicles should be examined by a physician.

What's Going On?   This is particularly true for *painless* lumps, which might be testicular cancer. Testicular cancer accounts for only about 1 percent of the cancers in men, but it's one of the most common cancers in men under thirty years of age. In recent years, testicular cancer has become quite treatable, with a ten-year survival rate of 85 percent—but only if it's diagnosed early.

On the other hand, most painless testicular lumps are *not* cancer. They may be any of several noncancerous growths: a fluid pocket ("hydrocele"), a sperm cyst ("spermatocele"), a varicose vein ("varicocele"), or a hernia within the scrotum (see HERNIA in Chapter 13).

Painful lumps suggest inflammation, infection, or possibly the conditions listed in the previous paragraph, which are usually painless but may, in some cases, cause pain.

Before You Call the Doctor.   The American Cancer Society urges all men to practice testicular self-exam monthly so they can detect the painless lumps that might be testicular cancer. Self-exam is particularly important for young men aged fifteen to thirty-five, because most testicular cancer strikes this age group.

The best place to examine your testicles is in the shower. Gently roll each testicle between your thumb and fingers. The testicles feel firm but slightly spongy, with a spongier area toward the rear, which is the collection of coiled sperm-storage tubes ("epididymis").

When to Call the Doctor.   If you feel a hard, painless, lump, nodule, or swelling, consult a physician promptly. None of the conditions which cause lumps in the testicles can be treated effectively at home, but physicians can treat all of them successfully—even testicular cancer if it's diagnosed early.

PAIN IN THE GROIN OR TESTICLES

(See also PROSTATITIS in this chapter, HERNIA in Chapter 13, and MUSCLE STRAINS in Chapter 15)

The pain may be sharp or dull and come on gradually or suddenly.

What's Going On?   In addition to prostatitis, hernia, or muscle strain, several other conditions may cause testicular pain:

• "Blue balls." This is the popular term for the dull aching caused by unreleased sexual arousal. Prolonged sexual excitement without ejaculation can leave the testicles feeling tender and achy.

• Epididymitis. The epididymis is the collection of sperm-storage tubes behind the testicles. This inflammation feels distinctly painful, as opposed to the dull aching of blue balls.

• Testicular torsion. Unusual rotation of a testicle can cut off its blood supply and cause considerable pain.

Before You Call the Doctor.   The traditional remedy for blue balls is a cold shower, but other approaches work better:

• Masturbate. The aching subsides shortly after sexual tensions have been released.

• Take a warm bath. As the body relaxes, the discomfort usually subsides.

When to Call the Doctor.   Consult a physician if you develop pain in the testicles. Epididymitis and testicular torsion require professional evaluation and treatment. Testicular torsion is an emergency requiring prompt surgery to prevent gangrene and save the testicle.

▶ **RED FLAGS**   Consult a physician promptly if:

• Discomfort does not subside within forty-eight hours.

• The dull ache becomes a sharper pain.

• The scrotum swells.

PAIN ON EJACULATION

(See PROSTATITIS in this chapter)

PAINFUL ERECTION

(See CIRCUMCISION in this chapter)

In addition to foreskin problems, other causes of painful erection include scar tissue in the penis and persistent erection that is not associated with sexual arousal ("priapism"). Priapism may be caused by sickle cell anemia, certain cancers (for example, leukemia), and a few prescription medications (for example, testosterone). These conditions cannot be self-treated, but they can be treated by urologists.

PENIS SIZE

Surveys show that most men consider their penises "too small."

What's Going On?   Concerns about penis size rank among the most frequently asked questions received by the *Playboy* Advisor, the nation's most widely read sexual advice column for men. And a survey by *Forum* magazine showed that "almost all respondents, with the exception of only the most extraordinarily endowed, expressed doubts about their sexuality based on their penile size."

Surveys of women show that few care about penis size, and those who do consider it much less important than a man's ability to listen, care, negotiate, compromise, be playful, share interests, and have a sense of humor. Nonetheless, most men would still like an extra inch or two, and the male-oriented sex magazines advertise devices which claim to be "penis enlargers."

For the record: The average soft ("flaccid") penis is three inches long when warm, and shorter when cold. The average erection measures about six inches. The vast majority of erections are about the same size. The smaller the flaccid penis, the greater the growth to erection. The larger the flaccid penis, the less the growth to erection.

When a man of average height compares himself to the average professional basketball player, he feels smaller, but not necessarily inferior because he knows that basketball players are unusually tall, and that most men are about his height. He has a basis for comparison. But when a man compares his penis to other men's he has considerably less basis for comparison. In locker rooms, men look *down* at their own penises but *across* at everyone else's. This difference in perspective makes a man's own penis look comparatively small, especially if he already believes he's "too small" to begin with.

The sex media compound the problem. It seems that every man who recounts his sexual exploits in the men's magazines has a telephone pole between his legs. Most men's magazine readers have no idea that these accounts are fiction.

Then there's pornography. Men see other men's penises in locker rooms, but most heterosexual men rarely, if ever, see other penises up close or erect. The only penises the average heterosexual man ever examines up close are those in pornography—penises selected to be unusually large to begin with, then magnified to truly awesome proportions with up-from-under photography. In other words, virtually every penis the average heterosexual man has an opportunity to examine closely looks a good deal larger than his own. After a few years of exposure to the sex media, a man is justified in concluding that he has one of the smallest penises he's ever seen.

Before You Call the Doctor. Forget the penis enlargers advertised in men's magazines. They are a case study in consumer fraud. The penis cannot be mechanically enlarged.

However, you *can* make the most of what you've got:

• Undress where it's warm. Temperature affects the "hang" of the penis and scrotum, particularly the scrotum, which hangs outside the body because the best temperature for sperm production is a few degrees cooler than body temperature. The warmer the scrotum, the looser it hangs. When it's cold, the scrotum hugs the body for warmth. The penis also reacts to temperature and hangs longer and fuller in a warm environment.

• Take a warm bath or shower before lovemaking. This helps warm the penis and scrotum. It's also relaxing, which enhances lovemaking.

• Stop worrying about penis size. Beyond physical warmth, the key to penis size is relaxation. When flaccid or erect, penis size depends on blood volume contained in its internal spongy tissues. The more blood, the larger the penis. Blood circulates through the penis all the time. When a man feels relaxed, blood tends to accumulate in the central body, which includes the genitals. However, fear or anxiety can trigger the body's "fight-or-flight" reflex, which directs blood away from the central body and out toward the limbs in preparation for self-defense or escape. Anxiety about penis size can initiate the fight-or-flight reflex, draining blood from the penis and, in effect, shrinking it.

When to Call the Doctor. A few men have extremely small penises due to hormonal or congenital disorders. Some of these problems may respond to treatment. If not, the man should have professional counseling.

PHIMOSIS

(See CIRCUMCISION in this chapter)

PROBLEMS WITH URINATION

(See PROSTATE ENLARGEMENT and PROSTATITIS in this chapter and DIFFICULT URINATION, EXCESSIVELY FREQUENT URI-

NATION, PAINFUL URINATION, URINARY INCONTINENCE, and URINARY TRACT INFECTION in Chapter 14)

PROSTATE ENLARGEMENT

Medically known as "benign prostatic hypertrophy" or BPH, this condition causes urinary difficulties: the feeling that you must urinate immediately ("urgency"), difficulty getting started ("hesitancy"), decreased flow, scant production, difficulty finishing ("dribbling"), and having to get up one or more times at night ("nocturia").

What's Going On? The prostate is a plum-sized, doughnut-shaped gland that sits a few inches above the rectum and produces some of the fluid in semen. The urine tube ("urethra") passes through the doughnut hole.

Most organs shrink with age, but for reasons that remain unclear, after about age forty, the prostate starts growing again. This growth may be prostate cancer, which is why men over forty years of age should have regular professional prostate exams, but it's usually noncancerous, or benign. As the prostate grows, its central doughnut hole shrinks, which pinches the urethra and causes all the urinary problems listed above. BPH symptoms occur in more than half of men by age fifty-five and in about 75 percent of men by age eighty.

Before You Call the Doctor. BPH can neither be prevented nor stopped once its symptoms begin to develop. However, it often helps to steer clear of certain medications that can make it worse: cold formulas and various drugs for ulcers, irritable bowel syndrome, depression, and high blood pressure ("hypertension"). If you're a man over fifty with BPH symptoms and take any of these medications, ask your pharmacist if they might aggravate BPH symptoms, and, if they do, whether other drugs might be substituted.

When to Call the Doctor. The most annoying aspect of BPH is the necessity to get up at night. Most men can live with getting up once or twice, but at a certain point, interrupted sleep interferes with quality of life, and men with BPH decide to have the condition treated.

Until quite recently, the only treatment for BPH was surgery, a procedure called a "transurethral resection of the prostate" or TURP. Entering the prostate through the urethra, the surgeon uses a flexible tube ("resectoscope") to snip away overgrown prostate tissues, allowing the urethra to return to its normal diameter. TURP is routine surgery, but it typically requires three days of hospitalization and a two-week recovery period.

The prostate tissue that's removed is then biopsied for cancer—and pathologists discover cancer in about 10 percent of cases. Fortunately, prostate cancer usually responds to treatment, and urolgists view TURPs as good cancer-screening opportunities.

TURPs typically provide long-term relief of BPH symptoms, but they cause erection impairment in about 10 percent of men (see ERECTION PROBLEMS in Chapter 19), and 60 to 70 percent of men lose the ability to ejaculate out the penis. Their orgasms remain as pleasurable as ever, but they ejaculate into the bladder ("retrograde ejaculation" or "dry orgasm").

Recently, several alternatives to TURPs have been introduced. Two nonsurgical drug treatments—finasteride and terazosin—are being tested, as are surgical procedures using ultrasound, balloons, and heat. As this book goes to press, these new treatments remain experimental, and TURP continues to be the standard of care. But BPH treatments are evolving rapidly. If you're getting tired of getting up at night, ask your urologist about recent advances in BPH therapy as well as TURP.

▶ **RED FLAG**   Consult a physician immediately if you experience any inability to urinate or any dramatic decrease in urinary ability.

PROSTATE SYNDROME

(See PROSTATITIS in this chapter)

PROSTATITIS

Prostatitis means inflammation of the prostate, the plum-sized gland a few inches above the rectum. Prostatitis causes pain or discomfort in the area behind the scrotum, and it frequently causes low-back pain and pain on urination or ejaculation. Fever, a general ill feeling ("malaise"), difficult urination, and a bloody or pus discharge are also possible.

What's Going On?   The prostate produces a good deal of the fluid in semen. It's a donut-shaped gland, and the urine tube ("urethra") passes through the donut hole. The prostate typically becomes infected when bacteria travel up the urethra into it. The infection produces pain or discomfort as well as fever and general malaise. The prostate also becomes swollen, which constricts the urethra and causes urinary difficulties.

The prostate can also become inflamed without bacterial infection. The major symptom is pain behind the scrotum or in the lower back. Chronic or recurrent pain in those areas, frequently mislabeled "chronic prostatitis," may actually be a condition called "prostate syndrome" or "prostatodynia," which simply means prostate pain with minimal inflammation. The pain and associated vague urinary problems result from excess tension in the pelvic floor muscles and/or congestion in the prostate gland itself. Prostate syndrome may begin with an episode of true prostatitis, but repeat episodes are often triggered by emotional stress.

Before You Call the Doctor.   Prostate infection requires professional diagnosis and antibiotics. But prostatodynia usually responds to self-care:

• Try hot baths, which help relax the muscles in the area and improve circulation.

• Eliminate chocolate, alcohol, tomato products, and caffeine (coffee, tea, colas, coffee-flavored items, and many over-the-counter drugs).

• Do Kegel exercises (see URINARY INCONTINENCE in Chapter 14).

• Practice stress-management techniques (see MANAGE YOUR STRESS LOAD in Chapter 1).

• Ejaculate frequently through lovemaking or masturbation.

• Take over-the-counter pain relievers: aspirin, acetaminophen, or ibuprofen. Aspirin and ibuprofen may cause stomach upset and should not be used by those with a history of ulcers or other gastrointestinal problems unless a doctor recommends it.

When to Call the Doctor.   Consult a physician if pain and any urinary difficulties do not improve significantly after a few days of self-treatment, if symptoms grow more severe, or if you develop a fever in addition to pain. Physicians treat prostatitis with antibiotics, and they generally recommend observation, pain relievers, and self-care for prostate syndrome, though some also prescribe muscle relaxants.

PROSTATODYNIA

(See PROSTATITIS in this chapter)

SWOLLEN TESTICLES

(See LUMP IN THE TESTICLES in this chapter)

CHAPTER 18

Sexually Transmitted Diseases

AIDS

AIDS stands for "acquired immune deficiency syndrome." It usually begins with weight loss, fever, night sweats, unusual infections, and/or a particular form of pneumonia. It progresses to collapse of the immune system and eventually death. Although AIDS is becoming more treatable, as this book goes to press, average life expectancy after diagnosis of full-blown AIDS is about three years, and few people survive longer than seven.

What's Going On? By the end of 1991, the World Health Organization estimated that more than 375,000 people worldwide had AIDS and that at least 5 million were infected with the human immunodeficiency virus (HIV) that causes it. WHO projects 40-million HIV-infected individuals by the year 2000.

Scientists believe AIDS originated in African green monkeys and spread to humans through bites or blood-to-blood contact. Examinations of the remains of people who died of mysterious causes in Africa, Europe, and the United States show that AIDS caused deaths as early as 1959. But the disease did not become a public health problem until 1981, when it was first identified in a cluster of gay sex partners in New York and Los Angeles. Since then, it has spread around the world, becoming the most serious new infectious disease identified in the late twentieth century.

HIV attacks and destroys certain white blood cells ("lymphocytes") known as "CD4 positive cells," "T4 cells," "T-helper cells," or simply "T cells," turning them into microscopic factories that churn out more virus. These white blood cells are crucial to the immune system, which protects the body from disease. Once HIV destroys these critical immune-system components, the body is open to all sorts of infections that people with healthy immune systems can easily fend off. These "opportunistic infections" may eventually cause death. Other AIDS-related causes of death include certain types of cancer and wasting away, which is apparently caused by the viral infection itself. HIV can also attack other types of immune cells as well as nerve cells, including those in the brain, causing loss of memory and other cognitive functions ("AIDS dementia").

It may take five to ten years for those infected with the AIDS virus to develop any symptoms of the disease ("incubation period"). They seem healthy but can spread the virus sexually or through blood-to-blood contact, particularly if they are intravenous (I.V.) drug users who share needles.

Fortunately, HIV cannot be transmitted by casual contact such as hugging or shaking hands with those who are infected, known medically as being "HIV-positive." AIDS experts say the virus spreads in only three ways: blood-to-blood contact, mother-to-fetus contact, and sexually. The most efficient method of transmission is through blood contact, which explains why intravenous drug users who share needles run such a high risk of contracting AIDS. In the U.S., I.V. drug users represent 21 percent of AIDS cases. Risk of infection from just one injection with an AIDS-contaminated needle is quite high. However, the amount of blood involved is also important. Health workers' risk of infection after an accidental stick with an AIDS-contaminated needle is less than one in 100 (about 0.4 percent). And the risk of infection during surgery by an HIV-infected surgeon is much less, about 1 in 84,000, approximately the risk of death from an automobile accident while driving to the hospital for the operation, and considerably less than the risk of death from general anesthesia complications.

Mother-to-fetus exposure is the second most efficient method of HIV transmission. An estimated one-third to one-half of babies born to HIV-positive mothers are infected. Few live beyond their second birthdays.

The risk of contracting the AIDS virus through one episode of unprotected sexual contact is about 1 percent. Condoms reduce that risk considerably but do not eliminate it entirely. The most hazardous type of lovemaking is anal intercourse, with the receiving partner at greatest risk, but any unprotected sexual contact can spread the virus.

Public hysteria about AIDS has fostered a number of myths about its transmission. Here's the truth:

• *Anyone can become infected with the AIDS virus.* Gay and bisexual men, I.V. drug users, children of I.V. drug–using mothers, and hemophiliacs are at highest risk, but the virus can be transmitted by heterosexual sex. Among heterosexuals, those at highest risk are women partners of I.V. drug users and bisexual men. But anyone can become infected, so everyone should learn how to protect themselves and take recommended precautions.

• *AIDS cannot be transmitted through casual contact.* HIV does not enter the body across intact skin and cannot be transmitted by touching, shaking hands, sharing utensils, living in the same household, or by being sneezed or coughed upon by an infected individual. The virus cannot be spread through tears, in showers or bath tubs, or on toilet seats, water fountains, phones, drinking glasses, or food touched by an HIV-infected individual. There is no evidence that AIDS can be spread by mosquitoes.

• *Wet kissing is controversial.* The AIDS virus has been detected in saliva, but its concentration is very low, too low according to many authorities to pose a threat of transmission. No study has ever shown kissing, even

"French-kissing" with exchange of saliva, to be a possible route of transmission. However, because the virus may be found in saliva, most AIDS groups list wet kissing as "risky." To be absolutely safe, don't do it with anyone who might be infected, especially if you have a cut or sore in your mouth.

• *You cannot become infected by donating blood.* Needles and equipment used in collection are disposable and never used more than once.

• *A history of other sexually transmitted diseases increases the risk of AIDS.* Other sexual infections injure the genital tract, increasing the likelihood of viral contact with blood.

• *Testing negative is no guarantee that people are not infected.* They could have become infected since they were tested. And people recently infected may test negative. It takes a few months for the infection to show up reliably in the current test.

Before You Call the Doctor. The only way to protect yourself from AIDS is to make sure you don't become infected. That means taking prevention and safe sex seriously in every sexual encounter with every sexual partner.

• Get to know sex partners before you have any intimate contact with them. Don't simply ask if they're infected. Many studies have shown that a considerable proportion of the public is less than truthful about their sexual histories. Get to know any potential partner well. Some authorities recommend not sleeping with anyone until you've met some of their friends and family members. Of course, when you have intercourse with another person is up to you, but AIDS authorities say careful partner selection is the single most important way to remain AIDS-free.

• If you feel embarrassed about raising the subject of AIDS or other sexually transmitted diseases, listen to the excellent audio tape "How to Talk to a Partner About Smart Sex" (see RESOURCES at the end of this chapter). This sixty-minute tape uses actors to play out the conversations many people find so intimidating. It also includes many witty come-backs to prospective lovers who don't want to use condoms.

• Limit your number of sexual partners. The fewer lovers you have, the fewer you have to worry about.

• During sexual intercourse, always use latex rubber condoms—not "skins" made of animal membrane. Latex condoms largely prevent transmission of the AIDS virus but do not provide perfect protection even when used properly. Skin condoms are less effective AIDS preventives.

• Oil-based lubricants, such as petroleum jelly or mineral oil, may cause condom deterioration. Use a water-based lubricant (KY jelly).

• Use spermicidal jellies and creams with nonoxynol-9 for extra protection. Studies show that nonoxynol-9 decreases the likelihood of AIDS infection if a condom breaks.

• Don't engage in unprotected mouth contact with the penis, vagina, or anus.

• Don't engage in extremely vigorous or unusual sexual activities that might cause cuts or tears in the penis, vagina, or rectum.

• Never use I.V. drugs. If you do, *never* share needles.

For free, confidential information about AIDS, call the National AIDS Hotline (see RESOURCES at the end of this chapter).

When to Call the Doctor.   AIDS cannot be cured. But drugs such as AZT, also called zidovudine (Retrovir), and antibiotics to prevent or control infections can improve quality of life and extend the lives of those who are infected. When used before symptoms develop, AIDS drugs can also postpone the onset of the disease. If you think you may have been exposed to the AIDS virus, get tested immediately. If you're HIV-positive, prompt treatment may postpone the disease. Knowing you're infected also allows you to take extra precautions to prevent transmitting the virus.

The AIDS test is an inexpensive blood test, the "enzyme-linked immunosorbent assay" or ELISA. A positive test is usually repeated to ensure accuracy. If the second test is positive, usually a more specific test, the Western blot, is performed to confirm the positive result.

AIDS testing is conducted confidentially and, in many communities, anonymously. You are identified not by name, only by a number, and no records are kept. Check with your county health department if you are concerned about insurance or employment problems that might arise if you are tested by your regular doctor. You can also call the National AIDS Hotline for other information about AIDS testing and anything having to do with HIV infection.

CHLAMYDIA

Chlamydia (pronounced kla-MID-ee-ah) is one of the most prevalent, yet least-publicized sexually transmitted disease. Four million Americans develop it annually. Chlamydia's initial symptoms, if any occur, are usually minor. But if this insidious infection remains untreated, it can threaten both men's and women's fertility, and women's very lives.

What's Going On?   Public health authorities consider chlamydia responsible for up to 50 percent of the cases of pelvic inflammatory disease (PID), a potentially life-threatening infection of women's reproductive organs and a major cause of fertility problems. In men, chlamydia is now considered responsible for more than half of nonspecific urethritis (NSU) infections (see NONSPECIFIC URETHRITIS in this chapter).

Chlamydia is caused by a virus-like bacterium called *Chlamydia trachomatis*. Like a bacterium, this microorganism has a cellular structure and can be killed with antibiotics. Like a virus, it depends on its human host for reproduction.

Chlamydia is usually spread by direct contact during vaginal or anal intercourse with an infected person. Occasionally, it is transmitted through eye secretions or from mother to child during birth. Doctors are still unsure whether or not chlamydia can be passed during oral sex.

When symptoms develop, they usually begin seven to fourteen days after exposure, although some people don't develop symptoms for several weeks.

An estimated 80 percent of women show no symptoms until the infection progresses to pelvic inflammatory disease (PID). PID often requires hospitalization and causes fertility impairment in up to 40 percent of cases. Among women who develop symptoms, the most common is a vaginal discharge. Other possible symptoms include painful urination, vaginal bleeding, bleeding after sex, and lower abdominal pain.

In men, the first symptom is a clear or whitish penile discharge, which may gradually disappear. This does not mean the infection has disappeared. Sometimes chlamydia also causes painful urination in men. In untreated men, the infection may progress into the testicles and impair fertility.

Based on available epidemiological data, you're at highest risk for chlamydia if you:
- Are a white male fifteen to twenty-four years of age.
- Have sex with multiple partners.
- Use oral contraceptives.
- Use an intrauterine device (IUD).

Before You Call the Doctor. If you're at risk for chlamydia, learn its symptoms, and don't delay seeking treatment for any unusual genital discharge or pelvic pain.

Men who notice a discharge have a special responsibility to encourage all their sex partners to get tested for chlamydia because of its potential severity in women.

Condoms usually prevent transmission. Use them. If you feel embarrassed suggesting condoms, listen to the excellent audio tape "How to Talk to a Partner About Smart Sex" (see RESOURCES at the end of this chapter). It includes many witty come-backs to prospective lovers who don't want to use condoms.

When to Call the Doctor.   Consult a physician for any unusual genital discharge or pelvic pain. Until a few years ago, chlamydia was difficult to detect. But recently, fast and accurate tests have been developed. If you're diagnosed with chlamydia, the treatment is tetracycline or another antibiotic. Pregnant women should be given erythromycin because tetracycline can stain the teeth of the developing fetus. *Both partners must be treated to avoid reinfection.* Partners should be treated whether or not they have symptoms. As with any antibiotic treatment, it's important to take all the prescribed medication, even if symptoms clear up before the end of the treatment course. During treatment, abstain from sexual intercourse.

If you are diagnosed with chlamydia, ask your doctor to test for gonorrhea and syphilis as well (see GONORRHEA and SYPHILIS in this chapter). Women should also have Pap smears to check for HPV infection (see VENEREAL WARTS in this chapter).

CONDYLOMA ACUMINATA

(See VENEREAL WARTS in this chapter)

GONORRHEA

In most men, gonorrhea causes burning pain on urination and a pus discharge from the penis. Women often develop no symptoms. But if women remain untreated, gonorrhea can cause pelvic inflammatory disease (PID), a potentially life-threatening infection of women's reproductive organs and a major cause of fertility problems.

What's Going On?   Gonorrhea is medically known as "GC" and colloquially as "the clap." More than 1.4 million cases are reported in the United States each year. Caused by the *Gonococcus* bacteria, gonorrhea is transmitted only sexually. The bacteria die a few moments after exposure to air, so the infection cannot be transmitted on toilet seats or through any other form of contact.

Gonorrhea can infect the throat ("gonococcal pharyngitis"), the rectum ("gonococcal proctitis"), the eyes ("gonococcal conjunctivitis"), and occasionally, it may even enter the circulatory system, becoming a "disseminated gonococcal infection," which may infect the heart valves and/or cause destructive arthritis.

In most men, gonorrhea symptoms are hard to miss: a thick, pus-like discharge from the penis, inflamed urethra, and burning or pain on urination. However, about 20 percent of men show no symptoms. Often, gonorrhea in men is confused with nonspecific urethritis (NSU) (see NONSPECIFIC URETHRITIS in this chapter), which is usually caused by chlamydia (see CHLAMYDIA in this chapter).

In women, gonorrhea often causes no symptoms or only mild symptoms, which most women ignore. If the cervix becomes infected (the most common site in women), examination may show a discharge, redness, and tenderness to touch or movement. If the urine tube ("urethra") is infected, urination may be painful. Gonorrhea that has progressed to the uterus and fallopian tubes may produce lower abdominal pain, vomiting, fever, and irregular menstrual bleeding. Untreated gonorrhea in women can progress to PID, which often requires hospitalization and causes fertility impairment in up to 40 percent of those who develop it.

If symptoms appear, they usually develop in both men and women within two days to three weeks of exposure.

Rectal gonorrhea infections cause irritation, discharge, and painful bowel movements.

If gonorrhea throat infection causes symptoms, they include swollen glands and/or sore throat.

Disseminated gonococcal infections are rare but cause rash, chills, fever, and joint pain and swelling.

Before You Call the Doctor. The best way to deal with gonorrhea is to prevent it. Get to know your sex partner(s) before becoming intimate. Gonorrhea often changes the taste of oral sex. If you notice any unusual taste, you and your partner should see a physician.

Condoms prevent gonorrhea transmission. Use them. If you feel embarrassed suggesting condoms, listen to the excellent audio tape "How to Talk to a Partner About Smart Sex" (see RESOURCES at the end of this chapter). It includes many witty come-backs to prospective lovers who don't want to use them.

When to Call the Doctor. If you develop any gonorrhea symptoms or learn that a sex partner has become infected, consult a physician promptly. Gonorrhea can be diagnosed with a simple test provided for free by most health departments. Be sure to alert the clinician to all the places you might be infected: genitals, throat, and/or rectum.

Until recently, the standard treatment for gonorrhea has been penicillin. However, penicillin-resistant gonorrhea has become a problem in recent years. Current treatment guidelines for uncomplicated gonorrhea call for a single-dose of another antibiotic, ceftriaxone (Rocephin), followed by a seven-day course of doxycycline to treat any chlamydia because gonorrhea and chlamydia often occur together (see CHLAMYDIA in this chapter). Erythromycin is less effective but may be given to pregnant women.

Sexual partners must be notified and treated as quickly as possible, even if they have no symptoms. If you are too embarrassed to notify your partners, your county health department will do it for you. Contact the Communicable Disease Office.

Gonorrhea treatment is almost always effective, but some people may become infected with antibiotic-resistant strains. Because of this possibility—and the risk of PID it entails—women should return four to six weeks after treatment for another gonorrhea test, and be re-treated if necessary.

If you are diagnosed with gonorrhea, ask your doctor to test for chlamydia and syphilis as well (see CHLAMYDIA and SYPHILIS in this chapter). Women should also have Pap smears to check for HPV infection (see VENEREAL WARTS in this chapter).

HERPES

(See also COLD SORES in Chapter 10)

Herpes causes painful, possibly recurring blister-like sores around the mouth and genitals. The mass media often call herpes "incurable," but this is terribly misleading. Herpes should be taken seriously, but there's no need to become hysterical or withdraw from sexuality because you're infected.

What's Going On?   Herpes infects about 500,000 Americans a year. It is caused by either of two closely related viruses: herpes simplex virus Type 1 (HSV-1) or Type 2 (HSV-2). Either one may infect the external sex organs or anal area, causing genital herpes, or the lips or mouth, causing cold sores or fever blisters.

Herpes is a "contact virus," spread by direct skin-to-skin contact with an infected person when a sore is visible or during the day or two before one erupts ("prodrome"). Oral herpes is usually passed during kissing or oral intercourse, genital herpes during oral, vaginal, or anal intercourse. The virus can live for up to a few hours outside the body, so this is one sexually transmitted disease you could conceivably pick up from a toilet seat. However, the virus needs warmth and moisture to survive, and most environments outside the body—including toilet seats—do not favor its survival.

Once infected, a characteristic sore ("lesion") develops. It's an open, red, tingling, itchy, painful blister or group of blisters surrounded by red skin, which lasts seven to ten days, then clears up on its own. If the sore is painless, it's not herpes, but probably syphilis (see SYPHILIS in this chapter). Initial herpes outbreaks might also cause fever, swollen glands, and a general ill feeling ("malaise"). The incubation period—the time from viral exposure to the development of symptoms—is extremely variable. It is possible to carry the virus for years before developing any lesions.

In women, genital lesions most likely occur on the vaginal lips, clitoris, or the area between the vagina and anus ("perineum"). Blisters may also occur on the cervix, buttocks, thighs, and vaginal wall.

In men, sores can appear on the head and/or shaft of the penis and/or on the foreskin, scrotum, perineum, buttocks, anus, and thighs.

The media have blown the supposed "incurability" of herpes way out of proportion. There is no drug that can eradicate the virus. It remains dormant in the body and may recur. But quite often, it never does. Many people suffer just one herpes outbreak and never have another. The reason they don't is that their immune systems attack the virus and effectively contain it. Researchers at the Centers for Disease Control estimate that thirty to thirty-five million Americans carry the herpes virus, but three out of four suffer only one outbreak, and quite a few don't even know they're infected.

People who experience recurrences usually get them in the same spot as the original eruption when they feel fatigued, stressed, tired, run down, or sick—which is why oral herpes ("cold sores") generally erupt in association with colds and flu. Many herpes sufferers have only one or two recurrences, then no more, as their immune systems get the better of the virus. Recurrences tend to be less painful and briefer than initial outbreaks.

If you get recurrent herpes, the day or two before the sore erupts you probably feel an odd itching or tingling. This is the prelude to an eruption, the "prodrome." Learn to recognize what your prodrome feels like. You're contagious—and should refrain from contact with uninfected partners or use condoms—from the moment your prodrome begins until the sore completely heals.

Before You Call the Doctor. The best way to deal with herpes is to prevent its transmission. Get to know your sex partner(s) before becoming intimate. Mention your concern about herpes and volunteer that you don't consider the infection a particular problem, as long as your partners are open and honest about it. Such forthrightness might encourage infected partners to declare any herpes history.

If partners have had herpes, ask if they've ever had recurrences. If not, or if they haven't had a recurrence in a few years, chances are they won't. But to be on the safe side, refrain from lovemaking or use a condom when any infected partner feels stressed or has another illness.

If your partners experience recurrences periodically, ask if they can recognize their prodromes, and discuss the need to refrain from lovemaking or use condoms from the moment the prodrome begins until any lesion entirely heals.

If you feel embarrassed asking a partner to use a condom, listen to the excellent audio tape "How to Talk to a Partner About Smart Sex" (see RESOURCES at the end of this chapter). It includes many witty comebacks to prospective lovers who don't want to use condoms.

Those with recurrent herpes may be able to prevent outbreaks. Eruptions often have triggers, such as job stress, certain drugs, colds and flu, menstruation, etc. Keep a herpes diary and try to track what occurred before any outbreaks. Once you know your herpes triggers, you may be able to prevent them—and the eruptions that follow them. And if not, at least you'll know what to expect and be able to take precautions against spreading the infection.

If you suffer herpes, these home remedies can help you deal with the pain and discomfort:

• Take aspirin, acetaminophen, or ibuprofen to reduce pain and any fever. Aspirin and ibuprofen can also help relieve the inflammation of herpes lesions. Acetaminophen has no anti-inflammatory effect. Aspirin and ibuprofen may cause stomach upset, and they should not be used by pregnant women or those with a history of ulcers unless a doctor recommends it.

• Apply cool compresses of Burow's solution (available at pharmacies) to genital sores four to six times a day.

• Try an over-the-counter anesthetic cream available at pharmacies—for example, Anbesol, Herpecin, Resolve, or Campho-Phenique.

• Numb the area with an ice pack. Wrap an ice cube in a plastic bag and wrap the bag in a clean cloth. Apply the ice pack for twenty minutes, then remove it for ten minutes before reapplying it. An ice substitute may also be used. Do not place ice directly on the skin. This can cause the equivalent of frostbite.

• Don't wear tight-fitting underwear or pants, which may irritate the genitals.

• Wear cotton underwear. Cotton allows air to reach the sores, which helps keep them dry and minimizes their pain and irritation.

• Keep the genitals clean and dry. Pat rather than rub yourself dry after bathing or use a hand-held hair dryer on the coolest setting. Use a separate towel for the genitals to prevent spreading the lesions to other parts of the body.

When to Call the Doctor.   If you've never had herpes before, see a doctor as soon as you suspect you're infected. The doctor can make a definitive diagnosis by culturing the virus—but only during a few days after the sores appear, so don't delay.

Herpes sores can resemble other sexually transmitted diseases, for example, venereal warts. If the sore you think is herpes does not clear up within two weeks, consult a physician. Venereal warts are treatable (see VENEREAL WARTS in this chapter).

In severe cases, the oral antiviral drug acyclovir (Zovirax) may be prescribed. It's particularly effective during the initial outbreak but less effective in treating recurrences (which are usually less severe anyway). Acyclovir cream is also available. For most people, it shortens the duration of sores only about one to two days, not enough for most people to justify its expense.

Some doctors prescribe daily acyclovir therapy for people with frequent or severe recurrences. Daily treatment should be discontinued after one year to reassess the need for the drug. After stopping daily acyclovir, many people experience one particularly severe outbreak.

▶ **RED FLAG**   Pregnant women who experience genital herpes eruptions close to term may transmit the virus to their newborn in the birth canal. Although herpes is not life-threatening in adults, the virus can kill newborns, and even if it doesn't it can cause brain damage.

Pregnant women should tell their obstetricians about any herpes history. Those who contract herpes during their last trimester are at the greatest risk of transmitting the infection. A cesarean delivery may be necessary. Babies born to mothers with herpes histories should be closely monitored by a physician for signs of infection.

NONSPECIFIC URETHRITIS

Nonspecific urethritis (NSU) is the most common and least publicized STD in men. It strikes 1.3 million men each year and causes pain on urination and a penile discharge.

What's Going On?   NSU, also known as nongonoccocal urethritis (NGU), is usually—though not always—caused by chlamydia (see CHLA-MYDIA in this chapter). Its symptoms resemble those of gonorrhea: mild burning or tingling during urination and a milky discharge. Most cases are sexually transmitted, but the infection may occur without sexual contact.

Before You Call the Doctor.   Drink plenty of nonalcoholic fluids. This may flush out the infection in mild cases or minimize burning.

Condoms prevent transmission. Use them. If you feel embarrassed asking a partner to use a condom, listen to the excellent audio tape "How to Talk to a Partner About Smart Sex" (see RESOURCES at the end of this chapter). It includes many witty come-backs to prospective lovers who don't want to use them.

When to Call the Doctor.   Because of the possibility that these symptoms are chlamydia or gonorrhea, it's important to consult a physician. Also, be sure to tell all your recent sexual partners to get checked.

To diagnose NSU, the doctor tests for gonorrhea and other sexually transmitted diseases. Once diagnosed, physicians treat NSU with antibiotics. Be sure to take the entire seven to ten-day course, even if symptoms clear up in a few days.

PENILE DISCHARGE

(See CHLAMYDIA, GONORRHEA, NONSPECIFIC URETHRITIS, TRICHOMONAS, and VENEREAL WARTS in this chapter and PROS-TATITIS in Chapter 17)

SYPHILIS

Initially, syphilis causes a painless sore or blister ("chancre"), which clears up with *or without* treatment within one to five weeks. About six months later, a whole-body rash develops—including on the palms and the soles of the feet—which comes and goes for several years and eventually goes away. Then, many years later, physically devastating symptoms develop, including heart and brain damage.

What's Going On?   The oldest and most destructive of the epidemic sexually transmitted diseases, syphilis was the AIDS of sixteenth and seventeenth century Europe. It is less common and severe today thanks to treatment, public education, and widespread preventive efforts, particularly premarital blood tests. But it has by no means been eradicated. Syphilis is still very much with us. It infects about 100,000 Americans a year, and in recent years that number has been increasing. If it remains untreated, it can become quite serious.

Syphilis is caused by a bacteria-like microorganism ("spirochete") that is transmitted sexually to the genitals, mouth, and/or anus. The spirochete cannot live outside the human body, so the disease cannot be contracted from doorknobs, toilet seats, etc.

Like gonorrhea, syphilis may not cause symptoms, especially in women, which makes it potentially quite insidious. But usually, from ten days to several months after infection, the characteristic chancre develops at the site of infection. Chancres may also appear elsewhere, for example, on the fingers or breasts. Because syphilitic chancres are painless, they often go unnoticed. (If the sore is painful, it's probably herpes and not syphilis.) The person may also develop swollen lymph nodes in the groin area. With or without treatment, the sore usually disappears within one to five weeks, but the infection remains.

Within six months, a rash or more sores typically develop, which may cover the entire body, including the palms and soles of the feet. Other possible symptoms include sores in the mouth and a sore throat. Again, these symptoms may be ignored, go unnoticed, or be confused with other conditions. These symptoms usually come and go sporadically for several years. During this stage, the disease may be passed through casual contact, for example, kissing or skin contact with any open sore.

Untreated syphilis then enters a latent, symptomless stage that often lasts several years. But eventually symptoms reappear, and during the late stage of the disease, symptoms are devastating, involving severe, potentially life-threatening damage to the heart and other major organs. Fortunately, few cases progress to this stage.

Before You Call the Doctor.   The best way to deal with syphilis is to prevent it. Get to know your sex partner(s) before becoming intimate. Learn the symptoms—particularly the painless genital sore and any unusual rash or group of sores on the hands—and if you notice them in any potential partners, encourage them to seek medical care.

Condoms usually prevent transmission. Use them. If you feel embarrassed asking a partner to use a condom, listen to the excellent audio tape "How to Talk to a Partner About Smart Sex" (see RESOURCES at the end of this chapter). It includes many witty come-backs to prospective lovers who don't want to use condoms.

When to Call the Doctor.   Because the early stages of syphilis may be misdiagnosed by doctors unfamiliar with the disease, it's best to visit a clinic that specializes in sexually transmitted diseases. During the initial stage, discharge from the syphilis sore should be examined under a special microscope.

Within a week or two of the sore's appearance (usually about six weeks after contact with the infected person) spirochetes enter the bloodstream and a blood test known as a "VDRL" or "RPR" reveals the disease. However, syphilis has a fairly long incubation period, and it may be necessary to have repeat blood tests over several months.

It's especially important for pregnant women to be diagnosed accurately and treated early. All women routinely have a blood test for syphilis during their first prenatal visit. If treated before the fourth month of pregnancy, fetal infection is unlikely. After the fourth month, treatment eradicates the infection but cannot reverse fetal damage already done.

The treatment for early syphilis is penicillin. Those with penicillin allergies should receive tetracycline or doxycycline. (Pregnant women should not receive tetracycline because it stains the developing fetus's teeth.)

For later-stage syphilis, penicillin is still the treatment of choice, but doctors should also test and monitor the fluid surrounding the brain and spinal cord ("cerebrospinal fluid"), especially if the person shows any signs of nerve damage.

If you are diagnosed with syphilis, ask the doctor to test for chlamydia and gonorrhea as well (see CHLAMYDIA and GONORRHEA in this chapter). Women should also have Pap smears to check for HPV infection (see VENEREAL WARTS in this chapter).

TRICHOMONAS

Trichomonas (trik-uh-MOAN-us) causes no symptoms in some women, but most develop a foul-smelling, frothy, yellowish discharge. If the bladder becomes infected, women may feel the need to urinate unusually frequently. In men, trichomonas typically does not cause symptoms and clears up by itself unless they keep getting reexposed by infected partners. However, men may experience painful urination, a clear discharge, and slight itching of the penis.

What's Going On?   Trichomonas, commonly called "trich" (pronounced "trick"), is caused by a single-celled animal ("protozoan"), the trichomonad. Trichomonas is not a classic sexually transmitted disease because it may develop or recur several years after sexual exposure. However, the infection is presumably sexually acquired because it doesn't occur in virgins. An estimated three million Americans develop it each year.

Before You Call the Doctor.   Trichomonads grow best in an alkaline environment. Acidifying the vagina cannot cure the infection, but it may relieve some symptoms. To do this, use a vinegar douche—three tablespoons of vinegar per quart of warm water. Do not squirt the douche. Simply let it flow into the vagina. Squirting may increase the risk of pelvic inflammatory disease, potentially life-threatening infection of the reproductive organs and a major cause of fertility problems (see DOUCHING in Chapter 16).

Condoms usually prevent transmission. Use them. If you feel embarrassed asking a partner to use a condom, listen to the excellent audio tape "How to Talk to a Partner About Smart Sex" (see RESOURCES at the end of this chapter). It includes many witty come-backs to prospective lovers who don't want to use them.

When to Call the Doctor.   To cure trichomonas, professional treatment is necessary. Consult a physician if you believe you've been exposed or if you develop any of the symptoms listed above. A doctor can easily diagnose trichomonas by examining the discharge under a microscope. Sometimes, trichomonads may be spotted during a routine Pap smear or in the sediment of a urine sample. Doctors usually treat trichomonas with a single dose of metronidazole (Flagyl). Persistent infections are treated with a seven-day course of the drug. To avoid reinfection, both partners must be treated, even if one has no symptoms.

▶ **RED FLAG**   If you take metronidazole be sure not to drink alcohol during treatment and for at least one day afterward. The combination of alcohol and metronidazole causes nausea, severe abdominal cramps, numbness in the arms and legs, and possibly seizures.

VAGINAL DISCHARGE

(See VAGINAL DISCHARGE in Chapter 16)

VENEREAL WARTS

Venereal warts are similar to other warts (see WARTS in Chapter 6). They may be flat or raised, single or multiple. They are often painless and may be quite small, so they may go unnoticed, increasing the risk of spreading the infection to others. On the other hand, they may also be large and easily noticeable.

In women, venereal warts often develop on the outer part of the vagina ("vulva"), inside the vagina, on the cervix, or on or near the anus. Women with internal warts (vaginal, anal, or cervical) sometimes notice a burning sensation or a change in their vaginal discharge. In men, venereal warts usually erupt on the penis, but they may also appear around the anus or inside the urine tube ("urethra"). Infection of the urethra may cause bleeding, discharge, and the need to urinate frequently.

What's Going On?   Venereal warts are also called "genital warts," and medically they are known as "condyloma" from the Greek for "knob." In recent years these sexually transmitted bumps have become a common sexually transmitted disease, particularly among young adults. About one million Americans develop venereal warts each year.

Venereal warts are caused by the human papillomavirus (HPV). While they may look similar to the warts that develop on the hands, feet, or other parts of the body, HPV warts are more serious because in women some strains have been associated with a high risk of cervical cancer.

They are spread only through sexual contact and usually develop two to three months after exposure to an infected person.

Before You Call the Doctor.   The best way to deal with venereal warts is to prevent them. Get to know your sex partner(s) before becoming intimate. If you notice any odd-looking bumps around their genitals, encourage them to seek medical care.

Sexual partners of those diagnosed with HPV should be checked for signs of the virus. Men may do this at home by wrapping the penis and scrotum in gauze or cloth soaked in white vinegar for about five minutes and then looking (preferably with a magnifying glass) for any areas that turn white, in which case they should consult a physician experienced with sexually transmitted diseases. Men may also ask a physician to perform the initial exam.

Condoms usually prevent transmission of venereal warts. Use them. If you feel embarrassed asking a partner to use a condom, listen to the excellent audio tape "How to Talk to a Partner About Smart Sex" (see

RESOURCES at the end of this chapter). It includes many witty come-backs to prospective lovers who don't want to use them.

When to Call the Doctor.   Sometimes a doctor can diagnose venereal warts simply by a visual exam. However, small or flat warts may go unnoticed or may be misdiagnosed. In some cases, accurate diagnosis requires a lighted magnifying device ("colposcope"), which allows the doctor to closely examine infected areas. A Pap test or biopsy may also be required.

Treatment depends on the severity and location of the warts. Some warts can be removed with caustic chemicals. Others must be burned off ("cauterized"). This technique requires local anesthesia. Some warts are frozen off with liquid nitrogen ("cryosurgery"). This technique can cause temporary blistering of nearby tissue. Laser surgery may be used for recurrent warts or for warts resistent to other methods.

Unfortunately, despite these treatments, venereal warts often recur, requiring repeat treatments, sometimes over several months.

Women exposed to lovers diagnosed with venereal warts should consult a physician for a Pap smear and pelvic exam. Women with a history of condyloma may need Paps more often than once a year. Discuss your follow-up schedule with your physician.

RESOURCES

The National AIDS Hotline. 1-(800)-342-2437. Provides free, confidential information about AIDS and referrals to testing and support organizations around the country.

"How to Talk to a Partner About Smart Sex." $11.95 from Focus International, 14 Oregon Dr., Huntington Station, NY 11746; 1-(800)-843-0305. Created by noted sexuality authorities Bernie Zilbergeld, Ph.D., and Lonnie Barbach, Ph.D., this sixty-minute audio cassette contains more than a dozen vignettes that dramatize conversations about safe sex and condom use. In some, the men are reluctant to practice safe sex; in others, the women are. If you've ever wanted to bring up safe sex and not felt able to, this empowering tape will help you raise the subject.

CHAPTER 19

Contraception and
Sex Problems

BIRTH CONTROL PILLS

SPERMICIDES—FOAM

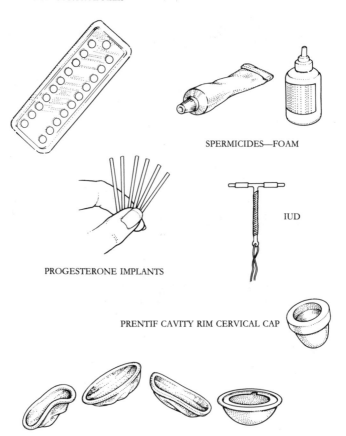

IUD

PROGESTERONE IMPLANTS

PRENTIF CAVITY RIM CERVICAL CAP

DIAPHRAGMS: ARCHING SPRING; COIL SPRING; FLAT SPRING; WIDE SEAL RIM

CONTRACEPTIVE SPONGE

CONDOM
(HOW TO PUT ON)

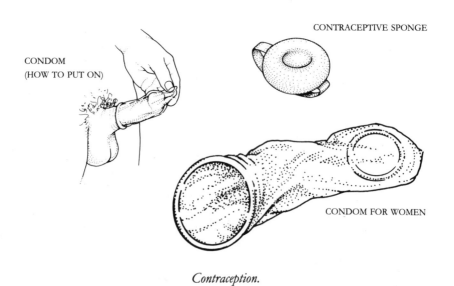

CONDOM FOR WOMEN

Contraception.

ABORTION

Pregnancy termination is very controversial, but more than one million legal abortions are performed in the United States each year, and women considering ending a pregnancy should be fully informed about all their options.

What's Going On? "Therapeutic abortion" is the deliberate removal of the embryo before it is able to survive outside the womb ("uterus"). Deciding to terminate a pregnancy is at best a difficult decision, one that should be made with great care and never impulsively. If possible, the woman should discuss her decision with her partner, family, trusted friends, a counselor, clergy, and/or doctor.

As this book goes to press, abortion is legal in the United States. During the first thirteen weeks after the last menstrual period ("first trimester"), the decision is entirely up to the woman and her physician. During the second thirteen weeks ("second trimester"), a state may impose some restrictions, for example, requiring abortions to be performed in hospitals. Abortion is very rarely performed after the twenty-fourth week of pregnancy because with the aid of current technology, fetuses may be viable at that age.

Most women (and usually their partners as well) feel mixed emotions about the decision to have an abortion. For some, the predominant feeling is relief. For others, it's profound loss. Studies show that first-trimester abortions cause the least psychological trauma and fewer medical complications than second-trimester abortions.

Abortion is certainly one of the nation's most explosive political issues. But not even those who champion a woman's right to choose abortion *like* it as a method of contraception. Some unplanned pregnancies occur truly accidentally. But many—perhaps most—occur because the lovers failed to use a reliable method of birth control properly every time they made love. Lovers should *always* discuss birth control and never risk an unplanned pregnancy. Once they decide on the best method for them, they should use it properly *every time* they have vaginal intercourse.

No single contraceptive is "best," and no single method is best for any couple all the time, or throughout life (see CONTRACEPTION in this chapter). But options abound, and today there's a reliable method to suit just about every couple's needs and sexual tastes (see BIRTH CONTROL PILLS, CERVICAL CAP, CONDOMS FOR MEN, CONDOMS FOR WOMEN, DIAPHRAGM, FERTILITY AWARENESS, MORNING-AFTER CONTRACEPTION, NONINTERCOURSE LOVEMAK-

ING AS BIRTH CONTROL, PROGESTERONE IMPLANTS, SPER-
MICIDES, SPONGE, TUBAL LIGATION, VASECTOMY, and
WITHDRAWAL in this chapter).

Before You Call the Doctor.   First, make sure you're clear about your
decision not to carry the pregnancy to term. Never rush into abortion
impulsively or under pressure. The vast majority of women learn they are
pregnant sometime during their third to eighth week of pregnancy. First-
trimester abortions can be obtained until the end of the twelfth week, so
most women can consider abortion decisions for several weeks without
jeopardizing their ability to obtain the simplest, most private type of
abortion. Talk to those who are important to you. If you have any
questions, contact a physician or family planning clinic near you.

Abortions *absolutely* require experienced doctors. *Never* attempt a self-
induced abortion or have an abortion performed by anyone other than a
qualified medical professional. Never take abortifacient herbs in an effort
to trigger abortion. Many plant oils, for example, pennyroyal oil, trigger
uterine contractions, but the abortifacient dose is also the *lethal* dose.
Within the last 100 years, about a dozen American women have died
shortly after ingesting as little as one teaspoon of pennyroyal oil for the
purpose of self-inducing abortion.

When to Call the Doctor.   Although pregnancy can now be detected
as early as ten days after conception, most clinicians advise women to wait
until two weeks after a missed period, or about six to eight weeks after the
last menstrual period, to ensure that the abortion procedure is successful.
Early abortion reduces the health risks to the mother, but abortions
performed before six weeks from the last menstrual period are more
painful and carry the risk of possibly not terminating the pregnancy.

In the United States, most abortions are surgical procedures:

• Vacuum curettage. The most widely used abortion procedure, vacuum curettage, also called "suction curettage" or "suction D&C," empties
the uterus through the cervix. Up until the sixteenth week of pregnancy,
the procedure can be performed in a doctor's office, provided that adequate medical backup is available. Most women receive a local anesthetic
("paracervical block") and possibly intravenous pain medication, but in
some cases, especially if the procedure takes place in a hospital, general
anesthesia may be used. The clinician places a clamp on the cervix to hold
it steady and then opens ("dilates") it using a series of metal rods with
increasing diameters. Some clinicians prefer to dilate the cervix with rods
of sterilized seaweed ("laminaria") inserted six to twenty-four hours

before the abortion. The seaweed rods absorb body fluid and swell, gently enlarging the cervical opening.

Once the cervix has been dilated enough to accommodate the vacuum tube, the doctor removes the contents of the uterus. Some women feel a slight tugging sensation during the procedure and cramping immediately following it as the uterus contracts. Afterward, the physician inserts a scraping instrument ("curette") to make sure all the fetal tissue has been removed.

After vacuum curettage, some women experience strong cramping. Others feel nauseous. With local anesthetic, most women are able to leave the medical facility within two hours. General anesthesia requires longer recovery.

• Dilation and curettage (D&C). This method substitutes a curette for the vacuum tube. The physician scrapes the curette around the uterus to loosen the tissue and then removes it with a forceps. Until the 1960s, D&C was the method of choice for first-trimester abortions. Today, it has largely been replaced by vacuum curettage, which is quicker and causes fewer complications. However, D&C is still used as a diagnostic test for other uterine problems.

• Dilation and evacuation (D&E). D&E is a second-trimester abortion procedure. Some clinicians use it through the twentieth week. Performed much like a D&C, the D&E uses special instruments to remove the larger volume of fetal and uterine tissue. Because the cervix must be dilated more than in a vacuum or D&C procedure, most clinicians use laminaria the day before surgery. Under a paracervical block or general anesthesia, the physician completes cervical dilation and removes the fetal tissue with a vacuum tube and other instruments. Most clinicians also administer oxytocin (Pitocin) intravenously, which stimulates uterine contractions and helps limit blood loss.

Drugs can also be used for second-trimester abortion. However, they are neither as safe nor as effective as first-trimester vacuum curettage:

• Prostaglandin E2. A vaginal suppository, this drug is inserted every three to four hours and causes intense uterine contractions that expel the fetus. Prostaglandin E2 is most successful when used with laminaria. Risks include fever and gastrointestinal distress.

• Prostaglandin F2. This drug is administered using a series of injections which trigger uterine contractions. Possible side effects include vomiting and diarrhea.

• Saline. "Saline" means salt water. After removing some amniotic fluid, the physician injects saline into the uterine cavity through the anesthetized skin of the abdominal wall. After six to eight hours, labor begins and the fetus and placenta are generally expelled within thirty-six hours. Sometimes the placenta must be removed through curettage. Possible complications include hemorrhage, retained placenta, and infection.

• Urea. Urea, a component of urine, is a natural chemical the body produces. Injected like saline, it, too, produces uterine contractions. Compared with saline, it causes fewer and less severe side effects, but it's also less effective. Urea is typically used in conjunction with one of the prostaglandins discussed above to increase effectiveness.

The newest method of abortion is a drug called RU486, the so-called "abortion pill." Developed in France in the late 1980s, this medication is administered orally within three weeks of a missed period. Studies to date show that RU486 is about 85 percent effective (more so if used within one week or used along with prostaglandin injections). It's also reasonably safe, though uterine bleeding is possible. As this book goes to press, RU486 is not available in the United States. Antiabortion activists hope to keep it that way. Meanwhile, some drug companies are exploring the possibility of applying for a license to market it. And several researchers are exploring RU486's potential value for other medical conditions. If it wins Food and Drug Administration approval for any purpose, U.S. physicians would be able to prescribe it for abortion.

Regardless of the type of abortion, a woman should follow her clinician's recommendations and:

• Rest for at least one day after the procedure.

• Avoid strenuous activity for seventy-two hours.

• Take any antibiotics as directed, and take the full course. Antibiotics reduce the risk of postabortion infection.

• Do not have intercourse for at least two weeks.

• Do not use tampons for three weeks.

• Have a follow-up exam two weeks after the abortion.

• Start using an effective method of birth control and use it properly during every sexual encounter.

▶ **RED FLAGS**   Consult a physician immediately if any of the following develop:

• Fever.

• Chills.

• Muscle aches.

• Persistent fatigue after seventy-two hours.

• Abdominal pain, cramping, or backache.

• Abdominal tenderness when you press on the lower abdomen above the pubic bone.

• Prolonged or heavy vaginal bleeding.

• Any foul-smelling vaginal discharge.

•No menstrual period within six weeks, especially if you still feel pregnant.

BIRTH CONTROL PILLS

Also known as "oral contraceptives" and "the Pill," birth control pills are small tablets which contain the female sex hormones produced by women's ovaries—estrogen and progesterone. (Actually they don't contain progesterone but one of a class of hormones known as "progestins" which are related to progesterone.)

What's Going On. For information about the effectiveness of this method compared with the others, see the CONTRACEPTION section of this chapter.

Birth control pills prevent pregnancy by preventing the release of eggs from women's ovaries. Birth control pills are available by prescription only, and regular clinic visits are necessary.

A woman on the Pill must take one pill a day, every day. If she misses a pill, she can take two the following day. If she forgets two pills, she can take two each day until she has caught up. But it's wise, in such cases, to use a backup form of contraception. If she misses three or more days in a row, she should stop taking the Pill and use another type of contraception until her next period, when she may return to taking her birth control pills.

Birth control pills come in two varieties: "combination" pills, which contain both estrogen and progestin, and progestin-only pills, known as "minipills." Minipills are slightly less effective than combination pills, but they can be used by women who cannot take estrogen for medical reasons. They can also be used by those who suffer severe side effects from combination pills—for example, nausea, breast swelling, and possible blood clots in the veins ("thrombosis"). Another alternative for those who suffer troubling side effects from older combination pills is the newer "triphasic combination Pill," which contains less progestin. Women considering birth control pills should discuss the various options with a family planning counselor or physician.

Before You Call the Doctor. Some women *should not* take birth control pills:
•Pregnant women, or women who suspect they might be pregnant. And women with any of the following:
•Liver disease (hepatitis, cirrhosis, or benign liver tumors).

• A history of heart disease, stroke, or angina (see ANGINA and HEART ATTACK in Chapter 12).

• A history of breast cancer.

Many other conditions make the Pill an iffy proposition. Your physician may advise against using the Pill if:

• You're a teenager whose menstrual cycle has not yet become firmly established.

• You smoke.

• You're breastfeeding.

• You're over thirty-five years of age.

• You have varicose veins (see VARICOSE VEINS in Chapter 12).

Or if you have any of the following:

• Migraines or other severe headaches (see HEADACHE in Chapter 7).

• High blood pressure (see HIGH BLOOD PRESSURE in Chapter 12).

• High cholesterol (see HIGH CHOLESTEROL in Chapter 12).

• Gallbladder disease (see GALLSTONES in Chapter 13).

• Diabetes (see DIABETES in Chapter 4).

• Uterine fibroids (see FIBROIDS in Chapter 16).

• Sickle cell anemia (see ANEMIA in Chapter 4).

• High risk of breast cancer (see BREAST LUMPS in Chapter 16).

• A family history of death from heart disease before age fifty.

Pill advantages include convenience and regularization of the menstrual cycle. Birth control pills typically decrease menstrual flow and cramping. They often help relieve acne, endometriosis, and ovarian cysts. Studies show that birth control pills also reduce the risk of ovarian and uterine ("endometrial") cancer. They also reduce the risk of pelvic inflammatory disease (PID), a potentially life-threatening infection of women's reproductive organs and a major cause of fertility problems. Finally, oral contraceptives reduce the risk of tubal ("ectopic") pregnancy, a serious medical problem.

However, oral contraceptives increase the risk of stroke, heart attack, high blood pressure ("hypertension"), and abnormal blood clotting.

Controversy surrounds the issue of whether the Pill is a risk factor for breast cancer. Estrogen, a major component of combination birth control pills, stimulates the growth of many breast tumors. Some studies have shown an increased breast cancer risk in Pill users. However, others have not. At this writing, the jury is still out, but women with a history of breast cancer or a family history of cancers diagnosed at an unusually early age (other than ovarian cancer) should not use the Pill.

Some women gain weight while taking birth control pills, which most women consider a disadvantage. Others notice an increase in breast size. Depending on the woman, this may be an advantage or disadvantage.

Other common side effects of the Pill include decreased sex drive, nausea, headaches, breast tenderness, depression, fatigue, irritability, and bleeding between periods ("spotting"). Minipills cause irregular periods in many women.

Birth control pills provide no protection against sexually transmitted diseases.

Finally, birth control pills are a relatively expensive form of contraception.

Women who stop using birth control pills typically return to ovulating normally within one to three months, but in some cases, ovulation does not return for up to six months.

When to Call the Doctor. If you decide to use the Pill, you'll need to have it prescribed by a physician.

•Make sure you understand all of its many effects.

•Make sure you have an annual physical exam while taking the Pill.

•Let your provider know about any changes in your medical status, particularly if you begin smoking, require a leg cast, or get diagnosed with cancer or any heart, blood pressure, or circulatory problem.

•Never share or borrow birth control pills.

▶ **RED FLAGS** Women taking the Pill should contact a physician immediately if they develop:

•Severe abdominal pain.

•Chest pain.

•Shortness of breath.

•Severe headaches.

•Blurred vision or vision loss.

•Severe leg pains.

CERVICAL CAP

(See also DIAPHRAGM and SPERMICIDES in this chapter)

The cervical cap is a small, thimble-shaped device that fits over the cervix and prevents sperm from entering the uterus.

What's Going On? For information about the effectiveness of this method compared with the others, see the CONTRACEPTION section of this chapter.

The cervical cap is one of several "barrier" contraceptives (see CONDOMS FOR MEN, CONDOMS FOR WOMEN, and DIAPHRAGM in this chapter). It fits over the cervix like a bottlecap. A combination of the cap's "fit" and natural suction hold it on the cervix. The cap is made of rubber and must be fitted by a clinician. In addition to serving as a physical barrier to sperm, it also holds spermicide.

Before You Call the Doctor.   Not all women can use cervical caps. The cap is not for you if:
- You're allergic to spermicides or rubber.
- Cervical abnormalities interfere with a good seal.
- You have a history of toxic shock syndrome (see TOXIC SHOCK SYNDROME in Chapter 16).

Cap advantages include:
- Small size. Some women who cannot use diaphragms comfortably can use cervical caps without problems.
- No serious side effects.
- Protection against sexually transmitted diseases.
- Can be used after age forty, when the Pill cannot.

Cap disadvantages include:
- Possible need to interrupt lovemaking to insert it.
- Objections to messiness.
- Difficulty inserting or removing it.
- Cervical irritation.
- Unpleasant odor if the cap is left in more than a day or two.
- An increased risk of urinary tract infections (see URINARY TRACT INFECTION in Chapter 14).

For reliable contraceptive protection, the cap should be left in for at least eight hours after your last intercourse. Caps may be left in for a day or two, so you might decide not to remove it during a weekend away. But authorities recommend against extended wear because it increases the risk of toxic shock syndrome. Cervical caps must be removed during menstruation.

When to Call the Doctor.   If you decide to use a cervical cap, you'll need to have one fitted during a pelvic exam. The cap is more difficult to insert than the diaphragm. The clinician should instruct you how to insert and remove it and check your insertion and removal technique.

Before inserting the cap, wash your hands with soap and water. Fill your cap with a half-tablespoon of spermicide. When you insert it, make sure you press it over the cervix and get a good seal.

Childbirth can change the size of the cervix, necessitating a refitting.

Before you start making love again after delivering, consult your clinician to check your cap's fit.

Depending on how frequently they are used, cervical caps can last up to a few years, but eventually they need to be replaced. Examine yours regularly and if you have any doubts about its integrity, visit your provider for a replacement.

If you notice any discomfort or unusual vaginal discharge or bleeding, consult your provider. Also contact your provider if you feel at all uncertain about your cap's fit or your ability to insert it properly.

▶ **RED FLAGS** Because the cervical cap may increase the risk of toxic shock syndrome, users should be able to recognize the signs of this potentially rapidly fatal infection. Call 911 or go to an emergency room immediately if you develop any of the following:

- Sudden high fever and chills.
- Vomiting with any other symptoms listed here.
- Diarrhea with any other symptoms listed here.
- Dizziness, faintness, and/or weakness.
- Sore throat with aching muscles and joints and other symptoms listed here.
- A sunburn-like rash.

CONDOMS FOR MEN

(See also SPERMICIDES in this chapter)

Condoms are disposable contraceptives, made from either latex rubber or sheep intestine ("skins"), which cover the erect penis during intercourse and prevent sperm from being deposited in the vagina.

What's Going On. For information about the effectiveness of this method compared with the others, see the CONTRACEPTION section of this chapter.

Condoms are one of the "barrier contraceptives" (see CERVICAL CAP, CONDOMS FOR WOMEN, and DIAPHRAGM in this chapter). Also known as "rubbers," "prophylactics," and "protection," condoms have enjoyed a resurgence in popularity since the mid-1980s because the latex rubber variety—not skins—have a major noncontraceptive benefit—protection against sexually transmitted diseases, including AIDS (see AIDS in Chapter 18). Condoms do not provide perfect protection against AIDS, but they are the best preventive available, and public health authorities urge all lovers who are nonmonogamous and/or at risk for AIDS to use condoms during every sexual encounter.

Condoms are relatively inexpensive and widely available without a prescription at pharmacies, many supermarkets, and by mail. There was a time when condoms were kept hidden behind pharmacy counters and boys died of embarrassment asking pharmacists for them. Today they are displayed openly, and women buy as many as men.

Latex condoms typically have a nipple at the head to catch the ejaculate. They come either straight-sided or contoured in the shape of the erect penis. The contoured variety provide a better fit, which some couples prefer for aesthetic reasons. Condoms also come unlubricated ("dry") or lubricated with a thin dusting of silicone powder. Most women prefer the lubricated kind because they are less likely to cause discomfort on insertion. Some condoms also come with spermicide. These provide extra protection against both pregnancy and AIDS.

Several myths continue to discourage men and couples from using condoms:

• "They're like taking a shower with a raincoat on." The myth that condoms dull sensitivity is an outgrowth of the idea that men's sexual pleasure happens only in the penis and only during intercourse. However, sex therapists agree that preoccupation with the penis is a major reason why men develop sex problems (see EJACULATION DIFFICULTIES, EJACULATION (INVOLUNTARY), and ERECTION PROBLEMS in this chapter). To enjoy high-quality lovemaking, sex experts urge men to cultivate an appreciation for whole-body sensuality, a massage approach to lovemaking that uses gentle touch to stimulate every square inch of the body.

Condom manufacturers have confused the sensitivity issue by claiming that their condoms deliver more sensitivity than anyone else's. Not so. All condoms are about the same. People may have personal preferences, but sexual pleasure is something lovers *create,* not something condoms *deliver.* Some condoms have "ribs" which supposedly enhance the pleasure of intercourse for women. If you like them, fine. But the ribs are virtually imperceptible, and while many women enjoy stimulation of the vaginal lips, most women derive the majority of their sexual pleasure from stimulation of the clitoris, which sits outside and above the vagina, an organ ribbed condoms never touch.

But what about condoms' effect on sexual pleasure in the penis? Imagine that you're watching a movie when suddenly your lover starts fondling between your legs. Many men would become highly aroused— despite the fact that several layers of thick clothing stand between those caressing hands and their penises. A shirt, pants, and underwear are approximately 5,000 times as thick as the average condom, yet they don't seem to get in the way of sexual enjoyment. How much sensation can a condom really block? Far from feeling like showering with a raincoat on, when used intelligently, condoms are more like showering with a ring on one finger.

•"They interrupt." Many lovers don't like taking a "time out" from lovemaking for the man to slip on a condom. Some men's erections also subside because of the hassle of donning the rubber. But condom use can easily be incorporated into lovemaking. Open the package beforehand to decrease "fiddling" time. And if the woman places it on the man while continuing to caress his penis, there's little if any interruption.

•"They break." This is possible, but the problem can easily be prevented.

•Never store condoms near a heat source. Heat deteriorates latex rubber.

•Don't keep them in wallets, pants pockets, or glove compartments. They're warm enough to cause heat damage.

•Open the condom beforehand so impatience doesn't get the better of you in the middle of lovemaking, resulting in a ripped condom.

•Roll the condom onto the penis slowly.

•Never insert a condom-covered penis (or an uncovered penis) into a vagina that is not sufficiently lubricated to allow easy insertion.

•If natural vaginal lubrication is insufficient, use saliva, vegetable oil, or a water-based over-the-counter lubricant, such as KY Jelly.

•Never use petroleum jelly as a lubricant with condoms. Petroleum jelly causes rubber deterioration and condom failure.

If a condom breaks, the woman should immediately insert some spermicide. However, despite immediate application of spermicide, sperm may still enter the uterus (see MORNING-AFTER CONTRACEPTION in this chapter). If a condom breaks, one thing a woman should *not* do is douche. Douching might push the sperm up into the uterus. Douching also increases the risk of pelvic inflammatory disease (PID), potentially life-threatening infection of women's reproductive organs and a major cause of fertility problems. (see DOUCHING in Chapter 16).

Before You Call the Doctor.   Follow the suggestions above for enjoyable condom use and reliable contraception. In addition:

•Beware of colored condoms. They may look festive, but some men are allergic to the dyes and suffer penile irritation.

•Never use a condom whose wrapper has come unsealed.

•Put it on before you put it in. Pre-ejaculatory fluid may contain sperm.

BEFORE YOU CALL THE DOCTOR

•Consider using a spermicide in addition. This increases condom effectiveness (see SPERMICIDES in this chapter).

•Use latex rubber condoms, not natural "skins," for best protection against sexually transmitted diseases. Latex blocks transmission of the viruses that cause AIDS, herpes, and venereal warts, but skins do not.

•Watch out for "lift-offs." Sometimes in the women-on-top position, the vaginal lips may lift a condom off the penis. Contoured penis-shaped condoms help prevent this. But in the woman-on-top position, the man should hold the condom on to the base of his penis. (In addition to securing the condom, the man can provide direct clitoral stimulation to the woman.)

•After ejaculation, hold the condom onto the base of the penis to keep from leaving an ejaculate-filled condom inside the vagina.

•Use condoms only once.

When to Call the Doctor.   If you develop penile or vaginal irritation from condoms, try changing your spermicide and/or lubricant. If irritation continues or gets worse, consider switching to another form of birth control.

If a condom breaks or comes off and you don't want to risk pregnancy, contact a physician immediately about morning-after contraception (see MORNING-AFTER CONTRACEPTION in this chapter).

CONDOMS FOR WOMEN

(See SPERMICIDES in this chapter)

As this book goes to press, the Food and Drug Administration has granted approval for the first female condom.

What's Going On?   Currently there is no reliable information about the effectiveness of this method. As a result, it is not included in the effectiveness chart in the CONTRACEPTION section of this chapter. However, clinical trials to date suggest a leakage-and-breakage rate that is similar to that of condoms for men.

Like traditional condoms, the female version, also called the vaginal pouch, is a barrier contraceptive (see CERVICAL CAP, CONDOMS FOR MEN, and DIAPHRAGM in this chapter). It should be used only once, and then discarded.

The female condom is a sheath that lines the vagina. About seven inches long, it is held in place by two plastic rings—an inner ring 1.5 inches in diameter which covers the cervix, and an outer ring about 2 inches in diameter, which rests on the vaginal lips. Insertion is similar to the procedure for a diaphragm (see DIAPHRAGM in this chapter). The inner ring tucks under the pubic bone.

While considered a contraceptive, the female condom was primarily developed to protect women against AIDS and other sexually transmitted diseases (see Chapter 18). Until the condom for women came about, condoms for men provided sexually active people their only real protection against sexually transmitted diseases. Since many women have had difficulty persuading their lovers to use traditional condoms, the condom for women gives them a way to protect themselves against these diseases.

Like the condom for men, the condom for women is more effective when used with spermicides.

At this writing, information about the female condom is sketchy. The manufacturer says the device will retail for about $2.00 apiece, considerably more than the cost of condoms for men. The manufacturer also claims that 65 percent of women and 80 percent of men have expressed satisfaction with the female condom. But independent studies to date suggest a lower satisfaction rate. Only 10 percent of men and 25 percent of women involved in one test said they would consider using the device as their primary method of contraception and sexual infection prevention.

The female condom's price, effectiveness, and consumer acceptance should become clearer in the future.

Before You Call the Doctor.   Follow package directions. In addition, review the CONDOMS FOR MEN section of this chapter. Many of the points are equally applicable to condoms for women.

When to Call the Doctor.   Consult a physician if you have problems inserting female condoms, or if you experience vaginal irritation as a result of using the device. If a female condom breaks, immediately insert some spermicide and call a doctor about morning-after contraception (see MORNING-AFTER CONTRACEPTION in this chapter).

CONTRACEPTION

(See also BIRTH CONTROL PILLS, CERVICAL CAP, CONDOMS FOR MEN, CONDOMS FOR WOMEN, DIAPHRAGM, FERTILITY AWARENESS, INTRAUTERINE DEVICES, MORNING-AFTER CONTRACEPTION, NONINTERCOURSE LOVEMAKING AS BIRTH CONTROL, PROGESTERONE IMPLANTS, SPERMI-

CIDES, SPONGE, TUBAL LIGATION, VASECTOMY, and WITH-DRAWAL in this chapter)

Contraception gives couples the freedom to plan their families and prevent undesired pregnancies. Contraception allows couples to make sure they're fully prepared—physically, emotionally, and financially—to assume the responsibilities of having children. It allows births to be joyous occasions, and not burdens.

For information on any method, see the discussion of that method. This section deals with more general issues that apply to all the methods: contraceptive responsibility and effectiveness.

• *Responsibility.*   Some methods are used by men—condoms, vasectomy, and withdrawal. Others are used by women—birth control pills, cervical caps, diaphragms, fertility awareness, intrauterine devices (IUDs), spermicides, the sponge, and tubal ligation. And some require both partners' involvement—nonintercourse lovemaking and the combination of condoms and spermicide. But no matter which partner "does" the birth control, both partners should share the responsibility for method selection, and both partners should share the responsibility to use the method properly every time they make love. Couples should also periodically reevaluate their method choice because needs and preferences change over time, and the method that was once best for you may not be after a while.

It's often not easy for couples to discuss birth control. Many people, particularly men, believe that sex should happen "spontaneously" and that contraception gets in the way, or that it is the woman's concern. Others, particularly women, believe that "being prepared" with birth control implies sexual eagerness that's unladylike, and they find it impossible to ask a man to use a condom.

But sexuality experts agree that using contraception *enhances* lovemaking. Good sex requires mutual comfort, relaxation, and undivided attention. If one or both of you feels at all anxious about the risk of pregnancy or the possibility of catching a sexually transmitted disease, you may not be able to relax and feel sufficiently comfortable to enjoy good sex. In addition, raising the subject of birth control helps nurture intimacy in the relationship, which also enhances lovemaking. If you take care of business before getting down to pleasure, you'll have more fun, better sex, and no regrets afterward.

To make contraceptive discussions easier:

• Never assume that women take care of birth control and men don't. Plenty of women use the "prayer method," and plenty of men are seriously concerned about preventing unplanned pregnancies.

• Visit a family planning clinic together. The more than 5,000 clinics around the country have counselors trained to help couples evaluate all the methods and decide which one fits most comfortably into their life-style.

• Raise the subject of birth control early in the relationship. When is the right time? As soon as you think any relationship might become sexual.

• Be matter-of-fact about your own concerns. Every intelligent American should be concerned about preventing unplanned pregnancies as well as the sexually transmitted diseases discussed in Chapter 18. Mention that these subjects are on your mind and ask if your prospective lover shares your concerns.

• Listen to a tape. The sixty-minute audio cassette program "How to Talk to a Partner About Smart Sex" contains more than a dozen vignettes that dramatize conversations about condom use for the prevention of sexually transmitted diseases and help people raise this sensitive subject. The opening lines and snappy come-backs can also be applied to contraception (see RESOURCES at the end of Chapter 18).

• Raise the subject periodically. Relationships evolve, and so do contraceptive needs. Check in about your birth control method periodically and see if you both still feel comfortable with the one you're using. If not, visit a family planning clinic and consider something else.

• *Effectiveness.* Many people feel confused by contraceptive effectiveness statistics. If a method is, say, 98 percent effective, does that mean that while using it you can expect two pregnancies every 100 times you make love? No, it doesn't.

Birth control effectiveness is measured by "100 couple years," which means the experience 100 couples could expect to have if they used the method for a year. An effectiveness of 95 percent means that if 100 couples used the method for a year, five of them could expect to become pregnant at some point during that year.

Contraceptive effectiveness statistics also attempt to measure *how well* couples use the various methods. The idea here is that even the most theoretically effective method can't work if it's not used properly.

The following chart lists two effectiveness statistics for all currently FDA-approved nonsterilization methods—one for couples who use it perfectly, the other for couples who feel committed to contraception but use it less than perfectly—in other words, the use-effectiveness for typical couples. For example, condoms are 98 percent effective when used perfectly—that is, two pregnancies could be expected among 100 couples who used them properly and religiously for a year. But condoms are only 88 percent effective when used less than perfectly—that is, twelve preg-

Birth Control Method	Effectiveness When Used Perfectly (%)	Effectiveness When Used Typically (%)
No method	15	15
Spermicides	97	79
Fertility awareness	98	80
Withdrawal	96	82
Cervical cap	94	82
Sponge:		
Woman has never had children	94	86
Woman has had children	91	72
Diaphragm with spermicide	94	82
Condom:		
No spermicide	98	88
With spermicide	98+	90+
IUD	98	97
Pill	99	97
Progesterone Implants	99	99

(Source: *Contraceptive Technology* Irvington Pubs., 522 E. 82nd St., Suite #1, NY, NY 10028 1990–1992)

nancies could be expected among 100 couples who meant to use them properly and religiously but slipped-up now and then.

For more information about contraception, consult a physician or family planning clinic.

DESIRE DIFFERENCES

(See also LOSS OF SEXUAL INTEREST in this chapter)
One wants to make love. The other doesn't.

What's Going On?   It's very rare—some would say impossible—for both people in a couple to have identical desires for sexual frequency.

Almost always, one person is more interested in making love than the other.

Sometimes the roles never change, and one person always wants to make love more often than the other. But sometimes, as people grow older or if other things in their lives change—for example, job pressures, physical and emotional health, and feelings about the relationship—the roles reverse and the one who used to say "no thanks" becomes the one making the overtures.

Despite their inevitability, desire differences become a problem in many relationships. The more sexually inclined partner tends to feel rejected, guilty, angry, unloved, resentful, controlled, abnormally "oversexed," and victimized and may develop doubts about his or her sexual attractiveness. Meanwhile, the less amorous partner tends to feel harassed, guilty, angry, resentful, abnormally "undersexed," and victimized and may feel like a sexual object.

To make matters worse, many couples descend into frustrated name-calling. Men may accuse comparatively uninterested women of being "frigid" or "ice maidens" and call comparatively amorous women "castrating" or "nymphomaniacs." Meanwhile, women may accuse more sexually inclined men of being "sex fiends" or "animals" and call less amorous men "passive" or "wimps."

There is no "normal" amount of sexual interest. Sexual desire is as individual as our fingerprints. What's "enough" for one person may be "too much" for another and "nowhere near enough" for someone else. There's a famous scene in *Annie Hall* where Woody Allen tells his psychotherapist, "I don't know what to do. We hardly ever do it. I can't stand it. She'll only make love with me three times a week." Cut to Diane Keaton who tells her psychotherapist, "I don't know what to do. He's all over me. I can't stand it. We're making love three times a week."

Before You Call the Doctor. Negotiating desire differences is no different from negotiating anything else in a relationship—except that most people don't have much practice discussing sex. But try not to let fears of being inarticulate stop you. When couples make sexual frequency discussions a regular part of their relationships, resentment, guilt, and name-calling tend to subside—and sometimes the desire differences do, too:

• Stop all name-calling immediately and forever. Name-calling precludes good communication. There are no "frigid bitches" or "nymphos." There are no "sex fiends" or "wimps." There are only people who would like to love and be loved according to their own unique desires.

• Apologize for past outbursts, and pledge to try to work things out without anger and recriminations in the future. Admit you understand that sexual desire is a matter of personal preference and has nothing to do with being "normal" or "abnormal." This may not resolve accumulated resentments, but it's a start.

• Set aside time to discuss your desire differences. Take a walk. Have a picnic. Do it after making love. Whenever you both feel comfortable and able to give the subject your undivided attention.

• Talk about your whole relationship, not just its sexual component. Some people say, "Good relationships leads to good sex." Others insist, "Good sex leads to good relationships." It's really a chicken-and-egg question. Clearly good sex and good relationships are connected, but the connection differs from person to person. Sometimes people who don't feel sufficiently cared for out of bed focus on sex instead of saying what's really bothering them.

• Both partners might write down all the things that turn them on and off, and then share the lists, either all at once or an item or two at a time.

• Cuddle more—but don't expect that all cuddling leads to intercourse. Surveys have asked, "What kind of loving behavior would you like more of in your relationship?" Both men and women often answer, "More cuddling when we watch TV." Many people also would like their partners to kiss them good morning, good night, and when they leave for and return from work.

• Spend more nonsexual time together in ways you both enjoy. Go out on dates. Rediscover the person you fell in love with. Court one another again.

• If you'd like to make love, ask for it directly. Never assume that "If he (or she) loved me, he (or she) would know." No one can read your mind. Ask for what you want. Understand that asking directly does not necessarily get you what you want, but at least your partner unequivocally knows what you want.

• Get away. Days off, weekend getaways, and vacations allow people to leave their daily cares behind for a while and focus on more intimate activities.

• Get more information. For free confidential answers to questions about sexuality, call San Francisco Sex Information (see RESOURCES at the end of this chapter). SFSI is a national service.

When to Call the Doctor. If you feel you've tried your best and are still getting nowhere, consider professional help. Few physicians are skilled in sex and relationship counseling. If you'd like help from a psychotherapist, couples counselor, or marriage counselor, call your religious organization or local mental health agencies. To find a certified sex therapist near you, contact the American Association of Sex Educators, Counselors and Therapists (see RESOURCES at the end of this chapter).

DIAPHRAGM

(See also CERVICAL CAP and SPERMICIDES in this chapter)

The diaphragm is a round, dome-shaped cup of soft plastic or rubber with a flexible metal spring rim that covers the cervix, holds a spermicide, and prevents live sperm from entering the uterus.

What's Going On?   For information about the effectiveness of this method compared with the others, see the CONTRACEPTION section of this chapter.

The diaphragm is one of the "barrier" contraceptives (see CERVICAL CAP, CONDOMS FOR MEN, and CONDOMS FOR WOMEN in this chapter). Its springlike rim allows the device to be folded in half for insertion. Once inside the vagina, it springs back to its original shape and covers the cervix, providing a physical barrier to sperm. More importantly, the diaphragm also holds spermicidal jelly or cream against the cervix, which kills sperm before they can enter the uterus.

To work properly, diaphragms must be fitted by a medical professional. If it's too small, it may slip away from the cervix. If it's too large, it can cause cramping, discomfort during intercourse, and an increased risk of recurrent urinary tract infections (see URINARY TRACT INFECTION in Chapter 14).

Before You Call the Doctor.   Not all women can use diaphragms. This method is not for you if:

• You're allergic to spermicides or rubber or plastic.
• Your vaginal structure interferes with a good fit.
• You have a history of toxic shock syndrome (see TOXIC SHOCK SYNDROME in Chapter 16).

Diaphragm advantages include:
• No serious side effects.
• Protection against chlamydia and gonorrhea.
• Can be used after age forty, when the Pill cannot.
• Easier to insert and remove than the cervical cap.

Diaphragm disadvantages include:
• Possible need to interrupt lovemaking to insert it.
• Objections to messiness.
• Difficulty inserting or removing it.

• No protection against AIDS, herpes, syphilis, or venereal warts.

• Vaginal irritation.

• An increased risk of urinary tract infections (see URINARY TRACT INFECTION in Chapter 14).

Diaphragm effectiveness depends on the use of a spermicide with the device. In fact, some authorities say the physical barrier the diaphragm provides is incidental to its effectiveness and that it works because it holds a relatively large amount of spermicide up against the cervix.

For reliable contraceptive protection, the diaphragm should be left in for at least eight hours after your last intercourse. Some women forget they're wearing diaphragms and leave them in for a day or two, but authorities recommend against this. Extended wear may cause cramping and increase the risk of toxic shock syndrome (see TOXIC SHOCK SYNDROME in Chapter 16).

When to Call the Doctor.   If you decide to use a diaphragm, you'll need to have one fitted during a pelvic exam. The clinician should instruct you how to insert and remove it and check your insertion and removal technique.

Before inserting your diaphragm, wash your hands with soap and water. Fill your diaphragm with a tablespoon of spermicide. When you insert it, make sure you position it over the cervix correctly.

If you notice any discomfort or unusual vaginal discharge or bleeding, consult your provider. Also contact your provider if you feel at all uncertain about your diaphragm's fit or your ability to insert it properly.

Childbirth or significant weight gain or loss can change the size of the back of the vagina, necessitating a refitting. Before you start making love again after delivering, or if you gain or lose ten pounds, consult your clinician to check your diaphragm's fit.

Depending on how frequently they are used, diaphragms can last up to a few years, but eventually they need to be replaced. Examine yours regularly and if you have any doubts about its integrity, visit your provider for a replacement.

▶ **RED FLAGS**   Because the diaphragm may increase the risk of toxic shock syndrome, users should be able to recognize the signs of this potentially rapidly fatal infection. Call 911 or go to an emergency room immediately if you develop any of the following:

• Sudden high fever and chills.

• Vomiting with any other symptoms listed here.

• Diarrhea with any other symptoms listed here.

• Dizziness, faintness, and/or weakness.

• Sore throat with aching muscles and joints and any other symptoms listed here.

• A sunburn-like rash.

EJACULATION DIFFICULTIES

(See also EJACULATION (INVOLUNTARY) in this chapter)

Difficulty ejaculating ranges from ejaculation only after an unusual amount of stimulation to an inability to ejaculate at all.

What's Going On?   Difficulty ejaculating is the flip side of involuntary ejaculation (see EJACULATION (INVOLUNTARY) in this chapter). Instead of coming before he'd like to, the man has trouble coming at all.

This problem is officially known as "retarded ejaculation" or "ejaculatory incompetence," but for many men, these labels imply problems that go far beyond problematic ejaculation. There is nothing "retarded" or "incompetent" about men with this problem. We use the term "difficulty ejaculating" because that's all it usually is.

Difficulty ejaculating is the least known of men's sex problems. Everyone has heard of erection problems and coming too soon, but most men have no idea that this sex problem exists. Men who develop difficulty ejaculating typically feel unnerved by the problem and believe they are the only one who has ever experienced it. Far from it. Ejaculatory difficulties may not be as prevalent as involuntary ejaculation or erection problems, but plenty of men share this concern.

Most men (and women) equate ejaculation and male orgasm because the two usually occur at the same time. However, orgasm and ejaculation are actually two distinct physiological events. It's possible to have orgasm without ejaculation ("dry orgasm"), and it's possible to produce semen with little or no feeling ("numb come"). But because ejaculation and male orgasm typically occur simultaneously, this discussion treats them as interchangeable, even though technically they are not.

Like erection problems, difficulty ejaculating can be caused by both physical ("organic") problems and by relationship and lovemaking issues. Physical factors include:

• Aging. As men grow older, their penises require more stimulation to trigger ejaculation. Many men over age forty experience a decreased urgency to ejaculate, prompting some sexuality authorities to assert that aging "cures" involuntary ejaculation. It doesn't. Men can come before they'd like to at any age. But after around age forty, most men notice that ejaculation requires more friction and fantasy than it used to.

• Drugs. Many of the drugs implicated in erection problems—particularly alcohol—may also cause difficulty ejaculating (see ERECTION PROBLEMS in this chapter). Bear in mind that taking any of these drugs in no way condemns you to erection problems or difficulty ejaculating. But if your problem developed shortly after increasing your alcohol consumption or after starting to take narcotics, hypnotics, barbiturates, antidepressants, antipsychotics, or ulcer or high blood pressure medication, suspect a drug cause. In fact, suspect a drug cause if your problem began shortly after starting to take *any* drug.

• Genital infections. Prostatitis, gonorrhea and nonspecific urethritis typically cause painful urination or ejaculation and may produce enough anticipatory anxiety about expected pain to make men hold back (see PROSTATITIS in Chapter 17 and GONORRHEA and NONSPECIFIC URETHRITIS in Chapter 18).

• Other diseases. Several diseases may cause difficulty ejaculating or prevent ejaculation altogether: multiple sclerosis, paraplegia, diabetes, and advanced syphilis (see DIABETES in Chapter 4 and SYPHILIS in Chapter 18).

• Prostate surgery. TURP, the operation used to treat benign prostate enlargement, usually changes how men ejaculate. Instead of ejaculating out the penis, they generally ejaculate up into the bladder ("retrograde ejaculation"). All sexual sensations remain the same. The man experiences orgasm normally, but no semen leaves the penis ("dry orgasm") (see PROSTATE ENLARGEMENT in Chapter 17).

• Stress. Work, job, parenting, and money problems are more likely to cause erection problems than ejaculatory difficulties, but stress might contribute to this problem.

Relationship and lovemaking problems can also cause difficulty ejaculating:

• Emotional withholding. Relationship doubts and problems can cause a man to "freeze up" emotionally, making it more difficult for him to ejaculate. Sometimes a man's ejaculatory response senses relationship problems before the man consciously realizes they exist. Any problems may or may not be serious. Sometimes even chronic minor annoyances can contribute to ejaculatory difficulties.

• Fundamentalist religious background. The research here is scanty, but many sex therapists have the impression that this problem is often associated with a strict religious upbringing which taught men sex is a "sin."

• Rushed lovemaking. As men grow older, especially after about age forty, rushed lovemaking may not provide enough stimulation to trigger ejaculation.

• Routine lovemaking. The same old moves can become boring and not provide enough stimulation to trigger ejaculation.

Before You Call the Doctor. The causes of ejaculatory difficulties point the way to many effective self-care solutions:

• Don't drink alcohol to excess before lovemaking. One beer, one glass of wine, or one mixed drink probably won't hurt your ejaculatory ability, but any more might.

• Beware of all drugs. When you fill any prescription or buy any over-the-counter drug, ask your pharmacist if it might cause difficulty ejaculating.

• Adjust to the effects of aging. You may have to ask for more vigorous and more extended penile stimulation. Lubricants often intensify sexual caresses. Try saliva, vegetable oil, or over-the-counter products: KY jelly, Astroglide, or Surgilube.

• Explore what turns you on. Most men who have difficulty ejaculating don't lose the ability altogether. Using masturbation, identify the kinds of caresses and fantasies that allow you to ejaculate. Either incorporate them into your lovemaking, or adjust your lovemaking toward your ejaculatory triggers.

• Don't fake orgasm. The myth is that only women do this, but in fact, many men who have difficulty ejaculating fake it as well. They often use condoms to hide the fact that they don't produce semen. Faking is always bad for the relationship. The faker becomes a victim of long-term sexual frustration and may grow to resent the lover who does not understand the situation intuitively. Meanwhile, when the deceived lover learns the truth, feelings of not being trusted are inevitable, and good relationships cannot be built on mistrust. If you have trouble ejaculating, mention it to your lover. Ask for the kinds of stimulation that turn you on the most, and ask that your lover be patient with you. Most women prefer lovemaking that proceeds slowly and are happy to be patient.

• Take a long hard look at your relationship. Is this the relationship you want? If not, what's wrong? What could be done to make things better? Make regular dates to check in about your feelings, identify problems and stressors, and attempt to work them out. Don't withhold your emotions. Express them, though, of course this may not be easy. If necessary, consult a counselor.

• Take a break from ejaculation. For a few lovemaking sessions, stop expecting yourself to come. Taking the pressure off allows you to refocus your sexual energy on whole-body sensuality. Every square inch of skin is capable of physical arousal. Caress each other everywhere. Breathe deeply during lovemaking. (See the discussion of whole-body sensuality in EJACULATION (INVOLUNTARY) in this chapter.)

• Vary your sexual routine. Make a date to make love in a different place, in a different way, or at a different time. Go away for the weekend. Use your imagination.

• Try reading *Sexual Solutions: For Men and the Women Who Love Them* (see RESOURCES at the end of this chapter).

When to Call the Doctor. If self-care approaches don't resolve the problem sufficiently within a few months, contact the American Association of Sex Educators, Counselors, and Therapists for a list of the sex therapists in your area (see RESOURCES at the end of this chapter).

EJACULATION (INVOLUNTARY)

Involuntary ejaculation is what most men call "coming too soon," or ejaculating before the man intends to.

What's Going On? The official name for this problem is "premature ejaculation," but it's misleading. Many men infer that their "premature" ejaculation means they are somehow *immature* and that the problem would clear up if only they could grow up and become more mature. But personal maturity has nothing to do with this problem. Resolving it means gaining voluntary control over something that's been involuntary, which is why we use the term "involuntary ejaculation."

According to Helen Singer Kaplan, M.D., Ph.D., Director of the Human Sexuality Program at the New York Hospital–Cornell Medical Center in New York City, more than 90 percent of men suffering involuntary ejaculation can be cured within fourteen weeks. All it takes is some information and a few adjustments in lovemaking.

Involuntary ejaculation usually starts in adolescence. Young men feel peer pressure to become sexual, and they fear their early partners may suddenly become unwilling, so they rush through sex. As time passes, men learn that women generally prefer to make love more slowly, and they want to, too, so they start trying to last longer. But men who ejaculate involuntarily have never learned to control their ejaculatory timing, so they come before they and their partners would like.

Involuntary ejaculation can be caused by medical problems—for example, a hormone imbalance—but this is rare. Experts estimate that 99 percent of men who ejaculate involuntarily are normal in every way. They simply come before they want to.

Most men assume the way to resolve the problem is to distract themselves during intercourse, believing that by thinking about other things they can trick themselves into lasting longer. But that only makes things worse.

To learn ejaculatory control, the man shouldn't tune out his body. He should *tune into it.* He must learn to recognize how it feels to approach his "point of no return" ("ejaculatory inevitability"). Then it's usually not difficult to make small adjustments that allow him to maintain a high level of sexual arousal but not go over the edge to ejaculation.

Before You Call the Doctor.   The vast majority of men—single or married—can learn to last as long as they'd like:

•Using masturbation, learn to recognize how it feels to approach your point of no return. Most men quickly learn that by varying how they caress their penises, they can stay highly aroused without coming. When they feel themselves approaching the point of no return, they learn they can back off a bit, touch themselves more gently, breathe deeply, and stay highly aroused without ejaculating. Then as they get a little distance from the point of no return, they can return to more vigorous self-stimulation. For most men, it doesn't take long to develop good ejaculatory control while alone.

•Learn to appreciate whole-body sensuality. Men often think sex happens only in the penis and only during intercourse. That view is a one-way ticket to uncontrolled ejaculation—and erection problems—and it may cause partners to lose interest in sex (see ERECTION PROBLEMS and LOSS OF SEXUAL INTEREST in this chapter). Men learning how to approach—but not arrive at—the point of no return need to understand the importance of whole-body sensuality, the pleasure gained from touching every square inch of the body. Think of whole-body sensuality as massage. It produces the type of relaxation you feel after a hot bath or shower. In fact, many sex therapists suggest couples begin lovemaking by bathing or showering together to help them both relax and begin to enjoy whole-body sensuality. Whole-body sensuality releases tension. Tense bodies that have no other outlet for pent-up stresses often find release through involuntary ejaculation. As men learn to appreciate sensual pleasure from head to toe, whole-body arousal takes the pressure off their penises, and it becomes easier to last longer.

•Breathe deeply. An easy way to stay relaxed during lovemaking is to breathe deeply. Many men are amazed at the improvement in their ejaculatory control when they begin consciously breathing deeply.

•"Stop" and "Start." Once a man recognizes the sensations leading to his point of no return and feels comfortable with deep breathing and whole-body sensuality, then it's time for the couple to start working together. First they prearrange "stop" and "start" signals. Either the man says the words, or he touches his partner in an easily recognizable way, for example, a light pinch.

Together in bed, the partner strokes the man's penis with one hand. The man lies still, but he should feel free to guide the hand to show what he likes best. When he approaches his point of no return, he gives the "stop" signal, and the partner simply holds his penis gently without caressing it. The man continues to breathe deeply and pays close attention to the sensations he's feeling. When he no longer feels close to ejaculation, he gives his partner the "start" signal, and his partner returns to stroking him.

Sex therapists differ on the number of stops and starts couples should incorporate into each practice session. A half-dozen over a fifteen-minute period works for most couples. Experiment and do what feels comfortable for you.

Some sex therapists also forbid intercourse during ejaculatory training, on the theory that a preoccupation with intercourse is part of the man's problem. They urge couples to take a break and learn to appreciate sensual pleasure without intercourse. Again, do what feels best for you. You might practice stop-start for a while, then get up and have a light snack, and return to bed and make love.

With stop-start, the focus is necessarily on the man and what he's feeling because he's the one learning the new skill. But the woman's sensual needs should not be forgotten. As part of each practice session, she might guide his hand over her to show him what *she* likes.

Once the man has gained good ejaculatory control when the woman arouses him by hand, then it's time to progress to oral caresses and intercourse (with the woman on top—see below). The procedure remains the same. The man lies still. The woman provides the stimulation. The man gives her the "stop" and "start" signals along the way.

Finally, the man starts moving, and the couple is making love again— only now the man has ejaculatory control.

• Woman-on-top. The man-on-top ("missionary") position can be fun for both men and women, but it makes ejaculatory control more difficult because the man must support his weight and be concerned about not crushing the woman. Ejaculatory control is easier when the woman is on top. Then the man can relax, which helps his control.

Many women also prefer being on top because they have greater freedom of movement, and this position leaves the man's hands free to caress them all over.

• Side-by-side. Compared with the missionary position, the side-by-side intercourse position also helps most men's ejaculatory control.

• Muscle relaxation. No matter which intercourse position you use, some men automatically tense their leg and buttocks muscles during lovemaking. Consciously relaxing them often enhances ejaculatory control.

• Kegel exercises. Named for the physician who popularized them, Kegel exercises tone the muscle that runs between the legs of both men and women ("pubococcygeus" or "PC"), a key muscle that contracts during orgasm. Toning it often improves ejaculatory control—and the pleasure of orgasm in both men and women. For Kegel directions, see URINARY INCONTINENCE in Chapter 14.

• Try reading *Sexual Solutions: For Men and the Women Who Love Them* (see RESOURCES at the end of this chapter).

When to Call the Doctor. If these suggestions don't lead to sufficient ejaculatory control within a few months, contact the American Association of Sex Educators, Counselors, and Therapists for a list of certified sex therapists in your area (see RESOURCES at the end of this chapter).

ERECTION PROBLEMS

Some men cannot raise erections or maintain them long enough to enjoy mutually satisfying lovemaking.

What's Going On? Erection problems are often called "impotence." But impotence is a terrible word. It implies that a man has lost all personal vitality, that he is a failure as a man. We use the term "erection problems" because that's usually all this condition entails—an inability to raise or maintain an erection.

Until about twenty-five years ago, most authorities believed erection problems were caused by deep psychological problems treatable only by psychoanalysis. But psychoanalysis had very limited success. Today we know that most erection difficulties are caused by physical ("organic") factors, relationship/lovemaking factors, or a combination of the two.

Many physical health problems can cause erection loss. But having one or more of the following conditions *in no way* condemns any man to this problem. Diabetes is a classic organic cause of erection loss, and when diabetic men learn this, quite frequently the news becomes a self-fulfilling prophecy. In one noted study, a large group of men with "diabetic erection loss" were treated with standard sex therapy. Most regained their erections. Biologically speaking, the purpose of life is to reproduce life, and erection plays a key role in that mission. The body wants to be able to have erections. Men who have diseases or take drugs known to cause it may suffer erection impairment, but then again, they may not.

That said, here are the physical factors that can cause or contribute to erection loss. The more you have, the more likely you are to experience difficulty:

• Drugs. Alcohol is one of the nation's leading causes of erection impairment. In small doses (one beer, one glass of wine, or one mixed drink), it can increase interest in lovemaking ("disinhibition"), but any more alcohol causes central nervous system depression and erection impairment. Any drugs that cause drowsiness or tranquilizing effects can impair erection: narcotics (Demerol, Percodan, methadone, heroin, codeine), hypnotics (Dalmane, Nembutal, Halcion, Placidyl), tranquilizers (Valium, Xanax, Ativan), and antipsychotics (Thorazine). Other possible erection deflators include many—but not all—high blood pressure medications; the anti-ulcer drug, cimetidine (Tagamet); antidepressants (Elavil, Tofranil); and beta-blockers (Inderal). In fact, so many common drugs—both prescription and over-the-counter—have been implicated in erection impairment that sexuality authorities say *every* drug should be considered a possible erection deflator until shown otherwise.

• Aging. Healthy men can have erections throughout life, but as men grow older, most notice that their erections are not as full or as firm as they used to be. This is normal, but some men mistake it for erection impairment.

• Stress. When a runaway truck is careening down a hill straight for you, the body triggers the "fight-or-flight" reflex, which sends blood away from the central body and out toward the limbs for escape or self-defense. This reflex has clear survival advantages, which is why it evolved within us. But the vast majority of stressors in the modern world are not the life-and-death variety. Rather, they encompass everything from minor hassles (unbalanced checkbook, not finding parking, etc.) to major life changes (getting fired, the death of a spouse, etc.). These modern stressors cause more subtle but potentially equally profound effects on the body. Sometimes the cumulative impact of everyday stress can trigger physiological changes equivalent to the fight-or-flight reflex, and as blood leaves the central body for the limbs, less is available to fill the penis and cause erection.

• Depression. Many modern stressors also cause depression—everything from the blues to serious suicidal crises. Any events or emotional changes that cause intense feelings of helplessness and hopelessness can contribute to erection problems. (Ironically, so can antidepressant drugs—see DEPRESSION in Chapter 5.)

• Acute illness. Don't expect your penis to stand up if you cannot. Any ailment, from a cold to more serious diseases, can cause loss of interest in lovemaking and erection impairment.

•Convalescence from illness. Once they're "better," many men expect an immediate return to full sexual functioning. But just as you can feel lethargic for a week or so after recovering from the flu, erections may not spring back right away.

•Chronic diseases. Many chronic diseases *may* cause erection impairment in some men. The list includes but is not limited to diabetes, chronic fatigue syndrome, mononucleosis, depression, heart disease, stroke, high blood pressure ("hypertension"), congestive heart failure, fatty deposits on artery walls ("atherosclerosis"), emphysema, kidney disease, multiple sclerosis, and severe low-back pain (see CHRONIC FATIGUE SYNDROME and DIABETES in Chapter 4, DEPRESSION in Chapter 5, STROKE in Chapter 7, EMPHYSEMA in Chapter 11, CONGESTIVE HEART FAILURE, HEART ATTACK and HIGH BLOOD PRESSURE in Chapter 12, and BACK PAIN (LOWER) in Chapter 15).

•Genital diseases. Any disease that causes pain in the penis, scrotum, or prostate or pain on urination and/or ejaculation can cause erection difficulties (see PAIN IN THE GROIN OR TESTICLES and PROSTATITIS in Chapter 17 and CHLAMYDIA, GONORRHEA, HERPES, and NONSPECIFIC URETHRITIS in Chapter 18).

•Paraplegia and quadraplegia. Spinal cord injuries may sever the nerves necessary for erection.

•Congenital factors. Some men are born with a condition that causes painful erections that bend off to one side ("chordee"). Men exposed before birth to the drug DES may suffer genital abnormalities that impair erection. DES was given to millions of U.S. women from the late 1940s until 1971 in the mistaken belief that it would prevent miscarriage. If you were born during this period and your mother had any miscarriages prior to conceiving you, ask if she took any medication to prevent miscarriage. If so, chances are it was DES.

•Hormone imbalances. An abnormally low testosterone level can interfere with both erection and sexual desire.

•Surgery. TURP, the operation typically performed to treat benign prostate enlargement, causes erection problems in about 10 percent of men (see PROSTATE ENLARGEMENT in Chapter 17). Other genital-area or lower-back operations may cause similar complications.

•Environmental factors. Smoking is associated with erection problems. So is occupational exposure to toxic chemicals, particularly lead and other heavy metals.

Relationship and lovemaking problems can also cause erection impairment:

• Troubled relationships. Sometimes the penis senses relationship turmoil before the man consciously realizes it's occurring. The problems may or may not be serious. Sometimes even chronic minor annoyances can contribute to erection difficulties.

• Preoccupation with the penis. Erection requires not only stimulation of the penis, but stimulation of the entire body ("whole-body sensuality"). Men who believe the penis is the only arousable part of a man's body put too much pressure on it. Eventually the penis can't take the psychological pressure, and it quits.

• Rushed lovemaking. "Quickies" often don't provide enough time for the penis to become fully aroused. And as men pass about forty, they usually require more time to become aroused.

• Routine lovemaking. Penises can get bored with the same old moves.

Before You Call the Doctor.   The causes of erection problems point the way to many effective self-care solutions:

• Don't drink alcohol to excess before lovemaking. One beer, one glass of wine, or one mixed drink probably won't hurt your erection, but any more might.

• Beware of all drugs. When you fill any prescription or buy any over-the-counter drug, ask your pharmacist if it might cause erection problems.

• Understand the effects of aging. Healthy men can have erections no matter how old they grow. But as men age, erections tend to become less firm and full and may subside and return during lovemaking. These changes are normal. Some men misinterpret these natural changes as signs that it's time to retire from sexuality. Not at all. It's simply time to evolve your expectations and make a few adjustments in your lovemaking.

• Stay as healthy as possible and manage your stress load (see Chapter 1). Exercise is particularly important because it reduces stress, serves as a natural antidepressant, and contributes to the health of the arteries that supply blood to the penis, a blood supply necessary for erection.

• Give yourself enough time to convalesce from illness. Be patient with your body, especially if you are over age forty.

• Disabilities and chronic diseases may require some sexual adjustments. Chronic diseases neither eliminate sexual desires nor preclude lovemaking. They may, however, force you to make some changes in bed. Contact the organizations related to any chronic disease you have and ask about sexual adjustments. Many chronic illness organizations, for example, the Arthritis Foundation and the American Lung Association, make a point of encouraging people to remain sexually active despite any disabilities. Not even spinal cord injuries which preclude erection need signal the end of sexuality. When there's a will, there's a way. And after people adjust to disabilities and chronic diseases, many report they enjoy lovemaking as much as they did when they were able-bodied—sometimes more.

• There's sex after heart attack. Everyone has heard stories about men who had fatal heart attacks during lovemaking. Some of these so-called "mistress's nightmares" may be true, but they obscure a greater truth. Sex is not particularly strenuous or taxing for the heart. Studies have shown that sex stresses the heart *less* than walking up two flights of stairs or merging into freeway traffic during rush hour, especially if the lover with heart disease is on the bottom. Obviously, men who have heart disease should consult with their physicians about acceptable amounts of exercise, including lovemaking, but the fear of death that causes some heart attack survivors' penises to call it quits is usually unfounded.

• Don't smoke. For help quitting, see RESOURCES at the end of Chapter 11.

• Raise erection concerns before consenting to any surgical procedure, particularly prostate, lower abdominal, and lower back surgery. If there's any risk of erection impairment, ask if nonsurgical treatment is possible.

• Minimize any exposures to environmental pollutants. Always wear recommended protective gear at work. Work with your union, employer, and if necessary the Occupational Safety and Health Administration (OSHA) to keep your workplace safe. Don't ignore exposures from hobbies. Many arts and crafts expose men to potentially erection-impairing chemicals—painting, ceramics, photography, woodworking, and wood finishing, among others.

• Take a long hard look at your relationship. Is this the relationship you want? If not, what's wrong? What could be done to make things better? Make regular dates to check in about your feelings, identify problems and stressors, and attempt to work them out. You don't have to be the world's most sensitive, articulate person to do this. The key is to do it regularly, honestly, and mutually respectfully. If necessary, consult a counselor.

• Take some responsibility off your penis. Don't be so preoccupied with it. The body is a sensual playground. Every square inch of skin is capable of physical arousal. Caress each other everywhere. Women generally prefer a leisurely, playful, massage-oriented, whole-body approach to lovemaking. Many penises prefer it, too. When your whole body feels aroused, the penis doesn't have to take so much responsibility for your sexual fulfillment, and it often works better.

• Slow down. Hurried lovemaking goes hand in hand with penis-preoccupied lovemaking. Slow down, and then slow down some more. Take the time to savor whole-body sensuality.

• Vary your sexual routine. Make a date to make love in a different place, in a different way, or at a different time. Go away for the weekend. Use your imagination.

• Try reading *Sexual Solutions: For Men and the Women Who Love Them* (see RESOURCES at the end of this chapter).

When to Call the Doctor.   If you've noticed changes in your erections or erective capacity since taking any prescription medications—especially drugs in any of the categories mentioned above—consult a physician and ask if another medication might be substituted that is less likely to cause erection impairment.

If you suspect that you have any illness that might contribute to erection problems, consult a physician for an examination and treatment.

If you have a chronic disease, discuss its sexual implications with a physician, and ask for referrals to specialists in your condition, who might know more about coping with its sexual effects.

Many men who develop erection difficulties seize on the idea that they need a shot of the male sex hormone, testosterone. Men (and women) who have clear hormonal deficiencies benefit from hormone replacement. However, testosterone deficiencies are very rare. It takes only a tiny amount of testosterone to fuel normal sexual functioning, and the only thing additional testosterone does is increase risk of prostate cancer.

If self-care and ruling out possible physical problems don't provide sufficient relief, contact the American Association of Sex Educators, Counselors, and Therapists for a list of the sex therapists in your area (see RESOURCES at the end of this chapter). Sex therapists enjoy about an 80 percent success rate treating erection problems.

If sex therapy does not provide sufficient relief, a physician might prescribe yohimbine. This recently-approved prescription drug is derived from the bark of an African tree, reputed for centuries to have aphrodisiac properties. Studies have shown that yohimbine helps restore some erections.

Another drug which produces erection is papaverine. However, it must be self-administered by injection directly into the penis, something most men are unwilling to do. Those who use it tend to be diabetics who are used to self-injection. However, papaverine is not currently recommended for more than about one year of use because of possible side effects.

If drug therapy doesn't work, surgical penile implants are another option. Under general anesthesia, the urologist removes some of the spongy erectile tissue inside the penis and inserts hydraulic cyclinders connected to a fluid reservoir implanted in the lower abdomen. To inflate the implant, the man pumps a squeeze bulb inserted into his scrotum. A valve deflates the implant and returns the penis to its soft ("flaccid") state. Implants generally work well, but they are complicated devices and require major surgery. Be sure you've exhausted all nonsurgical alternatives before considering an implant. For more information about penile implants, contact Potency Restored (see RESOURCES at the end of this chapter).

FERTILITY AWARENESS

Fertility awareness teaches women how to recognize the subtle but distinct signs of their own fertile and infertile days each menstrual cycle. It can be used to prevent pregnancy or to maximize the chances of getting pregnant.

What's Going On?   For information about the effectiveness of this birth control method compared with the others, see the CONTRACEP-TION section of this chapter.

Also known as "natural family planning" and the "symptothermal method," fertility awareness is a scientific—and much more reliable—version of the "rhythm method." Women are fertile for only part of each menstrual cycle. About two weeks before each monthly period, women release an egg ("ovulation"). Ovulation triggers hormonal changes that make the vagina more hospitable to sperm. Fertilization, the union of the egg and sperm, can occur on any of about nine days approximately halfway between menstrual periods. Once a woman learns how to recognize her infertile "safe" days, the couple need not use any contraception then. During fertile days, they can use condoms, a diaphragm, cap, spermicides, or nonintercourse lovemaking.

Three elements are involved in charting fertility: the calendar, basal body temperature, and cervical mucus. The calendar was the only element in the old rhythm method. It attempts to predict a woman's fertile days based on her menstrual history, the assumption being that her cycles are regular enough to give her a good idea of her fertile and infertile days. The woman uses a calendar to record the start of her periods for six to eight cycles. Each cycle begins on the first day of one period and ends on the first day of the next period. During this time, she should use another form of birth control (not the Pill, which artificially controls many women's menstrual cycles). By assuming that her longest and shortest cycles are her personal baselines, she can calculate when she's most likely to ovulate and, based on that, her fertile period. The shortest cycle gives the earliest day she may ovulate; the longest gives the latest day she may ovulate. Ovulation occurs thirteen to fourteen days before the next menstrual period.

The calendar method works well for women with extremely regular menstrual cycles. But many factors can affect cycle-length and ovulation, including travel, illness, drugs, fatigue, and emotional stress. That's why so many women experience unplanned pregnancies when they rely on the calendar alone. In fertility awareness, the woman watches not only the calendar, but also *herself.*

Basal body temperature means body temperature the moment you wake up in the morning. It's typically a few degrees below "normal" 98.6°, and it's measured with a special basal body thermometer, which has an expanded scale in the normal range. Once a woman becomes familiar with her basal body temperature, it's not difficult for her to recognize the sudden, approximately one-half degree increase in basal body temperature that follows ovulation (see chart for typical variations).

Finally, the cervical mucus or Billings method predicts ovulation by observing the changes in a woman's cervical mucus. The cervix, the entrance into the uterus which hangs down into the back of the vagina, secretes mucus continually. But the texture of cervical mucus changes predictably at certain times during the menstrual cycle. During a woman's safe period, cervical mucus is scant, white, and dry. During her fertile days, it's clear, thinner, more abundant, and stretchy.

By combining the three fertility indicators, fertility awareness can be quite effective. Using it, any woman can figure out when she's fertile and infertile each cycle, making this the only birth control method that can both prevent pregnancy and optimize the chances of conception.

However, women or couples interested in fertility awareness must invest six to eight months to learn the woman's fertility pattern and take a class to master the complexities of this method. A few books have been

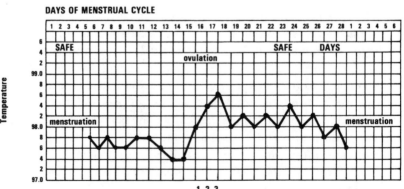

DAYS OF MENSTRUAL CYCLE

1 2 3

published about fertility awareness, but birth control experts strongly recommend taking a class to learn to chart properly and get all your questions answered. For a referral to a class, call a family planning provider.

Before You Call the Doctor.   Decide if you think this method might be a good one for you and your relationship. The advantages of fertility awareness include:

• No need for contraception for about ten days each month.

• The ability to be completely sexually spontaneous during infertile times.

• Decreased birth control hassles because you only use another method part of each cycle.

• Decreased risk of adverse effects from the other methods because they are only used part of each cycle.

Disadvantages include:

• The need to study the method to learn how to use it effectively. Books are available, but classes generally teach it better.

• The six- to eight-month lag time between beginning to chart fertility and being able to use the method reliably.

Fertility awareness generally works best for couples in monogamous relationships, and when men understand the method and support its use.

When to Call the Doctor.   If fertility awareness appeals to you, consult a physician or family planning clinic for a referral to a book or class that teaches this method.

IMPOTENCE

(See ERECTION PROBLEMS in this chapter)

INFERTILITY

If a couple desiring children does not become pregnant after one year of trying, authorities consider them infertile.

What's Going On?   Infertility affects an estimated 20 percent of married couples, and authorities generally agree that the problem is at an all-time high.

Couples who spend years hassling with birth control and fearing unplanned pregnancies are often surprised later to learn that it's not easy to become pregnant. Women must ovulate normally and have healthy fallopian tubes not scarred by infection. The uterine lining must be properly prepared to receive the fertilized egg. And the right amounts and types of hormones must be secreted at precisely the right times. Men must have normal erections and tens of millions of healthy sperm with enough energy to swim up the fallopian tubes and fertilize the egg. If any one of these factors malfunctions, the result might well be infertility. In about half of cases, the man is the one with the fertility problem, and in half, the woman is.

Normally each month, a woman's hypothalamus, a tiny gland at the base of the brain, secretes a small amount of a hormone ("gonadotropin-releasing hormone" or "GnRH"). In response, the nearby pituitary gland releases another hormone ("follicle-stimulating hormone" or "FSH"), which causes one of the egg follicles in the woman's ovaries to mature. It also stimulates the release of a third hormone ("luteinizing hormone" or "LH"), which triggers the release of the mature egg from the follicle. The egg then travels along the fallopian tube toward the uterus. In the tube, the egg meets sperm and becomes fertilized. If the egg isn't fertilized or if a fertilized egg fails to become implanted on the uterine wall, it's flushed out during menstruation, and the process begins anew the following month.

In addition to congenital abnormalities of the reproductive organs, many factors can impair fertility, especially among those born after World War II:

• People born after 1945 tend to have more sex partners than those born earlier. The more sex partners, the greater the risk of sexually transmitted diseases, particularly gonorrhea and chlamydia. These sexually transmitted diseases increase the risk of pelvic inflammatory disease (PID), a potentially life-threatening infection of women's reproductive organs that is believed to be a factor in as much as 50 percent of infertility in women.

• Intrauterine devices (IUDs), not available before the late 1960s, are associated with an increased risk of infertility.

• Female fertility decreases with age, and the trend toward delayed childbearing has taken its toll on women's ability to conceive. Only about 9 percent of women in their twenties have fertility problems. For women thirty-five to forty years of age, the figure jumps to more than 22 percent.

• Exposure to toxic environmental chemicals can threaten fertility in both men and women. These exposures, particularly on the job, have increased in the last twenty years as thousands of new chemicals have been introduced. Fertility-threatening chemicals are widely used in farming, dentistry, health care, dry-cleaning, pharmaceutical manufacturing, and electronics assembly. Other hazardous materials are used in hobbies, such as ceramics, painting, etching, jewelry-making, and color photography.

Other causes of infertility include:

• Weight loss. Women with anorexia nervosa don't ovulate, and any rapid significant weight loss can interfere with ovulation. With an estimated one-third of American women dieting to lose weight at any one time, some of them lose more than pounds.

• Exercise. Regular *moderate* exercise is good for you—in fact, crucial to health—but very strenuous exercise by women interferes with menstruation ("amenorrhea") and, therefore, impairs fertility.

• Alcohol abuse. Alcoholism affects an estimated 10 percent of the population. It impairs sexual desire in both men and women and erection ability and sperm quality in men. It is also a factor in irregular ovulation and menstruation.

• Cigarette smoking. Men who smoke produce fewer and less healthy sperm. Cigarettes are also associated with fertility problems in women (and low birth weight and other potentially serious problems in the children of women who smoke while pregnant).

• Marijuana. High doses of THC, the drug's active ingredient, impair ovulation. In men, marijuana has been shown to impair the health, motility, and number of sperm.

• DES. Physicians prescribed this drug ("diethylstilbestrol") to hundreds of thousands of women from the late 1940s to 1971 in the mistaken belief that it would prevent miscarriage. An estimated 50 percent of the daughters of these women ("DES daughters") suffer reproductive abnormalities.

• Tight underwear. The scrotum hangs outside the body because sperm thrive best at temperatures slightly lower than normal body temperature. Tight underwear holds the scrotum unnaturally close to the body and warms it, which temporarily reduces the number of healthy sperm.

• Hot tubs. Extended soaks in hot baths or hot tubs can raise scrotal temperature and temporarily reduce fertility.

Before You Call the Doctor.   There are plenty of things you can do to increase your chances of becoming pregnant:

• Women who plan to have children in the future should consider birth control methods other than IUD. IUDs increase the risk of pelvic inflammatory disease, which is strongly associated with infertility.

• Use barrier contraceptives—diaphragm, cervical cap, or condoms—or the sponge until you decide you want to become pregnant. Barrier contraceptives reduce the risk of contracting sexually transmitted diseases, which can cause pelvic inflammatory disease and impair fertility.

• Don't smoke anything. Women smokers have significantly lower rates of fertility than nonsmokers. Nonsmoking men have healthier sperm.

• Don't abuse alcohol.

• Maintain normal weight. Women who become too thin stop menstruating (see EAT AND DRINK RIGHT in Chapter 1).

• Exercise regularly, but keep it moderate. Superstrenuous workouts cause menstrual irregularity (see EXERCISE REGULARLY in Chapter 1).

• Men should not wear tight-fitting pants and underwear, which tend to increase scrotal temperature and impair sperm production.

• Men should avoid hot tubs, saunas, and extended hot showers while trying to conceive. Ideally, they should begin to do this a few months before the couple starts trying to conceive.

• After intercourse, women should remain on their backs for thirty minutes with knees drawn up and a pillow under the hips to retain as many sperm as possible.

• Do not use commercial sexual lubricants. They may kill sperm. If you need extra lubrication, use a vegetable oil.

• Do not douche. Douching increases the risk of pelvic inflammatory disease (see DOUCHING in Chapter 16).

For more information on dealing with infertility and coping with its emotional toll on relationships, contact Resolve, Inc. (see RESOURCES at the end of this chapter).

When to Call the Doctor.   Couples who do not become pregnant after six to eight months of trying should consult a physician. According to the American Fertility Society, 50 to 70 percent of infertile couples eventually conceive. The doctor should conduct a complete medical exam and take a complete medical history from both the man and woman, which should include information about past pregnancies, any sexual problems, areas of stress, menstrual problems, birth control history, alcohol and drug use, and diet and exercise habits.

The next step is a "fertility study" to determine why pregnancy isn't occurring. This includes a scrotal exam and semen analysis to determine the number, health, and motility of the man's sperm. Other sperm tests may also be performed.

Testing a woman's fertility is more difficult and time-consuming. Blood tests can determine if the levels of the various hormones are normal and whether ovulation has occurred. Tubal x-rays ("uterotubogram" or "hysterosalpingogram") may also be necessary to check for fallopian tube blockages or malformations.

Many treatments are available, everything from devices that lower scrotal temperature in men to high-tech in vitro fertilization, where eggs are removed from the woman's body, fertilized in a lab, and then implanted in the woman's uterus.

Although most infertile couples eventually conceive, many do not. And no matter what the ultimate outcome, infertility can have devastating emotional and relationship repercussions. Professional counseling may help. Contact Resolve, Inc., or a couples counselor (see RESOURCES at the end of this chapter).

INTRAUTERINE DEVICES (IUDS)

IUDs are small, flat plastic or plastic-and-copper objects inserted into the uterus.

What's Going On? For information about the effectiveness of this method compared with the others, see the CONTRACEPTION section of this Chapter.

IUDs are inserted semipermanently inside the uterus. A string attached to the device protrudes down through the cervix, which allows it to be removed. Unfortunately, microorganisms may ascend the string and infect the uterus and fallopian tubes, which is why IUDs are associated with an increased risk of pelvic inflammatory disease (PID), a potentially life-threatening infection of women's reproductive organs and a major cause of fertility problems.

Doctors aren't exactly sure how IUDs prevent pregnancy, but they suspect the device causes an inflammatory response in the uterus which prevents egg implantation or destroys the egg and sperm. Copper IUDs appear to interfere with sperm and egg metabolism and with implantation mechanisms in the uterus. Progesterone-secreting IUDs alter the cells of the uterine lining and apparently make them inhospitable to implantation.

During the 1970s, about 10 percent of women using contraception wore IUDs, primarily a model called the Dalkon shield. Then the Dalkon shield turned out to cause high rates of pelvic inflammatory disease and infertility, apparently because of its polyfilament string. The device was withdrawn from the market. In 1988, its manufacturer agreed to pay $2.4 billion in damages to Dalkon shield users. The scandal turned the nation away from IUDs, and today less than 1 percent of women who use birth control use this method. Two IUDs are currently available: a copper IUD

(ParaGard) and a progesterone-releasing IUD (Progestasert). Both of these IUDs use a monofilament string.

Many women cannot wear IUDs. Don't get one if you have:
• A known or suspected pregnancy.
• Any history of pelvic inflammatory disease.
• Active, recent, or recurrent gonorrhea or chlamydia.

You probably should not opt for an IUD if you have:
• A past history of ectopic pregnancy.
• Multiple sex partners.
• Plans to have children in the future.
• Lack of readily available emergency medical care.
• Heavy periods, anemia, or painful periods.
• Uterine fibroids, endometrial polyps, endometriosis, or an abnormal shape or size of the uterus or cervix.
• Cervical or uterine cancer or precancerous conditions.
• Valvular heart disease.
• Diabetes.
• Copper allergy (for copper-bearing IUDs).
• A history of IUD expulsion or pregnancy while using a previous IUD.

Before You Call the Doctor.   Decide if you think an IUD would fit safely and comfortably into your life and relationship.

The IUD's main advantage is convenience. Once inserted, it remains in place until it's removed by a clinician, usually once a year for Progestasert and every three or four years for ParaGard. However, women must check their IUDs regularly by feeling for the string that emerges into the vagina through the cervix. If an IUD user cannot feel her string, she should contact her family planning provider immediately.

IUD disadvantages include heavier, more painful periods and an increased risk of pelvic inflammatory disease.

When to Call the Doctor.   IUDs must be fitted by a medical professional. Improper insertion can cause expulsion of the device, which leaves the woman unprotected or results in the IUD perforating the uterus and becoming lodged in the woman's abdominal cavity, which is a medical emergency. IUD insertion requires a minimum of two office visits. The first visit should include a medical history, physical exam, blood test for anemia, Pap smear, pregnancy test, and tests for gonorrhea and chlamydia. A clinician counsels the woman, and she signs a consent form. If all tests are normal, on the subsequent visit, the clinician determines the size and shape of the uterus and inserts the IUD. The woman should be instructed how to feel for the string. After insertion, the woman may experience some cramping.

▶ **RED FLAGS**   Consult your physician or family planning provider immediately if:

•You cannot feel the IUD string.

•You feel any part of the hard plastic IUD itself in the cervix or vagina.

•You develop any signs of pelvic inflammatory disease: fever, pelvic pain or severe cramping, or an unusual vaginal discharge.

LOSS OF SEXUAL INTEREST

(See also DESIRE DIFFERENCES, ERECTION PROBLEMS, and ORGASM DIFFICULTIES in this chapter)

Loss of sexual interest ranges from minor declines in sexual desire to complete withdrawal from sexuality.

What's Going On?   In recent years, loss of sexual interest, professionally known as "disorders of desire," has become the leading reason why couples consult sex therapists. The problem itself is not new, but other changes in how our society views sexuality have resulted in a new emphasis on the issue of sexual interest. These changes include:

•The success of self-help methods to treat other sex problems. When the pioneering sex research of William Masters, M.D., and Virginia Johnson during the 1960s led to modern sex therapy in the 1970s, the major reasons people consulted sex therapists were lack of orgasm in women and involuntary ejaculation, erection problems, and difficulty ejaculating in men. But several books (see RESOURCES at the end of this chapter) have enabled many individuals and couples to resolve these problems on their own. Today, sex therapists tend to deal with relationship issues, chief among them loss of desire, and the related problem, desire differences (see DESIRE DIFFERENCES in this chapter).

•Changes in attitudes toward aging. Until recently, Americans assumed aging brought a loss of sexual interest. But now most people understand that after retirement, people can remain physically—and sexually—active, leading many to wonder why they're not.

•Changes in women's attitudes about sex. Until recently, most people assumed that men should be the initiators and women the "passive" ones. Few women ever made sexual overtures, and few men ever had to decide whether or not to accept them. But today, women are more likely to invite men into bed, and many men and women feel unnerved when men express any lack of interest.

• Changes in time commitments. In the 1950s, many futurists predicted the dawning of an Age of Leisure, when automation and labor-saving devices would leave Americans free to spend their time as they liked. In reality, today's Americans work longer and harder than ever. Two incomes are necessary to maintain a middle-class life-style, people commute longer distances in worse traffic, and the family dinner seems to have gone the way of auto tailfins. People have less time than ever and often feel that sex gets lost in the daily grind.

Now that loss of sexual interest has been identified as a problem—some say an "epidemic"—sexuality authorities have focused on its many causes:

• Two-career marriages. When two people work long hours, come home exhausted, and have to spend their evenings dealing with children, bills, grocery shopping, and all the other banal necessities of life, they often have little energy left for sex.

• Aging. Sexual desire generally—but not always—declines somewhat with age. But it rarely disappears. As Art Linkletter wrote in *Old Age is Not For Sissies,* "Older people enjoy sex just as much as younger people. But it changes. It's not like the Fourth of July anymore. It's more like Thanksgiving."

• Children. Hormonal changes associated with pregnancy cause many women to lose interest in sex. Diminished interest often continues through breastfeeding and sometimes afterward.

• Alcohol. Small amounts of alcohol (one beer, one glass of wine, or one mixed drink) promote relaxation and decrease sexual inhibitions, but at higher levels of consumption, alcohol is a central nervous system depressant, which decreases desire for sex and impairs its enjoyment. Alcohol is a leading cause of erection problems and ejaculation difficulties in men and loss of orgasm in women.

• Other drugs. Review the list of drugs associated with erection loss in ERECTION PROBLEMS in this chapter. Any of these drugs may also cause loss of interest in sex. In addition, some women experience decreased sexual interest while taking birth control pills. In addition to narcotics, barbiturates, hypnotics, antidepressants, antipsychotics, beta-blockers, and many other prescription drugs, quite a few over-the-counter products may also reduce sexual desire, notably antihistamines.

• Illness and chronic diseases. Few people want to make love while acutely ill, and chronic medical problems, which are increasingly prevalent, take a toll on sexual desire as well. In addition, a history of sexually transmitted diseases can make people wary of new sexual encounters. A history of unplanned pregnancies and/or abortions can have similar effects.

• Smoking. Smoking decreases general vitality, including energy for sex. Meanwhile, nonsmoking partners of smokers may become offended by the taste and smell of lovers who smoke.

• Mental health problems. Depression, anxiety problems, severe emotional stress, anorexia nervosa, bulimia, a history of rape or incest, and other mental health problems often contribute to loss of sexual interest (see Chapter 5).

• Surgery. Surgery on the reproductive organs—hysterectomy, prostate surgery, etc.—may diminish sexual interest. Any surgery that leaves a person scarred and/or feeling disfigured may cause a loss of self-esteem and a retreat from sexuality. In some cases, surgery may lead to hormonal changes that decrease sexual interest (see "Hormone problems" below). However, some operations may increase sexual interest—for example, certain cosmetic procedures, and voluntary sterilization, which eliminates the need for contraception and allows couples to be more spontaneous about lovemaking (see TUBAL LIGATION and VASECTOMY in this chapter).

• Hormone problems. Sex drive in both men and women is fueled by male sex hormones ("androgens"): testosterone in men and a similar hormone in women. (Both men and women also produce female sex hormones as well. Men produce more male sex hormones; women produce more female sex hormones.) Both sexes need only a minute amount of androgen to function normally sexually. Higher levels of male sex hormones don't do anything except increase the risk of prostate cancer in men and cause masculinizing effects in women, such as voice deepening and unwanted hair growth. But in some cases, male sex hormone deficiencies cause loss of sexual interest—for example, after surgical removal of the ovaries.

• Relationship problems. Troubled relationships are not conducive to good sex or frequent sex. When relationship tensions build, sex is often one of the first things to go.

• Nonsensual lovemaking. Women, in particular, tend to turn off to lovemaking focused primarily on genital caresses. And both sexes enjoy more intimacy and more fulfilling sex when lovemaking includes whole-body sensuality, a massage-oriented approach which stimulates every square inch of skin surface.

• Routine lovemaking. The same old thing can get boring.

Before You Call the Doctor.   First decide whether your loss of interest is a problem. If your relationship feels satisfying with less sex than you and your partner engaged in years ago and you both agree you feel no need for more, then there's no problem. But if you or your partner would like things to change, then you have some issues to discuss and perhaps some work to do. The suggestions here parallel some of the recommendations in DESIRE DIFFERENCES in this chapter, though some of the suggestions are different:

• Spend more nonsexual time together. Make dates. Have fun together. Rediscover the wonderful person you fell in love with. Absence may make the heart grow fonder, but just as often it does the opposite. Lovers who don't spend time together have difficulty maintaining intimacy and sexual interest in one another. The fires of passion must be stoked regularly by friendship and shared activities and interests. Enroll in a class together. Take up a hobby together. Try some weekend getaways and other vacations. Go out—just the two of you. Share some good laughs.

• Don't become tyrannized by your age. Okay, so most people notice some decrease in sexual desire after age forty or so. That doesn't mean the end of sexual desire or the beginning of a long slide into sexlessness. Lovemaking is a lifelong activity. Aging may require some adjustments, but no one is ever too old for sex or sexual desire.

• Don't become tyrannized by your children. There is sex after children, though some new parents have their doubts. Work your lovemaking around young children's nap schedules. Send your children to a babysitter from time to time to get more privacy.

• Cuddle more. Make a point of engaging in more nonsexual physical contact. Cuddling does not necessarily lead to intercourse—and don't expect that it should—but holding hands, kissing, hugging, and other little intimacies help people feel appreciated, loved, nurtured, and cared for, which often stokes the embers of desire back into flames.

• Write down all the things that turn you on and off, and then share the lists, either all at once or an item or two at a time.

• Drink less alcohol. Drink too much and all you'll do in the prone position is pass out.

• Beware of all drugs. Make a list of all the drugs you take—both prescription and over-the-counter—and ask a pharmacist if any might decrease interest in sex. In particular, beware of the drugs listed above and in ERECTION PROBLEMS in this chapter. (Drugs that cause erection problems in men often cause loss of sexual interest in women.)

• Give yourself time to convalesce from illness. It may take a while for sexual desire to return to normal.

• Don't smoke. For help quitting, see RESOURCES at the end of Chapter 11.

• Get more exercise. Moderate regular exercise helps relieve depression. It also increases vitality and makes people feel healthier, which increases self-esteem and generally boosts sexual desire and desirability.

• Work on your relationship. Talk about your *whole* relationship, not just its sexual component. Some people say, "Good relationships lead to good sex." Others insist, "Good sex leads to good relationships." It's really a chicken-and-egg question. Good sex and good relationships are clearly connected, but the connection differs from person to person. Sometimes people who don't feel sufficiently cared for out of bed focus on sex instead of what's really bothering them.

• Slow down. Women in particular generally dislike rushed lovemaking.

• Vary your routines. Make love at different times, in different ways, in different places. Add some music or scented massage oil. Use your imagination.

When to Call the Doctor.   If relationship problems seem to play a role in your loss of interest, consult a couples therapist.

Few people have hormone deficiencies severe enough to interfere with sexual desire, but this is possible. A physician can test you. If you've had a hysterectomy, discuss hormone replacement therapy with your physician. Some women who have had their ovaries removed require a little testosterone to restore lost libido, in addition to estrogen and progestin.

Before consenting to any surgery—particularly pelvic, prostate, lower abdominal, or lower back surgery—discuss its possible sexual implications with your surgeon.

Although most antidespressants diminish sexual interest, a recently introduced drug, bupropion (Wellbutrin), appears to have the opposite effect. In one study of men and women who sought sex therapy for lost sexual interest, a few months on bupropion returned them to what the researchers called "normal functioning." However, bupropion is not an "aphrodisiac." No one rips anyone else's clothes off. It takes several weeks to have any effect, and it works best in combination with professional sex therapy. If you're interested in bupropion, ask your physician about it.

MORNING-AFTER CONTRACEPTION

(See also "RU486" in the ABORTION section of this chapter)

As long as condoms break, IUDs get expelled, diaphragms and cervical caps become dislodged, women get raped or forget to take birth control pills, and sexual passions sweep people away, there will be a need for morning-after contraception.

What's Going On?   The average risk of pregnancy after unprotected intercourse is 15 to 25 percent. A woman is most likely to become pregnant if the intercourse occurs about midway between her periods. For many women, morning-after contraception is preferable to the risk of unwanted pregnancy.

Because of the political sensitivity of the abortion issue, no postcoital contraceptives have been officially licensed as such, but women still have several alternatives:

· Birth control pills. The regimen is two Ovral pills (a "combination" birth control pill) within seventy-two hours (preferably within twenty-four hours), then two more twelve hours later (see BIRTH CONTROL PILLS in this chapter).

· High-dose estrogen. The drug of choice used to be diethylstilbestrol (DES), but today physicians prescribe other estrogens (Femogen, Premarin).

· Morning-after IUD insertion. If inserted within a week of unprotected intercourse, an IUD prevents implantation of the fertilized egg in the uterine wall (see INTRAUTERINE DEVICES in this chapter).

Before You Call the Doctor.   If you don't want to get pregnant, use a reliable birth control method conscientiously so you don't have to opt for morning-after contraception.

When to Call the Doctor.   All postcoital contraceptives must be prescribed by a physician. Consult a physician or family planning clinic if you are concerned about pregnancy after unprotected intercourse.

NATURAL FAMILY PLANNING

(See FERTILITY AWARENESS in this chapter)

NONINTERCOURSE LOVEMAKING AS BIRTH CONTROL

"Nonintercourse lovemaking" means sex without vaginal intercourse.

What's Going On?   During oral or anal intercourse or mutual masturbation, no sperm are deposited in the woman's vagina, and pregnancy cannot occur.

Since the 1970s, sexuality surveys have shown that almost all American lovers engage in mutual masturbation and oral-genital caresses. Anal intercourse is a minority experience, practiced regularly by an estimated 5 to 10 percent of heterosexual lovers.

Before You Call the Doctor.   If you decide to use nonintercourse lovemaking as a form of birth control, refrain entirely from vaginal intercourse. Nonintercourse lovemaking might be combined with withdrawal, but authorities do not consider withdrawal a reliable form of contraception (see WITHDRAWAL in this chapter).

If you practice anal intercourse:

•Lubrication is crucial. Use vegetable oil or an over-the-counter sexual lubricant available at pharmacies: KY Jelly, Surgilube, or Astroglide.

•Insert very slowly. Women usually feel most comfortable guiding the penis in with their own hand.

•Do not penetrate deeply unless the woman says it's okay.

•Anything that has touched the anal area should be washed with soap and water before coming in contact with the vagina. Bacteria from the anal area that are introduced into the vagina may cause urinary tract infections (see URINARY TRACT INFECTION in Chapter 14).

•Be aware that those who engage in anal intercourse with men infected with the AIDS virus are at considerable risk of becoming infected themselves. Anyone who engages in anal intercourse should practice safe sex by using latex condoms.

ORGASM DIFFICULTIES

(See also EJACULATION DIFFICULTIES, ERECTION PROBLEMS, and PAINFUL INTERCOURSE in this chapter)

An estimated one-third to one-half of women do not regularly experience orgasm from vaginal intercourse, and many do not experience orgasm at all no matter how much sexual stimulation they receive.

Many men have difficulty ejaculating. Others ejaculate but do not experience pleasure ("numb come").

What's Going On?   An orgasm is an orgasm no matter if it's triggered by masturbation, direct oral or manual stimulation, intercourse, a vibrator, or some other kind of stimulation. In both men and women, orgasm results from wave-like contractions of the muscle that runs between the legs ("pubococcygeus" or "PC"). The same muscle helps control urination (see URINARY INCONTINENCE in Chapter 14). The typical orgasm lasts a few seconds.

In women, orgasm usually requires direct stimulation of the clitoris, though some women can experience it as a result of indirect stimulation provided by vaginal intercourse or as a result of other forms of stimulation. In men, orgasm usually requires direct stimulation of the head of the penis, though some men can experience it as a result of stimulation of the penile shaft, scrotum, anus or other forms of stimulation.

After orgasm, the vast majority of men and women experience physical release as their sexual arousal subsides and their breathing, pulse, and mental state return to normal. For the vast majority of men and women, some time must elapse before they feel interested in sex or able to become aroused again. However, some men, particularly young men, may be able to have another erection fairly quickly. And a small proportion of women do not experience postorgasm release but maintain a high level of arousal and can have another orgasm soon after the first. However, *very few* men are capable of immediate re-erection, and *very few* women are capable of multiple orgasm. No man should expect multiple orgasm in a woman. And no woman should expect rapid re-erection in a man.

Several physical problems can impair orgasm in both men and women:

• Central nervous system disorders. Spinal injuries or diseases such as multiple sclerosis, advanced syphilis, paraplegia, or diabetes can affect the nerves involved in orgasm.

• Other illnesses. Any significant illness, including such "minor" illnesses as colds, allergies, and sinus infections can interfere with sexual arousal and orgasm.

• Drugs. Alcohol is a central nervous system depressant. Large amounts impair sexual responsiveness in both men and women. Alcohol also impairs erection in men (see ERECTION PROBLEMS in this chapter). Other central nervous system depressants—narcotics, barbiturates, hypnotics (Valium, Halcion, Xanax), and sleep aids—have similar effects. Amphetamines, cocaine, and crack may heighten sexual arousal, but they impair orgasm. Many women find that birth control pills impair sexual arousal and orgasm. This list just scratches the surface of drugs that can affect sexuality. Many over-the-counter and prescription medicines impair sexual interest and ability.

• Everyday stresses. Any emotions that distract from the undivided attention lovemaking deserves can impair sexual responsiveness and orgasm. Common stresses include work, money, family, or relationship problems.

• A history of severe emotional trauma. Childhood physical or sexual abuse, rape, or other major emotional traumas can haunt people for years and contribute to inability to experience orgasm.

Beyond these possibilities, in most women, lack of orgasm ("anorgasmia") is caused by lack of sexual information and experience and by an inability to ask for direct clitoral stimulation:

• Some women have been brought up to believe that sex is "dirty" or that it's a "sin" to experience sexual pleasure unless the goal is procreation. Sex is not dirty, and though some religious leaders may disagree, we don't see anything wrong with two people who love each other making love simply to express that emotion.

• Some women have been brought up to believe that self-pleasuring ("masturbation") is "wrong." We don't think masturbation is wrong. On the contrary, it can be a powerful stress reliever, and sex therapists recommend it to help teach women how to have orgasms.

• Some women—and many men—don't fully appreciate the clitoris. This most sexually sensitive part of a woman's body sits outside and above the vagina near the junction of the vaginal lips.

• Some women have been accused of being "unresponsive" or "frigid." Typically the fault lies not with the woman but is a result of lack of information on the part of the couple. Men tend to become fully sexually aroused more quickly than women. Many men feel ready to have their orgasms long before most women have become sufficiently aroused to enjoy theirs. Men need to slow down and give women time to become fully aroused. Vaginal lubrication is a convenient sign of arousal. As women become sexually aroused, natural vaginal lubrication moistens their vaginal lips. Men should never try to insert their penises into vaginas unmoistened by vaginal lubrication. Furthermore, the mere presence of vaginal lubrication does not mean the woman is fully aroused. Men should wait a while *after* the woman's vaginal lips have become moist before attempting insertion.

• Many perfectly normal women simply do not have orgasms during vaginal intercourse no matter how long it lasts. For many women, vaginal intercourse does not provide enough clitoral stimulation. They need direct clitoral stimulation—by hand, mouth, or vibrator. One way to combine vaginal intercourse and direct clitoral stimulation is the woman-on-top position. With the woman on top, the man's hands are free to provide clitoral stimulation. Doggie-style intercourse—with the woman on her hands and knees, and the man behind her—also allows men to caress the clitoris during intercourse.

• Many women find it difficult to ask men to slow down or provide the kind of direct clitoral stimulation that brings them to orgasm.

• Some women fake orgasm to please the men in their lives or to make themselves appear "normal" and "responsive."

In men, orgasm is a two-part process. When they become sufficiently aroused, the prostate gland and seminal vesicles contract and empty semen into the urethra ("emission"), which men experience as the point of no return ("ejaculatory inevitability"). Shortly afterward, the PC muscle's wavelike contractions trigger orgasm and propel the semen down the urethra and out of the penis ("expulsion").

Most men don't distinguish between orgasm and ejaculation because they usually occur simultaneously. But in men who have had TURP surgery for benign prostate enlargement, orgasm occurs without ejaculation ("dry orgasm") (see PROSTATE ENLARGEMENT in Chapter 17). And depending on the man's use of medications and emotional commitment to the relationship, orgasm may not produce much pleasure ("numb come").

In addition to nervous system disorders, drugs, stress, and other illnesses, several other factors can interfere with men's ability to have orgasm:

• Erection problems and difficulty ejaculating (see ERECTION PROBLEMS and EJACULATION DIFFICULTIES in this chapter).

• Aging. Older men require more stimulation to raise and maintain erections and to experience orgasm. Older men's erections tend not to be as firm as they once were and their ejaculations often feel less forceful because age decreases pelvic muscle tone.

• Prostate problems and sexually transmitted diseases. These can make ejaculation painful and interfere with orgasm (see PROSTATITIS in Chapter 17 and GONORRHEA and NONSPECIFIC URETHRITIS in Chapter 18).

Before You Call the Doctor.   To experience and enjoy orgasm, both men and women should:

• Stay healthy. Review Chapter 1. Illness (even minor ones) and falling out of good physical condition can impair sexual functioning.

• Cut back on all drugs with adverse sexual effects. Drink less alcohol. Consider switching from birth control pills to another method. Make a list of every prescription and over-the-counter drug you use, take it to a pharmacist, and ask if any might have sexual effects. Read the labels of over-the-counter medicines. If it says, "May cause drowsiness," chances are it can impair orgasm.

• Deal with your everyday stressors (see MANAGE YOUR STRESS LOAD in Chapter 1).

• Take a look at your relationship. Relationship problems often affect sexual enjoyment. Check in with your lover and talk about your feelings for each other.

• Women who don't have orgasms or have difficulty experiencing them might:

• Read a good book. Several self-help books have been published to help women discover the orgasms within themselves. Most begin with a program that progresses from basic sexuality information, through non-sexual self-pleasuring and masturbation, to discovering how to be orgasmic with a supportive partner. These books may be obtained confidentially by mail from The Sexuality Library (see RESOURCES at the end of this chapter).

• Work on your relationship. Try to discuss anything that's bothering you. Work to reestablish any lost intimacy.

• Stop faking orgasm. Deception may solve some problems in the short run, but it compounds them in the long run. Ask specifically for the kinds of stimulation you would like. If you find it difficult to make direct requests, then simply use positive reinforcement. Say to your partner, "That feels wonderful," or make little appreciative noises when you receive caresses you enjoy, and simply remain silent when you don't. Or ask what kinds of touch your lover wants, and mention that you'd appreciate more of some moves and less of others. Try to be playful about making and granting intimate requests.

• Cultivate a whole-body, massage-oriented approach to lovemaking. Explore every square inch of each other's bodies. Use massage oils to increase skin sensitivity.

• Vary your routine. Try making love in new locations, at new times, and in other mutually agreeable ways that spice up the humdrum.

• Don't make love right before retiring when both of you feel fatigued and sleepy.

• Get professional help. For a referral to a psychotherapist or couples counselor, contact your local mental health agencies. For a list of the certified sex therapists in your area, write the American Association of Sex Educators, Counselors, and Therapists (see RESOURCES at the end of this chapter).

When to Call the Doctor. Most physicians are neither skilled in nor inclined toward sex therapy. But consult a doctor if you suddenly lose the ability to function sexually or suddenly enjoy sex less. Sudden sexual changes might mean illness. Also, consult a physician if you suspect your inability to experience orgasm has a physical cause.

PAINFUL INTERCOURSE

Pain or soreness during intercourse can affect either men or women, but it's usually a woman's problem.

What's Going On?   Medically, this problem is called "dyspareunia." Occasionally, men suffer painful intercourse caused by:
- Allergies to spermicides.
- Irritation from diaphragms, cervical caps, condoms, or the sponge.
- Irritation from attempts to enter unlubricated vaginas that are not ready to receive them.
- A tight foreskin in uncircumsized men (see PHIMOSIS in Chapter 17).

But usually it's women who complain of dyspareunia. Possible causes include:
- Attempts at intercourse without sufficient vaginal lubrication. Some men don't give women enough time or whole-body caresses to become sufficiently lubricated before attempting insertion.
- Vaginal or urinary tract infection infections (see URINARY TRACT INFECTION in Chapter 14, YEAST INFECTION in Chapter 16, and TRICHOMONAS in Chapter 18).
- Vaginal irritation because of estrogen deficiency related to breast-feeding, birth control pills, or aging (see ATROPHIC VAGINITIS in Chapter 16).
- Endometriosis (see ENDOMETRIOSIS in Chapter 16).
- Scarring from surgical procedures, such as episiotomy or vaginal hysterectomy.
- Involuntary contraction of the vaginal muscles with intercourse (see VAGINISMUS in this chapter).

Pain in the vaginal canal entrance ("introitus pain") usually indicates a vaginal problem. Pain that occurs only when the penis is fully inserted ("bump dyspareunia") suggests a uterine, tubal, or other pelvic problem.

Before You Call the Doctor.   A good deal of pain on intercourse for both men and women can be resolved if the couple postpones vaginal intercourse until the woman's vagina has become fully lubricated and ready to receive the penis. Compared with men, women tend to become fully aroused more slowly. Arousal depends not only on genital stimulation but on leisurely, playful, whole-body, massage-style caresses. For additional lubrication, try saliva, vegetable oil, or a commercial lubricant (KY jelly, Astroglide, Surgilube).

If a diaphragm, cervical cap, condom, or vaginal sponge causes penile irritation, the couple might try less vigorous, less deep penetration or switching to another birth control method.

If a spermicide sensitivity seems to cause the problem, try changing brands. If that doesn't work, consider switching birth control methods to one that does not require spermicide.

If the cause is recent childbirth or vaginal surgery, consider nonintercourse lovemaking until the vagina has completely healed. Then use slow, partial penetration and massage of the area between the vagina and anus ("perineum") to gradually soften the scar tissue in the area.

When to Call the Doctor. Consult a physician for suspected foreskin problems ("phimosis"), vaginal irritation or infection, urinary tract infection (UTI), endometriosis, or vaginismus. Physicians can prescribe antibiotics for vaginal infections and UTIs, hormone creams to relieve postmenopausal vaginal irritation, surgery for phimosis, a variety of treatments for endometriosis, and vaginal dilation, muscle relaxants, and counseling for vaginismus.

PREGNANCY AND CHILDBIRTH

A full discussion of pregnancy and childbirth is beyond the scope of this book. Ask your prenatal clinician, librarian, or bookseller to suggest good handbooks. However, we'll mention several key points:

• Adopt a healthy life-style even before you start to try to get pregnant. Prepare for pregnancy by reviewing Chapter 1 and reading the INFERTILITY section in this chapter.

• Prenatal care. Begin prenatal care as soon as a test confirms your pregnancy. This is particularly important for teens, women over thirty-five years of age, any woman with a preexisting medical condition (asthma, diabetes, etc.), and any woman with a history of miscarriage. Diabetics should start their prenatal care with an obstetrician *before* conception.

• Diet. During pregnancy, women's nutritional requirements increase dramatically. Pregnant women should make sure they get sufficient calcium, iron, and folic acid. Vitamin supplements are recommended during pregnancy even if you didn't take them before getting pregnant. Although vitamins are available over-the-counter, many do not contain sufficient folic acid. (Most contain 0.4 mg instead of the recommended 1.0 mg for pregnant women.) Recent studies indicate that early supplementation with 1.0 mg a day of folic acid helps prevent spinal ("neural tube") birth defects.

• Weight gain. Recommendations vary somewhat from clinician to clinician, but most suggest weight gain in the 30- to 35-pound range. Eat a low-fat, high-fiber diet based on whole grains and fresh fruits and vegetables. Women who eat a no-dairy ("vegan") vegetarian diet must pay particular attention to getting adequate protein and calcium. Beans and tofu are good sources. If you suffer from nausea ("morning sickness") during pregnancy try "grazing" throughout the day instead of eating big meals.

• Increase your fluid intake. Drink at least six glasses of water, unsweetened fruit juices, vegetable juices, or herb teas daily.

• Do not drink alcohol. Overuse of alcohol during pregnancy causes "fetal alcohol syndrome," a group of birth defects that includes mental retardation. Even one or two drinks a day can reduce a baby's birth weight.

• Exercise. Stay physically active. Don't do anything terribly strenuous like running long distances. Instead, take walks, garden, swim, do yoga, or enroll in a prenatal exercise class. If you have been doing aerobic exercise, you can continue, but with these modifications:

  ◦ Change to a non-impact activity—for example, racewalking instead of running.
  ◦ Keep your heart rate below 140 beats per minute. Higher rates divert blood away from the uterus.
  ◦ When performing toning exercises, be extra careful to avoid jerky motions or hyperextending. During pregnancy, the joint structures soften and loosen, making them more prone to injury.
  ◦ As you begin to show, modify abdominal exercises, emphasizing pelvic tilts and avoiding any moves in which the legs extend straight out.
  ◦ After the sixth month, don't lie flat on your back because the uterus tends to press on veins in the abdomen, which can interfere with blood return to the heart.
  ◦ Drink plenty of fluids before, during, and after exercising.
  ◦ If you feel fatigued, stop or slow down. If an activity or particular exercise feels painful, stop immediately.

• Get extra rest. Most women need more sleep during pregnancy. Many need naps and waking rest periods as well. Modify your schedule if necessary. Insomnia is common during the third trimester (see INSOMNIA in Chapter 4).

• Manage your stress. Pregnancy and a new baby are quite stressful. Plan ahead for increased stress. Ask your partner to take on more household chores. Ask friends and family to help you. Use a stress reduction technique, such as meditation, deep breathing, or music therapy, daily to reduce your stress level.

• Remember your relationships—including friends and family. Don't become obsessed with the baby. You have other important relationships that also deserve care and attention.

• Play it safe. Don't take any drugs (including tobacco!) during pregnancy unless they are prescribed by a physician. Don't drink alcohol. Beware of toxic chemicals on your job or in hobbies. Stay away from kitty litter if you're not certain you're immune to toxoplasmosis.

• Be attentive to physical complaints. Backaches, heartburn, varicose veins, and many other physical complaints are all part of pregnancy. Consult the appropriate section in this book, but don't use *any* medications without first consulting your physician.

PREMATURE EJACULATION

(See EJACULATION (INVOLUNTARY) in this chapter)

PROGESTERONE IMPLANTS

This new, recently approved birth control method, called Norplant, involves the surgical implantation of six match-stick size hormone rods in a woman's upper arm. This contraceptive provides safe, reliable, reversible contraception for five years.

What's Going On?   For information about the effectiveness of this method compared with the others, see the CONTRACEPTION section of this chapter.

Before You Call the Doctor.   Implants' advantages include:
• Extremely effective with a hormone dose significantly lower than conventional birth control pills or minipills.
• No interruption of lovemaking or sacrifice of sexual spontaneity. This method is not intercourse-related, so there's nothing to do to prepare for lovemaking.
• Minor side effects. Compared with the Pill or an IUD, the two other methods whose use is unrelated to intercourse, implants' side effects are less medically serious. There may be decreased menstrual cramping and lighter or no menstrual flow. Menstrual periods are usually irregular, especially during the first three to six months after insertion.

Implants' disadvantages include:

• Possible cosmetic problems. The hormone capsules may be visible on the woman's inner arm.

• Possible changes in menstrual pattern, including prolonged bleeding, spotting between periods, and irregular or missed periods.

• Initial cost. Implants cost more than other methods, about $400 for the capsules and $100 to $300 for their implantation. But over the implants' five-year life, this method may actually wind up costing less than the Pill or condoms.

• Surgery. Implants require minor surgery for insertion and removal.

• Still fairly new. Implants appear to cause few side effects, but some might turn up in the future.

When to Call the Doctor.   Women interested in progesterone implants should consult their family planning providers. The implantation procedure involves brief, minor surgery under local anesthesia. The physician inserts the six little implant tubes in a fan-shaped pattern on the inside of your upper arm. Once in place, the implants release a low dose of levonorgestrel, a progesterone-type hormone, which lasts five years, or until the capsules are removed. Once removed, fertility reliably returns.

RETARDED EJACULATION

(See EJACULATION DIFFICULTIES in this chapter)

SPERMICIDES

(See also CERVICAL CAP, DIAPHRAGM, and SPONGE, in this chapter)

Spermicides are over-the-counter contraceptives available in creams, jellies, foams, and suppositories. Creams and jellies are used in conjunction with diaphragms and cervical caps. Foams and suppositories may be used by themselves or with condoms.

What's Going On?   For information about the effectiveness of this method compared with the others, see the CONTRACEPTION section of this chapter.

Spermicides kill sperm. The term "spermicide" sounds a lot like "insecticide" and "pesticide," but unlike the chemicals used to control insects and agricultural pests, spermicides are not poisonous. They interact chemically with the outer membranes of sperm cells and disable sperm cells. Spermicidal chemicals include nonoxynol-9 and octoxynol-9. Spermicides have never been shown to damage vaginal tissue, nor to cause harm when small amounts are ingested during oral sex.

Spermicides used with diaphragms, cervical caps, and vaginal sponges are discussed in the DIAPHRAGM, CERVICAL CAP, and SPONGE sections of this chapter. The discussion that follows deals only with foams and suppositories.

Spermicidal foam comes in aerosol containers with plunger applicators. To be effective, you must insert an applicator-full no more than one hour before having vaginal intercourse. A new applicator-full must be inserted before every lovemaking episode that involves vaginal intercourse.

Spermicidal suppositories must be inserted at least ten minutes before intercourse to allow them time to melt. Twenty minutes is safer.

A woman should not douche or sit in a bathtub for at least six to eight hours after using a spermicide. (Women shouldn't douche at all unless a physician recommends it to treat a vaginal infection—see DOUCHING in Chapter 16.)

Before You Call the Doctor.   Decide if you think spermicides would fit safely and comfortably into your life and relationship.

Spermicide advantages include:

• They're available over-the-counter. No need to spend time and money on professional providers.

• They help prevent sexually transmitted diseases, including AIDS.

• They provide some backup protection if a condom breaks or if a man who intends to withdraw doesn't do so in time.

• They help provide additional lubrication during intercourse.

• They cause no serious side effects.

• You use them only when you make love.

Spermicide disadvantages include:

• Possible objections to insertion.

• Possible objections to messiness.

• Possible objections to the effervescence of vaginal suppositories. Many women feel a sensation of heat as they melt inside the vagina.

• Possible vaginal or penile irritation.

• Possible objections to their taste during oral sex.

When to Call the Doctor.   Consult a physician if spermicide-associated vaginal or penile irritation does not clear up within a few days after discontinuing spermicide use.

652 **BEFORE YOU CALL THE DOCTOR**

SPONGE

(See also SPERMICIDES in this chapter)

The vaginal sponge is a soft, dimpled, pillow-like polyurethane cup two-inches across, permeated with spermicide. The dimple is placed over the cervix, and the device may be left in place for twenty-four hours without adding additional spermicide.

What's Going On?   For information about the effectiveness of this method compared with the others, see the CONTRACEPTION section of this chapter.

The vaginal sponge (Today) was approved in 1983. It serves as a physical barrier to sperm but works primarily as a continuous-release source of spermicide. The spermicide used is nonoxynol-9 (see SPERMICIDES in this chapter).

One size fits all. Vaginal sponges are available over-the-counter and do not have to be fitted by a medical professional. Like condoms, sponges are discarded after removal.

The sponge has been implicated in a few cases of toxic shock syndrome and vaginal infections when used improperly (see TOXIC SHOCK SYNDROME and VAGINITIS in Chapter 16). Asthmatics and those sensitive to sulfites may develop respiratory difficulties because of a sulfiting agent, sodium metabisulfite, used as a preservative.

Before You Call the Doctor.   Decide if you think the sponge would fit safely and comfortably into your life and relationship.

Sponge advantages include:

• They're available over-the-counter. No need to spend time and money on professional providers.

• They help prevent sexually transmitted diseases, including AIDS.

• They cause no serious side effects.

• You use them only when you make love.

• Unlike spermicidal foam or suppositories, the sponge may be inserted as early as twenty-four hours before intercourse, and there is no need to add anything for repeated intercourse within the twenty-four hours that the sponge is in place.

Sponge disadvantages include:

• Possible difficulty inserting and removing them.

• Possible vaginal or penile irritation.

• Decreased effectiveness in women who have had children (see CONTRACEPTION in this chapter).

•Somewhat increased risk of toxic shock syndrome, vaginal infections, and sulfite reactions.

When to Call the Doctor. Women should consult a physician if they develop vaginal itching, burning, irritation, or an unusual discharge. If you cannot remove the sponge, or if it tears and you cannot remove all the pieces, see a physician promptly. Men should consult a physician if they develop any penile irritation that does not resolve within a few days of discontinuing sponge use.

▶ **RED FLAGS** Because the sponge may increase the risk of toxic shock syndrome, users should be able to recognize the signs of this potentially rapidly fatal infection. Call 911 or go to an emergency room immediately if you develop any of the following:
•Sudden high fever and chills.
•Vomiting with any other symptoms listed here.
•Diarrhea with any other symptoms listed here.
•Dizziness, faintness, and/or weakness.
•Sore throat with aching muscles and joints or with any other symptoms listed here.
•A sunburn-like rash.

STERILIZATION

(See TUBAL LIGATION and VASECTOMY in this chapter)

TUBAL LIGATION

(See also VASECTOMY in this chapter)
Tubal ligation is the sterilization operation performed on women. Sterilization is the most effective birth control method, but it's also permanent.

What's Going On? Sterilization for women involves blocking the tubes ("fallopian tubes") which connect the ovaries and the uterus. The fallopian tubes can be blocked by cutting ("ligation"), mechanical closure with clips, or removal of the uterus ("hysterectomy"). Tubal ligation is generally considered the most effective, least costly, and least physically traumatic alternative.

The standard procedure takes places under sedation and local or general anesthesia. An overnight hospital stay may be necessary. It involves a small incision at the top of the pubic hairline ("suprapubic minilaparotomy") and insertion of an instrument ("laparoscope"), which is used to cut the tubes.

Surgical complications develop in about 1 percent of cases. They include wound infections, anesthesia reactions, intestinal injury, and sterilization failure.

About 40 percent of tubal ligations are performed shortly after delivery of a child. In such cases, the surgeon uses a slightly different procedure which requires general anesthesia.

Tubal ligation is considered minor surgery, but it's more major—and more costly—than vasectomy (see VASECTOMY in this chapter).

Before You Call the Doctor.   If you have completed your family and no longer care to use other contraceptives, tubal ligation might be right for you. But before you have the operation, think long and hard about some difficult questions:

•Suppose you divorced or became widowed and then remarried. Would you want more children? What if your new husband wanted more children?

•Suppose your children were killed? Would you want to start a new family?

If you find yourself thinking: Well, I could always get it reversed, think again. There's no guarantee that any tubal ligation can be reversed, and no woman should have one if she thinks she might ever want it reversed.

When to Call the Doctor.   If you're quite certain you want to be sterilized, contact a physician.

VAGINISMUS

(See also PAINFUL INTERCOURSE in this chapter)

Vaginismus means involuntary contraction of the vaginal muscles, which makes intercourse painful and/or impossible.

What's Going On?   In this condition, the muscles of the outer third of the vagina suddenly contract involuntarily. Sometimes the cause is organic and the woman should be examined to rule out structural abnormalities. But most cases are associated with an emotional aversion to sexual intercourse, often with a history of sexual trauma—for example, rape, incest, or other forms of sexual abuse.

Before You Call the Doctor.   Both partners need to understand that vaginismus is involuntary. The woman cannot help herself. Women should try not to feel guilty or ashamed. Rather, they should try to look at the problem as a result of traumas they have suffered—traumas they need to work out in therapy. Men need to understand the traumatic roots of vaginismus and support the woman to get professional help.

Therapy for vaginismus may take some time, so both partners need to be patient. Couples counseling may be beneficial while the woman is in treatment. However, couples need not refrain from sex. Many women suffering from vaginismus enjoy nonintercourse lovemaking.

When to Call the Doctor.   Vaginismus requires professional therapy, which typically includes a combination of psychotherapy, sex therapy, muscle relaxants, and serial insertion of rods ("dilators") of increasing diameter. Frequently, therapy includes the woman and/or her partner inserting their fingers into her vagina as she works up to intercourse.

VASECTOMY

(See also TUBAL LIGATION in this chapter)

Vasectomy is the sterilization operation performed on men. Sterilization is the most effective birth control method, but those who opt for it should consider it permanent.

What's Going On?   Vasectomy is a minor surgical procedure which cuts the tubes that carry sperm out of the testicles.

Sperm are produced in the testicles, the two "nuts" in the scrotum. Once mature, they leave through a tube, one per testicle ("vas deferens"). The two vas tubes carry the sperm up to the prostate gland, where they combine with seminal fluid to form semen. Sperm account for about 2 percent of semen by volume.

Vasectomies are twenty-minute procedures performed under local anesthesia. The surgeon makes two tiny incisions in the upper scrotum, cuts the vas tubes, and seals their ends. After vasectomy, men usually feel some soreness and see some scrotal discoloration.

Surgical complications develop in about 1 percent of cases. They include wound infections, anesthesia reactions, and sterilization failure.

Most vasectomies are performed on Fridays. Afterward, men should take it easy on the weekend and not do any heavy lifting. Most feel fine by the following Monday.

Couples may resume lovemaking whenever they wish but *must* use another form of birth control until the man has been confirmed sterile. After vasectomy, men are *not* sterile. Typically, hundreds of millions of live sperm remain in the vas tubes above where the surgeon cuts. It usually takes about two dozen ejaculations to eliminate them. A few weeks after vasectomy, men return for follow-up appointments. They masturbate, and the physician examines their semen for live sperm. You're not sterile until the doctor says you are. Until then, continue to use another form of birth control.

After vasectomy the man's testicles continue making sperm, but they are reabsorbed into the body like other cells that outlive their usefulness.

Vasectomy is a more minor, less costly, less traumatic procedure than the woman's sterilization operation ("tubal ligation"—see TUBAL LIGATION in this chapter) because it does not require entering the abdominal cavity.

Recently, urologists have enjoyed increasing success reversing vasectomies. Using the latest microsurgical techniques, sperm return to semen in about 75 percent of cases, and impregnation occurs about half the time. But vasectomy reversal is major surgery. Instead of a twenty-minute office procedure, reversals take hours in a hospital under general anesthesia. Vasectomies cost a few hundred dollars, and health insurance pays for them. Reversals cost $5,000 to $10,000; few insurers cover them, and success cannot be guaranteed.

Before You Call the Doctor.   If you have completed your family and no longer care to use other contraceptives, vasectomy might be right for you. But before you have the operation, think long and hard about some difficult questions:

• Suppose you divorced or became widowed and then remarried. Would you want more children? What if your new wife wanted children?

• Suppose your children were killed? Would you want to start a new family?

If you find yourself thinking: Well, I could always get it reversed, think again. There's no guarantee that any vasectomy can be reversed, and no man should have one if he thinks he might ever attempt to have it reversed. (The vast majority of reversal attempts involve men who divorce, remarry, and want children with the new wife.)

Sterilization decisions should not be made impulsively. Studies of men's feelings after vasectomy show that those happiest with the operation thought about it for at least a year before having the surgery.

When to Call the Doctor.   If you're quite certain you want a vasectomy, contact a physician.

WITHDRAWAL

Withdrawal means that the man removes his penis from the woman's vagina before he ejaculates.

What's Going On?   For information about the effectiveness of this method compared with the others, see the CONTRACEPTION section of this chapter.

Theoretically, withdrawal, also known as "pulling out," makes sense. If the man doesn't ejaculate inside the vagina, the woman can't become pregnant. But in practice, things often don't work out that way, and authorities do not consider withdrawal a reliable form of contraception. The pre-ejaculatory lubricating fluid that emerges from the penis may contain sperm, and a man might deposit some of these sperm in the vagina before he pulls out. In addition, for this method to work properly, the man must have excellent ejaculatory control, a skill many men have not mastered (see EJACULATION (INVOLUNTARY) in this chapter).

On the other hand, withdrawal is considerably better than nothing, and after weighing the advantages and disadvantages of all the methods of contraception, some couples might decide to use it.

Before You Call the Doctor.   Withdrawal's advantages include:
- Nothing to buy.
- No devices to use.
- No visits to medical providers.
- No harmful side effects.

Withdrawal's disadvantages include:
- Considerable risk of pregnancy.
- Possible interference with the pleasure of lovemaking.

When to Call the Doctor.   If the man accidentally ejaculates in the vagina, the woman should consider consulting a physician or family planning clinic for a morning-after contraceptive (see MORNING-AFTER CONTRACEPTION in this chapter).

RESOURCES

American Association of Sex Educators, Counselors, and Therapists. 535 N. Michigan Ave., Suite 1717, Chicago, IL 60611; (312)

644-0828. Write for a free list of all the certified sex therapists in your state.

For Yourself: The Fulfillment of Female Sexuality by Lonnie Barbach, Ph.D. (New York: Signet, $5.95) An excellent self-help book for women who have difficulty having orgasms.

Sexual Solutions: For Men and the Women Who Love Them by Michael Castleman. (New York: Touchstone, $22.95) Self-help for men troubled by involuntary ejaculation, erection problems, and difficulty ejaculating. Send $14.95 postpaid to Self-Care Associates, P.O. Box 460066, San Francisco, CA 94146-0066. Discreetly packaged. Money-back guarantee. Mailing list never rented.

San Francisco Sex Information. (415) 621-7300. Operators are specially trained to provide accurate, confidential answers to questions about sexuality. The service is free. Call from anywhere in the U.S. or Canada 3:00 to 9:00 P.M. Pacific time.

The Sexuality Library. 1210 Valencia St., San Francisco, CA 94110; (415) 550-9112. An excellent source of helpful sexuality books and other resources. Send $2.00 for catalog. Discreetly packaged. Money-back guarantee. Mailing list never rented.

Resolve, Inc. 5 Water St., Arlington, MA 02174; (617) 643-2424. Resolve's fifty two chapters around the country provide information, support, and referrals to couples dealing with infertility. Contact the national office for a referral to the chapter nearest you.

Potency Restored. 8630 Fenton St., Suite 218, Silver Spring, MD; (301) 588-5777. Provides information about surgical penile implants and support for men before and after the operation.

INDEX

About the Authors

Anne Simons, M.D., is a board-certified family practitioner. She practices in a primary care clinic affiliated with the San Francisco Department of Public Health and is an Assistant Clinical Professor of Family and Community Medicine at the University of California's San Francisco Medical Center. She lives in San Francisco with her husband, co-author Michael Castleman, and their two children, Jeffrey and Maya.

Bobbie Hasselbring is a health and medical writer whose work has appeared in *Glamour, Women's Sports and Fitness, Pacific Northwest,* and many other publications. She is a health and fitness columnist for the *Portland Oregonian* newspaper and *Northwest* magazine. Her books include: *Aching for Love: The Sexual Drama of Adult Children of Alcoholics* (Harper and Row, with Mary Ann Klausner); *The Medical Self-Care Book of Women's Health* (Doubleday, with Sadja Greenwood, M.D., and Michael Castleman); and *Pregnancy and Childbirth* (World). She lives in Beavercreek, Oregon.

Michael Castleman is a San Francisco–based health and medical writer whose work has appeared in *The New York Times, Reader's Digest, Redbook, Glamour, Playboy, Self, Men's Health, Longevity,* and many other publications. His books includes: *Sexual Solutions: For Men and the Women Who Love Them* (Simon and Schuster); *Crime Free: The Community Crime Prevention Handbook* (Simon and Schuster); *Cold Cures: The Complete Guide to Preventing and Treating the Common Cold and Flu* (Ballantine); and *The Healing Herbs: The Complete Guide to the Curative Powers of Nature's Medicines* (Rodale).

Medical reviewer Elizabeth Johnson, M.D., is a board-certified family practitioner. An Assistant Clinical Professor of Family and Community Medicine at the University of California's San Francisco Medical Center, she is the medical director of a primary care clinic affiliated with the San Francisco Department of Public Health.